Created Equal

Created Equal

A History of the United States

THIRD EDITION

VOLUME I ■ TO 1877

Jacqueline Jones
Brandeis University

Peter H. Wood
Duke University

Thomas Borstelmann
University of Nebraska

Elaine Tyler May
University of Minnesota

Vicki L. Ruiz
University of California, Irvine

PEARSON
Longman

New York San Francisco Boston
London Toronto Sydney Tokyo Singapore Madrid
Mexico City Munich Paris Cape Town Hong Kong Montreal

Executive Editor: Michael Boezi
Assistant Development Manager: David B. Kear
Senior Development Editor: Marion B. Castellucci
Executive Marketing Manager: Sue Westmoreland
Media Editor: Melissa Edwards
Supplements Editor: Brian Belardi
Editorial Assistant: Vanessa Gennarelli
Director of Market Research: Laura Coaty
Production Manager: Ellen MacElree
Project Coordination, Electronic Page Makeup, Interior Design and Cartography: Electronic Publishing Services Inc., NYC
Cover Designer/Manager: Wendy Ann Fredericks
Photo Researcher: Photosearch, Inc.
Senior Manufacturing Buyer: Alfred C. Dorsey
Printer and Binder: Quebecor World/Dubuque
Cover Printer: Coral Graphics
Cover/Frontispiece Photo: 1861, Civil War Camp Life, 31st Pennsylvania Infantry of the Union Army at Queen's Farm, near Fort Slocum, Washington, D.C., © Rue des Archives/The Granger Collection, New York.

Library of Congress Cataloging-in-Publication Data

Created equal : a history of the United States / Jacqueline Jones . . . [et al.]. — 3rd ed.
    v. cm.
  Includes bibliographical references and index.
  ISBN-13: 978-0-205-58581-6 (complete ed.)
  ISBN-10: 0-205-58581-7 (complete ed.)
  1. United States—History. 2. United States—Social conditions. 3. United States—Politics and government.
4. Pluralism (Social sciences)—United States—History. 5. Minorities—United States—History. 6. Pluralism
(Social sciences)—United States—History—Sources. 7. Minorities—United States—History—Sources.
  E178.C86 2009
  973—dc22

                  2007045111

Please visit us at www.ablongman.com

ISBN 13: 978-0-205-58581-6 (Complete Edition)
ISBN 10:   0-205-58581-7 (Complete Edition)
ISBN 13: 978-0-205-58583-0 (Volume I)
ISBN 10:   0-205-58583-3 (Volume I)
ISBN 13: 978-0-205-58584-7 (Volume II)
ISBN 10:   0-205-58584-1 (Volume II)

1 2 3 4 5 6 7 8 9 10—QWD—11 10 09 08

To our own teachers, who helped set us on the historian's path, and to our students, who help keep us there. You have touched our intellects, our hearts, and our lives.

A nuestros propios maestros, quienes nos ayudaron a seguir en el sendero de historiador, y a nuestros estudiantes que ayudan a mantenernos allí. Usted han tocado nuestros intelectos, nuestros corazónes, y nuestras vidas.

Detailed Contents   ix

Maps   xvii

Figures   xix

Tables   xxi

Features

Interpreting History   xxiii

The Wider World   xxv

Envisioning History   xxvii

Preface   xxix

Supplements for Instructors and Students   xxxvii

Meet the Authors   xli

A Conversation with the Authors   xlv

Acknowledgments   li

Part One

North American Founders   2

1   First Founders   4
2   European Footholds in North America, 1600–1660   39
3   Controlling the Edges of the Continent, 1660–1715   70

Part Two

A Century of Colonial Expansion to 1775   102

4   African Enslavement: The Terrible Transformation   104
5   An American Babel, 1713–1763   136
6   The Limits of Imperial Control, 1763–1775   167

Part Three

The Unfinished Revolution, 1775–1803   198

7   Revolutionaries at War, 1775–1783   200
8   New Beginnings: The 1780s   233
9   Revolutionary Legacies, 1789–1803   268

Part Four

Expanding the Boundaries of Freedom and Slavery, 1804–1848   296

10   Defending and Expanding the New Nation, 1804–1818   298
11   Society and Politics in the "Age of the Common Man," 1819–1832   327
12   Peoples in Motion, 1832–1848   359

Part Five

Disunion and Reunion   392

13   The Crisis over Slavery, 1848–1860   394
14   "To Fight to Gain a Country": The Civil War   423
15   Consolidating a Triumphant Union, 1865–1877   457

Appendix   A-1
Glossary   G-1
Credits   C-1
Index   I-1

Maps   xvii

Figures   xix

Tables   xxi

Features

   Interpreting History   xxiii

   The Wider World   xxv

   Envisioning History   xxvii

Preface   xxix

Supplements for Instructors and Students   xxxvii

Meet the Authors   xli

A Conversation with the Authors   xlv

Acknowledgments   li

Part One
North American Founders   3

Chapter 1
First Founders   4

Ancient America   6
   The Question of Origins   5
   The Archaic World   7
   The Rise of Maize Agriculture   8

A Thousand Years of Change: 500 to 1500   9
   Valleys of the Sun: The Mesoamerican
     Empires   10
   The Anasazi: Chaco Canyon and
     Mesa Verde   11
   The Mississippians: Cahokia and
     Moundville   13

Linking the Continents   14
   Oceanic Travel: The Norse and the Chinese   15
   Portugal and the Beginnings of Globalization   16

The Wider World: The Lateen Rig: A Triangular Sail That
Helped to Conquer Oceans   17

   Looking for the Indies: Da Gama and
     Columbus   18
   In the Wake of Columbus: Competition and Exchange   19

Spain Enters the Americas   23
   The Devastation of the Indies   24
   The Spanish Conquest of the Aztec   25

Interpreting History: "These Gods That We Worship Give Us
Everything We Need"   27

   Magellan and Cortés Prompt New Searches   27
   Three New Views of North America   28

The Protestant Reformation Plays Out in America   31
   Reformation and Counter-Reformation
     in Europe   31

   Competing Powers Lay Claim to Florida   32
   The Background of English Expansion   34

Envisioning History: "The World as a Clover": Mapping for
Art, Religion, or Science   36

   Lost Colony: The Roanoke Experience   36

Conclusion   38

Chapter 2
European Footholds in North America, 1600–1660   39

Spain's Ocean-Spanning Reach   40

The Wider World: Freedom of the Seas: Grotius and Maritime
Law   41

   Vizcaíno in California and Japan   41
   Oñate Creates a Spanish Foothold in the
     Southwest   43
   New Mexico Survives: New Flocks Among Old
     Pueblos   44
   Conversion and Rebellion in Spanish Florida   45

**France and Holland: Overseas Competition
for Spain   47**
   The Founding of New France   48
   Competing for the Beaver Trade   50
   A Dutch Colony on the Hudson River   50
   "All Sorts of Nationalities": Diverse New
     Amsterdam   52

English Beginnings on the Atlantic Coast   53
   The Virginia Company and Jamestown   54
   "Starving Time" and Seeds of Representative
     Government   55
   Launching the Plymouth Colony   56

The Puritan Experiment   57
   Formation of the Massachusetts Bay Company   58
   "We Shall Be as a City upon a Hill"   59

Interpreting History: Anne Bradstreet: "The Tenth Muse,
Lately Sprung Up in America"   60

   Dissenters: Roger Williams and
     Anne Hutchinson   61
   Expansion and Violence: The Pequot War   63

The Chesapeake Bay Colonies   64
   The Demise of the Virginia Company   64
   Maryland: The Catholic Refuge   65
   The Dwellings of English Newcomers   66

Envisioning History: A Roof Overhead: Early Chesapeake
Housing   67

   The Lure of Tobacco   67

Conclusion   68

Chapter 3
Controlling the Edges of the Continent, 1660–1715   70

France and the American Interior   72
The Rise of the Sun King   72
Exploring the Mississippi Valley   74

Envisioning History: La Salle's Ship, the *Belle,* Is Raised from a Watery Grave   75

King William's War in the Northeast   75

Interpreting History: "Marry or do not marry"   76

Founding the Louisiana Colony   77

The Spanish Empire on the Defensive   78
The Pueblo Revolt in New Mexico   79
Navajo and Spanish on the Southwestern Frontier   81
Borderland Conflict in Texas and Florida   82

England's American Empire Takes Shape   83
Monarchy Restored and Navigation Controlled   83
Fierce Anglo-Dutch Competition   84
The New Restoration Colonies   85
The Contrasting Worlds of Pennsylvania and Carolina   86

Bloodshed in the English Colonies: 1670–1690   87
Metacom's War in New England   88
Bacon's Rebellion in Virginia   89
The "Glorious Revolution" in England   91
The "Glorious Revolution" in America   92

Consequences of War and Growth: 1690–1715   93
Salem's Wartime Witch Hunt   94
The Uneven Costs of War   95

The Wider World: William Dampier: The World Became His University   97

Storm Clouds in the South   98

Conclusion   100

Part Two
A Century of Colonial Expansion to 1775   102

Chapter 4
African Enslavement: The Terrible Transformation   104

The Descent into Race Slavery   105
The Caribbean Precedent   109

Ominous Beginnings   106
Alternative Sources of Labor   108

The Wider World: The Odyssey of Job Ben Solomon   109

The Fateful Transition   109

The Growth of Slave Labor Camps   110
Black Involvement in Bacon's Rebellion   111
The Rise of a Slaveholding Tidewater Elite   111
Closing the Vicious Circle in the Chesapeake   113

England Enters the Atlantic Slave Trade   114
Trade Ties Between Europe and Africa   114
The Slave Trade on the African Coast   115
The Middle Passage Experience   117
Saltwater Slaves Arrive in America   120

Survival in a Strange New Land   121
African Rice Growers in South Carolina   122
Patterns of Resistance   123

Envisioning History: Drums and Banjos: African Sounds in English Colonies   124

A Wave of Rebellion   125

The Transformation Completed   127
Second Class Status in the North   127

Interpreting History: "Releese Us out of This Cruell Bondegg"   128

Uncertain Voices of Dissent   128
Is This Consistent "with Christianity or Common Justice"?   128
Oglethorpe's Antislavery Experiment   130
The End of Equality in Georgia   133

Conclusion   134

Chapter 5
An American Babel, 1713–1763   136

New Cultures on the Western Plains   138
The Spread of the Horse   138
The Rise of the Comanche   139
Creation of Comanchería on the Southern Plains   140
The Expansion of the Sioux   141

Britain's Mainland Colonies: A New Abundance of People   143
Population Growth on the Home Front   143
"Packed Like Herrings": Arrivals from Abroad   144

Non-English Newcomers in the British
    Colonies   145

Interpreting History: "Pastures Can Be Found Almost
Everywhere": Joshua von Kocherthal Recruits Germans to
Carolina   146

The Varied Economic Landscape   148
    Sources of Gain in Carolina and Georgia   148
    Chesapeake Bay's Tobacco Economy   151
    New England Takes to the Sea   152

The Wider World: Solving the Problem
of Longitude   153

    Economic Expansion in the Middle Colonies   154
Matters of Faith: The Great Awakening   155
    Seeds of Religious Toleration   155
    The Onset of the Great Awakening: Pietism
        and George Whitefield   156
    "The Danger of an Unconverted Ministry"   157
    The Consequences of the Great Awakening   158
The French Lose a North American Empire   159
    Prospects and Problems Facing French
        Colonists   160
    British Settlers Confront the Threat
        from France   161
    An American Fight Becomes a Global Conflict   162

Envisioning History: Putting Mary Jemison on a
Pedestal   163

    Quebec Taken and North America Refashioned   164
Conclusion   165

Chapter 6
The Limits of Imperial Control,
1763–1775   167

**New Challenges to Spain's Expanded
Empire   169**
    Pacific Exploration, Hawaiian Contact   169

The Wider World: "Farther than Any Other Man": Cook's
Second Voyage   170

    The Russians Lay Claim to Alaska   171
    Spain Colonizes the California Coast   172
New Challenges to Britain's Expanded Empire   175

Envisioning History: William Hogarth's "The Times,"
1762   176

    Midwestern Lands and Pontiac's War for Indian
        Independence   176
    Grenville's Effort at Reform   177

The Stamp Act Imposed   179
The Stamp Act Resisted   180
"The Unconquerable Rage of the People"   182
    Power Corrupts: An English Framework
        for Revolution   183
    Americans Practice Vigilance and Restraint   184
    Rural Unrest: Tenant Farmers and Regulators   185

Interpreting History: "Squeezed and Oppressed": A 1768
Petition by 30 Regulators   186

A Conspiracy of Corrupt Ministers?   186
    The Townshend Duties   187
    Virtuous Resistance: Boycotting British
        Goods   188
    The Boston Massacre   189
    The *Gaspée* Affair Prompts Committees
        of Correspondence   190
Launching a Revolution   191
    The Tempest over Tea   191
    The Intolerable Acts   192
    From Words to Action   193
Conclusion   196

Part Three
The Unfinished Revolution, 1775–1803   198

Chapter 7
Revolutionaries at War, 1775–1783   200
"Things Are Now Come to That Crisis"   202
    The Second Continental Congress Takes
        Control   202

The Wider World: The Journey of Tom
and Sally Peters   203

    "Liberty to Slaves"   204
    The Struggle to Control Boston   205
Declaring Independence   206
    "Time to Part"   207
    The British Attack New York   208

Interpreting History: "Revoking Those Sacred Trusts Which Are
Violated": Proclaiming Independence in South Carolina, May
1776   210

    "Victory or Death": A Desperate Gamble
        Pays Off   212
The Struggle to Win French Support   213
    Breakdown in British Planning   213
    Saratoga Tips the Balance   214
    Forging an Alliance with France   216

Legitimate States, a Respectable Military 217
  The Articles of Confederation 217
  Creating State Constitutions 218
  Tensions in the Military Ranks 220
  Shaping a Diverse Army 220
  The War at Sea 222

The Long Road to Yorktown 223
  Indian Warfare and Frontier Outposts 223
  The Unpredictable War in the South 226
  The Final Campaign 227
  Winning the Peace 229

Envisioning History: Benjamin Franklin: The Diplomat
  in a Beaver Hat 230

Conclusion 231

Chapter 8
New Beginnings: The 1780s 233

Beating Swords into Plowshares 234
  Will the Army Seize Control? 235
  The Society of the Cincinnati 238
  Renaming the Landscape 238

Interpreting History: Demobilization: "Turned Adrift Like Old
  Worn-Out Horses" 236

  An Independent Culture 239

**Competing for Control of the Mississippi
Valley 240**
  Disputed Territory: The Old Southwest 241
  Southern Claims and Indian Resistance 242
  "We Are Now Masters": The Old
      Northwest 243
  The Northwest Ordinance of 1787 245

**Debtor and Creditor, Taxpayer and
Bondholder 247**
  New Sources of Wealth 248

The Wider World: John Ledyard's Wildly Ambitious
  Plan 250

  "Tumults in New England" 250
  Shay's Rebellion: The Massachusetts
      Regulation 251

Drafting a New Constitution 253
  Philadelphia: A Gathering of Like-
      Minded Men 253
  Compromise and Consensus 254
  Questions of Representation 255
  Slavery: The Deepest Dilemma 256

Ratification and the Bill of Rights 257
  The Campaign for Ratification 257
  Dividing and Conquering the
      Anti-Federalists 258
  Adding a Bill of Rights 260

Envisioning History: "Grand Federal Processions" 259

Conclusion 260

Chapter 9
Revolutionary Legacies, 1789–1803 268

Competing Political Visions in the New Nation 264
  Federalism and Democratic-Republicanism in Action 265

Envisioning History: President-Elect Washington Is Greeted by
  the Women and Girls of Trenton, New Jersey 266

  Planting the Seeds of Industry 267
  Echoes of the American Revolution: The Whiskey
      Rebellion 268
  Securing Peace Abroad, Suppressing Dissent at Home 269

People of Color: New Freedoms, New Struggles 271
  Blacks in the North 272
  Manumissions in the South 273

Continuity and Change in the West 274
  Indian Wars in the Great Lakes Region 275
  Patterns of Indian Acculturation 277
  Land Speculation and Slavery 278

**Shifting Social Identities in the Post-Revolutionary
Era 280**
  The Search for Common Ground 281
  Artisan-Politicians and Menial Laborers 283

Interpreting History: A Farmer Worries about the Power of
  "the Few" 284

  "Republican Mothers" and Other Well-Off Women 284
  A Loss of Political Influence: The Fate of Nonelite
      Women 287

The Election of 1800
  The Enigmatic Thomas Jefferson 290

The Wider World: Comparative Measures of Equality in the
  Post-Revolutionary World 291

  Protecting and Expanding the National Interest 291

Conclusion 293

Part Four
Expanding the Boundaries of Freedom
and Slavery, 1804–1848 296

Chapter 10
Defending and Expanding the New Nation,
1804–1818 298

The British Menace 300
  The Embargo of 1807 301
  On the Brink of War 302

The War of 1812   304
　　Pushing North   305
　　Fighting on Many Fronts   307

Envisioning History: A Government Agent Greets a Group of
Creek Indians   309

　　An Uncertain Victory   309
The "Era of Good Feelings"?   310
　　Praise and Respect for Veterans
　　　　After the War   311
　　A Thriving Economy   313
　　Transformations in the Workplace   314

Interpreting History: Cherokee Women Petition Against
Further Land Sales to Whites in 1817   312

　　The Market Revolution   317
The Rise of the Cotton Plantation Economy   318

The Wider World: Which Nations Transported Slaves
in 1800?   319

　　Regional Economies of the South   319
　　Black Family Life and Labor   320
　　Resistance to Slavery   322
Conclusion   325

Chapter 11
Society and Politics in the "Age of the Common Man," 1819–1832   327
The Politics Behind Western Migration   329
　　The Missouri Compromise   329
　　Ways West: The Erie Canal   331
　　Spreading American Culture—and
　　　　Slavery   334

The Wider World: The Global Trade in Cotton   335

　　Migration and Its Effects on the Western
　　　　Environment   335
　　The Panic of 1819 and the Plight of Western
　　　　Debtors   335
　　The Monroe Doctrine   337
　　Andrew Jackson's Rise to Power   338

Envisioning History: A Rowdy Presidential
Inauguration   339

Federal Authority and Its Opponents   340
　　Judicial Federalism and the Limits of Law   340
　　The "Tariff of Abominations"   342
　　The "Monster Bank"   343
Americans in the "Age of the Common Man"   344
　　Wards, Workers, and Warriors:
　　　　Native Americans   344
　　Slaves and Free People of Color   346

　　Legal and Economic Dependence: The Status
　　　　of Women   348

Interpreting History: Eulalia Perez Describes Her Work in a
California Mission   350

Ties That Bound a Growing Population   352
　　New Visions of Religious Faith   352
　　Literary and Cultural Values in America   354
Conclusion   456

Chapter 12
Peoples in Motion, 1832–1848   359
Mass Migrations   361
　　Newcomers from Western Europe   362
　　The Slave Trade   363

Envisioning History: An Owner Advertises for His Runaway
Slave   365

　　Trails of Tears   365
　　Migrants in the West   367
　　Government-Sponsored Exploration   368
　　The Oregon Trail   369
　　New Places, New Identities   371
　　Changes in the Southern Plains   373

The Wider World: The U.S. and Other Railroad Networks
Compared   374

A Multitude of Voices in the National Political Arena   374
　　Whigs, Workers, and the Panic of 1837   375
　　Suppression of Antislavery Sentiment   376
　　Nativists as a Political Force   378
Reform Impulses   380
　　Public Education   380
　　Alternative Visions of Social Life   382
　　Networks of Reformers   383
The United States Extends Its Reach   384
　　The Lone Star Republic   384
　　The Election of 1844   385
　　War with Mexico   386

Interpreting History: Senator John C. Calhoun Warns Against
Incorporating Mexico into the United States   388

Conclusion   390

Part Five
Disunion and Reunion   392

Chapter 13
The Crisis over Slavery, 1848–1860   394
Regional Economies and Conflicts   396
　　Native American Economies Transformed   397

Land Conflicts in the Southwest 398
Ethnic and Economic Diversity in the
    Midwest 399
Regional Economies of the South 400
A Free Labor Ideology in the North 401

Individualism Versus Group Identity 402
Putting into Practice Ideas of Social
    Inferiority 403

Interpreting History: Professor Howe on the Subordination
of Women 404

"A Teeming Nation"—America in
    Literature 404
Challenges to Individualism 406

The Paradox of Southern Political Power 407

Envisioning History: An Artist Renders County Election Day
in the 1850s 409

The Party System in Disarray 410
The Compromise of 1850 410
Expansionism and Political Upheaval 412
The Republican Alliance 413

The Deepening Conflict over Slavery 415
The Rising Tide of Violence 415

The Wider World: When Was Slavery
Abolished? 416

The *Dred Scott* Decision 417
The Lincoln-Douglas Debates 418
Harpers Ferry and the Presidential Election
    of 1860 418

Conclusion 421

Chapter 14
"To Fight to Gain a Country": The Civil War 423

Mobilization for War, 1861–1862 425
The Secession Impulse 425
Preparing to Fight 428

Envisioning History: A Civil War Encampment 429

Barriers to Southern Mobilization 430

Interpreting History: A Virginia Slaveholder Objects
to the Impressment of Slaves 432

Indians in the Service of
    the Confederacy 434
The Ethnic Confederacy 434

The Course of War, 1862–1864 436
The Republicans' War 436

The Ravages of War 438
The Emancipation Proclamation 441
Persistent Obstacles to the Confederacy's
    Grand Strategy 441

**The Other War: African American Struggles
for Liberation 442**
The Unfolding of Freedom 443
Enemies Within the Confederacy 444
The Ongoing Fight Against Prejudice 445

Battle Fronts and Home Fronts in 1863 446
Disaffection in the Confederacy 446
The Tide Turns Against the South 447

The Wider World: Deaths of Americans in Principal Wars,
1775–1991 448

Civil Unrest in the North 449
The Desperate South 449

**The Prolonged Defeat of the Confederacy,
1864–1865 450**
"Hard War" Toward African Americans
    and Indians 450
"Father Abraham" 452
Sherman's March from Atlanta to the Sea 452
The Last Days of the Confederacy 454

Conclusion 455

Chapter 15
Consolidating a Triumphant Union, 1865–1877 457

The Struggle over the South 459
Wartime Preludes to Postwar Policies 460
Presidential Reconstruction,
    1865–1867 460
The Southern Postwar Labor Problem 463

Interpreting History: A Southern Labor Contract 464

Building Free Communities 467
Landscapes and Soundscapes
    of Freedom 469
Congressional Reconstruction: The Radicals'
    Plan 469
The Remarkable Career of Blanche K. Bruce 472

Claiming Territory for the Union 473
Federal Military Campaigns Against Western
    Indians 474

Envisioning History: Two Artists Memorialize the Battle
of Little Big Horn 475

The Postwar Western Labor
    Problem 476

Land Use in an Expanding
Nation   478
Buying Territory for the
Union   480

The Republican Vision and Its Limits   481
Postbellum Origins of the Woman Suffrage
Movement   481

The Wider World: When Did Women
Get the Vote?   483

Workers' Organizations   484
Political Corruption and the Decline of Republican
Idealism   486

Conclusion   488

Appendix

The Declaration of Independence   A-3

The Articles of Confederation   A-5

The Constitution of the United States of America   A-8

Amendments to the Constitution   A-13

Presidential Elections   A-17

Present Day United States   A-20

Present Day World   A-22

Glossary   G-1

Credits   C-1

Index   I-1

1.1   The Earliest Americans   7
1.2   America in the Millennium Before Columbus,
       500–1500   10
1.3   Opening New Ocean Pathways Around the Globe,
       1420–1520   20
1.4   The Extent of North American Exploration by 1592   33

2.1   The Spanish Southwest in the Early Seventeenth Century   42
2.2   Sites of Catholic Missions in Spanish Florida in the
       Mid-Seventeenth Century   46
2.3   European and Native American Contact in the Northeast,
       1600–1660   53
2.4   Cultures Meet on the Chesapeake   65

3.1   France in the American Interior, 1670–1720   73
3.2   Changes in the Southwest   80
3.3   Metacom's War in New England, 1675–1676   89
3.4   Virginia and the Carolinas, c. 1710   98

4.1   Regions of the African Slave Trade in 1700   116
4.2   One Century in the Transatlantic Slave Trade (1700–1800):
       African Origins, European Carriers, American
       Destinations   118
4.3   Enslaved People Living in North America in 1750:
       Distribution by Colony, Percentage of Total
       Population   121
4.4   English–Spanish Competition and the Expansion of Slavery
       into Georgia   132

5.1   The Horse Frontier Meets the Gun
       Frontier, 1675–1750   142
5.2   Economic Regions of the British Colonies   149
5.3   The British Conquest of New France, 1754–1760   162

6.1   Russian Alaska   173
6.2   Spanish Exploration After 1760 and the Start of the
       California Missions   174
6.3   British North America, 1763–1766   181
6.4   British North America, April 1775   194

7.1   Overview of the Revolutionary War   202
7.2   The Revolutionary War in the North   209
7.3   Britain at War: The Global Context, 1778–1783   215
7.4   The Revolutionary War in the West   224
7.5   The Revolutionary War in the South   227

8.1   The Spread of Smallpox Across North
       America, 1775–1782   235
8.2   Southern Land Debates After 1783   242
8.3   Native American Ohio Before 1785   245
8.4   Settlers' Ohio, After 1785   246

9.1   The Northwest Territory   275
9.2   The Southwest in 1800   278
9.3   Western Land Claims of the States   279

10.1   Lewis and Clark 301
10.2   The Public Domain in 1810   304
10.3   War of 1812, The Northern Front   306

11.1   The Center of Population Moves West, 1790–1970   330
11.2   The Missouri Compromise   331
11.3   Principal Canals Built by 1860   332
11.4   Mexico's Far Northern Frontier in 1822   336
11.5   The Cherokee Nation After 1820   341

12.1   Population Change in Ireland, 1841–1851   362
12.2   Expansion of the Cotton Belt and Slave Trading Routes,
        1801–1860   364
12.3   Indian Removal   366
12.4   Western Trails   369
12.5   The U.S.-Mexican War   387

13.1   Territorial Expansion in the Nineteenth Century   397
13.2   The Underground Railroad   411
13.3   The Kansas-Nebraska Act, 1854   413

14.1   The Secession of Southern States, 1860–1861   426
14.2   Slavery in the United States, 1860   428
14.3   Mescalero Apache Battle Confederates, Central New
        Mexico, 1861   431
14.4   The Battle of Gettysburg, July 1–3, 1863   447
14.5   African Americans in Civil War Battles,
        1863–1865   450
14.6   Sherman's March to the Sea, 1864–1865   453

15.1   Radical Reconstruction   469
15.2   Plains Indian Wars, 1854–1890   474
15.3   The Compromise of 1877   487

        Present Day United States   A20
        Present Day World   A22

Figures

1.1 The Columbian Exchange 22

2.1 The Tough Choice to Start Over 54

4.1 Goods Traded in Africa 115

5.1 Comparison of Overall Population Structure by Gender and Age: British Mainland Colonies, 1760s, and United States, 2000 144

7.1 British Government Expenses on Armed Forces Throughout the World, 1775–1782 (in millions of pounds) 217

8.1 Concentration of Security Notes in the Hands of a Few: The Example of New Hampshire in 1785 252

9.1 Growth in the American Free Black Population, 1790–1860 272

9.2 Percentage of White Men Eligible to Vote in the United States, 1792 281

Distribution of Wealth in the United States and Europe, 1798 291

Volume of the Transatlantic Slave Trade by Nationality of Carrier, 1801–1825 319

Value of U.S. Cotton Exports, 1815–1860 335

11.1 Estimated Population of the United States, 1790–1860 352

12.1 How Indians Used the Buffalo 373

Comparative Railway Lengths, 1845–1860 374

14.1 Occupational Categories of Union and Confederate Soldiers 430

2.1 North American Colonies by Nationality, 1560–1660   48

9.1 The Election of 1796   269

9.2 Denominational Shares (%) of Religious Adherents in the United States, 1776 and 1850   282

9.3 The Election of 1800   289

10.1 The Election of 1804   300

10.2 The Election of 1808   303

10.3 The Election of 1812   305

10.4 The Election of 1816   311

11.1 The Election of 1820   337

11.2 The Election of 1824   338

11.3 The Election of 1828   340

11.4 The Election of 1832   343

12.1 Outfitting a Party of Four for the Overland Trail   370

12.2 The Election of 1836   375

12.3 The Election of 1840   377

12.4 The Election of 1844   386

13.1 U.S. Population, 1830–1860, by Region, Showing Nativity, Race, and Enslavement   408

13.2 The Election of 1848   410

13.3 The Election of 1852   412

13.4 The Election of 1856   414

13.5 The Election of 1860   421

14.1 Ohio Men Drafted for Military Service Who Reported for Duty or Hired Substitutes   437

14.2 The Election of 1864   452

15.1 Comparison of Black and White Household Structure in 27 Cotton-Belt Counties   468

15.2 The Election of 1868   471

15.3 The Election of 1872   486

15.4 The Election of 1876   488

Chapter 1 "These Gods That We Worship Give Us Everything We Need" 26

Chapter 2 Anne Bradstreet: "The Tenth Muse, Lately Sprung Up in America" 60

Chapter 3 "Marry or Do Not Marry" 76

Chapter 4 "Releese Us Out of This Cruell Bondegg" 128

Chapter 5 "Pastures Can Be Found Almost Everywhere": Joshua von Kocherthal Recruits Germans to Carolina 146

Chapter 6 "Squeez'd and Oppressed": A 1768 Petition by 30 Regulators 186

Chapter 7 "Revoking Those Sacred Trusts Which Are Violated": Proclaiming Independence in South Carolina, May 1776 210

Chapter 8 Demobilization: "Turned Adrift like Old Worn-Out Horses" 236

Chapter 9 A Farmer Worries About the Power of "the Few" 284

Chapter 10 Cherokee Women Petition Against Further Land Sales to Whites in 1817 312

Chapter 11 Eulalia Perez Describes Her Work in a California Mission 850

Chapter 12 Senator John C. Calhoun Warns Against Incorporating Mexico into the United States 388

Chapter 13 Professor Howe on the Subordination of Women 404

Chapter 14 A Virginia Slaveholder Objects to the Impressment of Slaves 432

Chapter 15 A Southern Labor Contract 464

Feature: The Wider World

Chapter 1 The Lateen Rig: A Triangular Sail That Helped to Conquer Oceans 17
Chapter 2 Freedom of the Seas: Grotius and Maritime Law 41
Chapter 3 William Dampier: The World Became His University 97
Chapter 4 The Odyssey of Job Ben Solomon 109
Chapter 5 Solving the Problem of Longitude 153
Chapter 6 "Farther than Any Other Man": Captain Cook's Second Voyage 170
Chapter 7 The Journey of Tom and Sally Peters 203
Chapter 8 John Ledyard's Wildly Ambitious Plan 250
Chapter 9 Comparative Measures of Equality in the Post-Revolutionary Period 291
Chapter 10 Which Nations Transported Slaves in 1800? 319
Chapter 11 The Global Trade in Cotton 335
Chapter 12 The U.S. and Other Railroad Networks Compared 374
Chapter 13 When Was Slavery Abolished? 416
Chapter 14 Deaths of Americans in Principal Wars, 1775–1991 448
Chapter 15 When Did Women Get the Vote? 483

Chapter 1 "The World as a Clover": Mapping for Art, Religion, or Science   36
Chapter 2 A Roof Overhead: Early Chesapeake Housing   67
Chapter 3 La Salle's Ship, the *Belle,* Is Raised from a Watery Grave   75
Chapter 4 Drums and Banjos: African Sounds in English Colonies   124
Chapter 5 Putting Mary Jemison on a Pedestal   163
Chapter 6 William Hogarth's "The Times," 1762   176
Chapter 7 Benjamin Franklin: The Diplomat in a Beaver Hat   230
Chapter 8 "Grand Federal Processions"   259
Chapter 9 President-Elect Washington Is Greeted by the Women and Girls of Trenton,
    New Jersey   266
Chapter 10 A Government Agent Greets a Group of Creek Indians   309
Chapter 11 A Rowdy Presidential Inauguration   339
Chapter 12 An Owner Advertises for His Runaway Slave   365
Chapter 13 An Artist Renders County Election
    Day in the 1850s   409
Chapter 14 A Civil War Encampment   429
Chapter 15 Two Artists Memorialize the Battle of Little Big Horn   475

> *"I have a dream that one day this nation will rise up and live out the meaning of its creed: 'We hold these truths to be self-evident: That all men are created equal'. . . ."*
>
> —*Dr. Martin Luther King, Jr., Washington, DC, August 28, 1963*

Since the First Edition of *Created Equal* was published in 2002, we have been overwhelmed by the enthusiastic response to the book and its theme—that the United States is a country with a history of diverse racial, ethnic, regional, economic, and political groups made up of immigrants and their descendants, African Americans, native-born peoples, women and men, people of different ages and sexual orientation, and the powerful and the oppressed, all staking their claims on an American identity. We have gratefully listened when users of the book suggested ways to make improvements; this Third Edition is based on the cumulative suggestions of more than 170 reviewers who helped us find ways to make the book a better fit for their own classrooms.

We began the preface to the previous edition by noting that one of our teammates, Professor Vicki L. Ruiz, took office in 2005 as the President of the Organization of American Historians (OAH). She became the first Latino American scholar to hold that one-year, elected leadership position, and she did an impressive job. In this preface for the Third Edition, we are pleased to announce that another *Created Equal* author, Professor Elaine Tyler May, will become the President of the OAH in 2009. We celebrate this major honor bestowed upon two members of our team. These laurels are a tribute to their outstanding accomplishments as historians, and to the progress of the OAH in integrating women fully into all ranks of the historical profession. This progress reminds us why we wrote *Created Equal*, and why we chose to highlight the rich diversity of the American people.

Centuries ago, when the American Continental Congress approved the Declaration of Independence with its preamble's lofty claim that "all men are created equal," not everyone was impressed or inspired. The English philosopher Jeremy Bentham immediately made fun of the "contemptible and extravagant" document. The preamble, he protested, "would be too ridiculous to deserve any notice." The clever philosopher could hardly have been more wrong. Over the centuries since its publication, the powerful phrases of the Declaration have inspired people in the United States and around the world. After all, it was revolutionary for its authors to assert, as a "self-evident" and undeniable truth, that all humans are "created equal; that they are endowed by their Creator with certain unalienable rights; that among these are life, liberty, and the pursuit of happiness." Granted, the Founding Fathers conceived of the new nation as a political community for white men of property. But for generations, diverse racial and ethnic groups, as well as people of different ages, genders, or sexual orientation, have stressed that *all* Americans are endowed with basic individual rights that cannot be taken away. Repeatedly, they have cited the Declaration in their struggles to achieve a more inclusive definition of American citizenship.

Thus *Created Equal* illuminates the story of various groups of men and women, rich and poor, all "created equal" in their common humanity, claiming a social and political identity for themselves as Americans. In tracing their worlds, *Created Equal* also explores diverse forms of engagement—political, diplomatic, cultural, military, and economic—between the United States and other countries and cultures over time.

What's New in the Third Edition

Our aim, in crafting the Third Edition, is to provide students with a solid understanding of the individuals and forces that have shaped our history, both within the nation's changing borders and also through America's complex and crucial relations with the rest of the world. In doing so, we are mindful that history is never static, and that we must be responsive to shifting classroom needs. Therefore, we have drawn on almost a decade of creative feedback about the first and second editions from colleagues, instructors, and students who have used the book, as well as our own classroom experiences. Our primary goal is to improve each reader's experience and to deepen student understanding of the American journey. To that end, this edition introduces a number of significant additions and substantive changes.

Two Unifying Themes Focus the Narrative

In preparing the Third Edition, we have elected to focus on two particularly significant themes. Both themes are durable and many-sided. Emphasizing them has allowed us to bring continuity and clarity to the rich American story. Throughout the text, we have included new material related to both of these themes:

- **Diversity and inclusion.** In considering the theme of diversity, we acknowledge the formation of social and political identity as a central element of the American story. We examine how individual Americans have understood and identified themselves by gender, religion, region, income, race, and ethnicity, among other factors, while using the ideal of "created equal" to push for inclusion in the American nation. American Indians, African Americans, Latinos, Asian immigrants, members of distinct religions and social classes, women of every background—all of these people have played major roles in defining what it means to be an American. At the same time, individuals' identities are by no means fixed or static. For example, Chapter 20 now opens with a brief profile of W. E. B. DuBois, who was born in Massachusetts in 1869. In 1895, DuBois became the first African American to receive a history doctoral degree from Harvard University. Over his long career, DuBois defied categorization, working as a sociologist, a journalist, an editor, a poet, and a fervent reformer. Known as a brilliant and productive scholar, he also embraced the role of activist on behalf of people of color, not only in the United States but also around the world. In his writings and speeches, DuBois repeatedly expressed the aspirations of all races "for equality, freedom and democracy."

- **Globalization.** By heralding universal, unalienable rights, the Founding Fathers implied that the principles expressed in the Declaration possessed a global reach. For centuries, America has not existed in isolation from the rest of the world. Since the earliest days of colonial settlement, Americans have traded goods, cultural practices, and ideas with peoples outside their borders. As an immigrant nation, the United States has developed ties of human kinship with cultures in all parts of the world. In the twenty-first century, our linkage to the entire globe is more evident than ever. Today, many of the foods we eat, the clothes we wear, and the cars we drive originate abroad. Whether considering matters of commerce, migration, religion, security, health, or the environment, citizens of the United States regularly encounter broad forces that transcend national boundaries. The dilemmas of globalization are not new, but they now confront us in unprecedented ways. As Americans, we are now more than ever obliged to examine and discuss the role of our country—past, present, and future—in the wider world.

These themes serve as the lenses through which we view the traditional narrative framework of American history. Readers of *Created Equal* will learn about the major political developments that shaped the country's past, as well as the roles of diverse groups in initiating and reacting to those developments. Chapter 13, for example, which focuses on the 1850s, includes a detailed account of the effects of the slavery crisis on Congress and the political party system, as well as a discussion of shifting group identities affecting Indians, Latinos, northern women, and enslaved and free blacks. Chapter 18, on the 1890s, covers the rise of the Populist party and stirrings of American imperialism, as well as a discussion of barriers to a U.S. workers' political party and challenges to traditional gender roles. Thus, *Created Equal* builds on the basic history that forms the foundation of most major textbooks and offers a lively and comprehensive look at the past by including the stories of many different kinds of Americans and by emphasizing the nation's global connections.

New Features Support the Themes and Broaden the Use of Historical Sources

To provide students with pertinent, in-depth treatment of global issues and show them how objects and visuals can tell us about the past, we have introduced two new features:

■ **"The Wider World"** is a new feature that strengthens the globalization theme and keeps it in the foreground throughout the book. "The Wider World" appears in each chapter, introducing a person, a graph, a table, or an image that helps students to place that era of American history within its international context. "The Wider World" provides an informative and helpful exercise in expansive historical thinking. Repeatedly, the feature enables readers to compare specific aspects of American society, culture, politics, and economy with foreign counterparts. Among "The Wider World" features are charts and graphs juxtaposing American statistics on a variety of subjects with comparable data regarding other countries. Topics include equality in post-Revolutionary America (Chapter 9), when women got the right to vote in various countries (Chapter 15), the number of immigrants who later went back home (Chapter 19) and the use of the death penalty worldwide (Chapter 30). Chapters 7 and 8 introduce several remarkable and contrasting world travelers from the eighteenth century: an African American couple named Tom and Sally Peters, and the unique global hiker, John Ledyard. This feature reminds readers that the country's complex relationship with foreign places and cultures is not simply a recent development. It has been an enduring theme throughout American history, and at every stage we can learn more fully about our past by considering its international dimensions. Each "The Wider World" feature concludes with questions that ask students to think critically about the relationship of the local and the global.

■ **"Envisioning History"** is a new feature that draws upon the visual sophistication of today's students, alerting them to the many types of sources that historians rely upon, including engravings, maps, banners, pieces of fine art, public monuments and enduring material objects. With the growth of underwater archaeology, even sunken ships are yielding valuable evidence to historians. In Chapter 3, for example, we describe how archaeologists on the Texas coast recently salvaged the submerged remains of a small vessel used by the French explorer La Salle in the 1680s. Exploring paintings, photographs, and political cartoons can also allow us to "envision" American history in new ways. In Chapter 10, a painting depicts a federal agent greeting a group of Creek Indians in the early nineteenth century. The agent looks approvingly at signs of the Indians' willingness to adopt elements of European American agriculture, such as plowing fields and raising livestock. In Chapter 21, a photo of immigrants selling tamales and ice cream in a Los Angeles suburb illustrates the ways in which newcomers served, and altered, the changing tastes and desires of middle-class consumers; while in Chapter 25 a picture of a family fallout shelter suggests the impact of the atomic age on domestic life. A political cartoon satirizing the complicated American voting system is used in Chapter 29 to prompt consideration of the confusion and problems that surrounded the contested presidential election of 2000. Each "Envisioning History" feature concludes with questions that help students analyze the artifact or graphic.

Pedagogical Features Help Students Master American History

Several new features enhance the book's accessibility for students and provide aids to studying.

- A new **focus question at the beginning of each major section** helps students to anticipate and understand the major points of the section as they read it. Taken together, a chapter's focus questions provide guidance for reviewing the chapter's important content.

- A new **chronology** of the period's most important events appears at the end of each chapter, helping students put historical developments in the proper sequence, thus providing a framework for understanding the broader themes of the period.

- Each presidential election is summarized in a new **election table,** providing students with a framework for understanding political developments over the years.

- New **For Review** questions at the end of each chapter help students to grasp major ideas and enter into discussion about larger issues. They encourage students to make connections among the different sections of the chapter and to other periods in American history.

Substantive Changes, Rewriting, and a New Design Improve the Text

Our retooling did not stop with new features. In every chapter, we took the opportunity to make **adjustments, small and large, in content, organization, and presentation, making sure that the standard topics of American history are covered well**. For many of these improvements, we took our cue from suggestions made by the many historians who reviewed the text. For instance, Chapter 4, on the "terrible transformation" to race slavery in colonial America, now contains fresh material on slavery in the North, and in Chapter 9, the discussion of the crucial Supreme Court decision, *Marbury v. Madison*, has been expanded. The last ten chapters have been particularly reworked. Of course, as each year passes, there is more to incorporate. Chapter 30 now stretches through the second election of the second President Bush. It covers the devastation caused by Hurricane Katrina in 2005, plus the midterm elections of 2006 that altered the balance of power in Congress. It deals with the extended wars in Iraq and Afghanistan. We also **sharpened the chapter introductions, rewrote sections of the text, and improved transitions within chapters, tightening and condensing** where possible.

Furthermore, we **redesigned the text** and introduced **new illustrations and maps**. An added bonus from all this work has been to **reduce the book's overall length,** making it more convenient and accessible, but no less comprehensive. Textbooks, like people, can often afford to lose a little weight these days (and use less paper), so we have tried to do our part! *Created Equal* is still hefty—American history remains a rich and expansive saga—but we hope you will agree that a shorter book is a better book, especially given the new features that appear in this new edition.

Chronological Organization

One of the challenges in writing *Created Equal* has been to emphasize the way major developments affect specific generations of Americans. Thus, the text is organized into ten parts, most of these covering a generation. Many textbooks organize discussions of immigrants, cities, the West, and foreign diplomacy (to name a few topics) into separate chapters that cover large time periods. In contrast, *Created Equal* integrates material related to a variety of topics within individual chapters. Although the text adheres to a chronological organization, it stresses coherent discussions of specific topics within that framework.

This chronological approach provides students with a richer understanding of events. Chapter 15, for example, which covers the years immediately following the Civil War, deals with Reconstruction in the South, Indian wars on the High Plains, and the rise of the women's and labor movements, stressing the relationships among all these developments. To cite another example, many texts devote a single chapter exclusively to America's post-World War II rise to global power. But this complex process spans more than two generations, so *Created Equal* integrates material related to that development in a sequence of chapters that stretch from 1945 to the present. Each of these seven chapters illustrates the effects of dramatic world developments on American social relations and domestic policy on a decade-by-decade basis. This approach reflects the way in which we lead our lives—and the way our parents and grandparents led theirs. It allows readers to appreciate the rich complexity of any particular time period and to understand that all major events occur within a social and political context that is specific and unique.

Other Special Features

To assist students and teachers alike, this book retains a number of special features from the second edition that are suitable to a variety of classrooms. They will help readers connect more readily to the American past, and they will encourage students to engage with unfamiliar and surprising aspects of American history on their own. These features include:

- **Parts.** As in previous editions, *Created Equal* consists of ten parts covering three chapters each. A two-page opening section that lays out basic themes and sketches key developments of the period introduces each part.

- **Chapter introductory vignettes.** Every chapter begins with a story that introduces the reader to groups and individuals representative of the themes developed in the chapter. In the Third Edition, we have included eight new chapter vignettes. For example, Chapter 7, covering the American Revolution, starts by sketching the war experience of families from one small village in New Hampshire: Peterborough. Chapter 19 profiles Upton Sinclair, the writer whose exposure of the meat packing industry led to food inspection laws; while Chapter 23 introduces the story of Frank Steiner, a young Jew from Vienna whose family perished in the Holocaust. Steiner managed to escape from the Nazis, going first to Shanghai, China, and then ending up in San Francisco. Chapter 27, on the 1970s, now begins with the story of Emily Howell Warner, a Coloradoan who became the nation's first female commercial airline pilot. Chapter 29, on the 1990s, introduces the increasing gap between rich and poor with a brief profile of Jack Welch, whose annual compensation as CEO of General Electric reached 123 million dollars

- **"Interpreting History."** This feature consists of a primary document on a topic relevant to the chapter's themes. The "Interpreting History" feature takes many different forms—letters, sermons, court decisions, labor contracts, congressional hearings, interviews, poems, and songs. Students thus have an opportunity to analyze primary documents and to better appreciate the historian's task—reading materials critically and placing them in their larger socio-historical context. Questions at the end of each document point students toward major issues and encourage them to analyze both the rhetoric and the larger meaning of the document. The Third Edition includes four new documents through which we hear the voices of a variety of Americans. In Chapter 9, a farmer worries that the wealthy "few" will upend the legacy of the American Revolution, to the detriment of the common folk. In Chapter 11, a woman records in detail her many duties as a housekeeper of a Spanish mission in early nineteenth-century California. In Chapter 20, an individual goes to court during World War I in an effort to reestablish the U.S. citizenship that had been taken from her when she married a British citizen. And in Chapter 30, President George W. Bush lays out the principles behind the "war on terror" in a speech to West Point graduates in 2002.

- **Glossary.** Located at the back of the book, the glossary is a list of hundreds of historical terms and significant events culled from the text and defined in a sentence or two. These entries include everything from court cases (*Plessy v. Ferguson*) and pieces of legislation (Alien and Sedition Acts) to political groups (Democratic-Republicans) and cultural designations (Victorians). In addition, the glossary defines words and phrases familiar to historians but unlikely to be found in a conventional dictionary. Examples include: middle ground, "Republican Mother," yellow journalism. All the terms presented in the glossary are highlighted in **boldface type** in the chapter text.

- **Maps, charts, photos, and artifacts.** Illustrations—photographs, tables, pictures of objects from the time period, and figures—enhance the narrative. Large maps offer great geographical detail and invite students to understand and discuss the relationship between geography and history.

- **MyHistoryLab.** Icons in the margin throughout the pages of the book identify assets on the Pearson U.S. history Web site—MyHistoryLab—that relate to the chapter content and themes. The icons indicate the kind of asset—document, map, image, video, or audio—and the title of each asset. These Web asset icons are representative of the thousands of additional resources on MyHistoryLab, including an e-book version of the entire text, history-related Web sites and other sites to visit, bibliographies, source documents, interactive maps, videos, audio clips, and history-related Web sites designed to enrich students' study of U.S. history.

The Third Edition of *Created Equal* remains true to the vision that first inspired us to craft this book. Its basic framework focuses on the political events and economic structures discussed in most American history textbooks. But the work is distinctive in several ways. It demonstrates a broad geographical scope and environmental awareness, from the very beginning of the narrative. Also, the text is consistently attentive to matters of economic, social, and political power; it suggests vividly how power has been acquired, used, challenged and redistributed over time. *Created Equal* lays out and sharpens the chronology of American history, while integrating a rich variety of groups and individuals into that framework. This Third Edition tells the dramatic, evolving story of America in all its complexity—the story of a diverse people "created equal" yet struggling creatively to achieve equality.

—The Authors

Supplements for Instructors and Students

FOR QUALIFIED COLLEGE ADOPTERS

Name of Supplement	Available in Print	Available Online	Instructor or Student Supplement	Description
Instructor's Resource Center (IRC)		✓	Instructor Supplement	Web site for downloading relevant supplements. Password protected. Please contact your local Pearson representative for an access code. *www.ablongman.com/irc*
MyHistoryLab		✓	Both	With the best of Longman's multimedia solutions for history in one easy-to-use place, MyHistoryLab offers students and instructors a state-of-the art interactive instructional solution for your U.S. history survey course. Built around a complete e-book version of this text, MyHistoryLab provides numerous study aids, review materials, and activities to make the study of history an enjoyable learning experience. Icons in the e-book link directly to relevant materials in context, many of which are assignable. MyHistoryLab includes several hundred primary source documents, videos, images, and maps, all with accompanying analysis questions. It also includes a History Bookshelf with 50 of the most commonly assigned books in U.S. history courses and a History Toolkit with guided tutorials and helpful links. MyHistoryLab is flexible and easy-to-use as a supplement to a traditional lecture course or to administer as a completely online course. *www.myhistorylab.com*
MyHistoryKit for American History		✓	Both	Online package of study materials, gradable quizzes and over 1,000 primary sources organized generically by typical American history themes to support your U.S. history survey text. Access code required. *www.myhistorykit.com*
American History Study Site		✓	Both	Online package of practice tests, Web links, and flashcards organized generically by major history topics to support your U.S. history survey text. Open access. *www.longmanamericanhistory.com*
Instructor's Manual	✓	✓	Instructor Supplement	Each chapter includes a chapter overview, lecture supplements, and questions for class discussion. Text specific.
Test Bank	✓	✓	Instructor Supplement	Contains thousands of conceptual, objective, and essay questions. Text specific.

(Continued)

Name of Supplement	Available in Print	Available Online	Instructor or Student Supplement	Description
Computerized Test Bank	✓	✓	Instructor Supplement	Includes all items in the printed test bank. Questions can be edited, and tests can be printed in several different formats. Text specific.
PowerPoint Presentation		✓	Instructor Supplement	*Created Equal* contains an outline of each chapter of the text and full-color images of maps and figures. Text specific. www.ablongman.com/irc
Digital Transparency Masters		✓	Instructor Supplement	*Created Equal* contains full-color images from the text. Available exclusively on the Instructor's Resource Center. Text specific. www.ablongman.com/irc
Comprehensive American History Digital Transparency Masters		✓	Instructor Supplement	Vast collection of American history transparency masters. Available exclusively on the Instructor's Resource Center. www.ablongman.com/irc
Discovering American History Through Maps and Views Digital Transparency Masters		✓	Instructor Supplement	Set of 140 full-color digital transparency masters includes cartographic and pictorial maps, views, photos; urban plans and building diagrams; and works of art. Available exclusively on the Instructor's Resource Center. www.ablongman.com/irc
History Digital Media Archive	CD		Instructor Supplement	Contains electronic images, interactive and static maps, and video. Available on CD only.
Visual Archives of American History, Updated Edition	CD		Instructor Supplement	Contains dozens of narrated vignettes and videos as well as hundreds of photos and illustrations. Available on CD only.
Study Guide	✓		Student Supplement	Contains chapter overviews, learning objectives, identifications, mapping exercises, multiple-choice and essay questions, and critical thinking exercises. Available in two volumes. Text specific.
Vango Notes		✓	Student Supplement	Downloadable MP3 audio topic reviews. Includes major themes, key terms, practice tests, and rapid reviews. www.vangonotes.com
Study Card for American History	✓		Student Supplement	Distills course information down to the basics, helping students quickly master the fundamentals and prepare for exams.
Research Navigator Guide	✓	✓	Student Supplement	A book that contains an access code to EBSCO ContentSelect, *The New York Times,* and "Best of the Web."

FOR QUALIFIED COLLEGE ADOPTERS

Name of Supplement	Available in Print	Available Online	Instructor or Student Supplement	Description
Longman American History Atlas	✓		Both	100 full-color maps.
Mapping America: A Guide to Historical Geography	✓		Student Supplement	18 exercises explore the role of geography in history.
Voices of *Created Equal*	✓		Student Supplement	Two-volume collection of primary sources, organized to correspond to the table of contents of *Created Equal*.
America Through the Eyes of Its People	✓		Student Supplement	Two-volume comprehensive anthology of primary sources expertly balances social and political history and includes up-to-date narrative material.
American History Timeline	✓		Student Supplement	Gives students a chronological context to help them understand important political, social, economic, cultural, and technological events.
Sources of the African-American Past	✓		Student Supplement	This collection of primary sources covers key themes in the African-American experience.
Women and the National Experience	✓		Student Supplement	Primary source reader contains both classic and unusual documents describing the history of women in the United States.
Reading the American West	✓		Student Supplement	Primary sources in the history of the American West.
A Short Guide to Writing About History	✓		Student Supplement	Teaches students to write cogent history papers.
American History Firsthand: Working with Primary Sources	✓		Student Supplement	This two-volume collection of loose leaf reproduced primary sources exposes students to archival research.
Longman Penguin Putnam Inc. Value Packs	✓		Student Supplement	A variety of Penguin-Putnam texts are available at discounted prices when bundled with *Created Equal*. Complete list of available titles at www.ablongman.com/penguin.
Library of American Biography Series	✓		Student Supplement	Renowned series of biographies that focus on figures who had a significant impact on American history. Complete list at www.ablongman.com/html/lab.

Jacqueline Jones was born in Christiana, Delaware, a small town of 400 people in the northern part of the state. The local public school was desegregated in 1955, when she was a third grader. That event, combined with the peculiar social etiquette of relations between blacks and whites in the town, sparked her interest in American history. She attended the University of Delaware in nearby Newark and went on to graduate study at the University of Wisconsin, Madison, where she received her Ph.D. in history. Her scholarly interests have evolved over time, focusing on American labor and women's, African American, and southern history. She teaches American history at Brandeis University, where she is Harry S. Truman Professor. In 1999, she received a MacArthur Fellowship.

Dr. Jones is the author of several books, including *Soldiers of Light and Love: Northern Teachers and Georgia Blacks* (1980); *Labor of Love, Labor of Sorrow: Black Women, Work, and Family Since Slavery* (1985), which won the Bancroft Prize and was a finalist for a Pulitzer Prize; *The Dispossessed: America's Underclasses Since the Civil War* (1992); and *American Work: Four Centuries of Black and White Labor* (1998). In 2001, she published a memoir that recounts her childhood in Christiana: *Creek Walking: Growing Up in Delaware in the 1950s*. She recently completed a book titled *Savannah's Civil War*, which spans the period 1854 to 1872 and chronicles the strenuous but largely thwarted efforts of black people in lowcountry Georgia to achieve economic opportunity and full citizenship rights during and after the Civil War.

Peter H. Wood was born in St. Louis (before the famous arch was built). He recalls seeing Jackie Robinson play against the Cardinals, visiting the courthouse where the *Dred Scott* case originated, and traveling up the Mississippi to Hannibal, birthplace of Mark Twain. Summer work on the northern Great Lakes aroused his interest in Native American cultures, past and present. He studied at Harvard (B.A., 1964; Ph.D., 1972) and at Oxford, where he was a Rhodes Scholar (1964–1966). His pioneering book *Black Majority* (1974), concerning slavery in colonial South Carolina, won the Beveridge Prize of the American Historical Association. Since 1975, he has taught early American history and Native American history at Duke University. The topics of his articles range from the French explorer LaSalle to Gerald Ford's pardon of Richard Nixon. He has written a short overview of early African Americans, entitled *Strange New Land*, and he has appeared in several related films on PBS. He has published two books about the famous American painter Winslow Homer and coedited *Powhatan's Mantle: Indians in the Colonial Southeast* (revised, 2007). His demographic essay in that volume provided the first clear picture of population change in the eighteenth-century South.

Dr. Wood has served on the boards of the Highlander Center, Harvard University, Houston's Rothko Chapel, and the Institute of Early American History and Culture in Williamsburg. He is married to colonial historian Elizabeth Fenn. His varied interests include archaeology, documentary film, and growing gourds. He keeps a baseball bat used by Ted Williams beside his desk.

Thomas ("Tim") Borstelmann, the son of a university psychologist, grew up in North Carolina as the youngest child in a family deeply interested in history. His formal education came at Durham Academy, Phillips Exeter Academy in New Hampshire, Stanford University (A.B., 1980), and Duke University (Ph.D., 1990). Informally, he was educated on the basketball courts of the South, the rocky shores of New England, the streets of Dublin, Ireland, the museums of Florence, Italy, and the high-country trails of the Sierra Nevada and the Rocky Mountains. He taught history at Cornell University from 1991 to 2003, when he moved to the University of Nebraska–Lincoln to become the first E. N. and Katherine Thompson Distinguished Professor of Modern World History. Since 1988 he has been married to Lynn Borstelmann, a nurse and hospital administrator, and his highest priority for almost two decades has been serving as the primary parent for their two sons. He is an avid cyclist, runner, swimmer, and skier.

Dr. Borstelmann's first book, *Apartheid's Reluctant Uncle: The United States and Southern Africa in the Early Cold War* (1993), won the Stuart L. Bernath Book Prize of the Society for Historians of Foreign Relations. His second book, *The Cold War and the Color Line: American Race Relations in the Global Arena,* appeared in 2001. At Cornell he won a major teaching award, the Robert and Helen Appel Fellowship. He is currently working on a book about the United States and the world in the 1970s.

Elaine Tyler May grew up in the shadow of Hollywood, performing in neighborhood circuses with her friends. Her passion for American history developed in college when she spent her junior year in Japan. The year was 1968. The Vietnam War was raging, along with turmoil at home. As an American in Asia, often called on to explain her nation's actions, she yearned for a deeper understanding of America's past and its place in the world. She returned home to study history at UCLA, where she earned her B.A., M.A., and Ph.D. She has taught at Princeton and Harvard Universities and since 1978 at the University of Minnesota, where she was recently named Regents Professor. She has written four books examining the relationship between politics, public policy, and private life. Her widely acclaimed *Homeward Bound: American Families in the Cold War Era* was the first study to link the baby boom and suburbia to the politics of the Cold War. The *Chronicle of Higher Education* featured *Barren in the Promised Land: Childless Americans and the Pursuit of Happiness* as a pioneering study of the history of reproduction. *Lingua Franca* named her coedited volume *Here, There, and Everywhere: The Foreign Politics of American Popular Culture* a "Breakthrough Book."

Dr. May served as president of the American Studies Association in 1996 and as Distinguished Fulbright Professor of American History in Dublin, Ireland, in 1997. In 2007 she became president-elect of the Organization of American Historians. She is married to historian Lary May and has three children, who have inherited their parents' passion for history.

Vicki L. Ruiz is a professor of history and Chicano/Latino studies and interim Dean for the School of Humanities at the University of California, Irvine. For her, history remains a grand adventure, one that she began at the kitchen table, listening to the stories of her mother and grandmother, and continued with the help of the local bookmobile. She read constantly as she sat on the dock, catching small fish ("grunts") to be used as bait on her father's fishing boat. As she grew older, she was promoted to working with her mother, selling tickets for the *Blue Sea II.* The first in her family to receive an advanced degree, she graduated from Gulf Coast Community College and Florida State University, then went on to earn a Ph.D. in history at Stanford in 1982. She is the author of *Cannery Women, Cannery Lives* and *From Out of the Shadows: Mexican Women in 20th-Century America* (named a Choice Outstanding Academic Book of 1998 by the American Library Association). She and Virginia Sánchez Korrol have coedited *Latinas in the United States: A Historical Encyclopedia* (named a 2007 Best in Reference work by the New York Public Library). Active in student mentorship projects, summer institutes for teachers, and public humanities programs, Dr. Ruiz served as an appointee to the National Council of the Humanities. In 2006 she became an elected fellow of the Society of American Historians. She is the past president of the Organization of American Historians and currently serves as president of the American Studies Association.

Active in student mentorship projects, summer institutes for teachers, and public humanities programs, Dr. Ruiz served as an appointee to the National Council of the Humanities. In 2006, she became an elected fellow of the Society of American Historians. She is a past president of the Organization of American Historians and the Berkshire Conference on the History of Women. She currently serves as president of the American Studies Association. The mother of two grown sons, she is married to Victor Becerra, urban planner, community activist, and gourmet cook extraordinaire.

> Created Equal *tells stories across generations, regions, and cultures, integrating the lives of individuals within the economic, political, cultural, global, and environmental vectors shaping their lives. We cherish the telling of stories, for it is within these tales that we remember the ánimo y sueños (spirit and dreams) of the American people.*
>
> —*Vicki L. Ruiz*

How Did You First Come to Write This Book?

Elaine: The challenge came from fellow teachers. We had a chance to watch a video recording of a lively conversation with a dozen first-rate history instructors from all across the country. They loved teaching American history, but they felt that current textbooks held them back. Listening to them talk showed me there was a real need for a book that was broad and lively, combining social and political history. When Longman asked if we would undertake such a book, we all agreed that the timing was right.

Jacqueline: I thought that writing a new kind of text would be a real intellectual challenge. We have the opportunity to rethink and reconfigure the traditional American history narrative, and that's exciting.

Peter: At the time, I was teaching one of those special classes, a group of history majors that really clicked. Four of the best students had parents from other countries—South Africa, Mexico, Haiti, Vietnam—and all four were fascinated by American history. I remember thinking, "I'd love to be part of a team of historians who developed a text that would excite the whole broad spectrum of young Americans."

Thomas: Writing a textbook was attractive because it's so complementary to what I do in the classroom, particularly teaching the introductory American history survey. Having the chance to try to tell the entire story of the American past was exciting as a balance to the other work we do.

Tell Us About the Title—*Created Equal.*

Jacqueline: The title reflects our commitment to be inclusive in our coverage of different groups and the part they played in shaping American history. Of course, we are invoking the Declaration of Independence: "We hold these truths to be self-evident, that all men are created equal." That document, and those words, have inspired countless individuals, groups, and nations around the world.

Peter: We all recognize the phrase "created equal" from the Declaration of Independence, but we rarely ponder it. For me, it represents an affirmation of humanity, the family of mankind. But it also raises the deepest American theme: the endless struggles over defining whose equality will be recognized. I suppose you could say that there is equality in birth and death, but a great deal of inequality in between. Many of those inequities—and their partial removal—drive the story of American history.

Tom Paine understood this in 1776 when he published *Common Sense*. Months before the Declaration of Independence appeared, Paine put it this way: "Mankind being originally equal in the order of creation, the equality could only be destroyed by some subsequent circumstance."

How and Why Did You Choose the Themes That Structure the Text?

Thomas: We have chosen to highlight two important and overlapping themes in *Created Equal*. One is American diversity and social inclusion over time; the other is increasing globalization and its implications over centuries. Selecting these twin themes reflects what we see as the current and future state of the field of U.S. history, but our choice is also meant to address the vital needs of an emerging generation of students. The prominence of multiculturalism in recent decades made clear that identity remains a central piece of the American story. But too much attention to how individual Americans understand and identify themselves (by religion, class, region, sex, race, or ethnicity) has often led to a discounting of the political and economic structures of American society. In exploring American cultural diversity, it is important to remember that who has material wealth and power at any time, and how they use it, is also fundamental in shaping the American story. Second, the increasing globalization of the U.S. economy and American society in recent decades (through rising immigration, for example, and changing trade patterns) has reminded us of how deeply the United States has always been engaged with the rest of the world. Because America is an immigrant nation and the modern world's superpower, America's foreign and domestic affairs have always been intertwined. And the deepening awareness in recent decades of the fragility of the earth's environment has added to our global awareness. Indeed, for a new generation of students, the environment itself represents the clearest example of the interconnectedness of American and international history.

Jacqueline: It was time to integrate recent scholarship related to the many different groups that have been part of the American story, and to open up that story to include all geographical areas. For far too long, U.S. history seemed to be a tale told from, and about, the eastern seaboard. Giving special attention to the nation's significant social and environmental diversity has allowed us to explore in fresh ways how American cultural, political, and economic developments have been influenced by the nation's natural resources and landscape—and vice versa. This approach helps students to understand that differences in political and material resources, in access to power, have played a significant part in shaping the country's history. We balance this perspective by showing how America emerged as a uniquely open and middle-class nation. The United States has attracted immigrants from all over the world throughout its history, making us a strikingly global nation. No other society has so many roots stretching all around the world.

Elaine: *Created Equal* brings together aspects of the nation's story that are usually examined separately. It demonstrates that the people who make change are not only those in major positions of power; they are also ordinary Americans from all backgrounds. We illuminate ways that diverse Americans have seized opportunities to improve their lives and their nation. We also address the ongoing interaction between the United States and the rest of the world, examining the nation in a truly global context. We started with an understanding that the North American land itself is a major player in the story—the environment, the different regions, and the ways in which people, businesses, public policies, and the forces of nature have shaped it. Our emphasis on the process of globalization over time helps to broaden that perspective. As American citizens inhabiting a "shrinking" planet, we are all learning to think harder than ever about complex links between the local and the global—past, present, and future.

How Is the Book Organized?

Peter: History is the study of change over time, so chronology becomes extremely important. We wanted to emphasize central themes, but we wanted to explore and explain how they related to one another at any given moment. So we made a conscious decision to be more chronological in our presentation than many recent texts. It makes for less confusion, less jumping back and forth in time, than when broad themes are played out separately. After all, this is the way we lead our own lives—sequentially.

Jacqueline: Most of the ten separate parts in the book cover about a generation each. The parts give students a sense of the big picture over a longer period—the way our themes fit together and the impact of major developments on a particular generation of Americans. The chronological organization of the book forces us to understand the "wholeness" of any particular period—to consider links among political, social, economic, and cultural developments. By maintaining a strictly chronological focus, we hope to show students how the events and developments of any one period are intertwined with each other. For example, for coverage of the period after the end of the Civil War, it is important to show links between the Indian wars in the West and the process of Reconstruction in the South. In most texts, those regional perspectives are separated into different chapters, but in *Created Equal*, these connections are presented together in Chapter 15.

How Has Teaching the Text Influenced You?

Jacqueline: In teaching the text I've learned more about what interests and challenges my students. One day we had a long discussion about a particularly gruesome photograph of a black man who was the victim of a lynching. Is there a place for such graphic and disturbing pictures in a survey text? We discussed whether students needed to see those images, and what they might learn from them. So after writing the material, putting together the features, and choosing pictures, I find it gratifying to see all those elements actually generate a great discussion in the classroom.

Peter: Even when you have been teaching for decades, you learn new things every year. That was especially true for me recently, when I decided to teach an overview of U.S. history in one fifteen-week term. I called it "One Nation—One Semester," and we zipped through *Created Equal* at a pace of two chapters per week. You would think that on such a fast-moving train, everything would become a blur. But it didn't work that way. Instead, it was more like a plane ride, where we could look down from a high altitude, moving fast but watching things unfold below us. Sure, some details were lost in our rapid ride, but students were able to make broad connections that they would not have seen otherwise. "I liked the chance to learn about specific trees," one of them told me, "but we got to see the whole forest, too."

Thomas: I love connecting the big picture to the smallest details of daily life. *Created Equal* does this, and teaching it forces me to think constantly about these connections. In my classroom we spend a lot of time wrestling with broad themes of diplomacy, globalization, national politics, cultural diversity, and economics. But the text helps us link these themes directly to everyday choices, from grocery shopping and music styles to how we read newspapers and the size of houses.

Elaine: During each particular time period, I find myself more aware of the connections among diverse themes. That reflects the way we wrote the book. I teach in a more layered way now, forging links among cultural, political, social, and economic developments rather than carving out those topics separately.

What Were Your Goals in Tackling a Major Revision for the Third Edition?

Thomas: We love lively writing. The first two editions were well written, but we were especially eager to use this major revision to make the text still more engaging and accessible for students. We have also worked very hard to draw even greater attention to the global connections in the American past. In the years since the first two editions, globalization has accelerated, and the Third Edition reflects that reality. Older, more narrow national histories are a thing of the past.

Vicki: For me, the contextualization of stories was important—to explain more clearly why these voices mattered and what they tell us about the American past. I understood the historical context, but at times I forget that students appreciate additional background so they can place individuals within their historical moments. I want our readers to take away from the text the messiness of the past—to challenge a paradigm of an inevitable "march of progress." So many disparate groups and regions have shaped our national history.

Jacqueline: I hoped to streamline the previous edition and at the same time retain those elements that are most appealing—the stories of individuals, the unique blend of social and political history. I was also eager to expand our coverage of foreign relations, broadly defined; it makes the book fresh and timely.

Elaine: History is not just the telling of events from the past. It is an interpretive art. The way we interpret history—making links, weighing priorities—is naturally shaped by the times in which we live. The world of today changes quickly – it has altered dramatically since we wrote the first and even the second edition of Created Equal. I wanted to consider the American past again through the interpretive lens of the present, attentive to the stories, themes, and events that have shaped the nation and the world we all inhabit.

What Do You Hope Students Will Get Out of the Book?

Peter: I want readers to connect. In a good history class, or a strong history book, you start to care about, argue with, and connect to the persons you are studying. Pretty soon, their tough choices and surprising experiences in life start to resemble our own in ways we never expected, even though their worlds are dramatically different from ours.

Jacqueline: Many texts only pay lip service to diversity. Non-elite groups are tacked on, marginalized, or segregated from the "real" story of America. In *Created Equal*, by presenting a more inclusive view of the past, we want to give students a fuller and more accurate account of American history.

As authors, we could not have completed this project without the loving support of our families. We wish to thank Jeffrey Abramson, Lil Fenn, Lynn Borstelmann, Lary May, and Victor Becerra for their interest, forbearance, and encouragement over the course of many drafts and several editions. Our children of all ages have been a source of inspiration, as have our many students, past and present. We remain grateful to scores of colleagues and friends who have helped shape this book, both directly and indirectly, in more ways than they know.

Special thanks are due to Steve Fraser for his insightful suggestions at a crucial time. Along the way, Rob Heinrich, Matthew Becker, Scott Laderman, Matt Basso, Chad Cover, Eben Miller, Andrea Sachs, Mary Strunk, Melissa Williams, Louis Balizet and Jason Stahl provided useful assistance; their aid was invaluable. Two dedicated teachers, Jim Hijiya and Hannah Page, each read the entire manuscript and offered many helpful comments that have made the Third Edition stronger. We are grateful for their hard work.

We thank all of the creative people at Longman (and there are many) who have believed in our project and have had a hand in bringing this book to life. From the start, Priscilla McGeehon, Betty Slack, and Sue Westmoreland offered us their expertise and friendship. Michael Boezi has embraced *Created Equal* and given it his full and effective support, encouraging, pushing, and humoring us in all the right ways. We are especially grateful to Marion Castellucci, who has overseen this new edition with such care and understanding. She has sharpened our thoughts, clarified our prose, and kept us on schedule with wonderful grace and good spirits.

We also wish to express our deep gratitude to our consultants and reviewers whose candid and constructive comments about the Second Edition text and the Third Edition manuscript contributed greatly to this revision. Collectively, they pushed us hard with their high standards, tough questions, and shrewd advice. The thoughtful criticisms and generous suggestions from these colleagues have helped improve the book.

Terry Alford,
Northern Virginia Community College

Marynita Anderson,
Nassau Community College

Melissa Anyiwo,
University of Tennessee, Chattanooga

Emily Blanck,
Rowan University

Rebecca Borton,
Northwest State Community College

J. D. Bowers,
Northern Illinois University

Kimberley Breuer,
University of Texas, Arlington

Charlotte Brooks,
State University of New York, Albany

Vernon Burton,
University of Illinois at Urbana-Champaign

Eduardo Canedo,
Columbia University

Nancy Carnevale,
Montclair State University

James S. Day,
University of Montevallo

Christian R. Esh,
Northwest Nazarene University

Barbara C. Fertig,
Armstrong Atlantic State University

Colin Fisher,
University of San Diego

Jennifer Fronc,
Virginia Commonwealth University

Jessica Gerard,
Ozarks Technical Community College

Traci Hodgson,
Chemeketa Community College

Charlotte Haller,
Worcester State College

Rose Holz,
University of Nebraska, Lincoln

Creed Hyatt,
Lehigh Carbon Community College

Michael Jacobs,
University of Wisconsin, Baraboo

Jeff Janowick,
Lansing Community College

John S. Kemp,
Truckee Meadows Community College

Cynthia Kennedy,
Clarion University of Pennsylvania

Michael Lansing,
Augsburg College

Chana Kai Lee,
University of Georgia

Kyle Longley,
Arizona State University

Eric Mayer,
Victor Valley College

Beth Ruffin McIntyre,
Missouri State University

Jennifer McLaughlin,
Sacred Heart University

Eva Mo,
Modesto Junior College

Sandy Moats,
*University of Wisconsin,
Parkside*

Carl H. Moneyhon,
*University of Arkansas
at Little Rock*

Matthew Mooney,
Santa Barbara City College

Daniel S. Murphree,
University of Texas, Tyler

Peter C. Murray,
Methodist University

C. Samuel Nelson,
Ridgewater College

Jason C. Newman,
Cosumnes River College

Ting Ni,
Saint Mary's University

Steven Noll,
University of Florida

David R. Novak,
Purdue University, Calumet

Daniel Prosterman,
Syracuse University

Nannette Regua,
Evergreen Valley College

Thomas Rowland,
*University of Wisconsin,
Oshkosh*

Leonard Sadosky,
Iowa State University

Carli Schiffner,
*Yakima Valley Community
College*

Cornelia F. Sexauer,
University of Wisconsin

David J. Silverman,
George Washington University

Melissa Soto,
Cuyahoga Community College

Robert A. Taylor,
Florida Institute of Technology

David Tegeder,
Santa Fe Community College

Emily Teipe,
Fullerton College

Gary E. Thompson,
Tulsa Community College

Michael M. Topp,
University of Texas, El Paso

Sylvia Tyson,
Texas Lutheran University

Anne M. Valk,
*John Nicholas Brown Center,
Brown University*

David Voelker,
*University of Wisconsin,
Green Bay*

Randall Walton,
New Mexico Junior College

Charles Westmoreland,
University of Mississippi

Larry C. Wilson,
San Jacinto College

David Wolcott,
Miami University

Jason Young,
*State University of New York,
Buffalo*

Finally, we also owe much to the many conscientious historians who reviewed the First and Second editions throughout many drafts and offered valuable suggestions. We acknowledge with gratitude the contributions of the following:

Ken Adderley,
Upper Iowa University

Leslie Alexander,
Ohio State University

John Andrew,
Franklin and Marshall College

Yvonne Baldwin,
Morehead State University

Abel Bartley,
University of Akron

Donald Scott Barton,
*Central Carolina Technical
College*

Mia Bay,
Rutgers University

Marjorie Berman,
Red Rocks Community College

Chris Bierwith,
*Treasure Valley Community
College*

Charles Bolton,
*University of Arkansas, Little
Rock*

Susan Burch,
Gallaudet University

Tommy Bynum,
Georgia Perimeter College

Robert B. Carey,
Empire State College, SUNY

Todd Carney,
Southern Oregon University

JoAnn D. Carpenter,
*Florida Community College,
Jacksonville*

Kathleen Carter,
Highpoint University

Jacqueline M. Cavalier,
*Community College of
Allegheny County*

Jonathan Chu,
University of Massachusetts

Amy E. Davis,
*University of California, Los
Angeles*

Judy DeMark,
Northern Michigan University

Ann Denkler,
Shenandoah University

James A. Denton,
University of Colorado

Joseph A. Devine,
Stephen F. Austin University

Paul E. Doutrich,
York College of Pennsylvania

Margaret Dwight,
*North Carolina Agricultural
and Technical University*

Susan Edwards,
Cy-Fair College

Ronald B. Frankum,
Millersville University

Nancy Gabin,
Purdue University

Lori Ginzberg,
Pennsylvania State University

Gregory Goodwin,
Bakersfield College

Amy S. Greenberg,
Pennsylvania State University

Mike Haridopolos,
Brevard Community College

Nadine Isitani Hata,
El Camino College

James Hedtke,
Cabrini College

Andrew M. Honker,
Arizona State University

Adam Howard,
University of Florida

Fred Hoxie,
University of Illinois

Tera Hunter,
Carnegie Mellon University

David Jaffe,
City College of New York

Jeremy Johnson,
Northwest College

Yvonne Johnson,
*Central Missouri State
University*

Kurt Keichtle,
University of Wisconsin

Anne Klejment,
University of St. Thomas

Dennis Kortheuer,
*California State University,
Long Beach*

Rebecca A. Kosary,
Texas Lutheran University

Michael L. Krenn,
Appalachian State University

Joel Kunze,
Upper Iowa University

Joseph Laythe,
*Edinboro College of
Pennsylvania*

Chana Kai Lee,
Indiana University

Kurt E. Leichtle,
*University of Wisconsin,
River Falls*

Dan Letwin,
*Pennsylvania State
University*

Gaylen Lewis,
Bakersfield College

Xiaobing Li,
*University of Central
Oklahoma*

Mike Light,
*Grand Rapids Community
College*

Kenneth Lipartito,
Florida International University

Kyle Longley,
Arizona State University

Edith L. Macdonald,
University of Central Florida

Michelle Espinosa Martinez,
St. Philip's College

Lorie Maltby,
Henderson Community College

Sandra Mathews-Lamb,
Nebraska Wesleyan University

Constance M. McGovern,
Frostburg State University

Henry McKiven,
University of South Alabama

James H. Merrell,
Vassar College

Earl Mulderink,
Southern Utah State University

Steven Noll,
University of Florida

Jim Norris,
North Dakota State University

Elsa Nystrom,
Kennesaw State University

Gaye T. M. Okoh,
*University of Texas, San
Antonio*

Keith Pacholl,
*California State University,
Fullerton*

William Pelz,
Elgin Community College

Melanie Perrault,
University of Central Arkansas

Delores D. Petersen,
Foothill College

Robert Pierce,
Foothill College

Louis Potts,
*University of Missouri,
Kansas City*

Sarah Purcell,
Central Michigan University

Niler Pyeatt,
Wayland Baptist University

Steven Reschly,
Truman State University

Arthur Robinson,
Santa Rosa Junior College

Robert E. Rook,

Fort Hays State University

Thomas J. Rowland,
*University of Wisconsin,
Oshkosh*

Steven Ruggles,
University of Minnesota

Christine Sears,
University of Delaware

Rebecca Shoemaker,
Indiana State University

Howard Shore,
Columbia River High School

James Sidbury,
University of Texas

Mike Sistrom,
Greensboro College

Arwin D. Smallwood,
Bradley University

Melissa Soto-Schwartz,
Cuyahoga Community College

Margaret Spratt,
*California University
of Pennsylvania*

Rachel Standish,
Foothill College

Jon Stauff,
St. Ambrose University

David Steigerwald,
Ohio State University, Marion

Kay Stockbridge,
*Central Carolina Technical
College*

Stephen Tallackson,
Purdue University, Calumet

Daniel Thorp,
Virginia Tech University

Michael M. Topp,
University of Texas, El Paso

Clifford Trafzer,
*University of California,
Riverside*

Deborah Gray White,
Rutgers University

Scott Wong,
Williams College

Bill Woodward,
Seattle Pacific University

Nancy Zens,
*Central Oregon Community
College*

David Zonderman,
North Carolina State University

Part One

North American Founders

Created
Equal

First Founders

CHAPTER OUTLINE

- Ancient America

- A Thousand Years of Change: 500 to 1500

- Linking the Continents

- Spain Enters the Americas

- The Protestant Reformation Plays Out in America

Illustration by Andy Buttram courtesy of the Illinois State Museum

■ The skeleton of Kennewick Man revealed an enlarged right arm, strengthened by hurling spears with the ancient throwing device known as an atlatl.

"This is real old C.S.I.," Hugh Berryman told reporters. As a forensic anthropologist, Dr. Berryman knew all about "crime scene investigation." He had come to Seattle in July 2005 as part of an eleven-member team to examine the bones of a deceased human. "It's the type of skeleton that comes along once in a lifetime," commented another member of the team.

In 1996, two outdoorsmen near the Columbia River in Kennewick, Washington, had stumbled on the bones of a middle-aged man. At first, authorities guessed they had the corpse of an early white settler. But tests revealed it to be much older—9,400 years old, in fact. That touched off years of legal wrangling over control of one of the most ancient skeletons ever found in the Americas.

When the team of experts finally won the right to examine Kennewick Man, they found him to be five feet nine inches tall, roughly forty years old, with early arthritis in his knees. Healed injuries to his head and ribs suggested a tough life. Years before his death, an enemy attack had embedded a stone point in his right hipbone. "This is like an extraordinary rare book," Berryman observed, "and we are reading it one page at a time."

The discovery of Kennewick Man followed a century of mounting study into when and how human beings first came to inhabit North America. In 1907, on the three-hundredth anniversary of Jamestown, amazingly little was understood about who had lived in North America before the first successful English colonists arrived. Everyone knew that the Italian explorer Christopher Columbus had reached the Caribbean while attempting to sail to the

Indies for Spain in 1492. They had learned in school that Columbus, thinking he had reached the Asian islands close to India and China ("the Indies"), mistakenly lumped America's peoples together as "Indians." But most Americans still knew very little about who the earliest North Americans really were.

In the past century, that has changed dramatically, as scholars have steadily learned more about the continent's first inhabitants. An expanding American history now stretches back in time far before the Jamestown settlement and reaches broadly from coast to coast. Its earliest roots lie with the ancient Indians of the continent over many millennia. In addition, the foreigners who suddenly intruded into portions of the Native American world in the sixteenth century— speaking Spanish, French, and occasionally English—also represent a significant beginning. All these people now number among America's first founders.

Ancient America

■ *What types of evidence are used to explain the arrival of humans in North America?*

Early in the twentieth century near Folsom, New Mexico, archaeologists found a man-made spear point resting between the rib bones of a type of ancient bison that had been extinct for 10,000 years. They named such thin projectile tips Folsom points, after the site. Their discovery proved that humans had lived and hunted on the continent far earlier than scientists had ever imagined. It sparked a revolution in North American archaeology. Soon after the Folsom find, amateurs at nearby Clovis, New Mexico, spotted some large, well-chipped spearheads. In 1932, collectors found more of these so-called Clovis points in the same vicinity, this time beside the tooth of an extinct mammoth. They lay underneath a soil layer containing Folsom points, so they were clearly even older.

IMAGE
Clovis Points

Since then, scientists have unearthed Clovis-like points throughout much of North America. According to the latest calculations, humans started creating these weapons roughly 13,900 years ago and ceased about 12,900 years ago. Between those early dates, therefore, people were hunting widely on the bountiful continent. Using scant remaining traces, such as spear tips, archaeologists continue to push back and refine the estimated date for the appearance of the first people in the Americas. Recently, they have unearthed evidence suggesting the possible presence of pre-Clovis inhabitants.

THE QUESTION OF ORIGINS

Like all other peoples, Native American societies retain rich and varied accounts of their own origins. No amount of scientific data can diminish or replace tribal creation stories that serve an important cultural purpose. In these powerful sagas, America's first human inhabitants emerge from the earth, are created by other animals, or receive life from the Great Spirit. At the same time, modern researchers continue to compile evidence about the origin and migrations of the diverse peoples who inhabited the Americas for thousands of years before the arrival of Christopher Columbus.

DOCUMENT
Iroquois Creation Story

Scientists have determined that the most recent ancestors of modern humans moved from Africa to spread across the Eurasian landmass, the area comprising Europe and Asia, scarcely 70,000 years ago. By 40,000 years ago some of these Stone Age hunter-gatherers had already reached Australia. Others lived on the steppes of central Asia and the frozen tundra of

■ Archaeologists digging at Cactus Hill, Virginia, and several other sites have unearthed artifacts that suggest human habitation before the arrival of hunters using Clovis points. The foreground objects are laid out clockwise by apparent age, with the most recent at the top. Clovis-like spearheads appear in the second group. The third and fourth groups, taken from lower layers of soil, are thought to be older items, some reaching back well beyond 14,000 years. With the most primitive tools, it becomes difficult to separate implements made by humans from natural rock fragments.

Kenneth Garrett/National Geographic Image Collection

Siberia. They had perfected the tools they needed to survive in a cold climate: flint spear points for killing mammoths, reindeer, and the woolly rhinoceros; and bone needles to sew warm, waterproof clothes out of animal skin.

Over thousands of years, bands of these northern hunters migrated east across Siberia in search of game. Eventually they arrived at the region where the Bering Strait now separates Russia from Alaska. The geography of this area has fluctuated over time because of dramatic changes in global climate. Between 25,000 and 11,000 years ago, cold conditions expanded arctic ice caps, trapping vast quantities of the earth's water in the form of huge glaciers. As a result, ocean levels sank by 300 feet—enough to expose a low bridge of land 600 miles wide between Asia and America.

The Bering land bridge formed part of a frigid, windswept region known as Beringia. Small groups of people could have subsisted in this cold landscape by hunting mammoths and musk oxen. As the climate warmed and the ocean rose again, some might have headed farther east onto higher ground in Alaska. If so, these newcomers would have been cut off permanently from Siberia as water once more submerged the land bridge. But the same warming process also eventually opened a pathway through the glaciers blanketing northern America.

This ice-free corridor along the eastern slope of the Rocky Mountains could account for the sudden appearance of Clovis hunters across much of North America nearly 14,000 years ago. Small bands of people, armed with razor-sharp Clovis points, spread rapidly across the continent, destroying successive herds of large animals that had never faced human predators before. According to this theory, generations of hunters known as **Paleo-Indians** moved swiftly south as local game supplies dwindled. They would have migrated as far as the tip of South America within several thousand years.

In recent decades, three new developments have complicated the picture. At Cactus Hill, Virginia, and other sites, archaeologists have uncovered artifacts suggesting the presence of immediate predecessors to the Clovis people. In addition, a provocative discovery in South America—a campsite at Monte Verde, Chile, dating back more than 14,000 years—suggests to some that small groups may have used simple boats on a coastal route around the North Pacific rim. Reaching the Northwest Coast, their descendants could have hugged the shoreline to reach South America by water in gradual stages. Finally, genetic comparisons of different peoples, present and past, are yielding increasingly specific, if controversial, details about

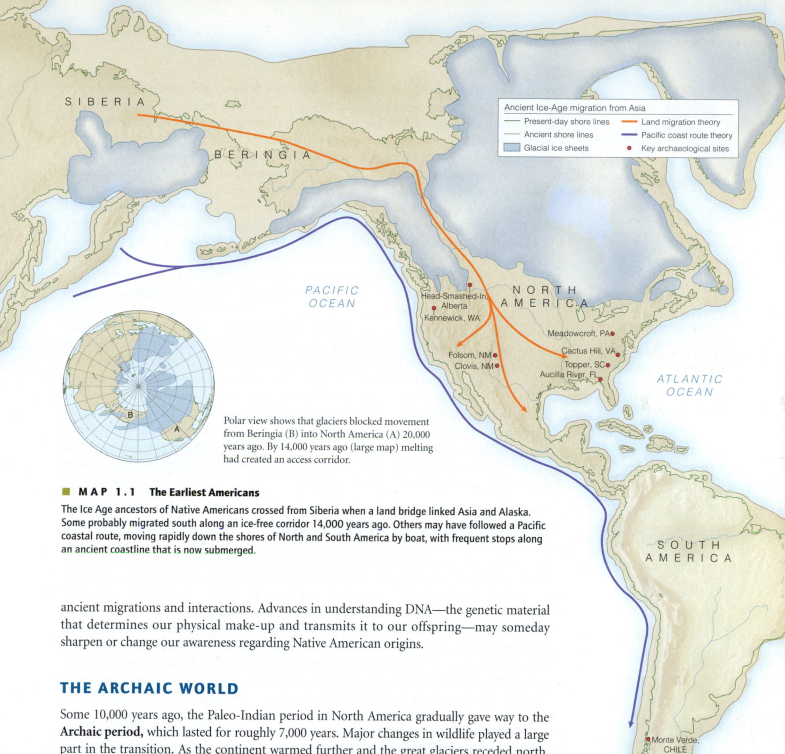

Polar view shows that glaciers blocked movement from Beringia (B) into North America (A) 20,000 years ago. By 14,000 years ago (large map) melting had created an access corridor.

■ MAP 1.1   The Earliest Americans

The Ice Age ancestors of Native Americans crossed from Siberia when a land bridge linked Asia and Alaska. Some probably migrated south along an ice-free corridor 14,000 years ago. Others may have followed a Pacific coastal route, moving rapidly down the shores of North and South America by boat, with frequent stops along an ancient coastline that is now submerged.

ancient migrations and interactions. Advances in understanding DNA—the genetic material that determines our physical make-up and transmits it to our offspring—may someday sharpen or change our awareness regarding Native American origins.

THE ARCHAIC WORLD

Some 10,000 years ago, the Paleo-Indian period in North America gradually gave way to the **Archaic period,** which lasted for roughly 7,000 years. Major changes in wildlife played a large part in the transition. As the continent warmed further and the great glaciers receded north, over one hundred of America's largest species disappeared. These included mammoths, mastodons, horses, camels, and the great long-horned bison. Researchers debate whether these large animals were hunted to extinction, wiped out by disease, or destroyed by climate change.

Whatever the causes—and probably there were many—human groups had to adapt to the shifting conditions. They developed new methods of survival. Inhabitants turned to the smaller bison, similar to modern-day ones, that had managed to survive and flourish on the northern plains. Archaic-era hunters learned to drive herds over cliffs and use the remains for food, clothing, and tools. One such bison jump is located in eastern Colorado. Another mass kill location, known as Head-Smashed-In, is in western Alberta; native peoples used this Canadian site for 7,000 years. A weighted spear-throwing device, called an atlatl, let hunters such as the Kennewick Man bring down medium-sized game. Archaic peoples also devised nets, hooks, and snares for catching birds, fish, and small animals. By 4,000 years ago, they were even using duck decoys in the Great Basin of Utah and Nevada.

Though genetically similar, far-flung bands of Archaic Indians developed diverse cultures as they adapted to very different landscapes and environments. Nothing illustrates this diversity more clearly than speech. A few early languages branched into numerous language families, then divided further into hundreds of separate tongues. Similar cultural variations emerged in everything from diet and shelter to folklore and spiritual beliefs.

All of these variations reflected local conditions, and each represented an experiment that might potentially lead to more elaborate social arrangements. Eventually in the Americas, as elsewhere, the cultivation of domesticated plants led to settled **horticultural** societies. A more stable food supply allowed the creation of surpluses, prompting larger permanent villages, wider trade, and a greater accumulation of goods. With this settled lifestyle, daily subsistence no longer required everyone's labor. With specialized tasks came greater social hierarchy—stratification into distinct classes—and the emergence of hereditary chiefdoms where one powerful extended family wielded political control.

> *Bands of Archaic Indians developed diverse cultures as they adapted to very different landscapes and environments.*

Frequently, a class of priests appeared near the top of the expanding hierarchy, mediating between the people and a god or gods who were intimately involved in human affairs. Slaves, unknown in hunting and gathering societies, appeared at the bottom of the hierarchy, since captives could be put to work for their conquerors. An expanded labor force not only produced more food; it created public works that showed (and enhanced) the power of the chiefs and priests. As populations grew and social structures became more complex, greater specialization ensued. This allowed the development of more extensive communities with more elaborate political and religious activities and greater concentrations of power. But such developments were slow and uneven, depending on local conditions.

THE RISE OF MAIZE AGRICULTURE

One condition remained common to all the various Archaic American groups, despite their emerging regional differences: they all lacked domesticated animals. Diverse peoples living in Eurasia had managed to domesticate five important species—sheep, goats, pigs, cows, and horses—by 6,000 years ago, leading to the creation of stable pastoral societies. But none of these mammals existed in the Americas, nor did camels, donkeys, or water buffalo, the other large animals that lend themselves to domestication. Archaic Indians, like their Asian forebears, did possess dogs, and settlers in the Andes domesticated the llama over 5,000 years ago. Herds of buffalo and deer could be followed, and even managed and exploited in various ways. But no mammal remaining in the Americas could readily be tamed to provide humans with milk, meat, hides, and hauling power.

Although their prospects for domesticating animals were severely limited, early Americans had many more options when it came to the domestication of plants. Humans managed to domesticate plants independently in five different areas around the world, and three of those regions were located in the Americas. First, across parts of South America, inhabitants learned to cultivate root crops of potatoes and manioc (also known as cassava, which yields a nutritious starch). Second, in **Mesoamerica** (modern-day Mexico and Central America), people gradually brought squash, beans, and maize (corn) under cultivation—three foods that complement one another effectively in dietary terms.

Maize agriculture became a crucial ingredient for the growth of complex societies in the Americas, but its development and diffusion took time. Unlike wheat, the Eurasian cereal crop that offered a high yield from the start, maize took thousands of years of cultivation in the Americas to evolve into an extremely productive food source. The differences between Mesoamerica and North America proved substantial when it came to mastering maize agriculture. Southwestern Indians in North America began growing thumb-sized ears of maize only about 3,000 years ago (at a time of increasing rainfall), well after the crop had taken hold in Mesoamerica. More than a thousand years later, maize reached eastern North America, where it adapted slowly to the cooler climate and shorter growing season.

In the East, a different agriculture had already taken hold, centered on other once-wild plants. This was the third zone where the independent domestication of plants occurred in the Americas. As early as 4,000 years ago, eastern Indians at dozens of Archaic sites were cultivating domesticated squash and sunflowers. These domesticated plants provided supplemental food sources for eastern communities that continued to subsist primarily by hunting and gathering until the arrival of maize agriculture in the eastern woodlands during the first millennium C.E.

About 3,000 years ago, as maize cultivation began in the Southwest and gardens of squash and sunflowers appeared in the Northeast, the first of several powerful Mesoamerican cultures—the Olmec—emerged in the lowlands along the southwestern edge of the Gulf of Mexico. Their name meant "those who live in the land of rubber," for they had learned how to turn the milky juice of several plants into an unusual elastic substance. The Olmec, considered the "mother culture" of Mesoamerica, grew maize and manioc in abundance, and their surplus of food supported a hierarchical society. They built large burial mounds and pyramids, revered the jaguar in their religion, developed a complex calendar, and played a distinctive game with a large ball of solid rubber. Since they traded widely with peoples across Mesoamerica, they passed on these cultural traits, which reappeared later in other societies in the region.

> *As early as 4,000 years ago, eastern Indians at dozens of Archaic sites were cultivating domesticated squash and sunflowers.*

Olmec traders, traveling by coastal canoe, may even have encountered and influenced the culture that existed in northeast Louisiana 4,200 to 2,700 years ago. The Poverty Point culture (named for a key archaeological site) involved trade networks on the lower Mississippi River and its tributaries. It stands as a mysterious precursor to the mound-building societies of the Mississippi Valley that emerged much later. Remnants of these more extensive Mississippian cultures still existed when newcomers from Europe arrived to stay, around 1500. In many parts of North America, smaller and less stratified Archaic cultures remained intact well into the era of European colonization. To subsist, they combined hunting for a variety of animals with gathering and processing local plant foods.

A Thousand Years of Change: 500 to 1500

■ *How did complex cultures arise in the Americas in the millennium before Columbus?*

The millennium stretching from the fifth century to the explorations of Columbus in the fifteenth century witnessed dramatic and far-reaching changes in the separate world of the Americas. In the warm and temperate regions on both sides of the equator, empires rose and fell as maize agriculture and elaborate irrigation systems provided food surpluses, allowing the creation of cities and the emergence of hierarchical societies.

On the coast of Peru, between roughly 100 and 800, the Moche people created delicate gold work, intricate pottery, and huge pyramids to honor the sun. In the 1400s, centuries after the Moche and their neighbors disappeared, the expansive Inca empire emerged in their place. Inca emperors, ruling from the capital at Cuzco, prompted the construction of a vast road system throughout the Peruvian Andes. Stonemasons built large storage facilities at provincial centers to hold food for garrisons of soldiers and to store tribute items such as gold and feathers destined for the capital. Until the empire's fall in the 1530s, officials leading pack trains of llamas ferried goods to and from Cuzco along mountainous roadways.

MAP

Pre-Columbian Societies of the Americas

■ MAP 1.2 America in the Millennium before Columbus, 500–1500
A number of distinctive cultures emerged in the Americas during the ten centuries before 1500. Most learned from their predecessors—Mississippians from Hopewell, and Aztec from Maya, for example—but debate continues over the full extent of trade and travel networks at any given time.

Similarly, Mesoamerica also saw a series of impressive civilizations—from the Maya to the Aztec—in the millennium spanning 500 to 1500 in the western calendar. Developments in North America in the same millennium were very different, but they bear enough resemblance to patterns in Mesoamerica to raise difficult questions about early contacts. Did significant migrations northward from Mesoamerica ever take place? And if not, were there substantial trade links at times, allowing certain materials, techniques, ideas, and seeds to reach North American peoples? Or did the continent's distinctive societies, such as the Anasazi in the Southwest and the Cahokia mound builders on the Mississippi River, develop almost entirely independently?

VALLEYS OF THE SUN: THE MESOAMERICAN EMPIRES

In Mesoamerica, the Maya and the Aztec established rich empires where worship of the sun was central to their religious beliefs. Mayan culture flourished between 300 and 900. The Maya controlled a domain stretching from the lowlands of the Yucatan peninsula to the highlands of what is now southern Mexico, Guatemala, Honduras, and El Salvador—an area half the size of Texas. They derived their elaborate calendar—a fifty-two-year cycle, with each year made up of twenty-day months—and many other aspects of their culture from the earlier Olmec, but they devised their own distinctive civilization. The Maya built huge stone temples and held ritual bloodletting ceremonies to appease their gods. Recently, researchers have deciphered the complex pictographs, or glyphs, that appear throughout Mayan art. New discoveries are pushing back the earliest dates for Mayan culture.

The Maya, like the Moche in Peru, declined rapidly after 750, and dominance in Mesoamerica moved farther west, where great cities had arisen in the highlands of central Mexico. The people who constructed the metropolis of Teotihuacan in the Mexican highlands remain an enigma. They appear to have traded with the Maya and perhaps with the Olmec before that. They laid out their immense city in a grid, dominated by the 200-foot Pyramid of the Sun. By 500, the city held more than 100,000 inhabitants, making it one of the largest in the world. But Teotihuacan's society declined fast, for unknown reasons, succeeded first by the Toltec and then by the Aztec.

The Aztec (or Mexica) had migrated to the central Valley of Mexico from the north in the twelfth century. Looked down on at first by the local people, they swiftly rose to power through strategic alliances and military skill. According to legend, the Aztec war god instructed Aztec priests to look for the place where a great eagle perched on a cactus. They found such a spot, on a swampy island in Lake Texcoco. By the 1400s the Aztec had transformed the island into Tenochtitlán, an imposing urban center, located on the site of modern Mexico City.

> *Looked down on at first by the local people, the Aztec swiftly rose to power through strategic alliances and military skill.*

The impressive city of Tenochtitlán, surrounded by Lake Texcoco and linked to shore by causeways, became the Aztec capital. Its architecture imitated the ruined temple city of Teotihuacan, which lay thirty-five miles to the north. The Aztec also adopted many other features of the cultures they had displaced. They used the cyclical fifty-two-year Mesoamerican calendar, and they worshipped the great god Quetzalcoatl, the plumed serpent associated with wind and revered by the Toltec, their predecessors in the Valley of Mexico. Constant military readiness, clear gender roles, strict civic order, and a pessimistic worldview characterized Aztec society.

Eager to expand their empire, the Aztec launched fierce wars against neighboring lands. But their primary objective was not to kill enemies or gain more territory. Instead, Aztec warriors demanded tribute and took prisoners from the people they subdued. They then sacrificed numerous captives at pyramid temples to placate the gods. These deities, they believed, would in turn protect them as they conducted further wars of capture, leading to more tribute and sacrifices.

Like the Inca of Peru, the Aztec imposed harsh treatment on the peoples they conquered, extracting heavy annual taxes. This stern policy caused outlying provinces to resent Aztec authority and made the centralized empire vulnerable to external attack. When a foreign assault prompted the empire's downfall in the early sixteenth century, the challenge came from a direction that Aztec priests and generals could not predict.

THE ANASAZI: CHACO CANYON AND MESA VERDE

The great urban centers of Peru and Mesoamerica had no counterparts farther north. The peoples inhabiting North America in the millennium before Columbus never developed the levels of **social stratification**, urban dynamism, architectural grandeur, astronomical study, or intensive corn agriculture that characterized the Maya, Inca, or Aztec. Yet elements of all these traits appeared in North America, especially in the Southwest and the Mississippi Valley, with the emergence of increasingly settled societies and widening circles of exchange. Could north–south movements back and forth have occurred? Recently, researchers have identified a north–south traffic in turquoise, highly prized in both Mexico and the Southwest.

David Muench

■ Cliff Palace, at Mesa Verde National Park in southwest Colorado, was created 900 years ago, when the Anasazi left the mesa tops and moved into more secure and inaccessible cliff dwellings. Facing southwest, the building gained heat from the rays of the low afternoon sun in winter. Overhanging rock protected the structure from rain, snow, and the hot midday summer sun. The numerous round kivas, each covered with a flat roof originally, suggest that Cliff Palace may have had a ceremonial importance.

Three identifiably different cultures were already well established in the North American Southwest by 500. The Mogollon occupied the dry, mountainous regions of eastern Arizona and southern New Mexico. Mogollon women were expert potters who crafted delicate bowls from the clay of the Mimbres River. Families lived in sunken pit houses that were cool in summer and warm in winter. The Hohokam, their neighbors to the west in south-central Arizona, did the same. The Hohokam also constructed extensive canal and floodgate systems to irrigate their fields from the Gila and Salt rivers. According to their Native American successors, who still dwell in the Phoenix area, the name *Hohokam* means "those who have gone."

Farther north, where Utah and Colorado meet Arizona and New Mexico, lived the people remembered as the Anasazi, or "ancient ones." By 750 the Anasazi inhabited above-ground houses of masonry or adobe clustered around a central ceremonial room dug into the earth. They entered this sunken religious chamber, known as a kiva, by descending a ladder through the roof. The climb back up symbolized the initial ascent of humans into the Upper World from below. European explorers later used the Spanish word for town, *pueblo,* to describe the Anasazi's complex multistory dwellings of masonry or adobe.

Beginning in the 850s, Chaco Canyon in the San Juan River basin of northwest New Mexico emerged as the hub of the Anasazi world. Wide, straight roads radiating out from Chaco let builders haul hundreds of thousands of logs for use as roof beams in the nine great pueblos that still dot the canyon. The largest, Pueblo Bonito, rose five stories high in places and had 600 rooms arranged in a vast semicircle.

After 1130, a prolonged drought gripped the area, and the turquoise workshops of Chaco Canyon fell silent. Many of the inhabitants headed north, where dozens of Anasazi communities with access to better farming conditions dotted the landscape. Gradually— with populations growing, the climate worsening, and competition for resources stiffening—the Anasazi moved into sheltered cliff dwellings such as Cliff Palace at Mesa Verde in southwestern Colorado, with its 220 rooms and 23 kivas. Reached only by ladders and steep trails, these pueblos offered protection from enemies and shelter from the scorching summer sun. But the environmental crisis proved too great; warfare intensified

■ The most striking Mississippian earthwork to survive is the enigmatic Serpent Mound, built in the eleventh century by the Fort Ancient people in southern Ohio. The snake (holding an egg in its mouth) has links to astronomy because its curves are aligned toward key positions of the sun. The serpent may even represent Halley's Comet, which blazed in the heavens in 1066. Completely uncoiled, the earthwork would measure more than a quarter-mile in length.

over scant resources. When another prolonged drought (1276–1299) forced the Anasazi to move once again, survivors dispersed south into lands later occupied by the Hopi, Zuni, and Rio Grande peoples.

THE MISSISSIPPIANS: CAHOKIA AND MOUNDVILLE

Earlier, in the Mississippi Valley, the Hopewell people had prospered for half a millennium before 500 C.E. (in the era of the Roman Empire in Europe). The Hopewell lived mainly in Ohio and Illinois. But their network of trade extended over much of the continent. Hopewell burial sites have yielded pipestone and flint from the Missouri River valley, copper and silver from Lake Superior, mica and quartz from Appalachia, seashells and shark teeth from Florida, and artwork made from Rocky Mountain obsidian and grizzly-bear teeth.

Hopewell trading laid the groundwork for larger mound-building societies, known as the Mississippian cultures, which emerged in the Mississippi Valley and the Southeast in roughly the same centuries as the great Mesoamerican civilizations and the Anasazi in the Southwest. The Mississippian tradition developed gradually after 500. Then after 900, it flourished broadly for six centuries, as centralized societies combined thriving agricultural economies with long-distance trade in scarce goods.

Shifts in technology and agriculture facilitated the rise of the Mississippians. Bows and arrows, long employed in arctic regions of North America but little known elsewhere, became widespread in the eastern woodlands around 700. At the same time, maize underwent a transformation from a marginal oddity to a central staple crop. Across the East, food supplies expanded as Native American communities planted corn in the rich bottomland soil along the

Reconstructed View of Cahokia

region's many rivers. With greater productivity, commercial and religious elites took advantage of farmers and asserted stronger control over the community's increasing resources.

Separate Mississippian mound-building centers have been found as far apart as Spiro, in eastern Oklahoma, and Etowah, in northern Georgia. The largest complex was at Cahokia on the American Bottom, the twenty-five-mile floodplain below where the Illinois and Missouri rivers flow into the Mississippi. On Cahokia Creek, near East St. Louis, Illinois, dozens of rectangular, flat-topped temple mounds still remain after almost a thousand years. The largest mound—indeed, the largest ancient earthwork in North America—rises 100 feet in four separate levels, covering 16 acres and using nearly 22 million cubic feet of earth. A log palisade with gates and watchtowers once enclosed this temple mound and its adjacent plaza in a 200-acre central compound. Nearby, residents used engineering and astronomy skills to erect 48 posts in a huge circle, 410 feet in diameter. This creation, now called Woodhenge after England's Stonehenge, functioned as a calendar to mark the daily progression of the sun throughout each year.

Cahokia's mounds rose quickly in the decades after 1050, as the local population expanded beyond 10,000. A succession of powerful leaders reorganized the vicinity's small, isolated villages into a strong regional chiefdom that controlled towns on both sides of the Mississippi River. These towns provided the chiefdom's centralized elite with food, labor, and goods for trading. The elaborate religious rituals and the wealth and power of the leaders are seen in a burial site opened by archaeologists in the 1970s. The body of one prominent figure, presumably a chief, was laid out on a surface of 20,000 shell beads. Near him lay six young adults who must have been relatives or servants sacri-

> *Mississippian mound-building centers have been found as far apart as Spiro, in eastern Oklahoma, and Etowah, in northern Georgia.*

ficed at the ruler's funeral. They were supplied with hundreds of stone arrowheads—finely chipped and neatly sorted—plus antler projectile points and numerous ceremonial objects. Around 1100, the population of Cahokia perhaps exceeded 15,000 people. It then waned steadily over the next two centuries as the unstable hierarchy lost its sway over nearby villages.

As Cahokia declined, other regional chiefdoms rose along other rivers. The most notable appeared at Moundville in west-central Alabama, fifteen miles south of modern Tuscaloosa. The site, with more than twenty flat-topped mounds, became a dominant ceremonial center in the thirteenth century. But by 1400, Moundville's Mississippian elites had started to lose their power. Throughout the prior millennium, societies had grown by linking agriculture and trade, only to suffer when they reached their environmental limits. A river could dry up or change course; a key local resource, such as timber or game, could diminish sharply. Also, trade could be interrupted or curtailed. When the Europeans first appeared, they would be welcomed by many Native Americans as potential trading partners.

Linking the Continents

■ *Why is the first voyage of Columbus in 1492 still viewed as such an earth-changing event?*

Estimates vary widely, but probably around one-sixth of the world's population—as many as 60 to 70 million people—resided in the Americas when Columbus arrived in 1492. Most of them lived in the tropical zone near the equator, where their ancient ancestors had developed efficient forms of agriculture. But roughly one-tenth of the hemisphere's population (6 to 7 million) dwelt in North America, spread from coast to coast.

We cannot rule out the occasional appearance in America of ancient ocean travelers. Around 400, Polynesian mariners sailed their double-hulled canoes from the Marquesas Islands in the South Pacific to the Hawaiian **archipelago.** Conceivably, in the millennium before 1500, one or two boats from Africa, Ireland, Polynesia, China, or Japan sailed—or were blown—to the American mainland. But any survivors of such a journey would have had little genetic or cultural impact, for no sustained back-and-forth contact between the societies occurred. Even the seafaring Norse from Scandinavia, known as Vikings, never established a lasting colony. Their brief Vinland settlement a thousand years ago at L'Anse aux Meadows in northern Newfoundland is now well documented, but they remained only a few years at this coastal site. Native American societies, therefore, knew nothing of the people, plants, animals, and microbes of the Eastern Hemisphere.

America's near isolation ended dramatically, beginning in the late fifteenth century, after innovations in deep-sea sailing opened the world's oceans as a new frontier for human exploration. Chinese sailors in the North Pacific or Portuguese mariners in the South Atlantic could well have been the first outsiders to establish ongoing contact with the peoples of the Western Hemisphere. Instead, it was Christopher Columbus, an Italian navigator in the service of Spain, who became the agent of this sweeping change. He stumbled upon the Americas by accident and misinterpreted what he had found. But his chance encounter with a separate realm sparked new patterns of human migration, cultural transfer, and ecological exchange that would reshape the modern world.

OCEANIC TRAVEL: THE NORSE AND THE CHINESE

Scandinavian settlers had colonized Ireland in the 830s and Iceland in the 870s. These seafarers—led by Erik the Red—reached Greenland in the 980s. When Erik's son, Leif, learned that Norse mariners blown off course had sighted land farther west, he sailed from Greenland to the North American coast. Here he explored a region near the Gulf of St. Lawrence that he named Vinland.

Around 1000, Leif Eriksson's relatives directed several return voyages to Vinland, where the Norse Vikings built an outpost called Straumfjord. The tiny colony of 160 people, including women and children, lived and grazed livestock in Vinland for several years until native peoples drove them away. The Greenlanders returned occasionally to cut timber, and they traded with inhabitants of northeastern Canada for generations. But by 1450, Norse settlements in Greenland had died out completely and the trade with Native Americans had stopped.

Whether sailors in Europe knew much about Norse exploits in the North Atlantic remains shrouded in mystery. What Europeans did know, vaguely, was the existence of the distant Chinese empire. They called the realm Cathay, a term used by Italian merchant Marco Polo, who journeyed from Venice across Asia along the fabled Silk Road in the 1270s. Polo returned to Italy in 1292 to publish his *Travels,* an account of adventures in China during the reign of Kublai Khan.

> *Chinese strength in overseas exploration and trade reached its height in the early fifteenth century under Admiral Zheng He.*

Marco Polo told of many things unknown to Europeans, including rocks that burned like wood (coal) and spices that preserved meat. Lacking winter fodder for their herds, Europe's farmers regularly slaughtered numerous cattle in the fall and pickled or salted the beef to preserve it. Asian spices such as nutmeg, cinnamon, pepper, ginger, and cloves, if they could be obtained, would offer new preservatives. When renewed Islamic power in the Middle East cut off the Silk Road to Cathay, Europeans searched for other ways to reach that far-off region.

The desire to obtain oriental spices at their source fueled European oceanic exploration, leading eventually to the transformation of the Americas. Yet it was China, not Europe, that first mastered ocean sailing on a large scale. Chinese strength in overseas exploration and trade reached its height in the early fifteenth century under Admiral Zheng He (pronounced "Jung Huh"). Between 1405 and 1433, this brilliant officer led seven large fleets to the Indian Ocean, sailing as far as east Africa. His immense treasure ships, 400 feet long and equipped with cannon, carried strange items—even giraffes—home to Asia.

Then, abruptly, China turned away from the sea, passing up its chance to become the first global maritime power. The Chinese, once poised to play a leading role in early oceanic trade, therefore lost an opportunity to shape the destiny of North and South America. Within a century of Zheng He's accomplishments, the royal court grew dismissive of foreign trade and turned inward. Chinese officials destroyed the logbooks of earlier voyages and curtailed production of oceangoing vessels. Instead of powerful China facing the Pacific, it was tiny Portugal, overlooking the Atlantic, which emerged as the leader in maritime innovation and exploration in the fifteenth century.

PORTUGAL AND THE BEGINNINGS OF GLOBALIZATION

Geography and religious zeal helped spur Portugal's unlikely rise to world prominence. The tiny maritime country faced the sea at the crossroads between Mediterranean commerce and the coastal traffic of northern Europe. This strategic location on the **Iberian** peninsula also exposed Portugal to the ongoing conflict between Christianity and Islam. The religion founded by Muhammad (born at Mecca in 570) had spread rapidly across North Africa from Arabia. By the eighth century, followers of Islam (known as Muslims, Moslems, or Moors) had crossed the Strait of Gibraltar to establish a kingdom in southern Spain. Centuries later, Spanish and Portuguese Christians rallied to force the Muslims out of the Iberian peninsula—a campaign that concluded in 1492—and to join other militant Europeans in fighting against Islamic power in the Middle East.

When Christian crusades to the holy land failed to defeat the Muslims and reopen overland trade routes to China, European strategists dreamed of skirting Africa by sea to reach Asia. The Portuguese were well positioned to lead this flanking movement around the areas under Muslim control. And if no such oceanic route to Asia existed, some speculated that Portuguese exploration south beyond Africa's Sahara Desert still might provide links to a strong Christian ally. For generations, Europeans had fostered legends of a wealthy kingdom somewhere in Africa ruled by a black Christian known as Prester John. Even if Prester John's realm could not be found, probes south from the Iberian Peninsula by ship might explore the extent of Islamic influence and seek out African converts to Christianity.

Intellectual and economic motives also existed for Portuguese ventures along the coast of sub-Saharan Africa. Such journeys, presenting new challenges in shipbuilding and navigation, could boost European knowledge of the unknown and open new markets. The first step involved an investment of leadership and resources, before early efforts could bear fruit and give the exploration process a momentum of its own.

Prince Henry of Portugal (1394–1460) provided these initial ingredients. In 1415 the young prince—later honored as "Henry the Navigator"—had crossed the Straits of Gibraltar to fight Muslims at Ceuta in North Africa. Committed to the campaign against Islam, Henry then waged a religiously inspired crusade-at-sea, building his headquarters at Sagres in southwest Portugal. The center overlooked the ocean near Cape St. Vincent,

■ Prince Henry of Portugal rarely went to sea himself. Instead, he established a base at Sagres, overlooking the Atlantic Ocean. From here, beginning in 1418, he sent mariners south along the African coast. They quickly laid claim to the islands of the eastern Atlantic, and by the 1440s they had initiated trade along the west African coast, carrying gold and slaves back to Portugal.

Courtesy, Algarve Tourism Board

The Lateen Rig: A Triangular Sail That Helped to Conquer Oceans

Viking ships and other medieval European sailing vessels used square sails that were only effective when traveling "with the wind." On a journey facing *into* the wind, it was often necessary to use oars instead of sail power. But Arab sailors on the Red Sea and the Indian Ocean had devised a solution. For more than a thousand years, they had been employing a "lateen rig" for their feluccas and dhows. The long wooden "yard" (a flexible beam attached to the mast) can be cumbersome, but it holds a triangular sail that offers mariners more options in directing their ships. The angled leading edge of the lateen sail allows a vessel to sail into the wind, tacking back and forth on a zigzag course against a prevailing breeze, as well as to sail downwind like a square-rigged ship.

In late medieval times, European sailors on the Mediterranean Sea adopted this innovation. (Scholars call this process "cultural diffusion," in which a valuable innovation passes from one society to another, rather than being invented separately.) Lateen sails appeared on the early Iberian caravels sent into the Atlantic by Prince Henry of Portugal. Aided by this novel rigging, later European sailors, including Columbus, could follow prevailing winds on long voyages without fear that they would be unable to sail home in the opposite direction. In the age of oceanic exploration, each journey brought increased knowledge of deep-sea

winds and currents. But it was the lateen sail that allowed mariners to explore the farthest reaches of the globe and still return safely, tacking steadily to make headway against opposing winds.

QUESTIONS

1. European acquisition of the lateen sail illustrates cultural diffusion. What are some other examples of one society borrowing a technological innovation from another?

2. Lateen rigs allowed ships to sail into the wind, so they no longer needed bulky oars and extra crewmen to row. What new advantages did this create for long ocean voyages?

---

the western tip of Europe. From there, his sailors launched a far-reaching revolution in human communication and trade, perhaps the most momentous single step in a **globalization** process that continues to the present day.

Henry's innovative ships, known as caravels, pushed south along the African coast. Their narrow hulls, deep keels, and high gunwales were well suited for ocean sailing. On the masts, their array of canvas usually included several lateen sails. These triangular sails, long used by Arab sailors on the Red Sea, helped mariners to maneuver against headwinds. Other innovations proved equally valuable. Henry's experts at Sagres drew on the work of Jewish cartographers from the island of Majorca to develop state-of-the-art charts, astronomical tables, and navigational instruments.

With these advantages, and years of experience, Henry's captains slowly mastered the winds and currents near West Africa. In the process, they located three island groups off northwest Africa: the Canaries, the Madeiras, and the Azores. Before midcentury, Portuguese settlers on the never-inhabited island of Madeira had burned off all the timber and started planting sugar for export. In the 1440s, Portuguese mariners began seizing people who lived on the coast of Africa and deporting them as slaves to the new Atlantic sugar island. In addition, Portuguese captains carried slaves back to Europe and sold them there to supplement the growing trade in ivory and gold from sub-Saharan Africa. Nevertheless, when Henry died in 1460, his mariners had still glimpsed only a small portion of the African coast, sailing as far as what is now Sierra Leone.

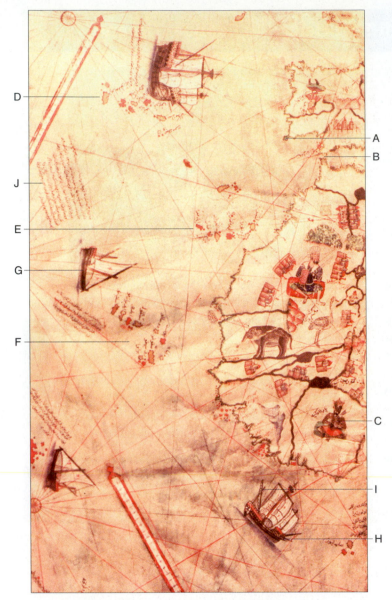

■ This Atlantic chart illustrates key aspects of Portuguese success in overseas exploration. Cape St. Vincent (A), where Prince Henry built his headquarters at Sagres, lies near the Strait of Gibraltar (B), the narrow entrance to the Mediterranean Sea. As Henry's mariners explored along the African coast for a sea passage to Asia, they also looked for possible allies such as Prester John, a mythical black king (C). They used the island groups of the eastern Atlantic to check their position: Azores (D), Madeiras (E), Canaries (F). Their small caravels (G) adopted the triangular lateen sail seen on traditional Arab boats in the Red Sea. Larger square-rigged ships that later sailed from Portugal to India (H) also incorporated lateen sails on a mast at the stern (I). A skilled Turkish navigator—who had never sailed on the Atlantic—made this unusual map in 1513. Piri Re'is used charts captured from a Christian ship in the Mediterranean; his inscriptions (J) are in Turkish.

LOOKING FOR THE INDIES: DA GAMA AND COLUMBUS

During the 1480s, following a war with Spain, the Portuguese renewed their African designs. In 1482 they erected a trading fort called Elmina Castle on the Gold Coast (modern Ghana) to guard against Spanish competition and to support exploration toward the east. Finally, in 1487, Bartolomeu Dias rounded the southernmost tip of Africa, the Cape of Good Hope, proving that a sea link existed between the Atlantic and Indian oceans. The Portuguese could now sail to India and tap into the rich spice trade flowing from the islands of Southeast Asia that Europeans vaguely called the Indies. Success came a decade later with the voyage of Vasco da Gama, who set out from Lisbon in 1497. After two years, his ship returned from India laden with pepper and cinnamon. The Portuguese had at last opened a southeastern sea route to the silk and spice markets of the East.

Meanwhile, the rulers of rival Spain gambled on finding a profitable *westward* route to the Indies. Ferdinand of Aragon had married Isabella of Castile in 1469, leading to the unification of Christian Spain under a single royal family. Pooling resources, they used force to reconquer portions of their realm still under Muslim control. In 1492, King Ferdinand and Queen Isabella finally succeeded in driving the Muslims from Spain by military means. The monarchs imposed Christian orthodoxy and forced Jews into exile. That same year, they agreed to sponsor an Atlantic voyage to the west by Christopher Columbus, a charismatic dreamer in his early forties whose arguments often relied on obscure passages in Christian scripture and conflicting ancient geography treatises.

It was the navigator's experience and knowledge that gained him the trust of Spain's king and queen, for he had practical familiarity with the Atlantic world. Born in Genoa, Italy, the son of a weaver, Columbus had gone to sea at age nineteen. He had visited the Madeiras, West Africa (Guinea), and perhaps even Iceland. His brother Bartholomew was a mapmaker, and both men had heard stories from sailors aboard English and Portuguese fishing vessels. They told of islands, real and imagined, which dotted the Atlantic. Columbus had tried unsuccessfully to convince various European monarchs, including Henry VII of England, that an alternative route to China could be found by sailing west.

On August 3, 1492, Columbus set out to test his audacious plan. Leaving Spain with ninety men aboard three small vessels, he headed for the Canary Islands, eluding

Portuguese caravels sent to stop him. From the Canaries, his ships sailed due west on September 6. After a voyage of three or four weeks, he expected to encounter the island of Cipangu (Japan), which Marco Polo had mentioned, or to reach the coast of Asia, where Polo had seen the court of the Great Khan. After weeks without sight of any land, his crew worried that they might not have enough supplies for the long return home. So Columbus gave out a false, reduced estimate of each day's headway, leading his sailors to believe they were still close to Europe. He recorded the much longer, more accurate distance in his own private log, but he harbored huge illusions regarding his actual whereabouts.

Why these misunderstandings? The mariner made several crucial mistakes. Like other Europeans, Columbus knew the world was round, not flat, and he accepted the idea of the ancient geographer Ptolemy that by using north–south lines, one could divide the globe into 360 degrees of longitude. But he questioned Ptolemy's estimate that each degree measures fifty nautical miles at the equator. (Each actually measures sixty miles.) Instead, Columbus accepted an alternative figure of forty-five miles, making the circumference of his theoretical globe 25 percent smaller than the real distance around the earth. Besides *under*estimating the world's circumference, he compounded his error by *over*estimating two other crucial distances: the breadth of the Eurasian landmass and the extent of Japan's separation from China. The first distance is actually 130 degrees of longitude, and the second is 20. Columbus used authorities who suggested 225 and 30 degrees, respectively. His estimates placed Japan 105 degrees closer to Europe, at the longitude that runs through eastern Lake Superior and western Cuba.

> *Early on October 12, the distressed sailors finally sighted a small island, naming it San Salvador after their Christian savior.*

Early on October 12, the distressed sailors finally sighted a small island, naming it San Salvador after their Christian savior. The inhabitants in the Bahamas proved welcoming, and Columbus recorded pleasure over the "gold which they wear hanging from their noses. But I wish to go and see if I can find the island of Cipangu." Within several weeks he located a large and beautiful island (Cuba, not Cipangu), and he estimated that the Asian mainland of the Great Khan was only "a 10 days' journey" farther west. He claimed a nearby island as La Isla Española, the Spanish island, or Hispaniola (current-day Haiti and the Dominican Republic). He noted stories of hostile islanders farther south called Caribs, or Caniba, who were said to devour their enemies. "I repeat," he asserted, "the Caniba are no other than the people of the Grand Khan." (Upon hearing of these fierce Caribs, Europeans soon fashioned the word *cannibal* and named the region the Caribbean.)

DOCUMENT

From the Journal of
Christopher Columbus

Bolstered by these encounters, the explorers returned hastily across the Atlantic on a more northerly route. They weathered a horrendous winter storm to reach Spain in March 1493. Columbus told the Spanish court that he had reached the Indies off the Asian coast, and he displayed several natives he called "Indians" to prove it. His three later voyages did not shake this belief, which he clung to until his death in 1506. The captain, one observer wrote in 1493, "has sailed . . ., as he believes, to the very shores of India, . . . even though the size of the earth's sphere seems to indicate otherwise." Columbus had not reached the lands he sought, but his initial voyage of 1492 would have immediate and extraordinary consequences.

IN THE WAKE OF COLUMBUS: COMPETITION AND EXCHANGE

Within months of Columbus's return, the pope in Rome issued a papal bull, or decree. This pronouncement, titled *Inter Caetera,* claimed the entire world as the rightful inheritance of Christianity. It brashly divided the globe between two Christian powers, Spain and Portugal, by drawing a line through the western Atlantic Ocean from the North Pole to the South Pole. For 180 degrees of longitude west of the line, the Spanish alone could

The largest Chinese vessels of Zheng He (400ft.) were nearly five times longer than Columbus's flagship (85ft.).

Major expeditions

- - - Marco Polo: from Venice (1271) to China along the Silk Road
— Zheng He: from China to East Africa with a fleet of huge ships (1420s)
— Prince Henry's ships: from Portugal as far as Sierra Leone (1420–1460)
— Columbus: first voyage west from Spain via Canary Islands (1492–1493)
— Da Gama: from Portugal to India via Cape of Good Hope (1497–1499)
— Magellan's circumnavigation, completed by his crew (1519–1522)

■ **MAP 1.3   Opening New Ocean Pathways Around the Globe, 1420–1520**

In the 1420s, ships from Portugal and China explored opposite coasts of Africa. But China withdrew from oceanic trade, and European mariners competed to explore the earth by sea. Within a century, Magellan's ship had circled the globe for Spain. The colonization in North America is a chapter in this larger saga of exploration.

continue to seek access to Asia. The Portuguese king claimed that east of such a line, on the other half of the globe, Portugal would have a monopoly in developing the route that Dias had opened around the Cape of Good Hope. The two Iberian powers affirmed this division of the earth in the Treaty of Tordesillas (1494).

That same year Columbus led a huge fleet back to Hispaniola, taking 1,200 men aboard seventeen ships. By employing only men to launch Spain's overseas empire, the 1494 expedition initiated a pattern of warfare against native Caribbean men and intermarriage with indigenous women. A mestizo, or mixed-race (Spanish/Indian), population emerged swiftly in Spanish settlements there. On his third Atlantic crossing (1498), Columbus glimpsed the wide mouth of Venezuela's Orinoco River. Given the huge volume of fresh water entering the sea, he knew he had reached a large landmass, perhaps a part of Asia. When Amerigo Vespucci, another Italian in the service of Spain, saw the same continent in 1499, he described it as a *Mundus Novus*, or New World. European geographers wrote his name, *America,* across their maps.

Meanwhile, a third Italian navigator—John Cabot (or Caboto)—obtained a license from the English king, Henry VII, to probe the North Atlantic for access to Cathay. Cabot knew that English mariners from the port of Bristol had been fishing in the waters off Newfoundland for decades. In 1497, Cabot sailed west from Bristol across the Atlantic to

Newfoundland and perhaps Nova Scotia, thinking he was viewing the coast of Asia. When Cabot died at sea during a follow-up voyage the next year, Henry VII, the founder of England's new Tudor dynasty lacked the resources to pursue the explorer's claims. Nevertheless, the ventures of Columbus had sparked widespread excitement and curiosity in European ports. Within a generation, navigators and cartographers began to comprehend the geographic reality that Columbus had so thoroughly misunderstood. Their increasing knowledge fueled greater transatlantic contact.

After thousands of years, the long separation of the hemispheres had been broken. The destinies of the world's most divergent continents swiftly became linked. Those links fostered human migrations of an unprecedented scale. Moreover, with European ships came transfers of seeds and viruses, bugs and birds, plants and animals that forever reshaped the world. Scholars call this phenomenon the **Columbian Exchange.** The phrase acknowledges Columbus as the crucial initiator, but it also underscores the two-way nature of the flow.

Within a matter of decades, this dramatic Columbian Exchange saw the movement west across the Atlantic of cows, sheep, pigs, chickens, and honeybees—all unknown in the Western Hemisphere. Horses, which had disappeared from the Americas thousands of years earlier, arrived once again aboard Spanish ships. So did Old World foods such as

IMAGE

Early Botanical Illustration—New World Plants

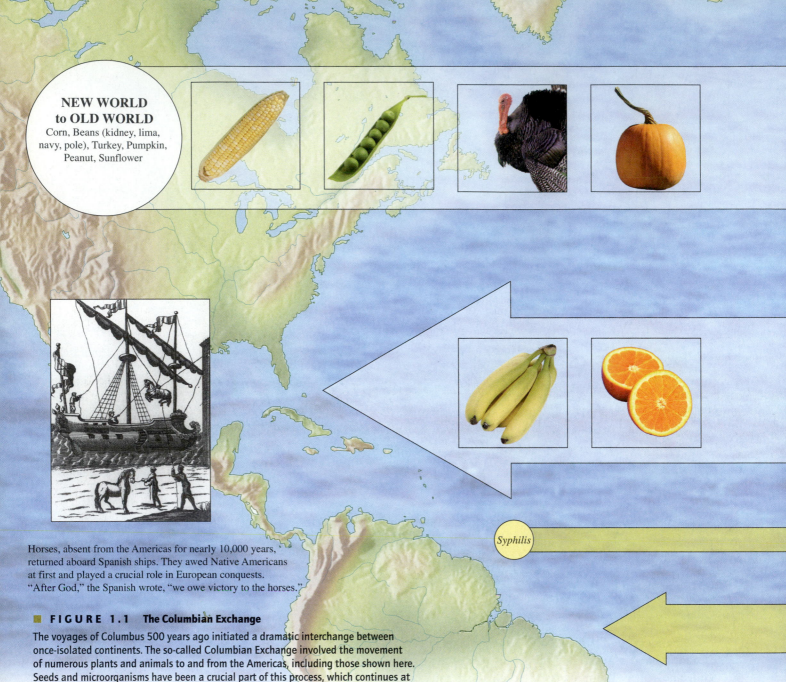

NEW WORLD to OLD WORLD

Corn, Beans (kidney, lima, navy, pole), Turkey, Pumpkin, Peanut, Sunflower

Syphilis

Horses, absent from the Americas for nearly 10,000 years, returned aboard Spanish ships. They awed Native Americans at first and played a crucial role in European conquests. "After God," the Spanish wrote, "we owe victory to the horses."

■ **FIGURE 1.1   The Columbian Exchange**

The voyages of Columbus 500 years ago initiated a dramatic interchange between once-isolated continents. The so-called Columbian Exchange involved the movement of numerous plants and animals to and from the Americas, including those shown here. Seeds and microorganisms have been a crucial part of this process, which continues at an ever-increasing rate.

All photos from photos.com, except horses: Courtesy, Bancroft Library, University of California, Berkeley (SF309 G7 M25 1769 pl.20)

sugar cane, coffee, bananas, peaches, lemons, and oranges. But westbound European ships also carried devastating diseases unknown in the Americas, such as smallpox, measles, malaria, and whooping cough. Returning east across the Atlantic, ships also carried a great deal in the opposite direction. Gradually they transported to the Old World such New World novelties as corn, potatoes, pumpkins, chili peppers, tobacco, cacao, pineapples, sunflowers, and turkeys. Many Europeans suspected that syphilis, the sexually transmitted disease which spread across Europe during the wars of the 1490s, had been introduced from America by Columbus's returning sailors. The ongoing Columbian Exchange had dimensions and implications few could imagine; the planet and all its inhabitants would never be the same again.

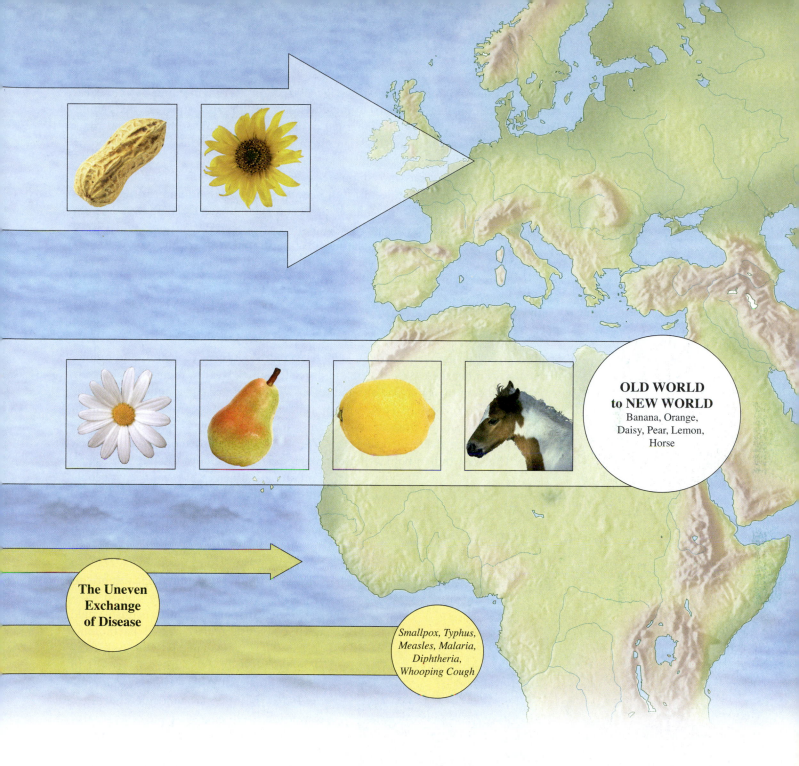

OLD WORLD
to NEW WORLD
Banana, Orange,
Daisy, Pear, Lemon,
Horse

The Uneven
Exchange
of Disease

Smallpox, Typhus,
Measles, Malaria,
Diphtheria,
Whooping Cough

Spain Enters the Americas

■ *What factors motivated and shaped Spain's rapid intrusion into sixteenth-century America?*

Throughout the sixteenth century, European mariners, inspired by the feats of Columbus and da Gama, risked ocean voyaging in hopes of scoring similar successes. Those who survived brought back novelties for consumers, information for geographers, and profits for ship owners. New wealth prompted further investment in exploration, and expanding knowledge awakened cultural changes for both explorers and the people they met.

The dynamic European era known as the Renaissance, or rebirth, owed much to overseas exploration. Returning mariners brought reports of surprising places and people. Their experiences challenged the inherited wisdom of traditional authorities and put a new premium on rational thought, scientific calculation, and careful observation of the natural world.

In turn, Europe's Renaissance stimulated ever wider exploration as breakthroughs in technology and navigation yielded practical results. Sailing south around Africa and then east, Portuguese caravels reached China by 1514 and Japan by 1543. Sailing west, Spanish vessels learned first that the Caribbean did not offer a passage to Asia and then in 1522—through Magellan's global voyage—that the ocean separating America and Asia was enormous. In the West Indies, and then elsewhere in the Western Hemisphere, Native Americans began to pay dearly for the exchange that ships from Spain had initiated.

THE DEVASTATION OF THE INDIES

Spanish arrival in the West Indies in 1492 triggered widespread ecological and human disaster within decades. Well armed and eager for quick wealth, the early colonizers wrought havoc on the Taino Indians and Caribs who inhabited the islands. The strange newcomers killed and enslaved native peoples and extracted tribute from the survivors in the form of gold panned from streams. Spanish livestock trampled or consumed native gardens, prompting severe food shortages. Worse, European diseases ravaged countless villages. The West Indian population plummeted. Island societies totaling more than 1 million lost nineteen of every twenty people within a generation.

This near-extinction had three consequences. First, devout Catholics back in Spain protested the loss of potential American converts. When Dominican friars reached Cuba in 1510, they denounced Spanish brutality as sinful. The Indians, they argued, possessed souls that only Christian baptism could save. A Spanish soldier named Bartholomé de Las Casas, who repented and joined the Dominican order, led the outcry for reform. In his scathing exposé titled *The Devastation of the Indies,* he opposed genocide and urged conversion.

Second, in response to the steep drop in population, Spanish colonizers began importing African slaves. The same Christians who bemoaned Native American enslavement justified this initiative to replace the decimated Indian workforce in mining for gold. A few enslaved Africans were brought from Seville to Hispaniola as early as 1502. After 1510, several dozen black workers were sent from Spain each year, mostly (in the words of Columbus's son) "to break the rocks in which the gold was found." But Spanish landowners in the West Indies soon saw the prospects for growing sugar cane with African labor, following the Portuguese precedent in Madeira and the

■ As the Indian population of the Caribbean plummeted in the face of new diseases and exploitation, the Spanish began importing Africans to the New World as slaves. Many were put to work mining precious metals. Here men are forced to dig for gold nuggets beside a mountain stream, then wash them in a tub and dry them over a fire, before handing them to their Spanish master to weigh in his hand-held scale.

The Pierpont Morgan Library/Art Resource, NY

Azores. By 1518, European investors had started to ship black slaves directly from Africa to the Caribbean.

Third, decimation in the islands prompted the Spanish to intensify their explorations. Captains looked for new sources of Indian labor, fresh lands to exploit, and easy passageways to the Pacific. They pushed out from the Caribbean in several directions. In 1510, they established a mainland outpost at Darien on the Atlantic coast of Panama. From there, Vasco Núñez de Balboa pressed south over the mountainous **isthmus** to glimpse the Pacific in 1513. That same year, Juan Ponce de León sailed northwest from Puerto Rico, where he had amassed a fortune as governor. Despite later tales that he sought a fountain of youth, he actually hoped the nearby land, which he named Florida, would yield new gold and slaves. But the peninsula's Indians were already familiar with Spanish raiders. They turned Ponce de León away after he claimed the region for Spain.

THE SPANISH CONQUEST OF THE AZTEC

By 1519, the Spanish had determined that the Gulf of Mexico offered no easy passage to Asia. They needed fresh alternatives. In Spain, crown officials sought someone to sail southwest, around the South American continent that Columbus and Vespucci had encountered. For this perilous task, they recruited a Portuguese navigator named Ferdinand Magellan, who had sailed in the Indian Ocean. On his epic voyage (1519–1522), Magellan located a difficult passage through the tip of South America—now called the Strait of Magellan. But the journey also revealed the vast width of the Pacific. The crew nearly starved crossing its enormous expanse, which covers one-third of the earth's surface. Warring factions in the Philippines killed Magellan and twenty-seven of his men shortly after they reached the islands. However, one of his ships, the *Victoria*,

The Newberry Library, Chicago

■ Cortés enclosed this map of Tenochtitlán in a letter to King Charles V (the Holy Roman Emperor and grandson of Ferdinand and Isabella). The map remained secret in Spain, but it was published in a 1524 Nuremberg edition of the letter, giving many Europeans their first glimpse of the defeated Aztec capital that was later rebuilt as Mexico City. The city plan shows the causeways over Lake Texcoco and the central square, with high temples where Aztec priests conducted human sacrifices. The flag with the double-headed eagle of Charles V's Hapsburg dynasty may mark Cortés's headquarters.

"These Gods That We Worship Give Us Everything We Need"

Interpreting History

Three years after Cortés captured Tenochtitlán in central Mexico, twelve missionaries from the Franciscan order arrived in the city to preach Christianity to the conquered Aztec. In several meetings with principal elders and priests, they explained their beliefs and laid out their plans through a translator. Similar talks would take place throughout America in later generations.

No transcript of the 1524 conversations exists, but another Franciscan, the famous preserver of Aztec culture Bernardino de Sahagún, gathered recollections of the encounter from both sides and reconstructed the dialogue. He published his version in 1564, creating parallel texts in Spanish and Nahuatl, the Aztec language. "Having understood the reasoning and speech of the twelve," Sahagún reports, the city leaders "became greatly agitated and fell into a great sadness and fear, offering no response." The next morning, they requested a complete repetition of the unsettling message. "Having heard this, one of the

The Bibliothèque Nationale, Paris

principal lords arose, asked the indulgence of the twelve, . . . and made the following long speech."

Our lords, leading personages of much esteem, you are very welcome to our lands and towns. . . . We have heard the words that you have brought us of the One who gives us life and being. And we have heard with admiration the words of the Lord of the World which he has sent here for love of us, and also you have brought us the book of celestial and divine words.

You have told us that we do not know the One who gives us life and being, who is Lord of the heavens and of the earth. You also say that those we worship are not gods. This way of speaking is entirely new to us, and very scandalous. We are frightened by this way of speaking because our forebears who engendered and governed us never said anything like this.

made it back to Spain via Africa's Cape of Good Hope, becoming the first vessel to circumnavigate the globe.

As news of Magellan's voyage raced through Spain in 1522, word also arrived that a Spanish military leader, or *conquistador,* named Hernán Cortés had toppled the gold-rich empire of the Aztec in central Mexico. Like other ambitious conquistadores, Cortés had followed Columbus to the Caribbean. In 1519, hoping to march overland to the Pacific as Balboa had done, Cortés sailed along Mexico's east coast and established a base camp at Vera Cruz. He quickly realized he had reached the edge of a powerful empire.

At Tenochtitlán the Aztec emperor, Moctezuma, reacted with uncertainty to news that bearded strangers aboard "floating islands" had appeared off his coast. Ominous signs—shooting stars, fierce storms, unknown birds—had foretold an extraordinary arrival. If the newcomers' leader was the returning god Quetzalcoatl, the court had to welcome him with the utmost care. The emperor sent basketloads of precious objects encrusted with gold to Cortés's camp. But the elaborate gifts only alerted Cortés and his men to the Aztec's wealth.

Although the Spanish numbered scarcely 600, they had several key advantages over the Aztec. Their guns and horses, unknown in America, terrified the Indians. When Cortés found coastal peoples staggering under heavy Aztec taxes, he recruited them as willing allies. A young Indian woman (christened Doña Marina, or La Malinche) acted as Cortés's translator and companion. In an aggressive show of force, Cortés marched directly to the capital and seized Moctezuma as his hostage.

The Spanish still faced daunting obstacles. But sickness worked decisively to their advantage. Smallpox was a disease the Aztec had never encountered before, so they lacked any immunity. The European illness reached the mainland with the invading army, and

On the contrary, they left us this our custom of worshiping our gods. . . . They taught us how to honor them. And they taught us all the ceremonies and sacrifices that we make. They told us that . . . we were beholden to them, to be theirs and to serve countless centuries before the sun began to shine and before there was daytime. They said that these gods that we worship give us everything we need for our physical existence: maize, beans, chia seeds, etc. We appeal to them for the rain to make the things of the earth grow.

These our gods are the source of great riches and delights, all of which belong to them. . . . They live in very delightful places where there are always flowers, vegetation, and great freshness, a place . . . where there is never hunger, poverty, or illness. . . . There has never been a time remembered when they were not worshiped, honored, and esteemed. . . .

It would be a fickle, foolish thing for us to destroy the most ancient laws and customs left by the first inhabitants of this land. . . . We are accustomed to them and we have them impressed on our hearts. . . . How could you leave the poor elderly among us bereft of that in which they have been raised throughout their lives? Watch out that we do not incur the wrath of our gods. Watch out that the common people do not rise up

against us if we were to tell them that the gods they have always understood to be such are not gods at all.

It is best, our lords, to act on this matter very slowly, with great deliberation. We are not satisfied or convinced by what you have told us, nor do we understand or give credit to what has been said of our gods. . . . All of us together feel that it is enough to have lost, enough that the power and royal jurisdiction have been taken from us. As for our gods, we will die before giving up serving and worshiping them. This is our determination; do what you will.

QUESTIONS

1. *Why would the Aztec priests fear an uprising of the common people under these circumstances? How would you respond to a similar situation?*

2. *As suggested near the end of this chapter, a similar religious confrontation was taking place in Europe in 1524, during the early years of the Protestant Reformation. Contrast and compare these two situations.*

Source: Kenneth Mills and William B. Taylor, *Colonial Spanish America: A Documentary History* (Wilmington: Scholarly Resources, 1998), 21–22.

a crushing epidemic swept the Aztec capital in 1521. The disaster let Cortés conquer Tenochtitlán (which he renamed Mexico City) and claim the entire region as New Spain.

MAGELLAN AND CORTÉS PROMPT NEW SEARCHES

Cortés's conquest of Mexico raised Spain's hopes of additional windfalls in the Americas. In 1531, Spanish raiders under Francisco Pizarro set sail from Panama's Pacific coast for Peru, with plans to overthrow the Inca empire. Pizarro had limited resources (180 men and 37 horses), but smallpox assisted him, as it had helped Cortés, and his invaders accomplished their mission. Marching overland to Cuzco in 1533, they killed the emperor, Atahualpa, and sacked the mountain capital for the gold it contained.

Meanwhile, inspired by the explorations of Magellan, Spanish mariners pressed across the Pacific from the west coast of Mexico. Cortés dispatched three ships for the Philippines, and one actually reached its destination. Still, not until the 1560s did Spanish cargo ships, known as galleons, accomplish the arduous round trip across the Pacific from Acapulco to the Philippines and back.

Balboa and Cortés had failed to find a water passageway near the equator that could link the Atlantic directly to the Pacific. And while Magellan had located a navigable strait at the tip of South America, his new route appeared extremely long and dangerous. Therefore, fresh interest emerged in Europe for finding a shorter passage to Asia somewhere in the northern hemisphere. In 1524, Italian navigator Giovanni da Verrazzano, sailing for the French, renewed the search initiated by John Cabot. Verrazzano reached North America near the Outer Banks of North Carolina; he wondered if Pamlico Sound, visible beyond Carolina's barrier islands, might be the Pacific. He then cruised north, entering New York harbor and exploring further along the coast before returning to France without finding a strait. In 1526, Lucas Vásquez de Ayllón led 500 men and women from the Spanish Caribbean to the Santee River region (near present-day Georgetown, South Carolina) to settle and explore. But Ayllón fell sick and died, and the colony proved short-lived.

In 1528, a rival of Cortés and Ayllón named Pánfilo de Narváez launched another ill-fated expedition from Cuba. Narváez landed near Florida's Tampa Bay with 400 soldiers, hoping to travel overland to find riches or a Pacific passageway. But disease, hunger, and Indian hostilities plagued the party's journey along the Gulf Coast. Only four men—three Spanish and one North African black named Esteban—survived to make an extended trek on foot across the Southwest from Galveston Bay to Mexico City. The leader of this tiny band, Álvar Núñez Cabeza de Vaca, wrote about their odyssey after he returned to Spain in 1537. Scholars now recognize Cabeza de Vaca's *Relation* (1542) as an early classic in North American literature.

THREE NEW VIEWS OF NORTH AMERICA

Even before Cabeza de Vaca published his narrative, Europeans initiated three more expeditions into North America. Each probed a separate region of the continent, hoping to gauge the land's dimensions, assess its peoples, and claim its resources. Together, the three enterprises made 1534 to 1543 the most extraordinary decade in the early European exploration of North America, for Native Americans and newcomers alike.

DOCUMENT

Jacques Cartier: First
Contact with the
Indians

In the Northeast, Frenchman Jacques Cartier visited the Gulf of St. Lawrence in 1534 and bartered for furs with the Micmac Indians. He returned the next year and penetrated southwest up the St. Lawrence River into Canada. (The name comes from *kanata*, the Huron-Iroquois word for "village.") After a friendly reception at the large Indian town of Hochelaga near modern Montreal, the French returned downriver to camp at Stadacona, the future site of Quebec. Following a hard winter, in which he lost twenty-five men to scurvy, the explorer and his remaining crew sailed for France.

Cartier returned again in 1541, building a fort on high ground overlooking the St. Lawrence River. (In 2006 archaeologists located the exact site near Quebec, tipped off by

> Cartier returned again in 1541, building a fort on high ground overlooking the St. Lawrence River.

a single shard of European pottery dating from the 1540s.) From this base, the explorer hoped to find precious minerals and signs of a water passage farther west to the Pacific Ocean. He found neither. When he returned to France, Parisians ridiculed his rock crystals as "Canada diamonds." In Cartier's wake came a colonizing party of several hundred in 1542, led by a nobleman named Roberval. It contained several hundred French settlers, including women for the first time. But again, scurvy and cold took a heavy toll at the Quebec campsite, and the weakening colony withdrew after a single winter. Despite a decade of contacts with Indians of the St. Lawrence valley, the French still had not established a beachhead in the New World. Nevertheless, they had demonstrated their resolve to challenge Spain's exclusive claim to American lands.

The Spanish, meanwhile, launched two intrusions of their own—one in the Southeast and one in the Southwest. News of Pizarro's 1533 triumph over the Inca in Peru helped renew the search for wealthy kingdoms to conquer. In 1537, Emperor Charles V of Spain granted one hardened veteran of the Peruvian campaign—Hernando de Soto—the right to explore and conquer in and beyond Florida, establishing a personal domain for himself and his descendants. The conquistador spent most of his fortune assembling a force of more than 600 soldiers that reached Tampa Bay in 1539. The enterprise included several women and priests, along with scores of servants and African slaves, plus 200 horses. De Soto had also brought along a herd of 300 pigs that multiplied rapidly and provided food during the long march through the interior.

Over the next four years, de Soto's party traveled across parts of ten southern states. They hoped to find a city as wealthy as Cuzco in Peru or Tenochtitlán in Mexico. Instead,

■ Two decades after Verrazzano's explorations, this 1547 chart shows the early claims of France in North America. It depicts the men and women of Roberval's short-lived colonizing expedition as they disembarked in 1542, watched by Native Americans. Perhaps to feature the large St. Lawrence River, the European mapmaker put North at the bottom and South at the top. Hence, the Atlantic coast seems upside-down to our eyes, with Florida appearing in the upper right-hand corner.

they encountered only scattered villages. Towns that refused to provide the intruders with porters or guides met with brutal Spanish reprisals that made use of attack dogs. At Mabila near modern-day Selma, Alabama, de Soto's mounted army, brandishing swords and lances, killed several thousand Native Americans who had dared to attack them with bows and arrows. Still, Spanish frustrations grew due to difficult terrain, stiff Indian resistance, and failure to find riches. After exploring beyond the Mississippi River, de Soto died of a fever in 1542. His disheartened followers escaped downstream to the Gulf of Mexico the next year, leaving epidemic sickness in their wake.

At the same time, another encounter was unfolding in the Southwest. By 1539, Spanish sailors voyaging up Mexico's western coast had explored the Gulf of California and skirted the Baja Peninsula. Over the next four years, similar expeditions cruised the coast of California and southern Oregon. Once again, they found no signs of a passage linking the Pacific and Atlantic oceans. In Mexico, speculation about gold in the north had intensified after the appearance of Cabeza de Vaca. His African companion, Esteban, guided a reconnaissance party north in 1539. Esteban was killed by the Zuni Indians, but exaggerated accounts of the region's pueblos prompted rumors about the seven golden cities known as Cibola.

The next year, aspiring conquistador Francisco Vásquez de Coronado set out from northern Mexico to reach these wealthy towns before de Soto could. He left his post as a frontier governor and assembled a huge expedition with more than 300 Spanish adventurers and 1,000 Indian allies. However, his grandiose expectations were quickly dashed. The pueblos of the Zuni, he reported, "are very good houses, three and four and five stories high," but the fabled "Seven Cities are seven little villages." Hoping to gauge his distance from the Pacific, Coronado sent explorers northwest. When they reached the amazing but impassable Grand Canyon, they realized they could go no farther and returned.

> *Spanish newcomers imposed a heavy burden on the Pueblo Indians, demanding food and burning helpless towns.*

Spanish newcomers imposed a heavy burden on the Pueblo Indians, demanding food and burning helpless towns. Desperate to get rid of Coronado, the Pueblo told him stories of a far-off, wealthy land called Quivira. They secretly recruited a Plains Indian to lead the Spaniards to some place where men and horses "would starve to death." In the spring of 1541, he guided Coronado's party northeast onto the Great Plains, repeating tantalizing tales of gold and silver. Coronado's soldiers became the first Europeans to see this rolling ocean of grass and its endless herds of buffalo. But when Quivira proved to be a Wichita Indian village in what is now central Kansas, the Spanish strangled their deceitful guide and made their way back south to New Spain. At one point, as they crossed northern Texas, they even came within 300 miles of de Soto's ill-fated party in eastern Arkansas. But neither de Soto nor Coronado—nor Cartier in the north—ever discovered wealthy cities or a sea passage to the Far East.

The British Library, Maps Division

■ European mapmakers learned quickly about the expeditions into the North American interior led by Cartier, de Soto, and Coronado. This 1566 Italian chart places New France, or Canada, in the North, and shows the Indian town of "Ochelaga" visited by Cartier. "La Florida," labeled twice, includes not only the crudely drawn peninsula but also all of the Southeast explored by de Soto. The imagined regions of Cibola and Quivira, sought by Coronado, appear in the Southwest. European hope of a Northwest Passage from the Atlantic to Asia continues, and the size of the North Pacific remains uncertain, so Japan (Giapan) is shown near the coast of California.

The Protestant Reformation Plays Out in America

■ *How did Europe's sharp religious split influence the early colonization of North America?*

In 1520, while Cortés vied with the Aztec for control in Mexico and Magellan maneuvered around South America, the pope excommunicated a German monk named Martin Luther. Three years earlier, Luther had nailed a list of ninety-five theses to the church door at Wittenberg, challenging long-standing church practices and papal authority. Luther's followers questioned lavish church spending—construction of the ornate St. Peter's Basilica was under way in Rome at the time—and the practice of selling religious pardons to raise money. They also rejected the church's elaborate hierarchy and criticized its refusal to translate the Latin Bible into modern languages.

Luther's reform movement triggered the division of western Christianity into competing religious camps, bitterly at odds. For their written protestations against the papacy, Luther and his fellow insurgents received the enduring name *Protestants*. Their movement became known broadly as the Reformation. Those who opposed it, siding with Rome, launched a Counter-Reformation to defend and revitalize the Roman Catholic Church.

For the first time in history, a controversy in Europe made waves that washed onto American shores. Throughout the remainder of the sixteenth century, European national and religious conflict played out in part overseas, a pattern that repeated itself in future centuries. France and Spain, Catholic powers competing for dominance in Europe, wrestled to claim control of Florida. England, an upstart island nation with a rising population, an expanding navy, and a monarchy at odds with the pope in Rome, seized control of Ireland and launched its first attempt to plant a colony in North America.

REFORMATION AND COUNTER-REFORMATION IN EUROPE

As zeal for Luther's religious reforms spread across Europe, it split communities and even sparked armed conflict. In Switzerland, a priest named Ulrich Zwingli led the revolt. He abolished the practice of confession, condemned the church calendar full of fasts and saints' days, and defied the tradition of a celibate clergy by marrying. Zwingli was killed in battle in 1531, but the Swiss Reformation soon found a new leader in John Calvin. A French Protestant, Calvin settled in Geneva and for more than two decades (1541–1564) ruled the city as a church-centered state.

Kings and queens gradually expanded court bureaucracies and asserted greater control over their subjects and economies.

Calvin imposed his own strict interpretation on Lutheranism and drew dedicated followers to his church. Offended by expensive vestments and elaborate rituals, he donned a simple black "Geneva" robe. He argued that faith alone, not "good works," would lead Christians to be saved. He preached that God alone determined salvation; it could not be bought by giving **tithes** to the church. Only a select few people, Calvin explained, were destined to be members of God's chosen elect. Moreover, only an informed clergy and the careful study of scripture could reveal signs of a person's status. Soon, Calvinist doctrine helped shape Protestant communities across northern Europe: Huguenots in France, Puritans in England, Presbyterians in Scotland, and the Dutch Reformed Church in the Netherlands.

The Protestant Reformation that Luther had ignited coincided roughly with another important change in Europe, the emergence of the modern nation-state. Kings and queens gradually expanded court bureaucracies and asserted greater control over their subjects and economies. They strengthened their armies, gaining a near monopoly on the use of force, and they took full advantage of the new medium of printing. As religious ferment spread and local allegiances gave way to a broader sense of national identity, strong sovereigns moved to distance themselves from papal authority in Rome.

The emergence of England as a nation-state under the Tudor dynasty (founded by Henry VII in 1485) illustrates this shift in power away from Rome. When Henry VIII succeeded his father in 1509, he married Catherine of Aragon, the youngest surviving daughter of Spain's royal couple, Ferdinand and Isabella. As queen, she suffered numerous miscarriages and was unable to produce a male heir, so in 1533 the restless monarch sought a divorce. When the pope refused to grant an annulment of the king's marriage, Henry VIII wrested control of the English church from papal hands and had Parliament approve his divorce and remarriage. The new Church of England, or Anglican Church, continued to follow much of the Catholic Church's doctrine. However, its "Protector and only Supreme Head" would now be the English monarch. During her long reign from 1558 to 1603, Henry VIII's daughter Queen Elizabeth I managed to steer the Church of England on a middle course between advocates of Catholicism and extreme Protestants.

Throughout Europe, as zealous believers on both sides of the debate staked out their positions, attempts to heal religious divisions gave way to confrontation. Reformation challenges to the pope in Rome, whether from local parishes or powerful monarchs, met with stiff resistance as Catholic leaders mobilized opposition. Their followers rallied to defend Roman Catholicism in a variety of ways. Taken together, these efforts are known as the Counter-Reformation.

A militant new Catholic religious order called the Society of Jesus, or the Jesuits, represented one dimension of the Counter-Reformation. Led by a Spanish soldier named Ignatius Loyola and willing to give their lives for their beliefs, these dedicated missionaries and teachers helped reenergize the Catholic faith and spread it to distant parts of the world. Another institution, the Inquisition, reflects a different side of the Counter-Reformation. In 1542, Catholic authorities established a new religious-judicial proceeding, known as the Inquisition, to help resist the spread of Protestantism. Heretics—individuals accused of denying or defying church doctrine—were brought before the Inquisition's strict religious courts. Those who refused to renounce their beliefs suffered severe punishment, including torture and execution. These heresy trials made clear to Inquisition leaders that the advent of printing was helping spread the works of Luther and his Protestant allies. In 1557, therefore, the pope issued an "Index" of prohibited books.

In Spain, King Philip II, who ruled from 1556 to 1598, led an Inquisition to root out Protestant heresy. The Spanish monarch came close to acquiring England as well. In 1588, he dispatched a fleet of warships—the Spanish Armada—in hopes of seizing control in London and restoring the Catholic faith as England's sanctioned religion. A sudden storm and hasty mobilization by the island nation foiled the Spanish king's invasion. But Philip II's confrontation with the navy of Queen Elizabeth I epitomized the sharp new division between Catholic and Protestant power in Europe. This deepening antagonism—religious, ideological, and economic—shaped events overseas in the second half of the sixteenth century. The struggle became especially clear in Florida, the vague region claimed by Spain that encompassed Indian lands from Chesapeake Bay to the Gulf of Mexico.

COMPETING POWERS LAY CLAIM TO FLORIDA

As Spain used force to obtain the dazzling wealth of New World societies, its European rivals looked on jealously. As early as 1523, French sea raiders had captured Spanish ships returning from Mexico with Cortés's bounty of Aztec gold, silver, and pearls. Ten years later, French pirates made a similar haul. To protect the flow of riches from America, the Spanish soon initiated a well-armed annual convoy to escort their wealth from Havana to Seville. Each year, Spain's huge West Indies treasure fleet made an enticing target as it followed the Gulf Stream along the Florida coast.

But France had its own designs on Florida, furthered by the special concerns of French Huguenots. Unsure of their future in a religiously divided country, these Protestants took a

■ MAP 1.4   The Extent of North American Exploration by 1592

By 1592, a century after Columbus's initial voyage, European explorers and colonists had touched the edges of North America, and a few had ventured far inland. But they had not found riches or a passageway to the Pacific, and only the Spanish had managed to establish a lasting foothold along the Florida Coast.

leading role in the colonization efforts of France. In 1562, French Huguenots established a settlement at Port Royal Sound (Parris Island, South Carolina), close to the route of Spain's annual treasure fleet. The effort lasted only two years and aroused Spanish suspicions of "Lutheran" intruders.

Undaunted, the French backed a larger colonizing effort to Florida in 1564. When French Protestants erected Fort Caroline on the St. John's River at present-day Jacksonville, the Spanish crown took swift action. In 1565, Philip II sent 300 soldiers and 700 colonists under Pedro Menéndez de Avilés to oust the French and secure Florida. Menéndez captured Fort Caroline and massacred hundreds of French settlers. The heretics, he feared, might attack the treasure fleet, forge alliances with Florida's Indians, or provoke revolt among slaves in the Spanish Caribbean. To prevent further French incursions on Florida's Atlantic coast, Menéndez established a new outpost at nearby St. Augustine. He also sent Juan Pardo north from Port Royal Sound to establish half a dozen forts in the interior.

With French threats defeated, the Spanish at St. Augustine attempted to plant strategic missions farther north to convert Native Americans to Christianity and secure Spain's land claims. In 1570, eight missionaries from Loyola's Society of Jesus sailed north from Florida to Chesapeake Bay. There, the Jesuits established a mission to convert local Indians and looked for "an entrance into the mountains and on to China." But the friars' rules and

Prom.Lupi.

Portus Regalis, siue F. S. Helenæ.

■ In 1562, French Protestants established a short-lived colony at Port Royal Sound on the South Carolina coast. "The commander, on landing with some soldiers, found the country very beautiful, as it was well wooded with oak, cedar, and other trees. As they went through the woods, they saw Indian peacocks, or turkeys, flying past, and deer going by." Traveling upstream beyond Parris Island, they surprised an encampment of Indians, "who, on perceiving the boats, immediately took flight," leaving behind the meat "they were roasting."

beliefs antagonized the Native Americans. By the time Menéndez visited the region in 1572, all the missionaries had been killed. Spain's failure to secure a foothold on Chesapeake Bay soon proved costly, as a new European rival appeared on the scene. Almost overnight, Protestant England emerged as a contending force in the Atlantic world. Now English adventurers began challenging Spanish dominance in the Caribbean and along North America's southeastern coast.

THE BACKGROUND OF ENGLISH EXPANSION

The voyages of John Cabot and the visits of Bristol fishing vessels to Newfoundland's Grand Banks had stimulated an early English interest in the Atlantic. But for several reasons this curiosity intensified after 1550. Henry VIII had used his power, plus the wealth he had seized from the Catholic Church, to build a sizable navy before he died in 1547. The merchant fleet grew as well, carrying English wool and cloth to Antwerp and other European ports. In addition, the English population, which had declined in the previous 150 years, grew steadily after 1500. Overall numbers more than doubled during the sixteenth century.

England's rising population created new pressure on limited resources, especially land. Tenants needed access to agricultural plots in order to subsist, but the growing market in English woolens made property owners eager to enclose pastures for sheep grazing, even if it involved pushing tenants off the land. This gradual squeeze, known as "the enclosure movement," set countless rural people adrift to seek work in towns and cities. London's population soared from 50,000 in 1500 to 200,000 a century later.

Emphasis on wool production had additional unforeseen effects. At midcentury, Europe's market in textile goods became saturated with cheap woolens and collapsed suddenly. English cloth exports fell 35 percent in 1551, prompting merchants to search for new avenues of foreign commerce. Starting in the 1550s, therefore, England's overseas exploration pushed in all directions. Investors in the new Muscovy Company sent ships north around Scandinavia through the Arctic Ocean, but they failed to find a northeastern route above the Asian landmass to China. Other English vessels sailed south to Morocco and the Gold Coast, challenging the Portuguese monopoly of the African trade. English mariner John Hawkins conducted three voyages to West Africa during the 1560s. Horning in on the growing transatlantic slave traffic, he purchased Africans and then sold them in Caribbean ports to Spanish buyers.

Philip II, having driven the French out of Florida, had had enough of Protestant interlopers. A Spanish fleet forced Hawkins and his young kinsman Francis Drake out of Mexican waters in 1568. But thereafter, English sea rovers, with quiet support from Elizabeth, stepped up their challenges to Spain on the high seas. Drake proved the most wide-ranging and successful. On a voyage to the Pacific (1577–1580), he plundered Spanish ports in Peru and landed near San Francisco Bay. He claimed California for England as New Albion and then sailed around the globe. In the 1580s, Drake continued, in his words, "to singe the Spaniard's beard." He sacked ports in the West Indies, encouraged slave uprisings against the Spanish, and attacked the settlement at St. Augustine. He also captured numerous treasure ships, sank two dozen enemy vessels in their home port at Cadiz, and helped defeat Philip's Spanish Armada in 1588.

England's anti-Catholic propagandists made Drake a national hero. Moreover, they painted Spanish cruelties toward Indians in the New World in the worst possible terms. To bolster their case, they translated the vivid tracts of Las Casas into English. Writers loyal to the Counter-Reformation rejected this smear tactic as a "black legend," while Protestants in England countered that Las Casas was a firsthand witness and conscientious reformer, not a fabricator of lies. Whatever the later verdict on Spain's early conduct overseas, the English themselves proved far from innocent. In the Elizabethan years, they established their own pattern of violence during their brutal conquest of Ireland. Many who played leading roles in this bloody takeover came to view a colony in America as the next logical step in England's aggressive overseas expansion.

British Museum/Bridgeman Art Library, New York

■ Painter John White accompanied Martin Frobisher on a search for the Northwest Passage in 1577. When the English captured several inhabitants of Baffin Island, the young artist painted an Eskimo mother and her baby, with attention to her warm clothing and the way she carried the child. White later took part in several voyages to Roanoke Island. His striking pictures were widely copied in Europe, but the original watercolors only become known in the twentieth century.

"The World as a Clover": Mapping for Art, Religion, or Science

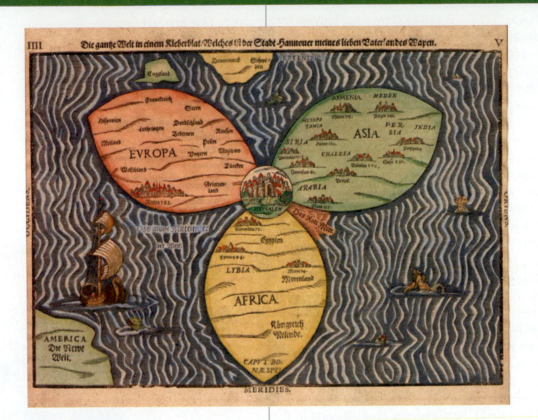

Every map is a work of art, reducing a three-dimensional world to two dimensions. In any age, some charts have a scientific or commercial purpose, while others offer symbolic or spiritual meaning. World maps drawn in medieval Europe had a religious origin and use, so they highlighted the holy city of Jerusalem at the center. As oceanic exploration increased, Europeans developed sophisticated navigational charts that emphasized practical information rather than artistic symbolism. But the older tradition of allegorical maps continued, as shown by this fanciful world diagram created in Germany in 1582.

This depiction was made later than the other sixteenth-century maps that appear in this chapter. The creator came from Hanover, a city that used a three-leafed clover on its crest, so he portrayed "The Whole World as a Clover Leaf." The Christian holy land is at the center, while England and the Red Sea are clearly visible. Scandinavia and America float at the edges of the chart, and strange sea creatures populate the oceans. Portraying a symmetrical clover enhances the map's aesthetic appeal, but it also vastly exaggerates the relative size of Europe in comparison to Africa and Asia.

QUESTIONS

1. Compare this 1582 map with the other sixteenth-century charts in this chapter. In each case, who might have commissioned such a map, and for what potential uses?

2. Specifically, how does this map reflect the slowness of Europeans to cope with new geographical knowledge provided by Marco Polo, Columbus, da Gama, and Magellan?

LOST COLONY: THE ROANOKE EXPERIENCE

Sir Humphrey Gilbert, who had served in Ireland, was one Elizabethan with an eye on America. In 1576, Gilbert published his *Discourse for a Discovery for a New Passage to Cathay.* In it, he speculated on a short northwestern route to China. Martin Frobisher, another veteran of the Irish campaign, undertook voyages to locate such a route. He mistakenly thought he had found the passage, or strait, to Asia. As evidence, he brought back members of an Eskimo family he believed to be Chinese, and English artist John White drew their pictures. The next year, writing an essay on "How Her Majesty May Annoy the King of Spain," Gilbert proposed a colony in Newfoundland. The queen granted him a patent—a license giving him exclusive rights—for such a project. But shipwrecks and desertions doomed the venture to failure. When Gilbert died at sea on the homeward voyage, his half-brother, Walter Raleigh, obtained a similar patent to plant a colony in North America.

In 1584, Raleigh sent explorers to the Outer Banks, the string of coastal barrier islands below Chesapeake Bay that Verrazzano had glimpsed sixty years earlier. They brought back two Indian informants and positive reports about the land near Roanoke Island. The next month, Richard Hakluyt, England's foremost advocate and chronicler of overseas expansion, handed Elizabeth an advisory paper entitled "Western Planting." The document called for the establishment of a strategic outpost on the North American coast, where the English could launch attacks against Spanish shipping, hunt for useful commodities, and convert Indians to Protestant Christianity.

Raleigh's three efforts to establish such an outpost failed in rapid succession. In 1585, he first sent Ralph Lane, a hardened veteran of the Irish campaigns, to build a fort at Roanoke Island. Like other Europeans who had preceded him to America, Lane anticipated "the discovery of a good mine, or a passage to the South Sea." But storms in mid-ocean scattered his ships, and most of Lane's initial force never arrived. Those who did, including artist John White, fared badly because of scarce food, bad discipline, and hostile relations with the Indians. Francis Drake, arriving in 1586 after harassing the Spanish in the West Indies and Florida, expected to find a thriving enterprise. Instead, he carried the disheartened soldiers back to England. They had paid a price, Hakluyt commented, "for the cruelty and outrages committed by some of them against the native inhabitants of that country." A second expedition diverted to the Caribbean to prey on enemy shipping, after leaving a few men at Roanoke, who did not survive.

In May 1587, John White led a third English venture to America, with 110 people, including women and children. They planned to settle on Chesapeake Bay, but a contentious captain refused to carry them farther north after an initial stop at Roanoke Island. In August the settlers sent White back to England for more supplies; they would leave a message for him if they moved. When he finally returned in 1590—delayed by England's clash with the Spanish Armada—he found the site deserted. The word *Croatoan* carved on a post suggested that survivors had joined the nearby Croatan Indians, but the Lost Colony's fate remains a source of endless speculation. The Spanish, worried by the English foray, drew up plans for a fortification at Chesapeake Bay, but warfare between Spain and England kept both countries preoccupied elsewhere until Philip II and Elizabeth I died.

© The British Museum

■ John White made valuable firsthand drawings of Native Americans living in what is now coastal North Carolina, including the wife and daughter of a local leader. The woman kept her "haire trussed opp in a knott," had tattoos on her arms, wore "a chaine of great pearles," and often carried "a gourde full of some kinde of pleasant liquor." The girl holds an English doll, for Indian children "are greatly Deligted with puppetts . . . brought oute of England."

CHRONOLOGY: 14,000 YEARS AGO TO 1590 C.E.

14,000 years ago	Early Paleo-Indians in Florida and Pennsylvania regions, and also in Monte Verde, Chile.
13,900 to 12,900 years ago	Clovis hunters spread across North America.
10,000 to 3,000 years ago	Archaic Indians flourish in diverse settings.
4,200 to 2,700 years ago	Poverty Point culture exists in Louisiana.
300 to 900 C.E.	Mayan culture flourishes in Mesoamerica.
500 to 600	Teotihuacan in central Mexico becomes one of the world's largest cities.
900 to 1100	Anasazi culture centers in Chaco Canyon in Southwest.
1000	Norse explorers establish a Vinland colony in Newfoundland.
1100	Cahokia in Illinois becomes one focus of Mississippian culture.
1400	Aztec build capital at Tenochtitlán (site of modern Mexico City).
1405 to 1433	Chinese fleet of Admiral Zheng He reaches Indian Ocean and Africa's east coast.
1418 to 1460	Prince Henry of Portugal sends ships to explore Africa's west coast.
1492	First voyage of Columbus.
1494	Treaty of Tordesillas arranges division between overseas claims of Spain and Portugal.
1517	Martin Luther launches Protestant Reformation.
1519	Cortés invades Mexico.
1519 to 1522	Magellan's ship circumnavigates the globe and returns to Spain.
1534 to 1543	Expeditions of Cartier (Canada), de Soto (Southeast), and Coronado (Southwest) probe North America.
1565	Spanish establish St. Augustine.
1585 to 1590	English attempt to establish Roanoke colony fails.

Conclusion

For approximately 150 centuries, people descended from distant Asian ancestry had explored and settled the bountiful Western Hemisphere. In every region of North America, from the arctic north to the semitropical Florida Keys, they had adapted and multiplied, building distinctive and durable ways of life over countless generations. Then suddenly, in a single century, unprecedented intrusions brought newcomers from foreign lands to the coasts of the Americas, in wooden castles that floated on the sea. At first, local inhabitants retained the balance of power; the fate of a colonizing effort could hinge on Indian relations. But the number of foreigners only increased with time. In the next century, the contest for European control of the Atlantic seaboard began in earnest.

For Review

1. How has our awareness about the earliest human societies in the Western Hemisphere changed over the past century?

2. Why did complex societies develop in Mesoamerica and Peru, close to the equator?

3. Amerigo Vespucci called the Western Hemisphere a "New World" in 1499. What reasons can you offer for or against using this term today in discussing North and South America after 1500?

4. If you lived in Madrid, Spain, in 1525, how might your understanding of world geography differ from your grandparents' views fifty years earlier?

5. Discuss the paradox that English charges of Spanish cruelty in the Americas ("the black legend") may be both valid and exaggerated. Can you cite a similar paradox among other countries in modern times?

6. After reading this chapter, where would you mark the beginning of American history? How would you defend your choice in comparison to other options for an earlier or later starting point?

7. Describe at least three ways in which the Columbian Exchange dramatically altered history in North America and elsewhere by 1600.

Created Equal Online

For more *Created Equal* resources, including suggestions on sites to visit and books to read, go to **MyHistoryLab.com**.

Chapter 2

European Footholds in North America, 1600–1660

■ A *Mayflower* replica is now part of the restored Plymouth Colony site.

CHAPTER OUTLINE

■ Spain's Ocean-Spanning Reach

■ France and Holland: Overseas Competition for Spain

■ English Beginnings on the Atlantic Coast

■ The Puritan Experiment

■ The Chesapeake Bay Colonies

In the summer of 1621, an Englishman and an Indian left Plymouth Village on foot to visit a Native American leader named Massasoit and secure his support for the struggling English colony. During their forty-mile journey, Stephen Hopkins and Squanto saw numerous signs of a wave of disease that had swept the New England coast four years earlier, killing thousands of Indians. Skulls and bones still lay aboveground in many places. The two men who encountered these grim scenes had come together from strikingly different backgrounds.

Back in 1609, Hopkins had left England in a fleet heading for Jamestown in Virginia. When a storm wrecked his ship on the uncharted island of Bermuda, he and others rebelled against their official leader. Accused of mutiny and sentenced to hang, Hopkins pleaded his case and narrowly escaped the noose. Hopkins made it back to England and started a family, but in 1620 he decided to return to America. At the English port of Plymouth, Hopkins, his pregnant wife, Elizabeth, and several children and servants became paying passengers on a ship called the *Mayflower*. The vessel had been chartered to carry a group of English Protestants to America from their exile in Holland.

During the arduous passage, tensions mounted. Hopkins was among those who muttered "mutinous speeches" and argued that "when they came ashore, they should use their own libertie, for none had power to command them." But after Elizabeth gave birth, Hopkins joined the other forty men aboard in signing the Mayflower Compact. The agreement bound all the passengers together in a "Civil Body Politic" to be governed by laws "most meet and convenient for the general good." They reached New England in early winter, and Hopkins and others laid out the village of Plymouth in the snow. There, the newcomers met Squanto, a Native American with a command of English who helped them negotiate with local Indians.

Squanto had also endured Atlantic travel. He remembered the first French and English fishing vessels, which had appeared when he was a small boy. In 1614 Squanto was among twenty-seven Indians taken hostage aboard an English ship and sold into slavery in Spain. Escaping, he spent time in England and Newfoundland before returning home in 1619, only to find his entire village swept away by disease.

The *Mayflower* pilgrims, arriving a year after Squanto's return, also suffered heavy losses. Of the 102 settlers who had begun the voyage, half of them died in Plymouth Colony by the next spring. But in New England, as elsewhere in America, death seemed to play favorites in the following years. As colonization continued, recurrent epidemics took a particularly heavy toll on Native Americans, who lacked immunity when exposed to foreign diseases for the first time. In 1622, Squanto fell sick and died of a fever, leaving no relatives behind. In contrast, Stephen and Elizabeth Hopkins lived on to see numerous children and grandchildren thrive.

Near Cape Cod and Chesapeake Bay, local Indians had initially welcomed newcomers from England as potential military allies. But by the middle of the seventeenth century, arriving settlers had taken over Indian land in both Massachusetts and the Chesapeake region. The success of these English-speaking colonists would exert a lasting influence on the future direction of American society. But their stories unfolded as part of a far wider North American drama that included a diversity of European groups and embraced both the Atlantic and the Pacific shores. Whether confronting newcomers from Spain, France, Holland, or England, scores of Native American communities faced new challenges that altered traditional Indian ways of living and sometimes threatened their very survival.

Spain's Ocean-Spanning Reach

■ *What motivated Spain to extend the northern borders of its New World empire?*

In 1580, Spain's Philip II laid claim to the throne of Portugal, unifying Europe's two richest seaborne empires. But this consolidation, which endured until 1640, created problems. First, combining with Portugal put huge additional burdens on the overstretched Spanish bureaucracy. Second, the global success of the combined Iberian empires invited challenges from envious rivals in northern Europe. The new international competition came from France, Holland, and England, aspiring naval powers with imperial ambitions that touched the Pacific as well as the Atlantic.

In 1598, for example, ten ships from Amsterdam found their way to the Pacific, defying Spanish claims for control of that ocean. One of these Dutch vessels, piloted by Englishman Will Adams, ended up in Japan, where the new Tokugawa dynasty (1600–1868) was consolidating its control. Adams visited Edo—the rising military town that would grow into modern-day Tokyo—and even built a ship for the *shogun* (ruler). Adams's experiences (which inspired the 1975 bestseller *Shogun*) serve as a reminder that by 1600, competition for oceanic control had stretched far beyond the Atlantic. Who would dominate Pacific sea-lanes to America?

Freedom of the Seas: Grotius and Maritime Law

In our era, air travel has given rise to the growing field of air and space law. Similarly, in the sixteenth century, the expansion of oceanic travel led to legal conflicts and the growth of international maritime law.

In 1494, a treaty had divided the world equally between Spain and Portugal, and in 1580 those two kingdoms were combined under Philip II, creating a global monopoly. That same year, Spain's ambassador in England complained to Elizabeth I about the recent incursion of Francis Drake into Pacific waters. The queen replied that everyone had equal access to the sea and the air. Her clever retort would be given legal strength in the next generation by the great Dutch jurist and humanist Hugh de Groot, best known by his Latin name, Hugo Grotius (1583–1645).

Grotius grew up in the Netherlands at a time when Dutch, French, and English ships were challenging Spain's monopoly on the high seas. Seventeenth-century seafarers stood to make huge profits, but they faced intense competition and few rules. As a Dutch poet put it: "Wherever profit leads us, to every sea and shore, for love of gain the wide world's harbors we explore." After studying a case in which a Dutch vessel seized a Portuguese ship in Asian waters, Grotius, a gifted young lawyer, drafted a treatise putting such incidents in a broader context. In 1609, at age twenty-six, he published *Mare librum*, underscoring the freedom of the seas.

Grotius lived an eventful life, enduring prison and surviving a shipwreck. He was a pioneer in framing international law and exploring the rules of warfare. But his argument that the sea could not be the property of any country proved

■ This 1633 pamphlet is a reprint of an earlier essay on the freedom of the seas by Hugo Grotius, the Dutch legal expert who helped shape modern maritime law.

controversial, as rival maritime nations claimed control over neighboring waters. Eventually, however, Grotius's farsighted argument that the oceans should be free for all to use gained acceptance, paving the way for expanding networks of trade that continue to the present day.

QUESTIONS

1. How would Grotius's argument for freedom of the seas benefit rising European countries committed to overseas trade, such as England and the Netherlands?

2. If expanding oceanic trade gave rise to international maritime law, what developments might give birth to new areas of law in our own time?

VIZCAÍNO IN CALIFORNIA AND JAPAN

In April 1607, a letter from the king of Spain reached Mexico City. The king commanded his viceroy in charge of affairs in Mexico (New Spain) to create an outpost on California's Monterey Bay. Spanish galleons returning through the North Pacific from Manila (Spain's recently established port in the Philippines) desperately needed a coastal haven after crossing the immense ocean. Monterey Bay was well supplied with water, food, and timber. The sheltering harbor would provide a perfect way station, where ships could take on supplies and make repairs before heading south.

But the viceroy in Mexico City had other ideas. He diverted the necessary funds into a search for the fabled North Pacific isles of Rica de Oro (Rich in Gold) and Rica de Plata (Rich in Silver). To hunt for the mysterious islands, the viceroy chose a seasoned navigator who had already explored the California coast and taken part in the Pacific trade. Sebastián Vizcaíno had sailed to Manila from Acapulco on Mexico's west coast. His ships had carried Mexican chocolate to the Philippines and brought back silks and spices from Asia. Dispatched in 1611, Vizcaíno found no isles of gold and silver, but he did visit Japan. When he finally returned across the Pacific in 1613 aboard a vessel built in Japan, he brought

Spanish exploration by land and sea

- Spanish territory, 1610
- Juan de Oñate, 1598–1601
- Juan de Oñate, 1604–1605
- Sebastián Vizcaíno, 1602–1603
- Sebastián Vizcaíno, 1611–1613

Present state boundaries provided for orientation

■ **MAP 2.1**   **The Spanish Southwest in the Early Seventeenth Century**

180 Japanese with him to Mexico. This unique delegation was bound for Spain and Italy to open doors between East and West. However, the Tokugawas soon began to persecute the European traders and Christian missionaries who had been allowed in the Japanese islands for a generation, so the frail link between Europe and Japan through Mexico never developed further.

Tokugawa officials, it seems, feared that tolerating foreigners in Japan's ports might "propagate the doctrine of the Catholics" and undermine their supremacy. Moreover, developing Japanese fleets might bring guns to warlords and disrupt hard-won peace. "No Japanese ship or boat whatever, nor any native of Japan, shall presume to go out of the country," a government edict declared in 1638. It added, "whoso acts contrary to this shall die, and the ship with the crew and goods aboard shall be sequestered till further order. All Japanese who return from abroad shall be put to death."

So Japan passed up an opportunity for naval expansion, just as Ming China had done two centuries earlier after the voyages of Zheng He. Instead, the new dynasty adopted a policy of commercial and cultural isolation that lasted for more than 200 years. Had Japanese society followed another route, co-opting Western technologies and aggressively exploring and colonizing the Pacific, the subsequent history of North America and the world would almost certainly have taken a very different path.

For the Spanish, Vizcaíno's Pacific adventure consumed crucial funds, and the possibility of a Spanish settlement at Monterey quickly disappeared. Concerned that their empire had already become overextended, Spanish officials postponed plans to colonize California's coast. In addition, Spain wondered whether to maintain its existing North American colony in Florida and its newest frontier province: New Mexico.

OÑATE CREATES A SPANISH FOOTHOLD IN THE SOUTHWEST

In 1598, Juan de Oñate renewed the northern efforts of Coronado's expedition several generations earlier. Setting out from New Spain, he led 500 men, women, and children north into the upper Rio Grande valley to create the province of New Mexico. Oñate was a wealthy man—his father had discovered a major silver mine at Zacatecas—and he had bold ambitions. Aided by Franciscan friars (organized followers of St. Francis loyal to the pope), Oñate and his mixed-race colonists expected to convert the Indians to Christianity. Expanding outward from the compact apartment-like native towns, or pueblos, the intruders hoped to open a vast new colonial realm. It would be a "new world," they proclaimed, "greater than New Spain."

DOCUMENT

Don Juan de Oñate, Letter from New Mexico to the Victory

But Oñate drastically underestimated the difficulties. When embittered Indians at Acoma pueblo killed eleven of his soldiers in 1599, he retaliated by bombarding the mesa-top citadel, killing 800 inhabitants and enslaving nearly 600 others. Hearing of the brutal repression of the residents of Acoma, neighboring pueblos reluctantly submitted to Spanish demands for labor and food. Colonial reinforcements arriving in 1600 were dismayed by the harsh conditions; Oñate needed new discoveries for the colony to prosper. In 1601, he launched an expedition east onto the Great Plains, but the venture proved as futile as Coronado's earlier march had been.

> Oñate's new "Mexico" remained isolated and impoverished, with the newcomers strapped for clothing and food.

To make matters worse, a drought gripped the Rio Grande valley, and many of the recent settlers departed, complaining that the region lacked woods, pastures, water, and suitable land. When Oñate returned from the plains, he found that two-thirds of his tiny colony had given up and returned to Mexico. Foiled on the east and weakened along the Rio Grande, Oñate next pressed west to seek a link to the Pacific. When he reached the Gulf of California in 1605, he mistook it for the great ocean and envisioned a possible link to the Pacific trade.

In fact, however, Oñate's new "Mexico" remained isolated and impoverished, with the newcomers strapped for clothing and food. The colonists, desperate to survive, pressed hard on the native peoples. They demanded tribute in the form of cotton blankets, buffalo hides, and baskets of scarce maize. In winter, ill-equipped Spanish-speaking soldiers stripped warm robes off the backs of shivering women and children; in summer, they scoured each pueblo for corn, torturing residents to find out where food was hidden.

Meanwhile, a few hundred Pueblo Indians—intimidated by the Spanish, desperate for a share of the food they had grown, and fearful of attacks by neighboring Apache—began to accept Christian baptism and seek Spanish protection. By 1608, when the crown threatened to withdraw support from the struggling province, the colony's Franciscan missionaries appealed that their converts had grown too numerous to resettle and too dependent to abandon. Their argument may have been exaggerated, but it caught the attention of authorities.

Besides, England and France were launching new colonies in Virginia and Canada. Since mapmakers still could not accurately calculate longitude (east-west position on the globe), no one was sure whether these bases created by international rivals posed

■ Acoma, often called Sky City, sits atop a high sandstone mesa west of Albuquerque, New Mexico. The name means "place that always was," and the pueblo has been continuously inhabited for roughly 1,000 years. Acoma's Native American community survived a devastating attack by Spanish colonizers in 1599.

a threat that was dangerously close at hand. Worried Spanish officials finally agreed with the Franciscan friars that New Mexico must carry on. They replaced Oñate with a new governor and asserted royal control over the few dozen settlers who remained in the colony.

NEW MEXICO SURVIVES: NEW FLOCKS AMONG OLD PUEBLOS

The Spanish decision to hold on in New Mexico reshaped life for everyone in the region. At least 60,000 Indians living in nearly sixty separate pueblos found their world transformed and their survival threatened over the next half-century. In 1610 the new governor, ruling over scarcely fifty colonists, created a capital at the village of Santa Fe. Within two decades, roughly 750 colonists inhabited the remote province, including Spanish, Mexican Indians, Africans, and mixed-race children.

The racial and ethnic diversity of New Mexico repeated the colonial pattern established in New Spain, where Iberians had been intermarrying with Indians and Africans for several generations. Similarly, labor practices and religious changes also followed models established after the conquest of the Aztec in Mexico. As in New Spain, certain privileged people in the new colony received **encomiendas;** such grants entitled the holders (known as an *encomenderos*) to the labor of a set number of Native American workers. With labor in short supply throughout the Spanish colonies, other settlers led occasional raids against nomadic Plains Indians, keeping some captives and shipping others south to toil as slaves in the Mexican silver mines.

Meanwhile, the number of Franciscan missionaries rose rapidly. They forbade traditional Pueblo celebrations, known as **kachina** dances, and destroyed sacred kachina masks. Their combination of intense zeal and harsh punishments prompted many Indians to learn Spanish and become obedient converts. However, it also drove the Indians' own religious practices underground—literally, into the hidden, circular kivas that had long been a focal point for Native American spiritual activities in the region. There, people kept their traditional faith alive in secret and passed sacred rituals along to the next generation.

The Spanish brought more than Christianity to New Mexico. The newcomers also transferred novel crops (wheat, onions, chilies, peas) and planted new fruits (peaches, plums, cherries). Settlers introduced metal hoes and axes, along with donkeys, chickens, and other domesticated animals previously unknown to the native inhabitants. Horses and cattle, led north from New Spain in small herds, eventually revolutionized life across the North American West. But the most immediate impact came from Spanish sheep, well suited to the semi-desert conditions. Each friar soon possessed a flock of several thousand, and Pueblo artisans wove wool into cloth.

© Jerry Jacka Photography

■ The Spanish made Santa Fe the capital of their New Mexico colony in 1610 and built the church of San Miguel there in 1626. Though destroyed in the Pueblo Revolt of 1680, it was rebuilt and has remained in use. "The floor is bare earth," wrote an eighteenth-century observer, "the usual floor throughout these regions."

But the Pueblo world, like Squanto's world, was eroding under the onslaught of new European diseases. The large Pueblo population, cut in half in the sixty years since Coronado's appearance, still numbered more than 60,000 in 1600, after the arrival of Oñate's colonizing expedition. Yet sickness, along with warfare and famine, cut this number in half again by 1650 and in half once more by 1680.

CONVERSION AND REBELLION IN SPANISH FLORIDA

By 1600, Spanish Florida also disappointed imperial officials. Dreams of gold-filled kingdoms and a strategic passage from the Southeast to the Orient had never materialized. The Spanish government regarded the outpost at St. Augustine as an undue burden and planned to disband the colony. But Franciscan missionaries won the day, as in New Mexico. They argued that scores of Indian towns appeared ready to receive Christianity. By 1608, the crown had decided to let the colony continue.

A handful of missionaries fanned out among the Indians of northern Florida, erecting small churches and mission schools. They recruited Indian students aggressively, without regard to age or sex. In 1612, Francisco de Pareja published an illustrated, bilingual confessional in Castilian Spanish and Timucuan, the earliest text in any North American Indian language. The book enabled wary friars to ask villagers, "Have you said suggestive words?" and "Have you desired to do some lewd act with some man or woman or kin?"

Contact with Christian beliefs and books came at a steep price, for each inland village was expected to help feed the colonial garrison and settlement at St. Augustine. Native women neglected their own household crops to grow additional maize and grind it into meal. Annually, Spanish officials requisitioned Indian men from each village to transport the cornmeal overland to the Atlantic coast and return to the mission carrying supplies for the

**Florida missions in the
mid-seventeenth century**

— Camino Real

✝ Missions

■ **M A P 2 . 2**   **Sites of Catholic Missions in Spanish Florida in the Mid-Seventeenth Century**

Franciscans. Imported candles, communion wine, and mission bells all had to be hauled inland. The trip to and from the coast lasted several weeks. After 1633, when missions appeared in the western province of Apalachee (near modern Tallahassee), the treks from the Atlantic Coast along the *camino real,* or "royal road," took even longer.

Friars and Indian bearers traveling to the interior also carried sickness from St. Augustine. Epidemics of foreign diseases—measles, bubonic plague, malaria, typhus, smallpox, and influenza—took a devastating toll on the Native Americans. Harsh work conditions and poor diets lowered people's resistance to illness. Indians expired more rapidly than the Spanish could convert them, and friars hastened to baptize the dying and claim their souls for Christ. In a letter to the Spanish king in 1617, a Franciscan reported that the local population had been cut in half in the five years since his arrival "on account of the great plagues and contagious diseases that the Indians have suffered." But he reassured his majesty that "a very rich harvest of souls for heaven has been made in the midst of great numbers of deaths."

MAP

**Native American
Population Loss,
1500–1700**

As whole villages disappeared, Hispanic entrepreneurs began to expand cattle ranching across the newly vacated lands of northern Florida. Faced with encroaching farms, crushing labor demands, and frightful mortality, local native leaders saw their power reduced and their communities depleted. These conditions sparked a short-lived revolt by Indians at Apalachee in 1647. Nine years later, when the governor at St. Augustine feared a possible attack by English ships, a wider Native American uprising shook Timucua in north-central Florida.

In the end, the English threat to Spanish Florida did not materialize in 1656, but the rumor underscored how much had changed in the preceding half-century. Two generations earlier, in 1600, no European power besides Spain had possessed a solid foothold in any portion of the Americas. But over the next six decades, France, Holland, and England all asserted claims on the American mainland. These rivals challenged Spain not only in the Atlantic but in the Pacific as well.

Mission San Luis, Florida Division of Historical Resources

■ The Spanish found that glass beads, colorful and easy to transport, made fine gifts and trade items in their contacts with Florida Indians. Chiefs often received special quartz crystal beads and pendants to retain their loyalty.

France and Holland: Overseas Competition for Spain

■ *How did the expanding beaver trade shape the French and Dutch colonies before 1660?*

At the turn of the seventeenth century, interlopers from Holland challenged Spanish colonizers in the Philippines and Portuguese traders in Japan. These Dutch efforts illustrated the growing competition among European powers for control of the world's oceans. In London, commercial leaders received a royal charter to create the English East India Company in 1600, and merchants in Amsterdam took a similar step. Hoping to capture Portugal's lucrative Asian trade, they established the Dutch East India Company in 1602. Over the next half-century, Dutch sailors reached Australia, Tasmania, and New Zealand. They took Malacca (near Singapore) from the Portuguese in 1641 and charted the coast of northern Japan in 1643. By 1652, they had also founded a Dutch colony at Cape Town, on the southern tip of Africa.

The united powers of Spain and Portugal proved even more vulnerable in the Atlantic. To be sure, annual Spanish convoys continued to transport Mexican gold and silver to Europe, along with Asian silks and spices shipped to Mexico via the Pacific. Portuguese vessels carried Africans to the New World at a profit. But ships from rival European nations preyed on these seaborne cargoes with increasing success. Defiantly, these competitors also laid claim to numerous islands in the Caribbean.

By 1660, the English had taken control of Barbados, Providence Island, Antigua, and Jamaica; the Dutch had acquired St. Maarten, St. Eustacius, Saba, and Curaçao; and the French had claimed Guadeloupe, Martinique, Grenada, and St. Lucia. For France, however, the most promising Atlantic prospects lay farther north, in Canada. There, Spanish power was absent, hopes for a Northwest Passage persisted, and French imperial claims stretched back generations.

TABLE 2.1

North American Colonies by Nationality, 1560–1660

European Power (Catholic/Protestant)	North American Colony (date founded–ended)	Largest Town (date founded)
Spain (C)	Florida (1565)	St. Augustine (1565)
	New Mexico (1598)	Santa Fe (1610)
France (C)	Port Royal (SC) (1562–1653)	Charlesfort (1562)
	St. John's River (FL) (1564–1565)	Fort Caroline (1564)
	New France (1603)	Quebec (1608)
Holland (P) (The Netherlands)	New Netherland (1609)	New Amsterdam (1626) (now New York, NY)
Sweden (P)	New Sweden (1637–1655)	Fort Christina (1637) (now Wilmington, DE)
England (P)	Roanoke (NC) (1585–1590)	Roanoke (1585)
	Virginia (charter issued 1606)	Jamestown (1607)
	Maryland (charter issued 1632)	St. Mary's (1634)
	Popham (Sagadahoc) (on Kennebec River in ME) (1607–1608)	Fort St. George (1607)
	Plymouth (1620)	Plymouth (1620)
	Massachusetts Bay (charter issued 1629)	Boston (1630)
	Rhode Island (charter issued 1644)	Providence (1636)
	New Haven (1643–1664; then absorbed into CT)	New Haven (1637)
	Connecticut (Fundamental Orders 1639; charter granted in 1662)	Hartford (1636)

THE FOUNDING OF NEW FRANCE

Since the time of Jacques Cartier, fishing boats from the coast of France had crisscrossed Newfoundland's Grand Banks. One old French salt claimed to have made the voyage for forty-two consecutive years. The trade increased after 1580, as crews built seasonal stations for drying codfish along the American coast. These stations prompted greater contact with Indians; soon Europeans were exchanging metal goods for furs on terms that pleased all. A Native American could trade a worn-out robe made from beaver skins for a highly valued iron kettle. European artisans could remove the soft underlayer of fur from the pelts and mat the short hairs into felt for making fashionable and waterproof beaver hats. One robe yielded felt for six to eight expensive hats, so dealers could pocket a profit and still purchase scores of kettles and knives for the next year's exchange.

As North Atlantic fishing and trading expanded, the domestic situation in France improved. In 1598, King Henry IV issued the Edict of Nantes, a decree granting political rights and limited toleration to French Protestants, or Huguenots. With religious wars curtailed, the king could contemplate new colonization initiatives in America. An experienced French soldier and sailor named Samuel de Champlain emerged as a key leader in this effort. Between 1599 and 1601, Champlain scouted Spain's New World empire and brought back suggestions to Paris for overseas advancement of French interests. He even offered a proposal to create a canal across the Isthmus of Panama. But from 1602 until his death in 1635, Champlain devoted himself to the St. Lawrence River region, where Acadia on the Atlantic coast and Canada along the extensive river valley made up the anticipated realm of New France.

In 1608, Champlain and several dozen other men established the outpost of Quebec, where Cartier and Roberval had wintered generations earlier. In June 1609, Champlain joined a band of Algonquin and Huron Indians in a raid on the Iroquois in what is now upstate New York. When they engaged their Iroquois enemies in battle, Champlain fired his gun—a novelty in the region—killing several war chiefs and sparking a rout. For the powerful **Iroquois League** south of the St. Lawrence (the Five Nation confederation composed of the Seneca, Cayuga, Onondaga, Oneida, and Mohawk Indians), the defeat sparked decades of warfare against the French. For the newcomers from France, the victory sealed good relations with the Algonquin and Huron, ensuring the survival of Quebec and spurring unprecedented commerce. Within fifteen years, Native Americans were trading 12,000 to 15,000 beaver pelts annually via the St. Lawrence River valley.

In 1627, the powerful first minister in France, Cardinal Richelieu, pressed for greater French settlement in Canada through a new private company. He banned Huguenots from participating and pushed to make sure that only Roman Catholics were allowed to migrate to Canada. But his expansive policies alarmed rival England, which captured Quebec briefly in 1629. When restored to French control several years later, the tiny outpost contained fewer than 100 people. In an effort to expand the meager settlement and populate the fertile valley upriver from Quebec, French authorities began granting narrow strips of land with river frontage to any Catholic lord who would take up residence there and bring French tenants to his estate. By 1640, the small colony of 356 inhabitants, with 116 women, included 64 families, 29 Jesuits, and 53 soldiers.

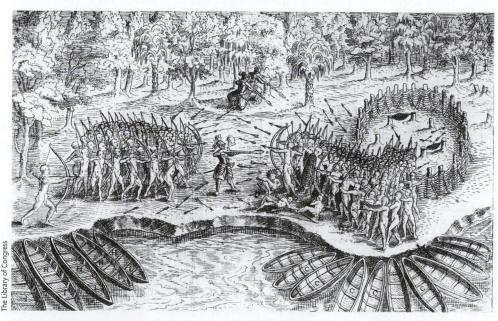

■ Champlain's drawing of the battle on Lake Champlain, 1609.

COMPETING FOR THE BEAVER TRADE

Cardinal Richelieu's power in France epitomized the ongoing Counter-Reformation. This outpouring of Catholic zeal reached as far as North America. In 1635 Jesuits founded a college in Quebec, and in 1639 six nuns arrived to begin a hospital and a school for Indian girls. Other religious workers established a station farther west in 1641 in territory recently dominated by the Iroquois. This strategic outpost, where the Ottawa River joined the St. Lawrence, marked the beginnings of Montreal. From there, the French planned to control the beaver trade as it expanded west. They also hoped to prevent the Iroquois League from diverting furs south to Holland's new colony on the Hudson River.

But the desperate Iroquois nations, facing collapse, took a stand. Increasing contact with Europeans and their contagious diseases had brought catastrophic epidemics to the Iroquois homelands below Lake Ontario. Beginning in 1633, sicknesses that were new to the region swept away some 10,000 people and cut the Five Nations' population in half within a decade, emptying the distinctive longhouses that made up Iroquois villages. According to Iroquois tradition, survivors must swiftly replace deceased individuals with new captives to maintain the community's strength and continuity. Pressed by grieving families, Iroquois warriors initiated a generation of violent campaigns intended to capture and absorb neighboring groups. These so-called mourning wars are also remembered as the Beaver Wars because they included a clear economic as well as cultural motive. Besides captives, the Iroquois aggressors sought furs. If they could seize pelts before the valuable items reached the French, they could trade them to the Dutch for guns and powder. Well armed, they could then engage in further wars for captives and furs.

This spiral of aggression put the Iroquois on a collision course with the Huron and their allies, a small band of Jesuit missionaries willing to risk martyrdom in New France. Eager for Native American converts, the Jesuits focused their attention on Huronia, the region east of Lake Huron and Georgian Bay. There, 30,000 Huron Indians lived in large, settled villages. The Jesuits erected chapels at four of these towns and constructed a central base at St. Marie near Georgian Bay. Having volunteered for hardship, they witnessed far more of it than they ever imagined.

First came the same foreign epidemics that had wasted the Iroquois; smallpox cut down roughly two-thirds of the Huron population, or 20,000 people, between 1635 and 1640. Then came the Iroquois themselves, bent on capturing Huron women and children to revitalize their longhouses, swept empty by disease in the 1630s. Armed by Dutch traders eager for furs, 1,000 Iroquois warriors descended on the weakened Huron in March 1649. They burned villages, secured captives, tortured several priests to death, and seized large stocks of pelts. The Iroquois then launched raids on the St. Lawrence River valley, disrupting the fur trade and frightening the several thousand French inhabitants. By 1660, it seemed that New France—thinly settled, weakly defended, and poorly supplied—might face the same extinction that the much older and larger Huronia community had suffered. (See Map 2.3 on p. 53.)

A DUTCH COLONY ON THE HUDSON RIVER

The Dutch traders who supplied firearms to the Iroquois in exchange for furs owed their start to English-born navigator Henry Hudson. In 1609, sailing for the Dutch East India Company, Hudson crossed the Atlantic in search of a western passage to the Orient. He visited Chesapeake Bay and Delaware Bay, and in September he rediscovered modern-day New York harbor, the bay that Verrazano had entered in 1524. Flying the Dutch flag above his vessel, the *Half Moon*, Hudson sailed north up the broad river that now bears his name. Along the way, he obtained food and furs from Algonquin Indians in exchange for knives and beads. He noted that saltwater ocean tides pushed sixty miles upstream—Indians called the river "the water that flows two ways." But no channel to the Pacific materialized.

The Dutch moved quickly to gain a foothold in the area, calling it New Netherland. Ships from Amsterdam appeared far up the Hudson, exchanging metal goods for beaver

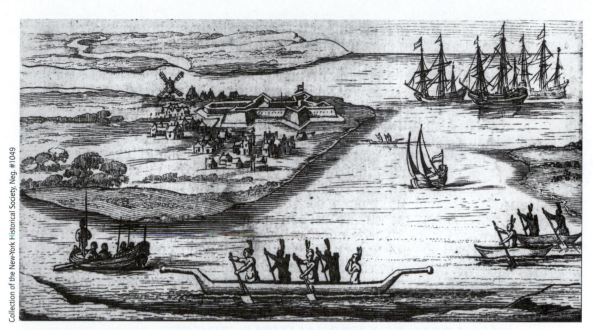

■ When the Dutch erected the village and fort of New Amsterdam beside the Hudson River in the late 1620s, a traditional windmill became a strange new part of Manhattan Island's skyline.

pelts and occasionally leaving men behind to trade with the Indians. Soon the Dutch had established a year-round trading post at Fort Orange, near present-day Albany. Mohawk traditions recall how the Indians "Planted the Tree of Good Understanding" with the Dutch newcomers, whom they called *Kristoni*, for "I am a metal maker."

In 1621, responsibility for New Netherland—the region claimed between the Delaware and Connecticut rivers—fell to the newly chartered Dutch West India Company (DWIC). Modeled on the Dutch East India Company, this enterprise made Holland a formidable force in the Atlantic, especially after the spectacular Dutch capture of the Spanish silver fleet off Cuba in 1628. The DWIC concentrated on piecing together an empire in the South Atlantic. Dutch ships seized part of sugar-rich Brazil (1632), the island of Curaçao near Venezuela (1634), and Portugal's African outpost at Elmina, on the coast of modern-day Ghana (1637). But the DWIC also laid plans for a North American colony.

To begin, the company transported a group of poor, would-be settlers to New Netherland in 1624, offering as an inducement "the profit that each can make for himself." To secure the boundaries of the province, officials sent colonists far up the Hudson to Fort Orange and deposited several farm families along the Connecticut and Delaware rivers. However, Peter Minuit, the colony's director from 1626 to 1631, saw danger in this dispersal. He worried that the widely scattered newcomers lacked defenses, trade, and community ties. To consolidate settlement, he purchased Manhattan Island—the eventual site of New York City—from the local Indians in 1626. The island's southern tip, where Minuit erected a small fort, overlooked a spacious harbor at the mouth of the Hudson. Like Amsterdam itself, the promising location—named New Amsterdam—combined shelter from the sea with easy access to interior settlements and to ocean trade.

By 1630, the village of New Amsterdam already boasted several windmills and 270 settlers, clustered in cottages near the fort. When the Dutch built a wall around their village to protect against Indian attacks, the road inside this palisade became known as Wall Street. Next, the DWIC granted huge estates along the Hudson to wealthy *patroons* (patrons), similar to the French land grants along the St. Lawrence. Hoping that private investment would strengthen their colony, the company gave a wilderness tract to any wealthy investor who could send fifty people to farm there as tenants. An Amsterdam diamond merchant named Kiliaen van

Rensselaer formed the first and most lucrative of these patroonships near Fort Orange. But this effort to promote migration faltered, and new conflicts began to appear on several fronts.

When the company threw open the Indian trade to others besides its own agents, the careless and greedy actions of unregulated traders sparked violence. The bloodshed known as Kieft's War (1643–1645) was sanctioned by the brash Indian policies of Willem Kieft, the colony's incompetent director general. In 1643, without public approval, Kieft ordered a midnight raid by company soldiers against tribute-paying Indians on both sides of the Hudson. Native retaliation for the massacre nearly destroyed New Netherland before Kieft's welcome removal in 1645.

The nearby colonies of rival powers also posed problems. The Dutch squabbled constantly with settlers from neighboring New England over fur-trading rights and other matters. To the south, the small colony of New Sweden materialized on the west side of the Delaware River in 1637. The several hundred Scandinavians who built Fort Christina (now Wilmington, Delaware) were Swedes and Finns hoping to establish their own trade with the Indians. The English too had designs on the region, as awareness grew that the river stretched far to the north and its owners could cut into New Netherland's western fur trade. But in 1655, these rivals were obliged to surrender the Delaware valley to a Dutch fleet.

"ALL SORTS OF NATIONALITIES": DIVERSE NEW AMSTERDAM

The symbol of Dutch power in the region, and the commander of the fleet that seized New Sweden, was Peter Stuyvesant. The son of a Calvinist minister, he had served as governor of Dutch Curaçao in the Caribbean, losing his right leg in a battle with the Spanish at age thirty-four. Recuperating in Holland, he married Judith Bayard, the Huguenot woman who nursed him back to health. In 1647, she was pregnant with their first child when the couple sailed from Amsterdam for New Netherland, in the service of the DWIC. There, Stuyvesant would rule aggressively for several decades, before England seized the colony in 1664.

Stuyvesant limited beer and rum sales, fined settlers for promiscuity and knife fighting, and established a nine-member night watch. When a group of English Quakers, members of the newly formed Society of Friends, arrived at New Amsterdam in 1657, Stuyvesant attempted to expel the radical Protestants and fine any who gave them shelter. However, Dutch residents of Flushing, on Long Island, defied his ban and signed a public letter of objection stressing religious toleration.

To address the colony's chronic labor shortage, Stuyvesant endorsed trade in African slaves and used his Caribbean connections to expand this traffic. When the Portuguese forced Holland out of Brazil in 1654 and closed that sugar colony to Dutch slave vessels, some of the ships brought their cargoes to New Amsterdam instead. Like the Dutch-speaking blacks already living in the colony, most of these newcomers were enslaved for life. But the DWIC, the largest importer and owner of slaves in New Netherland, granted "half-freedom" to some whom it could not employ year-round. These people, in return for an annual fee, could travel freely and marry, acquire property, and hire out their labor. By 1664, African arrivals made up more than 10 percent of New Netherland's population and 20 percent of New Amsterdam, the colony's capital.

New Amsterdam, home to fewer than 2,000 people, also had a small Jewish contingent, the first in mainland North America.

New Amsterdam, home to fewer than 2,000 people, also had a small Jewish contingent, the first in mainland North America. In 1654, twenty-three Sephardic Jews reached Manhattan, forced out of Brazil by the Portuguese. Stuyvesant, strident in his anti-Semitism, claimed such "blasphemers of the name of Christ" would "infect and trouble this new colony." But the DWIC, which included Jewish stockholders and was eager for newcomers of all kinds, overruled the governor's request to expel the refugees. In the end, colony officials authorized a Jewish ghetto, or segregated neighborhood, where the newcomers could pray together freely in private. At first, however, they were not allowed to construct a synagogue for public worship.

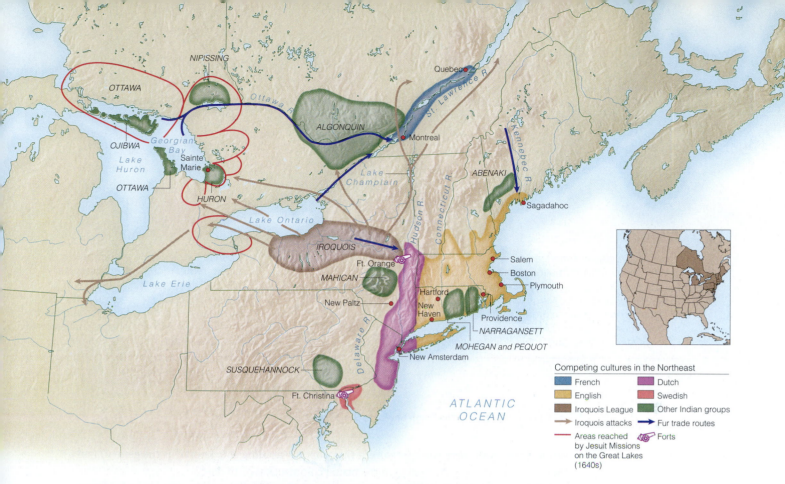

■ **MAP 2.3** **European and Native American Contact in the Northeast, 1600–1660**

French and English colonization efforts brought devastating diseases to the Five Nations of the Iroquois League. Eager to take captives and profit from the growing trade in furs, the Iroquois ranged north and west to make war on the French and their Huron Indian allies.

In the early 1660s, the colony continued to grow more diverse, "slowly peopled by the scrapings of all sorts of nationalities," as Stuyvesant complained. The accents of Danes, Bavarians, and Italians could already be heard on the streets of New Amsterdam. Huguenots occupied New Paltz near the Hudson; farther north, other newcomers founded Schenectady in 1661. Swedes and Finns continued to prosper along the Delaware, and numerous English had settled on Long Island. Compared with New France, New Netherland seemed far more populous, prosperous, and ethnically diverse. But while the French colony to the north endured for another century, the Dutch enterprise was soon absorbed by England. For despite a slow start, the English managed to outdistance all their European rivals and establish thriving North American colonies in the first half of the seventeenth century.

English Beginnings on the Atlantic Coast

■ *What factors worked for and against the early English colonization efforts in America?*

When Queen Elizabeth I passed away in 1603, several important elements were already in place to help England compete for colonial outposts. The trade in wool had prompted many large landholders to fence in their fields and turn to raising sheep. This "enclosure" movement pushed thousands of tenants off the land, and these uprooted people flocked to urban centers in search of work, forming a supply of potential colonists. Also, the country had an expanding fleet of English-built ships, sailed by experienced mariners. In addition, England had a group of seasoned and ambitious leaders. A generation of

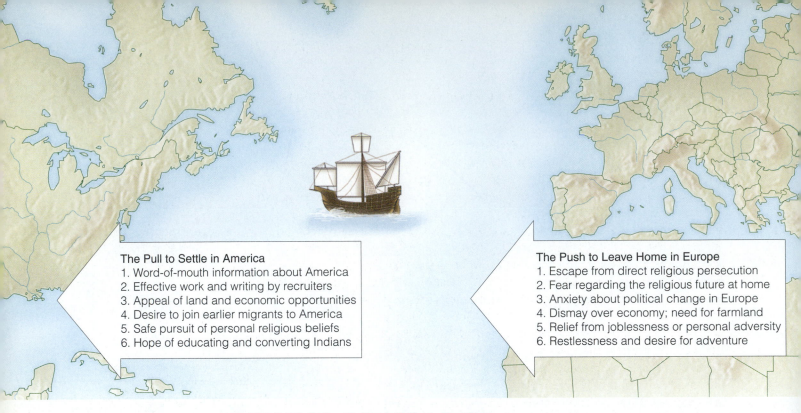

The Pull to Settle in America
1. Word-of-mouth information about America
2. Effective work and writing by recruiters
3. Appeal of land and economic opportunities
4. Desire to join earlier migrants to America
5. Safe pursuit of personal religious beliefs
6. Hope of educating and converting Indians

The Push to Leave Home in Europe
1. Escape from direct religious persecution
2. Fear regarding the religious future at home
3. Anxiety about political change in Europe
4. Dismay over economy; need for farmland
5. Relief from joblessness or personal adversity
6. Restlessness and desire for adventure

■ **FIGURE 2.1**   **The Tough Choice to Start Over**

soldiers (many of them younger sons of the property-holding elite known as the gentry) had fought in Europe or participated in the brutal colonization of Ireland.

Because Elizabeth I died without heirs, the king of Scotland, James Stuart, succeeded her as ruler. During the reigns of James I (1603–1625) and his son Charles I (1625–1649), religious and economic forces in England prompted an increasing number of people to consider migrating overseas. With the expansion of the country's Protestant Reformation, religious strife escalated toward civil war, which erupted in 1642. During the tumultuous 1630s, English public officials were glad to transplant Puritans and Catholics alike to foreign shores. In turn, many ardent believers—weary of conflict or losing hope for their cause at home—welcomed the prospect of a safe haven abroad. Economically, the development of joint stock organizations enabled merchants to raise capital and spread the high risk of colonial ventures by selling numerous shares to small investors. At the same time, the fluctuating domestic economy threatened family stability and prompted many disadvantaged people to seek their fortunes elsewhere.

THE VIRGINIA COMPANY AND JAMESTOWN

For Richard Hakluyt, England's leading publicist for overseas expansion, the proper focus seemed clear: "There is under our noses," he wrote in 1599, "the great & ample countrey of Virginia." Great and ample, indeed, especially before the rival Dutch established New Netherland. On paper, the enormous zone that England claimed as Virginia stretched north to south from the top of modern-day Vermont to Cape Fear on Carolina's Outer Banks. From east to west, it spanned North America from the Atlantic to the Pacific, however narrow or wide the continent might prove to be.

In 1606, James I chartered the Virginia Company as a two-pronged operation to exploit the sweeping Virginia claim. Under the charter, a group of London-based merchants took responsibility for colonizing the Chesapeake Bay region. Meanwhile, merchants from England's West Country, based in the seaports of Plymouth, Exeter, and Bristol, took charge of developing the northern latitudes of the American coast. In 1607, two ships from Plymouth deposited roughly a hundred settlers, led by George Popham, at the Sagadahoc (Kennebec) River in Maine. The settlers built houses and erected a fortress (Fort St. George) at the mouth of the river. They even constructed a small sailing vessel called the *Virginia*, the first of hundreds of ships that the

English would build from American forests. But frostbite, scurvy, and dwindling supplies forced the Popham colony to retreat home in 1608, two decades after the Roanoke failures.

A parallel effort by the Londoners proved more enduring—but just barely. In April 1607, three ships bearing 105 men sailed into Chesapeake Bay. Their leaders carried instructions to hunt for Roanoke survivors (they found none) and to search for gold. They were also to look westward from high hills in search of the Pacific Ocean. (After all, longitude remained a mystery, and the width of the continent was unknown. In the previous century, Verrazano claimed to have spied an arm of the Pacific from the Atlantic, and Drake, sailing into San Francisco Bay at the same latitude as the Chesapeake, had claimed that region for the English as New Albion.) The new arrivals in Chesapeake Bay disembarked on what appeared to be a secluded island near a broad river. Within months, these subjects of James I had named the waterway the James River and established a fortified village beside it called Jamestown. In June, hoping for quick rewards, they shipped to London various stones that they thought contained precious gems and gold ore.

Mural of Jamestown Settlement

When the rocks proved worthless, the colonists' dreams of easy wealth evaporated. So did their fantasies about pushing west to the Pacific. During Jamestown's first winter, a fire destroyed the tiny settlement, and death from hunger, exposure, and sickness cut the garrison's population in half. The governor and council appointed by the Virginia Company bickered among themselves, providing poor leadership. Fully one-third of the early arrivals claimed to be gentlemen, from England's leisure class—a proportion six times higher than in England—and most proved unaccustomed to hard manual labor. Moreover, all the colonists were employees of the company, so any profits from their labor went to repay London investors.

> *During Jamestown's first winter, death from hunger, exposure, and sickness cut the garrison's population in half.*

Despite the unsuitable make-up of the garrison, conditions improved briefly with the emergence of John Smith as a vigorous leader. He dealt brazenly with the local Powhatan Indian confederation, numbering more than 13,000 people. Captain Smith soon reached a tenuous accommodation with the paramount chief, Powhatan, who had been steadily expanding his power across the Tidewater region. (Later, Smith claimed to have been assisted and protected by Powhatan's young daughter, Pocahontas.) Still, the Jamestown colony limped along with meager support, living in fear of Spanish attacks.

With hopes of a swift bonanza dashed, the London merchants decided to alter their strategy. They would salvage the venture by attracting fresh capital; then they would recoup their high initial costs by recruiting new settlers who could produce staple products suited for export—perhaps grapes, sugar, cotton, or tobacco. In 1609, amid much fanfare, the company began to sell seven-year joint stock options to the English public. Subscribers could invest money or they could sign on for service in Virginia. Company officials promised such adventurers at least a hundred acres of land when their investment matured in 1616. In June 1609, 500 men and 100 women departed for the Chesapeake aboard nine ships.

"STARVING TIME" AND SEEDS OF REPRESENTATIVE GOVERNMENT

When the battered fleet reached Jamestown, the new arrivals found insufficient supplies. Moreover, the first settlers had failed to discover a profitable staple crop. The colonists depended heavily on the Native Americans for food, and Powhatan's Confederacy proved increasingly unwilling and unable to share its harvest. In a grim "starving time," the ill-equipped newcomers scavenged for berries and bark. Extreme hunger drove a few to cannibalize the dead before dying themselves. By the spring of 1610, seven of every eight people had died; scarcely sixty remained alive.

John Smith, "The Starving Time"

In June, these survivors abandoned their ghost town altogether. But as they set sail for England, they encountered three long-overdue ships entering Chesapeake Bay with fresh

National Geographic Society. © 1998 Photo by Steve Rawls

■ Inexperience prompted initial English difficulties at Roanoke and Jamestown, but so did poor weather. Scientists studying the region's bald cypress trees have recently shown (from certain narrow rings) that terrible droughts struck the coastal area in the late 1580s and again from 1606 through 1612. These two sequences of narrow annual rings are visible under the magnifying glass.

supplies and 300 new settlers. Reluctantly, they agreed to try again. More years of harsh discipline, Indian warfare, and chronic mismanagement followed. Another force—a severe local drought—also conspired against the hapless newcomers. Indian and English crops alike shriveled from 1607 through 1612.

Relief came from an unexpected quarter: the "bewitching vegetable" known as Orinoco tobacco. This plant, grown in parts of the West Indies and South America, had captured English taste in the previous generation. Sales of this New World product in England sent profits to the Spanish crown, prompting James I to launch a vigorous antismoking campaign in 1604. In his tract titled *Counterblaste to Tobacco*, the king condemned inhaling the noxious weed as a dangerous, sinful, and enfeebling custom, "lothsome to the eye, hatefull to the Nose, harmefull to the braine, daungerous to the Lungs."

John Rolfe, reaching Jamestown in 1610, promptly joined in the colonists' search for a viable staple. He found that local Indians cultivated an indigenous tobacco plant, but it proved "poor and weake, and of a byting tast." Rolfe, a smoker himself, suspected that sweet-flavored Orinoco tobacco could prosper in Virginia soil. Within a year, Rolfe had somehow managed to obtain seeds, and by 1612 his patch of West Indian tobacco was flourishing. The next year, he grew a sample for export. Desperate settlers and impatient London investors were delighted by Rolfe's successful experiment. Soon production of the leaf soared at Jamestown, to the neglect of all other pursuits.

During Virginia's initial tobacco boom, recently starving settlers saw handsome profits within reach. Because land was plentiful at first (a novelty for the English), the only limitations to riches were the scarcity of workers and the related high cost of labor. Any farmer who could hire half a dozen field hands could increase his profits fivefold, quickly earning enough to obtain more land and import more workers. The company transported several shiploads of apprentices, servants, and London street children to the labor-hungry colony. When a Dutch captain delivered twenty enslaved blacks in 1619, settlers eagerly purchased these first Africans to arrive in English Virginia. They also bid on the 100 women who disembarked the same year, shipped from England by the company to be sold as wives and workers. Still, men continued to outnumber women more than three to one for decades to come.

To encourage English migration further, the Virginia Company offered transportation and fifty acres to tenants, promising them ownership of the land after seven years of work. Men who paid their own way received fifty acres, plus an additional **headright** of fifty acres for each household member or laborer they transported. The Virginia Company went out of its way to assure its colonists of access to such established English freedoms as the right to trial by jury and a representative form of government. The company established civil courts controlled by English common law, and it instructed Virginia's governor to summon an annual assembly of elected **burgesses**—the earliest representative legislature in North America. First convened in 1619, the House of Burgesses wasted no time in affirming its commitment to fundamental English rights. The governor, the house said, could no longer impose taxes without the assembly's consent.

LAUNCHING THE PLYMOUTH COLONY

To attract additional capital and people, the Virginia Company began awarding patents (legal charters) to private groups of adventurers to "build a town and settle . . . there for the advancement of the general plantation of the country." The newcomers would live independently on a large tract, with only minimal control from the governor and his council. Two such small colonies originated among English Protestants living in exile in Holland because their separatist beliefs did not allow them to profess loyalty to the Church of England. The first group of 180, based in Amsterdam, departed for America late in 1618 on a crowded ship. Winter storms, sickness, and a shortage of fresh water destroyed the venture; scarcely fifty survivors straggled ashore in Virginia.

A second group of English Separatists, residing in the smaller Dutch city of Leiden, fared better. Most had migrated to Holland from northeast England in 1608. This group openly opposed the hierarchy, pomp, and inclusiveness of the Church of England. Instead, they wanted to return to early Christianity, where small groups of worthy (and often persecuted) believers formed their own communities of worship. After a decade in Holland, many of them had wearied of the foreign culture. They were dismayed by the effect of worldly Leiden on their children, and they also sensed, correctly, that warfare would soon break out in Europe. A few families pushed for a further removal to America, despite the obvious dangers of such a journey.

Possible destinations ranged from South America to Canada. Dutch entrepreneurs suggested the Hudson River. But in the end, still loyal to England, the Separatists decided to use a patent granted by the Virginia Company to a group of English capitalists. On the negative side, the migrants had to work for these investors for seven years. They also had to take along paying passengers who did not share their beliefs. On the positive side, they received financial support from backers who paid to rent a ship. Moreover, instead of having their daily affairs controlled from London, they could elect their own leader and establish civil authority as they saw fit. In short, they had the power to govern themselves.

In September 1620, after costly delays, thirty-five members of the Leiden congregation and additional Separatists from England departed from Plymouth, along with other passengers. They were crowded aboard the *Mayflower*, a 160-ton vessel bound for Virginia. But a stormy two-month crossing brought them to Cape Cod (in modern-day Massachusetts), which was no longer considered part of the Virginia Company's jurisdiction. Sickly from their journey and with winter closing in, they decided to disembark at the spot they called Plymouth rather than push south to Chesapeake Bay. Earlier, they had signed a solemn compact aboard the *Mayflower* binding them together in a civil community.

> *"They had now no friends to welcome them . . . . Besides, what could they see but a hideous and desolate wilderness."*

William Bradford, the chronicler and longtime governor of Plymouth Colony, later recalled their plight: "They had now no friends to welcome them nor inns to entertain or refresh their weather-beaten bodies. . . . Besides, what could they see but a hideous and desolate wilderness." Bradford could scarcely exaggerate the challenge. His own wife drowned (an apparent suicide) shortly after the *Mayflower* dropped anchor. And by the time the ship departed in April, an illness had swept away half the colonists. Those remaining planted barley and peas, but the English seeds failed to take hold.

Still, settlers had abundant fish and wildlife, along with ample Indian corn, and soon reinforcements arrived from England, bringing needed supplies. The newcomers also brought a legal patent for the land of Plymouth Plantation. With Squanto's aid, the settlers secured peaceful relations with Massasoit's villages. When survival for another winter seemed assured, they invited Massasoit and his followers to join in a three-day celebration of thanksgiving so that, according to one account, all might "rejoice together after we had gathered the fruit of our labors."

LISTEN

"Plymouth Colony"

The Puritan Experiment

■ *How were the Puritans strengthened or weakened by seeing themselves as God's chosen people?*

After more than a generation of costly colonization attempts, England still had little to show for its efforts when Charles I inherited the throne in 1625. Then two forces prompted rapid change: positive publicity about America and negative developments at home. John Smith, long a key promoter of overseas settlement, drew inspiration from the early efforts at Jamestown and Plymouth. In 1624, he published a best-seller predicting future success for these regions. Smith's *Generall Historie* went through six printings in eight years. Ironically, the book's popularity depended in large part on the grim religious, political, and economic conditions in England that suddenly gave such literature a broad appeal.

FORMATION OF THE MASSACHUSETTS BAY COMPANY

European Christianity had taken a number of different forms since the religious upheaval sparked by Luther a century earlier. The first Protestants had demanded a reformation of the Roman Catholic Church and had questioned papal authority over Christians. Now many non-Catholic English worshippers doubted whether the Church of England (also known as the Anglican Church) had gone far enough toward rejecting the practices of Rome. They lamented what they saw as the church's bureaucratic hierarchy, ornate rituals, and failure to enforce strict observance of the Christian Sabbath each Sunday. Puritans scoffed at the gaudy vestments of Anglican bishops, elaborate church music, and other trappings of worship unjustified by biblical scripture. Instead, they praised the stark simplicity that John Calvin had brought to his church in Geneva.

As English Calvinists grew in number, their objections to the Church of England increased. They protested that the Anglican Church, like the Catholic Church, remained inclusive in membership rather than selective. They argued for limiting participation only to the devout, and they insisted that the Church of England should be independent and self-governing rather than tied to the monarchy. This keen desire for further cleansing and purity, so common to reformers, spurred the ongoing movement known as Puritanism.

> *Puritans scoffed at the gaudy vestments of Anglican bishops, elaborate church music, and other trappings of worship unjustified by biblical scripture.*

Some of the most radical members of this broad religious coalition became known as Separatists (including Bradford and the Plymouth pilgrims), because they were committed to an extreme position: complete separation from what they saw as the corrupt Church of England. But many more Puritans (including most of the reformers who migrated to Massachusetts Bay) resisted separation. They hoped to stay technically within the Anglican fold while taking increased control of their own congregations—a practice known as congregationalism. Unwilling to conform to practices that offended them, these nonseparating Congregationalists remained determined to save the Anglican Church through righteous example, even if it meant migrating abroad for a time to escape persecution and demonstrate the proper ways of a purified Protestant church.

An emphasis on instructive preaching by informed leaders lay at the heart of the Puritan movement. Translation of scripture from Latin and its publication into everyday languages the people spoke or read, using the newly invented printing press, had been a central theme of the Reformation. An improved English translation of the Bible in 1611, known as the King James Version, provided further access to scripture for all who could read or listen. But James and his bishops, realizing that a "priesthood of all believers" threatened their power, moved to control who could preach and what they could say. A 1626 law prohibited preaching or writing on controversial religious topics such as the conduct of the clergy, the nature of church hierarchy, and the interpretation of scripture. "There should be more praying and less preaching," wrote one royal supporter, "for much preaching breeds faction, but much praying causes devotion."

Puritans believed that the sermon should form the center of the Christian worship service. Their churches resembled lecture halls, emphasizing the pulpit more than the altar. In preaching, Puritans stressed a "plain style" that all listeners could understand. Moreover, they urged listeners to play an active role in their faith—to master reading and engage in regular study and discussion of scripture. In response to mounting public interest in these practices, Puritan ministers intensified their preaching and published their sermons. In effect, they dared authorities to silence them.

Reprisals came swiftly, led by William Laud, bishop of London, whom Charles I elevated to archbishop of Canterbury in 1633. Laud instructed all preachers to focus their remarks on biblical passages and avoid writing or speaking about controversial religious matters. The bishop's persecution of Puritan leaders who appeared to disobey these orders only broadened their movement at a time when the king himself was arousing Protestant suspicions. In 1625, Charles I had married Henrietta Maria, Catholic sister of the French king, and had granted freedom of worship to English Catholics, disturbing a wide array of Protestants in the realm. When the House of Commons refused to approve finances for his policies, he arrested its leaders and disbanded Parliament in 1629. He governed on his own for eleven years by levying taxes without parliamentary approval.

As England's church grew more rigid and its monarchy more controlling, the nation's economy took a turn for the worse. The cost of rent and food had risen more rapidly than wages, and workers paid dearly. Jobs became more scarce after 1625, and unemployed workers staged local revolts. In 1629, entrepreneurs who viewed New England as a potential opportunity teamed up with disaffected Puritans to obtain a charter for a new entity: the Massachusetts Bay Company. Through a generation of costly trial-and-error experiments, the English had amassed great expertise in colonization. Given the worsening conditions at home, especially among the Puritan faithful, proposals for overseas settlement attracted widespread attention.

"WE SHALL BE AS A CITY UPON A HILL"

During the next dozen years, more than 70,000 people left England for the New World. Two-thirds of them sailed to the West Indies, attracted by the prospect of a warmer climate and a longer growing season. But a large contingent of Puritans embarked from England for the new colony at Massachusetts Bay adjacent to the Plymouth settlement. A loophole in the king's grant permitted them to take the actual charter with them and to hold their company meetings in America. This maneuver took them out from under the usual control of London investors and let them turn the familiar joint stock structure into the framework for a self-governing colony. By 1629 advance parties had established a post at Salem for people who "upon the account of religion would be willing to begin a foreign plantation."

In England, meanwhile, a Puritan squire named John Winthrop assumed leadership of the Massachusetts Bay Company. "God will bring some heavy Affliction upon this lande," he predicted to his wife, but the Lord "will provide a shelter & a hidinge place for us and others." In exchange, God would expect great things from these chosen people, as from the Old Testament Israelites. "We are entered into covenant with him for this work," Winthrop told his companions aboard the *Arbella* en route to America in 1630.

Winthrop laid out this higher Calvinist standard in a memorable shipboard sermon titled "A Model of Christian Charity." The values that others merely profess, he explained, "we must bring into familiar and constant practice," sharing burdens, extending aid, and demonstrating patience. "For this end, we must be knit together in this work as one," regardless of social rank. If we fail, he warned, "the Lord will surely break out in wrath against us, and make us know the price of the breach of such a covenant."

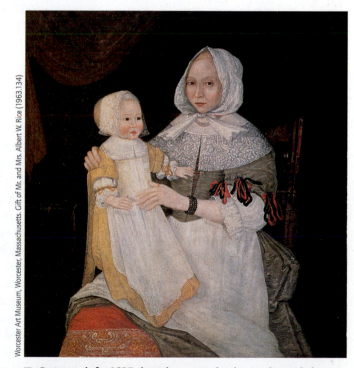

Worcester Art Museum, Worcester, Massachusetts. Gift of Mr. and Mrs. Albert W. Rice (1963.134)

■ Port records for 1635 show that groups leaving London varied markedly, depending on their colonial destination. Young children were common aboard ships heading for New England, as were women and girls. Among passengers for New England, eight of every twenty were female. In contrast, females made up only three in twenty of those going to Virginia and one in twenty among people heading for Barbados.

Anne Bradstreet: "The Tenth Muse, Lately Sprung Up in America"

Interpreting History

The Puritans who migrated to America stressed literacy and education as part of their faith. They left extensive court records, sermons, and diaries, but few of these surviving documents come from the pens of women. The poems and reflections of Anne Bradstreet provide a notable exception. "Here you may find," she told her children shortly before her death in 1672, "what was your living mother's mind."

The lifelong poet was born Anne Dudley in Lincolnshire, England, in 1612. She already "found much comfort in reading the Scriptures" by age seven. "But as I grew to be about 14 or 15," she recalled, "I found my heart more carnal, and . . . the follies of youth took hold of me. About 16, the Lord . . . smote me with the smallpox . . . and again restored me." That same year, she married Simon Bradstreet, the son of a minister. Two years later, despite a frail constitution, she sailed for Massachusetts Bay with her husband and her father (both future governors of the colony) aboard the *Arbella*.

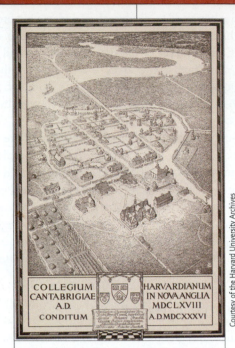

Courtesy of the Harvard University Archives

COLLEGIUM CANTABRIGIAE A.D. CONDITUM   HARVARDIANUM IN NOVA ANGLIA MDCLXVIII A.D.MDCXXXVI

■ Cambridge looked something like this in the 1660s. The large building in the foreground is Harvard College, founded in 1636, and the smaller brick building beside it is the Indian College, built in 1655. The village was even smaller when Anne Bradstreet resided there briefly after her arrival in Massachusetts Bay.

Anne Bradstreet was alert to all that seemed strange and different in America. When I "came into this country," she related, "I found a new world and new manners." The young couple set up housekeeping in the town of Cambridge, on the Charles River, but life was difficult at first. Anne suffered from "a lingering sickness like a consumption." Moreover, "It pleased God to keep me a long time without a child, which was a great grief to me and cost me many prayers and tears." Finally, she bore a son in 1633, and seven more children followed.

As the family grew and moved about, "Mistress Bradstreet" wrote poems and meditations, although detractors hinted that she should put down her quill pen and take up a sewing needle. "If what I do prove well, it won't advance," she lamented in rhyme; "They'l say it's stol'n, or else it was by chance." Nevertheless, a book of her poems was published in England in 1650, hailing her as "The Tenth **Muse**, Lately Sprung Up in America."

As a writer, Anne Bradstreet was more interested in spiritual improvement than literary grace. "Many speak well," she observed, "but few can do well." Throughout

Far from hiding in obscurity, dedicated Puritans must set a visible example for the rest of the world, Winthrop concluded. "We shall be as a city upon a hill."

The *Arbella* was one of seventeen ships that brought more than 1,000 people to New England in 1630. The English newcomers chose Winthrop as governor and established Boston as their port. They colonized Indian lands depopulated by recent epidemics. By the time civil war erupted in England in 1642, nearly 20,000 people had made the journey, eager to escape the religious persecution and governmental tyranny of Charles I. Whole congregations migrated with their ministers; other people (more than 20 percent) crossed as servants. But most came as independent families with young children. On average, of every 100 newcomers, roughly half were adults (thirty men to twenty women); the other half were all under age eighteen, divided about evenly between boys and girls.

Earlier settlers traded food, lodging, and building materials to fresh arrivals in exchange for textiles, tools, money, and labor. When new groups of church members wanted to establish a village, they applied for land to the General Court, a legislature made up of representatives elected from existing towns. Well before 1640, English settlements dotted the coast and had sprung up inland along the Connecticut River, where smallpox had decimated the Indians in 1633. There, English outposts rose at Hartford and Springfield; newcomers hoped to farm the fertile river valley and also attract part of the inland fur trade away from the French and Dutch. In 1639, some of the new towns along the navigable river agreed to a life, she followed a simple creed: "There is no object that we see; no action that we do; no good that we enjoy; no evil that we feel or fear, but we may make some spiritual advantage" of it. Nothing epitomizes this belief more clearly than "some verses upon the burning of our house, July 10th, 1666." Bradstreet composed the lines on an unburned scrap of paper as she groped to make sense of the calamity. The poem helped her to mourn her loss, take stock of her blessings, and renew her faith. In part, it reads,

In silent night when rest I took,
For sorrow neer I did not look,
I waken'd was with thundring nois
And Piteous shreiks of dreadfull voice ....

I, starting up, the light did spye,
And to my God my heart did cry ....
Then coming out beheld a space
The flame consume my dwelling place.

And, when I could no longer look,
I blest his Name that gave and took,
That layd my goods now in the dust:
Yea so it was, and so 'twas just ....

When by the Ruines oft I past,
My sorrowing eyes aside did cast,

And here and there the places spye
Where oft I sate, and long did lye.

Here stood that Trunk, and there that chest;
There lay that store I counted best:
My pleasant things in ashes lye,
And them behold no more shall I ....

Then streight I gin my heart to chide,
And did thy wealth on earth abide?
Didst fix thy hope on mouldring dust,
The arm of flesh didst make thy trust? ....

Thou hast a house on high erect
Fram'd by that mighty Architect ....
The world no longer let me Love,
My hope and Treasure lyes Above.

QUESTIONS

1. *How might Anne Bradstreet's eventful life before age twenty have shaped her into a poet?*

2. *Imagine losing your home and belongings in a storm, flood, or fire. Would it deepen or weaken your religious beliefs? How about your need for material possessions?*

rudimentary government, known as the Fundamental Orders (though Connecticut waited a generation before gaining its formal colonial charter in 1662).

The sheer number of land-hungry settlers drove the rapid expansion. So did friction among newcomers, who competed for scarce resources and complained about price controls and other economic constraints intended to impose civic order. In his initial call to "work as one," Winthrop had worried that migrants would neglect the duties of spiritual regeneration. However, the sharpest dissents came from zealous people who feared that the religious experiment had not gone far enough. Challenging authority lay at the heart of radical Protestantism, for its practitioners stressed inner conviction and personal belief over outward conformity and deference to wealth and status. The more seriously New England's believers took their "errand into the wilderness," the more contentious they became about the proper ways to fulfill their covenant with God.

DISSENTERS: ROGER WILLIAMS AND ANNE HUTCHINSON

Like the biblical Hebrews before them, the Puritans—self-appointed saints—believed that God had chosen them for a special mission in the world. The Almighty, they believed, would watch carefully, punish harshly, and reward mightily. Inevitably, some devout people, raised to question authority in England, continued to dissent in New England, and some were drawn to the more tolerant and open Dutch colony on the Hudson. Their stormy careers illustrate that not all Puritans accepted the idea that women should defer to men, or that the English should dominate the Indians.

Strong-willed Deborah Moody, for example, was an aristocratic Puritan who migrated to New England in her fifties. Offended by the "conceite" and "bickering" in her Massachusetts congregation, she joined other dissidents, known as Anabaptists, who protested that children too young to understand the faith should not receive baptism. When authorities denounced Lady Moody as a "dangerous" woman, she led a group to New Amsterdam. The Dutch governor, eager for settlers, gave the newcomers land south of Breukelen (Brooklyn) on eastern Long Island. There, near what is now Coney Island, they established the first North American settlement directed by a woman. Though Deborah Moody remains obscure, two other early dissenters—Roger Williams and Anne Hutchinson—are remembered as effective challengers to the leadership of the Massachusetts Bay colony.

When Williams arrived in Boston, his Separatist leanings angered Bay Colony authorities, who still hoped to reform the Anglican Church rather than renounce it. The recent graduate of Cambridge University had other ideas that proved equally distressing. The young minister argued that civil authorities, inevitably corrupt, had no right to judge religious matters. Williams even pushed for an unprecedented separation of church and state—to protect the church. He also contended that the colony's land patent from the king had no validity. The settlers, he said, had to purchase occupancy rights from the Native Americans. Unable to silence him, irate magistrates banished Williams from Massachusetts Bay in the winter of 1635. Moving south, he took up residence among the Narragansett Indians and built a refuge for other dissenters, which he named Providence. Still subject to arrest in Boston, he sailed home to England by way of tolerant New Amsterdam in 1643. Once back in London, he persuaded leaders of England's rising Puritan Revolution to grant a charter (1644) to his independent colony of Rhode Island.

A more explosive popular challenge centered on Anne Hutchinson. The talented eldest daughter of an English minister, she had grown up in England with a strong will, a solid theological education, and a thirst for spiritual perfection. She married a Lincolnshire textile merchant and took an active part in religious discussions while also bearing fifteen children. When her Puritan minister, John Cotton, departed for New England, Hutchinson claimed that God, in a private revelation, had instructed her to follow. In 1634, the family migrated to Boston, where Hutchinson attended Cotton's church and hosted religious discussions in her home. The popularity of these weekly meetings troubled authorities, as did her argument that the "Holy Spirit illumines the heart of every true believer." Hutchinson downplayed outward conformity—modest dress or regular church attendance—as a route to salvation. Instead, she stressed direct communication with God's inner presence as the key to individual forgiveness.

> Winthrop sentenced Hutchinson to banishment as "a woman not fit for our society."

Most Puritans sought a delicate balance in their lives between respected outer works and inner personal grace. Hutchinson tipped that balance dangerously toward the latter. To the colony's magistrates, especially Winthrop, such teaching pointed toward anarchy—more troublesome when it came from a woman. These officials labeled Hutchinson and her followers as Antinomians (from *anti*, "against," and *nomos*, "law"). But the vehement opposition faction grew, attracting merchants who chafed under economic restrictions, women who questioned men's domination of the church, and young adults who resented the strict authority of their elders. By 1636, this religious and political coalition had gained enough supporters to turn Winthrop out as governor.

Challenged by this Antinomian Crisis, members of the Puritan establishment fought back. They divided the opposition to win reelection for Winthrop, they established Harvard College to educate ministers who would not stray from the fold, they staged a flurry of trials for contempt and sedition (the crime of inciting resistance to lawful authority), and they made a special example of Hutchinson herself. After a two-day hearing in which she defended herself admirably, Winthrop sentenced Hutchinson to banishment as "a woman not fit for our society." Forced into exile, Hutchinson moved first to Rhode Island and later to New Netherland, living at Pelham Bay near the estate of Joseph Bronk (now called the Bronx). There, she and six of her children, plus nine of her followers, were killed in an Indian attack in 1643. A river and a parkway in New York still bear her name.

EXPANSION AND VIOLENCE: THE PEQUOT WAR

Immigration to New England slowed during the 1640s because of religious and political upheaval at home. In England, Puritans and supporters of Parliament formed an army and openly challenged royal authority during the English Civil War. After seizing power, these revolutionaries beheaded Charles I in 1649, abolished the monarchy, and proclaimed England a republican commonwealth. Settlers in Massachusetts Bay struggled to square such sweeping developments in England with Winthrop's earlier assurance that the eyes of God and humankind would be fixed on New England. Making matters worse, religious and economic controversies intensified as the next generation quickly came of age. Needing new farmland and intellectual breathing room, fresh congregations began to "hive off" from the original settlements like swarms of bees. By 1640, New Hampshire, Rhode Island, and Connecticut each had at least four new towns that would provide the beginnings for independent colonies.

But the northeastern forest was not an empty wilderness, any more than the Chesapeake tidewater, the Florida interior, or the mesas of New Mexico had been. As the Hutchinsons discovered, newcomers who pushed inland were co-opting the land of long-time residents. Pressure on New England's Native Americans erupted in armed conflict in the Pequot War of 1637, at the height of the Antinomian Crisis. The Pequot Indians, English allies recently weakened by smallpox, resided near the mouth of the Connecticut River. Unfortunately, Puritan settlers, led by John Winthrop's son, were attempting to launch a town at Old Saybrook in the same vicinity. From Boston, Governor Winthrop fanned fears that the Pequot "would cause all the Indians in the country to join to root out all the English."

Recruiting Narragansett and Mohegan Indians to the English side, the colonists unleashed all-out war against the Pequot. The campaign culminated in a dawn raid on a stockaded Pequot town that sheltered noncombatants. The invaders torched the village (at Mystic, Connecticut) and shot or put to the sword almost all who tried to escape. Some 400 Indian men, women, and children died. The Puritans' Indian allies were shocked by the wholesale carnage. English warfare, they protested, "is too furious, and slaies too many men." Chastened by this intimidating display of terror and weakened by recurrent epidemics, the tribes of southern New England negotiated away much of their land over the next generation, trading furs to the expanding colonists and seeking to understand their perplexing ways.

Having gained the upper hand, the Bible-reading English made gestures to convert their Native American neighbors. The Massachusetts General Court encouraged missionary work, forbade the worship of Indian gods, and set aside land for "praying towns" to encourage "the Indians to live in an orderly way amongst us." In Cambridge, the Reverend John Eliot labored to create and print a 1,200-page Indian Bible, using English words when terms such as "horse," "brass," "book," and "psalm" did not exist in the Massachusett language. At Harvard, officials committed by their charter to the "education of the English and Indian youth of this Country" erected a well-publicized Indian College.

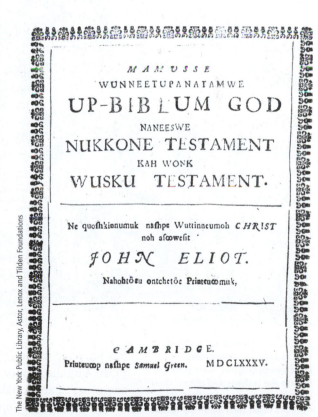

The New York Public Library, Astor, Lenox and Tilden Foundations

■ John Eliot and several Indian assistants translated the Old and New Testaments into the Massachusett language, printing 1,000 copies of their thick Indian Bible in 1663. This title page appeared on the second edition in 1685.

The Chesapeake Bay Colonies

■ *In what ways did the rapid spread of tobacco help or hurt the Chesapeake colonies?*

On Chesapeake Bay, settlers' relations with the Indians remained strained at best during the first half of the seventeenth century. In 1608, in an effort to secure the support of Indian leadership, the English performed an elaborate ceremony granting a scarlet cloak and a copper crown to Chief Powhatan. But two years later, suspicious that he was harboring runaway colonists, the English burned the nearest Indian villages and unthinkingly destroyed much-needed corn. A wife of one Indian leader, taken captive, watched English soldiers throwing her children in the river and shooting them in the head before she herself was stabbed to death.

For both sides, hopes of reconciliation rose briefly in 1614 with the match between Pocahontas, daughter of Powhatan, and John Rolfe, the prominent widower who had introduced tobacco. But the marriage proved brief; Pocahontas died in England three years later, after bearing one child. Leaders intended the wedding alliance as a diplomatic gesture toward peace. But it did little to curtail the settlers' bitterness over their lingering dependence on Indian supplies. For their part, the Native Americans resented the encroaching tobacco fields and belligerent tactics of the new settlers.

Courtesy of the John Carter Brown Library at Brown University

■ Captain John Smith boasted that in 1608 he intimidated Opechancanough with his pistol to disarm the Indians and obtain their corn. The insult was not forgotten; decades later, the Pamunkey leader launched two major attacks on the Jamestown colony. This image of the early incident appeared in Smith's popular *Generall Historie* of 1624.

THE DEMISE OF THE VIRGINIA COMPANY

Powhatan's death in 1618 brought to power his more militant younger brother, Opechancanough, the leader of the Pamunkey tribe. His encounters with the English had been frequent and unfriendly. John Smith had even taken him captive at gunpoint to extort food supplies. By 1618, the English were taking Indian land to grow tobacco, and more newcomers were arriving annually. Over the next three years, forty-two ships brought 3,500 people to the Chesapeake colony. The influx disheartened the Indians, and Opechancanough and his followers in the Powhatan Confederacy sought ways to end the mounting intrusion. Briefly, disease seemed to work in the Indians' favor. Immigrants who made the long sea voyage with poor provisions often fell ill in the swampy and unhealthy environment of Jamestown. By 1622, the colony's inhabitants were dying almost as rapidly as newcomers arrived. Sickness had carried off 3,000 residents in the course of only three years.

Opechancanough sensed a chance to deliver the finishing blow. He planned a sudden and coordinated offensive along the lower James River. On March 22, 1622, his forces attacked the English, surprising the outlying settlements and sparing no one. Of the 1,240 colonists, nearly 350 lost their lives. Warned by an Indian, Jamestown survived the uprising, but hope for peaceful relations ended. In London, word of the attack fueled opposition to the Virginia Company among disgruntled investors. In 1624, King James annulled the company's charter, making Virginia a royal colony controlled by the crown. In the colony's first seventeen years, more than 8,500 people, almost all of them young, had embarked for the Chesapeake. By 1624, only fifteen of every 100 remained alive.

The surviving colonists placed a bounty on Opechancanough's head, but attempts to ambush or poison him failed. The Indian leader lived on, nursing his distrust of the English. In 1644, he inaugurated a second uprising that killed some 500 colonists. But the English

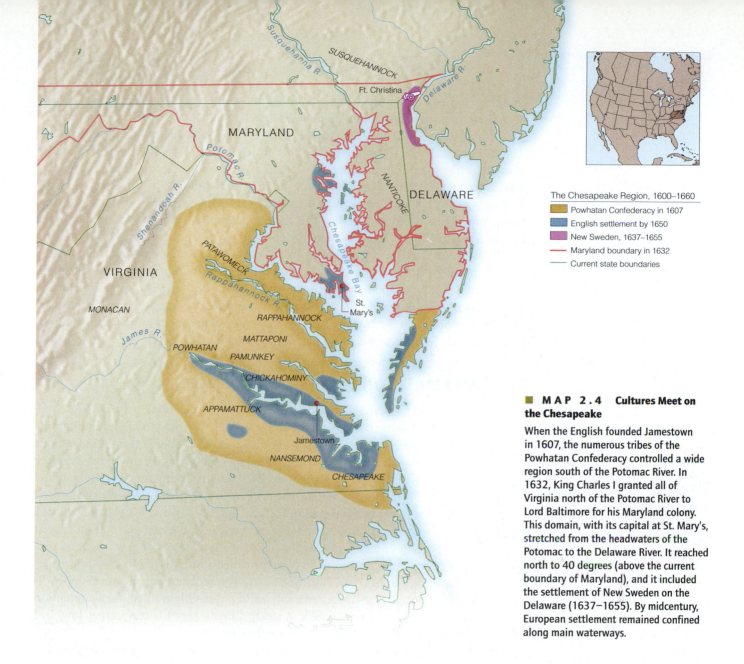

MAP 2.4 Cultures Meet on the Chesapeake

When the English founded Jamestown in 1607, the numerous tribes of the Powhatan Confederacy controlled a wide region south of the Potomac River. In 1632, King Charles I granted all of Virginia north of the Potomac River to Lord Baltimore for his Maryland colony. This domain, with its capital at St. Mary's, stretched from the headwaters of the Potomac to the Delaware River. It reached north to 40 degrees (above the current boundary of Maryland), and it included the settlement of New Sweden on the Delaware (1637–1655). By midcentury, European settlement remained confined along main waterways.

settlement had grown too large to eradicate. By this time old age forced the "Great General" to be carried on a litter. When the English finally captured him and brought him to Jamestown in 1646, Opechancanough was too old to walk unassisted. Still, he remained defiant until shot in the back by one of the Englishmen guarding him.

After two years of brutal warfare, the Pamunkey and their allies in the Powhatan Confederacy conceded defeat and submitted to English authority. From then on, they would pay a token annual tribute for the privilege to remain on lands that had once belonged to them. With the way cleared for Chesapeake expansion, land-hungry English settlers appeared in ever-increasing numbers in Virginia and the smaller and younger Maryland colony.

MARYLAND: THE CATHOLIC REFUGE

Maryland owed its beginnings to George Calvert, a respected Catholic member of England's government. He was named the first Baron of Baltimore, in Ireland, in 1625. Calvert, now Lord Baltimore, had a keen interest in colonization, and in 1632 he petitioned Charles I for land in the Chesapeake. The king granted him 10 million acres adjacent to Virginia, to be named Maryland in honor of the Catholic queen, Henrietta Maria. The Maryland charter

DOCUMENT

The Charter of Maryland (1632)

gave the proprietor and his heirs unprecedented personal power, especially in the granting of lands to colonists without limitations based on religious belief.

Because Calvert died before the royal charter took effect, his eldest son, the second Lord Baltimore, took charge of the settlement effort. In 1634, the *Ark* and the *Dove* carried more than 200 settlers—both Protestants and Catholics—to the new colony. There, they established a capital at St. Mary's, near the mouth of the Potomac River. With the execution of the king in 1649 and the creation of an anti-Catholic commonwealth in England, the Calvert family provided a haven in Maryland for their coreligionists. However, Catholics never became a majority in the Chesapeake colony.

In 1649, Maryland's assembly passed an Act Concerning Religion, guaranteeing toleration for all settlers who professed a belief in Jesus Christ. This assertion of religious toleration, though limited, proved too broad for many to stomach. In the 1650s, supporters of the English Puritan cause seized power in Maryland, repealed the act, and briefly ended the Calverts' proprietorship. But by 1660, with the restoration of the Stuart monarchy in England, proprietary rule returned to the prosperous farming colony.

THE DWELLINGS OF ENGLISH NEWCOMERS

By 1660, Virginia and Maryland totaled roughly 35,000 settlers, scattered along the edges of the bay and its adjoining tidewater rivers. In New England, where far fewer immigrants had arrived, the overall numbers were still somewhat smaller—perhaps only 25,000. But in the northeast, early marriage and long life expectancy prompted a rapidly rising population. From the start, Puritans embarking for New England had generally set out as families. The presence of thousands of wives and daughters led to the swift formation of stable households, and the balance between the sexes soon proved almost even. New England women took on crucial aspects of domestic production, cooking, baking, weaving, sewing, and gardening. Their numerous children provided additional hands, hauling water, making candles, and churning butter where labor was in short supply. In contrast to New England, the Chesapeake still could not maintain its colonial population without steady infusions of newcomers. A sickly climate kept life expectancy low, and men continued to outnumber women by more than two to one.

> *In both New England and the Chesapeake, initial crude shelters gave way to small frame houses.*

In both regions, housing was a primary concern, and newcomers brought English building traditions with them. But contrasting climates and differing priorities prompted the evolution of different architectural styles. In both New England and the Chesapeake, initial crude shelters gave way to small frame houses, usually with clapboard walls, as arrivals took advantage of the ample wood supply. At first, roofs were made of thatch—bundles of grass and straw. But as nails became more abundant, thatch yielded to lighter and less flammable wooden shingles.

Large New England families, facing longer winters indoors, needed warmer dwellings with more interior space. Many added another room at the gable end of a frame house, surrounding the external stone chimney and turning the cooking hearth into a central fireplace. Digging a cellar, building thick walls, and adding a second story made efficient use of heat from the log fire. New Englanders often linked additional storage rooms and animal sheds to the house for warmth as well.

Early Chesapeake houses, in contrast, were less solid and substantial. Most structures remained one story high, a simple wooden frame set on posts, with mortise-and-tenon joints and a dirt or plank floor. Oiled paper or wooden shutters covered most windows, as glass was rare. Since skilled bricklayers were few, most chimneys used wattle-and-daub construction, a simple weave of sticks and vines, covered with clay daubing. Tidewater residents built chimneys outside the house to help dissipate heat, and additional spaces were spread out, rather than being centralized under one roof. "All their drudgeries of cookery, washing, dairies, etc.," reported one Virginian, are done in small buildings "detached from the dwelling houses which by this means are kept cool and sweet."

A Roof Overhead: Early Chesapeake Housing

Lumber was plentiful in the Tidewater region, but labor was scarce and tools were crude. As a result, most structures were small and insubstantial, and seventeenth-century Chesapeake settlers lived in cramped quarters. This cutaway drawing illustrates the construction and floor plan of a house for "ordinary beginners," described in a pamphlet for potential migrants. The entire frame rested on sunken posts above an earth floor and was held together with wooden pegs inserted into mortise-and-tenon joints. A livable cottage often took less than two months to build.

During this period, only a few fashionable homes used brick construction. Thomas Jefferson, a Virginian who had an eye and pocketbook suited for grander architecture, noted with dismay in the 1780s that "the private buildings are very rarely constructed of stone or brick, much the greatest portion being of scantling and boards, plastered with lime. It is impossible to devise things more ugly, uncomfortable, and happily more perishable." Not surprisingly, only half a dozen structures built before 1660 still survive in Virginia and Maryland.

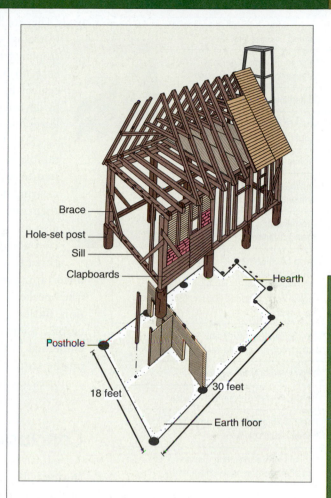

QUESTIONS

1. Which factors had the largest effect on early Chesapeake housing design: materials, climate, labor, or cultural traditions?

2. Thomas Jefferson asserted that it would be impossible to devise anything more ugly or uncomfortable than an early Chesapeake cottage. How does your own notion of what is beautiful and comfortable in a house or apartment differ from the ideas of your grandparents, your friends, or Jefferson?

THE LURE OF TOBACCO

Chesapeake residents spent most of their time out of doors, clearing land and tending fields. They readily adopted corn as a subsistence crop, and their imported livestock flourished. But early efforts to find a marketable export product met with disappointment. Hope for silk production disappeared when rats ate a supply of imported silkworms. Seeds of Mexican cotton, brought from southern Europe in 1621, failed to take hold. Experiments with oranges, pineapples, and grapes led nowhere. Chesapeake lumber sold well at first, but it was John Rolfe's tobacco plant that emerged as the tidewater's unlikely crop of choice.

Virginia's annual tobacco exports grew from a total weight of 2,000 pounds in 1615 to 500,000 in 1626. By 1630, saturated markets and stiff taxes led to slumping tobacco prices, so Virginians diversified their efforts. The beginning of the Massachusetts Bay colony created a demand for food that Chesapeake farmers met with well-timed coastal shipments. In 1634, they reported selling to "their zealous neighbours of New England tenne thousand bushels of corne for their releefe, besides good quantities of beeves, goats and hoggs, whereof this country hath great plentie." Such diversification proved brief, however. By 1640, London was receiving almost 1.4 million pounds of tobacco annually.

CHRONOLOGY: 1598–1660

1598	Spanish colonize New Mexico.
1607	England's Virginia Company launches colony at Jamestown.
1608	Champlain establishes Quebec
1610	Santa Fe becomes capital of Spanish New Mexico.
1619	Virginia creates an elected assembly.
1620	*Mayflower* passengers establish Plymouth Colony.
1622	Opechancanough leads surprise attack on Jamestown colonists.
1626	Dutch establish New Amsterdam on Manhattan Island.
1630	English Puritans found Massachusetts Bay Colony.
1636	Antinomian Crisis stirred by Anne Hutchinson divides Massachusetts Bay.
1637	Pequot War in New England.
1641	Montreal established in New France.
1644	Roger Williams obtains charter for his Rhode Island colony.
1649	Parliament executes King Charles I and abolishes the monarchy during England's Civil War.
1660	Restoration of monarchy in England under Charles II.

Though tobacco prices remained low throughout much of the seventeenth century, newcomers to Virginia and Maryland still managed to eke out a profit. They could grow the plants amid stumps in partially cleared fields. They could learn the many necessary procedures—planting, weeding, worming, suckering, topping, cutting, stripping, and curing—as the crop progressed. In short, it took hard work, but little farming experience, to bring cured tobacco to waterfront docks. Since captains charged by volume rather than weight, planters reduced shipping costs by devising a uniform barrel size and developing ways to press more leaves into each cask.

Still, the problems were formidable. Tobacco depleted the soil rapidly, so crop yields dwindled after several years. Then farmers had to leave their plots fallow, allowing them to recover, while clearing new fields for planting. This time-consuming task forced them onto marginal land that was poorly drained and less fertile. It also moved them away from navigable rivers, raising transportation costs. Storms, droughts, and crop diseases posed constant threats, and dependence on a single product in a distant and uncertain overseas market created added risks. By midcentury, Chesapeake planters worried about market saturation and overproduction. But by then, for better or worse, growing the noxious weed had become a way of life. Virginia and Maryland farmers found themselves enmeshed in the high-risk world of tobacco production. Dependence on the troublesome crop would expand across the upper South for centuries to come.

Conclusion

During half a century, the French, Dutch, and English had all moved to challenge Spanish claims in North America. By 1660, all four of these maritime powers of western Europe had taken aggressive steps to establish permanent footholds on the fringes of the enormous continent. In each instance, the European colonizers benefited first from the presence of knowledgeable Native Americans and then from the sharp decline of those same people through warfare and the onslaught of new diseases.

Granted, warfare with foreign invaders and death from unfamiliar illnesses had become a part of Native American history in the preceding century. But the sixteenth century was an era of tentative European exploration. In contrast, the first half of the seventeenth century saw Europeans move beyond occasional forays to permanent colonization. Spain, France, Holland, and England each had formidable assets in Europe and on the high seas. By 1660 all had sponsored colonial settlements that had endured for several generations, and each had begun to taste the seductive fruits of empire in America and elsewhere.

The English, slowest to become involved in overseas colonization, had caught up with their competitors by 1660. Among European countries, England had proven the most aggressive in forming expansive family-based colonies rather than military garrisons or trading outposts. As a result, by 1660 the population of England's North American settlements had already outstripped those of its imperial rivals. Indeed, fledgling English communities were growing at an increasing pace, thanks in particular to the rapid expansion in New England. This emerging superiority in numbers would prove advantageous in the imperial clashes that lay ahead.

French explorations

	La Sa
uette, 1673	Ibervi
1682	St. De
onists	La Ha
35	Frenc
s 1716–1717	Span
aries provided for orienta	

her party set out from Montreal on April 30, 1704, making their way up river and passing through Lake Ontario and Lake Erie. After more than a year, they reached Kaskaskia in southern Illinois and began to descend the Mississippi River. Marguerite's brother and a daughter died before the travelers finally reached their destination. When the survivors arrived at Mobile in August 1705, more bad news awaited them: the voyage of the *Pelican* had met with disaster.

Marguerite's husband had boarded the ship in France, joining missionaries, soldiers, and potential brides recruited to go to Mobile. But during a stopover in Cuba, Pierre-Charles and others caught yellow fever and died before the immigrants reached Mobile. The town—home to just 160 men and a dozen women—hardly had enough food and shelter for the sickly newcomers, and yellow fever spread quickly. The epidemic swept away forty residents in two months and decimated nearby Indian villages.

Still, life at the outpost persisted. Townsmen welcomed the *Pelican*'s eligible young women, ages fourteen to eighteen, and priests celebrated thirteen marriages within the first three weeks. New children were being born to these couples by the late summer of 1705, when Marguerite arrived from Montreal. Though distraught by news of Pierre-Charles's death, the young widow moved her children into the house he had built for them. She resumed her maiden name, Marguerite Messier, and determined to begin a fresh chapter of her life in the new Louisiana colony.

The changes taking place in North America during Marguerite Messier's lifetime occurred within a broad international context. In the second half of the seventeenth century, European maritime powers were caught up in a global race to expand and protect their overseas empires, and the chessboard was constantly changing. For example, by the 1670s, Dutch authorities had been forced to withdraw entirely from North America. As the Dutch departed, the Spanish, French, and English intensified their competition, starting towns wherever possible in order to stake their claims.

In the East, England expanded the number and size of its coastal colonies. English port towns multiplied along the Atlantic seaboard. English newcomers also pressed inland along numerous rivers to found towns. Many of these towns (such as William Byrd's trading post that became Richmond, Virginia) appeared at the "fall line," the point where waterfalls blocked passage upstream and provided waterpower to run gristmills. Farther inland, conflicts with hard-pressed Native Americans became more intense.

Pushing up from the south, meanwhile, Spain struggled to retain its foothold in Florida and New Mexico and to lay claim to parts of Arizona and Texas as well. New Spanish towns appeared at Albuquerque, El Paso, and Pensacola. Of the three competing powers, only France, pressing west and south from the St. Lawrence Valley, managed to penetrate the interior of the continent extensively. Its government created a string of forts from the Great Lakes to the Gulf of Mexico: Detroit, Peoria, and Mobile all came into being under the French flag.

One fundamental question recurred in numerous places during the decades after 1660: who has the right to govern? Often, boundaries were vague and structures of control were weak; religious dissenters and political rebels who felt excluded or exploited could openly question the legitimacy of those in charge. In congregations, towns, and whole colonies, challenges to authority arose repeatedly. Disruptions and violence became familiar experiences for thousands of people inhabiting North America.

For Review

1. What relevance did Spain's access to the Pacific have to its ambitions for colonization in the New World?

2. Why was Dutch New Netherland more culturally diverse than French Canada?

3. Among the forces shaping early migration to America shown in Figure 2.1 on page 54, which proved most important in colonizing Virginia? New England?

4. Why did the differing ideas of Anne Hutchinson and Roger Williams pose such a challenge to Puritan authorities in New England?

5. For Chesapeake colonists who survived past 1620, what large forces (often beyond their control) shaped their settlement over the next four decades?

6. How did religious views, demographic factors, and geography shape the success of European empires in North America after 1600?

Created Equal Online

For more *Created Equal* resources, including suggestions on sites to visit and books to read, go to **MyHistoryLab.com**.

Chapter 3

Controlling the Edges of the Continent, 1660–1715

CHAPTER OUTLINE

- France and the American Interior

- The Spanish Empire on the Defensive

- England's American Empire Takes Shape

- Bloodshed in the English Colonies: 1670–1690

- Consequences of War and Growth: 1690–1715

■ French fort at Mobile, 1705

In April 1704, Marguerite Messier Le Sueur, joined by her five children, loaded a large canoe on the Montreal waterfront. She worked with her brother, Jean-Michel Messier, and a guide to prepare for an immense inland journey to a new French outpost on the Gulf of Mexico. There she planned to meet her husband, explorer-trader Pierre-Charles Le Sueur. At age twenty-eight, Marguerite had already been married half her life, having wed Pierre-Charles in 1690 when he was thirty-four and she had just turned fourteen.

Marguerite was deeply involved, through family ties, in the dramatic changes taking place throughout the vast North American hinterland claimed by France. Her cousin, an adventurous Canadian named Pierre Le Moyne d'Iberville, had established the French colony of Louisiana near the mouth of the Mississippi River in 1699, and three years later Iberville and his younger brother Bienville had started the village of Mobile (near present-day Mobile, Alabama) to serve as the first capital. In 1702, Marguerite's husband, long active in Canada's far-flung western trade, had paddled down the Mississippi, taking furs to the new outpost at Mobile. After building a house for his family there, he accompanied Iberville back to France.

In 1704, confident about the future success of the Louisiana venture, Le Sueur sent word to his wife in Montreal to start the inland expedition of nearly 2,000 miles to Mobile. Pierre-Charles himself departed from France aboard the *Pelican* for the same destination, hoping to reunite with his family. With the ice gone from the St. Lawrence, Marguerite and

---

France and the American Interior

■ *Why did France gain access to North America's interior before other Europe*

The potential wealth of the North American interior had long intrigued gover isters in France. If Canadian fur traders could explore this vast domain and Indian inhabitants, France might control some of the continent's most fertile fa keep its extensive natural assets out of the hands of European rivals. If the Fr recruit enough Native Americans as loyal allies, they might even threaten the ri the Spanish empire in Mexico and challenge the growing English colonies lying t the Appalachian mountains. But for France to realize such wide ambitions, the I Louis XIV, would need to make North American colonization a national prior extent of his commitment remained uncertain.

THE RISE OF THE SUN KING

King Louis XIV stood at the center of France's expanding imperial sphere. Inde seemed to revolve around him that he became known as the "Sun King." He ha the French throne in 1643, as a child of five, and in 1661, at age twenty-two, he a sonal control of a realm of 20 million people. During most of his long rule—fron death in 1715 at age seventy-seven—Louis dominated European affairs. Always monuments, he expanded the Louvre in Paris and then dazzled the French r clergy with his opulent new palace at Versailles.

In religion, the Sun King challenged the authority of the Catholic pope on o suppressed the dissent of French Protestants (known as Huguenots) on the other he centralized the monarchy's power as never before. His administration cons laws of France, strengthened the armed forces, and expanded commerce. His ministries foreshadowed the power of modern nation-states by regulating in moting road building, and imposing tariffs and taxes.

■ Louis XIV, the Sun King.

Throughout Louis XIV's reign, his officials followed a set of po as **mercantilism,** a system in which a government stressed eco sufficiency and a favorable balance of trade. By avoiding foreig drawing in valuable resources from its competitors and its ow state could pay for wars abroad and costly projects at home. mercantilist strategy was to exploit labor efficiently and impor als cheaply, while exporting expensive manufactured produ glassware, wine, silk, and tapestries, in exchange for foreign go France's colonists, like those of Spain and England, were expecte much-needed natural resources and to serve as eager consur mother country's manufactured goods.

In Paris, finance minister Jean-Baptiste Colbert emerged architect of this strategy of aggressive mercantilism. At home he ta imports, removed domestic trade barriers, and improved internal tion. Moreover, he reduced worker holidays and outlawed strikes. toward colonial expansion, Colbert improved France's ports and create regulate maritime shipping. He expanded the naval fleet and pressed French its service. Pushing still harder, he organized overseas trading companies a insurance for their expensive ventures. In addition, he sanctioned France's i in the African slave trade. Colbert yearned to acquire new territory to i empire's self-sufficiency and keep overseas resources out of enemy hands. he and his successors encouraged French exploration of North America on dented scale.

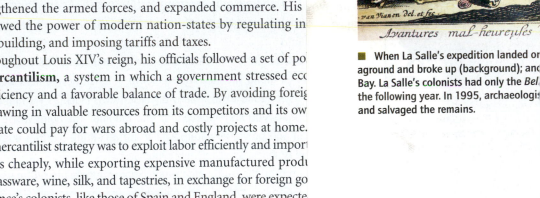

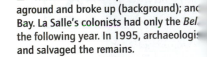

■ When La Salle's expedition landed or aground and broke up (background); and Bay. La Salle's colonists had only the *Bel* the following year. In 1995, archaeologi and salvaged the remains.

inasmuch as I was preventing his daughter from obeying him, he would also prevent her from going to the chapel. That very night her father gathered the chiefs of the four villages, and told them that, since I prevented the French from forming alliances with them…he earnestly begged them to stop the women and children from coming to the chapel.

I thought I should not remain silent after so great an insult had been offered to God. I went to the commandant of the fort, . . . who answered in an insulting manner that I had drawn all this upon myself, through my stubbornness in not allowing the girl to marry the Frenchman, who was then with him. [The Jesuit demanded that the commandant support him against the chiefs. The French leader] replied coldly that he would speak to the chiefs; but, instead of assembling them at once, he waited until the afternoon of the following day, and even then I had to return to him from the purpose. [Then Gravier advised Marie:] My daughter, God does not forbid you to marry; neither do I say to you: 'Marry or do not marry.' If you consent solely through love for God, and if you believe that by marrying you will win your family to God, the thought is a good one.

Marie, age sixteen, married Accault and bore two sons before he died. By 1704, she had married another French trader, Michel Philippe, and moved to the new town of Kaskaskia. There Philippe turned to farming and amassed a sizable estate, including an Indian servant and five black slaves. Marie raised six

more children before her death in 1725. Her will, dictated in French and then translated into the Illinois language, withheld property from one son who continued to live as an Indian. Her priest, Father Gravier, had been shot in the arm by an Indian in 1705. The arrowhead could not be removed, and he died three years later.

QUESTIONS

1. *Regarding the Rouensa-Accault marriage, can you explore the differing motives of Marie, her parents, Michel Accault, and Father Gravier?*

2. *Can you recreate an argument in 1720 at Kaskaskia between Catholic Marie and the son remaining loyal to the ways of Chief Rouensa?*

FOUNDING THE LOUISIANA COLONY

Even before new hostilities erupted in Europe in 1701, Louis XIV and his ministers took steps to secure French claims in the Gulf of Mexico, despite Spain's naval dominance in the area. By renewing La Salle's plan for a Louisiana colony, France could strengthen its hand in the impending war over succession to the Spanish throne. A colony on the Gulf of Mexico would provide a southern outlet for the French fur trade and a strategic outpost to counter Spain's new fort at Pensacola in western Florida.

England also saw advantages to establishing a base on the lower Mississippi. Such a post could challenge Spanish and French claims to the Gulf region and increase English trade with the Chickasaw and other southern Indians. In 1698, a London promoter quietly made plans to transport a group of Huguenot refugees to the mouth of the Mississippi. Catching wind of this scheme, the French naval minister, Comte de Pontchartrain, organized his own secret expedition to the Gulf of Mexico under an aspiring Canadian officer, Pierre Le Moyne d'Iberville.

Coming from a large and well-connected Montreal family, the Le Moynes, Iberville quickly drew several siblings into the gulf colonization plan, including his teenage brother, Bienville. Iberville and his party sailed for the Gulf of Mexico from the French port of Brest in 1699. Their ship entered the mouth of the Mississippi in time to repel the English expedition at a site on the river still known as English Turn. They also managed to build a fort at nearby Biloxi Bay before returning to France.

The two brothers were now well on their way to creating the Gulf Coast colony that La Salle and his followers had failed to establish. A second voyage let Iberville conduct further reconnaissance of the lower Mississippi. On a third trip, in 1702, he established Fort Louis, near Mobile Bay, giving French traders access to the Choctaw Indians. Young Bienville, placed in charge of Fort Louis, labored to sustain the tiny outpost at Mobile. Iberville himself left to pursue other schemes and died an early death in 1706.

Enmeshed in the War of Spanish Succession, France ignored its new Gulf colony. Epidemics reduced Louisiana's newcomers and took a far heavier toll on Indian neighbors. Settlers drawn from Canada, with prior wilderness experience, maintained close ties with local Native Americans and resented the incompetence and haughtiness of colonists sent from France. The latter complained about the poor living conditions and looked down on the uneducated Canadians. However, despite social friction and a chronic lack of supplies from France, the small community at Mobile survived, including the widow Marguerite Messier and her children.

Far to the north, additional posts reinforced French territorial claims, fostered the fur trade, and protected neighboring Indians against Iroquois raids. The village of Peoria sprang up on the Illinois River in 1691. Not far away, Catholic missions appeared nearby at Cahokia (1697) and Kaskaskia (1703). Fort de Chartres took shape in southern Illinois in 1719. Farther north, the French established two other strategic posts. In 1689, they laid out a garrison where Lake Huron joins Lake Michigan. In 1701, they created a lasting town, Detroit, on the strait (*le détroit* in French) connecting Lake Erie to Lake Huron. The founder of this village, Monsieur Cadillac, foresaw a prosperous future for the new trading post, since Detroit would be accessible "to the most distant tribes which surround these vast sweet water seas."

> *Over two generations, the French had established a solid claim on the American interior.*

In 1712 the French crown, its resources depleted by a decade of warfare in Europe, granted control over Louisiana to a powerful Paris merchant, Antoine Crozat. Drawing Cadillac from Detroit to serve as Louisiana's governor general, Crozat hoped to develop connections to mineral-rich Mexico and to discover precious metals in the Mississippi watershed. But probes on the upper Mississippi, the Missouri, and the Red rivers yielded no easy bonanza. Instead, explorers established three new trading posts among the Indians: Natchitoches on the Red River, Fort Rosalie on the Mississippi (at Natchez), and Fort Toulouse (near modern Montgomery, Alabama).

When Louis XIV died in 1715, the colonial population of Canada's St. Lawrence Valley had crept up to nearly 25,000, but fewer than 1,000 colonists lived in Lower Louisiana and the Illinois Country combined. Nevertheless, over two generations, the French had established a solid claim on the American interior. Their position was an ongoing challenge to English and Spanish competitors. The crescent of wilderness outposts arcing north and then east from the Gulf Coast offered a useful network for additional exploration, Indian trade, and military conquest. French control of the Mississippi Valley remained a real possibility until the era of Thomas Jefferson and Napoleon Bonaparte nearly a century later.

The Spanish Empire on the Defensive

■ *How did Indian experiences with the Spanish vary in Arizona, New Mexico, and Florida?*

Whereas France's power expanded during Louis XIV's reign, Spain's overextended empire continued to weaken. This decline opened the door for Louis to maneuver his own grandson onto the Spanish throne in 1700 as Philip V. Meanwhile, Spanish colonizers struggled to defend vast territorial claims in North America that spread—on paper—from the Gulf of California to the Florida peninsula.

In Spain's remote colonies of New Mexico and Florida, local administration often proved corrupt, and links to imperial officials at home remained weak and cumbersome.

For several generations, the Indian majority had resented the harsh treatment and strange diseases that came with colonial contact. Now, cultural disruptions and pressures from hostile Indian neighbors fanned the flames of discontent. In the late seventeenth century, a wave of Native American rebellions swept the northern frontier of New Spain.

THE PUEBLO REVOLT IN NEW MEXICO

The largest and most successful revolt took place in New Mexico, where soldiers, settlers, and priests, sent north by Spanish authorities at the beginning of the century, had staked out a remote colony along the upper Rio Grande. There, Pueblo Indians from dozens of separate communities (or pueblos) united in a major upheaval in August 1680. They murdered twenty-one of the forty friars serving in New Mexico, ransacked their churches, and killed more than 350 settlers. After laying siege to Santa Fe, the rebels drove the remaining Spanish colonists and their Christian Indian allies south out of the province and kept them away for more than a decade. Several thousand stunned survivors took refuge in what is now El Paso and soon began questioning Indian informants to find an explanation for the fearsome uprising.

DOCUMENT

Pedro Hidalgo, Legal Statement (1680)

Diverse factors, stretching back over decades, had combined to ignite the Pueblo Revolt of 1680. First, a five-year drought beginning in 1666 inflicted a famine with long-lasting effects on the peoples of New Mexico. Second, around the same time, neighboring Apache and Navajo stepped up their hostilities against the small colonial population and the numerous Pueblo Indians who had been linked with the Spanish for several generations. The attackers were embittered by colonial slave raids that took Indian captives to work in Mexican silver mines. In retaliation, these raiding parties, riding stolen Spanish horses, killed livestock and seized scarce food. When colonial soldiers proved unable to fend off the hit-and-run attacks, their credibility among the Pueblo Indians living alongside the colonists weakened.

Third, a smoldering controversy over religion flared during the 1670s. When an epidemic struck in 1671, Spanish missionaries could not stem the sickness through prayers. In response, traditionalist Indian priests revived age-old Pueblo religious customs. Horrified, the Spanish friars and government officials united to punish what they saw as backsliding within a Pueblo population that seemed to have accepted key elements of the Catholic faith. At Santa Fe in 1675, they hanged three Indian leaders for idolatry and whipped and imprisoned forty-three others—including a militant leader from San Juan pueblo named Popé. Before the captives could be sold into slavery, armed Indians successfully demanded the release of Popé and the other prisoners.

Popé withdrew to Taos, the northernmost pueblo in New Mexico. From there, he negotiated secretly with like-minded factions in other pueblos, unifying resistance to Spanish domination and forging an underground movement. In part, he built support around widespread resentment of the Spanish **encomienda** system (requiring Indian communities to supply labor or pay tribute) and toward the Catholic Church (which forbade traditional Indian religious ceremonies). Indian women whom Spanish priests or soldiers had abused took Popé's side in this cultural clash. The movement also received secret support from numerous **mestizos** and **mulattos,** mixed-race people whose dark skin and lack of "pure" Spanish blood cost them any chance for advancement. Popé sent runners to each conspiring pueblo to fix the date for the rebellion. When the time came, his Pueblo warriors swiftly overcame their adversaries. Unified in triumph, the zealous victors smeared excrement on Christian altars and bathed themselves to remove the stigma of baptism.

> *Pueblo Indians from dozens of separate communities (or pueblos) united in a major upheaval in August 1680.*

But initial cohesion gave way to friction. The successful rebels soon quarreled over who should hold power and how best to return to ancient ways. Kivas would replace churches, and the cross would give way to the **kachina.** But what other parts of the imported culture should the Indians abandon? Various Pueblo groups could not agree on which Spanish words, tools, and customs to discard or which foreign crops and animals to retain.

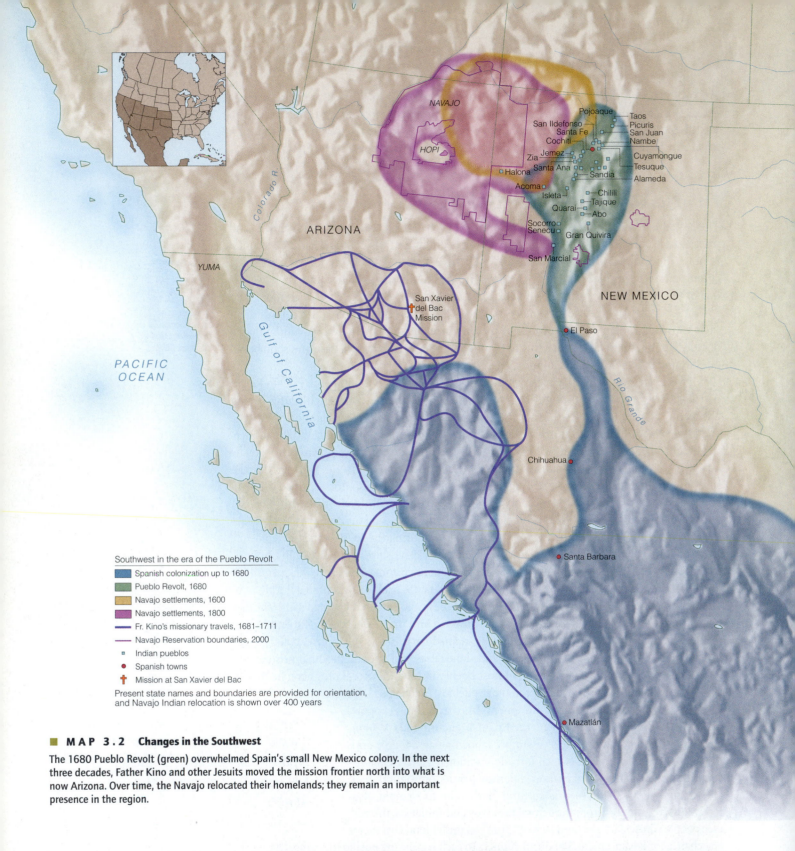

Southwest in the era of the Pueblo Revolt

- ■ Spanish colonization up to 1680
- ■ Pueblo Revolt, 1680
- ■ Navajo settlements, 1600
- ■ Navajo settlements, 1800
- ── Fr. Kino's missionary travels, 1681–1711
- ── Navajo Reservation boundaries, 2000
- ■ Indian pueblos
- ● Spanish towns
- ✝ Mission at San Xavier del Bac

Present state names and boundaries are provided for orientation, and Navajo Indian relocation is shown over 400 years

■ **MAP 3.2** **Changes in the Southwest**

The 1680 Pueblo Revolt (green) overwhelmed Spain's small New Mexico colony. In the next three decades, Father Kino and other Jesuits moved the mission frontier north into what is now Arizona. Over time, the Navajo relocated their homelands; they remain an important presence in the region.

In 1681, the Pueblo fended off a Spanish attempt at reconquest. But they remained divided among themselves and more vulnerable than ever to Apache raids. Within a decade, rival factions had deposed Popé, and another Spanish colonial army, under Governor Diego de Vargas, had entered New Mexico. It took the new governor several years to subdue the province, and the Pueblo managed another full-scale rebellion in 1696. But Vargas anticipated the revolt and crushed the opposition, just as Oñate had done a century earlier. In 1706, several soldiers and their families established the town of Albuquerque on its present site. Learning from prior mistakes, Spanish officials did not reimpose the hated *encomienda* system. A new generation of Franciscan missionaries tolerated indigenous Pueblo traditions as long as the Indians also attended Catholic mass.

NAVAJO AND SPANISH ON THE SOUTHWESTERN FRONTIER

The repercussions of rebellion and reconquest along the upper Rio Grande echoed throughout the Southwest. To the north, Pueblo refugees joined the Navajo and brought valuable experience as corn farmers. Corn, already known to the Navajo, now became an increasingly important food and sacred symbol for them. Moreover, the new arrivals had learned from the Spanish how to plant peach orchards and raise sheep. Navajo women—the weavers in their society—soon owned large flocks and wove wool blankets on their traditional portable looms. The Pueblo also brought more Spanish horses, a key asset that let the Navajo spread their domain west into fine grazing country in what is now northeast Arizona. Farther north, the Ute and Comanche also acquired horses after the Pueblo Revolt. Eventually, the Comanche pressed southeast onto the Texas plains.

After the Pueblo Revolt, officials in Mexico City worried about further upheavals along New Spain's wide northern frontier. Despite limited resources, authorities sent a few missionary-explorers north near the Gulf of California to spread Christianity and pacify hostile Indians. Year by year, these friar-explorers edged toward what is now southern Arizona, reaching the cactus-studded Sonoran Desert by the 1690s.

Eusebio Kino, a tireless Jesuit missionary born in Italy and educated in Germany, spearheaded the early exploration of the Arizona region. In 1701, he visited the large Indian village of Bak, located near the Santa Cruz River. There, among more than 800 inhabitants, he established the mission of San Xavier del Bac, near modern Tucson, Arizona. Kino's endless travels on horseback prompted additional missions farther south and west, but these outposts languished after his death in 1711. Warfare and sickness eroded the local population of Pima Indians, and attacks by Apache raiders destabilized the entire frontier region. Spain finally reinstalled priests at San Xavier del Bac and other missions along the Santa Cruz River in 1732. Four years later, a

Harald Sund/Getty Images

■ Horses and sheep arrived in the Southwest with the Spanish, and both became central to the Navajo (or Diné) culture in northern Arizona and New Mexico. Navajo women continue to herd sheep and weave their wool into rugs and blankets, as they have done for more than three centuries.

silver strike at "Arizonac," near present-day Nogales on the U.S.-Mexican border, provided a new name for the region, which would eventually become the state of Arizona.

BORDERLAND CONFLICT IN TEXAS AND FLORIDA

The encounters on Spain's other North American borderland frontiers took different forms, in part because European rivals appeared on the scene. Conflict with the French led the Spanish to found missions in Texas, a land they named after the local Tejas Indians. At first, responding to news about La Salle's ill-fated French colony, the Spanish made a brief attempt to establish a Texas mission in 1690, departing again in 1693. They renewed their effort two decades later, after Louisiana's Governor Cadillac (the founder of Detroit) sent explorers from Louisiana across eastern Texas to forge ties with Spanish communities south of the Rio Grande. Eager to open trade with the Spanish, the French visitors reached San Juan Bautista, below the modern U.S.-Mexican border, in 1714.

> The Indians of Florida, like the Pueblo in New Mexico, debated whether to reject generations of Spanish rule.

Spanish authorities, taken by surprise, dusted off plans for colonizing Texas. By 1717, they had established half a dozen small missions near the Sabine River, the boundary between modern Texas and Louisiana. The next year, to expand their missionary activities and secure the supply route from San Juan Bautista to these distant outposts in east Texas, the Spanish built a cluster of settlements beside the San Antonio River, at a midpoint on the trail from Mexico. Within two decades a string of missions stretched along the river. Indian converts tended herds of cattle and sheep and constructed aqueducts to irrigate new fields of wheat and corn. The earliest mission, San Antonio de Valero (1718), provided a nucleus for the town of San Antonio. Later known as the Alamo, the mission also strengthened Spanish claims to Texas against threats of French intrusion.

During the second half of the seventeenth century, the Indians of Florida, like the Pueblo in New Mexico, debated whether to reject generations of Spanish rule. The Columbian Exchange had altered their lives in dramatic ways. They ate new foods such as figs, oranges, peas, cabbages, and cucumbers. They used Spanish words—*azucár* (sugar), *botija* (jar), *caballo* (horse)—and metal hoes from Europe allowed them to produce more corn. But expanded contact with colonizers created major problems as well. By 1660 devastating epidemics had whittled away at Florida's Native American towns. The Indians still outnumbered the newcomers more than ten to one, but they had to expend enormous energy raising, processing, and hauling food for the Spanish. When colonists grew fearful of French and English attacks after 1670, they forced hundreds of Indians to perform even more grueling labor: constructing the stone fortress of San Marcos at St. Augustine.

Nothing proved more troubling to Florida's Indians than the spread of livestock farming. St. Augustine's elite had established profitable cattle ranches on the depopulated savannas of Timucua, near present-day Gainesville in north-central Florida. These entrepreneurs ignored requirements to keep cows away from unfenced Indian gardens, and they enforced harsh laws to protect their stock. Any Florida Indian who killed cattle faced four months of servitude; people caught raiding Spanish herds had their ears cut off.

Resentment grew in Florida's scattered mission villages. Restless Indian converts wondered whether the English, who had founded their Carolina colony in 1670, might make viable allies. The English seemed eager to trade for deerskins, and they offered the Native Americans a steadier supply of desirable goods than the Spanish could provide. Several Indian communities moved closer to Carolina to test this new alternative for trade. But when France and Spain joined forces against the English after 1700, Florida's Indians suddenly found themselves caught up in a struggle far larger than they had bargained for.

Ever since the days of Francis Drake, the English had schemed to oust the Spanish from St. Augustine. In 1702, led by South Carolina governor James Moore, English raiders and their Indian allies rampaged through the Florida town. Yet the new stone fortress of

San Marcos held firm, protecting the inhabitants. Two years later, Moore invaded Apalachee (near modern Tallahassee), accompanied by 50 Englishmen and 1,000 Creek Indians. His troops crushed the mission towns, killing hundreds and carrying away more than 4,000 Indian captives. Most of them were women and children, whom the English sold as slaves in Carolina and the Caribbean. By 1706 the mission villages in Apalachee and Timucua lay in ruins. "In all these extensive dominions," lamented a Spanish official from St. Augustine, "the law of God and the preaching of the Holy Gospel have now ceased."

England's American Empire Takes Shape

■ *What are the varied origins of England's Restoration-Era American colonies?*

In 1660, as Louis XIV began his long reign in France and Spanish missionaries labored in New Mexico and Florida, England experienced a counterrevolutionary upheaval that dramatically influenced American colonial affairs. In the 1640s, amid violent civil war, rebels supporting Puritans and the Parliament had overthrown the ruling Stuart family, beheaded King Charles I, and abolished hereditary monarchy altogether.

For a brief period, England became a republican commonwealth without a king. But Oliver Cromwell, the movement's dictatorial leader and self-styled Lord Protector, died in 1658. Pressures quickly mounted to undo the radical Puritan Revolution and *restore* monarchical government. In May 1660, a strong coalition of conservative interests welcomed the late king's son back from exile and placed him on the throne as King Charles II. With monarchy restored in England, the renewed Stuart dynasty ruled from 1660 until 1688. The period is remembered in English politics and culture as the **Restoration Era.**

> *Many who had fought to end monarchy and strengthen Parliament sought refuge in the American colonies.*

The shift in London's political winds could hardly have been more sudden. Charles II moved quickly in 1660 to underscore the end of England's Puritan experiment. He ordered the execution of those who had beheaded his father in 1649. Many who had fought to end monarchy and strengthen Parliament sought refuge in the American colonies when their religious and political beliefs abruptly fell out of favor at home. Other elements of colonial demographics—early marriage, high birthrates, and a low level of mortality in most places— did even more to prompt expansion up and down the Atlantic coast.

MONARCHY RESTORED AND NAVIGATION CONTROLLED

Because most English colonists still lived within fifty miles of the Atlantic, an increase in people steadily broadened the opportunities for seaborne trade. Growing ship traffic, in turn, sparked government desires to regulate colonial navigation to bring mercantilist advantages to the restored monarchy. In 1660, Parliament passed a major new law designed to promote British shipping and trade.

The Navigation Act of 1660 laid out important conditions that shaped England's colonial commerce for generations. First, merchants could not conduct trade to or from the English colonies in foreign-owned ships. Second, key non-English products imported from foreign lands—salt, wine, oil, and naval stores (the tar, pitch, masts, and other materials used to build boats)—had to be carried in English ships or in ships with mostly English crews. Third, the law contained a list of "enumerated articles" produced overseas. The items listed—tobacco, cotton, sugar, ginger, indigo, and dyewoods—could no longer be sent directly from a colony to a foreign European port. Instead, merchants had to ship them to England first and then reexport them, a step that directly boosted England's domestic economy. Another Navigation Act, in 1663, required that goods moving from the European continent to England's colonies

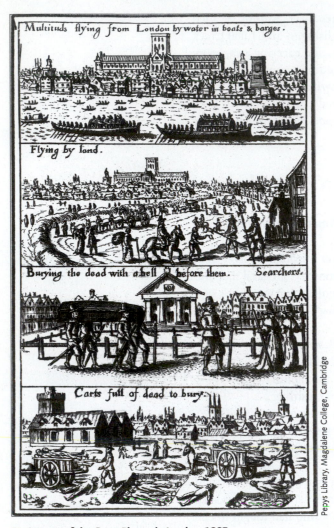

Multituds flying from London by water in boats & barges.

Flying by land.

Burying the dead with a bell before them.   Searchers.

Carts full of dead to bury.

Pepys Library, Magdalene College, Cambridge

■ Images of the Great Plague in London, 1665.

also needed to pass through the island. Moreover, they had to arrive and depart on English ships.

A later measure—the Plantation Duty Act of 1673—tried to close loopholes regarding enumerated articles. The new act required captains to pay a "plantation duty" before they sailed between colonial ports with enumerated goods. Otherwise, colonial vessels carrying such goods had to post bond before leaving harbor to ensure that they would sail directly to England. To enforce these rules, the government sent customs officers to the colonies for the first time. Backed by the Navigation Acts, England's fleets grew, and colonial trade became a major sector in England's economy.

Even the Great Plague, which swept England in 1665, could not blunt this mercantile growth. And when a catastrophic fire destroyed most of London the next year, the huge loss also provided an opportunity. Planners redesigned the city with the broad streets and impressive buildings that suited the prosperous hub of an expanding empire. The fashionable coffee shops that sprang up as a novelty in late-seventeenth-century London became common meeting places for exchanging news and views about England's increasingly profitable activities overseas. Much of what transpired in English North America was hashed out here, over pipes filled with Virginia tobacco.

DUTCH NEW NETHERLAND BECOMES NEW YORK

At the beginning of his reign, Charles II knew he had to build loyalty and strengthen an economy weakened by civil war. But the new monarch had expensive tastes and a depleted treasury. He soon found that he could reward loyal family members and supporters, at no cost to the crown, by granting them control over pieces of England's North American domain. With this prospect in hand, the king and his ministers sought to bolster foreign trade, expand the royal navy, and outstrip England's commercial rivals. They focused first on the Dutch.

As London stepped up its search for new profits, English officials moved to strengthen control over existing colonies and establish (or seize) new ones wherever possible. The Navigation Acts cut sharply into the Dutch carrying trade and spurred a decade of renewed warfare between England and Holland. For the most part, these intermittent Anglo-Dutch Wars ended in stalemate. But at the final Peace of Westminster in 1674, the English emerged with several gains in Africa and America that had lasting significance.

In West Africa, the English captured and held several key coastal outposts: an island at the mouth of the river Gambia (renamed James Fort for the Duke of York) and Cape Coast Castle on the Gold Coast (near Elmina, the African headquarters of the Dutch West India Company). This encroachment challenged Dutch dominance in the commerce for African gold and ivory. It also gave England the footholds it needed to force its way into the Atlantic slave trade. Charles II had already moved to take advantage of the situation. He granted a monopoly to the Royal Adventurers into Africa (1663) and then the Royal African Company (1672) to exploit the grim but highly profitable slave traffic. Within several generations, this ruthless initiative reshaped England's American colonies at enormous human cost.

Across the Atlantic, the English had seized the Dutch colony of New Netherland and its poorly defended port of New Amsterdam. Charles II claimed that the land had belonged to England from the time his grandfather endorsed the Virginia Company in 1606. The English king, eyeing the lucrative trade in beaver pelts that made New Netherland prosperous, used his royal prerogative to regain control of that domain. In 1664, he issued a charter putting the entire region between the Delaware and Connecticut rivers under the personal control of his brother James, Duke of York. That same year, James sent a fleet to claim his prize. When Governor Peter Stuyvesant surrendered the Dutch colony without a fight, the province and its capital on Manhattan Island each received the name *New York*. Fort Orange on the Hudson became Albany because England's traditional name was *Albion*. A Dutch fleet recaptured Manhattan briefly in 1673, but a treaty returned the colony to the English the following year.

> *Married women living in New Netherland lost ground in the transition to English rule.*

The Duke of York controlled an enormous domain (including the Dutch and English settlements on Long Island), and he wielded nearly absolute powers over his new dukedom. James never visited New York, but as proprietor, he chose the colony's governor. That official ruled with an appointed council and enforced "the Duke's Laws" without constraint by any assembly. English newcomers to the colony resented the absence of an elected legislature, and the governor finally authorized an elected body in 1683. But when the new assemblymen approved a Charter of Liberties endorsing government by consent of the governed, the Duke of York disallowed the legislature.

Married women living in New Netherland lost ground in the transition to English rule. Dutch law codes had ensured their full legal status, allowing them to hold property, make contracts, and conduct business. In contrast, English common law assigned wives to an inferior status known as **coverture.** They could not own property or keep control over money they earned, and they lacked any independent standing before the law.

As the English asserted political control over New York, the Dutch presence remained evident everywhere. Many English married into Dutch families and worshipped in the Dutch Reformed Church. The village of Harlem built a proper road to lower Manhattan in 1669, but an effort to change the town's Dutch name to Lancaster failed. English-speaking New Yorkers borrowed such Dutch words as *waffle, cookie, coleslaw,* and *baas* (boss). Anyone who was bilingual, such as Albany merchant Robert Livingston, had a special advantage. Livingston, an immigrant from Scotland, had learned to speak Dutch in Holland in his youth. His marriage in Albany to a prosperous young widow, Alida Schuyler Van Rensselaer, linked him to powerful Dutch families in the Hudson Valley, and much of his early wealth came from his ability to translate commercial documents between English and Dutch.

DOCUMENT

Church Record of a Marriage Conflict, Broaoklyn (1663)

THE NEW RESTORATION COLONIES

Charles II had spurred England's seizure of New Netherland by issuing a charter for control of the contested region to his brother, the Duke of York. To reward supporters, the king continued issuing royal charters granting American land, hoping to expand trade and colonization at no cost to the crown. In 1670, for example, he granted a charter to the Hudson's Bay Company. The deal gave the company's proprietors a monopoly on trade, minerals, and land across northern Canada. Farther south, Charles used charters to redistribute control along major portions of the Atlantic coast. His actions prompted an unprecedented scramble for colonial property and profits. Within decades, the English launched important settlement clusters in two regions: the Delaware River valley and the Carolina coast. Each depended upon lucrative royal charters offered to a small network of friends.

Most of these well-placed people belonged to the Councils for Trade and Plantations in London. Created in 1660, these advisory groups linked England's powerful merchants with crown officials. When Charles II issued a charter for Carolina in 1663, five of its eight initial proprietors served on those councils. In 1665, two of these same eight men became the proprietors of New Jersey. In addition, three of the eight played an active role in the Royal African Company, four became founders of the Hudson's Bay Company, and five became initial proprietors of the Bahamas. But Charles reached beyond this small group as well. In 1679, he made New Hampshire a proprietorship (an ill-fated experiment that lasted to 1708). In 1681, he paid off a debt to Quaker aristocrat William Penn by granting him a charter for Pennsylvania. (The generous arrangement included the "Lower Counties" that became Delaware in 1704.)

Penn's "holy experiment" to create a Quaker refuge benefited from earlier colonization south of New York. Dutch and Swedish settlers had inhabited the lower Delaware Valley for more than a generation. In 1665, the Duke of York carved off a portion of his vast proprietorship, granting the area between the Delaware and the Hudson to two friends: Lord John Berkeley and Sir George Carteret. They named the area New Jersey because Carteret had been born on the Isle of Jersey in the English Channel. Berkeley and Carteret promptly announced liberal "Concessions"—a representative assembly and freedom of worship—to attract rent-paying newcomers from England and the existing colonies. But their plans for profit made little headway.

In 1674, the proprietors divided these fertile lands into two separate provinces. East Jersey—where Newark was established in 1666—attracted Puritan families from New England, Dutch farmers from New York, and failed planters from Barbados. West Jersey was sold to members of the Society of Friends (including William Penn) who inaugurated a Quaker experiment along the Delaware River. Filled with egalitarian beliefs, the Quakers created a one-house **unicameral legislature,** used secret ballots, and gave more power to juries than to judges. West Jersey's "Concessions and Agreements" of 1677 barred taxation without the consent of the governed. This forward-looking document introduced a sunshine law, opening the doors of governmental meetings to all citizens. It also assured that no one could settle Native American land without consulting Indian leaders and obtaining their approval. The Quakers' idealistic effort foundered within decades, and by 1702 all New Jersey came under crown control as a royal colony. But by then, the Quakers had established a foothold in the neighboring colony of Pennsylvania.

> *West Jersey's "Concessions and Agreements" of 1677 barred taxation without the consent of the governed.*

THE CONTRASTING WORLDS OF PENNSYLVANIA AND CAROLINA

Proprietor William Penn laid out his capital for the Pennsylvania colony in 1682, naming it Philadelphia. Within two decades, this market center and "greene countrie towne" already had more than 2,000 inhabitants. An earnest Quaker, Penn professed pacifism and implemented many of the same policies tried in West Jersey. He emphasized religious toleration, and a growing stream of German Protestants and others facing persecution in Europe began to flow into Pennsylvania after 1700. Penn also made it a point to deal fairly with the Lenni-Lenape (Delaware) Indians. After purchasing their land, he resold it on generous terms to English, Dutch, and Welsh Quakers who agreed to pay him an annual premium, called a **quitrent.**

DOCUMENT

William Penn, Description of Pennsylvania (1681)

Penn drew inspiration from James Harrington, the English political philosopher. Harrington's book *Oceana* (1656) argued that the best way to create an enduring republic was for one person to draft and implement its constitution. After endless tinkering, Penn devised a progressive "Frame of Government" that allowed for trial by jury, limited terms of office, and no use of capital punishment except in cases of treason and murder. But he remained ambivalent about legislative democracy. Settlers resented his scheme for a lower house that could approve acts drafted by the governor but could not initiate laws. In a new Charter of Privileges in 1701, Penn agreed to the creation of a unicameral legislature with full lawmaking powers. Disillusioned, Penn then departed for England, writing, "The Lord forgive them their great ingratitude." Penn's expansive proprietorship belonged to his descendants until colonial rule ended in 1776.

In contrast to Pennsylvania, different development plans shaped the new Carolina colony—which split into North and South Carolina a generation later. Anthony Ashley-Cooper, leader of the Carolina proprietors, also drew inspiration from Harrington, but for a very different undertaking. *Oceana* had stressed that distribution of land determined the nature of any commonwealth, and Ashley-Cooper (later the first earl of Shaftesbury) was eager to establish a stable aristocratic system. With his young secretary, John Locke (later an influential political philosopher), he drew up a set of "Fundamental Constitutions" in 1669. They proposed a stratified society in which hereditary nobles controlled much of the land and wealthy manor lords employed a lowly servant class of "leetmen." Their unrealistic document tried to revive the elaborate feudal hierarchy of medieval times.

The new government framework also endorsed racial slavery, declaring that "Every Freeman of Carolina shall have absolute Power and Authority over his Negro Slaves." This endorsement was not surprising, given the proprietors' involvement with England's new slave-trading monopoly in Africa and their initial recruitment of settlers in 1670 from the sugar island of Barbados. When Carolina colonists founded Charlestown (later Charleston) between the Ashley and Cooper rivers in 1680, the proprietors had already modified aspects of their complicated scheme, setting aside feudalism to encourage greater immigration. Nevertheless, their endorsement of slavery shaped the region's society for hundreds of years.

Bloodshed in the English Colonies: 1670–1690

■ *To what degree was colonial violence after 1670 sparked by internal tensions or affairs in England?*

The appearance of isolated English settlements along the Atlantic coast did little, in most places, to alter traditional rhythms. Year after year, the daily challenges of subsistence dominated American life for Indians and colonists alike. The demanding seasonal tasks of clearing fields, planting seeds, and harvesting crops remained interwoven with the incessant chores of providing clothing, securing shelter, and sustaining community.

Over time, however, changing circumstances in America and Europe introduced new pressures up and down the Atlantic seaboard. On occasion after 1670, familiar routines gave way to episodes of bloodshed that threatened to tear whole colonies apart. Elsewhere in North America, Pueblo rebels were resisting the Spanish in New Mexico, and Iroquois warriors were challenging the French in Illinois Country. The English, with their larger numbers, posed an even greater cultural and economic problem for Native American inhabitants.

In 1675, embittered Wampanoag Indians and their allies rose up across southern New England in Metacom's War (or King Philip's War). The next year, frontier tensions in Virginia sparked the upheaval known as Bacon's Rebellion. A decade later, events in England prompted further tremors. Mounting opposition forced the unpopular King James II, who ruled from 1685 to 1688, to surrender the English throne to William of Orange. Parliament emerged from this transition (known in England as the "Glorious Revolution") with enhanced powers. In America, the end of rule by the Stuart dynasty was punctuated by controversy and violence in one colony after another.

> *After 1670, familiar routines gave way to episodes of bloodshed that threatened to tear whole colonies apart.*

METACOM'S WAR IN NEW ENGLAND

By 1675, the Native Americans of southern New England, like the Pueblo in New Mexico, had endured several generations of colonization. Yet they disagreed over how much English culture they should adopt. Many used English words for trading, English pots for cooking, and English weapons for hunting. Some had converted to Christianity, living in protected "praying towns." Several young men had enrolled in Harvard's Indian College, where they learned to write English, Latin, and Greek with an eye toward entering the ministry.

> Colonists now outnumbered the remaining 20,000 Indians in southern New England by more than two to one.

Massasoit, the Wampanoag **sachem** (leader) who had assisted the Pilgrims at Plymouth, made sure that his two sons, Wamsutta and Metacom, learned English ways. The two men raised pigs and fired guns, and the colonists called them Alexander and Philip, after the kings of ancient Macedon. But when Wamsutta died in the 1660s, shortly after succeeding his father, Metacom (now called King Philip) suspected foul play by the English. And Metacom had other grievances. Colonial traders made the Indians drunk and then cheated them. English livestock trampled Wampanoag corn, and if Indians shot the cattle, colonial courts imposed punishments. Land-hungry colonists now outnumbered the remaining 20,000 Indians in southern New England by more than two to one, and missionaries were drawing hundreds of Indians into Christian enclaves known as "praying towns."

One such convert was John Sassamon, who grew up among the colonists, learned to read and write English, and then taught school among other Indians. He became one of the first Native Americans to attend Harvard College and later preached the Gospel. Early in 1675, this respected go-between passed rumors of an impending Indian uprising to officials at Plymouth. When Sassamon died mysteriously days later, a jury of English and Indians blamed the revenge murder on three high-ranking Wampanoags. Their executions by the colonists in June outraged Metacom and triggered a long-expected conflict.

Metacom's warriors ravaged towns along the Connecticut River valley and near the coast, using the victories to recruit additional Indian allies. The colonists, unprepared after forty years of peace and unchallenged dominance, were caught off guard. Distrusting even the Christian Indians, Massachusetts officials relocated whole praying towns of Indian converts to windswept Deer Island in Boston Harbor.

By December, the Connecticut and Rhode Island colonies, terrified of being wiped out, united with Plymouth and Massachusetts Bay to create a force of more than 1,000 men. An Indian captive led them to a stronghold of the still-neutral Narragansett in a remote swamp a dozen miles west of Newport, Rhode Island. The colonists surprised and overwhelmed the fortified village, setting it ablaze during the fierce fighting. Indian survivors fled, leaving behind more than 600 dead. Many of the men, women, and children were "terribly Barbikew'd," minister Cotton Mather later recorded.

This "Great Swamp Fight," reminiscent of an earlier battle in the Pequot War, infuriated the Narragansett survivors, who joined Metacom's growing alliance. During the late winter of 1676, this loose confederacy continued to wreak havoc on New England villages. But as spring arrived, the coalition weakened and the tide turned. Sickness broke out among the fighters, who lacked food and gunpowder. The powerful Mohawk of the Iroquois Confederacy opposed Metacom from the west. Numerous Christian Indians joined the colonial forces, despite their painful internment at Boston's Deer Island.

With Metacom facing defeat, defections increased. In August, a former ally betrayed the resistance leader, shot him, and delivered his head to the English. As the struggle ground to a close, the colonists captured Metacom's wife and child, selling them into slavery in the West Indies along with hundreds of other prisoners of war. New England's remaining Indians became second-class inhabitants, confined to enclaves in the areas they had once dominated, while the colonists soon rebuilt and extended their domain.

■ MAP 3.3 Metacom's War in New England, 1675–1676

In fourteen months of war, New England Indians destroyed more than two dozen colonial towns and suffered their own heavy losses. The brutal conflict ended after the death of Metacom (the Wampanoag leader, also known as King Philip), near Mt. Hope, on August 12, 1676.

BACON'S REBELLION IN VIRGINIA

While smoke still billowed over New England, new flames broke out in Virginia. Social unrest had been growing under the stern governorship of Sir William Berkeley. England's wars with the Dutch cut into the tobacco trade and drew enemy ships into Chesapeake Bay. Unfree tobacco workers—more than 6,000 indentured Europeans and nearly 2,000 enslaved Africans—chafed against their harsh treatment. On the frontier, colonists resented the dependent Indians (Occaneechi, Pamunkey, and others) who traded furs in exchange for protection from other tribes. Settlers also feared the well-armed Susquehannock living near the Potomac River. "Consider us," Berkeley wrote to the king in 1667, "as a people press'd at our backes with Indians, in our Bowills with our Servants . . . and invaded from without by the Dutch."

By 1676, tensions in Virginia reached the breaking point. Officials had increased taxes to pay for fortifications, servant plots and mutinies abounded, and corruption ran rampant among Berkeley's close associates. The aging governor ruled from Green Spring, his huge estate near the capital, Jamestown. Fearing the hostile views of free men who did not own property, Berkeley had revoked their right to vote. He had not dared to call an election in fourteen years. He also dreaded outspoken preachers, free schools, and printing presses. "How miserable that man is," he wrote, "that Governes a People where six parts of seaven at least are Poore Endebted Discontented and Armed."

Benjamin Henry Latrobe, *View of Greenspring House*, 1796. Courtesy of The Maryland Historical Society, Baltimore, Maryland (1960.108.1.2.33).

■ Green Spring, the largest mansion in Virginia at the time of Bacon's Rebellion, symbolized the autocratic rule of Governor William Berkeley and his "Green Spring faction." The estate was seized by Bacon's forces in 1676 and later restored by Berkeley's widow.

DOCUMENT

Declaration against
the Proceedings of
Nathaniel Bacon
(1676)

Even wealthy newcomers such as Nathaniel Bacon had trouble gaining access to Berkeley's inner circle. When Bacon arrived from England in 1674 at age twenty-seven, he received a council seat because of his connections and money. But rivals denied the ambitious gentleman a license to engage in the profitable fur trade. Impatient, Bacon soon condemned Berkeley's ruling Green Spring faction as sponges who "have sukt up the Publique Treasure." When frontier tensions erupted into racial violence, Bacon threw himself into the conflict, challenging Berkeley's leadership and launching aggressive campaigns. His frontier followers, eager for Indian land, killed friendly Occaneechi as well as hostile Susquehannock.

The governor, aware of the damage that Metacom's War had inflicted on New England, refused to sanction these raids. He feared "a Generall Combination of all the Indians against us." But Bacon's army continued to grow, as backcountry leaders joined landless poor and runaway workers—both black and white—to support his anti-Indian cause. When the desperate governor called for a rare election to assert his strength, Bacon's supporters dominated the new House of Burgesses. Berkeley retreated across Chesapeake Bay and hid on Virginia's eastern shore.

Throughout the summer of 1676, rumors swirled that Bacon might join with malcontents in Maryland and in the newly settled Albemarle region of northeastern North Carolina to carve out an independent enclave and seek aid from the Dutch or the French. The new assembly quickly restored the vote to propertyless men and forbade excessive fees. It limited sheriffs to one year in office and passed other measures to halt corruption and expand participation in government. As an incentive for enlistment in the frontier war, the assembly granted Bacon's recruits the right to sell into slavery any Indians they captured.

For their part, slaves and indentured servants took advantage of the breakdown in public controls to leave their masters and join Bacon. Networks of "news wives" (women who used facts and rumors to fan worker discontent) spread stories of oppressive conditions. In June rebel soldiers talked openly of sharing estates among themselves, and in August they took over Green Spring Plantation, where Berkeley kept sixty horses and 400 head of cattle. A month later, Bacon's army burned Jamestown to the ground.

But by October, the tide had turned. Bacon was dead, struck down by dysentery, and reinforcements for Berkeley were on the way from England. With armed vessels patrolling the rivers, Berkeley worked up enough nerve to return from the eastern shore. Soon propertied men who had joined with Bacon were changing sides again and receiving amnesty from the governor.

The revolt had been crushed, but the impact of the tumult proved huge. On the frontier, Bacon's violent campaign against the Indians had killed or enslaved hundreds and fostered bitter hatreds. In the Tidewater, the uprising had raised a frightening prospect for wealthy tobacco planters: a unified and defiant underclass of white and black workers. From then on, Virginia's gentry applied themselves to dividing the races and creating a labor force made up of African slaves. In London, the recently formed Royal Africa Company stood ready to further such a design.

THE "GLORIOUS REVOLUTION" IN ENGLAND

No sooner had peace returned to New England and Virginia than Stuart policies brought a new round of turmoil on both sides of the Atlantic. In England, debate revived over who would succeed Charles II on the throne. The irreligious Charles, an Anglican in name only, had no legitimate children. Therefore, his brother James, a convert to Catholicism, was first in line to inherit the crown.

In 1678, rumors spread regarding a "Popish Plot" by Catholics to kill the king so that James could take power. The House of Commons, fearful of rule by a Catholic king, urged that James be excluded from the line of succession. Instead of James, House members argued, why not consider James's Protestant daughters by his first marriage: either Mary (recently wedded to her Dutch cousin, William of Orange) or Anne? Angered by such interference, Charles II dissolved Parliament in 1681 and ruled on his own for the last four years of his life.

When Charles II died in 1685, the traditional rule of succession prevailed: James II took over the English throne. In France that same year, Louis XIV revoked the Edict of Nantes, which had protected French Protestants. Fear spread among England's Protestant majority that their country's new Catholic ruler, James II, might also sanction persecution of non-Catholics. These concerns mounted when James disbanded Parliament, raised a standing army, and placed a Catholic in command of the navy. Then in 1688, James's queen gave birth to a male heir. Protestant anxieties about a pending Catholic dynasty erupted into open resistance.

United by their fear of Catholicism, rival factions among England's political elite (known for the first time as "Whigs" and "Tories") temporarily papered over their differences. They invited the Protestant William of Orange, James's Dutch son-in-law, to lead an army from Holland and take the English crown. In November 1688, William crossed the English Channel with 15,000 men, prompting James to abdicate the throne and escape into exile. William and Mary were proclaimed joint sovereigns in 1689, accepting a Bill of Rights that limited royal power.

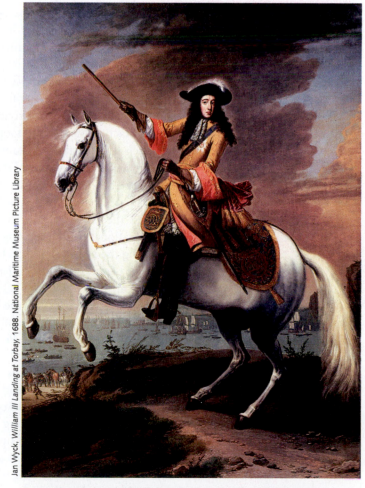

Jan Wyck, *William III Landing at Torbay*, 1688. National Maritime Museum Picture Library

■ Protestants in England and America opposed to King James II welcomed news that William of Orange (above) had arrived from Holland with his army in 1688 to take over the English throne.

Its position now enhanced, Parliament moved to grant toleration to Protestant dissenters, establish limited freedom of the press, and ensure regular parliamentary sessions. It also imposed limits on any permanent, paid military forces, known as standing armies, because they could accrue their own power and jeopardize civil authority. The English had thus preserved Protestantism and curtailed royal absolutism, all without bloodshed. Parliament hailed King William III as "our great Deliverer from Popery and Slavery." The propertied classes, who benefited most from the peaceful transition, hailed it as the "Glorious Revolution."

THE "GLORIOUS REVOLUTION" IN AMERICA

The succession of James II in 1685 did not bode well for England's American colonies. The new king not only professed the Catholic faith but also cherished absolute monarchy and distrusted elected assemblies. In colonial affairs, James favored revenue-generating reforms and direct obedience to the crown. He detested the powerful leaders in Massachusetts, for, as Congregationalists, they believed in a decentralized Protestant church. James also resented the fact that they disobeyed the Navigation Acts and asserted their right to self-rule, even after the crown revoked their charter in 1684. Moreover, he rejected the notion that colonists possessed the precious right claimed by the English at home: not to be taxed without giving their consent. The king envisioned an extensive reorganization of the American colonies.

> The success of William and the demise of the Dominion of New England did not end royal efforts to tighten imperial control over New England.

When James assumed the throne, his own colony of New York automatically became a royal province. Convinced of his divine right to set policy, the king nullified the charters of certain colonies in order to bring them under his control. As the cornerstone of his reorganization plan, James linked the New England colonies (plus New York and New Jersey in 1688) into one huge *Dominion of New England*. This consolidation, under an appointed governor general, would make it easier for England to suppress dissent, enforce shipping regulations, and defend the Dominion's frontiers—at least in theory.

In practice, the effort to forge a Dominion of New England proved a disaster. The move met such stiff resistance in America that a similar design for England's southern colonies never materialized. Control of the Dominion went to a military officer, Sir Edmund Andros. The heavy-handed Andros attempted to rule from Boston through a council he appointed, made up of loyal associates, without aid or interference from any elected legislature. He asserted the crown's right to question existing land patents, and he requisitioned a Congregational church for Anglican services. Worse, he offended local leaders by strictly enforcing the Navigation Acts to collect revenue. When participants in democratic town meetings raised objections, he jailed the leaders.

Colonists seethed with resentment toward this revival of Stuart absolutism, which claimed total obedience to the king and his officers as a divine right for the monarchy. Rumors of French invasions and Catholic plots swirled among staunch Protestants. In April 1689, welcome news that the Protestant William of Orange had invaded England inspired a revolt in Boston. Mobs showed public support for overthrowing the Stuart regime, and local leaders threw Governor Andros in jail.

The success of William and the demise of the Dominion of New England did not end royal efforts to tighten imperial control over New England. The new Massachusetts charter of 1691 consolidated neighboring Plymouth and Maine into the Massachusetts Bay colony. Moreover, it proclaimed that future governors would be appointed by the monarchy, as in other colonies. The men of Massachusetts, who had elected their own governor since the days of John Winthrop, would no longer have that right.

Emboldened by Boston's actions in 1689, New Yorkers ousted their own Dominion officials and set up a temporary government headed by Jacob Leisler. This German-born militia captain was a staunch Calvinist and hostile to the town's growing English elite. In Leisler's Rebellion, long-standing ethnic and religious rivalries merged with vague class hostilities: Leisler's supporters resented their treatment at the hands of the rich. They freed imprisoned debtors and attacked the houses of leading merchants. After a new governor arrived to take charge in 1691, the elite fought back. They lowered artisan wages and pressured the governor into hanging Leisler, on the grounds that his rebel followers were "growing dayly very high and Insolentt."

> *In Leisler's Rebellion, long-standing ethnic and religious rivalries merged with vague class hostilities.*

Similar tremors shook the Chesapeake region. In Maryland, where the Catholic proprietor ruled over a large and restive Protestant population, the governing Calvert family waited too long to proclaim its loyalty to King William. Fearing a "Popish" plot, assemblyman John Coode and a force of 250 armed Protestants marched on St. Mary's City and seized the government by force. The "happy Change in England" had replaced divine right rule with a more balanced constitutional monarchy, and Maryland settlers were determined to show their support.

Consequences of War and Growth: 1690–1715

■ *How did worldly success and wartime profits contribute to colonial unrest after 1690?*

The success of the Glorious Revolution hardly brought peace to England or its empire. On the contrary, warfare marked the reign of William and Mary and also that of Mary's sister, Queen Anne, who ruled from 1702 until her death in 1714. William immediately became involved in bloody campaigns to subdue highland clans in Scotland and overpower Catholic forces in Ireland. Moreover, English involvement against France in two protracted wars on the European continent had implications for colonists and Indians living in eastern North America. The War of the League of Augsburg in Europe became known to English colonists in America as King William's War (1689–1697), and the protracted War of Spanish Succession was experienced in America as Queen Anne's War (1702–1713).

Nowhere was the impact of these imperial wars more evident than in the rapidly growing colonies of the Northeast. Indeed, the earlier bloodshed of Metacom's (King Philip's) War, starting in 1675, had already aroused consternation and soul-searching. Bible-reading New Englanders viewed the violent decades that followed as a harsh test, or a deserved punishment, sent from the Almighty. They believed that God had watched closely over the initial Puritan "errand into the wilderness." Could it be, ministers now asked from the pulpit, that the Lord had some special controversy with the current generation? As communities grew more prosperous and became caught up in the pursuit of worldly success, were church members forgetting their religious roots and leading less pious lives? Invoking the Old Testament prophet Jeremiah, New England clerics interpreted most personal and collective troubles as God's punishment for the region's spiritual decline.

DOCUMENT

Benjamin Wadsworth, from *A Well-Ordered Family* (1712)

But such a sweeping explanation of misfortune only raised deeper questions. New Englanders could see clearly that the consequences of rapid change were not spread equally among all towns, congregations, and families. As in most war eras—and moments of economic and demographic growth—certain people and localities seemed to benefit while others fell behind. Some anxious believers saw the hand of Satan in the day-to-day struggles of village life. Others argued that the worldly success and wartime profits of an expanding elite had undermined the community ideals of earlier generations. While flames engulfed isolated Massachusetts communities such as Deerfield and portions of the Maine frontier, fiery passions were also being aroused in older settlements, such as Salem and Boston.

SALEM'S WARTIME WITCH HUNT

One of the most memorable disruptions, the Salem witch hunt, occurred in Essex County, Massachusetts, a two-day ride on horseback from the embattled Maine frontier. In 1692, an outburst of witchcraft accusations engulfed the farm community of Salem Village. The strange episode remains one of the most troubling in American history.

Among European Christians, a belief in witches with a supernatural power to inflict harm stretched back for centuries. In the 1600s, witchcraft trials abounded in Europe, and in New England zealous believers had executed several dozen people in isolated cases. Three-fourths of those accused (and even more of those executed) were women. Most were beyond childbearing age, often poor or widowed, with limited power to protect themselves in the community. But the hysteria in Salem went far beyond other colonial witchcraft incidents, with more than 200 people accused and twenty put to death.

Early in 1692, more than half a dozen young women in Salem Village, ranging in age from nine to twenty, began to suffer violent convulsive fits. With reduced appetites and temporary loss of hearing, sight, and memory, they also experienced choking sensations that curtailed their speech. Vivid hallucinations followed. Elders noted that some of those stricken had spent time with Tituba, a slave woman brought from Barbados who lived in the local minister's household. By April, the adolescents had accused ten adults of being witches. Then some of the ten named others in their elaborate confessions, and the hysteria snowballed.

In a world where people considered satanic influence very real, frightened authorities seriously weighed the young women's stories of people appearing to them as devilish specters and apparitions. Overriding tradition, jurists allowed such "spectral evidence" in court, and convictions mounted. The court ordered public executions of the condemned on Gallows Hill, and the hangings (fourteen women and five men) continued through September. One poor and elderly farmer, Giles Cory, was pressed to death under heavy stones. Another man and three additional women died in jail. Only when accusations reached too high in the social hierarchy and when several accusers recanted their stories did the new governor finally intervene. He emptied the jails, forbade further imprisonments, and pardoned the surviving accused until the tremor could subside.

> *The hysteria in Salem went far beyond other colonial witchcraft incidents, with more than 200 people accused and twenty put to death.*

Why this terrible outburst? Some historians argue that strained relations between farm families and the more prosperous urban residents in the nearby port of Salem Town may have influenced the craze. Some emphasize the zeal and gullibility of those first assigned to investigate. Still others speculate that the absence of central authority, until Governor Phips arrived in the colony in May, allowed a troubled situation to spin out of control. Finally, commentators stress a perverse psychological dynamic that arises in any witch hunt, ancient or modern. In such cases, accused suspects often can save their own lives by supplying damaging and vivid confessions implicating others rather than by offering heartfelt denials of guilt. One or more of these factors surely came into play.

Yet devastation on the Maine frontier also contributed to what happened in Salem Village. The little Massachusetts town had numerous links to the war zone. A recent minister, George Burroughs, much disliked in the village, had come from Maine. He had returned there when the contentious parish refused to pay him. Traumatized survivors from King

William's War—the current conflict against the Abenaki and French—had trickled into the community. Significantly, more than half the young women who accused others of witch-craft had lost one or both parents in the brutal frontier wars. On February 5, just weeks before the first accusations, 150 Indian attackers had burned the Maine village of York 80 miles north of Salem, killing forty-eight people and taking seventy-three captives. Word of the raid no doubt triggered shocking memories among Salem's war refugees, especially the orphans who worked as servants in local households.

Fears deepened in April when one of the accused confessed that the Devil had tempted her while she had been living in Maine. Then it was reported that the specter of Reverend Burroughs "appeared" to an accuser. Charged with promoting witchcraft and encouraging the hostile Indians (whom the colonists saw as Satan's helpers), Burroughs was arrested in Maine and hanged on Gallows Hill. A servant named Mercy Short, who had been captured and orphaned by Indians, recalled disturbing dreams of the Devil. She told minister Cotton Mather that in her dreams Satan and his minions (who had "an Indian colour") had made "hideous assaults" upon her. Much of what Mather and others recorded as the work of Satan may actually have been posttraumatic stress in a frayed community during wartime.

DOCUMENT

Ann Putnam,
Deposition (1692)

THE UNEVEN COSTS OF WAR

Throughout the 1690s and beyond, King William's War and Queen Anne's War made conflict a constant element of colonial life, but the burdens fell unevenly. For many colonial families, incessant warfare brought only death and dislocation. But for others, it offered new opportunities as the colonial economies expanded. Farmers with access to port towns shifted away from subsistence agriculture and grew crops for commercial sale. In doing so, they exposed themselves to greater financial risks, given transportation costs and market fluctua-tions. But they hoped to reap large profits.

Overseas trade and wartime smuggling offered investors even higher gains and larger risks. These activities, in turn, boosted demand for sailing vessels. Boston alone supported more than a dozen busy shipyards. They employed numerous shipwrights, caulkers, and other skilled workers who crafted hulls, ropes, masts, and sails. Military campaigns, such as the successful ones against the French at Port Royal in Acadia in 1690 and again in 1710, engaged hundreds of colonial soldiers and sailors. When an English fleet of sixty warships carrying 5,000 men docked at Boston in 1711, local provisioners (those who sold food and other provisions) reaped the rewards.

The crews of **privateers** (boats licensed to harass enemy shipping in wartime) made money if they captured a foreign vessel as a prize. But when peace returned, many refused to enter the ranks of the unemployed on land. Instead, hundreds became buccaneers, pirates who operated for their own gain while avoiding the arm of the law. After all, poor work conditions, brutal discipline, and low pay were the rule aboard merchant ships. Therefore many sailors, when stopped by pirates on the high seas, chose to join their ranks. During the brief heyday of piracy in the generation before 1725, the number of buccaneers reached several thousand—enough to create a crisis in Atlantic shipping—and many had colonial ties. Englishman Edward Teach (known as Blackbeard) won notoriety as a privateer-turned-pirate, haunting the Carolina coast until his death in 1718.

> *For many colonial families, inces-sant warfare brought only death and dislocation. But for others, it offered new opportunities.*

Everywhere, poorer families were most likely to sink under the burdens of war. Regressive taxes, requiring the same amount from a poor carpenter as from a rich merchant, obviously hurt impoverished people the most. So did high wartime prices for food and other necessities. Furthermore, many of the poor men recruited by the military became casualties of combat or disease, increasing the number of widows

The New York Public Library, Astor, Lenox and Tilden Foundations

■ For protection, the pirate Blackbeard often brought his ship into the shallow waters behind the barrier islands that form North Carolina's Atlantic coast. There, his crew bartered stolen goods at Ocracoke Island and reveled on the beach with local inhabitants.

living in poverty. As New England's port towns expanded, the growing distance between rich and poor struck local residents. The moral ties and community obligations—known as the social covenant—that Puritan elders had emphasized two generations earlier were loosening. In their place emerged a focus on secular priorities and a new, individualistic spirit.

In Boston, troubled ministers decried the hunger and poverty that they saw deepening in their parishes alongside unprecedented displays of wealth. Between 1685 and 1715, the share of all personal wealth in the town controlled by the poorest 60 percent of the population fell from 17 percent to 13 percent. At the same time, the portion controlled by the richest 5 percent climbed from 26 percent to 40 percent. Angry writers published irate pamphlets encouraging working people to take political action. They charged once-respected elites with studying "how to oppress, cheat, and overreach their neighbours."

No Bostonian wielded more economic power than Andrew Belcher, who first made money by supplying provisions to troops during Metacom's War. Each succeeding war brought Belcher larger contracts and greater profits. To the dismay of devout churchgoers and the working poor, he built a mansion on State Street and rode in an imported coach, attended by black slaves dressed in fancy livery. He owned twenty-two ships and invested in many more. He also repeatedly cornered the wartime grain market, spawning food shortages and raking in inflated profits as prices rose.

In 1710, Belcher asserted his right to ship 6,000 bushels of grain on the open market rather than sell flour at home, where people desperately needed bread. Indignant residents rebelled against Belcher's outright defiance of traditional community values. In the dark of night, they disabled his ship by sawing through the rudder. A grand jury declined to indict the protesters. Did ambitious and aggressive merchants such as Belcher cause the city's calamities, or did the townsfolk bring on their own troubles? Using a refrain that recurred in later generations, one godly conservative pointed a finger at the poor and implied they must be sinful if they could not subsist. "There was Corn to be had," he argued; "if they had not impoverished themselves by Rum, they might buy Corn." Only "the Devil's people" lacked food.

William Dampier: The World Became His University

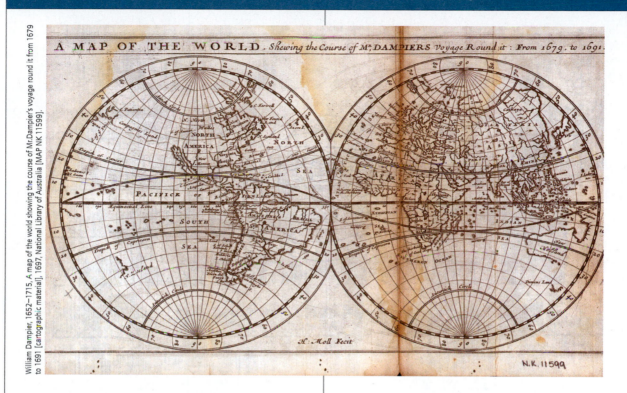

William Dampier, 1652–1715, A map of the world showing the course of Mr.Dampier's voyage round it: from 1679 to 1691 [cartographic material], 1697, National Library of Australia [MAP NK 11599].

The Wider World

In July 1682, William Dampier sailed into Chesapeake Bay aboard a pirate ship. The remarkable naturalist, scarcely thirty-one, had already spent half of his life at sea. The son of an English tenant farmer, Dampier was apprenticed to a shipmaster after his mother died in the Great Plague of 1665. He first joined a pirate band in 1679, "more to indulge my curiosity than to get wealth."

The Chesapeake provided many safe havens for buccaneers, but it seemed too tame for the restless Dampier. He stayed in Virginia only thirteen months. "That country is so well known to our nation," he wrote, "that I shall say nothing of it." For Dampier, there was a wider world to be seen, and he eagerly renewed his travels.

Over the next nine years, Dampier sailed from ocean to ocean, taking copious notes on everything he saw. He dined on flamingo tongues in the Cape Verde Islands and cruised along Australia's remote north coast, where a bay now preserves his name. To assist English colonists "in our *American* Plantations," he recorded detailed notes on the various uses for coconuts that he encountered in the East Indies.

Dampier made his way back to England in 1691. Travel tales, both real and imagined, were flooding the European market. In 1697, therefore, the observant ex-pirate published his own best-seller: *A New Voyage Round the World*. He was one of the first to introduce such diverse words as *chopsticks* and *barbecue* into the English language.

Two years later, Dampier's gripping account was already in its fourth edition when the English Admiralty chose him to command its first South Seas voyage of exploration. Before he died in 1715 at age sixty-four, he had circumnavigated the world three times, and he had done more to inform English readers about the wider world than any writer of his generation.

QUESTIONS

1. In the late seventeenth century, why was it so difficult for European readers to distinguish between false travel tales and real accounts, such as Dampier's?

2. What are the advantages in gaining "knowledge and experience" by roaming the world rather than by seeking a formal education? What are the disadvantages?

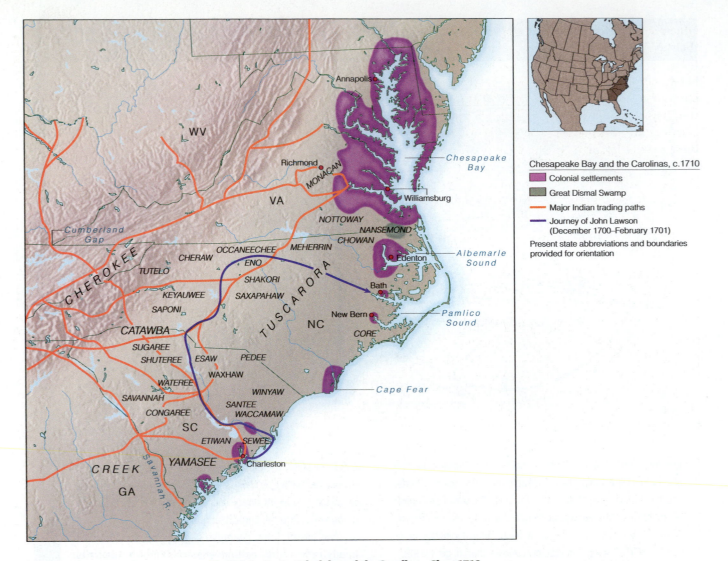

■ MAP 3.4   Virginia and the Carolinas, Circa 1710
After John Lawson made a 1,000-mile journey through the Carolina interior (1700–1701), he became an
advocate for colonial growth. The expanding settlements of North Carolina and South Carolina pressed the
Tuscarora and Yamasee Indians, who staged wars of resistance after 1710.

STORM CLOUDS IN THE SOUTH

Peace returned to New England's frontier villages and port towns in 1711, as negotiations
began for ending Queen Anne's War in America and the related War of Spanish Succession in
Europe. British diplomats gained favorable terms from France and Spain when they signed a
treaty at Utrecht two years later. (The formal union of England and Scotland in 1707 under
the name *Great Britain* had transformed the *English* empire into the *British* empire.) But
London officials could not prevent fresh violence in North America, given the expansion of
their British colonies. The Wampanoag, Narragansett, and Abenaki Indians had attempted
to roll back the advancement of northeastern settlers in Connecticut, Massachusetts, and
Maine. Now Native Americans in the Southeast sought to counter the encroachments of
newcomers along the Carolina coast.

By the 1660s, settlers were drifting into the pine wilderness that would become the
colony of North Carolina. Some were radicals fleeing the Restoration in England.

Others, such as John Culpeper, had moved north from the Carolina settlement on the Ashley River, where they disapproved of the hierarchical plans drawn up by Shaftesbury and Locke that gave the Carolina proprietors firm control over the new colony. Still others were runaway servants from Virginia and refugees escaping the aftermath of Bacon's uprising. In 1677, these newcomers, led by Culpeper, seized control in the Albemarle region just south of Virginia's Great Dismal Swamp. The proprietors suppressed "Culpeper's Rebellion," but in 1689 they agreed to name a separate governor for the portion of Carolina "That Lies north and east of Cape Feare." Another disturbance, "Cary's Rebellion" in 1710, led to official recognition of "North Carolina, independent of Carolina," the next year. (Surveyors marked off the dividing line with Virginia in 1728.)

In 1680, Native Americans still outnumbered newcomers in eastern North Carolina by two to one, but within thirty years that ratio had been reversed. The Naval Stores Act of 1705, passed by Parliament to promote colonial production of tar and pitch for shipbuilding, drew a stream of settlers to the pine forests of eastern North Carolina. By 1710, English communities existed on Albemarle Sound, at what is now Edenton, and on Pamlico Sound, at Bath (where Blackbeard and other pirates were frequent visitors). No one promoted the region more than John Lawson, who had made an extensive tour of Carolina in 1700, living among the Indians and assessing the land for colonization. The young explorer-naturalist returned to England in 1709 to publish an account of his travels, *A New Voyage to Carolina.*

THE BEASTES OF CAROLINA.

Courtesy, Dartmouth University Library

■ Frontispiece from John Lawson's *A New Voyage to Carolina* (London, 1709).

While in London, Lawson arranged to sell North Carolina land to a party of more than 600 Protestant immigrants from Bern, Switzerland. After a perilous Atlantic crossing—half the company died at sea—he led the survivors to the site of a Native American village at the mouth of the Neuse River. Lawson surveyed lots along the riverfront, and they "planted stakes to mark the houses and to make the principal streets." Within eighteen months, "sickness, want, and desperation" gave way to "a happy state of things," and Lawson headed inland from New Bern to eye more land for future settlement.

All this was too much for the Tuscarora Indians. Frustrated by corrupt traders and land encroachment, they launched a war in 1711 to drive out the intruders. They took Lawson prisoner, put him to death, and devastated the Swiss at New Bern. But they had waited too long. Within two years, the settlers—aided by a South Carolina force of several dozen whites and nearly 500 Yamasee Indians—had crushed Tuscarora resistance. Most of the Tuscarora survivors migrated north, where they became the sixth nation within the powerful Iroquois Confederacy.

Yamasee warriors from the Savannah River region helped British colonists quell the Tuscarora uprising. But in 1715, the Yamasee led their own rebellion. They too were troubled by encroaching settlers and aggressive traders, plus South Carolina's practice of exporting Native American captives to the West Indies as slaves. The Yamasee received support from

CHRONOLOGY: 1660–1715

1660	Restoration of monarchy in England under Charles II.
1664	Charles II grants a charter to his brother James, Duke of York, sanctioning the takeover of the Dutch New Netherland colony and the creation of New York.
1675 to 1676	Metacom's War in New England.
1676	Bacon's Rebellion in Virginia.
1680	Pueblo Revolt in New Mexico.
1681	Quaker William Penn receives charter for Pennsylvania.
1682	La Salle explores the Mississippi River and claims Louisiana for France.
1689	Dutch leader William of Orange and his wife Mary become joint English sovereigns in the Glorious Revolution, replacing King James II.
1692	Witchcraft trials in Salem, Massachusetts.
1699	Iberville begins colony in French Louisiana.
1711 to 1715	Tuscarora Indians in North Carolina, and then the Yamasee in South Carolina, resist English colonial expansion.

neighboring Creek Indians, Spanish-speaking colonists in Florida, and French traders at the new Alabama outpost of Fort Toulouse. The still-powerful Cherokee in southern Appalachia opted not to join in the Yamasee War. Otherwise, the Indians might have overwhelmed the South Carolina colony.

Conclusion

Inspired by the exploits of LaSalle and a generation of fur traders and missionaries, the French had made inroads into the heart of the continent, the huge Mississippi Valley. But most European intrusions remained confined to the fringes of the vast continent. The French established themselves in Louisiana, and small numbers of Spanish held onto footholds in New Mexico and Florida, while venturing into parts of Arizona and Texas.

The English newcomers, far more numerous, remained clustered along the Atlantic seaboard. When their rising numbers prompted expansion up local river valleys away from the coast, warfare with Native American inhabitants ensued. Along the length of eastern North America, from the Kennebec River to the Savannah, hundreds of settlers and Indians died violently during the half-century before 1715. Often the frontier struggles became entwined with wider conflicts between the rival European empires. These wilderness skirmishes seem minor compared with the battles raging in Europe at the same time. Despite the small scale of the conflicts in North America, however, Europe's imperial wars had started to influence developments in the English colonies.

Another element of Europe's expansion overseas—the transatlantic slave trade—had also begun to alter the shape of England's North American colonies. What had seemed only a small cloud on the horizon in the early seventeenth century had grown into an ominous force, with a momentum of its own, by the early eighteenth century. The storm hit hardest along the Southeast coast, where the arrival of thousands of Africans soon shaped a distinctive and repressive world of enslavement and exploitation that endured for generations. No sooner had the English gained control along the Atlantic edge of North America than they orchestrated a "terrible transformation" that placed thousands in bondage and altered the shape of American history.

For Review

1. What made the Pueblo Revolt of 1680 the most successful uprising against a colonizing power in the early history of North America?

2. How did Catholic missionaries aid, or hinder, the North American colonizing efforts of Spain and France?

3. How did the restoration of the monarchy in London in 1660 influence the evolution of England's American colonies over the next two generations?

4. Can you single out colonial incidents of ethnic, racial, political, religious, and class violence in this era? Or are these elements too thoroughly intertwined? Explain.

5. Carolina explorer John Lawson observed that by 1710 the Indians had been "better to us than we are to them." Do you agree?

6. Were developments during the half-century after 1660 as important to the future of North America as the earlier founding of Virginia and the New England colonies? Explain.

Created Equal Online

For more *Created Equal* resources, including suggestions on sites to visit and books to read, go to **MyHistoryLab.com.**

Part Two

A Century of Colonial Expansion to 1775

CHAPTER 4
African Enslavement: The Terrible Transformation

CHAPTER 5
An American Babel, 1713–1763

CHAPTER 6
The Limits of Imperial Control, 1763–1775

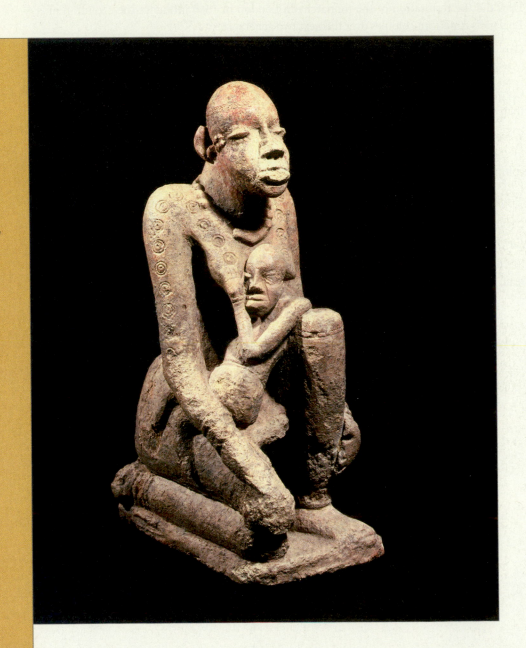

On April 19, 1775, New England farmers battled British soldiers at Concord Bridge. The confrontation marked the start of the American Revolution. (Each spring in Massachusetts, the date is still set aside as Patriots' Day and celebrated with the running of the Boston Marathon.) But how did colonies that were weak outposts before 1700 become strong enough to challenge the power of the British empire in the second half of the eighteenth century? The answer is not a simple one. Life changed in dramatic ways during the century before 1775, not only in New England but throughout much of North America.

The rapid spread of Spanish horses across the West allowed Native Americans, such as the Comanche and Sioux, to become mounted buffalo hunters on the Great Plains. The arrival of Russian fur traders disrupted traditional cultures on the Aleutian Islands and the coast of Alaska. At the same time, the gradual success of the new Louisiana colony gave France access to much of the Mississippi River valley. But the potential for a dominant French-speaking empire in America evaporated with the stunning defeat of French forces by the British in the Seven Years' War. As that global conflict ended in 1763, the Spanish also lost ground in North America. After claiming Florida for 200 years, they finally ceded the peninsula to the British, even as they began to extend Spanish missions up the coast of California.

Other changes were even more dramatic. In the eighteenth century, race-based slavery became an established aspect of colonial society in North America. The English had come late to the transatlantic slave trade, but by the 1660s they became aggressive participants in the lucrative traffic in human beings. English colonizers fashioned harsh slave-based societies in the Caribbean, then in the Chesapeake colonies of Virginia and Maryland, next in North and South Carolina, and finally, after 1750, in the recently established colony of Georgia.

Race slavery transformed the mainland colonies in terrible ways and had far-reaching results. Thousands of Africans arrived in North American ports in the eighteenth century. Strikingly, they were only a small fraction of the much greater transport of Africans to the Caribbean and Central and South America. Nevertheless, by 1750 there were nearly 250,000 African Americans living in North America. Most lived in the South, and most were enslaved, including several hundred in Spanish East Florida and several thousand in French Louisiana. By 1775, the number exceeded half a million. By then,

blacks made up more than 20 percent of the population of the British colonies, and the legal and social constraints that shackled their world remained tighter than ever.

Newcomers from Europe, as well as from Africa, altered the make-up of Atlantic colonies that had once been almost entirely English. Many of these newly arrived Europeans, unable to afford the cost of passage, had to pledge their labor for a period of years. But in contrast to the Africans, most European migrants came to America voluntarily and were free from obligations within a few years. The Atlantic crossing could be harrowing, of course, but for thousands the long-term advantages outweighed the short-term drawbacks. Artisans of all kinds were in high demand, and land was cheap. Colonial governments ruled with a light hand in comparison to the monarchies of Europe, and they competed with one another to attract newcomers. This competition for new arrivals bred relative religious and ethnic tolerance.

Pushed by events in Europe and drawn by opportunities in America, families flocked to Britain's North American colonies. This new flow from Europe and the British Isles, combined with the African slave trade, quickly generated a far more diverse colonial society on the foundations laid by earlier English immigrants. Prior generations of colonists had laid out towns, formed governments, and founded the rudimentary institutions of colonial social life. They had established an ambivalent pattern of interaction with Native Americans that involved warfare and displacement as well as trade and intermarriage. Also, they had located harbors, carved out roads, and started to build an economic infrastructure.

As numbers rose and diversity increased, a series of regional economies emerged along the eastern seaboard. Each sustained the local inhabitants while also serving the wider needs of the British empire. For much of the eighteenth century, the British crown promoted economic growth in the colonies through a workable combination of protectionist controls and benign neglect.

But the British victory over the French brought drastic new problems to eastern North America after 1763. Native Americans lost a valued trading partner and military ally when the French withdrew. Britain faced an enormous war debt and looked to its burgeoning colonies as a source of much-needed revenue. Within little more than a decade, Britain's North American colonists went from resentment and resistance to overt rebellion in the Atlantic world's first anticolonial war of independence.

Chapter 4

African Enslavement: The Terrible Transformation

CHAPTER OUTLINE

- The Descent into Race Slavery

- The Growth of Slave Labor Camps

- England Enters the Atlantic Slave Trade

- Survival in a Strange New Land

- The Transformation Completed

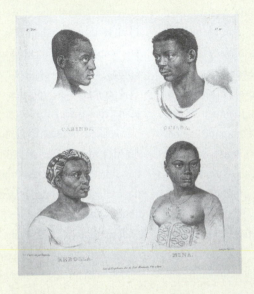

■ Africans arriving in America often had ornamental scarification (known as "country marks") on their bodies, as well as brands inflicted by slave traders and physical scars from the middle passage.

On a wintry day in January 1656, a mulatto servant named Elizabeth Key went before the local court in Northumberland County, Virginia. She was twenty-five years old. The late Colonel John Mottrom, a justice of the peace, had held Elizabeth as a slave, kept in perpetual bondage. She objected strongly, and she wanted to sue the executors of Mottrom's estate for her freedom and back pay. Bess, as she was known, presented a three-fold argument. First, as the daughter of a free man, she should inherit her father's legal status according to English law. Second, as a baptized Christian, she should not be enslaved. And third, she could produce a document showing that as a small child she had been "put out" to work until she was fourteen, following local custom. Such contracts for apprenticing a child for a fixed number of years were common in America, where labor was in short supply. But her term of work had expired long ago.

Key was accompanied in court by her white attorney and lover, William Greensted. They had had two children together and would marry six months later, when they finally won a favorable verdict. The executors of Mottrom's estate, eager to show that Bess's father was neither free nor Christian, implied that a Turkish crewman off a visiting ship was the woman's father. But the young couple produced witnesses who testified that Bess was the daughter of Thomas Key, a white man serving in the Virginia General Assembly, and his "Negro woman." One witness told the jury that Bess's mother had lived openly with Thomas Key and had said that the girl was Key's daughter.

Further testimony established that in 1636, not long before he died, Key had bound little Bess to Humphrey Higginson, a member of the Council of State. Higginson "promised to use her as well as if shee were his own Child"; that is, "more Respectfully than a Comon servant or slave." He even stood as her godfather when Bess was christened.

To be raised in a Christian church was no small matter at a time when Europeans viewed non-Christians captured in wars to be uniquely vulnerable to legal enslavement. For Bess, this circumstance helped her cause greatly, for she proved "able to give a very good account of her fayth." Furthermore, she produced clear evidence that her father had sold her to Higginson for nine years. Mr. Key had demanded that Higginson not dispose of her to any other person, such as to Colonel Mottrom. Rather, he was to give her the usual "freedom portion" of corn and clothes "and lett her shift for her selfe," either in England or Virginia, when her term expired.

The local jury accepted Elizabeth Key's three-part argument and pronounced her free. But the General Court overturned the verdict on appeal, only to be overruled in turn by a committee of the General Assembly. In the end, the committee determined that "Elizabeth ought to bee free." The assemblymen also argued that her last master owed her a "freedom portion," plus back pay "for the time shee hath served longer than Shee ought to have done." Still, the matter generated debate among settlers. In fact, several decades later, Elizabeth's case would have been decided differently. Moreover, the courts of Virginia might well have enslaved her children for life. And their offspring would have inherited slavery status as well.

A terrible transformation was under way in English colonial culture that would warp American society for centuries to come. It spread gradually, like a cancer, revealing a different pace and pattern in each mainland colony. During the 1620s and 1630s, a few black servants were working alongside white servants. But well before the end of the century, the grandchildren of those workers had been separated by skin color and physical appearance, according to emerging notions of "race." Free blacks persisted in the English colonies, but in most communities they became anomalies, for the tide was flowing against them. From now on, people of African ancestry were to be legally enslaved for life. Elizabeth Key and her children and grandchildren experienced the painful transition firsthand.

The Descent into Race Slavery

■ *How important was precedent in the English shift to hereditary enslavement of Africans?*

Some grim transitions in human affairs evolve slowly, even imperceptibly. Nothing shaped colonial cultures more forcefully than the European colonists' gradual commitment to the legalized enslavement of hundreds of thousands of people and their descendants. It is important to examine the slippery slope that led to perpetual servitude based on race.

THE CARIBBEAN PRECEDENT

The roots of race slavery in the Americas extend back to the era of Columbus, when warfare, sickness, and exploitation quickly decimated the native populations of the Caribbean after 1492. Hungry for human labor, the Spanish intruders began to import people from Africa to grow crops and dig for gold in the Caribbean islands. As the native population declined sharply through epidemics, the traffic in black newcomers expanded.

Spanish pressure for labor in the New World intensified further with the discovery of additional mines in Mexico and Peru. To meet the growing demand, Spain's king issued a contract (called the **asiento**) that allowed other European powers—such as Portugal, France, or the Netherlands—to import African slaves to the Spanish colonies. High profits drew eager participation. In the half-century between 1590 and 1640, more than 220,000 people arrived in chains from Africa at the Spanish empire's ports in Central and South America.

Meanwhile, the Portuguese purchased enslaved Africans to work their own expanding sugar plantations. They imported more than 75,000 slaves, mostly from the Congo River region of West Central Africa, to the Atlantic island of São Tomé in the sixteenth century. When Portuguese sugar production spread to coastal Brazil, so did the exploitation of African labor. By 1625, Brazil imported the majority of slaves crossing the Atlantic each year and exported most of the sugar consumed in Europe.

Long before the 1660s, therefore, Europeans had set a precedent for exploiting African workers in New World colonies. Religious and secular authorities frowned on actively enslaving people, especially if they were fellow Christians, but purchasing so-called infidels (those who followed other religions or opposed Christianity) could be tolerated, particularly if slavery had already been imposed on them by someone else. These West African victims were non-Christians, and most had already been enslaved by others, captured by fellow Africans in war.

Confident in this rationale, the Spanish and Portuguese adapted their laws to accept the enslavement of Africans. Moreover, the condition would be hereditary, with children inheriting at birth their mother's legal status. The Catholic Church backed the new labor system, though priests occasionally worked to alleviate suffering among Africans in the Americas. The pope did nothing to condemn the growing traffic, nor did the Protestant Reformation have a dampening effect. On the contrary, the rising Protestant sea powers of northern Europe proved willing to assist in the slave trade and take part in the dramatic "sugar revolution," growing sugar on a massive scale for expanding Atlantic markets.

The Dutch, for example, ruled Brazil for a generation in the first half of the seventeenth century, importing slaves to South America and exporting sugar. When the Portuguese regained control of Brazil at midcentury, they pushed out Dutch settlers. These outcasts took their knowledge about managing sugar plantations to the islands of the Caribbean. Some appeared in the new English possessions of Barbados and Jamaica, and soon they were directing African slaves in cutting, pressing, and boiling sugar cane to make molasses. The thick molasses could then be processed further to make rum and refined sugar for export. By the 1650s, slavery and sugar production were engulfing England's West Indian possessions, just as these twin features had already become central to the New World colonies controlled by Spain and Portugal. A looming precedent had been set. But as late as 1660, it was not at all clear that African slavery would gain a prominent place, or even a lasting foothold, in any of the North American colonies.

Anonymous, *Vue du Cap Francais et Du nvr La Marie Seraphique de Nantes*, 1772–1773. Le jour de l'Ouverture de sa Vente, Troisieme Voyage d'Angole. Musée du Château des Ducs de Bretagne (950.4.3)

■ This summary of an African slave-trading voyage shows wealthy planters boarding a French ship upon its arrival in the West Indies in order to buy slaves newly arrived from Angola. The crew has used an iron fence dividing the deck to protect against revolt during the voyage. The captain conducts business under an awning in the stern.

OMINOUS BEGINNINGS

As far back as the sixteenth century, African men had participated in Spanish explorers' forays into the Southeast, and some had remained, fathering children with Indian women. African slaves had helped establish the small Spanish outpost at St. Augustine in 1565, but a century later no additional coastal colonies had yet appeared on the mainland anywhere south of Chesapeake Bay.

Granted, Africans were present farther north in the fledgling settlements of the French, Dutch, and English. But their numbers remained small—several thousand at most—and few of these newcomers had come directly from Africa. Instead, most had lived for years in the Caribbean or on the mainland, absorbing colonial languages and beliefs. So they and their children, like Bess Key, were not viewed as complete outsiders by the European colonists. The legal and social standing of these early African Americans remained vague before the 1660s. Local statutes regarding labor were crude and contradictory; their interpretation and enforcement varied widely. Everywhere, workers were in demand, and most black newcomers found themselves laboring alongside European servants.

In the Massachusetts Bay colony, early Puritan settlers, casting about for sources of labor and for markets, exchanged goods for slaves in the Caribbean. In 1644, seafaring New Englanders even attempted direct trade with Africa. But the following year, Massachusetts authorities ordered a New Hampshire resident to surrender a black worker he had purchased in Boston. They argued that the man had been stolen from Africa, not captured in war, and should be returned to his home. For the earliest handful of black New Englanders, their standing proved uncertain in a region where religious status mattered far more than language, dress, or outward physical appearance. In 1652, Rhode Island passed a law limiting all involuntary service—whether for Europeans or Africans—to no more than ten years.

© Nik Wheeler/CORBIS

■ West Africans still grow gourds and carve them into bowls, dippers, and musical instruments. Earlier Africans, deported as slaves, used American gourds to expand this tradition.

Along the Hudson River, the Dutch colonists had close ties with the sugar islands of the West Indies, where race slavery was already an accepted system. In New Netherland, therefore, the laws discriminated against black workers and limited their rights. But the statutes also provided loopholes that permitted social and economic advancement to the community's Africans, most of whom spoke Dutch. When an African woman named Anna van Angola obtained a tract of farmland on Manhattan in the 1640s, the governor made clear that there were no limitations on this "true and free ownership."

Chesapeake Bay lay even closer to the main routes of the Atlantic slave traffic. In 1619, a Dutch warship brought to Virginia more than twenty African men and women acquired as slaves in the Caribbean. Like people deported from England to the Chesapeake, they were put up for sale as servants. Terms of service varied, and some black newcomers earned their freedom quickly and kept it. But others saw their terms extended arbitrarily. In 1640, Virginia's General Court considered punishment for "a negro named John Punch" and two other servants who had escaped to Maryland. When apprehended, the Dutchman and the Scotsman each received four additional years of service, but the African was sentenced to unending servitude "for the time of his natural life." That same year, Virginia passed a law that prevented blacks from bearing arms. And a 1643 law taxing productive field hands included African American women but not white women.

These early efforts to separate Africans from Europeans by law set an ominous precedent in the use of skin color as a distinguishing marker. Still, rules governing the lives of people of color and their offspring remained ambiguous for several decades, and (as the case of Bess Key makes clear) efforts at exploitation could often be undone in court. But new forces would come into play in the mainland American colonies after 1660, consolidating the transition to hereditary African slavery.

ALTERNATIVE SOURCES OF LABOR

The legal status of African newcomers to English North America became distinctly clearer and less hopeful in the decades after 1660. The transatlantic slave trade, already more than a century old, provided certain English colonies with a ready source of African workers at a time when more obvious streams of inexpensive labor—captured Native Americans and impoverished Europeans—were dwindling.

For labor-hungry colonists, Native Americans were close at hand and knew the country well. They took captives when fighting one another, so colonists could buy Indian prisoners or seize them in frontier warfare. Europeans felt they could enslave such people in good conscience, since they were non-Christians who had been taken captive in war. But Native American numbers were declining steadily, owing to epidemics. And those who did become enslaved knew the countryside well enough to escape. Besides, traffic in Indian slaves disrupted the profitable deerskin trade, undermined wilderness diplomacy, and sparked conflict on the frontier.

Efforts to maintain a steady flow of cheap labor from Europe ran into different problems. The Great Plague of 1665 devastated the English population, and the London Fire the following year created a new need for workers of all kinds to rebuild the capital. England's labor surplus, which had been a boon to the first colonies half a century earlier, rapidly disappeared. Those who made their living in English ports by procuring labor for America were forced to nab youngsters off the streets. But even this practice (called by the new word *kidnapping*) was soon outlawed.

What persisted, however, was the widespread use of **indentures.** These contracts allowed poor individuals to pay for their Atlantic passage by selling their labor for a fixed length of time. When these men and women reached America, they were obliged to work for several years in return for food and shelter. Still, the prospect of an independent future appealed to newcomers arriving without property. As an incentive to draw additional immigrants, colonial officials made clear that servants who completed their indenture could expect "freedom dues" (clothes, tools, and food from their former master) and their own land to farm. Established planters sensed three drawbacks: the indenture system created high labor turnover; it put added pressure on limited land resources; and it constantly created additional competing farmers.

> *England's labor surplus, which had been a boon to the first colonies half a century earlier, rapidly disappeared.*

Equally important, when indentured servants were mistreated, they had little difficulty in relaying their complaints home to other potential workers. The flow of ships back and forth between Europe and North America grew steadily in the century after 1660, so word of places where indentured servants were regularly abused or swindled quickly reached the other side of the Atlantic. As Europeans mulled over private letters, coffeehouse gossip, and sailors' reports, they could adjust their own plans for migration. Depending on what they heard or read, they might postpone a voyage or seek a more promising destination.

In contrast, the African slave trade lacked any similar "feedback loop." People swept up in the growing stream of unfree African labor had no access to information regarding New World conditions. A mere handful, among hundreds of thousands of enslaved Africans, ever managed to communicate with their homeland. As a result, the brutal treatment of black

The Odyssey of Job Ben Solomon

Job Ben Solomon, age twenty-nine, was kidnapped near the Gambia River in March 1731. He was a Muslim slave trader and herder from the Bondou region. Job had just traded two slaves for twenty-eight cattle when he was captured near the coast by Mandingo men. Before he could be rescued, they sold him aboard the English slave ship *Arabella*, bound for the Chesapeake Bay. At Annapolis, Captain Pyke turned over his cargo to Vachell Denton, the Maryland agent for London slave trader William Hunt. Denton sold Job to Alexander Tolsey for forty-five pounds, and the Maryland tobacco planter changed Job's name to Simon.

Like others from the *Arabella* and thousands of enslaved workers around him, Job's fate seemed sealed. By the 1730s, the British slave trade had become a vast and efficient machine. Once drawn into its iron grip, no African could ever hope to return home. Defying the odds, Job Ben Solomon escaped from the slave labor camp and made his way back to Africa, by way of London. A memoir of his exceptional experience was published in 1734, and sixteen years later an issue of *Gentleman's Magazine* in London featured his story, complete with a portrait.

Like many "saltwater slaves," Job ran away shortly after he was first sold. But he was soon captured and confined to the local jail, located at the back of a tavern in Queen Anne's County. While there, an African-born slave who could speak Wolof, Job's native language, explained the full nature of his grim situation. His one hope lay in the fact that he was well educated and could read and write Arabic with ease. Borrowing pen and paper, he drafted a brief letter describing his plight and arguing that he had been enslaved by mistake. The letter (which still survives in the British Library) was passed to Denton, who forwarded the curiosity to Hunt in London.

Soon a professor at Oxford University, fluent in Arabic, translated the note, and members of the Royal African Company decided to locate and ransom Job Ben Solomon. Hunt sent instructions to Denton to buy the slave back from his owner, and early in 1733 the fortunate Muslim was on board a ship to London, learning basic English during his weeks at sea. The Royal

African Company treated him well, assuring him that they would not take Muslim slaves in the future and arranging his passage home on a company ship. In return, he agreed to help the British compete against the French for trade in the Gambia region, including gold and non-Muslim slaves. Returning to his African homeland in 1734, Job "wept grievously...for the misfortunes of his country," according to the company's local agent. Friends and family were overwhelmed by his return. After all, he observed, "I was gone to a land" from which no one had "ever yet returned."

QUESTIONS

1. Why would Job Ben Solomon, a slave trader forced into slavery, agree to take part in the ongoing Atlantic slave trade after his return to Africa?

2. The phrase "banality of evil" described the methodical Nazi bureaucracy that implemented the Jewish Holocaust in the 1940s. How does this term apply to the Atlantic slave trade?

workers never had a chance, through accurate feedback across the Atlantic, to influence the future flow of captives from Africa.

THE FATEFUL TRANSITION

In general, powerful Chesapeake tobacco planters were encouraged in 1660 by news of the Restoration of Charles II, since England's new king was likely to support their interests and reward their loyalty. These men had noticed the rising profits that sugar growers were making by using slaves in the Caribbean. In Virginia and Maryland, therefore, planters passed a series of laws that sharpened distinctions between servants working for a fixed period and slaves consigned to labor for life.

In shaping new legislation, local leaders even challenged long-standing English legal traditions, such as the right of children to inherit their father's status. In 1662, Virginia's General Assembly considered whether any child fathered "by an Englishman upon a negro woman should be slave or Free." In a crucial reversal of precedent, the legislature said that in such cases "all children borne in this country" shall be "held bond or free *only according to the condition of the mother*." From now on, the infant of any female slave would be enslaved from birth, an obvious boon for masters who wanted additional long-term labor at little cost. Slavery was becoming a hereditary condition.

But what about a child born to a free white woman, whether "English or other Christian," married to an enslaved man? The gentry in Maryland's assembly answered that question when they adopted the colony's first slave code in 1664. Not only would all blacks serve lifetime terms, but from now on any free woman who married a slave "shall Serve the master of such slave dureing the life of her husband [and] all the Issue of such freeborne woemen soe marryed shall be Slaves as their fathers were."

Could enslaved persons receive their freedom if they accepted Christianity, as sometimes happened in Spanish colonies? The Maryland law of 1664 closed off that prospect. The act made clear that the legal status of non-Christian slaves did not change if they experienced religious conversion. Three years later, Virginia's government agreed that "the conferring of baptisme doth not alter the condition of the person as to his bondage." By taking religion out of the question, legislators shifted the definition of who could be enslaved from someone who was not Christian to someone who did not look European. In 1680, Reverend Morgan Godwyn observed that the "two words, *Negro* and *Slave*," had already "by custom" grown interchangeable in Virginia. Because nobody could alter their skin color but anyone could change faith, planters moved to categorize colonial workers by their appearance rather than their religion.

In scarcely a generation, black bondage had become a hereditary institution, and the conditions of life had grown markedly worse for African Americans. Europeans receiving wages for work could pay fines for misbehavior; servants indentured for a term could be required to work additional months or years as a punishment. But enslaved Africans, condemned to unpaid labor for life, had no money or time to give up when disciplined for misdeeds, whether real or imagined. Therefore, increasingly they faced corporal punishments: whippings, torture, and even mutilation. In the generation after Elizabeth Key, black slaves—and often free blacks as well—lost their right to accuse, or even testify against, a white person in a court of law. "And further," stated Virginia's formative slave law of 1680, "if any Negro" so much as raises a hand, even in self-defense, "against any Christian, he shall receive thirty lashes, and if he absent himself . . . from his master's service and resist lawful apprehension, he may be killed."

The Growth of Slave Labor Camps

■ *What factors created a vicious circle that sealed the fate of African workers in Virginia?*

Over two generations, beginning in the late seventeenth century, tobacco growers in the Chesapeake and rice producers in the new colony of South Carolina embraced the system of hereditary race slavery that had developed in the Caribbean. Traditionally, historians describe this change as "the rise of plantation agriculture." But for those forced to cut the trees, drain the swamps, and harvest the crops, the shift in production strategy represented—in modern terminology—the emergence of slave labor camps. These people received no wages for their labor, had no legal rights, and could be moved to some other location at any time. This deterioration in conditions occurred first, and most dramatically, in Virginia, where several thousand African Americans lived and labored by the 1670s.

BLACK INVOLVEMENT IN BACON'S REBELLION

Nothing did more to consolidate Virginia's slide toward race slavery than Bacon's Rebellion, the major uprising that shook the Chesapeake region in 1676 (see Chapter 3). The episode pitted aspiring gentry, led by Nathaniel Bacon, against hard-pressed Indian groups on the frontier and an entrenched elite in Jamestown. The rebellion underscored the dilemma created by Virginia's reliance on a steady flow of white indentured servants to cultivate tobacco. That labor supply was uneven at best, and large-scale planters constantly needed new recruits, since terms of service lasted only several years. Workers who earned their freedom—hundreds every year— were predominantly young, armed men who demanded property of their own. Whether they had to take it from rich landholders or neighboring Indians made little difference to them.

> A letter reaching London that fall suggested that at the height of the rebellion Bacon had "proclaimed liberty to all Servants and Negroes."

Free men, would-be farmers in search of land, made up part of Bacon's following, but diverse unfree workers also proved eager recruits. Such ill-treated people remained legally bound to large landholders for varying terms, and many of the Africans were undoubtedly bound for life. Together, they raised much of the colony's annual tobacco crop. The backbreaking labor prompted frequent unrest. These ragged workers, however long their term of service might be, had the most to gain and the least to lose from Bacon's revolt. According to the Virginia Assembly, "many evill disposed servants . . . taking advantage of the loosenes of the tymes . . . followed the rebells in rebellion." When Bacon fell ill and died in October 1676, many of his wealthier supporters reasserted their loyalty to the colonial government. But bound workers who had escaped from their masters continued the fight.

A letter reaching London that fall suggested that at the height of the rebellion Bacon had "proclaimed liberty to all Servants and Negroes." Clearly, the widespread unrest had given hope to the most downtrodden tobacco pickers, about a quarter of whom were black. As a Royal Commission put it, "sundry servants and other persons of desperate for-tunes" had "deserted their masters and run into rebellion on the encouragement of liberty." When military reinforcements arrived in Chesapeake Bay from England in November, their commanding officer, Captain Thomas Grantham, found hundreds of laborers still in active revolt.

Impressed by their strength, Grantham chose to use deceit when he met with 800 heavily armed rebels, both white and black, at their headquarters near the York River. By distributing brandy and making vague promises regarding pardons and freedom, he per-suaded most of the white men to surrender and return home. Only about "Eighty Negroes and Twenty English . . . would not deliver their Armes." According to Grantham, they threatened to kill him, asserting that they wanted "their hoped for liberty and would not quietly laye downe their armes." But when these last holdouts boarded a sloop to head downriver, Grantham disarmed the rebels and chained them below decks for return to their masters.

THE RISE OF A SLAVEHOLDING TIDEWATER ELITE

With Bacon's death and the arrival of British ships, propertied Virginians had narrowly averted a successful multiracial revolution, fueled from below by workers who resented their distressed condition. But clearly some future revolt might succeed, so the great planters of

■ A small minority of enslaved Africans became house servants to wealthy families in England and America. Though set apart from the black community and denied entry into white society, many traveled widely and described the outside world to fellow slaves confined to field labor.

the Chesapeake region moved to tighten their hold on political and economic power. After Bacon's Rebellion, a strategy of divide and conquer seemed in order. They moved to improve conditions for poor whites in ways that would reduce tension between classes and ensure deference and racial solidarity among Europeans. At the same time, they further reduced the legal status of blacks, solidifying their enslavement for life and increasing penalties for any show of opposition or dissent.

For precedent, the planters had the model provided by slavery-based colonial societies in the West Indies, including the English sugar island of Barbados. Their uneasiness continued over importing non-Christian strangers who spoke little, if any, English. But such doubts were more than offset by the prospect of laying claim to the children of slaves and to the lives and labor of all generations to come. Every child of every enslaved African woman became an additional worker, acquired by the master at no extra cost. These same women, moreover, were often more familiar with agricultural tasks than European servant women. Besides, planters could exploit black women and men more ruthlessly than they could whites, since there was no feedback to Africa affecting future labor supplies.

Increasing life expectancy in the Chesapeake region, resulting from sturdier dwellings and more stable living conditions, further motivated planters to move away from a workforce of indentured servants. For a self-interested planter, longer lives meant that a white indentured person, after serving only a few years, would become yet another long-term competitor in the crowded tobacco market. In contrast, Africans enslaved for life would yield profitable service for an increasingly long time. And they would be more likely than ever to produce healthy offspring. Boys and girls who survived childhood could then be forced to clear more land to grow additional crops.

Among a circle of wealthy investors, the enticement of such an economic bonanza overcame any cultural anxieties. The sudden lure of enormous gain outweighed any moral or religious scruples. Seizing the moment, these aggressive entrepreneurs established themselves as the leading families of Virginia. William Byrd was an apt example. The son of an English goldsmith, Byrd took over his uncle's trading post near the falls of the James River at age eighteen and soon married into a prominent family. As a frontier resident, he joined briefly in Bacon's uprising. But by the 1680s, he occupied a seat on Virginia's council and held several high financial posts. With his salary, he bought up his neighbors' tobacco and shipped it to England. He then used the proceeds to purchase cloth, kettles, muskets, and beads for the Indian trade. After exchanging these goods for deerskins, he exported the skins at a profit. In return, he imported trade goods from London and slaves and rum from the Caribbean, all of which he sold to small planters for more tobacco so the lucrative cycle could begin again.

In the 1690s, Byrd moved his operations closer to the seat of power, which remained at Jamestown until the capital shifted to nearby Williamsburg in 1699. He established a large estate at Westover, on the north bank of the James River, where he used scores of imported slaves to expand his assets and launch a family dynasty. By the 1730s, Byrd's son, like other wealthy slave owners, came to fear a "servile war" so violent that it would "tinge our rivers, as wide as they are, with blood."

For early merchant-planters such as the Byrds, the enormous profits offered by slavery outweighed the calculated risks. These ambitious men expected that the English-speaking Africans already present could assist in teaching newcomers to receive orders. They also assumed that slave laborers from diverse African societies could not communicate well enough with one another to cause dangerous disturbances. And of course, having now made skin color a determining feature of social order, they knew that black runaways could be spotted and apprehended readily in the free white community.

> *Wealthy slave owners came to fear a "servile war" so violent that it would "tinge our rivers, as wide as they are, with blood."*

CLOSING THE VICIOUS CIRCLE IN THE CHESAPEAKE

As the profitability of slavery increased, so did its appeal. By 1700, some 4,500 people were enslaved in Maryland in a total population of 35,000. And the colony's assembly was taking further measures to encourage the importation of slaves. Growing demand meant that merchants and sea captains who had only occasionally dabbled in the transportation of slaves now devoted more time and larger ships to the enterprise. Expansion of the slave-trading infrastructure made African workers readily available and affordable.

As the supply of enslaved black newcomers grew larger, planters eager to strengthen their position manipulated the established headright system. Traditionally, under this system, the colonial government granted to any arriving head of household fifty acres for every family member or hired hand he brought into the colony. The incentive was intended to spur migration from Europe, expand the free population, and develop the land through the establishment of family farms. But the wealthy planters who saw African slavery as a profitable labor source also controlled Virginia's legal system. For their own benefit, therefore, they extended the headright system so that a land bonus also went to anyone who purchased an African arrival as a lifelong slave. Thus, before the seventeenth century closed, a Virginia investor buying twenty slaves could also lay claim to headrights worth 1,000 acres of land.

To consolidate their new regime, planters worked through the church and the legislature to separate whites from blacks socially and legally. They undermined the position of free blacks and stigmatized interracial ties. A 1691 Virginia statute decried the "abominable mixture and spurious issue" that resulted from "Negroes, mulattoes and Indians intermarrying" with English or other white people. All such couples were "banished from this dominion forever." It also prohibited masters from freeing any black or mulatto unless they paid to transport that person out of the colony within six months.

Virginia's Negro Act of 1705 further underscored the stark new boundaries. It mandated that white servants who were mistreated had the right to sue their masters in county court. Slaves, in contrast, had no such right. Any enslaved person who tried to escape could be tortured and even dismembered in hopes of "terrifying others" from seeking freedom. When masters or overseers killed a slave while inflicting punishment, they were automatically free of any felony charge, "as if such accident had never happened." And if slaves were killed or put to death by law, the owners would be paid public funds for the loss of their "property." In scarcely forty years, prominent whites had used the law to transform the labor system of the Chesapeake, entrapping Africans and their descendants in perpetual slavery.

DOCUMENT

Of the Servants and
Slaves in Virginia
(1705)

England Enters the Atlantic Slave Trade

■ *Why did England, once suspicious of the trade, become a leader in transporting enslaved Africans?*

The Atlantic slave trade was the largest and longest-lasting deportation in human history. In nearly four centuries, more than 10 million people were torn from their homelands against their will and transported to the Caribbean and to Central, South, and North America. Several million more perished in transit. By 1700, more Africans than Europeans had already crossed the Atlantic to the Western Hemisphere. Their numbers grew over the following century as the commerce reached its height. As for the importation of Africans to *North* America, that part of the traffic expanded after 1700, but it remained a small portion of the overall Atlantic slave trade.

England took little part in the trade at first. However, the development of Barbados as a lucrative sugar colony and the expansion of English overseas ambitions changed matters quickly after 1640. In 1652, Prince Rupert, a nephew of the late Charles I, visited Gambia in sub-Saharan Africa and saw profits to be made. With the restoration of the English monarchy in 1660, Rupert's cousin Charles II immediately granted a monopoly on African trade to a small group of adventurers, and in 1672 he chartered the powerful new Royal African Company (RAC).

The RAC dispatched a steady flow of merchant ships along a triangular trade route. The first leg took captains to English outposts along the coast of West Africa, where they exchanged textiles, guns, and iron bars for gold, ivory, and enslaved Africans. After a transatlantic **middle passage** of one to three months, the captains sold slaves and took on sugar in the West Indies before returning to England on the final leg of the triangle.

> By 1700, more Africans than Europeans had already crossed the Atlantic to the Western Hemisphere.

The lure of profits prompted interlopers to horn in on the RAC traffic with increasing success. When the company's monopoly ended officially in 1698, English slave trading ballooned. In the mainland colonies, boat builders and ship owners from Boston to Charleston sought out a portion of the trade, concentrating first on links to the Caribbean. In 1713, England obtained the *asiento*, the lucrative contract to deliver Africans to Spain's colonies in America. By the 1730s, British ships controlled the largest share of the Atlantic slave trade. They continued to dominate the traffic for the next seventy years.

TRADE TIES BETWEEN EUROPE AND AFRICA

By the 1680s, it had been two centuries since Portuguese sailors had visited Africa's western shores and established a post at Elmina, in modern-day Ghana. Dozens of these depots, controlled by rival European powers and their local allies, dotted the sub-Saharan coastline. (They became known as *factories*—an early use of the word—since a factor, or manager, ran each imperial trading post.) This string of European outposts began at the mouth of the Senegal River, just above Cape Verde, the continent's westernmost point; it ended below the mouth of the Congo River, in present-day Angola. In between, the coastline curved some 5,000 miles. It embraced diverse geographic environments—from open savannas to thick forests—and scores of distinctive cultures. All along this coastline, villagers caught fish and gathered salt for trade with herders and farmers living farther inland.

Generations of contact with oceangoing ships brought new pressures and opportunities to African coastal communities. Local merchants formed alliances with European partners to trade gold and ivory to sea captains for imported textiles and alcohol. People with links to several cultures became crucial to this competitive commerce. Just as outsiders occupied posts on the African coast to learn local ways, an important African occasionally traveled north by ship to gain knowledge of European languages, ideas, and religion. For example, Aniaga, the brother of the king of Guinea, was sent to France around 1680.

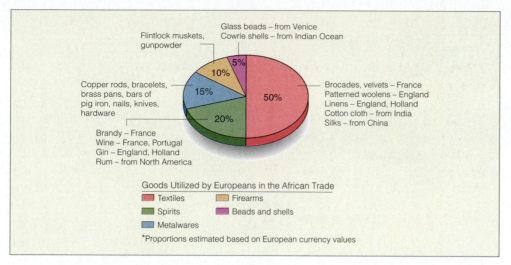

Glass beads – from Venice
Cowrie shells – from Indian Ocean

Flintlock muskets,
gunpowder

Copper rods, bracelets,
brass pans, bars of
pig iron, nails, knives,
hardware

5%

10%

15%

50%

20%

Brocades, velvets – France
Patterned woolens – England
Linens – England, Holland
Cotton cloth – from India
Silks – from China

Brandy – France
Wine – France, Portugal
Gin – England, Holland
Rum – from North America

Goods Utilized by Europeans in the African Trade

- Textiles
- Spirits
- Metalwares
- Firearms
- Beads and shells

*Proportions estimated based on European currency values

■ FIGURE 4.1
Goods Traded in Africa

As European ship captains expanded trade along the African coast, they tailored their cargoes to suit the demands of local markets.

When the African prince reached Paris, Louis XIV "was pleas'd to have him Educated, Instructed and Baptiz'd." Aniaga eventually became a respected captain in the French military, but after several decades he expressed a desire to return home. He promised to promote the work of French traders and missionaries, so "his Majesty loaded him with Presents, and order'd a Ship to carry him back to Guinea." In later years, Europeans complained that Aniaga "no longer remember'd he had been baptiz'd." Still, the prince often "express'd much Gratitude for the Kindness that had been shewn him in France." As an important local figure, he became a courteous and influential visitor aboard French ships reaching the Guinea coast.

THE SLAVE TRADE ON THE AFRICAN COAST

As sugar production expanded across the Atlantic, well-connected African traders responded to the growing demand for human labor. They consolidated their positions near suitable harbors and navigable rivers. From there, they bartered local servants and war captives to white agents (factors). In return, they obtained linen, beads, metal wares, and muskets, items that enhanced their prestige and let them extend their inland trading networks.

■ Slaves were held as prisoners in the interior before being marched to the African coast in groups known as coffles.

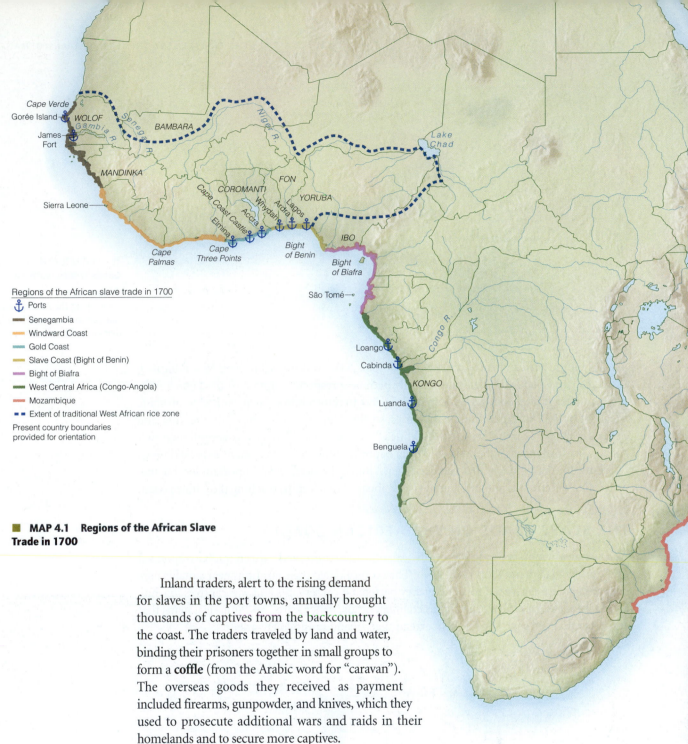

Regions of the African slave trade in 1700
⚓ Ports
━━ Senegambia
━━ Windward Coast
━━ Gold Coast
━━ Slave Coast (Bight of Benin)
━━ Bight of Biafra
━━ West Central Africa (Congo-Angola)
━━ Mozambique
▪▪▪ Extent of traditional West African rice zone
Present country boundaries
provided for orientation

Map labels: Cape Verde, Gorée Island, James Fort, WOLOF, Gambia R., Senegal R., BAMBARA, Niger R., Lake Chad, MANDINKA, Sierra Leone, Cape Coast Castle, COROMANTI, FON, YORUBA, Whydah, Ardra, Accra, Lagos, Elmina, Cape Palmas, Cape Three Points, Bight of Benin, IBO, Bight of Biafra, São Tomé, Loango, Cabinda, KONGO, Congo R., Luanda, Benguela

■ **MAP 4.1** **Regions of the African Slave Trade in 1700**

Inland traders, alert to the rising demand for slaves in the port towns, annually brought thousands of captives from the backcountry to the coast. The traders traveled by land and water, binding their prisoners together in small groups to form a **coffle** (from the Arabic word for "caravan"). The overseas goods they received as payment included firearms, gunpowder, and knives, which they used to prosecute additional wars and raids in their homelands and to secure more captives.

By the 1660s and 1670s, the pace of deportation across the Atlantic had reached an average rate of nearly 15,000 people each year. It rose steadily to a high of more than 65,000 people per year a century later. As the traffic grew, it became increasingly organized, competitive, and routine. Shrewd African traders played one European vessel against another for the best deals and hid illness among captives. When they saw that a ship was eager to depart, they increased their prices. Hardened European agents stockpiled the wares that African traders most wanted. They also learned to curry favor with local officials and to quell unrest among captives, confined in the holding pens known as **barracoons**. Experienced captains timed their ventures to avoid the months when sickness was most rampant in the tropics. Through repeated voyages, improved charts, and accumulated lore, they came to differentiate and exploit half a dozen major slaving regions along Africa's Atlantic coast. Occasionally, they even ventured to Mozambique in southeast Africa and the nearby island of Madagascar.

The closest market where Europeans bargained for goods and slaves was Senegambia, or the northern parts of Guinea, between the Senegal River and the Gambia River. Gorée Island, off the coast of Senegal, and James Fort, located in the mouth of the Gambia, served as slave trading centers. The long Windward Coast extending to the southeast beyond Sierra Leone became known for its pepper and grain and for ivory in the south beyond Cape Palmas. To the east, from the area of Cape Three Points and Elmina to the factory at Accra, stretched the Gold Coast. There, the Portuguese had established Elmina to draw trade from the Asante gold fields in the interior. Farther east, the Slave Coast reached along the Bight of Benin to the huge delta of the Niger River. Trading depots at Whydah, Ardra, and Lagos drew captives from secondary ports in between. Beyond the Niger, where the African coast again turns south near Cameroon, lay the Bight of Biafra. English captains quickly learned the preferences for trade goods in each district, carrying textiles to the Gold Coast, cowrie shells to the Slave Coast, and metals to the Bight of Biafra.

The largest and most southerly slave-trading region along Africa's Atlantic coast was known as Congo-Angola or West Central Africa. Here, Catholic missionaries established footholds, and Portuguese traders exported slave labor for sugar production in Brazil and the Caribbean. Before 1700, more than half of all Atlantic slaves departed from West Central Africa. In the eighteenth century, the proportion remained over one-third, as French and English interests came to dominate the slave traffic out of Loango and Cabinda, north of the Congo River. South of the great waterway, the Portuguese continued to hold the upper hand at Luanda and Benguela. During the entire span of the slave trade, the Congo-Angola hinterland furnished roughly 40 percent of all African deportees to the Americas: more than 4.5 million men, women, and children.

THE MIDDLE PASSAGE EXPERIENCE

For every person the exodus was different. Harrowing individual stories depended on the particulars of how old the captives were, where they had lived, and how they were captured. Nevertheless, the long nightmare of deportation contained similar elements for all who fell victim to the transatlantic trade. The entire journey, from normal village life to enslavement beyond the ocean, could last a year or two. It unfolded in at least five stages, beginning with capture and transport to the African coast. The initial loss of freedom—the first experience of bound hands, harsh treatment, and forced marches—was made worse by the encounters with strange landscapes and unfamiliar languages. Hunger, fatigue, and anxiety took a steady toll as coffles of young and old were conveyed slowly toward the coast through a network of traders.

The next phase, sale and imprisonment, began when a contingent reached the sea. During this stage, which could last several months, African traders transferred "ownership" of the captives to Europeans. Many buyers subjected their new property to demeaning inspections and burned brands into their skin. Then they were put in irons alongside hundreds of other captives and guarded in a secure spot to prevent escape. For example, the underground dungeon at Cape Coast Castle on the Gold Coast had walls fourteen feet thick. A visitor in 1682 observed that the RAC's fortress provided "good security . . . against any insurrection."

Werner Forman Archive/Art Resource, NY

■ England's Royal African Company maintained more than a dozen small posts along the Gold Coast. Each outpost funneled slaves to this strong seventy-four-gun fortress known as Cape Coast Castle. Cut into rock beneath the parade ground, the vaulted dungeon inside could "conveniently contain a thousand Blacks...against any insurrection."

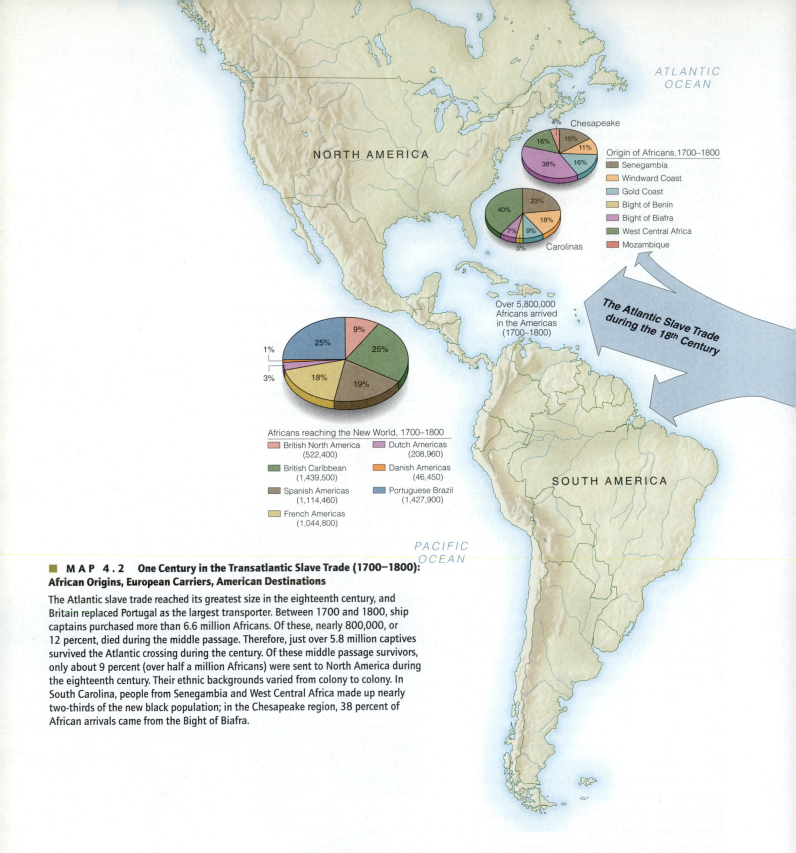

■ MAP 4.2   One Century in the Transatlantic Slave Trade (1700–1800): African Origins, European Carriers, American Destinations

The Atlantic slave trade reached its greatest size in the eighteenth century, and Britain replaced Portugal as the largest transporter. Between 1700 and 1800, ship captains purchased more than 6.6 million Africans. Of these, nearly 800,000, or 12 percent, died during the middle passage. Therefore, just over 5.8 million captives survived the Atlantic crossing during the century. Of these middle passage survivors, only about 9 percent (over half a million Africans) were sent to North America during the eighteenth century. Their ethnic backgrounds varied from colony to colony. In South Carolina, people from Senegambia and West Central Africa made up nearly two-thirds of the new black population; in the Chesapeake region, 38 percent of African arrivals came from the Bight of Biafra.

When a ship arrived, canoes transported the captives through the surf to the waiting vessel. Once aboard, prisoners might languish in the sweltering hold for weeks while the captain cruised the coast in search of additional human cargo. According to one English trader, "the negroes were so wilful and loth to leave their own country, that they often leap'd out of the canoos, boat and ship, into the sea, and kept under water till they were drowned." Crewmembers sometimes raised nets surrounding the deck to prevent attempts at escape or suicide.

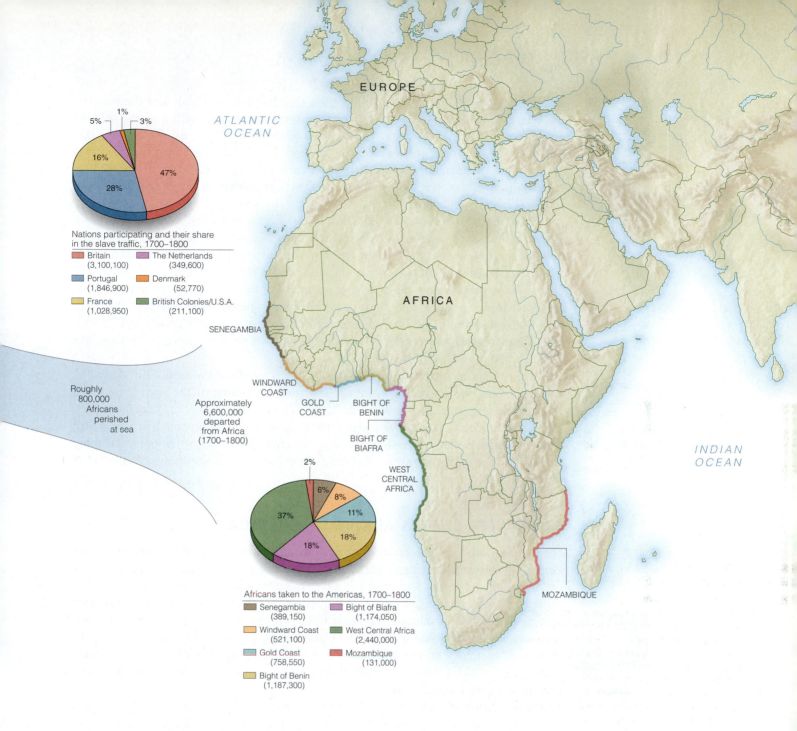

ATLANTIC
OCEAN

EUROPE

AFRICA

INDIAN
OCEAN

Nations participating and their share
in the slave traffic, 1700–1800

■ Britain (3,100,100)	■ The Netherlands (349,600)	
■ Portugal (1,846,900)	■ Denmark (52,770)	
■ France (1,028,950)	■ British Colonies/U.S.A. (211,100)	

1%
3%
5%
16%
28%
47%

SENEGAMBIA

Roughly
800,000
Africans
perished
at sea

Approximately
6,600,000
departed
from Africa
(1700–1800)

WINDWARD
COAST

GOLD
COAST

BIGHT OF
BENIN

BIGHT OF
BIAFRA

WEST
CENTRAL
AFRICA

MOZAMBIQUE

2%
6%
8%
11%
18%
18%
37%

Africans taken to the Americas, 1700–1800

■ Senegambia (389,150)	■ Bight of Biafra (1,174,050)	
■ Windward Coast (521,100)	■ West Central Africa (2,440,000)	
■ Gold Coast (758,550)	■ Mozambique (131,000)	
■ Bight of Benin (1,187,300)		

The ship's captain decided when to begin crossing the Atlantic, the harrowing third phase that constituted the actual middle passage. If he lingered too long to obtain more slaves at lower prices, he risked depleting his food supplies and raising the death toll among his crew and prisoners. If he departed too soon in an effort to shorten the voyage and preserve lives, including his own, he risked missing a drop in prices or a new contingent of slaves that could absorb his remaining stock of trade goods and bring more profits. He had to balance the danger of late summer hurricanes in the Caribbean against the need to arrive in America when harvests were complete—the time when planters had crops to send to Europe and money or credit to invest in African workers.

The Africans aboard each ship knew nothing of such calculations. Even those who had spent time serving as slaves among fellow Africans or fishing in coastal waters now faced an utterly alien plight, trapped in a strange wooden hull. When the crew finally raised anchor and unfurled the vessel's huge sails, the captives could only anticipate

**Diagram of a Slave Ship
Filled for Middle
Passage**

DOCUMENT

Alexander
Falconbridge, the
African Slave Trade
(1788)

the worst. Already the crowded hold of the ship had become foul, and the wooden buckets used as latrines had taken on a loathsome smell. The rolling of the ship on ocean swells brought seasickness and painful chafing from lying on the bare planks. Alexander Falconbridge, who sailed as a surgeon on several slave ships, recorded that "those who are emaciated frequently have their skin and even their flesh entirely rubbed off, by the motion of the ship, from the . . . shoulders, elbows and hips so as to render the bones quite bare."

Historians have documented more than 27,000 slave voyages, and an array of variables shaped each Atlantic crossing. Factors included the exact point of departure, the planned destination, the season of the year, the length of the journey, the supplies of food and fresh water, the navigational skills of the captain and crew, the condition of the vessel, the health and resolve of the prisoners, the vagaries of piracy and ocean warfare, and the ravages of disease. A change in weather conditions or in the captain's mood could mean the difference between life and death. The *Emperor*, crossing from Angola to South Carolina in 1755 with 390 Africans aboard, encountered a storm that lasted for a week. By the time the heavy seas subsided, 120 people had died in the hold.

While the grim details varied, the overall pattern remained the same. Ship after ship, year after year, the attrition continued. The constant rolling of the vessel; the sharp changes in temperature; the crowded, dark, and filthy conditions; and the relentless physical pain and mental anguish took a heavy toll. Pregnant mothers gave birth or miscarried; women were subjected to abuse and rape by the crew. Sailors threw the bodies of those who died to the sharks or, worse still, used them as bait to catch sharks, which they fed to the remaining captives.

DOCUMENT

Olauda Equiano, The
Middle Passage (1788)

SALTWATER SLAVES ARRIVE IN AMERICA

For the emaciated survivors of the Atlantic ordeal, two further stages remained in their descent into slavery: the selling process and the time called "seasoning." The selling process on American soil varied widely and could drag on for weeks or months after the ship dropped anchor. Prospective owners examined and prodded the newcomers in dockside holding pens. Those purchased were wrenched away from their compatriots and the shipmates with whom they had formed strong links during their shared miseries at sea. Slaves often were auctioned off in groups, or parcels, to ensure sale of the weak along with the strong. Then another journey brought them to the particular plantation where they were fated to work and probably to die.

IMAGE

Sale Notice

Most newcomers did not begin their forced labor immediately. Instead, they entered a final stage, known as seasoning, which lasted several months or longer. The strangers were distinguished as "saltwater slaves"—in contrast to "country-born slaves" who had grown up in America from birth. Seasoning gave them time to mend physically, regain their strength, and begin learning a new language. Inevitably, many suffered from what we now describe as posttraumatic stress syndrome.

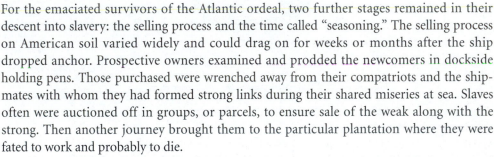

The strangers were distinguished as "saltwater slaves"—in contrast to "country-born slaves" who had grown up in America from birth.

As adults and children recovered from the trauma of the middle passage, they faced a series of additional shocks. Around them they found other Africans who had survived earlier voyages and still spoke their traditional languages. In conversation, they gradually learned where they were and what lay in store for them. They confronted strange foods, unfamiliar tasks, and even new names. They faced alien landscapes and unfamiliar diseases. Worst of all, they encountered a master or his overseer who made every effort to break the wills of these fresh arrivals and to turn them into compliant bondservants. Repeatedly, the powerful stranger used arbitrary force to demand the newcomers' obedience, destroy their hope, and crush any thoughts of resistance.

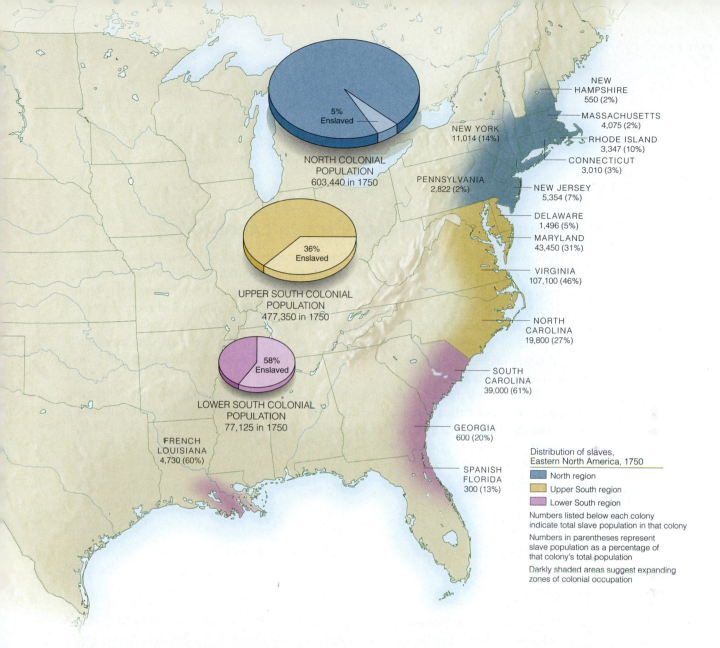

North region

NEW HAMPSHIRE
550 (2%)

MASSACHUSETTS
4,075 (2%)

RHODE ISLAND
3,347 (10%)

CONNECTICUT
3,010 (3%)

NEW YORK
11,014 (14%)

PENNSYLVANIA
2,822 (2%)

NEW JERSEY
5,354 (7%)

DELAWARE
1,496 (5%)

MARYLAND
43,450 (31%)

VIRGINIA
107,100 (46%)

NORTH CAROLINA
19,800 (27%)

SOUTH CAROLINA
39,000 (61%)

GEORGIA
600 (20%)

SPANISH FLORIDA
300 (13%)

FRENCH LOUISIANA
4,730 (60%)

5% Enslaved

NORTH COLONIAL POPULATION
603,440 in 1750

36% Enslaved

UPPER SOUTH COLONIAL POPULATION
477,350 in 1750

58% Enslaved

LOWER SOUTH COLONIAL POPULATION
77,125 in 1750

Distribution of slaves, Eastern North America, 1750

- North region
- Upper South region
- Lower South region

Numbers listed below each colony indicate total slave population in that colony

Numbers in parentheses represent slave population as a percentage of that colony's total population

Darkly shaded areas suggest expanding zones of colonial occupation

■ **M A P 4 . 3** **Enslaved People Living in North America in 1750: Distribution by Colony, Percentage of Total Population**

By 1750, nearly a quarter of a million people lived as slaves in eastern North America—more than 21 percent of the colonial population. Almost all were Africans or the descendants of Africans, along with a few thousand Native American and mixed-race slaves. In the North, slaves made up a small fraction of a large population. By far the greatest number of slaves lived in the Chesapeake area, where they made up more than a third of the total population. Enslaved people were less numerous but much more concentrated in the lower South, making up a clear majority of the overall inhabitants. White settlers had already smuggled several hundred slaves into the fledgling colony of Georgia, even though the exploitation of slave labor did not become legal there until 1751.

Survival in a Strange New Land

■ *How did diverse Africans find common ground for resistance as slaves in America?*

By 1700, race slavery was accepted throughout the mainland colonies. Africans found themselves scattered from northern New England to Gulf Coast Louisiana. But their distribution was far from even. Among roughly 247,000 slaves in the colonies in 1750, only 30,000 (or 12 percent) resided in the North, where they made up just 5 percent of the overall population from Pennsylvania to New Hampshire. More than one-third of these northerners (11,000) lived in the colony of New York, where they constituted 14 percent of the non-Indian inhabitants. All the rest of the people of African descent in North America—some 217,000 men, women, and children by the mid-eighteenth century—lived and worked in the Chesapeake region and the lower South. Fewer than 500 of these black southerners were in Spanish Florida, and fewer than 5,000 resided in French Louisiana.

AFRICAN RICE GROWERS IN SOUTH CAROLINA

Throughout the eighteenth century, by far the most North American slaves lived in Virginia or Maryland: 150,000 African Americans by 1750. But the highest *proportion* of enslaved workers lived in South Carolina, where Africans began outnumbering Europeans as early as 1708. By 1750, this black majority (40,000 people) constituted more than 60 percent of the colony's population. Almost all had arrived through the deepwater port of Charleston. Sullivan's Island, near the entrance to the harbor, with its **pest house** to quarantine incoming slaves and reduce the spread of shipborne disease, has been called the Ellis Island of black America.

What explains the emergence of South Carolina's slave concentration? For one thing, the colony was closer than Virginia to Africa and to the Caribbean. Moreover, it had been founded in 1670, just as the English were embracing plantation slavery and the African trade.

Alive Ravenel Huger Smith, *The Threshing Floor with a Winnowing-House (The Carolina Rice Plantation Series)*, Gibbes Museum of Art/California Art Association (37.09.22)

■ Rice plantations that emerged in coastal South Carolina around 1700 became labor camps where enslaved blacks were confined for generations, without wages or legal rights. In the 1850s, distant descendants of the region's first African workers were still being forced to plant, harvest, and process the huge rice crops that made their masters rich.

Indeed, some of the colony's original proprietors owned stakes in the Royal African Company. Also, some of Carolina's influential early settlers came directly from Barbados, bringing enslaved Africans and planter ambitions with them.

In the earliest days of colonization in South Carolina, newcomers lacked sufficient labor to clear coastal forests and plant crops. Instead, they let their cattle and pigs run wild. With easy foraging and warm winters, the animals reproduced rapidly. The settlers slaughtered them and shipped their meat to the Caribbean, along with firewood for boiling sugar cane and wooden barrels for transporting sugar. Ship captains also carried enslaved Native Americans to the West Indies and brought back African slaves.

The arriving Africans understood South Carolina's subtropical climate, with its alligators and palmetto trees, better than their European owners did. Many of these enslaved newcomers were already familiar with keeping cattle. Others, obliged to feed themselves, began growing rice in the fertile swamplands just as they had in West Africa. Half a century before, a brief experiment with rice in the Chesapeake region proved short lived. But a Virginia observer in 1648 had noted that the southern soil and climate seemed "very proper" for the cultivation of rice, "as our Negroes affirme," adding that rice "in their Country is most of their food."

South Carolina slave owners quickly realized that this plant, unfamiliar to much of northern Europe, held the answer to their search for a profitable staple crop. Soon, people who had tended their own irrigated rice crops near the Gambia River were obliged to clear cypress swamps along the Ashley and Cooper rivers to grow rice for someone else. Women who had prepared small portions of rice daily for their families in West Africa—pounding the grains with a wooden pestle to remove the husks, then tossing them in a broad, flat basket to winnow away the chaff—now had to process vast quantities of rice for export.

Before long, people in England had developed a taste for rice pudding, and London merchants were shipping tons of Carolina rice to other European countries, where it proved a cheap grain for feeding soldiers, orphans, and peasants. By the middle of the eighteenth century, South Carolina's white minority had the most favorable trade balance of any mainland colonists. Their fortunes improved even more when indigo, another African crop, joined rice as a profitable export commodity. Outnumbered by their enslaved workers, South Carolina's landowners passed strict Negro Acts patterned on those of the Caribbean. Legislation prohibited slaves from carrying guns, meeting in groups, raising livestock, or traveling without a pass. Statutes controlled everything from how they dressed to when they shoveled the dung off of Charleston streets. Everywhere, mounted patrols enforced the regulations with brutal severity.

> *The arriving Africans understood South Carolina's subtropical climate better than their European owners did.*

PATTERNS OF RESISTANCE

In South Carolina and elsewhere, enslaved African Americans pushed against the narrow boundaries of their lives. Like any other imprisoned population, they pressed to relieve their condition in any possible way. Time and again, they spread rumors, refused to work, broke tools, feigned illness, or threatened violence. In response, their owners tried to divide them in order to control them. Masters rewarded workers who acted obedient and diligent or who informed on fellow slaves. They imposed harsh punishments—whipping, mutilation, sale, or death—on those suspected of taking food, sowing dissent, or plotting revolt. And they encouraged the formation of black families, not only to gain another generation of laborers at no cost but also to create the emotional ties that they knew would hold individuals in check for fear of reprisals against loved ones.

Owners confined residents in the slave labor camps with curfews and pass systems and kept them from learning to read and from communicating freely with neighbors and

Drums and Banjos: African Sounds in English Colonies

■ Few African instruments survive from the colonial era. This Virginia slave drum resembles Ashanti drums in Ghana. African banjoes became common in the South.

In every area of life, the earliest African Americans blended remembered portions of diverse African cultures with strange new variations acquired from Europeans and Native Americans in the New World. Despite the harsh conditions of enslavement, this pattern of combining new and old applied to food and clothing, language and movement, housing and hairstyles. This mixing of worlds also appeared in the realm of music.

Once in America, Africans recreated cherished instruments they had left behind. Drums such as this slave drum from Virginia, which is similar to Ashanti drums in Ghana, reappeared quickly, and

Africans who had used drums to convey messages shared this skill with others. Conch shells and cow-horn trumpets could also send signals. In 1740, anxious South Carolina legislators outlawed slaves from "using or keeping drums, horns, or other loud instruments, which may call together, or give sign or notice to one another of their wicked designs and purposes." The Virginia militia, however, recruited free blacks "as Drummers and Trumpeters."

The most prominent African instrument was the banjo. "The instrument proper to them," Jefferson observed, "is the banjar, which they brought hither from Africa." A Maryland minister recalled, "the favorite and almost only instrument in use among the slaves there was a bandore; or, as they pronounced the word, banjer. Its body was a large hollow gourd, with a long handle attached to it, strung with catgut, and played on with the fingers."

Eventually, white musicians began making and playing their own banjos, just as black musicians soon took up the European violin. John Marrant, a young free black in colonial Charleston, remembered spending most evenings with older musicians. "My improvement was so rapid that in a twelve-month's time I became master of both the violin and the French horn." African American fiddlers became common in the South, playing African and English melodies, and much that lay in between.

QUESTIONS

1. How did musical traditions as different as spirituals, jazz, and blues eventually emerge from the African American experience?

2. How would music have assisted African Americans in resisting the most corrosive effects of generations of forced bondage?

relatives. They also refused to allow any impartial system for expressing grievances or appealing arbitrary punishments. Faced with such steep odds, many slaves submitted to the deadening routine of the prison camp to survive. But others resorted to diverse strategies to improve their situation or undermine their masters' dominance. Running away, even for a brief period, provided relief from forced work and deprived owners of the labor they depended on. Because arson created serious damage and was difficult to detect, some slaves burned down barns at harvest time. Others succeeded in killing their masters or overseers. Such acts of pent-up rage usually proved suicidal, but they also confirmed slave owners' worst fears. Realizing that many Africans could communicate using drums and could concoct poisons from herbs, white planters became even more fearful of blacks.

Above all, the prospect of open rebellion burned in the minds of prisoners and jailers alike. Often, therefore, it is hard to untangle episodes of white paranoia from incidents of actual revolt. Many innocent slaves were falsely accused. But countless others did discuss plans for resistance, and a few freedom fighters avoided detection or betrayal long enough to launch serious uprisings. Word of one upheaval, real or imagined, could spark others.

An early wave of slave unrest erupted in the dozen years after 1710, highlighted by violence in New York City in the spring of 1712. The leaders of the conspiracy were "Coromantee," or Akan people from Africa's Gold Coast region. Several dozen enslaved Africans and Indians, determined to obtain their freedom and kill all the whites in the town, set fire to a building. As citizens rushed to put out the blaze, the rebels attacked them with guns, clubs, pistols, staves, and axes, killing eight and wounding more. When the militia finally captured the insurgents, six of them committed suicide. Authorities executed eighteen, burning several at the stake, hanging others and leaving their bodies on display. Eager to curtail slavery following such unrest, the governor called for "the Importation of White Servants." New York's elected colonial assembly, expressing growing racial hatred, chastised free blacks and prohibited freed slaves from owning property.

A WAVE OF REBELLION

A second wave of black resistance swept the mainland colonies after 1730, fueled by the largest influx of Africans to date. In Louisiana, the French had moved their capital to the new town of New Orleans on the Mississippi River (1722) and had joined their Choctaw allies in a devastating war to crush the Natchez Indians and seize their lands (1729–1731). As French landowners staked out riverfront plantations, they also imported African slaves. The several thousand black workers soon outnumbered European settlers.

Fearful of attack, Louisiana's whites broke up two presumed slave plots in 1731. One involved a scheme to rebel while Catholic colonists attended a midnight mass on Christmas. Another apparent plot was revealed by the careless boast of a black servant woman in New Orleans. It included several hundred Bambara newcomers from Senegal who aspired to massacre whites, enslave other Africans, and take control of the region. The leader was a man known as Samba Bambara, a former interpreter at Galam on the Senegal River. Bambara had lost that post and been deported to Louisiana, where he became a trusted slave, supervising workers owned by the French Company of the Indies. When torture by fire failed to force confessions from the key suspects, officials hanged the servant woman. Then Bambara and half a dozen other men were "broken on the wheel" (put to death slowly by being tied to wagon wheels and having their bones broken).

The largest slave uprising in colonial North America broke out in 1739 near the Stono River, twenty miles southwest of Charleston. Several factors fueled the Stono Rebellion. By 1739, blacks exceeded whites nearly two to one among South Carolina's 56,000 people. The proportion of recently imported slaves had reached an all-time high. In addition, working conditions had worsened steadily as rice production expanded. Moreover, for several decades the Spanish in Florida had been luring slaves from South Carolina, knowing that the promise of freedom might destabilize Carolina's profitable slave regime. More than a hundred fugitives had escaped to Florida by 1738, when Florida's governor formed them into a free black militia company at St. Augustine. Hoping to win more defections, he allowed thirty-eight African American households to settle north of the city and build a small fortress—Fort Mose.

DOCUMENT

James Oglethorpe, The Stono Rebellion (1739)

Courtesy, Florida Museum of Natural History. Photo by James Quine

■ Archaeologists have recently excavated the site of Fort Mose, near St. Augustine, Florida. Dozens of slaves who escaped from South Carolina received their freedom from the Spanish and established an outpost there in the 1730s.

Meanwhile, the wider commercial rivalries of the British and Spanish continued elsewhere, leading to open warfare between the two Atlantic empires in 1739. The slave uprising at Stono erupted just after word reached Charleston that war had broken out between Spain and Britain. Other factors may also have influenced the rebels' timing. An epidemic in Charleston had disrupted public activities, and a new Security Act requiring all white men to carry arms to church was to take effect before the end of September.

Early on Sunday, September 9, 1739, twenty slaves from a work crew near the Stono River broke into a local store. There they seized weapons and executed the owners. Led by a man named Jemmy, they raised a banner and marched south, beating drums and shouting "Liberty!" The insurgents burned selected plantations, killed a score of whites, and gathered more than fifty new recruits. But armed colonists overtook them near the Edisto River and blocked their escape to St. Augustine. Dozens of rebels died in the ensuing battle. In the next two days, militia and hired Indians killed twenty more and captured an additional forty people, whom they immediately shot or hanged.

South Carolina officials displayed the heads of slain rebels on poles, stepped up night patrols, and passed a harsher Negro Law. Yet even these reprisals could not quell black hopes. In June 1740, several hundred slaves plotted to storm Charleston and take arms from a warehouse. However, a comrade revealed the plan. According to a report, "The next day 50 of them were seized, and these were hanged, ten a day, to intimidate the other negroes." In November, a great fire of suspicious origin consumed much of Charleston.

Fire also played a role in hysteria that broke out in New York City in 1741. Britain's ongoing conflict with Spain (1739–1743) fanned wild Protestant fears that Jesuit spies and Catholic slaves planned to burn the major towns in British North America. In March, a blaze consumed the residence of New York's governor and a local fort. Other fires soon focused suspicions on a white couple, John and Sarah Hughson, who had often entertained blacks at their alehouse. The Hughsons—thought to fence stolen goods for a black crime ring—were accused of inciting working-class unrest. In exchange for her freedom, a sixteen-year-old Irish indentured servant at the Hughsons' tavern testified that she had overheard the planning of an elaborate "popish plot."

In a gruesome spiral of arrests and executions, New York authorities put to death thirty-four people (including the Hughsons and two other whites) and banished seventy-two blacks. On one hand, the debacle recalled the Salem witch trials, as a fearful community engaged in judicial proceedings and killings on the basis of rumors and accusations. On the other hand, the New York Slave Plot recalled Bacon's Rebellion, for evidence emerged of cooperation between impoverished blacks and whites eager to see a redistribution of property. According to his accusers, a slave named Cuffee had often observed that "a great many people had too much, and others too little." He predicted that soon his master "should have less, and that he [Cuffee] should have more." Instead, he was burned at the stake.

The Transformation Completed

■ *What prevented antislavery ideas from gaining a stronger foothold in the American colonies?*

The mechanisms for extorting labor from tens of thousands of people were firmly in place. But to maintain the slave labor system, local governments had to be vigilant and repressive, prompting debates within the white population. At a time of growing humanitarian concerns in Enlightenment Europe, it took great effort to maintain the rationale for enslavement in America. Some colonists saw slavery as too morally degrading and physically dangerous to maintain. Powerful supporters of the institution, however, found it too rewarding to give up and suggested modifications instead. This was even true in the North, where the number of blacks, both enslaved and free, remained relatively small.

Stakes were highest in the South, where most African Americans lived. As race-based slavery came to shape the entire nature of early southern society, leaders argued over the troublesome presence of free blacks, including many with mixed racial ancestry. Increasingly, white southerners treated the continuing presence of free blacks as a contradiction and a threat. As early as 1691, the Virginia assembly passed an act restricting **manumissions** (grants of individual freedom by masters) because "great inconvenience may happen to this country by setting of negroes and mulattoes free." According to the act, such people fanned hopes of freedom among enslaved blacks by their mere presence. By 1723, additional Virginia statutes prevented free people of color from voting, taxed them unfairly, and banned them from owning or carrying firearms. Lawmakers went on to prohibit all manumissions, except when the governor rewarded "meritorious service," such as informing against other enslaved workers.

> *Increasingly, white southerners treated the continuing presence of free blacks as a contradiction and a threat.*

Farther south, the contrasting colonies of South Carolina and Georgia conducted their own debates. Following the Stono uprising, for example, legislators in Charleston imposed a heavy import duty on new African arrivals for several years, hoping to increase the ratio of whites to enslaved blacks in the South Carolina lowcountry. But free people who went further, challenging the existence of slavery, met stiff resistance from those with vested interests, as the experience of the new colony of Georgia demonstrates.

MAP

African Slave Trade, 1500–1870

SECOND-CLASS STATUS IN THE NORTH

While southern planters labored to intimidate their enslaved population and weaken or contain local free black communities, African Americans in the North faced related challenges. Northern slave populations, though very small in comparison to those in the southern colonies, were growing steadily. As the North's involvement in the Atlantic slave trade expanded, its economic and legal commitment to race slavery increased. Rhode Island's slave ranks jumped from 500 in 1720 to more than 3,000 in 1750. Everywhere, new laws made manumission more difficult and African American survival more precarious. Free blacks in northern colonies faced growing discrimination in their efforts to hold jobs, buy land, obtain credit, move freely, and take part in civic life. Only in the century after 1760 did northern free black communities gain the numerical and social strength to offer effective opposition to enslavement.

Whereas free blacks lacked the means to oppose slavery, prominent white Christians lacked the will. Even in Massachusetts, where religion remained a dominant force at the turn of the century and the number of slaves had scarcely reached 1,000 people, many leaders already owned black servants. They used them more to flaunt their prosperity than to expand their wealth. When Boston merchants purchased black attendants to serve as coachmen, few citizens objected.

"Releese us Out of This Cruell Bondegg"

Interpreting History

As researchers pay increasing attention to African bondage in the colonial era, new pieces of evidence continue to appear. This appeal, written in Virginia in 1723 by a mulatto Christian slave, was rediscovered in a London archive in the 1990s and transcribed by historian Thomas Ingersoll. It is addressed to Edward Gibson, the newly appointed bishop of London, whose position gave him religious oversight over all the Anglican parishes in England's American colonies, including Virginia. Gibson, through his pamphlets, had shown an interest in the Christianization of enslaved Africans, but like many contemporary church leaders, he had less interest in the liberation of slaves. This heartfelt document, prepared with great labor and at enormous risk, was simply filed away with the bishop's vast correspondence. It never received a response or prompted any further inquiry into conditions in Virginia.

George Morland, *Traite Des Negres*, 1790–1791. Colonial Williamsburg Foundation

■ When abolition of the slave trade finally became a public issue in England in the 1780s, British artists painted scenes criticizing the traffic. But two generations earlier, pleas from New World slaves aroused no response, even from the Bishop of London, who supervised the Church of England in the American colonies.

The protests that did appear were ambivalent at best, including the one offered in 1700 by Samuel Sewell of Massachusetts. He had taken part in the 1692 witchcraft trials at Salem (later apologizing for his role), and he would become the chief justice of the colony. In a tract titled *The Selling of Joseph*, Judge Sewell questioned African enslavement, suggesting that no one should carelessly part with liberty "or deprive others of it."

But even as Sewell questioned the institution of race slavery, he also revealed his sense of superiority. His pamphlet expressed skepticism that blacks could play a part in "the Peopling of the Land." African Americans, the judge commented, "can seldom use their freedom well; yet their continual aspiring after their forbidden Liberty, renders them unwilling servants." Reverend Cotton Mather, a slave owner who once berated Sewell as one who "pleaded much for Negroes," held a more adamant view. In *The Negro Christianized* (1706), the influential Puritan stressed that conversion and Christian instruction, far from earning African slaves their freedom, would make them into "better servants."

IS THIS "CONSISTENT WITH CHRISTIANITY OR COMMON JUSTICE"?

The conversion and instruction of slaves, rather than the abolition of slavery, became a mission for English philanthropist Thomas Bray, a pious, well-to-do Anglican committed to religious education and prison reform. In 1699, Bray founded the Society for Promoting Christian Knowledge to organize libraries in the fledgling colonies. The following year, the

August the forth 1723

to the Right Raverrand father in god my Lord arch Bishop of Lonnd . . . .

this coms to sattesfie your honour that there is in this Land of verJennia a Sort of people that is Calld molatters which are Baptised and brouaht up in the way of the Christian faith and followes the ways and Rulles of the Chrch of England and sum of them has white fathars and sum white mothers and there is in this Land a Law or act which keeps and makes them and there seed SLaves forever. . . .

wee your humbell and poore partishinners doo begg Sir your aid and assisttancce in this one thing...which is that your honour will by the help of our Sufvering [i.e., sovereign] Lord King George and the Rest of the Rullers will Releese us out of this Cruell Bondegg. . . ./ and here it is to bee notd that one brother is a SLave to another and one Sister to an othe which is quite out of the way and as for mee my selfe I am my brothers SLave but my name is Secrett/

wee are commandded to keep holey the Sabbath day and wee doo hardly know when it comes for our task mastrs are has hard with us as the Egypttions was with the Chilldann of Issarall. . . . wee are kept out of the Church and matrimony is deenied us and to be plain they doo Look no more upon us then if wee ware dogs which I hope when these Strange lines comes to your Lord Ships hands will be Looket in to. . . .

And Sir wee your humble perticners do humblly beg . . . that our childarn may be broatt up in the way of the Christtian faith and our desire is that they may be Larnd the Lords prayer the creed and the ten commandements and that they may appeare Every Lord's day att Church before the Curatt to bee Exammond for our desire is that godllines Shoulld abbound amongs us and wee desire that our Childarn be putt to Scool and Larnd to Reed through the Bybell

my Riting is vary bad. . . . I am but a poore SLave that writt itt and has no other time butt Sunday and hardly that att Sumtimes. . . . wee dare nott Subscribe any mans name to this for feare of our masters for if they knew that wee have Sent home to your honour wee Should goo neare to Swing upon the gallass tree.

QUESTIONS

1. *In 1723, do these mulatto petitioners identify more closely with their African and non-Christian relatives who are enslaved or with their European and Anglican relations who are free? Explain.*

2. *Using the same kind of phonetic spelling and good logic, draft a paragraph or two that might further strengthen this petition and prevent the bishop of London from setting it aside.*

Source: Thomas N. Ingersoll, "'Releese Us out of This Cruell Bondegg': An Appeal from Virginia in 1723," *William and Mary Quarterly*, 3rd Series, 51 (October 1994): 776–782.

bishop of London sent Bray to Maryland. He soon returned to England with a desire to train better ministers and to spread the Anglican faith in America among Europeans, Indians, and Africans. In 1701, Bray established the Society for the Propagation of the Gospel in Foreign Parts (SPG). The SPG strengthened the Church of England abroad in the eighteenth century by providing dozens of ministers to serve in the colonies.

But this Anglican foothold came at a steep price. Southern planters made SPG ministers agree that any promise they offered to slaves regarding heavenly salvation would not include hints of earthly freedom. With few exceptions, the Anglican clergy gave in, strengthening religious support of race slavery. In 1723, a heartfelt petition from a mulatto slave to the bishop of London, in which the author protested "Cruell Bondegg" in Virginia, went unanswered. That same year, Bray set up a trust of "Associates" to carry on his work. With limited success, they focused on converting blacks in the British plantation colonies.

By the 1730s, only a few whites in Europe or America dared to press publicly for an end to slavery. Christian Priber, who arrived in the South in 1735, was one such activist. The idealistic German hoped to start a utopian community in southern Appalachia. But his radical proposal for a multiracial "Paradise" uniting Indians, Africans, and Europeans posed a huge threat to South Carolina authorities. "He enumerates many whimsical Privileges and natural Rights, as he calls them, which his citizens are to be entitled to," wrote a scornful detractor, "particularly dissolving Marriages and allowing Community of Women and all kinds of Licentiousness." Worst of all, according to the coastal elite, this egalitarian haven at the "Foot of the Mountains among the Cherokees" was to be "a City of Refuge for all Criminals,

Debtors, and Slaves who would fly thither from [the] Justice of their Masters." Priber's brief career as a social agitator challenging the status quo ended in 1743, when he was arrested and brought to jail in Charleston. He died—or was killed—before his case could be heard in court.

At the same time, a New Jersey tailor and bookkeeper named John Woolman posed a less defiant but more enduring threat to race slavery. In 1743, at age twenty-three, this shy Quaker began to question his role in writing out bills of sale when his fellow Quakers purchased slaves. It struck him forcefully that "to live in ease and plenty by the toil of those whom violence and cruelty have put in our power" was clearly not "consistent with Christianity or common justice." Woolman traveled widely to Quaker meetings, north and south, pressing an issue that most Quakers preferred to ignore. "The Colour of a Man avails nothing," Woolman insisted, "in Matters of Right and Equity." When he drafted *Some Considerations on the Keeping of Negroes* (1754), members of the Quaker Yearly Meeting in Philadelphia published his booklet and circulated it widely in several editions. Four years later, led by Anthony Benezet, this group outlawed slaveholding among its local members. They set a precedent that many Quakers followed in the next generation, and they challenged other denominations to do the same.

OGLETHORPE'S ANTISLAVERY EXPERIMENT

The most sustained early challenge to the slavery system in the American South came in the Georgia colony, named after King George II. In 1732, a group of well-connected London proprietors (known as trustees) obtained a twenty-year charter for the region between English South Carolina and Spanish Florida. Ten of the twenty-one initial trustees were members of Parliament, and one, James Oglethorpe, had recently organized a "committee on jails" to investigate the condition of debtors in English prisons.

William Hogarth, *To Inquire into the State of the Gaols of This Kingdom.* © The National Portrait Gallery, London (NPG926)

■ In 1729, James Oglethorpe (seated, right front) chaired a parliamentary committee exposing the harsh conditions in English jails. When William Hogarth portrayed the committee's visit to Fleet Street Prison, the artist showed Oglethorpe's concern for a dark-skinned prisoner, a hint of Oglethorpe's future opposition to slavery in Georgia.

The trustees foresaw three related purposes—charitable, commercial, and military—for their experimental colony. Georgia would provide a haven for England's worthy poor, selected members of the neediest classes who could be transported across the Atlantic and settled on small farms. These grateful newcomers would produce warm-weather commodities—olives, grapes, silk—to support the empire, and their prosperity in turn would create a growing market for English goods. Finally, their presence would provide a military buffer to protect South Carolina from further warfare with the Yamasee and Creek Indians and from possible invasion by the Spanish in St. Augustine.

With Oglethorpe as their governor, an initial boatload of 114 settlers arrived in 1733 and began building a capital at Savannah. By 1741 the town, located on a bluff fifteen miles up the Savannah River, boasted more than 140 houses. It also had a wharf, a jail, a courthouse (which doubled as a church), and a building for receiving delegations of neighboring Indians. By then, more than a thousand needy English, plus 800 German, Swiss, and Austrian Protestants, had journeyed to Georgia at the trustees' expense. Another thousand immigrants had paid their own way. Like earlier colonizers, Georgia's first arrivals had trouble adjusting to a strange environment. Alligators, rattlesnakes, and hurricanes tested their resolve. Tension over governance only deepened their discouragement.

The idealistic trustees in London declined to accumulate property and profits for themselves in the colony, but they felt justified in controlling every aspect of Georgia's development. For example, they knew that gin was becoming a source of debt and disruption in Europe and that rum and brandy sold by traders was poisoning colonial relations with southeastern Indians. So in 1735 they outlawed the use of every "kind of Spirits or Strong Waters" while still allowing consumption of wine and beer. Georgia's early experiment with prohibition of hard liquor proved difficult to implement, and officials quietly stopped enforcing the law in 1742.

DOCUMENT

James Oglethorpe, Establishing the Colony of Georgia (1733)

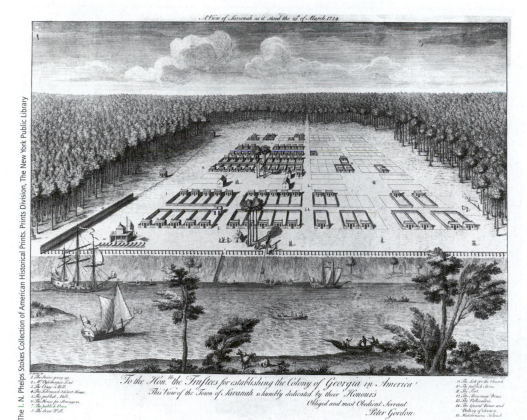

A View of Savanah as it stood the 29th of March 1734

To the Hon.ble the Trustees for establishing the Colony of Georgia in America
This View of the Town of Savanah is humbly dedicated by their Honours
Obliged and most Obedient Servant
Peter Gordon.

■ Savannah, the capital of Oglethorpe's Georgia, was one year old when this view was sketched in 1734. The following year, Georgia's trustees officially outlawed slavery, creating a sharp contrast with the other British colonies in North America, especially neighboring South Carolina on the opposite bank of the Savannah River.

Other efforts at control from above went further. The trustees refused to set up a legislature or to let settlers buy and sell land. Instead, they gave fifty acres of farm land to each family they sent over, plus a house lot in a local village, so all new towns could be well defended. But they parceled out land with little regard for variations in soil fertility. They also stipulated that owners could pass land on to sons only. Denying daughters the right to inherit, the trustees reasoned, would prevent men from creating large estates simply by marrying women who were likely to inherit big tracts of land. To prevent the concentrations of wealth that they saw developing in other colonies, the trustees said that no one could own more than 500 acres. Prohibiting massive estates would allow for thicker settlement and therefore greater manpower to defend the colony militarily.

But the most important prohibition, by far, involved slavery. Oglethorpe began his career as a deputy governor of the Royal African Company, but he died in 1785 opposing the slave trade. His sojourn in Georgia turned him against slavery. In neighboring South Carolina, he saw firsthand how the practice degraded African lives, undermined the morals of Europeans, and laid that colony open to threats of revolt and invasion. So Oglethorpe persuaded the trustees to create a free white colony, convincing them to enact a law in 1735 that prohibited slavery and also excluded free blacks. He believed that this mandate would protect Georgia from the corruptions of enslavement while also making it easier to apprehend black runaways heading to Florida from South Carolina.

In 1739, the Stono Rebellion and the outbreak of war between England and Spain strengthened Oglethorpe's belief that slavery undermined the security of the English colonies by creating internal enemies who would support any foreign attackers. He saw further evidence in 1740, when he failed in a wartime attempt to capture St. Augustine from Spain. Unable to take the Florida stronghold, the governor managed to seize neighboring Fort Mose, which had been erected by anti-English slaves who had escaped from Carolina.

MAP 4.4 English–Spanish Competition and the Expansion of Slavery into Georgia

The Spanish and the British had competing land claims along the southeast coast after 1670. Creation of the Georgia colony in 1732 intensified the rivalry. The Spanish in Florida offered freedom to any slaves who escaped from South Carolina to St. Augustine, sparking the Stono Revolt in 1739. During the war between Britain and Spain (1739–1743), Georgians defeated the Spanish at Bloody Marsh and secured the disputed "Sea Island" region for the British. Within a decade, slavery became legal in Georgia, and scores of new labor camps appeared between the Savannah and the St. Mary's River, producing rice for export.

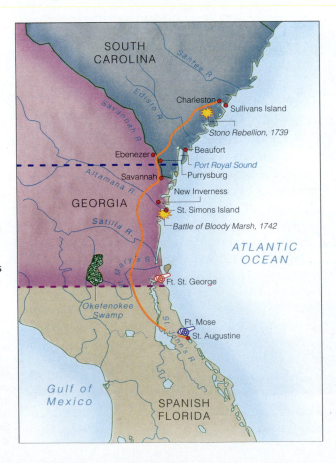

English-Spanish competition and the expansion of slavery into Georgia

- ■ Southern extent of British slavery regime before 1751
- ■ Southern extent of British slavery regime, 1751–1763
- – – Northern limit of Spanish claim in 1670
- – – Southern limit of British claim in 1736
- — Path from Charleston to St. Augustine
- ☀ Major battles
- Fort St. George, a British lookout post
- Fort Mose, Spanish outpost made up of escaped South Carolina slaves

When a Spanish force retook Fort Mose, relying heavily on Indian and African American fighters, Oglethorpe saw the intensity with which ex-slaves would fight the English, their former masters.

The next year, fearing a counterattack, Oglethorpe issued a warning to imperial officials. He predicted that if Spanish soldiers captured Georgia, a colony inhabited by "white Protestants and no Negroes," they would then send agents to infiltrate the vulnerable colonies farther north and stir black rebellion. The Spanish, he argued, understood that the thousands of embittered slaves "would be either Recruits to an Enemy or Plunder for them." No sooner had he written his wartime prediction in 1741 than suspicious fires broke out in New York and Charleston.

THE END OF EQUALITY IN GEORGIA

As Britain's war with Spain continued, few whites could deny the Georgia governor's assertion that slavery elsewhere in British America was a source of internal weakness and strategic danger. In 1742, as the governor had predicted, Spain pushed from Florida into Georgia with an eye toward destabilizing the colonies farther north. Oglethorpe's troops repulsed the invading Spanish force in the crucial Battle at Bloody Marsh on St. Simons Island. The victory reduced the immediate threat to Britain's North American colonies, especially neighboring South Carolina, where Oglethorpe and his idealistic policies had numerous powerful opponents. These opponents now joined a group of so-called Malcontents in Savannah to question Georgia's continued prohibition against slavery. When this coalition challenged the trustees' antislavery stance, it prompted the first protracted North American debate about enslavement.

> Oglethorpe warned that the proslavery lobby seemed bent on "destroying the Agrarian Equality" envisioned in Georgia's initial plan.

In the face of numerous ills—including a sickly climate, poor soil, restrictive land policies, and lack of representative government—a well-organized Georgia faction argued that slavery was the one thing needed for the colony to prosper, since it would provide profits to slave owners regardless of Georgia's many drawbacks. Not everyone agreed. In 1739, Scottish Highlanders living at Darien on the Altamaha River had contacted Oglethorpe to lay out their practical arguments against importing Africans. Their petition expressed shock "that any Race of Mankind, and their Posterity, Should be sentenced to perpetual slavery." Immigrants from Salzburg, Germany, residing at Ebenezer on the Savannah River drafted a similar statement. But Georgia's Malcontents pushed back, demanding the right to import slaves. They drew encouragement and support from powerful merchant-planters in South Carolina. Eager to expand their trade in slaves from Africa and to open up new lands for profitable plantations, these well-to-do Carolinians dreamed of extending their successful rice operations into coastal Georgia.

Oglethorpe warned that the proslavery lobby, hungry to create large estates, seemed bent on "destroying the Agrarian Equality" envisioned in Georgia's initial plan. But the colony's trustees in London grew less unified, committed, and informed over time. Eventually, the persistent efforts of the proslavery pamphleteers bore fruit. In 1750, the trustees gave in on the matter of land titles. They allowed acreage to be bought and sold freely in any amount, which opened the door for the creation of large plantations. From there, it was just one more step to allowing slavery. The trustees finally gave in on the question of bondage, letting Georgians exploit slave labor after January 1, 1751. The 1750 law permitting slavery made futile gestures to ensure kind treatment and Christian education for slaves, but the dam had broken. Hundreds of slave-owning South Carolinians streamed across the Savannah River to invest in land. In 1752, the trustees disbanded, their patent expiring, their vision undone. By 1754, Georgia had become a royal colony.

Some argued that Georgia should simply be incorporated into South Carolina. In a sense it was: slave labor camps producing rice and indigo for export soon dotted the low-country on both sides of the Savannah River. Georgia's assembly passed a harsh slave code in

1755, based on South Carolina's. Two years later, it legislated a system of patrols to keep the brutal new regime in place. Georgia's effort to counter race slavery in North America had failed, a case of too little too late. After holding out for nearly two decades, the colony fell victim to the same divisive institution that had already taken root elsewhere.

Conclusion

From the outset, Africans in America offered determined resistance against slavery, and white colonists occasionally voiced dissent. But their efforts proved no match for soaring Atlantic commerce. Bit by bit, the slavery system gained a firm foothold in North America during the century after 1660. In southern colonies the system shaped the entire economy and social structure, creating a society based on race slavery. Farther north, where the institution never dominated, it still persisted as a disturbing element of colonial life.

These North American developments, involving thousands of lives, still represented only a small portion of the gigantic African slave traffic. Two final observations provide a broader Atlantic context. First, for the people swept up in the North American portion of the trade, their odyssey began comparatively late, for this dimension of the trade did not expand rapidly until after the 1670s. In the larger history of North American immigration, of course, their forced migration from Africa came relatively early. (Indeed, the proportion of blacks in the colonial population on the eve of the American Revolution—over 20 percent—was higher than it has ever been in the United States since then.) But in terms of the entire African slave **diaspora,** or dispersion, the influx to English North America occurred long after the traffic to Mexico, Brazil, and the Caribbean was well established.

Second, even at its height, the North American trade remained marginal in relation to the wider Atlantic commerce in African labor. For example, whereas roughly 50,000 enslaved men and women reached all the docks of North America between 1721 and 1740, the small West Indian islands of English Barbados and French Guadeloupe *each* received more than 53,000 Africans during the same period. In the next two decades, while Britain's mainland colonies purchased just over 100,000 Africans, Caribbean Islands such as English Jamaica (120,000) and French Saint Domingue (159,000) absorbed many more slaves.

During this single forty-year span (1721–1760), Brazil bought 667,000 African workers—more than would reach North America during the entire slave trade. All told, scholars currently estimate that some 650,000 Africans were brought to North America over several centuries. They represented roughly 6 percent of the total Atlantic commerce in enslaved people. Still, the number of North American slaves expanded from scarcely 7,000 in 1680 to nearly 29,000 in 1700 and to more than 70,000 in 1720. Half a century later, in 1770, because of importation and natural increase, 470,000 individuals were confined to enslavement from New Hampshire to Louisiana.

A century had passed since Elizabeth Key's generation saw the terrible transformation begin. Relative openness had given way to systematic oppression, and slavery's corrosive effects were felt at every level of society. An English visitor to the South in 1759 found provincial planters "vain and imperious," subject "to many errors and prejudices, especially in regard to Indians and Negroes, whom they scarcely consider as of the human species." It took another century before pressures developed that could unseat race slavery, sanctioned by law, as a dominant institution in the land.

CHRONOLOGY: 1672–1751	
1672	Royal African Company (RAC) formed in London.
1676	Virginia and Maryland slaves join in Bacon's Rebellion.
1705	Virginia approves Negro Act.
1712	New York City slave revolt.
1713	British receive the contract *(asiento)* to supply African slaves to Spanish colonies.
1734	James Oglethorpe launches Georgia as a nonslave colony.
1739	Slave revolt in Stono, South Carolina.
1741	Alleged slave plot in New York City.
1751	Slavery is legalized in Georgia.

For Review

1. What role did the English Restoration of 1660 play in the establishment of African slavery in England's North American colonies?

2. What evidence exists that enslaved Africans, stripped of so much in the Middle Passage, still brought knowledge, skills, and cultural values with them to the New World?

3. If you had been an enslaved person, how would you have responded to harsh, arbitrary treatment? Why?

4. Though the evidence remains slim, how do you assess the idealistic multiracial experiment for a utopian southern community proposed by Christian Priber in 1735?

5. "In retrospect, the best time and place to halt and reverse the 'Terrible Transformation' would have been. . . . " How would you complete this thought?

6. In what ways can the destructive, uncontrollable African slave trade created by competing European powers be compared to the modern nuclear arms race?

Created Equal Online

For more *Created Equal* resources, including suggestions on sites to visit and books to read, go to **MyHistoryLab.com**.

to the Spanish settlements of northern New Mexico, where they could trade buffalo hides for additional horses at Taos and Santa Fe. The Spanish noted the Shoshone-speaking arrivals in 1706, referring to them as Comanche in their records.

Officials in Santa Fe, fearful about their own defenses, looked for ways to halt Comanche aggression. They also hoped to convert the Apaches to Christianity and stop French traders from moving onto the Plains. In 1714, a French adventurer named Etienne Bourgmont had traveled up the Missouri River as far as the mouth of the Platte, near modern Omaha. In 1720, the Spanish sent soldiers northeast from Santa Fe to check the latest rumors of a French advance. But they pushed too far. An Indian war party, with French support, routed the force somewhere near present-day North Platte, Nebraska.

Seizing the advantage, Bourgmont pushed west onto the Nebraska Plains again in 1724, hoping to lure local tribes (such as the Pawnee and Padouca) away from their trade with the Spanish. "It is true that we go to the home of the Spaniards," a chief told him, "but they trade to us only some horses, a few knives, and some inferior axes; they do not trade in fusils [guns], or lead, or gunpowder, or kettles, or blankets, or any of the goods that the great French chief has given us. Thus the French are our true friends." But the French, far from their source of supply, were unable to sustain this trade advantage on the plains. Instead, the Comanche benefited most from the Spanish defeat in 1720, gaining greater access to markets in New Mexico. Comanche bands stepped up raids on Apache and carried captives to Santa Fe for sale as slaves at the annual *rescate,* or ransoming.

THE CREATION OF COMANCHERÍA ON THE SOUTHERN PLAINS

At first, New Mexico resisted the additional trade in slaves. The colony had not been able to protect Apache families or convert them; now it was being asked to buy them.

Comanchería roughly equaled all the English settlements on the Atlantic coast in size.

But in the 1740s, officials in Santa Fe discovered that if they turned away Comanche traders, they faced the increasing power of Comanche war parties. So they granted the Comanche access to the *rescate* at Taos in exchange for assurances of peace. With a secure market for their hides, meat, and captives, the Comanche could now focus their raids on central Texas, where their hard-pressed Apache enemies had sealed a pact with the Spanish in 1749.

Not long after they buried the horse in the plaza at San Antonio, the Spanish began planning a mission and presidio (military post) among their new Apache allies. The outpost would lie 150 miles northwest of San Antonio on the San Saba River, near present-day Menard, Texas. But the post had been established for less than a year when an attack by 2,000 Indian warriors overwhelmed the little log mission in 1758. Comanche, many firing French-made guns, led the violent raid, and they returned the next year to capture 700 horses. "The heathen of the north are innumerable and rich," exclaimed a Spanish officer at San Saba. "They dress well, breed horses, [and] handle firearms with the greatest skill." A Spanish counterattack northward to the Red River did not stop the Comanche onslaught. Their continuing attacks finally forced the Spanish to withdraw from San Saba in 1767.

In less than two decades, the Comanche had overrun most of Texas. By the 1770s, mounted Comanche warriors commanded respect and fear across a vast domain. Their territory stretched south nearly 600 miles from western Kansas to central Texas, and it spanned 400 miles from eastern New Mexico to what is now eastern Oklahoma. This area, known as Comanchería, roughly equaled all the English settlements on the Atlantic coast in size. The Comanche continued to absorb smaller Native American groups and swell in numbers. By 1780, they had grown into a proud Indian nation of more than 20,000 people. Comanchería remained a powerful entity in the Southwest for decades.

THE EXPANSION OF THE SIOUX

Comanche strength depended not only on mounted warfare but also on trading horses to obtain guns. Because Spanish policy prohibited the sale of firearms to Native Americans, the Comanche looked east for weapons. They quickly discovered that by selling horses to their eastern allies, such as the Wichita Indians, they could receive French muskets from Louisiana in return. But the Comanche were not alone; the Sioux Indians also took advantage of the gun frontier as it inched steadily west.

By 1720, the French had established settlements at Peoria, Cahokia, and Kaskaskia in Illinois and at New Orleans, Natchez, and Natchitoches in Louisiana. French traders at these sites provided guns and other metal goods to Indians in exchange for salt, deerskins, beaver pelts, horses, and war captives. Native American groups that took advantage of this trade included the Tunica beside the lower Mississippi, the Caddo and Wichita along the Red and Arkansas rivers, and the Osage, Pawnee, and Omaha tribes near the Missouri.

> *By midcentury on the northern Great Plains, the horse frontier moving from the southwest had met the gun frontier moving from the east.*

Farther north, muskets carried west from French posts on the Great Lakes and south from English bases in subarctic Canada proved especially important among the Sioux peoples, who trapped game and gathered wild rice by the lakes of their northern Minnesota homeland. The Comanche had mastered horses and then acquired guns; the Sioux, given their different location, first absorbed firearms and then adopted the horse. The results proved equally dramatic.

When the Sioux first encountered a gun from French voyageurs in the mid-seventeenth century, they called it *mazawakan*, meaning "mysterious or sacred iron." Initially, they used the few muskets they could obtain to fight their less well-armed Indian neighbors. By 1700 French traders, moving from the east, had established direct trade with the Sioux, offering a steady supply of guns and powder in exchange for furs.

For a generation, several Sioux bands (the Teton and Yanktonai) walked between two worlds. In the summers, they followed the buffalo onto the prairies, with dogs pulling travois and women carrying heavy burdens. As cold weather approached, they retreated to the edge of the woodlands to gather firewood and hunt beaver. In the spring, after trading meat and pelts to the French for guns and ammunition, they returned to the edge of the plains. They glimpsed their first horses not long after 1700. But it was several generations before the western Sioux had acquired enough mounts and developed sufficient confidence to drop their old customs and adopt a horse-centered way of life.

By midcentury on the northern Great Plains, the horse frontier moving from the southwest had met the gun frontier moving from the east. Saukamappee, a Cree Indian living with the Blackfoot, remembered vividly the surprise of the initial encounter. When he was a young man, his war party—well armed and on foot—had gone into battle against the Shoshone. "We had more guns and iron headed arrows than [ever] before," he recalled years later. "But our enemies . . . and their allies had Misstutim (Big Dogs, that is, Horses) on which they rode, swift as the Deer."

Indian women remembered the arrival of the horse and the gun with ambivalence. These new assets improved food supplies and made travel less burdensome, but the transition also brought disadvantages. Violent raids became more common. Young men who fought as warriors gained status in the community compared to older men and women. The

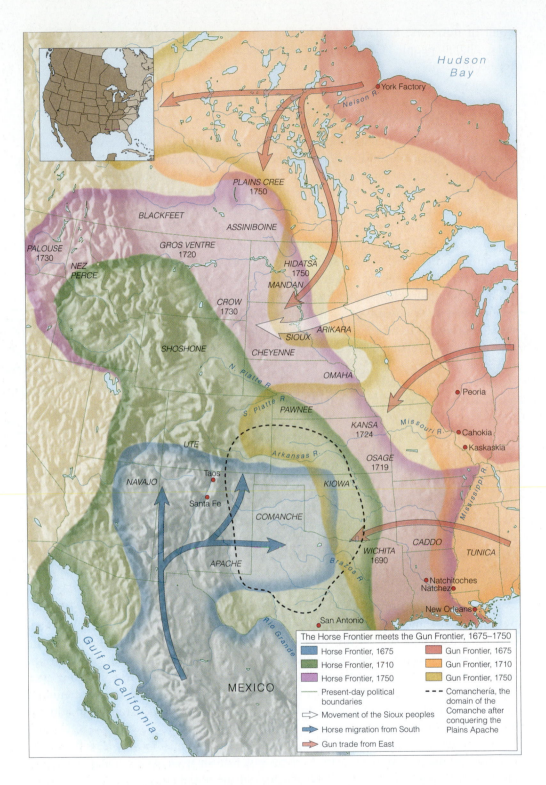

■ MAP 5.1   The Horse Frontier Meets the Gun Frontier, 1675–1750

difficult task of processing slain buffalo increased, creating new work for women even as it provided fresh resources for the whole community.

As the overlap of horse and gun proceeded after 1750, Sioux men bearing muskets continued to acquire mounts and fight for control of the buffalo grounds. Their competitors, all of whom had recently acquired horses, now had guns as well. Within several decades, the Sioux had pushed their domain west to the Missouri River. Like the Comanche farther south, they had emerged as a dominant power on the Great Plains—a force to be reckoned with in the century ahead.

Britain's Mainland Colonies: A New Abundance of People

■ *In what ways did Britain's North American colonies become "less English" after 1700?*

West of the Mississippi, horses and guns brought dramatic shifts as the eighteenth century progressed. But east of the Appalachian Mountains, a different force prompted striking change: population growth. Several factors came together to push the demographic curve upward at an unprecedented rate after 1700. From our vantage point in the twenty-first century, the colonial seaports and villages appear tiny, and rural settlement seems sparse. But by the mid-eighteenth century, the coastal colonies represented the largest concentration of people that had ever occupied any portion of the continent.

Population growth characterized eighteenth-century life on both sides of the North Atlantic. In Europe, improvements in agriculture led to larger harvests and more fodder for keeping livestock alive through long winters. These changes prompted better diets. Improvements in food distribution and sanitation also stimulated population growth. But while European numbers rose at a gradual pace, the population of Atlantic North America surged. England in 1700 had 5.1 million people, a figure that increased a mere 14 percent to 5.8 million by 1750. In contrast, during the same half-century, the colonial population in British North America more than quadrupled, from 260,000 to nearly 1.2 million.

During these same decades, the Atlantic seaboard colonies made a permanent and dramatic shift away from a population that was almost entirely of English origin. Never before had North America seen such extensive ethnic and racial diversity. As the numerous cultures and languages indigenous to western Europe, western Africa, and eastern North America mixed and mingled, they gave rise to an American Babel.

POPULATION GROWTH ON THE HOME FRONT

Natural increase—more births than deaths—played an important role in colonial population growth. People married young, and the need for labor spurred couples to have large families. Benjamin Franklin, who became the best-known colonist of his generation, was born in Boston in 1706. He grew up in a household of seventeen children. Large families had long been commonplace, to compensate for frequent deaths among children. What made the Franklin family unusual was that all the children survived childhood and started families of their own.

A high birthrate typified most preindustrial cultures. It was the low death rate and long average life span that pushed up American population numbers. With no huge urban centers, colonial epidemics proved less devastating than in Europe. Food was plentiful, and housing improved steadily. Newborns who survived infancy could live a long life. (Franklin himself lived eighty-four years.) The 1720s and 1730s were peaceful, so soldiering did not endanger the lives of men of military age. For women, death related to pregnancy and childbirth still loomed as a constant threat. (Franklin's own mother was his father's second wife; the first wife died after bearing seven children.) Yet women still outnumbered men among people living into their sixties, seventies, and eighties.

Elderly grandparents were common, but the overall society was remarkably young, with well over half the population below the age of twenty. (See Figure 5.1.) The reasons seem clear. The ratio between men and women was becoming more even over time, the marriage rates for women remained extremely high, and there was no effective means of contraception. Women could only avoid pregnancy through sexual abstinence or by nursing their infants for a long period (since lactation reduces the chances of conception). Not surprisingly, children abounded.

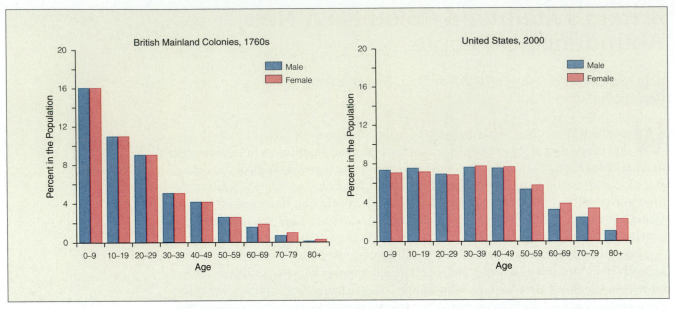

■ FIGURE 5.1   Comparison of Overall Population Structure By Gender and Age: British Mainland Colonies, 1760s, and United States, 2000

In the mid-eighteenth century, more than half of all people in the British mainland colonies were under age twenty, and fewer than two in ten were forty or older. In contrast, among all the living Americans at the start of the twenty-first century, fewer than three in ten are under twenty, and more than four in ten are age forty or older.

"PACKED LIKE HERRINGS": ARRIVALS FROM ABROAD

Frequent births and improving survival rates were only part of the population story. Immigration—both forced and free—also contributed mightily to the colonies' growth. The unfree arrivals came in two different streams from two separate continents and faced very different prospects. The largest flow of unfree arrivals came from Africa, and these forced migrants faced a bleak new life with few options for improvement. Well before the 1720s, the system of race-based slavery was sanctioned by law. By the 1730s, the expanding transatlantic slave trade brought at least 4,000 Africans to the colonies every year, and the rate increased steadily. In 1756, Charleston, South Carolina, received more than 2,200 slaves aboard fourteen ships (including vessels that bore grimly ironic names such as *Relief, Hope,* and *Success*).

A separate stream of unfree laborers came to the colonies from Europe. It included prisoners removed from crowded jails and indentured servants unable to pay their own way to America. Compared with enslaved Africans, these European migrants faced long-term prospects that were far more promising. Every year, hundreds of detainees in British jails were offered transportation to the colonies and a term of service laboring in America as an alternative to prison time or execution.

Deported felons joined the larger flow of unfree migrants from Europe: poor people, unable to pay their own passage, who accepted transportation to America as indentured servants. All were sold to employers to serve as workers, with scant legal rights, until their indenture expired, usually after three to six years. In the 1720s, Philadelphia shippers devised a variation on indentures known as the redemption contract. Under this **redemption system,** agents in Europe recruited migrants by contracting to loan them money for passage and provisions. On arrival in America, the recruits could then sign a pact with an employer of their own choosing. That person agreed to pay back the shipper, "redeeming" the original loan that had been made to the immigrant. In exchange, the newcomer (called a redemptioner) promised to work for the employer for several years,

DOCUMENT

Gottlieb Mittelberger,
The Passage of
Indentured Servants
(1750)

receiving no more than room and board. After that, the redemptioners were on their own, and their prospects usually improved.

Besides Africans who remained unfree for life and Europeans who gained freedom after a period of service, a smaller stream of newcomers involved free families arriving from Europe who could pay their own way. Poor conditions at home pushed these risk-takers to try their luck in the New World. Glowing descriptions of abundant land at bargain rates caught their attention. American land speculators hoped to rent forest tracts to immigrant farmers who would improve the value of the land by clearing trees and building homes. In turn, Britain's imperial administrators sought to recruit non-English migrants from the European continent. Their immigrant settlements near the American frontier could bolster colonial defenses against foreign rivals and provide a buffer to ward off Indian attacks. In one of many pamphlets for German immigrants, Joshua von Kocherthal explained how South Carolina's proprietors would give a sixty-five-acre plot to each head of household, with the promise of more land if they needed it or if they came with a large group.

Even for those newcomers who paid for their own crossing, the Atlantic passage was a life-threatening ordeal. "The people are packed densely, like herrings," Lutheran minister Gottlieb Mittelberger recorded after a voyage to Pennsylvania. "During the journey the ship is full of pitiful signs of distress—smells, fumes, horrors, vomiting, various kinds of sea sickness, fever, dysentery, headaches, heat, constipation, boils, scurvy, cancer, mouth-rot, and similar afflictions." Despite such hardships, newcomers found economic opportunities awaiting them in America. They often wrote home glowing accounts of colonial life, and their letters helped boost the rising population further. In 1773, English customs officials quizzed twenty-nine-year-old Elizabeth McDonald about why she was departing for Wilmington, North Carolina. The unmarried Scottish servant replied that she was setting out "because several of her friends, having gone to Carolina before her, had assured her that she would get much better service and greater encouragement in Carolina than in her own country."

DOCUMENT

Elizabeth Sprigs, Letter to Her Father (1756)

NON-ENGLISH NEWCOMERS IN THE BRITISH COLONIES

Colonies that were thoroughly English at their origin became decidedly more varied after 1700. By far the largest and most striking change came from North America's increasing involvement in the Atlantic slave trade. By 1750, some 240,000 African Americans made up 20 percent of the population of the British colonies. Native Americans had been drawn into the mix in small numbers as slaves, servants, spouses, and Christian converts. But roughly four out of five colonists were of European descent. Among them, as among the Africans and Indians, many spoke English with a different accent, or as a second language, or not at all.

The New England colonies remained the most homogenous, but even there, 30 percent of the residents had non-English roots by 1760. The new diversity was most visible in New York because of the colony's non-English origins. A 1703 census of New York City shows that the town had no single ethnic majority. It remained 42 percent Dutch, with English (30 percent) and Africans (18 percent) together making up nearly half the population. The rest of the population included a small Jewish community (1 percent) and a growing number of French Protestants, or Huguenots (9 percent).

The French New Yorkers had fled to America after Louis XIV ended protection for the Protestant minority of France. When the king revoked the long-standing Edict of Nantes in 1685, he also prohibited Huguenot emigration, but

John Wollaston, *Mary Spratt Provoost Alexander*, undated. Museum of the City of New York, Gift of William Hamilton Russell (50.215.4)

■ Like many New Yorkers of her generation, shopkeeper Mary Spratt Provoost Alexander (1693–1760) spoke both Dutch and English. Her Dutch mother had married a Scottish immigrant, and Mary was the wife of a local attorney who also came from Scotland.

"Pastures Can Be Found Almost Everywhere": Joshua von Kocherthal Recruits Germans to Carolina

Interpreting History

Joshua von Kocherthal grew up in southern Germany and trained to be a Lutheran minister. On a visit to London at the start of the eighteenth century, he learned of England's desire to recruit settlers to its American colonies. Because fellow Germans faced hard times at home, he led several groups to New York, where they established Neuberg (Newburgh) on the Hudson River. In 1706, Kocherthal published a German-language tract promoting migration to South Carolina. The popular booklet went through several editions in his homeland.

The winter of 1708–1709 was especially harsh east of the Rhine River. In the spring of 1709, a stream of German refugee families migrated north along the Rhine and then west to England. From there, they hoped to obtain passage across the Atlantic to South Carolina. Many carried Kocherthal's simple pamphlet, and they focused on the numerous advantages outlined in his brochure, especially the abundance of land. According to Kocherthal, the colonial government registered all land grants "to prevent errors or future arguments," and it exempted newcomers from taxes for several years. Best of all, food was plentiful, no feudal obligations or serfdom existed, and members of Protestant denominations had "freedom of religion and conscience."

South Carolina is one of the most fertile landscapes to be found . . . preferable in many respects to the terrain in Germany, as well as in England. . . . Game, fish, and birds, as well as waterfowl such as swans, geese, and ducks, occur there in such plentiful numbers that . . . newcomers can sustain themselves if

necessary . . . until they have cleared a piece of land, sown seeds, and gathered in a harvest. . . . Among other things, there can be found in the wild so-called "Indian chickens" [turkeys], some of which weigh about 40 pounds or even more. These exist in incredible numbers. . . .

Hunting game, fishing, and bird-catching are free to anyone, but one shouldn't cross the borders of neighbors or of the Indians [who] live in complete peace and friendship with our families. In addition, their number decreases while the number of our people (namely the Europeans) increases. . . . Lumber can be found there in abundance, especially the most beautiful oaks, but also many of the nicest chestnuts and nut trees which are used by many for building and are considered better than oaks. One can also find beeches, spruces, cypresses, cedars, laurels, myrtle, and many other varieties.

Hogs can be raised very easily in great numbers at little cost, because there are huge forests everywhere and the ground is covered with acorns. . . . Above all, the breeding of horses, cows, sheep, hogs and many other kinds of domestic livestock proceeds excellently, because pastures can be found almost everywhere, and the livestock can remain in the fields the whole year, as it gets no colder in Carolina in the middle of winter than it does in Germany in April or October. . . . Because of the multiplication of livestock, almost no household in Carolina (after residing there a few years) can justifiably be called poor.

As far as vegetables and fruits are concerned, Indian corn predominates, thriving in such a way that one can harvest it twice a year and grow it wherever one wants to. Our local cereals such as wheat,

several thousand French Protestants escaped illegally and sought refuge in America. They established small communities such as those at New Rochelle in New York and along South Carolina's Santee River. South Carolina's governor protested against the Huguenots' early political activity: "Shall the Frenchmen, who cannot speak our language, make our laws?" But everywhere, they intermarried with the English and prospered in commerce. By the 1760s, several families with humble Huguenot origins—among them the Faneuils in Boston and the Laurenses, Manigaults, and Ravenels in Charleston—had amassed enormous fortunes.

At a time when France and Great Britain were at war, another infusion of French-speaking refugees, the Acadians, fared less well. In 1755, authorities evicted French colonials from Acadia in British Nova Scotia, fearing they might take up arms for France. Officials burned their homes and deported more than 6,000 of them to the various coastal colonies farther south. Mistreated for their Catholicism and feared as enemies during wartime, the Acadians struggled to get by. Resented in their new homes, many moved on to French Louisiana, where the Acadians, or **Cajuns,** became a lasting cultural force.

Scotland provided a much larger flow of migrants than France, stemming from two different sources. A growing stream of families, at least 30,000 people by 1770, came from Scotland itself. They were pushed by poverty, land scarcity, famines, and a failed political rebellion in 1745. In addition, a larger group known as the Scots-Irish came from Ulster in

LONDON: Printed for J. Baker, at the Black-Boy in Pater-Noster-Row. 1710.

■ In 1709, roughly 13,000 German immigrants seeking passage to America encamped for months at Blackheath, near London. The British government supplied them with tents, blankets, bread, and cheese, and churchgoers prayed for their welfare. But other Britons protested that the German strangers took "bread out of the mouths of our native handicraft men and laboring people, and increase the number of our poor which are too many and too great a burden to our nation already." Most of the refugees reached North America, serving as the vanguard for later German migration.

Courtesy, Dartmouth University Library

seeds. . . . There can already be found different kinds of our local apples. . . . As far as cabbage, beets, beans, peas, and other garden plants are concerned, not only do our local plants grow very well, but there are also many other varieties with excellent taste that are completely unknown to us. . . . Newcomers will do well to acquire all sorts of iron tools and bring these along. . . . If someone has lived in Carolina for a time and he wants to go to another country, he may do so freely at any time.

QUESTIONS

1. *Study the picture and caption regarding German refugees near London. Is that situation similar to, or different from, conditions in a modern refugee camp that you have read about or seen in the news? Be specific.*

2. *Do any of Kocherthal's observations about the natural world relate to the ongoing Columbian Exchange described in Chapter 1?*

Source: Translations by Dorothee Lehlbach from Joshua von Kocherthal, *Ausfuehrlicher und umstaendlicher Bericht von der beruehmten Landschaft Carolina, in dem engellaendischen American gelegen* (Frankfurt: Georg Heinrich Oehrling, 2nd ed., 1709), in the Special Collections Library of Duke University.

rye, barley, and oats do well, but above all, rice thrives there as excellently as in any other part of the world, and it grows in such amounts that it can be loaded on ships and transported to other places. And as the inhabitants use rice so much and make much more profit from it than any other cereal, they are most keen on growing rice and there has been very little cultivation of other cereals.

All kinds of our fruits can be planted there, but . . . future arrivals would do well to bring along seedlings of any kind, or at least the

Northern Ireland. The British had encouraged these Scottish Presbyterians to settle in Ireland in the seventeenth century, displacing rebellious Irish Catholics. In Ulster the Scottish newcomers soon faced commercial and political restrictions from Parliament and the Anglican Church. By 1770, nearly 60,000 Scots-Irish had left Ireland for America.

Another stream, German-speaking immigrants, nearly equaled the combined flow of Scots and Scots-Irish settlers. They began to arrive shortly after 1700 as religious persecution, chronic land shortages, and generations of warfare pushed whole communities out of southern Germany and neighboring Switzerland. Roughly 30,000 migrated in the 1750s; by 1770 the total had reached 85,000. These refugees generally came as whole families, and they usually took up farmland on the fringes of the colonies. Germans occupied the Mohawk Valley in New York and Virginia's Shenandoah Valley, and they fanned out from Germantown across the rich farmland of Pennsylvania. Swiss founded New Bern, North Carolina, in 1710. Migrants from Salzburg established New Ebenezer near Savannah, Georgia, in 1734.

Almost all of the white, non-English newcomers, including several thousand migrants from Wales, were Protestant Christians. Many clung to their language and traditions. But most arrivals learned English, and their children intermarried with English settlers. A French visitor described a typical American "whose grandfather was an Englishman, whose wife is Dutch, whose son married a French woman, and whose present four sons have now four wives of different nations."

The Varied Economic Landscape

■ *What role did geography play in shaping the emerging regional colonial economies?*

Population growth had consequences, and the changes began at the water's edge. Ships carrying newcomers docked most often at Boston, New York, Philadelphia, or Charleston. Each of these deepwater ports grew from a village to a bustling commercial hub, absorbing manufactured goods from Britain and shipping colonial produce abroad. All four towns spawned secondary ports located on neighboring rivers. In contrast, Chesapeake Bay had no single dominant port. There, Annapolis, Alexandria, and Norfolk all expanded, joined by the new town of Baltimore. But given the bay's many rivers, Atlantic ships often visited riverside plantations and villages to conduct separate business.

Colonial Products

In Chesapeake Bay and elsewhere, inland commerce was conducted by boat wherever possible. Hartford and Springfield on the Connecticut River, Kingston and Albany on the Hudson, Wilmington and Trenton on the Delaware, and Savannah and Augusta on the Savannah all became active riverside trading centers. Richmond, Virginia, which began as a trading post at the falls of the James River, already had 250 inhabitants when it incorporated as a town in 1742. Trails and former Indian paths connected these river-based communities, easing the way for travelers in the hinterland. By the 1740s, a pathway known as the Great Wagon Road headed southwest from Philadelphia to Winchester in Virginia's Shenandoah Valley and then south through gaps in the Blue Ridge Mountains to the Piedmont region of Carolina.

Widening networks of contact, using boats and wagons, extended inland from the primary seaports. Expanding fleets of ships tied each major hub to distant Atlantic ports. As a result, farmsteads and villages that had been largely self-sufficient before 1710 gradually became linked to wider markets. Local production still met most needs.

> *As local commercial systems gained coherence and strength, a string of regional economies developed along the Atlantic seaboard.*

But increasingly, the opportunity existed to obtain a new tool, a piece of cloth, or a printed almanac from far away. The new possibility of obtaining such goods lured farmers to grow crops for market rather than plant only for home consumption.

As local commercial systems gained coherence and strength, a string of regional economies developed along the Atlantic seaboard. Coastal vessels and a few muddy roads linked them tenuously to one another. But geographical and human differences gave each a character of its own. Migration patterns reinforced this diversity, since arrivals from Europe often sought out areas where others already spoke their language or shared their form of worship. The influx of German farmers through Philadelphia, for example, gave unique traits to Pennsylvania. (Because the newcomers spoke German, or *Deutsch,* they became known as Pennsylvania Dutch.) The rising importation of Africans helped shape the economy and culture of Chesapeake Bay, and of coastal South Carolina. Besides the diversity among arriving peoples, American ecological differences also played a role. Variations in land and climate contributed to the emergence of five distinctive economic regions along the Atlantic coast.

SOURCES OF GAIN IN THE CAROLINAS AND GEORGIA

Two related but distinctive regions took shape along the southeastern coast, linked respectively to the two Carolina colonies. The larger one centered on the lowcountry of coastal South Carolina and Georgia. There, the warm current of the Gulf Stream moving north

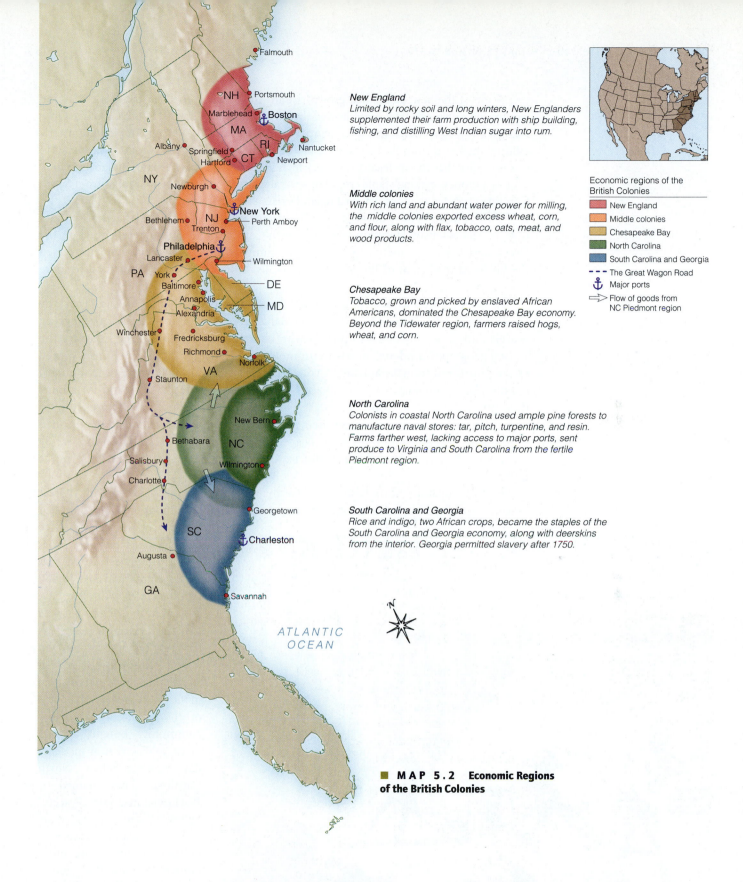

New England
Limited by rocky soil and long winters, New Englanders supplemented their farm production with ship building, fishing, and distilling West Indian sugar into rum.

Middle colonies
With rich land and abundant water power for milling, the middle colonies exported excess wheat, corn, and flour, along with flax, tobacco, oats, meat, and wood products.

Chesapeake Bay
Tobacco, grown and picked by enslaved African Americans, dominated the Chesapeake Bay economy. Beyond the Tidewater region, farmers raised hogs, wheat, and corn.

North Carolina
Colonists in coastal North Carolina used ample pine forests to manufacture naval stores: tar, pitch, turpentine, and resin. Farms farther west, lacking access to major ports, sent produce to Virginia and South Carolina from the fertile Piedmont region.

South Carolina and Georgia
Rice and indigo, two African crops, became the staples of the South Carolina and Georgia economy, along with deerskins from the interior. Georgia permitted slavery after 1750.

Economic regions of the British Colonies

- New England
- Middle colonies
- Chesapeake Bay
- North Carolina
- South Carolina and Georgia
- The Great Wagon Road
- Major ports
- Flow of goods from NC Piedmont region

■ **M A P 5 . 2   Economic Regions of the British Colonies**

from Florida along the Sea Islands provided a long growing season. It also assured mild winters, in contrast to Europe, meaning that cattle and hogs could forage in the woods unattended for most of the year. As livestock multiplied, lowcountry settlers sold meat, barrel staves, and firewood to the sugar islands of the West Indies, purchasing African slave labor in return.

Some of the newcomers had grown rice in Africa before their enslavement. Planting rice for their own use, they soon showed that the crop could thrive in South Carolina. Once African know-how made clear the potential for rice cultivation, a system of plantation agriculture, imported from Barbados, took hold quickly after 1700. Rice production spread to Georgia after that colony legalized slavery in 1751. Another African plant, indigo, also took root as a money-making staple crop. For several generations after 1740, indigo from South Carolina provided the blue dye for England's rising textile industry.

On Charleston's busy docks, casks of deerskins piled up beside the barrels of rice and indigo. The extensive deerskin trade in South Carolina and Georgia depended on the Creek and Cherokee men who hunted the animals and the women who processed the hides. At the height of the trade in the 1730s, Indian and white hunters killed more than a million deer per year.

In North Carolina, a second regional economy evolved. North of Cape Fear, the sandy barrier islands known as the Outer Banks prevented easy access for oceangoing vessels and gave protection to pirates who harassed Atlantic shipping. Because the coastal geography hindered efforts to promote staple crop agriculture, colonists turned to the pine forest to make a living. A wide band of longleaf pine bordered the southern coastal plain from Virginia to Texas. In North Carolina it stretched inland for a hundred miles. With labor, this pine forest yielded an abundance of naval stores: the tar and pitch used by sailors to protect their ships and rigging. Workers hauled the finished products to Wilmington on the Cape Fear River, the colony's best outlet to the sea. By the 1770s, the port was well known for exporting naval stores, and a dozen sawmills dotted the river.

Farther inland, Scots-Irish and German families moved down the Great Wagon Road after 1740 to carve out farms across the Carolina Piedmont on lands controlled largely by several absentee owners in Britain. By 1763, Ben Franklin estimated that Pennsylvania had lost 10,000 families to North Carolina. Typical of this migration were the Moravians, a German-speaking religious group who established towns at Nazareth and Bethlehem, Pennsylvania, in the 1740s. In 1753, members of the expanding Moravian community bought a tract of 100,000 acres near modern-day Winston-Salem, North Carolina. They named it Wachovia, meaning "Peaceful Valley." Within several years they had developed prosperous farms, a pottery shop, and a tannery around their initial settlement, called Bethabara. The newcomers bartered seeds and tools with one another and shipped extra produce overland to South Carolina and Virginia.

Schomburg Center for Research in Black Culture, New York Public Library

■ In North Carolina, black workers cut pine trees and then burned the wood in closed ovens to turn pine resin into tar and pitch. These so-called naval stores were sealed into barrels and used by sailors to protect the ropes on ships.

John Moale, engraving, 1752. The I. N. Phelps Stokes Collection, The New York Public Library

BALTIMORE IN 1752,

■ In 1729, Maryland planters founded Baltimore to provide a port on Chesapeake Bay for shipping tobacco. The town had only 50 homes and 200 inhabitants when this 1752 sketch was made, but the seaport grew rapidly after that.

CHESAPEAKE BAY'S TOBACCO ECONOMY

North of the Carolinas, farmers in the colonies bordering Chesapeake Bay committed to tobacco production in the seventeenth century. They clung to that staple crop despite a long decline in its market price. After 1710, demand for tobacco revived and prices rose again, in part because snuff (pulverized tobacco inhaled through the nostrils) became popular among Europeans. Tobacco continued to dominate the Chesapeake economy.

However, local conditions in parts of Virginia and Maryland prompted crop diversification as the century progressed. Constant tobacco planting depleted the soil. Moreover, most farms lay far from any navigable river, and rolling huge casks of tobacco many miles to market proved expensive. Wheat and corn thus became important secondary staples. These new crops, along with flax, hemp, and apples for making cider, provided a buffer against poor tobacco harvests and spurred related activities such as building wagons, making barrels, and constructing mills. These trades, in turn, produced widening networks of local exchange and prosperity for white yeoman families, with or without slaves.

Before 1700, all the mainland colonies could be described as *societies with slaves.* After that, the northern colonies continued to allow enslavement, but they never relied on it. In contrast, the southern colonies, except for certain inland farmlands settled from the north, shifted early in the eighteenth century to become something different: full-fledged *slave societies,* tied economically and culturally to slavery. By midcentury, plantation owners remained less wealthy than their counterparts in the West Indies who lived off the profits of slave-grown sugar. But on average, members of the southern elite controlled far more wealth than their counterparts in the North. The profits of the plantation system spread widely through the rest of the European American community. By the 1770s, whites in the South averaged more than twice as much wealth per person as whites in the North. An estimate for 1774 puts the average white Southerner's net worth at £93, a sharp contrast to the comparable figure for counterparts in the middle colonies (£46) and New England (£38).

NEW ENGLAND TAKES TO THE SEA

North of Chesapeake Bay, two overlapping economic regions emerged: the long-established New England colonies and the somewhat newer and more prosperous middle colonies.

> *In timber-rich New England, shipbuilding prospered. Colonists established shipyards at the mouth of nearly every river.*

New England faced peculiar disadvantages, beginning with the rocky soil. Ancient glaciers had strewn stones across the landscape, and it was tedious work to haul them off the fields to build endless stone walls. As imports from London increased, New Englanders found no staple crop that could be sold directly to Britain to create a balance of trade. All the beaver had been hunted, and much of the best land had been occupied. The region's farm families had adapted well to the challenging environment and short growing seasons. Both men and women worked on handicrafts during the long, hard winters, and networks of community exchange yielded commercial prosperity in many towns. But with a rapidly growing population, successive generations had less land to divide among their children.

Increasingly, young men with little prospect of inheriting prime farmland turned to the sea for a living. In timber-rich New England, shipbuilding prospered. Colonists established shipyards at the mouth of nearly every river, drawing skilled carpenters and willing deckhands to the coast. By 1763, Marblehead, Massachusetts, with a fleet of a hundred ships, had grown to 5,000 people. That made it the sixth largest town in the thirteen colonies, behind only Philadelphia, New York, Boston, Charleston, and Newport, Rhode Island. Providence, at the top of Narragansett Bay, opened its first shipyard in 1711 and soon became a competing seaport.

By 1770, three out of every four ships sailing from New England to a British port were owned by colonial residents. In contrast, in the southern colonies from Maryland to Georgia, the proportion was only one in eight.

On Nantucket Island off Cape Cod, whaling became a new source of income. For generations, the islanders had cooked the blubber of beached whales to extract oil for lamps. In 1715, they outfitted several vessels to harpoon sperm whales at sea and then return with the whale blubber in casks to be rendered into oil. In the 1750s, they installed brick ovens on deck and began cooking the smelly blubber at sea in huge iron vats. This change turned the whaling vessel into a floating factory, and it prompted longer voyages in larger ships. By the 1760s, Nantucket whalers were cruising the Atlantic for four or five months at a time and returning loaded with barrels of whale oil.

LISTEN

"The Connecticut Peddler"

The fishing industry also prospered. All along the coast, villagers dispatched boats to the Grand Banks, the fishing grounds off Newfoundland. When the vessels returned, laden with fish, the townspeople graded, dried, and salted the catch. The colonists sent the best cod to Europe in exchange for wine and dry goods. Yankee captains carried the lowest grade to the Caribbean sugar islands, where planters bought "refuse fish" as food for their slaves. In return, skippers brought back kegs of molasses to be distilled into rum. By 1770, 140 American distilleries, most of them in New England, produced 5 million gallons of rum annually. Much of it went to colonial taverns and Indian trading posts. But some also went to Africa, aboard ships from Britain and New England. American rum, along with various wines and spirits from Europe, made up one-fifth of the total value of goods used to purchase African slaves.

As the New England economy stabilized, it became a mixed blessing for women. On the farm, their domestic labors aided the household economy and helped to offset bad

Solving the Problem of Longitude at Sea

■ **English clockmaker John Harrison, the son of a carpenter, revolutionized global navigation in the 1760s with a reliable timepiece that allowed captains to calculate their longitude at sea.**

Even before Columbus, sailors could determine their latitude, or north–south position, from the stars. But finding one's exact longitude, or east–west position, on the trackless ocean remained far more elusive. It depended on measuring time accurately, but pendulum clocks were no use on the rolling sea, and early pocket watches could be thrown off by changes of temperature and humidity. Again and again, mistakes in estimating longitude at sea proved disastrous. By the turn of the eighteenth century, Europeans considered this problem the greatest single barrier to the expansion of overseas trade.

Then in 1707, a dense autumn fog blanketed five British troop ships as they sailed north past the coast of France toward the west coast of England. The admiral was sure his course lay well to the west of the Scilly Isles, which protrude dangerously from the southwest tip of Britain. Indeed, when a sailor questioned the accuracy of their position, the commander ordered him hanged for insubordination. But hours later, on the night of October 22, the fleet foundered on the sharp rocks of the Scillies. Four huge ships broke up and sank; 2,000 men died in the pounding surf.

The scope of this disaster pushed British officials to redouble efforts to solve "the longitude problem." In 1714, Parliament passed the Longitude Act, establishing a Board of Longitude and offering £20,000 (roughly $12 million in today's money) to anyone who could devise a reliable way to determine longitude at sea. After four decades of experimentation, an English clockmaker named John Harrison (1693–1776) came up with a viable answer. Harrison devised a seaworthy and compact pocket watch that maintained accurate time over long periods, allowing navigators to determine longitude.

Using Harrison's chronometer, captains could set the time at the Royal Observatory in Greenwich, England, before departing. Then at sea months later, if the timepiece indicated midnight "Greenwich time" when the sun showed high noon locally, they knew they were halfway around the world, at a longitude of 180 degrees from Greenwich. Soon mariners everywhere on the globe computed their longitude east or west of Greenwich, which came to mark the prime meridian, or zero longitude, on later maps.

QUESTIONS

1. *Why was knowledge of exact longitude so important to sea captains who had no access to our modern global positioning system (GPS)?*

2. *What is the longitude of your own town? When it is noon at your home, what time is it in Greenwich, England?*

harvests. Mothers continued to teach their daughters to spin yarn, weave cloth, sew clothes, plant gardens, raise chickens, tend livestock, and churn butter. The products from these chores could be used at home or sold in a nearby village to buy consumer goods. While the husband held legal authority over the home, a good wife served as a "deputy husband," managing numerous household affairs, or perhaps earning money as a midwife to help make ends meet. She took charge entirely if her husband passed away or went to sea.

But for all their labors, women seemed to lose economic and legal standing to men as New England towns became larger and more orderly. Networks of local officials, consisting entirely of men, drafted statutes and legal codes that reinforced male privileges. Women found it difficult to obtain credit or receive a business license, and the law barred married women from making contracts, limiting their chance for activities outside the home. Gradually, male apothecaries and physicians with a smattering of formal training pushed traditional midwives away from the bedside. Even in the port towns, where women outnumbered men, their rights were limited, and poor women faced particular scrutiny. Selectmen and overseers of the poor had the power to remove children from a widowed mother and place them in the **almshouse.**

ECONOMIC EXPANSION IN THE MIDDLE COLONIES

The fifth regional economy, the one that flourished in the middle colonies between New England and Chesapeake Bay, improved upon these two neighboring worlds. The Europeans who resettled Indian lands in Delaware, Pennsylvania, New Jersey, and New York found a favorable climate, rich soil, and numerous millstreams. Unlike New Englanders, they developed a reliable staple by growing an abundance of grain. They exported excess wheat, flour, and bread as effectively as Southerners shipped tobacco and rice. But unlike the planters in Virginia and South Carolina, middle-colony farmers did not become locked in the vicious cycle of making large investments in enslaved workers and exporting a single agricultural staple. Instead, they developed a more balanced economy, using mostly free labor. Besides grain products, they also exported quantities of flaxseed, barrel staves, livestock, and pig iron. Large infusions of money from Britain during its long war against France in the 1750s further boosted this prosperous economy.

Whereas the Chesapeake had no dominant seaport, the middle colonies boasted two major ports of entry. Hundreds of Europeans, skilled in a craft and unwilling to compete with unpaid slave artisans in the South, flocked to the middle-colony seaports instead. Both Philadelphia and New York grew faster than rival ports in the mid-eighteenth century, passing Boston in size in the 1750s. Each city doubled its number of dwellings in the two decades after 1743, as brick structures with slate roofs replaced older wooden homes covered with inflammable cedar shingles. But new houses could not meet the ever increasing demand. By 1763, Philadelphia had more than 20,000 people, New York had nearly as many, and both cities faced a set of urban problems that had already hit Boston.

As the port towns grew, they became more impersonal, with a greater economic and social distance between rich and poor. Large homes and expensive imports characterized life among the urban elite. In contrast, the poorest city dwellers lacked property and the means to subsist. By the 1760s, Philadelphia's almshouse and the new Pennsylvania Hospital for the Sick Poor were overflowing. In response, Philadelphia's Quaker leaders established a voluntary Committee to Alleviate the Miseries of the Poor, handing out firewood and blankets to the needy. They also built a "Bettering House," patterned on Boston's workhouse, that provided poor Philadelphians with food and shelter in exchange for work.

In an effort to limit urban poverty, authorities in New York and Philadelphia moved newcomers to the countryside, where Dutch and German settlers had already established an efficient farming tradition. As immigration rose after 1730, the burgeoning region slowly expanded its economy far up the Hudson Valley, east into Connecticut and Long Island, and south toward Maryland.

The farm frontier pushed west as well. The acquisitive Thomas Penn had inherited control of Pennsylvania from his more idealistic father, founder William Penn. In 1737, the young proprietor defrauded the Delaware Indians out of land they occupied west of the Delaware River. In the infamous Walking Purchase, Penn claimed a boundary that could be walked in a day and half. Then Penn's men cleared a path through the woods and sent horsemen along to assist his runners, who covered more than fifty-five miles in thirty-six hours. In all, the fast-moving agents took title to 1,200 square miles of potential farmland near modern Easton and Allentown, Pennsylvania. Land-hungry settlers pressed the reluctant Delaware west toward the Allegheny Mountains and occupied the rich river valleys of eastern Pennsylvania. Land agents and immigrant farmers called the fertile region "the best poor man's country."

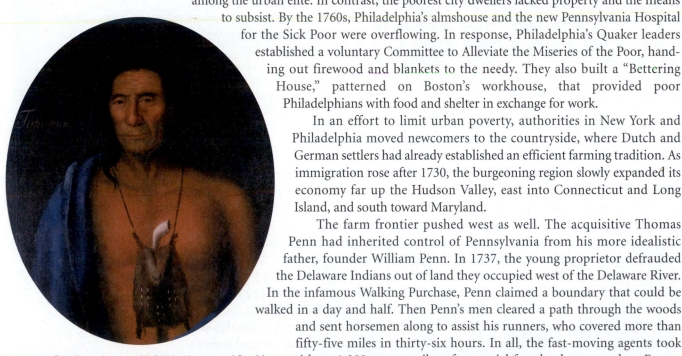

■ Soon after the Delaware chief Tishcohan posed for this 1735 portrait, his people lost valuable land due to Pennsylvania's notorious Walking Purchase.

Matters of Faith: The Great Awakening

■ *Why did economic and demographic growth go hand in hand with fresh religious intensity after 1730?*

Philadelphia epitomized the commercial dynamism of the eighteenth-century British colonies. The city was a hub in the fastest-growing economic region on the Atlantic seaboard. Ben Franklin, arriving there in 1723 at age seventeen, achieved particular success. Within seven years he owned a printing business. Within twenty-five years he was wealthy enough to retire, devoting himself to science, politics, and social improvement. He created a lending library, developed an efficient stove, promoted schools and hospitals, supported scientific and philosophical organizations, and won fame in Europe for his experiments with electricity.

The outburst of scientific inquiry and religious skepticism spreading through the Atlantic world at the time became known as the Enlightenment, and its spirit of rational questioning and reason was greatly aided by the printing press. In America, Franklin and his fellow printers personified the new Age of Enlightenment. By 1760, the British mainland colonies had twenty-nine printing establishments, more presses per capita than in any country in Europe. These presses squeezed out eighteen weekly newspapers and countless public notices, fostering political and business communication throughout the colonies. American printers also published an array of religious material, for the colonial spirit of worldly enterprise existed uneasily beside a longing for spiritual community and social perfection. The story of another Pennsylvania printer offers an apt example.

> *The colonial spirit of worldly enterprise existed uneasily beside a longing for spiritual community and social perfection.*

In 1720, three years before Franklin arrived in Pennsylvania, Conrad Beissel migrated to Philadelphia from Germany. He lived and preached in nearby Germantown; in 1738 he withdrew farther west to lead a life of unadorned simplicity. Soon other men and women joined him at his retreat near modern-day Lancaster, Pennsylvania. There they created Ephrata Community, the earliest of many wilderness utopias in North America. The communal experiment lasted for more than a generation, supporting itself by operating a printing press. Although Beissel pursued the same trade as Franklin, his experience as a dedicated seeker of spiritual truth represents a very different and important side of colonial life.

In the first half of the eighteenth century, colonists witnessed surprising breakthroughs in religious toleration but also bitter controversies within the ministry. In addition, they experienced a revivalist outpouring, with roots in Europe and America, that later became known as the **Great Awakening.** This stirring began in the 1730s, and it gained momentum through the visits from England of a charismatic preacher named George Whitefield (pronounced Whitfield). In most colonies, the aftershocks of the Awakening persisted for a full generation.

SEEDS OF RELIGIOUS TOLERATION

The same population shifts that made Britain's mainland colonies more diverse in the eighteenth century also created a new Babel of religious voices that included many non-Christians. Africans, the largest of all the new contingents, brought their own varied beliefs across the Atlantic. Some slaves from Portuguese Angola had had exposure to Catholicism in their homeland. But most Africans retained as much of their traditional religions and cultures as possible under the circumstances. At first, they were skeptical toward Christianity. An Anglican missionary recalled one black South Carolinian saying that he "preferred to live by what he could remember" from Africa. Christian efforts to convert Native Americans also had mixed results. A minister living near the Iroquois reported that Indians would beat a drum to disrupt his services and then "go away Laughing."

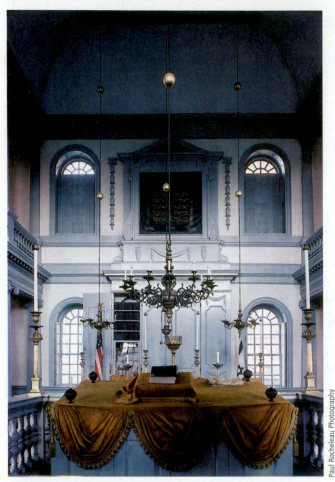

Paul Rocheleau Photography

■ Members of the Jewish community in Newport started Touro Synagogue in 1759, a century after the first arrival of their ancestors in the Rhode Island seaport. Completed in 1763, this gem of colonial architecture is the oldest existing synagogue in the United States.

Another non-Christian contingent, Jewish immigrants, remained few in number, with only several hundred families by 1770. Merchants rather than farmers, they established communities in several Atlantic ports, beginning in Dutch New Amsterdam (1654) and Newport (1658). Most were Sephardic Jews; that is, their ancestral roots were in Spain and Portugal. They came by way of the Caribbean, reaching Charleston in 1697, Philadelphia after 1706, and Savannah in 1733. A few of their children merged into the Protestant culture, but more than 80 percent of Jewish young people (including a handful of Ashkenazi Jews with ties to central Europe) found partners within their own small communities.

The majority of eighteenth-century newcomers to the British colonies were Christians. A few, such as the Acadians, were Catholics, but the rest had some Protestant affiliation. In the two centuries since the Reformation, numerous competing Protestant denominations had sprung up across Europe. Now this wide array made itself felt in America, as Presbyterians, Quakers, Lutherans, Baptists, Methodists, and smaller sects all increased in numbers. To attract immigrant families, most colonies abolished laws that favored a single "established" denomination. Nevertheless, New England remained firmly Congregational, and the southern gentry (plus merchant elite everywhere) concentrated increasingly within the Anglican Church.

Rhode Island had emphasized the separation of church and state from the start, and Pennsylvania had likewise favored toleration, both as a matter of principle and as a practical recruitment device to attract new settlers. Since migration from Europe was a demanding ordeal, those who took the risk were often people with strong religious convictions. Such newcomers looked for assurances that they could practice their religion freely, and colonies competed to accommodate them. In many places, religious tests still limited who could hold public office, but tolerance for competing beliefs was expanding.

Many felt that if any institution threatened the growing religious toleration in the colonies, it was, ironically, the British king's own denomination. The monarch headed the Anglican Church, and it had influential American members, including almost every colonial governor. Repeated talk by the Church of England about installing a resident bishop in America aroused suspicions among colonists who worshipped in other denominations. This was especially true in New England, where Congregationalists had long opposed ideas of religious hierarchy. In 1750, Boston, which had eighteen churches, rose up against a plan for an Anglican bishop. In a passionate sermon, Reverend Jonathan Mayhew preached that the town must keep "all imperious bishops, and other clergymen who love to lord it over God's heritage, from getting their feet into the stirrup."

THE ONSET OF THE GREAT AWAKENING: PIETISM AND GEORGE WHITEFIELD

As relative toleration became a hallmark of the British colonies, no one benefited more than German-speaking Protestant groups. Numerous religious sects, such as the Moravians, Mennonites, Schwenkfelders, and Dunkers, were fleeing persecution and poverty at home. As their numbers multiplied after 1730, hymns in German became a common sound on

Sabbath day. In 1743, before any American printer produced an English-language Bible, a press in Pennsylvania put out a complete German edition of Luther's Bible, using type brought from Frankfurt.

Collectively, these newcomers were part of a European reform movement to renew piety and spiritual vitality among Protestant churchgoers in an age of increasing rationalism and worldliness. Pietism, as this "Second Reformation" was called, had roots in eastern Germany and stressed the need to restore emotion and intensity to worship that had become too rational, detached, and impersonal. The German pietists reached out after 1700 to inspire Huguenots in France and Presbyterians in Scotland. They influenced reformers in the Church of England such as John Wesley, the founder of Methodism and a teacher at Oxford University. Through Wesley, pietist ideas touched George Whitefield during his time at Oxford in the class of 1736. Over the next decade, "the boy parson" became the first transatlantic celebrity. Hailed as a preaching prodigy, he sparked a widespread religious awakening in the American colonies.

As a boy growing up in England, George Whitefield left school at age twelve to work in the family tavern. But he still managed to attend college, and at Oxford he discovered Wesley and the pietists. He also discovered two other things: the lure of America and his calling to be a minister. His mentor, Wesley, had preached briefly in Georgia. So in 1738, at age twenty-three, Whitefield spent several months in the new colony, where he laid plans for an orphanage near Savannah.

Arriving back in England, Whitefield quickly achieved celebrity status. He drew large crowds with fiery sermons that criticized the Anglican Church. The evangelist's published *Journals,* priced at only sixpence, went through six editions in nine months. He also recruited an experienced publicist. In 1739, word of his popularity preceded him when he returned to America for an extended tour, the second of seven transatlantic journeys during his career. Building on religious stirrings already present in the colonies, Whitefield preached to huge and emotional crowds nearly 350 times in 15 months. He made appearances from Savannah to Boston, something no public figure had ever done.

The timing was perfect. Whitefield's brother was a wine merchant who understood the expanding networks of communication and consumption in the British Atlantic world. Whitefield realized that in America, as newspapers multiplied and roads increased, he could advertise widely and travel extensively. Other ministers from England had remarked in frustration that most colonists knew "little of the nature of religion, or of the constitution of the church." At times, each person seemed to hold to "some religious whim or scruple peculiar to himself." Whitefield thrived on this vitality and confusion. He had little taste for Protestant debates over church organization and sectarian differences. Instead, he believed that an evangelical minister should simply preach the Bible fervently to a wide array of avid listeners. Everywhere he went, Whitefield served as a catalyst for religious activity.

Courtesy, Winterthur Museum (63.639)

■ When George Whitefield visited America in 1739, his preaching spurred the Great Awakening. "God shews me," he wrote in his journal, "that America must be my place for action."

"THE DANGER OF AN UNCONVERTED MINISTRY"

The heightened commotion in American churches had local origins as well. The same tension felt in European parishes—between worldly, rational pursuits and an emotional quest for grace and salvation—also troubled colonial congregations. Occasional local revivals had taken place in America for decades. The most dramatic one occurred in Northampton, Massachusetts, in 1734–1735, spurred by a talented minister named Jonathan Edwards. As the colonies' most gifted theologian, Edwards anticipated Whitefield's argument that dry, rote "head-knowledge"

IMAGE

Jonathan Edwards

made a poor substitute for "a true living faith in Jesus Christ." "Our people do not so much need to have their heads stored," Edwards observed, "as to have their hearts touched."

DOCUMENT

Edwards, "Sinners in the Hands of an Angry God"

In a fast-growing society, who would prepare suitable church leaders for the next generation? Candidates for the ministry could train at Harvard College (founded 1636), William and Mary (1693), Yale (1707), or one of several small academies. But these institutions could not instruct sufficient numbers. The shortage of educated ministers, combined with steady geographic expansion, meant that pulpit vacancies were common. A minister might oversee several parishes. Even if he tended only a single one, the great distances separating parishioners made it hard for any pastor to travel widely enough to address their needs. Feeling neglected, people voiced their dissatisfaction over the shortage of ministers.

Problems in the pulpit included quality as well as quantity. Many college graduates had too much "head-knowledge" and too little common touch. Their fluency in Latin and Greek often earned them more disdain than respect from down-to-earth congregations. Most foreign-born ministers, such as Anglicans sent from England and Presbyterians from Scotland, had failed to find good positions at home. Too often, they showed limited appreciation for the local church members who paid their salaries, and they resented those who criticized their ministries.

One such critic was William Tennent, a Scots-Irish immigrant who arrived in Pennsylvania with his family in 1716. Dismayed by the cold, unemotional outlook of Presbyterian ministers, Tennent opened a one-room academy in a log house to train his four sons and other young men for the ministry. Local Presbyterian authorities challenged his credentials and disparaged the teachings of his "Log College." Eventually, the school moved and grew, becoming linked to the new College of New Jersey in 1746, which later evolved into Princeton University. But before this happened, Tennent's preacher sons allied themselves with Whitefield and managed to shake the colonial religious establishment to its roots.

One of Tennent's sons, Gilbert, eventually led a Presbyterian church in Philadelphia created by Whitefield's supporters. In 1740, at the time of Whitefield's triumphal tour, young

Gilbert Tennent delivered a blistering sermon entitled "The Danger of an Unconverted Ministry" that became a manifesto for the revival. Cutting to the heart of the matter, he condemned the "sad security" offered by incompetent, uncaring, and greedy ministers. "They are as blind as Moles, and as dead as Stones," he charged, "without any spiritual Taste and Relish." He argued that congregations should turn away from these "Orthodox, Letter-learned . . . Old Pharisee-Teachers" and listen to traveling preachers instead. It was "an unscriptural Infringment on Christian Liberty," Tennent proclaimed, "to bind men to a particular Minister, against their Judgement and Inclinations."

THE CONSEQUENCES OF THE GREAT AWAKENING

Whitefield hailed Gilbert Tennant and his brothers as "burning and shining lights" of a new kind. All the ministers and worshipers who joined in the movement began to call themselves "New Lights." Opponents, whom they dismissed as "Old Lights," continued to defend a learned clergy and emphasized head-knowledge on the difficult road to salvation. The Old Lights opposed the disruptions caused by so-called "itinerant ministers" who traveled freely from parish to parish without invitation. The New Light ministers, in contrast, appealed to people's emotions and stressed the prospect of a more democratic salvation open to all. They defended their wanderings, which made them more accessible to a broader public and less likely to become set in their ways. "Our Blessed Saviour was an Itinerant Preacher," they reminded their critics; "he Preach'd in no other Way."

Just as New Light preachers moved readily across traditional parish boundaries, they also transcended the lines between different Protestant sects. Their simple evangelical message reached across a wide social spectrum to diverse audiences of every denomination. Moreover, their stress on communal singing, expressive emotion, and the prospects for personal salvation drew special attention from those on the fringes of the culture, such as young people, women, and the poor. Not surprisingly, New Light ministers also made headway in spreading Christianity within various African American and Native American communities.

Members of the religious establishment, once secure as unchallenged leaders within their own church communities, now confronted a stark choice. Some powerful churchmen acknowledged their New Light critics and reluctantly welcomed the popular renegades into the local pulpits. Such a strategy might blunt the thrust of the revival, and it would surely raise church attendance. Other Old Lights, however, took the opposite approach: they clung to tradition and stability, challenging their new rivals openly. They condemned itinerancy and disputed the interlopers' right to preach. They mocked the faddish popularity of these overemotional zealots and even banned the New Light itinerants from local districts for the good of the parishioners.

> *Zealous New Light men and women tried to transcend the competing denominations and create a broad community of Protestant believers.*

In the end, neither tactic stemmed the upheaval, which peaked in the North in the 1740s and in the South during the 1750s and 1760s. Its long-term consequences were mixed. Zealous New Light men and women tried to transcend the competing denominations and create a broad community of Protestant believers. But for all their open-air preaching, the reformers could never create such unity, and they left behind no new set of doctrines or institutional structures. Nevertheless, they created an important legacy. First, they infused a new spirit of piety and optimism into American Christianity that countered older and darker Calvinist traditions. Second, they established a manner of fiery evangelical preaching that found a permanent place in American life. Most importantly, they underscored democratic tendencies in the New Testament gospels that many invoked in later years when faced with other apparent infringements of their liberties.

The French Lose a North American Empire

■ *What key factors undermined the French position in America in the decades after 1740?*

In 1739, while George Whitefield launched his tour of the English colonies and the Stono slave rebellion erupted in South Carolina, the French dreamed of expanding their American empire. When Pierre and Paul Mallet set out up the Mississippi River from New Orleans that year, the two French Canadians suspected that the Missouri River, the Mississippi's mightiest tributary, stretched to New Mexico. If so, they hoped to claim a new trading route for France. Pausing in Illinois to gather seven French Canadian recruits, the Mallet brothers pushed up the Missouri, hoping it flowed from the southwest.

But the river flowed from the northwest instead. Disappointed, the party left the river in Nebraska, purchased horses at an Omaha Indian village, and set off across the plains, reaching Santa Fe in July. After a nine-month stay, most of them returned east across the southern plains the next year. When the Mallets completed their enormous circuit and returned to New Orleans, they brought word from the West of Indian and Spanish eagerness to engage in greater trade. From their perspective, the future of France in America looked bright indeed. But the promise disappeared entirely within their lifetimes.

Veue et Perspectiue de la nouuelle Orleans 1726

FLEVVE   DE   St LOVIS   OV MISSISSIPI

Jean-Pierre Lassus, Vue et Perspective de la Nouvelle-Orleans, 1726. C.A.O.M. Aix-en-Provence (France) DFC Louisiane 71 (pf6B)

■ By 1726, New Orleans, with 100 cabins and nearly 1,000 inhabitants, was receiving shipments of trade goods from France and distributing them up the Mississippi River and its tributaries. Following a Louisiana hurricane in 1722, the levees along the waterfront were expanded, but flooding remains a threat to the low-lying city even today, as the huge devastation of Hurricane Katrina in 2005 made clear.

PROSPECTS AND PROBLEMS FACING FRENCH COLONISTS

In 1740, French colonists had grounds for cautious optimism. France already claimed a huge expanse of North America. Its wilderness empire ran strategically through the center of the continent. The potential for mineral resources and rich farmland seemed boundless, as French pioneers in the Illinois region already realized. No Europeans had shown greater skill in forging stable and respectful relations with Native Americans. A chain of isolated French forts stretched northward along the Mississippi River and then east to the lower Great Lakes and the St. Lawrence Valley. These posts facilitated trade with Native Americans and secured ties between Canada and Louisiana. With Indian support, more outposts could be built farther east near the Appalachian mountain chain to contain the English settlers and perhaps one day to conquer them.

At least three problems marred this scenario. First, the French population in America paled in comparison to the large number of English settlers. Canada still had fewer than 50,000 colonial inhabitants in 1740, whereas Britain's mainland colonies were rapidly approaching 1 million. Louisiana contained only 3,000 French people, living among nearly 4,000 enslaved Africans and 6,000 Native Americans. Second, French colonists lacked sufficient support from Paris to develop thriving communities and expand their Indian trade. The importation of goods from France was still meager and unpredictable. Finally, an ominous trickle of British hunters and settlers was beginning to cross the Appalachian chain. Carolina traders already had strong ties with the Chickasaw Indians living near the Mississippi River, and Virginia land speculators were eyeing lands in the Ohio Valley.

What seemed a promising situation for the French in 1740 was soon put to the test. Britain and France had long been on a collision course in North America. Colonial subjects of the two European superpowers had already clashed in a series of wars, with Indian allies playing crucial roles. After several decades of peace, warfare was about to resume. Two more contests, King George's War (1744–1748) and the French and Indian War (1754–1763) preoccupied colonists and Native Americans alike over the next two decades. In 1763, the Treaty of Paris ended the French and Indian War, part of a far broader conflict known in Europe as the Seven Years' War.

At that point, less than a quarter-century after the Mallet brothers' optimistic journey through the heartlands, the expansive French empire in North America suddenly vanished.

BRITISH SETTLERS CONFRONT THE THREAT FROM FRANCE

These colonial conflicts of the mid-eighteenth century, generally linked to wider warfare in Europe, had a significant impact on everyone living in the British mainland colonies. A few people took advantage of the disturbances to become rich. They provisioned troops, sold scarce wartime goods, sponsored profitable privateering ventures, or conducted forbidden trade with the enemy in the Caribbean. But many more people paid a heavy price because of war: a farm burned, a job lost, a limb amputated, a husband or father shot in battle or cut down by disease. From London's perspective, the Americans made ill-disciplined and reluctant soldiers. From the colonists' viewpoint, the British offered them too little respect and inadequate assistance.

Adding insult to injury, a hard-won victory on North American soil could be canceled out at the peace table in Europe. In 1745, during King William's War, Massachusetts called for an attack on Louisburg, the recently completed French fortress on Cape Breton Island that controlled access to the St. Lawrence River and nearby fishing grounds. After a long siege, the New England forces prevailed. But British diplomats rescinded the colonial victory, handing Louisburg back to France in 1748 in exchange for Madras in India.

Whatever their differences, the American colonists and the government in Britain saw potential in the land west of the Appalachian Mountains, and both were eager to challenge French claims there. In 1747, a group of colonial land speculators formed the Ohio Company of Virginia, seeking permission to develop western lands. Two years later the crown granted them rights to 200,000 acres south of the Ohio River if they would construct a fort in the area. Moving west and north, the Virginians hoped to occupy a valuable spot where the Monongahela and Allegheny rivers come together to form the Ohio River. The French had designs on the same strategic location (modern-day Pittsburgh, Pennsylvania) controlling the upper Ohio.

> *Throughout the British colonies in 1754, fears spread about the danger of French attacks and the loyalty of Native American allies.*

In 1753, the Virginia governor sent an untested young major in the colonial militia named George Washington—at age twenty-one already regarded as a promising officer—to warn the French to leave the area. The next spring, Virginia workers began erecting a fort at the Fork of the Ohio, but a larger French force drove them off and constructed Fort Duquesne on the coveted site. When Major Washington returned to the area with troops, he probed for enemy forces. In a skirmish on May 28, 1754, near modern Uniontown, Pennsylvania, his men killed ten French soldiers, the initial casualties in what eventually became history's first truly global war. With 450 men and meager supplies, Washington fortified his camp, calling it Fort Necessity, and dug in to prepare for a counterattack.

Throughout the British colonies in the early summer of 1754, fears spread about the danger of French attacks and the loyalty of Native American allies. Officials in London requested that all the colonies that had relations with the Iroquois send delegates to a special congress in Albany, New York, to improve that Indian alliance. Seven colonies sent twenty-three representatives, who hoped to strengthen friendship with the Iroquois nations and discuss a design for a union of the colonies.

With these goals in mind, the delegates to the Albany Congress adopted a proposal by Benjamin Franklin that called for a colonial confederation empowered to build forts and repel a French invasion. The colonies would be unified by an elected Grand Council and a president general appointed by the crown. The delegates hoped the design would be debated by colonial assemblies and implemented by an act of Parliament. But no colonial legislature ever ratified Franklin's far-sighted Albany Plan. "Everyone cries, a union is necessary," Franklin wrote, "but when they come to the manner and form of the union, their weak noodles are perfectly distracted."

■ **MAP 5.3** **The British Conquest of New France, 1754–1760**

British conquest of New France

- French settlements
- British settlements
- Iroquois settlements
- - - Land claimed by the Ohio Company of Virginia
- French victories
- British victories
- French forts
- British forts

1 Washington gives up Ft. Necessity to French, July 3–4, 1754

2 Braddock's army destroyed near Ft. Duquesne, July 9, 1755

3 British yield Ft. William Henry to Montcalm, Aug. 9, 1757

4 British capture French fort at Louisburg, July 26, 1758

5 British take Ft. Frontenac from the French, Aug. 27, 1758

6 Johnson captures Ft. Niagara from the French, July 25, 1759

7 Wolfe defeats Montcalm, Plains of Abraham, Sept. 13, 1759

8 Amherst accepts French surrender of Montreal, Sept. 8, 1760

The main distraction came from Pennsylvania. On July 3, word arrived that the French had defeated Washington's small force at Fort Necessity. But the British were not willing to give up their claims to the Ohio Valley without a fight. Taking the lead, the Virginia government asked for help from Britain in conducting a war against the French and their Native American allies. The crown responded by dispatching General Edward Braddock and two regiments of Irish troops to America. Early in 1755, his force arrived in Virginia, where preparations were already under way for a campaign to conquer Fort Duquesne. Washington accepted an unpaid position as an aide to Braddock, and in June the combined British and colonial army of 2,500 began a laborious march west to face the French.

AN AMERICAN FIGHT BECOMES A GLOBAL CONFLICT

The early stages of the war in America could hardly have been more disastrous for Britain or more encouraging for France. According to his own secretary, the aging Braddock was poorly qualified for command "in almost every respect." A French and Indian force ambushed his column in the forest near Fort Duquesne, cutting it to pieces in the most

Putting Mary Jemison on a Pedestal

In 1910, near the Genesee River east of Buffalo, New York, a statue was erected to commemorate the unusual life of Mary Jemison (1743–1833). Like all historical statues, this one connects two stories: the actual life of the individual, plus the worldview of the benefactor erecting the monument and the artist creating the work.

In 1743, Mary Jemison was born at sea, aboard a ship bound for Philadelphia. She was the fourth child of immigrants from northern Ireland, Jane and Thomas Jemison. The Scots-Irish family carved out a frontier farm in central Pennsylvania. Thomas's brother died in George Washington's defeat at Fort Necessity when the French and Indian War erupted in 1754. Four years later, Shawnee and French raiders destroyed the

Jemison farm, killing and scalping most of their captives during a forced march to the Ohio River. They spared fifteen-year-old Mary, and she was adopted into the Seneca tribe of the powerful Iroquois Confederacy.

Jemison soon became the wife of a Delaware Indian in Ohio and the mother of a son named Thomas. But with the war ending and her husband dead, she trekked more than 600 miles on foot, carrying her infant in a cradle board on her back, to the Seneca homeland in western New York. Staying there by choice, she remarried and became a respected Iroquois parent, landowner, and negotiator. Her descendants remain members of the Seneca nation.

At age eighty, still speaking English fluently, Jemison recounted her personal history to a frontier doctor named James Seaver. He published *A Narrative of the Life of Mary Jemison* (1824), and her first-person account went through numerous editions, making her an American folk figure. Half a century later, the book inspired the Buffalo businessman and philanthropist William Letchworth. A friend and benefactor of the Seneca, Letchworth had Jemison's remains buried at his estate on the scenic Genesee River (now a state park), and he commissioned a statue to mark her grave. The sculptor, H. K. Bush-Brown, studied moccasins, buckskins, and cradle boards in Native American museums and then cast his bronze figure of "the white woman of the Genesee," striding through the wilderness with her child strapped to her back. The powerful but ambiguous monument was unveiled shortly before Letchworth's death in 1910.

QUESTIONS

1. *Why did Mary Jemison's* Narrative *have such lasting appeal? Is the 1910 bronze by Bush-Brown intended to be realistic or idealized—or a bit of both?*

2. *Think of a statue you have encountered portraying a famous person. Does it matter when it was created, or by whom? What ideas or values was it intended to convey?*

thorough defeat of the century for a British army unit. Elsewhere, Indian raids battered the frontiers, spreading panic throughout the colonies. With the local militia away at war, fears of possible slave uprisings swept through the South. The French commander, the Marquis de Montcalm, struck into New York's Mohawk Valley from Lake Ontario in 1756, then pushed south down Lake Champlain and Lake George in 1757. After a seven-day siege, he took 2,000 prisoners at Fort William Henry. In an episode made famous in *The Last of the Mohicans,* France's Huron Indian allies killed more than 150 men and women after their release from the fort.

The change in British fortunes came with the new ministry of William Pitt, a vain but talented member of the House of Commons. Pitt was an expansionist committed to the growth of the British Empire at the expense of France. He brought a daring new strategy to the war effort, and he had the determination and bureaucratic skill to carry it out. Stymied in Europe by the military might of the French army, the British would now concentrate their forces instead on France's vulnerable and sparsely populated overseas colonies. Under Pitt, the British broadened the war into a global conflict, taking advantage of their superior naval power to fight on the coasts of Asia and Africa and in North America as well. By 1758, Britain had undertaken a costly military buildup in America, with nearly 50,000 troops.

MAP

The Seven Years' War

To win colonial support for his plan, Pitt promised to reimburse the colonies generously for their expenses. In the South, guns, ammunition, and trade goods flowed freely to Britain's Native American allies. In the North, France lost Louisburg again in July 1758. Fort Frontenac on Lake Ontario fell in August. In November, the French destroyed and abandoned Fort Duquesne. The British seized the strategic site at the Fork of the Ohio, erecting a new post (aptly named Fort Pitt) and laying out the village of Pittsburgh beside it. In Canada, autumn brought a poor harvest, followed by the harshest winter in memory. Ice in the St. Lawrence, plus a British blockade, cut off overseas support from France. The Marquis de Montcalm huddled in the provincial capital at Quebec with his ill-equipped army.

In the spring of 1759, the British pressed their advantage, moving against Canada from the west and the south. As Britain's superintendent of Indian affairs in the region, Sir William Johnson had lived among the Iroquois nations for twenty years. His Mohawk Indian wife, Molly Brant, was the sister of Chief Joseph Brant. As British successes mounted, the Mohawks and other Iroquois became increasingly eager to support the winning side in the war. Sensing this, Johnson recruited 1,000 formerly neutral Iroquois to join 2,000 British regulars on the shores of Lake Ontario. With Johnson in command, they laid siege to Fort Niagara. The fort fell in July, a British victory that effectively isolated enemy posts farther west and obliged the French to abandon them. In August, a British force under Jeffery Amherst captured Ticonderoga and Crown Point on Lake Champlain. The stage was set for an assault on Quebec.

QUEBEC TAKEN AND NORTH AMERICA REFASHIONED

In London, William Pitt knew that capturing Quebec would conquer Canada. Months earlier, he had ordered James Wolfe "to make an attack upon Quebeck, by the River St. Lawrence." Wolfe's **flotilla,** with 8,500 troops, anchored near the walled city in late June. But the French held their citadel despite weeks of heavy shelling. Desperate and sick, Wolfe resorted to a ruthless campaign against the countryside that left 1,400 farms in ruins. Even this strategy failed to draw Montcalm's forces out to fight.

> *The future of the continent and its inhabitants hinged on a pitched battle between opposing European armies.*

As a last resort, Wolfe adopted a risky plan to climb a steep bluff by the river and attack the vulnerable west side of the city. On the night of September 12, 1759, he dispatched troops in small boats to float quietly past French sentries and scale the formidable cliffs. At daybreak, twelve British battalions emerged on a level expanse known as the Plains of Abraham. The future of the continent and its inhabitants hinged on a pitched battle between opposing European armies. Montcalm and Wolfe staked everything in the clash, and both lost their lives in the encounter. By nightfall, the British had won a decisive victory, and four days later the surviving French garrison surrendered the city of Quebec.

Montreal fell to Britain the following year, and fighting subsided in America. But Pitt continued to pour public money into the global war, and one military triumph followed another. The British conquered French posts in India, took French Senegal on the West African coast, and seized the valuable sugar islands of Martinique and Guadeloupe in the French West Indies. When Spain came to France's aid in 1762, British forces captured the Philippines and the Cuban city of Havana. But British taxpayers resented the huge costs of

John Webber, *A View of Kealakekua Bay, c. 1781–1783. Dixson Library, State Library of New South Wales (3.293)*

■ When Captain Cook anchored at Hawaii's islanders crowded aboard his two vessels and p of others swam around the ships, along with "a is visible in the foreground.

The Hawaiians mistook Captain Co and treated him with hospitality and res captain observed. During the next twelv America. Two centuries after Francis D passage through North America that m Asia. But Cook encountered a solid coa way, he traded with Northwest Coast In

Cook's vessels returned south in the big island of Hawaii. But admirat their welcome, and an angry crowd o After the captain's death, his two slo sold their furs at a huge profit. Then the money to be made selling North also confirmed a disturbing rumor Pacific traffic.

THE RUSSIANS LAY CLAI

In 1728, Vitus Bering, a Danish capta pleted a three-year trek east across S Pacific Ocean, he built a boat and sa strait that bears his name today. The linked to North America. On a seco mainland and claimed it for Russia. H on a frozen island.

Bering's crew finally returned to round trips between Russia and Ame generation, Russian merchants sent s furs that they traded with the power Alaska's Aleutian Island chain in 175 foxes, and 840 fur seals.

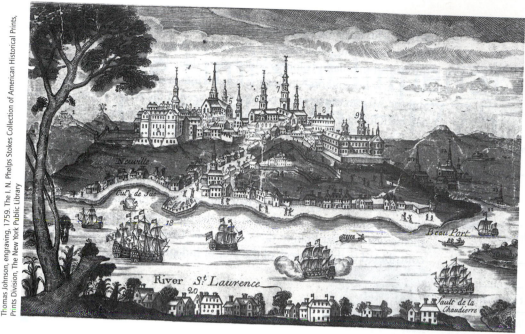

Thomas Johnson, engraving, 1759. The I. N. Phelps Stokes Collection of American Historical Prints, Prints Division, The New York Public Library

■ *Quebec, the Capital of New France,* by Thomas Johnson. A New England printer, eager to celebrate the fall of Quebec in 1759, copied an old image of the city from a French map. The sketch emphasizes the Catholic churches and seminaries that Louis XIV had promoted in the previous century. But in fact, British cannon fire during the siege of 1759 had devastated much of the town.

the war. Many also worried that the effort to humiliate France and Spain and undo their empires could spark retaliation in the years ahead. Rising criticism pushed Pitt from office, and peace negotiations began.

In a matter of months, the European powers redrew the imperial map of North America. Their complex swaps constituted the largest single rearrangement of territory in the history of the continent. First, France ceded to Spain the port of New Orleans and all of the Louisiana territory west of the Mississippi River. Then, in the 1763 Treaty of Paris, Spain turned over East Florida to Britain, receiving back Havana and the Philippines in return. France gave Britain its holdings between the Appalachians and the Mississippi River as well as the parts of Canada not already claimed by the Hudson's Bay Company. In exchange for this vast acquisition, the British returned the sugar islands of Martinique and Guadeloupe to the French, and they allowed France to retain fishing rights off Newfoundland.

In North America, this "first global war" had involved far more than the British versus the French. Diverse colonists drawn from Europe and Africa had a substantial part in the struggle, and for Indian societies caught between French and English forces, the stakes were particularly high. Ironically, the Paris peace treaty made no mention of the thousands of Native Americans whose homelands were being reassigned. The final results were striking. Britain emerged as the world's leading colonial power. After two centuries, France's North American empire disappeared abruptly, inviting further expansion by English colonists and making political independence from Britain a viable possibility.

Conclusion

For half a century, the complex currents of colonial life had recalled the ancient tale of Babel, as told in the Book of Genesis in the Bible. A confusion of voices, interests, and cultures competed and interacted over a wide expanse in North America. In the process, a string of related economic regions emerged along the eastern seaboard. The British colonies that composed these regions varied in ethnic make-up, but they were all expanding rapidly in population. This unprecedented demographic growth would alter the power and the place of the Atlantic colonies.

"Farther than Any Oth

The Wider World

The Ice Islands on the 9th January 1773, engraved by B. T. Pouncy, 31st Feb 1777 (engraving) (b/w photo), Hodges, William (1744–97) (after)/Private Collection/The Bridgeman Art Library

■ In January 1773, Captain Cook'
explorer wrote, "we could not procee

James Cook (1728 –1779) had made
naval surveyor during the British sie
he commanded an expedition to explo
observe the transit of Venus between t
sun. Cook and his crew charted the i
Island of New Zealand, and the east c
returning around the globe to England

Two more voyages followed. The t
was killed in the Pacific in 1779–is th
early exploration of Hawaii, careful c
Northwest Coast, and the profitable
in Canton, China. But some have calle
journey, a circumnavigation of th
1775, "the greatest single voyage in
This memorable expedition from Brita
for its unprecedented three-year len
Cook's breakthroughs in navigation,
diets for sailors.

During the previous decade a fe
maker John Harrison, had perfect
allowed captains to determine longit
Cook carried a replica of Harrison's ti
accuracy. Armed with "our never fail
probed toward the South Pole in the
the Pacific. His ship, the *Resolution*,

"Squeez'd and Oppressed": A 1768 Petition by 30 Regulators

Interpreting History

In the 1760s, corruption prevailed among appointed officials in central North Carolina. Often holding numerous offices at once, these men managed elections, controlled courts, and gathered taxes. Apparently not all the tax money they collected made it to the public treasury. Nevertheless, any farmer who resisted paying might lose the plow horse or the milk cow that sustained the family. It could be "seized and sold" to cover a small tax payment or minor debt, with "no Part being ever Return'd" from the proceeds.

Banding together to better regulate their own affairs, angry farmers sought relief through every possible legal means. By 1768, these organized Regulators had exhausted most avenues of peaceful protest. The western counties where they resided were badly underrepresented in the colonial assembly. As a new session prepared to convene, they fired off a final round of petitions, assuring legislators that they were law-abiding citizens willing to pay their legal share of taxes. In this message of October 4, 1768, thirty Regulators begged for the appointment of honest public officials.

Photo courtesy of Tryon Palace Historic Sites and Gardens

■ Tryon's Palace, the governor's home in New Bern, North Carolina, built in 1768.

To the Worshipful House of Representatives of North Carolina

Your Poor Petitioners [have] been Continually Squez'd and oppressed by our Publick Officers both with Regard to their fees as also in the Laying on of Taxes as well as in Collecting. . . . Being Grieved thus to have our substance torn from us [by] . . . such Illegal practices, we applied to our public officers to give us some satisfaction . . . which they Repeatedly denied us.

With Regard to the Taxes, . . . we labour under Extreem hardships. . . . Money is very scarce . . . & we exceeding Poor & lie at a

---

A Conspiracy of Corrupt Ministers?

■ *Did the Boston Massacre highlight deep, justifiable colonial grievances, or was it a provoked attack, exploited by colonial dissidents?*

Numerous sharp divisions—some leading to armed conflict—continued to separate colonists of different classes and regions. But ill-timed steps by successive administrations in London attracted widening attention throughout British America, prompting uneasy new alliances. Colonists familiar with the dire warnings of Real Whig pamphleteers asked themselves a question: in the weak and short-lived ministries that succeeded Grenville's, were the leaders simply ill-informed, or were they corrupt? Colonists wondered whether there was some official conspiracy to chip away at American liberties. Even loyal defenders of the crown expressed frustration with new policies, fearing that they were too harsh to calm irate colonists, yet too weak to force them into line. "It's astonishing to me," wrote a beleaguered supporter from Boston, "after the Warning and Experience of the Stamp Act Times, that any new Impositions should be laid on the Colonies," especially "without even so much as a single Ship of Warr" to back up new measures.

Parliament's first new imposition after repealing the Stamp Act was the Revenue Act of 1766. This act further reduced the molasses duty, from threepence per gallon to a single great distance from Trade which renders it almost Impossible to gain sustenance by our utmost Endeavours. . . .

To Gentlemen Rowling in affluence, a few shillings per man may seem triffling. Yet to Poor People who must have their Bed and Bedclothes, yea their Wives Petticoats, taken and sold to Defray, how Tremenious [tremendous] . . . must be the Consequences. . . . Therefore, dear Gentlemen, to your selves, to your Country, and in Pity to your Poor Petitioners, do not let it stand any longer to Drink up the Blood and vitals of the Poor Distressed.

After seeking relief from existing taxes, the petitioners went on to question new burdens, such as the law imposing an additional tax "to Erect a Publick Edifice" for Governor Tryon in New Bern.

Good God, Gentlemen, what will become of us when these Demands come against us? Paper Money we have none & gold or silver we can Purchase none of. The Contingencies of Government Must be Paid, and . . . we are Willing to Pay, [even] if we [must] sell our Beds from under us. And [yet] in this Time of Distress, it is as much as we can support. . . . If, therefore, the Law for that Purpose can be happily Repealed, . . . May the God of Heaven Inspire you with sentiments to that Purpose.

We humble Begg you would . . . Use your Influence with our Worthy, Virtuous Governor to discontinue . . . such Officers as would be found to be ye Bane of Society, and [instead to] Put in the Common Wealth [officials willing] to Encourage the Poor

and . . . to stand [up] for them. This would Cause Joy and Gladness to Spring from every Heart. This would cause Labour and Industry to prevail over Murmuring Discontent. This would Raise your poor Petitioners . . . to a flourishing Opulent and Hoping People. Otherwise . . . disatisfaction and Melancholy must Prevail over such as Remain, and Numbers must Defect the Province and seek elsewhere an Asylum from Tyranny and Oppression. . . .

We leave it to you . . . in your great Wisdom . . . to pass such Act or Acts, as shall be Conducive to the welbeing of a whole People over Whose welfare ye are plac'd as Guardians. . . . For the Lords Sake, Gentlemen, Exert your selves this once in our favour.

QUESTIONS

1. *How, specifically, do the tone and content of this petition reflect the widespread political outlook, combining vigilance and restraint, described in Cato's Letters?*

2. *Pick some current issue that concerns you deeply and draft a brief, impassioned petition to your legislators. In compelling language, lay out your best arguments for action. Then, see if thirty people will sign your petition.*

Source: William S. Powell, James K. Huhta, and Thomas J. Farnham, eds., The Regulators of North Carolina: A Documentary History, 1759–1776 (Raleigh: State Department of Archives and History, 1971), pp. 187–189. Some corrections have been made for readability.

penny, to discourage smuggling and raise revenue. Colonial merchants accepted this measure as an external tax designed to regulate imperial trade. Most paid the new duty, and customs revenues rose. But Real Whig warnings reminded them that compliance with seemingly innocuous legislation could set a dangerous precedent. The skeptics had a point, for Parliament soon imposed new hard-line measures.

THE TOWNSHEND DUTIES

The new statutes were set in motion by Charles Townshend, the chancellor of the Exchequer (or chief finance minister). He hoped Americans would accept "regulations of trade" intended to raise funds for colonial affairs. Townshend died suddenly in 1767, before his central measure took effect, but the bill carried his name. Passage of the Townshend Revenue Act sparked angry responses from colonists. The most telling came from John Dickinson, a moderate Philadelphia lawyer. He drafted a series of widely circulated "Letters from a Farmer in Pennsylvania," urging colonists to respond "peaceably—prudently—firmly—jointly." He dismissed any distinction between external and internal taxation, and he also rejected the idea that Americans had "virtual" or implicit representation in Parliament. "We are taxed without our own consent," Dickinson proclaimed to his readers. "We are therefore—SLAVES."

DOCUMENT

John Dickinson, Letters from a Farmer in Pennsylvania

The Revenue Act obliged colonists to pay duties for the importation of any glass, paint, lead, paper, and tea. Proceeds were to be spent in the colonies for "the administration of justice, and the support of civil government," a seemingly benevolent gesture. But Dickinson and other colonists pointed out what these two phrases actually meant. "The administration of justice" cloaked expanded searches of American homes and shops in which customs officers used hated "writs of assistance" to ferret out smuggled goods. "The support of civil government" ensured that governors and appointed office holders could draw their pay directly from the new duties instead of depending on an annual salary grant from the local assembly. In short, the new act removed from colonial legislatures one of their strongest bargaining tools in dealing with the crown: the power to pay or withhold the yearly salaries of key officials sent from Britain.

Similar acts and instructions followed. Asserting its sovereignty, Parliament disciplined the New York Assembly for its "direct disobedience" in refusing to comply with the Quartering Act of 1765. The crown instructed governors in America, now less dependent for their salaries on colonial lower houses, to disapprove any further measures from legislatures asserting their traditional control over how members were chosen, what their numbers should be, and when they would meet.

Equally galling, the Customs Act of 1767 established a separate Board of Customs for British North America. Ominously, the commissioners would live in Boston rather than London. To strengthen the board's hand, in 1768 Britain expanded the number of vice-admiralty courts in North America from one to four. It supplemented the court in Halifax (established by the Sugar Act of 1764) with new courts in Boston, Philadelphia, and Charleston. Furthermore, to look after its troublesome mainland colonies, the British government created a new American Department. It was to be overseen by the Earl of Hillsborough, a former president of the Board of Trade who became the first secretary of state for the American colonies. It also began to move British troops in America from remote frontier outposts to major Atlantic ports, both as a cost-cutting measure and as a show of force.

Americans found these measures threatening, especially when considered as a whole. In February 1768, the Massachusetts legislature, led by forty-six-year-old Samuel Adams, petitioned the king for redress. The legislators circulated a call to other colonial assemblies to voice similar protests. Condemning the Townshend Revenue Act as unconstitutional, they argued that it imposed taxation without representation. By removing control of the governors' salaries from colonial legislatures, they said, Parliament set the dangerous precedent of making royal officials "independent of the people." Lord Hillsborough demanded an immediate retraction of this provocative "Circular Letter" and ordered the dissolution of any other assembly that took up the matter.

VIRTUOUS RESISTANCE: BOYCOTTING BRITISH GOODS

In June, just as word arrived of the Wilkes Riot in London, events in Boston took a more radical turn. Defying Hillsborough, the Massachusetts assembly voted against rescinding its circular letter. On June 5, a dockside crowd faced down a "press-gang" from a British warship and protected local sailors from being forced (or "pressed") into naval service. Five days later, customs officials seized John Hancock's sloop, *Liberty,* and demanded that he pay import duties for a cargo of Madeira wine. This move sparked a huge demonstration, as citizens dragged a small customs boat through the streets and burned it on Boston Common. "Let us take up arms immediately and be free," Sam Adams was heard to say; "We shall have thirty thousand men to join us from the Country."

Emotions ran high. But most leaders sensed that any escalation of the violence would be premature and perhaps suicidal. They reined in demonstrations and instead initiated a massive boycott of British goods. Nonimportation plans called upon colonists to refrain from buying imported luxuries. Instead, they were to opt for virtuous self-sufficiency, buying locally and making more of what they needed. This strategy for resistance seemed broad-based, moderate, and nonviolent, so it held wide appeal. Since colonial women usually managed household affairs and family purchases, it drew them into the growing political debate.

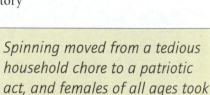

LISTEN

"The Liberty Song"

As the nonimportation movement expanded, women of all ranks, self-proclaimed Daughters of Liberty, made, sold, and dressed in homespun garments. Anna Winslow (age eleven, of Boston) wrote proudly, "I chuse to wear as much of our own manufactory as pocible." Spinning moved from a tedious household chore to a patriotic act, and females of all ages took part in spinning bees to encourage household frugality. Newspaper editors urged them on, promising that women who were competing "with each other in their skill and industry" would also "vie with the men in contributing to the preservation and prosperity of their country and equally share in the honor of it."

> *Spinning moved from a tedious household chore to a patriotic act, and females of all ages took part in spinning bees.*

Local associations sprang up, pledging to forgo imported tea and London fashions. A dozen colonial assemblies voted to halt importation of selected goods. In New York, the value of imports from Britain shrank from £491,000 to just £76,000 in a single year. The damage to English shipping proved substantial. Britain was losing far more revenue in colonial trade than it was gaining through the expanded customs duties.

Soon influential exporters in Britain were pressing their government for relief. When Baron Frederick North, who had succeeded Townshend, established a new ministry in January 1770, he received the king's consent to work toward a better arrangement with the colonies. On March 5, 1770, Lord North persuaded Parliament to repeal all the Townshend Duties except the one on tea. The move defused the colonial boycott, but it offered too little too late. Like the earlier Declaratory Act, this measure reaffirmed Parliament's disputed right to tax the colonists at will. Moreover, it came on the exact day that violence and bloodshed were escalating in Boston.

IMAGE

Women Signing an Anti-Tea Agreement

THE BOSTON MASSACRE

After the *Liberty* riot in June 1768, tensions had mounted in Boston, especially with the arrival in October of two regiments of British soldiers, well armed and dressed in their traditional red coats. Paul Revere, a local silversmith and member of the Sons of Liberty, crafted an ominous engraving entitled "British Ships of War Landing Their Troops." According to Real Whig beliefs, any appearance by a standing army in peacetime constituted danger. The issue of housing and feeding unwanted troops quickly became a political hot button. The soldiers pitched their tents on Boston Common, a central gathering place for boisterous crowds. Artisans in a sluggish economy welcomed the increased business that the men in uniform generated, but numerous unemployed workers resented the soldiers' "moonlighting," trying to earn extra pay by applying for local jobs.

With 4,000 armed men encamped in a seaport of scarcely 16,000, confrontation seemed inevitable. When rowdy American youths harassed the intruders as "redcoats" and "lobsterbacks," British officers ordered their men not to retaliate. Their refusal to fight only prompted more taunts. Affairs "cannot long remain in the state they are now in," wrote one observer late in 1769; "they are hastening to a crisis. What will be the event, God knows."

DOCUMENT

Boston Gazette, Description of the Boston Massacre

In March 1770, protesters took to the streets after a run-in between local workers and job-seeking soldiers. Rumors spread about a larger confrontation, and on March 5, around 9 p.m., a crowd gathered outside the customs house. When a harassed sentry

The Library of Congress

■ In Paul Revere's image of the 1770 Boston Massacre, soldiers defend the hated customs house by moonlight, while a sniper fires from a window clearly labeled "Butcher's Hall." The partisan engraving spread an anti-British view of the bloody event.

struck a boy with his rifle butt, angry witnesses pelted the guard with snowballs. As seven fellow soldiers pushed through the mob to assist him, firebells summoned more townspeople to the scene. The British loaded their rifles and aimed at the crowd, their bayonets fixed.

Into this tense standoff marched several dozen sailors, waving banners and brandishing clubs. Their leader was Crispus Attucks, an imposing ex-slave who stood six feet two inches. The son of a black man and an Indian woman, he had run away from his master two decades earlier and then taken up a life at sea. The scene was described later, at the trial resulting from the incident. John Adams, who assumed the unpopular task of defending the British soldiers, told the court: "Attucks appears to have undertaken to be the hero of this night." Damning the soldiers and daring them to fire, Attucks pressed his band of colonial sailors to the front, waving a long stick in the moonlight.

A slave witness named Andrew, who had climbed a post to get a better view, testified that Attucks "threw himself in, and made a blow at the officer," shouting, "kill the dogs, knock them over." Adams later showed the court how with one hand the sailor "took hold of a bayonet, and with the other knocked the man down." In the mayhem, a British gun went off, prompting a volley of fire from the other soldiers. The crowd recoiled in disbelief at the sight of their dead and wounded neighbors lying in the street, but they stayed past midnight to demand that the soldiers be jailed for murder. According to a printed report, Attucks and four others had been "killed on the Spot." The anti-British cause had its first martyrs.

By grim coincidence, the bloody episode in New England occurred only hours after Lord North addressed the House of Commons to urge removal of most Townshend Duties. His effort at reconciliation immediately became lost in a wave of hostile publicity. In Boston, Paul Revere captured the incident in an inflammatory engraving that circulated widely. The Sons of Liberty quickly named the evening violence of March 5 the Boston Massacre and compared its martyred victims to the Wilkes demonstrators who had perished in London during the Massacre at St. George's Field. "On that night," John Adams remarked, "the foundation of American independence was laid."

THE *GASPÉE* AFFAIR PROMPTS COMMITTEES OF CORRESPONDENCE

The overzealous conduct of customs officers gave colonists further cause for distrust. As traffic with Britain revived, after the repeal of most Townshend Duties and the end of the colonial boycott of English goods, so did the likelihood of conflict between merchants and customs inspectors. In the Delaware River region, local residents thrashed and jailed a customs collector in 1770. The next year, protesters stormed a customs schooner at night, beat up the crew, and stole their sails. Tensions ran especially high in Rhode Island. In 1769, Newport citizens seized the sloop *Liberty*—which crown agents had confiscated from John Hancock the year before and converted into a customs vessel—and scuttled it. In June 1772, the *Gaspée*, another customs boat said to harass local shipping, ran aground near Pawtuxet. In a midnight attack, more than sixty raiders descended on the stranded schooner in eight longboats, driving off its crew and setting fire to the vessel.

The destruction of the *Gaspée* renewed sharp antagonisms. The irate Lord Hillsborough sent a royal commission from London to investigate and to transport suspects to England for trial. But many of the attackers, such as John Brown of Providence, came from important Rhode Island families. Even a £500 reward could not induce local inhabitants to name participants. Besides, many viewed the order to deport accused citizens to England as a denial of their fundamental right to trial by a jury of their peers.

When the colonists took action, Virginia's House of Burgesses again led the way, as it had in the Stamp Act crisis. In March 1773, Patrick Henry, Thomas Jefferson, and Richard Henry Lee pushed through a resolution to set up a standing committee to look into the *Gaspée* affair and to keep up "Correspondence and Communication with our sister colonies" for the protection of rights. Following Virginia's example, ten other colonial legislatures promptly established their own Committees of Correspondence. In Massachusetts, people formed similar committees, linking individual towns. Within months a new act of Parliament, designed to rescue the powerful East India Company from bankruptcy, gave these emerging communication networks their first test.

Launching a Revolution

■ *Could the British, through a more creative response to the Boston Tea Party, have averted the ensuing escalation toward violence?*

In 1767, before Parliament imposed the Townshend Duties, Americans had imported nearly 870,000 pounds of tea from England. But the boycott movement cut that annual amount to less than 110,000 pounds by 1770, as colonists turned to smuggling Dutch blends and brewing homemade root teas. When nonimportation schemes lapsed in the early 1770s, purchase of English tea resumed, although a duty remained in effect.

Encouraged by this apparent acceptance of parliamentary taxation, Lord North addressed the problem facing the East India Company. The ancient trading monopoly owed a huge debt to the Bank of England and had 18 million pounds of unsold tea wasting in London warehouses. Many MPs held stock in the East India Company, so in May 1773 Parliament passed a law designed to assist the ailing establishment.

THE TEMPEST OVER TEA

The Tea Act of 1773 let the struggling East India Company bypass the expensive requirement that merchants ship Asian tea through England on its way to colonial ports. Now they could send the product directly to the colonies or to foreign ports, without paying to unload, store, auction, and reload the heavy chests. Any warehouse tea destined for the colonies would have its English duty refunded. These steps would reduce retail prices and expand the tea market. They would also quietly confirm the right of Parliament to collect a tea tax of threepence per pound.

The company promptly chose prominent colonial merchants to receive and distribute more than 600,000 pounds of tea. These consignees would earn a hefty 6 percent commission. But wary colonists in port towns, sensing a repetition of 1765, renewed the tactics that had succeeded against the Stamp Act. Sons of Liberty vowed to prevent tea-laden ships from docking, and crowds pressured local distributors to renounce participation in the scheme. "If they succeed in the sale of that tea," proclaimed New York's Sons of Liberty, "then we may bid adieu to American liberty."

> *"If they succeed in the sale of that tea," proclaimed New York's Sons of Liberty, "then we may bid adieu to American liberty."*

The Bostonians Paying the Excise-Man, or Tarring and Feathering (1774). The Library of Congress

■ A 1774 London cartoon expressed anger that Boston's Sons of Liberty, defying British authority, could overturn the Stamp Act, tar and feather revenue agents, dump East India Company tea, and use their "Liberty Tree" to hang officials in effigy.

In Boston, where tea worth nearly £10,000 arrived aboard three ships in late November, tension ran especially high. The credibility of Governor Thomas Hutchinson, who had taken a hard line toward colonial dissent, had suffered in June when Benjamin Franklin published private correspondence suggesting the governor's willingness to trim colonists' rights. When two of Hutchinson's sons were named tea consignees, the appointments reinforced townspeople's suspicions. The governor could have signed papers letting the three vessels depart. But instead he decided to unload and distribute the tea, by force if necessary. One could scarcely buy a pair of pistols in Boston, a resident observed on December 1, "as they are all bought up, with a full determination to repel force by force."

On December 16, the largest mass meeting of the decade took place at Boston's Old South Church. A crowd of 5,000, including many from other towns, waited in a cold rain to hear whether Hutchinson would relent. When word came in late afternoon that the governor had refused, the cry went up, "Boston Harbor a teapot tonight!" Following a prearranged plan, 150 men, disguised as Mohawk Indians and carrying hatchets, marched to the docks and boarded the ships.

As several thousand supporters looked on, this disciplined crew spent three hours methodically breaking open hundreds of chests of tea and dumping the contents overboard. The well-organized operation united participants representing all levels of society—from merchants such as John Hancock to artisans such as George Hewes. News of the event spurred similar acts of defiance in other ports. "This destruction of the Tea is so bold, so daring, so firm," John Adams wrote in his diary the next day, "it must have so important Consequences, and so lasting, that I can't but consider it as an Epocha in History." Sixty years later, as one of the oldest veterans of the Revolution, George Hewes still recalled with special pride his role in "the destruction of the tea."

THE INTOLERABLE ACTS

"The crisis is come," wrote British general Thomas Gage, responding to the costly Tea Party in Boston Harbor; "the provinces must be either British colonies, or independent and separate states." Underestimating the strength of American resolve, Parliament agreed with King George III that only stern measures would reestablish "the obedience which a colony owes to its mother country." Between March and June 1774, it passed four so-called Coercive Acts to isolate and punish Massachusetts.

The first of the Coercive Acts, the Boston Port Act, used British naval strength to cut off the offending town's sea commerce—except for shipments of food and firewood—until the colonists paid for the ruined tea. By the Administration of Justice Act, revenue officials or soldiers charged with murder in Massachusetts (as in the Boston Massacre) could have their trials moved to another colony or to Great Britain. The Quartering Act gave officers more power to requisition living quarters and supplies for their troops throughout the colonies. Most importantly, the Massachusetts Government Act removed democratic elements from the long-standing Massachusetts Charter of 1691. From now on, the assembly could no longer elect the colony's Upper House, or Council. Instead, the governor would appoint council members, and any town meetings would require his written permission.

Lord North's government went even further. It replaced Hutchinson with Gage, installing the general as the governor of Massachusetts and granting him special powers and three additional regiments. It also secured passage of the Quebec Act, new legislation to address nagging problems of governance in Canada after a decade of English rule. The act accommodated the Catholic faith and French legal traditions of Quebec's inhabitants. Moreover, it greatly expanded the size of the colony to draw scattered French settlers and traders under colonial government. Suddenly, Quebec took in the entire Great Lakes region and all the lands north of the Ohio River and east of the upper Mississippi River.

Expanding the province of Quebec to the Ohio River might extend British government to French wilderness outposts and help to regulate the Indian trade. But the move also challenged the western claims of other colonies. The Quebec Act appeared to favor Canada's French Catholics and Ohio Valley Indians—both recent enemies of the crown—over loyal English colonists. Resentment ran especially high in New England, where Protestants had long associated Catholicism with despotism. The Quebec Act, which denied the former French province a representative assembly and jury trials in civil cases, set an ominous precedent for neighboring colonies.

The Coercive Acts and the Quebec Act—lumped together by colonial propagandists as the Intolerable Acts—brought on open rebellion against crown rule. Competing pamphlets debated the proper limits of dissent. In *A Summary View of the Rights of British America,* Thomas Jefferson went beyond criticisms of Parliament to question the king's right to dispense land, control trade, and impose troops in America. Within months, Massachusetts had called for a congress of all the colonies. It also established its own Provincial Congress at Concord, a small village that lay seventeen miles west of Boston. Out of reach of British naval power, this de facto Massachusetts government reorganized the militia into units loyal to its own Committee of Public Safety. These farmer-soldiers became known as Minutemen for their quick response to Gage's repeated efforts to capture patriot gunpowder supplies.

FROM WORDS TO ACTION

While Massachusetts chafed under these new restrictions, shifting coalitions in each colony, ranging from conservative to radical, vied for local political control. Extralegal committees, existing outside the authorized structure of colonial government, took power in hundreds of hamlets. In Edenton, North Carolina, fifty-one women signed a pact to abstain from using imported products, including tea. London cartoonists mocked the action as the "Edenton Ladies' Tea Party," but women in other colonies made similar agreements to boycott British tea and textiles. During the summer, all colonies except Georgia selected representatives to the First Continental Congress.

During the summer, all colonies except Georgia selected representatives to the First Continental Congress.

In September 1774, fifty-six delegates convened at Carpenters Hall in Philadelphia. Most had never met before, and they differed as much in their politics as in their regional manners. At first the delegates disagreed sharply over how best to respond to the Intolerable Acts. Joseph Galloway, a wealthy lawyer and commercial land speculator from Pennsylvania, urged a compromise with Britain modeled on the Albany Congress of 1754. His plan called for the creation of a separate American parliament, a grand council with

■ MAP 6.4 British North America, April 1775

Rising colonial unrest brought strong countermeasures. The British government organized regional vice-admiralty courts to punish smugglers; it greatly expanded Quebec in 1774; and it reallocated troops to the Boston area. When warfare erupted there in April 1775, the news spread throughout the colonies within weeks.

delegates elected by the colonial legislatures. The less conservative delegates opposed this idea for a colonial federation, under a president-general appointed by the king. Led by Patrick Henry of Virginia, they managed to table the Galloway Plan by a narrow vote.

When Paul Revere arrived from Boston on October 6, bearing a set of militant resolves passed in his own Suffolk County, further rifts appeared. Southern moderates, while expressing sympathy for Massachusetts, still resisted calls for a nonexportation scheme that would withhold American tobacco, rice, and indigo from Great Britain. But by the time the Congress adjourned in late October, it had issued a Declaration of Rights and passed a range of measures that seemed to balance competing views. On one hand, the Congress endorsed the fiery Suffolk Resolves, which condemned the Coercive Acts as unconstitutional and spoke of preparation for war. On the other, it humbly petitioned the king for relief from the crisis and professed continued loyalty. But in practical terms, Galloway and the more conservative members had suffered defeat. Most importantly, the delegates signed an agreement to prohibit British imports and halt all exports to Britain except rice. They called for local committees to enforce this so-called Association, and they set a date—May 10, 1775—for a Second Congress.

Before delegates could meet again in Philadelphia, the controversy that had smoldered for more than a decade on both sides of the Atlantic erupted into open combat. Predictably, the explosion took place in Massachusetts. The spark came in the form of secret orders to General Gage, which he received April 14, 1775. The confidential letter from his superiors in London urged him to arrest the leaders of the Massachusetts Provincial Congress and regain the upper hand before the strained situation grew worse. He was to use force, even if it meant the outbreak of warfare.

On April 18, Gage ordered 700 elite troops from Boston to row across the Charles River at night, march ten miles to Lexington, and seize John Hancock and Sam Adams. Next, the soldiers were to proceed seven miles to Concord to capture a stockpile of military supplies. Alerted by signal lanterns, express riders Paul Revere and William Dawes eluded British patrols and spurred their horses toward Lexington along separate routes to warn Hancock and Adams. Bells and alarm guns spread the word that the British were coming. By the time the British soldiers reached Lexington, shortly before sunrise, some seventy militiamen had assembled on the town green. When the villagers refused to lay down their arms, the redcoats dispersed them in a brief skirmish that left eight militiamen dead.

From Lexington, the British column trudged west to Concord and searched the town for munitions. Four hundred Minutemen who had streamed in from neighboring communities advanced on the town in double file, with orders not to shoot unless the British fired first. At the small bridge over the Concord River, British regulars opened fire. "The shot heard

DOCUMENT

Warren, "Account of the Battle of Lexington"

Amos Doolittle, "The Battle of Lexington, Plate I," 1775. Connecticut Historical Society, Hartford, CT (Acc. #1844.10.1)

■ **The shots fired at dawn by British troops, dispersing local militia from Lexington's town green, were the opening volley of the American Revolution. Amos Doolittle, a Connecticut soldier who responded to the alarm, later depicted the events of April 19, 1775. The date is still honored in New England as Patriots' Day.**

CHRONOLOGY: 1763–1775

1763   Treaty of Paris ends the French and Indian War.

Proclamation Line limits westward expansion of British colonies.

Pontiac's Rebellion.

1764   Sugar Act; Currency Act.

1765   Quartering Act; Stamp Act.

Virginia Resolves; Stamp Act demonstrations.

Tenant riots in Hudson Valley.

1766   Stamp Act repealed.

Declaratory Act.

Bougainville explores the South Pacific.

1767   Townshend Acts.

1768   James Cook makes first of three voyages to explore the Pacific.

Massachusetts Circular Letter.

1770   Boston Massacre.

1771   Battle of Alamance ends the Regulator Movement in North Carolina.

1772   Burning of the *Gaspée*.

1773   Boston Tea Party.

1774   Intolerable Acts.

First Continental Congress meets.

Suffolk Resolves.

1775   Battles of Lexington and Concord.

'round the world" killed two men. The Americans loosed a volley in return, killing three. By noon, exhausted British forces were retreating in disarray. The redcoats made easy targets for the more than 1,000 Americans who shot at them from behind stone walls. A relief party prevented annihilation, but the British suffered severe losses: seventy-three killed and 200 wounded or missing. They encamped briefly at Bunker Hill, but lacking the foresight and strength to retain that strategic height, they soon returned to Boston. The Americans, with only forty-nine dead, had turned the tables on General Gage, transforming a punitive raid into a punishing defeat.

Conclusion

For the British, festering administrative problems in America had suddenly become a military emergency. A decade of assertive but inconsistent British policies had transformed the colonists' sense of good will toward London into angry feelings of persecution and betrayal. Britain's overseas empire, which had expanded steadily for two centuries, now seemed on the verge of splitting apart.

The years of incessant argument and misunderstanding reminded many, on both sides of the Atlantic, of watching a stable, prosperous household unravel into mutual recrimination. A once-healthy family was becoming increasingly dysfunctional and troubled. The assertive children grew steadily in strength and competence; the aging parents chafed at their diminished authority and respect. Predictably, authorities in London found the once-dependent colonists to be ungrateful, intemperate, and occasionally paranoid. With equal assurance, the American subjects saw Parliament, government ministers, and eventually the king himself as uninformed, selfish, and even deceitful.

As the limits of imperial control in North America had become more evident, colonists worked to overcome the regional and ethnic differences that had long been a fact of eighteenth-century life. Political independence no longer seemed implausible. With effort, class hostilities and urban-rural divisions could also be overcome. Redirecting old local resentments toward the distant and powerful British crown could increase the sense of unity among people with different personal backgrounds and resources.

Nor would British colonists be alone if they mounted a rebellion. On one hand, they could make the unlikely choice of liberating half a million slaves, empowering colonial women, and embracing the anti-British cause of Pontiac and numerous Native Americans. Such revolutionary moves would increase their strength dramatically in one direction. On the other hand, they could also take a more cautious and less democratic route. If men of substance could gain control of the forces that were being unleashed, they might curb potential idealism among slaves, women, tenant farmers, and the urban poor, giving precedence instead to policies that would win vital support from the continent of Europe in an American fight for independence. France, recently evicted from North America, and Spain, anxious about British designs in the Pacific, might both be willing allies, despite their commitment to monarchy. Such an alliance, if it ever came about, could push the limits of British imperial control to the breaking point.

For Review

1. Was the creation of Spanish missions in California a milestone, or a footnote, in early American history? Explain.

2. "By challenging the expansion of British military power in his homeland, Pontiac set an example for American colonists." Discuss.

3. Using Map 6.3, argue that the seeds of conflict in British America were already present by 1766.

4. How does the Regulator upheaval in North Carolina relate, if at all, to wider patterns of American resistance?

5. "By demanding 'obedience' in 1774, King George III treated his American colonies as unruly children, not as grown family members." Explain.

6. List (and prioritize) four main factors that explain how so many British colonists made the rapid shift from loyal subjects to irate rebels.

Created Equal Online

For more *Created Equal* resources, including suggestions on sites to visit and books to read, go to **MyHistoryLab.com.**

Part Three

The Unfinished Revolution, 1775–1803

CHAPTER 7
Revolutionaries at
War, 1775–1783

CHAPTER 8
New Beginnings:
The 1780s

CHAPTER 9
Revolutionary
Legacies,
1789–1803

Unidentified Artist, *Jonathan Knight*, c. 1797. Collection of American Folk Art Museum, New York, Promised gift of Ralph Esmerian (P1.2001.3). Photo Courtesy Sotheby's, New York

In 1775, Great Britain still possessed all of North America east of the Mississippi River, from Hudson Bay to the Gulf of Mexico. If the British could suppress the troublesome rebellion along the Atlantic seaboard, their prospects for expansion in America looked promising. Farther west, Spain had recently acquired the vast Louisiana Territory from France. The Spanish retained their dominance in the Southwest, and they were finally beginning to expand their claim to California by building a series of new missions and presidios.

By 1803, however, the broad picture had changed markedly. In the Pacific Ocean, Europeans had encountered the Hawaiian Islands for the first time, Russian fur traders had consolidated their hold in Alaska, and Spanish vessels along the Pacific coast faced increasing competition from the ships of rival nations. The British still held Canada and Florida, but the thirteen rebellious colonies had become an independent republic and had started to acquire new territories. The most spectacular acquisition was the Louisiana Territory, which the United States purchased in 1803, after Spain returned the region to France.

Few could have foreseen such an unlikely series of events in such a brief span of time. Thomas Jefferson drafted the Declaration of Independence in 1776 at age thirty-three. His generation had reluctantly become the effective leaders of a revolutionary movement by the mid-1770s. They contended ably with those who pushed for greater democratization, those who desired the stability of military rule, and even those who longed for the protection of the British monarchy.

These unlikely revolutionary leaders were by no means united in all their views and actions. They argued fervently over constitutional issues, domestic policies, and foreign alignments. Most reaped personal rewards from the new society's collective success. And they saw to it that these rewards reached far beyond their own households. Urban artisans, frontier farmers, and immigrant newcomers benefited from the removal of monarchy.

Such positive developments inspired optimism for many, both at home and abroad. Yet although the revolutionary era fulfilled the expectations of numerous citizens, it failed to meet the hopes and aspirations of other Americans. Many merchants and planters, indebted to British interests before 1776, gained by the separation from Great Britain and became creditors and investors in the new society. Many frontier farmers and army veterans, on the other hand, faced burdensome debts after the Revolutionary War.

Women worried that the numerous written constitutions of the period were unresponsive to their interests. In 1776, only New Jersey gave the vote among property holders to "all free inhabitants," including women. But this provision was undone a generation later,

in 1807, when New Jersey men objected to the idea of women having the right to vote. From New Hampshire to Georgia, committed "Daughters of Liberty" had made possible colonial boycotts through their industry and had managed families, farms, and businesses during the dislocations of war. Female access to education and the courts improved somewhat in the last quarter of the eighteenth century, but for most American women the advances were more symbolic than real.

For African Americans the disappointments were greater still. British offers of freedom prompted thousands of southern slaves to take up the Loyalist cause at great personal risk. Other free blacks and slaves, primarily in the North, shouldered arms for the Patriots, drawn by the rhetoric of liberty and the prospect of advancement. Even though they had chosen the winning side, they reaped few benefits. Although the number of free blacks increased after the Revolutionary War, the African slave trade to the United States resumed and received official protection. Slavery itself gained renewed significance with the transition to cotton production in the South and a federal constitution that sanctioned the power of slaveholders. Even in the North, where gradual emancipation became the norm by the end of the century, free blacks found their welcome into white churches and schools to be so half-hearted that many began organizing their own separate institutions.

Eastern Indians, like African Americans, had good reason to distrust the Revolution and its leaders. The majority, including most Iroquois and Cherokee warriors, sided with the British and paid a steep price in defeat. Throughout the Mississippi Valley, Native Americans who remembered the benefits of French trade and British military support faced relentless pressure as American speculators, soldiers, and settlers dissected their homelands. After 1803, government officials promised that the newly acquired lands beyond the Mississippi would become an Indian Territory, providing lasting refuge for displaced eastern tribes. If so, what was to become of the Native American nations that already inhabited these same western plains?

Like most political upheavals, the American Revolution left many questions unanswered and much business unfinished. Even the new federal government, in operation for little more than a decade by 1803, remained a work in progress. The specific roles and relative power of the government's three separate branches spurred endless debate, as did the proper place of the military and the most suitable direction for foreign policy. The Constitution ratified in 1789 seemed promising, but it remained an uncertain and largely untested framework.

Chapter 7

Revolutionaries at War, 1775–1783

CHAPTER OUTLINE

- **"Things Are Now Come to That Crisis"**

- **Declaring Independence**

- **The Struggle to Win French Support**

- **Legitimate States, a Respectable Military**

- **The Long Road to Yorktown**

North Carolina Museum of Art, Raleigh, Purchased with funds from the State of North Carolina (52.9.25).

■ In April 1775, riders spread word across New England that violence had erupted near Boston. William Ranney's history painting *First News of the Battle of Lexington* (1847) shows a small town preparing to send reinforcements. The ominous storm clouds suggest impending war.

The shots fired at Concord Bridge, Massachusetts, in April 1775 resounded immediately through all the villages of New England. In Peterborough, New Hampshire, a storekeeper promptly recruited a company of reinforcements to shoulder their rifles and march toward Boston. In his town of 549 people, not everyone was eager to join the risky fight. In fact, the Presbyterian chaplain deserted to the British as soon as the new company reached Massachusetts. However, before the long Revolutionary War ended in 1783, most of Peterborough's adult men had performed some sort of Patriot military service.

In Peterborough, as in countless other American towns, reasons for enlisting differed, and length of service varied greatly. At a moment of regional crisis, such as when General Burgoyne's British army threatened to isolate New England by thrusting down the Hudson Valley in 1777, most able-bodied men in Peterborough, young and old alike, entered the militia for several months, until the enemy had been stopped. But in Peterborough, as elsewhere, the most established merchants and farmers generally served least. They remained close to home and handled local affairs, while fewer than two dozen men, driven by poverty, ambition, or patriotic zeal, did most of the town's fighting.

No one in the community saw more action than William "Long Bill" Scott, a thirty-three-year-old husband and father when the war began. "I was a Shoemaker, & got my Living by my Labor." In April 1775, when Scott enlisted in the local militia company headed by his cousin, he refused to serve as a private. Convinced that his own "Ambition was too great for so low a Rank," he talked his relative into granting him a lieutenant's commission.

At Bunker Hill in June, Lieutenant Scott was severely wounded and left bleeding on the battlefield overnight. Taken captive the next morning, the prisoner hid his convictions from the British, claiming that he had no stake in the conflict except personal advancement. "If I was killed in Battle," he told a Tory interviewer, that would be "the end of me, but if my Captain was killed, I should rise in Rank, & should still have a Chance to rise higher." As to the "Dispute between Great Britain and the Colonies," Scott supposedly added, "I know nothing of it; neither am I capable of judging whether it is right or wrong."

If detached and skeptical at first, Long Bill Scott stayed the course, in contrast to many whose initial zeal for the cause faded quickly. Scott was deported to Halifax, Nova Scotia, when the British evacuated Boston, but he escaped and fought at New York the following year, only to be captured again. Newspapers told of his next dramatic escape: tying his sword around his neck and pinning his watch to his hat, he swam across the Hudson River at night. Scott returned to Peterborough in 1777 to recruit a company of his own, serving for several more years before old wounds made marching difficult. He finished the war as a volunteer on a navy frigate.

In all, a dozen Scott relatives from Peterborough gave forty years in wartime service to the army, the navy, and the state and local militias. In addition to Long Bill, his father and many of his cousins saw action, as did several of his sons, one of whom died of camp fever after six years of service. Long Bill himself sustained nine wounds and was captured twice, but his rewards proved slim. He sold his farm in 1777 to cover debts, but the notes he received in payment lost 98 percent of their worth within three years, and his military pay also depreciated sharply in value. He lost the down payment on another farm, and he was unable to care for his own children when his wife died. Destitute, he returned to army service in the mid-1790s. He died at Fort Stanwix in New York in 1796, at age fifty-four.

Despite his early disclaimers, Long Bill Scott's commitment to the Patriot cause proved unwavering. For most, the War of American Independence was not a clear, two-sided struggle in which colonists unified to oppose the English monarchy. Within each small community, and within the Atlantic theater as a whole, alliances often proved the old adage that "My enemy's enemy is my friend." Powerful merchants like John Hancock and Henry Laurens threw in their lot with the people in part because they had grown disillusioned with Parliament's political and commercial controls. Many enslaved blacks, eager for liberty from their masters, escaped to join the British. On the international scale, the monarchies of France and Spain swallowed their dislike for America's republican rhetoric, joining in a war that allowed them an opportunity to attack their long-standing rival, Britain. On the other hand, many Cherokee and Iroquois Indians, disillusioned by contact with land-hungry settlers, cast their lot with the British forces from overseas.

Not all Indian warriors or enslaved Africans sided with the British, and by no means all New England farmers or Virginia planters embraced the Patriot cause. In a landscape marked by uncertainty, large numbers of people at all levels of society opted for cautious neutrality as long as they could, while others shifted their allegiance as the winds changed. The final outcome of the conflict, therefore, remained a source of constant doubt. Looking back, Americans often view the results of the Revolutionary War as inevitable, perhaps even foreordained. In fact, the end result—and thus independence itself—hung in the balance for years.

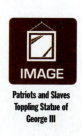

IMAGE

Patriots and Slaves
Toppling Statue of
George III

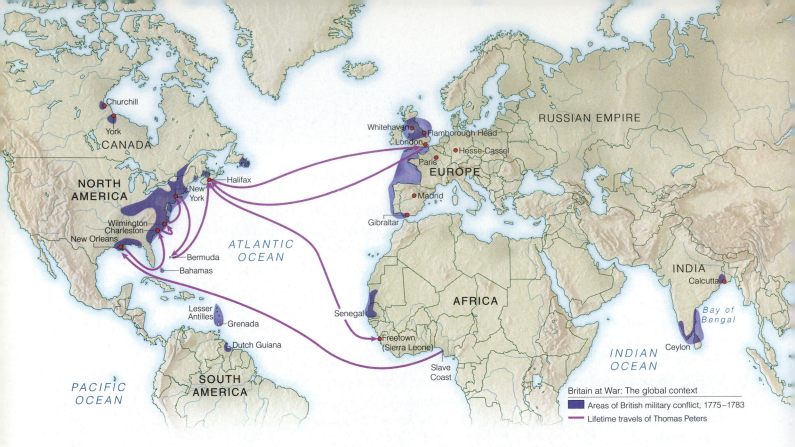

■ **MAP 7.1** **Britain's American War Viewed in a Global Context**

War is always a source of rapid dislocation and movement, as in the remarkable case of African-born Thomas Peters, whose lifelong Atlantic journey is traced here (see The Wider World, page 203). For Britain, the colonial war that began in 1775 expanded within three years into a worldwide conflict against rival European powers. By 1783, the British lost American colonies while expanding their hold in India. General Cornwallis, for example, went on to serve the British in India after his defeat at Yorktown in 1781.

"Things Are Now Come to That Crisis"

■ *How were the Americans able to drive British forces out of Boston in March 1776, less than a year after the Battle of Lexington?*

Royal Proclamation of Rebellion (1775)

New England's Minutemen had rallied swiftly at Lexington and Concord. In the ensuing months, while George III prepared a proclamation declaring the colonists to be in open rebellion, Congress took the initial steps to form the Continental Army. It also launched efforts to force the British out of Boston and to pull Canada into the rebellion. If these predominantly Protestant rebels hoped to draw the French Catholics of Quebec into their revolt, would free whites also be eager to include the blacks of Boston, Williamsburg, and Charleston in the struggle for liberty? Or would it be the British who recruited more African Americans and furnished them with arms? The answers to such questions became clear in the fifteen months between the skirmish at Lexington and the decision of Congress to declare political independence from Britain in July 1776.

THE SECOND CONTINENTAL CONGRESS TAKES CONTROL

Enthusiasm ran high in Philadelphia in May 1775 as the Second Continental Congress assembled amid cheers and parades. Delegates moved quickly to put the beleaguered colonies on a wartime footing. They instructed New York to build fortifications. They also paid for a dozen new companies of riflemen—recruited in Pennsylvania, Maryland, and Virginia—to be sent north to aid the Minutemen surrounding Boston. They created

The Journey of Tom and Sally Peters

The Wider World

In 1760, a young Yoruba-speaking man, age twenty-two, had been taken from what is now Nigeria and shipped to Louisiana aboard the slave ship *Henri Quatre*. Forced to cut sugar cane, he rebelled so often that he was sold to a prosperous Scottish immigrant in Wilmington, North Carolina, and put to work operating a gristmill. The African took an English name, Thomas Peters, and started a family with a young woman named Sally.

During the fifteen years between Peters's abduction from Africa and the outbreak of hostilities between America and Britain in 1775, nearly 225,000 people had poured into the British mainland colonies. Of these, two in five (or 85,000 individuals) had been purchased in Africa and were enslaved in the coastal South. As open warfare erupted, Tom and Sally Peters, even more than most people in British North America, experienced hardships, opportunities, and enormous dislocations.

Late in 1775, word reached Wilmington that Virginia's governor, Lord Dunmore, had offered freedom to slaves who would take up arms for the British. So when ships of the Royal Navy arrived at the Cape Fear River in March, Tom and Sally Peters risked arrest to gain their personal liberty by bolting to the British vessels. Peters was with the British when General Clinton's forces tried to take Charleston, South Carolina, in June 1776.

Throughout the war, Peters served the British in a unit called the Black Pioneers. Wounded twice, he rose to the rank of sergeant and earned the promise of a farm in Canada. In 1783, as defeated Loyalists left New York City at the end of the war, he and his family joined other ex-slaves aboard the *Joseph James*, bound for Nova Scotia. Departing in November, the ship was blown off course by foul weather. Tom and Sally, with their twelve-year-old daughter Clairy and eighteen-month-old son John, spent the winter sheltered at Bermuda before finally joining 3,500 other black Loyalists in Nova Scotia in May 1784.

But the odyssey of the Peters family did not end in Nova Scotia. In 1790, after he and others had been denied the promised farmland, Thomas ventured to London as an advocate

■ Escaped slave Tom Peters was with the British fleet that attacked Charleston in June 1776. A South Carolina soldier sketched the American victory.

for these former slaves. He protested their treatment, petitioned for relief, and met with British abolitionists planning a colony of former slaves in West Africa. Eager for his family to join the effort, he returned to Canada and led 1,200 African Americans to Sierra Leone, where he died at Freetown in 1792. During a life that began and ended in Africa, Peters had seen New Orleans, Wilmington, Charleston, Philadelphia, New York, Bermuda, Halifax, and London. He had survived sixteen years of enslavement and fought his own war for the freedom and safety of family and friends.

QUESTIONS

1. Follow the journey of Tom Peters and his family on Map 7.1. In what ways does his life reflect the title for Part Three: "The Unfinished Revolution"?

2. If the Revolutionary War brought Tom and Sally Peters "hardships, opportunities, and enormous dislocations," how was their experience typical, or exceptional?

an Army Department under the command of a New York aristocrat, General Philip Schuyler, and approved an issue of $2 million in currency to fund the military buildup.

In late May, word arrived from Lake Champlain in New York of a victory for the Green Mountain Boys (farmers led by Ethan Allen, from the area that became Vermont) and soldiers under Benedict Arnold of Connecticut. They had captured Fort Ticonderoga, along with its cannons, and the new Army Department badly needed all such heavy arms. This initiative not only secured the Hudson Valley against a British attack from the north; it also allowed Schuyler to propose a strike against Montreal and Quebec via Lake Champlain and the Richelieu River. Congress approved the assault, to be led by General Richard Montgomery. It also approved a daring scheme submitted by Arnold. He planned to lead separate forces up the Kennebec River. They would assist Montgomery in seizing Quebec and winning Canada before the region could become a staging ground for British armies.

> *Putting a slaveholder in command signaled the beginning of an important alliance between the well-to-do regional leaders of the North and South.*

No single action by Congress had greater implications for coalition building among the colonies than the one taken on June 15, 1775. That day, members voted unanimously to appoint George Washington, a forty-three-year-old delegate from Virginia, "to command all the continental forces." Colonel Washington already headed a committee that was drawing up regulations to run the new army, and he had notable military experience. But among his strongest assets may have been his southern roots. Northern delegates—especially John Adams, who had nominated Washington—sensed the need to foster colonial unity by placing a non–New Englander in charge of the army outside Boston. For their part, Southerners sensed keen regional differences, particularly over slavery. They appeared jealous, as one delegate noted, "lest an enterprising New England general, proving successful, might with his victorious army" enforce control over "the southern gentry."

In military and political terms, the selection of Washington proved auspicious. The tall, imposing planter from Mount Vernon emerged as a durable and respected leader in both war and peace. But putting a slaveholder in command also closed certain radical options. It signaled the beginning of an important alliance between the well-to-do regional leaders of the North and South. Although no one could foresee it at the time, this alliance would contribute to the particular form of the federal Constitution a dozen years later. The bond endured, shaping the governing of the country until the middle of the next century.

"LIBERTY TO SLAVES"

The selection of Washington sent a strong message to half a million African Americans, increasing their skepticism about the Patriot cause and spurring many of them to risk siding with the British. For their part, the British sensed an opportunity to undermine rebellious planters. In June 1775, the British commander in America, Thomas Gage, wrote to London: "Things are now come to that crisis, that we must avail ourselves of every resource, even to raise the Negros, in our cause." One Lutheran minister who spoke to black house servants near Philadelphia the next year noted that they "secretly wished that the British Army might win, for then all Negro slaves will gain their freedom. It is said that this sentiment is almost universal among the Negroes in America."

In the South, rumors of liberation swept through the large African American community during 1775. Slaveholding rebel authorities countered with harsh measures to quell black unrest. In Charleston that spring, they deported an African-born minister, David Margate, for preaching a sermon that hinted at equality. Also, they focused their attention on a prominent free black man named Thomas Jeremiah, who had prospered as a skilled pilot guiding vessels between treacherous sandbars into the busy South Carolina port. In April, Jeremiah supposedly told an enslaved dockworker of a great war coming and urged slaves to prepare to seize the opportunity. Weeks later, nervous Patriot planters made the well-known free black into a scapegoat, accusing him of involvement in a plot to smuggle guns ashore from British ships to support a slave uprising. In August 1775, despite a lack of hard evidence against him, Jeremiah was publicly hanged and then burned.

That September, a Georgia delegate to Congress made a startling comment. He predicted that if British troops were to land on the Georgia and South Carolina coast with a supply of food and guns, offering freedom to slaves who would join them, then 20,000 blacks would swiftly materialize. In November, the beleaguered royal governor of Virginia, Lord Dunmore, attempted just such a scheme. Dunmore issued a proclamation granting freedom to the slaves of rebel masters who agreed to take up arms on behalf of the king. Hundreds responded to Dunmore's proclamation. They formed the Ethiopian Regiment and wore sashes proclaiming "Liberty to Slaves."

THE STRUGGLE TO CONTROL BOSTON

In the North, British forces had been confined in Boston ever since the Battle of Lexington. They would remain isolated on the town's main peninsula for nearly a year, supported by the Royal Navy. In early July 1775, Washington arrived at nearby Cambridge to take up his command and oversee the siege of Boston. He quickly set out to improve order among his men. He tightened discipline, enforced sanitation, calmed regional jealousies, and removed nearly a dozen incompetent officers.

Washington also wrote scores of letters to civilian political leaders and the president of Congress to muster support for his meager army. The Massachusetts legislature alone received thirty-four messages from the new commander. He made clear that nearly everything was in short supply, from tents and uniforms to gunpowder, muskets, and cannons. He dispatched twenty-five-year-old Henry Knox, a former bookseller and future general, to retrieve the cannons captured at Ticonderoga. The Patriots' siege, he informed Congress, could not succeed without heavy fieldpieces to bombard the city from the heights at Dorchester and Charlestown, across the water from Boston.

Even before Washington's arrival, the British and the Americans had vied for control of these strategic heights. Indeed, the British General Gage drew up plans to secure Charlestown peninsula by seizing its highest point, Bunker Hill. But the Patriots learned of the scheme. On the night of June 16, 1775, they fortified Breed's Hill, a smaller knoll 600 yards in front of Bunker Hill. The next afternoon, 1,500 well-entrenched but inexperienced Patriot volunteers confronted the full force of the British army as thousands watched from the rooftops of Boston.

Gage might easily have sealed off Charlestown peninsula with his naval power. Instead, he used 2,500 British infantry, weighed down by heavy packs, to launch three frontal attacks up Breed's Hill from the shoreline. The first two uphill charges fell back before withering volleys at close range. Finally, with adjoining Charlestown ablaze and rebel powder supplies exhausted, a third assault overran the hill and dislodged the Americans. Mistakenly, the engagement became known as the Battle of Bunker Hill. Although it was technically a British victory, success came at a terrible price. The encounter left 42 percent of British troops (1,054 men) wounded or dead—the worst casualty figures of the entire war. Gage lost his command and was replaced in October by General William Howe. The Royal Army no longer appeared invincible.

As Washington organized his rudimentary army near Boston during the second half of 1775, Henry Knox pursued his mission to retrieve the British ordnance captured at Ticonderoga. Using oxen, sledges, and local volunteers, he managed to haul forty-three heavy cannons east, across trails covered with snow and ice, from the Hudson Valley to the Massachusetts coast. His men delivered the guns in late winter, finally giving Washington the advantage he needed. If he could move the cannons to high ground and protect them, he knew they had enough range to bombard the enemy

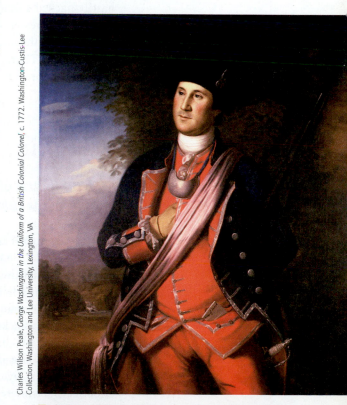

Charles Willson Peale, *George Washington in the Uniform of a British Colonial Colonel*, c. 1772. Washington-Custis-Lee Collection, Washington and Lee University, Lexington, VA

■ In June 1775, Congress selected a wealthy Virginia planter to command its army. The choice of George Washington reassured southern slave owners and disappointed blacks and whites in the North who saw slavery as a contradiction in the struggle for freedom.

huddled in Boston. In March 1776, the general designed an operation to secure Dorchester Heights. The Americans made their surprise move at night, as they had at Breed's Hill. But that maneuver had occurred in warm June weather. This time, in contrast, the ground was frozen solid, and they knew they had no possibility of digging in to protect the exposed position.

Planning ahead, Washington had his men prepare thousands of bundles of sticks and saplings, known as fascines. They also constructed large timber frames, a dozen feet wide, called chandeliers. When moved into place and filled with fascines and bales of hay, these wooden frames created a redoubt that could withstand cannon fire or a ground assault. On the night of March 4, several thousand American soldiers, using 300 wagons and oxcarts, hauled these barriers into place on Dorchester Heights. Behind them, the troops placed the cannons Knox had hauled overland from Fort Ticonderoga. By morning, the Herculean task was complete. On the fifth anniversary of the Boston Massacre, the exhausted but jubilant troops took up their new position and prepared to combat an assault such as the one at Breed's Hill nine months earlier. This time, they were determined to hold their strategic height at all costs, and they agreed that anyone who retreated would be "fired down upon the spot."

> A British officer remarked that the Americans had done more in one night than most armies could do in months.

But the assault never came. Shocked by the transformation under cover of darkness, a British officer remarked that the Americans had done more in one night than most armies could do in months. Suddenly confronted with Washington's commanding guns, the forces in Boston could not stay put; they had to attack or withdraw. At first, General Howe prepared to advance by boat and storm the heights. But he lost his nerve, perhaps because he had commanded the charges at Breed's Hill and seen the devastation. Instead, he drew back from an assault on Dorchester Heights and began evacuating his army by sea. Officers hastily packed soldiers and supplies, along with goods plundered from Boston homes, aboard naval vessels in the harbor. They left behind numerous horses, too cumbersome to transport. By the end of March, the entire British force had retreated by ship to Halifax, Nova Scotia. There, Howe made plans to attack the rebels again at New York, where Loyalist support was stronger.

Declaring Independence

■ *In the context of the entire year 1776, why was Washington's successful crossing of the Delaware River on December 25 so significant?*

As Washington laid siege to Boston, other Americans had converged on British forces in Canada. General Montgomery's troops seized Montreal in November 1775. They then descended the St. Lawrence River to join Benedict Arnold's men near Quebec. Arnold's troops had struggled north through Maine's rugged Kennebec Valley and crossed into Canada under brutal winter conditions. Their combined force, under Montgomery, attacked the walled city of Quebec during a fierce snowstorm on the night of December 30. But the assault failed, and Montgomery perished in the fighting. Smallpox had already broken out in the American ranks, and it spread to new arrivals during the next five months. When British reinforcements reached Quebec in May, the Americans hastily retreated toward Lake Champlain. They left behind most of their baggage and hundreds of sick companions.

Hundreds more died of smallpox during the withdrawal of the shattered army. Others spread the deadly virus when they returned to their New England homes. "I got an account of my johns Death of the Small Pox at Canada," one New Hampshire father scrawled in his diary after learning that his twenty-four-year-old son had died while fighting against the King's forces. "He was shot through his left arm at Bunker Hill." Now, "in defending the just Rights of America," John had been taken "in the prime of life by means of that wicked Tyranical Brute (Nea worse than Brute) of Great Britan." In thousands of American households, strained loyalty was turning to explosive anger.

"TIME TO PART"

In January 1776, Thomas Paine's brilliant pamphlet *Common Sense* captured the shifting mood and helped propel Americans toward independence. Paine, a former corsetmaker, had endured a long series of personal and economic failures in England before sailing to Philadelphia in 1774 at age thirty-seven. To this passionate man, with his gift for powerful and accessible prose, America represented a fresh start. Arriving late in 1774, Paine poured his energy into bold newspaper essays. In one, he argued that African American slaves deserved freedom and ample land to become productive citizen-farmers.

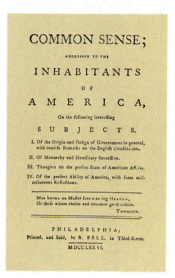

Paine's *Common Sense* sold an amazing 120,000 copies in three months, reaching all sorts of readers. The author promised to lay out "simple facts, plain arguments, and common sense" on the precarious American situation. He lambasted "the so much boasted constitution of England," and he went on to attack hereditary monarchy and the divine right of kings. "One honest man," Paine proclaimed, is worth more to society "than all the crowned ruffians that ever lived." He urged the creation of an independent constitutional republic that could become "an asylum for all mankind." "Reconciliation is now a fallacious dream," he argued: "'TIS TIME TO PART."

Paine's avid readers agreed. In the spring of 1776, one colony after another instructed its representatives to the Second Continental Congress to vote for independence. But many among the well-to-do had strong social and economic ties to London. They feared the loss of British imperial protection and the startling upsurge of democratic political activity among the lower orders. At first, Congress vacillated. Finally, with no sign of accommodation from England, most members agreed with Robert Livingston of New York that "they should yield to the torrent if they hoped to direct its course." In early June, Livingston, age thirty, joined the committee assigned to prepare a formal statement declaring independence from Great Britain. The Committee of Five also included Benjamin Franklin, John Adams, Roger Sherman, and the second youngest member of the Continental Congress, Thomas Jefferson.

DOCUMENT

John Adams to Abigail Adams (July 3, 1776)

The thirty-three-year-old Jefferson had recently returned to Philadelphia from Virginia, where his mother had died suddenly in March. Personally independent for the first time, he willingly took responsibility for crafting the document. He framed a stirring preamble, drawing on British philosopher John Locke's contract theory of government. Locke (1632–1702) believed that the sovereign power ultimately resided not in government but in the people themselves, who chose to submit voluntarily to civil law to protect property and preserve basic rights.

According to Locke, rulers possessed conditional, not absolute, authority over the people. Citizens therefore held the right to end their support and overthrow any government that did not fulfill its side of the contract. For any people facing "a long train of abuses," Jefferson wrote, "it is their right, it is their duty, to throw off such government and to provide new guards for their future security." He went on to catalogue the "repeated injuries and usurpations" committed by King George III. Meanwhile, on July 2, Congress voted on a statement affirming that "these United Colonies are, and of right, ought to be, Free and Independent States." Twelve colonies approved, with the New York delegation abstaining until it could receive further instructions from home. Having made the fundamental decision, the delegates then considered how to "declare the causes" behind their momentous choice to separate from Great Britain.

Over the next two days, all the Congress members edited the draft declaration submitted by the Committee of Five. They kept Jefferson's idealistic assertion that "all

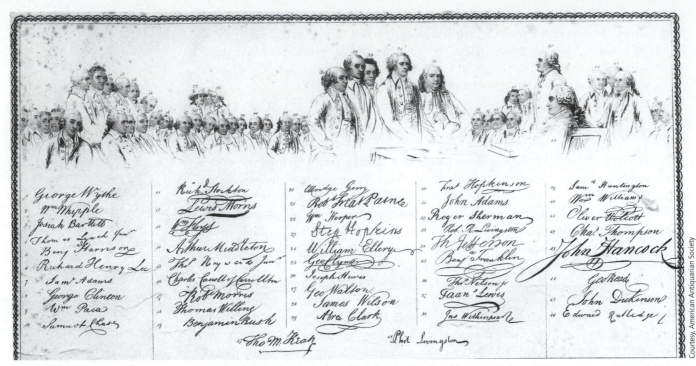

■ John Trumbull spent years gathering portraits for his famous painting *The Declaration of Independence*. This engraving identifies individuals in the painting with their signatures. The artist placed the Drafting Committee in the center (31–35). He omitted signers for whom he had no likeness, and he included several nonsigners, such as John Dickinson.

men are created equal." But they removed any reference to slavery, except for the charge that the king had "excited domestic insurrections amongst us," a veiled reference to the Thomas Jeremiah debacle in Charleston and to Lord Dunmore's proclamation. With other changes in place, they finally voted to approve the revised Declaration of Independence on July 4, 1776.

John Hancock, the president of the Congress, signed the document with a flourish, and printers hastily turned it into a published broadside. The other signatures (contrary to folklore) came two weeks later, after New York had finally offered its approval. That last endorsement meant that fifty-six delegates could gather to sign their names to "The *unanimous* declaration of the thirteen United States of America." They did so at great risk. As they endorsed the document with their signatures, they knew that they were opening themselves to face charges of treason, punishable by death.

IMAGE

Signing of the
Declaration of
Independence

THE BRITISH ATTACK NEW YORK

While the Continental Congress debated whether to declare independence, the British maneuvered to suppress the rebellion. Strangling the revolt with a naval blockade appeared impossible, given the length of the American coastline. But two other strategies emerged— one southern and one northern—that shaped British planning throughout the conflict.

The southern design rested on the assumption that loyalty to the crown remained strongest in the South. If the British could land forces below Chesapeake Bay, support from white loyalists and enslaved blacks might enable them to gain the upper hand and push north to reimpose colonial rule elsewhere. In June 1776, troops under General Henry Clinton arrived off the Carolina coast with such a mission in mind. But Loyalists had already lost a battle to the Patriots at Moore's Creek Bridge near Wilmington, North Carolina, in February, and the British ships sailed to South Carolina instead. On June 28, they bombarded Sullivan's Island,

Quebec, 1775

Montreal, 1775

Ft. Ticonderoga, 1775

Saratoga, 1777   Bennington, 1777

Ft. Stanwix, 1777   Boston, 1775

Newtown, 1777

Princeton, 1777   New York, 1776
Monmouth, 1777
Trenton, 1777
Brandywine, 1777   Germantown, 1777

Vincennes, 1779

Charlottesville, 1781
Yorktown, 1781   Naval Battle, 1781

St. Louis, 1780

Kaskaskia, 1778

Guilford Courthouse, 1781

Moore's Creek
Bridge, 1776

King's Mountain, 1780   Fishing
Creek, 1780

Cowpens, 1781   Camden, 1780

Charleston, 1780

Savannah, 1779

Natchez, 1778   Mobile, 1780

Pensacola, 1781

ATLANTIC
OCEAN

Mississippi

Overview of the Revolutionary War

✴ British victories
✴ Patriot victories

■ **M A P   7 . 2**   **Overview of the Revolutionary War**

at the mouth of Charleston harbor. But the Americans' cypress-log fortress withstood the cannon fire, and the attackers withdrew. The British did not renew their southern design for several years, concentrating instead on a separate northern strategy.

According to Britain's northern plan, troops would divide the rebellious colonies in two at the Hudson River valley, seizing New York City and advancing upriver while other forces pushed south from Canada. Then, having sealed off New England, they could finally crush the radicals in Massachusetts who had spearheaded the revolt and then restore the loyalties of inhabitants farther south. Lord George Germain, the aggressive new British cabinet minister in charge of American affairs, favored this plan. An overwhelming strike, he asserted, could "finish the rebellion in one campaign."

"Revoking Those Sacred Trusts Which Are Violated": Proclaiming Independence in South Carolina, May 1776

*T**hroughout the late spring of 1776, provincial assemblies, town meetings, and grand juries in the thirteen colonies began issuing their own pronouncements regarding a break with Great Britain. The authors drew on historical precedent, legal tradition, and emotional sentiment. They mixed lofty theory and Real Whig ideology with local concerns. They also incorporated rhetoric and ideas from current pamphlets, speeches, and newspaper essays.*

At least ninety of these proclamations survive. Most are more impressive for their strong feelings than for their literary merit. But taken together, they suggest the sentiments, arguments, and words that were in the air when Jefferson drafted the Declaration of Independence. This document

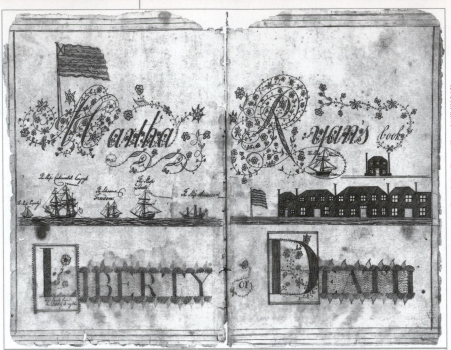

Southern Historical Collection, the University of North Carolina at Chapel Hill (#1940)

■ Young Martha Ryan used her cipher-book to do more than practice writing. She also drew American ships and flags and embellished the popular rallying cry "Liberty or Death."

was drawn up and signed by fifteen members of the Cheraw District grand jury during their regular court session in Long Bluff, South Carolina, May 20, 1776.

The Presentments of the Grand Jury of and for the Said District

I. When a people, born and bred in a land of freedom and virtue . . . are convinced of the wicked schemes of their treacherous rulers to

fetter them with the chains of servitude, and rob them of every noble and desirable privilege which distinguishes them as freemen,—justice, humanity, and the immutable laws of *God*, justify and support them in revoking those sacred trusts which are so impiously violated, and placing them in such hands as are most likely to execute them in the manner and for the important ends for which they were first given.

Early in 1776, Germain set out to generate a land and sea offensive of unprecedented scale. He prodded the sluggish admiralty for ships, and when he could not raise troops swiftly at home, he rented them from abroad. Russia declined a request for 20,000 soldiers, but the German states produced 18,000 mercenaries. Eventually, 30,000 German troops traveled to America, so many of them from the state of Hesse-Cassel that onlookers called all of them Hessians. Canada, having already repulsed Montgomery's American invasion, could provide a loyal staging ground in the north. "I have always thought Hudson's River the most proper part of the whole continent for opening vigorous operations," observed "Gentleman Johnny" Burgoyne, the dapper and worldly British general who arrived at Quebec with reinforcements in May 1776.

But plans for a strike south from Canada had to wait. Britain made its first thrust toward the mouth of the Hudson River by sea, using nearly 400 ships. In June, a convoy under General William Howe sailed from Halifax to Staten Island, New York, with 9,000 soldiers. By August, the general had received 20,000 reinforcements from across the Atlantic. His brother, Admiral Richard Howe, hovered nearby with 13,000 sailors aboard seventy naval vessels.

II. The good people of this Colony, with the rest of her sister Colonies, confiding in the justice and merited protection of the King and Parliament of *Great Britain,* ever . . . esteemed such a bond of union and harmony as the greatest happiness. But when that protection was wantonly withdrawn, and every mark of cruelty and oppression substituted; . . . self-preservation, and a regard to our own welfare and security, became a consideration both important and necessary. The Parliament and Ministry of *Great Britain,* by their wanton and undeserved persecutions, have reduced this Colony to a state of separation from her . . . as the only lasting means of future happiness and safety. . . . Cast off, persecuted, defamed, given up as a prey to every violence and injury, a righteous and much injured people have at length appealed to *God!* and, trusting to his divine justice and their own virtuous perseverance, taken the only and last means of securing their own honour, safety, and happiness.

III. We now feel every joyful and comfortable hope that a people could desire in the present Constitution and form of Government established in this Colony; a Constitution founded on the strictest principles of justice and humanity, where the rights and happiness of the whole, the poor and the rich, are equally secured; and to secure and defend which, it is the particular interest of every individual who regards his own safety and advantage.

IV. When we consider the publick officers of our present form of Government now appointed, as well as the method and duration of their appointment, we cannot but declare our entire satisfaction and comfort; as well in the characters of such men, who are justly esteemed for every virtue, as their well-known abilities to execute the important trusts which they now hold.

V. Under these convictions, . . . we . . . recommend it to every man . . . to secure and defend with his life and fortune a form of Government so just, so equitable, and promising; . . . that the latest posterity may enjoy the virtuous fruits of that work, which the integrity and fortitude of the present age had, at the expense of their blood and treasure, at length happily effected.

VI. We cannot but declare how great the pleasure, the harmony, and political union which now exists in this District affords; and having no grievances to complain of, only beg leave to recommend that a new Jury list be made for this District, the present being insufficient.

And lastly, we beg leave . . . that these our presentments be printed in the publick papers.—PHILIP PLEDGER, Foreman [and fourteen other signatures]

QUESTIONS

1. *While Thomas Jefferson was preparing the Declaration of Independence (see the text of the document in the Appendix), many local proclamations were in circulation. How does the South Carolina example compare in form, content, emotion, and clarity to Jefferson's document?*

2. *If many ideas and arguments present in the Declaration of Independence were indeed commonplace in the colonies early in 1776, how does this information enhance or alter your understanding of Thomas Jefferson's accomplishment?*

Source: Pauline Maier, American Scripture: Making the Declaration of Independence (New York: Knopf, 1997), 229–231.

On orders from Congress, General Washington moved south to defend New York City, a difficult task made harder by ardent Loyalist sentiment. Rumors swirled of a Loyalist plot to kidnap the general or even take his life. A bodyguard named Thomas Hickey, implicated in the Tory scheme, was hanged before a huge crowd of anxious onlookers in late June. Short on men and equipment, the general weakened his position further by dividing his troops between Manhattan and Brooklyn Heights on nearby Long Island.

A month after members of Congress signed the Declaration of Independence, the commander nearly lost his entire force—and the cause itself. General Howe moved his troops by water from Staten Island to the Brooklyn area and then outflanked and scattered the poorly trained Americans in the Battle of Long Island on August 27. Remarkably, the British leader called off a direct attack that almost certainly would have overrun the American batteries on Brooklyn Heights. When his equally cautious brother failed to seal off the East River with ships, rebel troops escaped disaster by slipping back to Manhattan in small boats under cover of night and fog.

"VICTORY OR DEATH": A DESPERATE GAMBLE PAYS OFF

New York Burning
(1776)

Washington's narrow escape to Lower Manhattan from Long Island in August 1776 was only the first of numerous retreats. His army left New York City on September 15. The rebels withdrew from upper Manhattan and Westchester in October and from Fort Washington and Fort Lee on the Hudson—with heavy losses—in November. The Americans "fled like scared rabbits," one Englishman wrote. "They have left some poor pork, a few greasy proclamations, and some of that scoundrel Common Sense man's letters, which we can read at our leisure." With winter at hand, the Continental forces retreated southwest toward Philadelphia.

Desertions and low morale plagued the ragged American army as it withdrew from New York late in 1776. But General William Howe repeatedly failed to press his advantage. The British commander and his brother had received a commission from Lord North, who headed the government in London, permitting them to negotiate a peace settlement with the Americans whenever possible. They hoped that a strong show of force, without a vicious offensive that might alienate civilians, could bring the enemy to terms. Howe's troops offered pardons to repentant rebels and encouraged desertions from Washington's army. In early December, the dwindling American force hurried through Princeton, New Jersey, and slipped across the Delaware River into Pennsylvania. Confident of victory, the British again failed to pursue them, instead making camp at Trenton. Washington realized that unless circumstances changed quickly, "the game will be pretty well up."

William Mercer, *Battle of Princeton*, date unknown. Courtesy of the Historical Society of Pennsylvania (HSP) Collection, Atwater Kent Museum of Philadelphia

■ This picture showing the noise and movement of the American victory at the Battle of Princeton was created by deaf painter William Mercer, whose father, Brigadier General Hugh Mercer, died in the battle.

Distressed by civilian talk of surrender, Tom Paine again took up his pen. In the *Pennsylvania Journal* for December 19, he launched a new series of essays (*The American Crisis*) that began with the ringing words "These are the times that try men's souls." Paine mocked "the summer soldier and the sunshine patriot" who shrank from extreme trials. "Let it be told to the future world, that in the depth of winter, when nothing but hope and virtue could survive," vigilant citizens, "alarmed at one common danger, came forth to meet and to repulse it."

Action soon followed words. On Christmas Day 1776, Washington issued a new code phrase for sentinels: "Victory or Death." He ordered Paine's words read aloud to the troops. Then, after dark, his men recrossed the windswept Delaware River in a driving snowstorm and advanced on Trenton. Holiday festivities and foul weather had left the enemy unprepared for this desperate maneuver, and intelligence of the impending attack seems to have been ignored. The Americans inflicted a startling defeat, killing several dozen and capturing more than 900 Hessian soldiers.

Most American troops had signed up to serve for a brief term and return home, and many had joined the previous January for a one-year stint. Washington knew that numerous enlistments expired on December 31 and that men would leave if the brief offensive halted. So he advanced again on December 30. Howe sent fresh troops forward under Charles Cornwallis to confront the rebels, pinning them down at Trenton. But when the British paused before attacking, the Americans left their campfires burning and slipped out of reach. They then circled behind Cornwallis to surprise and defeat his reinforcements at Princeton on January 3. It was not the last time that Washington bested Cornwallis.

DOCUMENT

Letter from
a Revolutionary
War Soldier

The Struggle to Win French Support

■ *Why did the French crown support the cause of the American Republic even though the new confederation had renounced the concept of hereditary monarchy?*

The successes at Trenton and Princeton restored a glimmer of hope for the tattered Continental Army and its supporters. As American forces took up winter quarters at Morristown, Howe withdrew his army from much of New Jersey to await the spring campaigns. As a result, anxious civilians in the region who had sworn their loyalty to the crown felt deserted. Public sentiment again swung toward the rebels. More importantly, news of the victories spurred support overseas for the American cause. French officials, eager to see their European rival bogged down in a colonial war, dispatched secret shipments of munitions to aid the revolutionaries.

One young aristocrat, the idealistic Marquis de Lafayette, was already on his way from France to volunteer his services to General Washington. But drawing forth an official French commitment to the American cause would take a larger show of success. That triumph finally came at the end of the next campaign season, with the Americans' stunning victory at Saratoga, deep in the Hudson Valley, 185 miles north of New York City.

BREAKDOWN IN BRITISH PLANNING

Among the Americans, two years of grim conflict had dampened the zeal that had first prompted citizens to enlist. Washington believed that the armed resistance could scarcely continue unless many more men made longer commitments to fight. He also insisted that his soldiers needed tighter discipline and better pay. In response, Congress expanded his disciplinary powers and offered a bonus to those who enlisted for a three-year term.

In a slumping economy, numerous recruits answered the call, including farmhands, immigrants, and unemployed artisans. All lacked training, supplies, and experience. Also, many of Washington's rural recruits had never been exposed to smallpox, so they lacked immunity to the devastating disease. When smallpox broke out among the American soldiers at Morristown, the commander promptly ordered mass inoculation. It proved to be one of General Washington's most shrewd decisions. Inoculation brings on a mild case of the disease, so the Virginian anxiously counted the days until his recuperating army could be ready to fight. "If Howe does not take advantage of our weak state," Washington commented in April 1777, "he is very unfit for his trust."

Despite American vulnerability, the British were slow to move. Lord North's ministry had fallen victim to its own contradictions. By seeking a decisive blow *and* a negotiated settlement in 1776, the British had achieved neither objective. They had also underestimated the persistence of Washington's army. During the 1777 campaigns, the British learned further hard lessons about the difficulty of their task and the need for coordinated plans.

General Burgoyne, returning to London for the winter, won government support for a major new offensive. He planned to lead a large force south from Canada via Lake Champlain, using the Hudson Valley to drive a wedge through the rebellious colonies. In support, a combined British and Indian force would strike east from Lake Ontario, capturing Fort Stanwix (east of modern-day Syracuse, New York) and descending eastward along the Mohawk River to meet Burgoyne at Albany. William Howe would push north from New York City to complete the design.

But General Howe had formed a different plan. Assuming Burgoyne would not need his help in the Hudson Valley, he intended to move south against Philadelphia. The two generals never integrated their separate operations, and the results were disastrous. In one six-month span, the British bungled their best chance for victory and handed their enemies an opening that permanently shifted the course of the war.

SARATOGA TIPS THE BALANCE

The isolated operations of Burgoyne and Howe got off to slow starts in late June 1777. Howe took two months to move his troops by sea from New York harbor to the headwaters of Chesapeake Bay. This delay gave the Americans time to march south, but an engagement at Brandywine Creek on September 11, 1777, failed to check Howe's advance north toward Philadelphia. The British finally entered the city in late September only to find that the rebel Congress had retreated to York, Pennsylvania.

At Germantown, just north of Philadelphia, Washington launched a surprise attack against the large Hessian garrison on October 4, but morning fog created so much confusion that the inexperienced Patriot troops allowed victory to slip away. Yet, as the battered army took up winter quarters at nearby Valley Forge, the defeats at Brandywine and Germantown seemed worth the price. The Americans had gained combat experience and had made Howe pay heavily for his hollow capture of Philadelphia. "Now," Washington wrote, "let all New England turn out and crush Burgoyne."

> *The Americans had gained combat experience and had made Howe pay heavily for his hollow capture of Philadelphia.*

Moving south from Canada in late June, "Gentleman Johnny" saw little likelihood of being crushed. His army consisted of 7,200 soldiers, with 1,500 horses to haul baggage and heavy equipment. British officers, foreseeing little danger, allowed nearly 2,000 women to accompany the huge force. General Burgoyne even brought his mistress along on the campaign. Weakened by tensions in their own command and knowing the British were on the march, the Americans fell back from Crown Point and Ticonderoga on Lake Champlain.

But as British supply lines lengthened, the crown's army grew less certain of victory. Burgoyne's soldiers expended valuable time cutting a roadway through the wilderness. Also, the reinforcements anticipated from the west had been turned back by Benedict Arnold

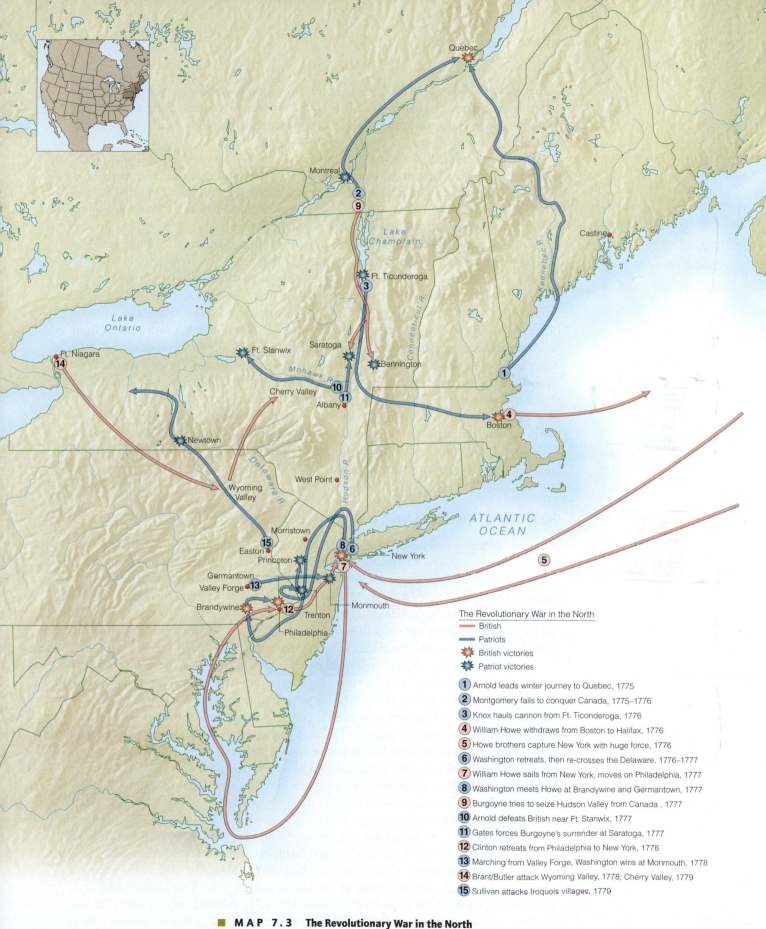

The Revolutionary War in the North
- British
- Patriots
- ✹ British victories
- ✹ Patriot victories

1. Arnold leads winter journey to Quebec, 1775
2. Montgomery fails to conquer Canada, 1775–1776
3. Knox hauls cannon from Ft. Ticonderoga, 1776
4. William Howe withdraws from Boston to Halifax, 1776
5. Howe brothers capture New York with huge force, 1776
6. Washington retreats, then re-crosses the Delaware, 1776–1777
7. William Howe sails from New York, moves on Philadelphia, 1777
8. Washington meets Howe at Brandywine and Germantown, 1777
9. Burgoyne tries to seize Hudson Valley from Canada , 1777
10. Arnold defeats British near Ft. Stanwix, 1777
11. Gates forces Burgoyne's surrender at Saratoga, 1777
12. Clinton retreats from Philadelphia to New York, 1778
13. Marching from Valley Forge, Washington wins at Monmouth, 1778
14. Brant/Butler attack Wyoming Valley, 1778; Cherry Valley, 1779
15. Sullivan attacks Iroquois villages, 1779

■ **M A P   7 . 3**   **The Revolutionary War in the North** at Fort Stanwix. Even worse, American militia near Bennington badly mauled a British unit of 600 sent to forage for corn and cattle. With cold weather approaching and supplies dwindling, Burgoyne pushed toward Albany, unaware that Howe would not be sending help up the Hudson to meet him.

As Burgoyne's situation worsened, the American position improved. An arrogant British proclamation demanding submission from local residents only stiffened their resolve and drew out more rebel recruits. The Americans' strength grew to nearly 7,000 in September after Congress gave command in the Hudson Valley region to Horatio Gates. The new general was an ambitious English-born officer who harbored resentments toward his American superior, Washington, and toward the much-admired Benedict Arnold. While Burgoyne's army crossed to the Hudson River's west bank at Saratoga, Gates's American forces dug in on Bemis Heights, ten miles downstream.

> An arrogant British proclamation demanding submission from local residents only stiffened their resolve and drew out more rebel recruits.

On September 19, 1777, Patriot units under two aggressive officers, Benedict Arnold and Daniel Morgan, confronted the enemy at Freeman's Farm, not far from Saratoga. In the grueling battle, British forces suffered 556 dead or wounded, nearly twice the American losses. Gates's refusal to commit reinforcements prevented the Patriots from achieving total victory. Nevertheless, the American ranks swelled with new recruits who sensed a chance to inflict losses on Burgoyne's forces. On October 7, the beleaguered British tried once more to smash southward, only to suffer defeat in a second battle at Freeman's Farm. Morgan and Arnold once again played key roles, though Arnold suffered a crippling leg wound. When Burgoyne's entire army of 5,800 surrendered at nearby Saratoga ten days later, Gates took full credit for the stunning triumph.

FORGING AN ALLIANCE WITH FRANCE

Ever since declaring independence, Congress had maneuvered to win international recognition and aid for the new nation. Success came first with the Dutch. Although the Dutch Republic claimed neutrality, its colonial merchants supplied gunpowder for the rebellion through the West Indian island of St. Eustatius. When a ship flying the American flag approached the island in November 1776, Dutch officials fired cannons in salute—the first foreign acknowledgment of American sovereignty. Weeks later, Benjamin Franklin arrived in France as part of a commission sent to seek wider European support.

It was one thing for the Dutch Republic to recognize fellow republicans; it was quite another for the French king, Louis XVI, to endorse a revolution that opposed monarchy. Some in France, like the young Marquis de Lafayette, felt enthusiasm for the American cause as an expression of rational Enlightenment beliefs. But others, such as France's foreign minister, Comte de Vergennes, saw the colonists' revolt as an opportunity to avenge old grievances against Britain and undermine British power. Uncertain about the rebellion's chances for success, especially after the fall of Philadelphia, the government in Paris moved cautiously. It confined itself to substantial but covert assistance in the form of money and arms.

Word of the American victory at Saratoga suddenly gave Franklin greater leverage. When he hinted to the French that he might bargain directly with London for peace, Vergennes moved immediately to recognize American independence. France agreed to renounce forever any claim to British land in North America, and Franklin promised that the Americans would help defend French holdings in the Caribbean. Both parties pledged to defend the liberty of the new republic, and each agreed not to conclude a separate peace with Great Britain or to cease fighting until U.S. independence had been ensured by formal treaty. In May 1778, the Continental Congress approved this alliance. The next month, France entered the war, adding its enormous wealth and power to the American cause. A year later, Spain—unwilling to ally itself directly with the upstart republic but eager to protect its vast American assets from Great Britain—entered the war on the side of France.

For the British, what had been a colonial brushfire swiftly flared into a global conflict reminiscent of the Seven Years' War. These new hostilities with France meant possible invasions at home and inevitable attacks on outposts of Britain's empire. French ships seized Senegal in West Africa, took Grenada in the West Indies, and burned trading posts on Hudson Bay in Canada. London's annual war expenditures climbed from £4 million in 1775 to £20 million in 1782.

As war costs mounted in Britain, domestic opposition to the conflict in America intensified. Some members of Parliament pushed for a swift settlement. In 1778, a peace commission led by Lord Carlisle offered concessions to the Continental Congress, hoping to tear the French alliance apart. But the Carlisle Commission failed to win reconciliation. Other Britons went further in opposing the American war. Their diverse reasons included fear of French power, desire for American trade, disgust over war profiteering, ties to friends in America, and idealistic belief in the revolution's principles. Many drank toasts to General Washington and openly supported the American cause.

Faced with growing economic and political pressure, the king and his ministers briefly considered withdrawing all troops from the rebellious colonies and focusing on the French threat. Instead, when General Howe resigned as commander in chief in America, they instructed his successor, Sir Henry Clinton, to retreat from Philadelphia to New York and devote his main resources to attacking the French in the Caribbean. Over the next four years, discontent within Britain continued to escalate, and no strategy proved sufficient to pacify the Americans or to crush their rebellion.

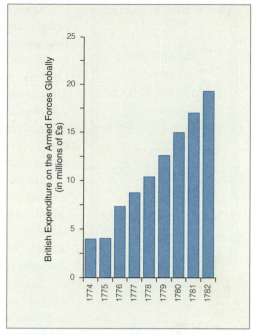

FIGURE 7.1 British Government Expenses on Armed Forces Throughout the World, 1775–1782 (in Millions of Pounds)

Britain's war budget soared after France entered the conflict in 1778, but major resources flowed toward India and the Caribbean, limiting the share available for North America.

Legitimate States, a Respectable Military

■ *If Americans were so fearful of centralized authority, how did they coordinate a successful political and military revolt against the powerful British Empire?*

Even with the new French alliance, the rebellious American states faced serious challenges on both the civilian and military fronts. They had thrown out their colonial governors and embarked on a dangerous war, but two fundamental questions still confronted them. First, how would the once-dependent colonies now be governed? And second, how could they shape a military force strong enough to defend themselves but not so powerful and unchecked as to seize control of their new civil governments?

THE ARTICLES OF CONFEDERATION

The Continental Congress had taken prompt initiative. Without clear authority, it had declared independence, raised an army, issued currency, borrowed money from abroad, and negotiated an alliance with France. Then it moved to bring greater stability and legitimacy to its work. In November 1777, one month after the victory at Saratoga, it approved the Articles of Confederation and presented this formal plan for a lasting and unifying government to the states for ratification. In every region, citizens were debating how much authority each new state government would have in relation to the larger federation. Who would have the power to levy taxes, for example, and who would control the distribution of land?

DOCUMENT

The Articles of
Confederation (1777)

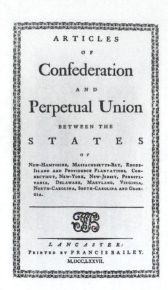

The Articles declared "The United States of America" to be a "firm league of friendship" between the thirteen former colonies. The final document proposed a weaker confederation than the one outlined in an earlier draft by John Dickinson. In the finished charter, each state would retain all independent rights and powers not "expressly delegated" to the Confederation Congress. Indeed, ties between the states seemed so loose that France considered sending thirteen separate ambassadors to America, and several European proposals to end the war suggested negotiating individually with each state.

According to the Articles, Congress could not collect taxes or regulate trade; it could only requisition funds from the states. Proportions would vary depending on each state's free population. Moreover, the Confederation had no separate executive branch; executive functions fell to various committees of the Confederation Congress. In addition, to the dismay of land speculators, the Congress would not control the western domains that several large states had claimed. Maryland, a small state without western claims, protested this arrangement and refused to ratify. To win the required approval from all thirteen states, drafters changed the plan and granted the Confederation control of western lands. After four years, the Articles finally won ratification in 1781.

Given the importance of the states, the task of designing new state governments seemed a higher priority to many than inventing a confederation structure. Some leaders in the Continental Congress returned home to help implement this state-level process. In May 1776, for example, two of Jefferson's friends in the Virginia delegation in Philadelphia departed for Williamsburg. They left their younger colleague behind, but they carried his written draft for a possible state constitution. Those already at work in Virginia accepted Jefferson's proposed preamble, and on June 29, 1776, Virginia led the way, adopting the first republican state constitution.

Virginia had already pioneered in another respect. Two weeks earlier, Virginia representatives approved a Declaration of Rights drawn up by George Mason. He affirmed the revolutionary concepts that all power derives from the people and that magistrates are their servants. He went on to endorse trial by jury, praise religious freedom, and condemn hereditary privilege. Over the next eight years, each state adopted a similar bill of rights to enumerate the fundamental limits of government power.

CREATING STATE CONSTITUTIONS

Though diverse, the thirteen states shared practical needs. Each had removed a functioning colonial government and needed to reestablish the rule of law under a new system. Britain possessed no written constitution, but the colonists had been ruled under published charters, and they shared a belief in the value of such clear and open arrangements. Thus they readily envisioned an explicit controlling document, or constitution, for each new state. Besides, the novel idea that government flowed from the people—as an agreement based on the consent of the governed—called for some all-encompassing, written legal contract.

A new written constitution, whether for a state or a union of states, represented something more fundamental and enduring than a regular law. It needed to be above day-to-day legal statutes and political whims. Somehow, the people, through chosen representatives, had to prepare a special document that citizens would affirm, or ratify, only one time. After the new government structure was in place, the constitution itself would be difficult, though not impossible, to change.

In 1779, Massachusetts legislators, under pressure from the public, fixed upon a method for providing the elevated status and popular endorsement for such a new document. Local voters in town meetings chose representatives for a specific constitution-drafting convention. These delegates, building on a model suggested by John Adams, crafted a suitable document, and their proposed constitution was then submitted to all the state's free men (regardless of race or property) for ratification. This widened constituency was intended to give special weight to the endorsement process.

Approval of the Massachusetts document was hotly debated. Many objected to the limits on popular power that were part of Adams's novel design. A reluctant revolutionary, Adams had dismissed Tom Paine as "ignorant, malicious, short-sighted." He had even composed a tract titled *Thoughts on Government* to counter the democratic enthusiasm of Paine's *Common Sense*. In his pamphlet, Adams argued that "interests" (like-minded groups), rather than people, should receive equal representation. In addition, he proposed sharing legislative responsibilities between a lower house, a senate, and a chief executive. Property requirements for these offices were steep, so wealthy interests would have power far beyond their numbers. The Massachusetts state constitution, ratified by a narrow margin, implemented these ideas. They signaled a turn away from the strongest popular radicalism of 1776 and foreshadowed the more conservative balance of interests that James Madison championed in the federal Constitution drafted in 1787.

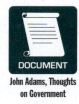

DOCUMENT

John Adams, Thoughts on Government

This extended experiment in constitution writing was exhilarating and unprecedented. Never before in history, John Adams observed, had several million people had numerous opportunities "to form and establish the wisest and happiest government that human wisdom could contrive." Initial state efforts yielded varied results as the minority of white male citizens debated novel approaches to self-government. By 1780, the desire of prominent and well-established elites to rein in democratic power was evident. Yet, in comparison to the overseas monarchy they had rejected, even the most conservative of the new governmental designs seemed risky and bold.

At least three common threads ran through all the state constitutions. First, fearing executive might, drafters curtailed the rights of state governors to dismiss assemblies, raise armies, declare war, fill offices, or grant privileges. Colonial governors had been appointed from above, by proprietors or the crown, and they could serve terms of any length. In contrast, state governors would now be elected annually, usually by the assembly. Moreover, their service was subject to impeachment and controlled by term limits. In Pennsylvania, the most radical of the new constitutions did away with a single governor altogether, placing executive power in the hands of a twelve-member council elected by the people.

Second, drafters expanded the strength of legislatures and increased their responsiveness to the popular will. They made elections more frequent, and they enlarged the size of assemblies to allow greater local involvement. They also reduced property requirements for holding office and changed limits on the right to vote to allow wider participation.

Third, the constitution-makers feared the possible corruptions that came when people held more than one office at the same time. Having experienced these glaring conflicts of interest firsthand, they stressed the separation of executive, legislative, and judicial posts. The decision to prevent members of the executive branch from also holding a legislative seat removed any prospect for a cabinet-style government along the lines of the British model.

John Singleton Copley, *John Adams*, 1783. Courtesy of the Harvard University Portrait Collection, Bequest of Ward Nicholas Boylston to Harvard College, 1828. Photograph by Photographic Services. © President and Fellows of Harvard College (H74)

■ After independence, Americans had to create their own governments, and states experimented with new forms. John Adams of Massachusetts was part of a unique generation of lawyers who became skilled in the art of constitution-making.

TENSIONS IN THE MILITARY RANKS

A new republican order, whatever its nature, could not defend itself without a suitable fighting force. Just as defunct colonial administrations gave way to new state governments after much debate, colonial militia companies transformed into state militia amid serious arguments. In the state militias and in Washington's army, which was controlled and paid by the Continental Congress, tensions emerged from the start. Animated discussions erupted as to what constituted equitable pay, appropriate discipline, suitable tactics, and a proper distribution of limited supplies. Others argued over whether wealth, popularity, vision, military experience, political savvy, European training, or influential ties should play a role in determining who received, or retained, the cherished right to command.

> *Wealthy gentry assumed that they would command the state militias, while citizen soldiers demanded the right to choose their own leaders.*

One heated topic involved the election of officers. Wealthy gentry assumed that they would command the state militias, while citizen soldiers demanded the right to choose their own leaders. Another source of tension concerned the right of a prosperous individual to buy exemption from military service or to send a paid substitute. In 1776, as Washington's army retreated into Pennsylvania, militia in Philadelphia had chastised "Gentlemen who formerly Paraded in our Company and now in the time of greatest danger have turn'd their backs." They asked whether state authorities meant "to force the poorer kind into the field and suffer the Rich & the Great to remain at home?"

Three years later, some of these same Philadelphia militia, bitter that the burdens of the war always fell disproportionately on the poor, took part in what became known as the Fort Wilson Riot. Staging a demonstration in October 1779 spurred by soaring food prices, they intentionally marched past the stately home of James Wilson, where wealthy Patriots had gathered. "The time is now arrived," the demonstrators' handbill proclaimed, "to prove whether the suffering friends of this country, are to be enslaved, ruined and starved, by a few overbearing Merchants, . . . Monopolizers and Speculators." Shots were exchanged, and six died in the melee at "Fort Wilson." (Wilson himself went on to become a leader of the 1787 Constitutional Convention.)

Subtle class divisions also beset the Continental Army, where jealousies over rank plagued the status-conscious officer corps. Congressional power to grant military commissions, often on regional and political grounds, only intensified disputes. Also, Americans representing Congress abroad were empowered to promise high military posts to attract European officers. Some of these recruits served the American cause well, such as Johann de Kalb and Friedrich von Steuben (both born in Germany), and Thaddeus Kosciusko and Casimir Pulaski from Poland. In France, at age nineteen, the Marquis de Lafayette secured a commission to be a major general in America, and he assisted Washington impressively throughout the war.

In contrast, other foreign officers displayed arrogance and spread dissension. Irish-born Thomas Conway, for example, courted congressional opponents of Washington and encouraged the desires of General Horatio Gates to assume top command. Whether or not a concerted "Conway Cabal" ever existed, Washington managed to defuse tensions from Valley Forge during the hard winter of 1777–1778. His numerous letters helped consolidate his position with Congress and patch frayed relations with Gates.

Another rival for command of the army, English-born Charles Lee, met disfavor several months later, when Washington ordered him to attack the rear guard of Clinton's army as it withdrew from Philadelphia to New York. Lee mismanaged the encounter at Monmouth, New Jersey, on June 28, 1778, and only Washington's swift action stopped a premature retreat. The Battle of Monmouth ended in a draw, but American troops claimed victory and took pride in their swift recovery and hard fighting.

SHAPING A DIVERSE ARMY

The army's improved effectiveness came in large part from the efforts of Friedrich von Steuben, a European officer recruited by Benjamin Franklin after charges of homosexuality

■ More than a century after the grim winter at Valley Forge, artist Edwin Abbey composed this mural of Steuben drilling Washington's soldiers in February 1778.

disrupted his German military career. He had arrived at Valley Forge in February 1778, offering to serve without pay. There he found soldiers with poor food, scant clothing, and limited training. Many Americans still wanted to see a more democratic citizen army, with elected officers and limited hierarchy. But Washington hoped to mold long-term soldiers into a more "Europeanized" force, and Steuben suited his needs. Shouting in several languages—he spoke no English—the newcomer worked energetically to drill soldiers. A written drill manual was drawn up, so that newly trained soldiers could drill others. Alexander Hamilton, who observed Steuben's strict training, gave him credit "for the introduction of discipline in the Army."

IMAGE

George Washington at Valley Forge

New discipline helped boost morale. Still, terms of service and wage levels remained sources of contention. So did the disparities in treatment and pay between officers and enlisted men. There were other grievances: inept congressional committees overseeing the war effort, incompetent officers filling political appointments, and a frustrating shortage of new recruits. Arguments also persisted over whether women or African Americans could serve in the army.

Women organized in diverse ways to assist the war effort, making uniforms and running farms and businesses for absent husbands. A few American women disguised themselves as men and fought. Deborah Sampson, for example, joined the Fourth Massachusetts Regiment, under the assumed name of Robert Shurtleff, and was wounded during her service. More commonly, women accompanied the troops to cook and wash in the camps. Earning scant pay, they carried water to the weary and wounded on the battlefield. Serving in these capacities, they formed a significant presence in both armies.

An estimated 20,000 women, many of them wives, may have accompanied the American army during the war. Washington reluctantly accepted the presence of women in camp, reasoning that they freed men for "the proper line of their duty." Mary Hays, the wife of a Pennsylvania soldier, endured the winter at Valley Forge, and later "Molly" Hays hauled pitchers of water on the battlefield and came to embody women's effort and commitment to the cause. When her husband was wounded at Monmouth, she is said to have set down her jug and joined his gun crew, earning folk-legend status as the cannon-firing "Molly Pitcher."

■ Exploring near the Altamaha River in Georgia, John Bartram and his botanist son William found "several curious shrubs, one bearing beautiful good fruit." They named it the Franklin tree after their scientist friend in Philadelphia, Benjamin Franklin. William painted a watercolor of the rare plant and saved seeds to protect the species.

© The Natural History Museum, London

American landscape. He promoted exploration, tested new crops, and tried his hand at archaeology by excavating ancient Indian mounds. In *Notes on the State of Virginia* (1785), Jefferson detailed his region's geography, society, and natural history.

In 1782, Hector St. John de Crèvecoeur, a Frenchman who lived in America, published *Letters from an American Farmer*. In the book's most famous essay, "What Is an American?" the author proclaimed that poor European immigrants became revitalized "in this great American asylum." According to Crèvecoeur, free people flourished in America not only because of "new laws" but also because of "a new mode of living, a new social system" that nurtured community growth. Societies for bettering jails, assisting debtors, and building libraries had existed before independence, but after the war Crèvecoeur watched a new generation creating voluntary associations at an unprecedented rate.

Earnest reformers launched more than thirty new benevolent organizations between 1783 and 1789. Some provided relief for the physically and mentally ill. Others aided strangers and immigrants. Still others granted charity to the poor and disabled or lobbied to reform harsh penal codes. In 1785, prominent New Yorkers John Jay and Alexander Hamilton joined like-minded citizens to form a Society for the Promotion of the Manumission of Slaves. Society members decried slavery as "disgraceful" and "shocking to humanity." In Connecticut, citizens banded together to stop the abuse of liquor. Members of this early **temperance** organization protested that the state's residents consumed 400,000 gallons of rum annually and that communities paid dearly in both financial and moral terms.

Similar efforts to reform and improve the new nation sprang up everywhere. The new Massachusetts Humane Society dedicated itself to assisting people in "suspended animation" between life and death, whether from drowning, drinking, heatstroke, or other causes. The society provided crude lifesaving equipment along waterfronts. It also constructed huts, stocked with food and firewood, to aid shipwreck survivors on isolated coastlines. Amid such general optimism, no sooner had the former colonists disentangled themselves from the British Empire than they began to speak of shaping an expansive empire of their own.

Competing for Control of the Mississippi Valley

■ *Why did control of the Mississippi Valley matter so much to Americans after the Revolution?*

I t has ever been my hobby-horse," John Adams wrote in 1786, "to see rising in America an empire of liberty, and a prospect of two or three hundred millions of freemen, without one noble or one king among them. You say it is impossible. . . . I would still say, let us try the experiment." Westward expansion became a persistent American theme. During the postwar decade, interest and activity centered on the area between the eastern mountains and the Mississippi River. This huge region had been reserved for Indians in 1763, when King George III prohibited colonial settlement west of a line along the Appalachian crest. The domain beyond that "Proclamation Line" was divided in two at the Ohio River into a northern and a southern district, until the British ceded the entire region to the United States at the end of the Revolution.

Both north and south of the Ohio, Indians now faced a flood of newcomers. The area from the Ohio River to the Gulf of Mexico (which eventually became known as the Old Southwest) immediately became a magnet for southern pioneer families in search of land. Following an old buffalo trail and Indian trading path, they pushed west through Cumberland Gap, where southwest Virginia now touches Kentucky, and spread out across fertile portions of the lower Mississippi River valley. These aspiring homesteaders promptly faced resistance from Native American inhabitants and their Spanish supporters.

North of the Ohio River, other Americans flocked to claim rich woodland farms, pushing into the area between Ohio and Wisconsin often known as the Old Northwest. These migrants also met stiff opposition from Native Americans defending their homelands and from the Indians' British allies in neighboring Canada. By 1787, the Continental Congress had designated this region as the Northwest Territory and was busy revising an elaborate plan to establish a territorial government that could draw this domain into the union. Looking first south, then north, from the banks of the Ohio, it is possible to see two distinctive stories unfold after 1783.

> *Looking first south, then north, from the banks of the Ohio, it is possible to see two distinctive stories unfold after 1783.*

DISPUTED TERRITORY: THE OLD SOUTHWEST

For a generation, Spain had been rebuilding its position north of the Gulf of Mexico and east of Texas in the Old Southwest, as part of wider reforms within its American empire. The Spanish had acquired Louisiana from France in 1763 and had conquered West Florida. In a 1783 treaty, Britain returned East Florida to the Spanish and agreed that Spain would retain West Florida. The Spanish occupied St. Augustine, Pensacola, New Orleans, and Natchez, as well as St. Louis farther north.

Because the Spanish controlled both banks of the lower Mississippi, they determined who could use the huge river for trade. Since 1763, they had let British subjects navigate freely on its waters, so trans-Appalachian fur traders had become accustomed to using this thoroughfare. Louisiana merchants paid for goods in Spanish silver, and settlers upriver needed such hard currency. During the Revolutionary War, Americans had retained access to the river, and the Spanish in New Orleans depended on produce from the north. Still, Spanish authorities feared American expansion into the Mississippi Valley. They debated whether to resist migrants pushing from the east, or to welcome such newcomers and profit from their trade.

In 1783, Spain was shocked when Britain, through its separate treaty with the United States, granted the Americans a generous southern boundary: the thirty-first parallel. The treaty terms also included the right of Americans to navigate on the Mississippi. The Spanish believed that they alone should decide whose boats had access to the river. Moreover, Spain had good reason to claim that its West Florida province stretched north *above* 31 degrees, at least to the mouth of the Yazoo River and perhaps as far as the Tennessee River.

For its part, the new Confederation had the force of numbers working to its advantage. The threat of Indian attacks had dammed up westward expansion since 1775. After the war, Americans migrated by the thousands to three existing centers of Anglo settlement in the Old Southwest. By 1785, 10,000 recent migrants clustered along the Holston, Watauga, and French Broad rivers above Knoxville. Nearly three times that many newcomers had already staked claims to the rich land south of the Ohio River between Lexington and Louisville. Another 4,000 were clearing farms along the Cumberland River around Nashville. Aggressive Americans talked about pushing even farther west. They imagined establishing a foothold on the Mississippi at Chickasaw Bluffs (modern Memphis) or perhaps seizing Natchez or New Orleans.

In New Hampshire, by 1785, securities valued at nearly £100,000 belonged to just 4.5 percent of the state's adult male population: 1,120 men among approximately 25,000. A mere 3 percent of this group—thirty-four men—controlled more than a third of this vast speculative investment. Most of these men had close ties to the current state government, situated in Exeter, near the coast. When farmers organized conventions to voice their economic grievances, merchants infiltrated and disrupted their meetings. In September 1786, 200 citizens, many of them armed war veterans, marched on Exeter to demand money reforms before conditions "drive us to a state of desperation." Officials organized cavalry units to confront the furious citizens, arresting their leaders from the crowd "as a butcher would seize sheep in a flock." As soon as the state's governor, General John Sullivan, had suppressed the dissenters, he issued a proclamation forbidding further conventions. He then wrote to the Massachusetts governor, James Bowdoin, offering to help crush similar unrest in the neighboring state.

DOCUMENT

Military Reports on Shays' Rebellion

Early in 1786, the Commonwealth of Massachusetts had imposed a heavy direct tax on its citizenry. Farmers in western Massachusetts lacked sufficient cash and already faced a wave of foreclosures for debt. They protested the tax law at town meetings and county conventions. When their complaints fell on deaf ears, they took actions into their own hands, "regulating" events as the North Carolina Regulators had done two decades earlier. The Massachusetts Regulation became known as Shays' Rebellion when Daniel Shays, a revolutionary officer who had served with distinction under Lafayette, emerged as one of its popular leaders. At first, these New England Regulators focused on closing the courts. In August 1786, 1,500 farmers marched against the Court of Common Pleas in Hampshire County and shut it down. The next month, another band closed the court in Worcester.

The confrontation escalated as winter set in. By January more than 1,000 Shaysites, knowing that their allies in New Hampshire had been defeated, moved to seize the federal arsenal in Springfield. But Governor Bowdoin had mobilized an army, financed largely by wealthy merchants in Boston. This private militia overpowered the westerners and forced all who did not flee to sign an oath of allegiance. Disarmed but not silenced, the dissidents succeeded in extracting some relief from the legislature. They also managed to defeat Bowdoin in the next election and replace him with a more popular governor, John Hancock.

The unrest in New England played into the hands of those advocating a stronger national government. (Rumors even circulated that nationalists had helped provoke the violence to rally support for their cause.) In a typical letter, Henry Knox expressed fear to his fellow general, John Sullivan, that "we are verging fast to anarchy." Writing in May 1787, he urged Sullivan to send delegates from New Hampshire to a crucial meeting that was about to begin in Philadelphia.

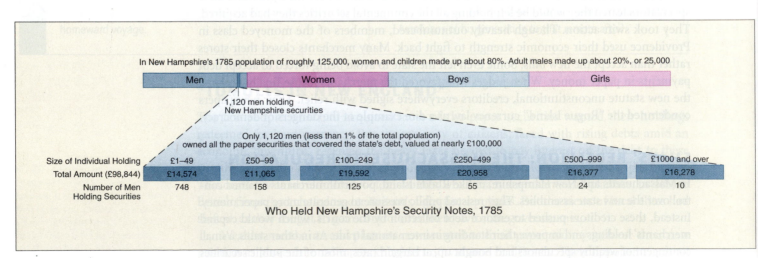

In New Hampshire's 1785 population of roughly 125,000, women and children made up about 80%. Adult males made up about 20%, or 25,000

| Men | Women | Boys | Girls |

1,120 men holding New Hampshire securities

Only 1,120 men (less than 1% of the total population) owned all the paper securities that covered the state's debt, valued at nearly £100,000

Size of Individual Holding	£1–49	£50–99	£100–249	£250–499	£500–999	£1000 and over
Total Amount (£98,844)	£14,574	£11,065	£19,592	£20,958	£16,377	£16,278
Number of Men Holding Securities	748	158	125	55	24	10

Who Held New Hampshire's Security Notes, 1785

■ **FIGURE 8.1 Concentration of Security Notes in the Hands of a Few: The Example of New Hampshire in 1785**

Drafting a New Constitution

■ *How did nationalist leaders use their political skills to bring about the Constitutional Convention in Philadelphia?*

Even before Yorktown, Alexander Hamilton, Washington's youthful Caribbean-born aide-de-camp, had proposed a convention to restructure the national government. Now he worked with another young nationalist, James Madison, and their energetic supporters to bring it about. Congress had made earnest efforts toward reform, but any changes to the Confederation's governing articles required approval from all thirteen states. Thus, vital amendments—which would let Congress regulate commerce, raise revenue, and establish a judiciary, for example—proved nearly impossible. For some powerful leaders, especially merchants and creditors, a major political revision seemed in order.

"Many Gentlemen both within & without Congress," wrote Madison, desire a "Convention for amending the Confederation." Still, it would take impressive leadership—Madison provided much of it—to seize the initiative and then generate enough momentum to change the rules of national government. Extensive compromise, both between elite factions and toward resistant popular forces, would be necessary at every stage along the path. After all, it would take an enormous push to engineer such a convention, to guide it to restructure the government along nationalist lines, and finally to persuade voting Americans to ratify the proposed changes and accept their legitimacy. To begin such a task, would-be reformers needed to convince the Confederation Congress to allow their revision plans to move forward. For that, they needed to recruit the enormous prestige of George Washington.

Alexander Hamilton – Portrait

PHILADELPHIA: A GATHERING OF LIKE-MINDED MEN

The path began at Mount Vernon in 1785 when Washington hosted commissioners appointed by Maryland and Virginia to resolve state boundary disputes regarding the Potomac River. During the gathering, these men (including James Madison) scheduled a broader meeting on Chesapeake trade for the next year at Annapolis, Maryland. They invited all the states to send representatives. Only twelve delegates from five states showed up at Annapolis in September 1786, but news of the serious unrest in New England prompted talk of a more extended meeting.

Mount Vernon

Alexander Hamilton, as a representative from New York, persuaded the other delegates at the Annapolis meeting to call for a convention in Philadelphia the following May to discuss commerce and other matters. Madison won endorsement for the proposal from the Virginia legislature and then from Congress. Reform-minded congressmen, such as James Monroe, saw an opportunity to amend and improve the existing Confederation structure. But when the states sent delegates to Philadelphia the following spring, many of the appointees believed that amendments might not be enough. They were open to the more sweeping changes that Madison and other nationalists had in mind. The gathering that had been called to consider commercial matters and propose improvements to the Articles of Confederation soon became a full-fledged Constitutional Convention, a private meeting to design and propose an entirely new structure for governing the United States.

Madison reached Philadelphia in early May 1787. He immediately began drafting plans for drastic change and lobbying delegates, some of whom came early to attend a secret gathering of the Society of the Cincinnati. On May 25, when representatives from seven states had arrived, they launched the convention and unanimously chose Washington as the presiding officer. Participants agreed that they would operate behind closed doors and each state delegation would have one vote. There would be no public discussion or official record of the proceedings. Soon, delegates from twelve states had joined the gathering. Only Rhode Island did not send representatives.

> *The gathering that had been called to propose improvements to the Articles of Confederation soon became a full-fledged Constitutional Convention.*

The fifty-five delegates had much in common. All were white, male, and well educated, and many already knew one another. These members of the national elite included thirty-four lawyers, thirty public creditors who had bought up war securities, and twenty-seven members of the Society of the Cincinnati. More than a quarter of the participants owned slaves, and nearly a dozen had done personal business with financier Robert Morris of the Pennsylvania delegation. Not surprisingly, all seemed to agree that the contagion of liberty had spread too far. Elbridge Gerry of Massachusetts called the current situation "an excess of democracy."

> *Most delegates agreed with this novel system of checks and balances, intended to add stability and remove corruption.*

Specifically, these men feared recent legislation that state assemblies had adopted to assist hard-pressed citizens: laws that delayed tax collection, postponed debt payments, and issued paper money. Most delegates hoped to replace the existing Confederation structure with a national government capable of controlling finances and creating creditor-friendly fiscal policy. To be effective, they believed, a strengthened central government must have greater control over the states. Only Robert Yates and John Lansing of New York and Luther Martin of Maryland staunchly resisted expanding central power.

Many delegates, especially those from heavily populated states, thought the national legislature should be based on proportional representation according to population rather than each state receiving equal weight regardless of its numbers. Also, most wanted to see the single-house (unicameral) Congress of the Confederation replaced by upper and lower houses that would reflect the views and values of different social classes. John Adams had helped create such a two-house (bicameral) system in the Massachusetts constitution, thereby limiting pure democracy and giving more political power to propertied interests.

Besides calling for checks within the legislative branch itself, Adams had also laid out strong arguments for separating, and checking, the powers of each competing branch of government. For a sound and lasting government, Adams had argued, there should be **separation of powers;** the legislative branch should be balanced by separate executive and judicial branches that are equally independent. Most delegates agreed with this novel system of **checks and balances,** intended to add stability and remove corruption.

COMPROMISE AND CONSENSUS

The Philadelphia gathering, which lasted through the entire summer, would later be known as the Constitutional Convention of 1787. Even as a general consensus emerged within the small meeting, countless personal, practical, and philosophical differences persisted. Hamilton delivered a six-hour speech in which he staked out an extremely conservative position. He underscored "the imprudence of democracy" and stressed a natural separation between "the few and the many"—the "wealthy well born" and the "turbulent and changing" people. Hamilton's conservative oration called for the chief executive and the senators to be chosen indirectly, by elected representatives rather than by the people themselves, and he recommended that these high officials should serve for life. Such ideas undoubtedly appealed to many of his listeners, but all of the delegates knew that a majority of citizens would never accept such proposals. Pierce Butler of South Carolina, invoking ancient Greece, urged members to "follow the example of Solon, who gave the Athenians not the best government he could devise but the best they would receive."

This attentiveness of convention members to what the public would accept is illustrated by their approach to voting rights. Even delegates who wanted to limit the vote to property holders realized that various state constitutions, responding to popular pressure, had already distributed **suffrage** (the right to vote) more broadly. Property ownership was no longer a universal voting requirement, and states varied on whether religion, race, or gender could determine eligibility. James Wilson of Pennsylvania, second only to Madison in working to build a practical nationalist majority in the convention, pointed out that "it would be very hard and disagreeable" for any person, once enfranchised, to give up the right to vote. Accordingly, the delegates proposed that in each state all those allowed to vote for the "most numerous branch of the state legislature" would also be permitted to cast ballots for members of the House of Representatives. But they shied away from accepting direct election for the Senate or the president. Members deferred other difficult suffrage matters, saying that the rules for carrying out elections in each state should be worked out by the state legislature.

Time and again during the sixteen-week convention, these like-minded men showed their willingness to bargain and compromise. Lofty principles and rigid schemes often gave way to balancing and improvisation. For example, delegates who differed over the length for the chief executive's term of office and right to run for reelection also disagreed on the best method of presidential selection. Some of them suggested that ordinary voters should elect the president; others proposed that the state governors, or the national legislature, or even electors chosen by state legislators should choose the chief executive.

Finally, the aptly named Committee on Postponed Matters cobbled together an acceptable system: a gathering (or "college") of chosen electors from each state would cast votes for the presidency. This **electoral college** plan had little precedent, but it managed to balance competing interests. Under the scheme, state legislatures would set the manner for selecting electors. The least populous states would get a minimum of three electoral votes, and states with more people would choose more electors in proportion to their numbers, giving them added weight in the decision. The people could also participate in the voting process, though only if their state legislatures called for it. If no candidate won a majority in the electoral college, the House of Representatives would determine the president, with each state's delegation having one vote. The system was far from elegant or democratic, but it placated varied interests, and it won prompt approval.

QUESTIONS OF REPRESENTATION

As deliberations stretched across the long, hot summer of 1787, two central issues threatened to unravel the convention: political representation and slavery. Questions of representation pervaded almost every discussion, pitting large states such as Virginia, Pennsylvania, and Massachusetts against the less populated states. Madison's well-organized Virginians offered a comprehensive blueprint outlining a new national government that would have three separate branches. This design, called the "Virginia Plan," recommended a bicameral national legislature with proportional representation in each body. The House of Representatives would be chosen by popular election. Then members of the House would elect the Senate, choosing among persons nominated by the state legislatures.

Madison's system clearly favored populous states. Not surprisingly, a coalition of small-state delegates led by William Paterson of New Jersey submitted an alternative "New Jersey Plan." This less sweeping revision built on the existing Articles of Confederation. It called for a continuation of the current unicameral legislature, in which each state received an equal vote. A committee chaired by Benjamin Franklin broke the impasse. The idea of an upper house, or Senate, would be retained, and each state, whatever its size, would hold two senate seats. Seats in the House of Representatives would be determined proportionally, according to the relative population of each state. This lower house would initiate all bills dealing with finance and money matters.

> *To implement proportional representation in a fast-growing society, the delegates provided for a national census every ten years.*

To implement proportional representation in a fast-growing society, the delegates provided for a national census every ten years. No European country had attempted a regular periodic headcount, so the census represented a radical innovation at the time. This in turn raised a thorny question. Should slaves—people enumerated in the census yet denied the rights of citizens—be counted in determining a state's proportional representation in the national government? Slaveholding states wanted their human property to count because that would give those states more representation. The convention resolved this dilemma in mid-July with a "three-fifths" formula that Madison had proposed in earlier legislation. The odd recipe made every five enslaved people equivalent to three free people in apportionment matters.

In an ironic twist, the same week the Constitutional Convention delegates approved the notorious **three-fifths clause,** the existing government of the United States leaned in the opposite direction. Meeting in New York, members of the Confederation's Congress passed the Northwest Ordinance of 1787, which outlawed slavery in the new territory above the Ohio River. Because there was much contact between the two meetings, some scholars speculate that powerful Southerners agreed to give away the prospect of slavery north of the Ohio River in exchange for more support of slavery within the new plan taking shape in Philadelphia.

SLAVERY: THE DEEPEST DILEMMA

During the debate over the three-fifths clause, Madison commented that the greatest division in the United States "did not lie between the large & small States: it lay between the Northern & Southern," owing to "the effects of their having or not having slaves." This highly charged issue simmered beneath the surface for most of the summer.

In late August, with most other matters resolved, delegates could no longer postpone questions surrounding slavery. Yet again, a committee deliberated, and a bargain was struck. This time, hundreds of thousands of human lives were at stake. Planter delegates from Georgia and South Carolina refused to support any document that regulated the slave trade or curtailed slavery itself. They asserted that such a charter could never win acceptance at home. In part they were bluffing. In fact, constraints against slavery had wide popular appeal in the expanding backcountry of the Deep South, where independent farmers outnumbered planters, ministers questioned slavery, and pioneers wanted national support in confronting powerful Indians.

Yet few delegates challenged the proslavery posture, possibly because strong antislavery opinions could have prolonged or even deadlocked the convention. Weary participants were eager to complete their work and fearful of unraveling their hard-won consensus. Rather than force the matter, even those who disapproved of slavery rushed to compromise, heaping a huge burden on future generations. Southern delegates dropped their protests against giving Congress the power to regulate international shipping. In exchange, the framers approved a clause protecting the importation of slaves for at least twenty years. They also added a provision governing fugitive slaves that required the return of "any person held to service or labor." Through a calculated bargain, delegates had endorsed slavery and drawn the South into the union on terms that suited that region's leaders. The word *slave* never appeared in the finished document.

In early September, the convention members put the finishing touches on their proposal and wondered whether Americans would accept it. Winning state-by-state approval would involve an uphill battle, especially given the absence of a bill of rights. George Mason, who had drawn up Virginia's Declaration of Rights eleven years earlier, reminded members that such a set of guarantees "would give great quiet to the people." But in the convention's closing days, many delegates resisted the notion, and all were eager to adjourn. They overwhelmingly voted down Mason's suggestion.

Without a bill of rights, Mason, Elbridge Gerry of Massachusetts, and Edmund Randolph of Virginia refused to endorse the final document. Other delegates who dissented had already departed. Of the seventy-four delegates chosen at the convention's outset, fifty-five actually attended the proceedings, and only thirty-nine agreed to sign the finished plan. These small numbers made it more important than ever to end on a note of unanimity. By polling the state delegations instead of individual delegates, the document's authors shrewdly hid the three dissenting votes. This allowed them to assert, in Article VII, that their task—framing a new constitution for the United States—had been approved "by the unanimous consent of the States present" on September 17, 1787.

■ In a crucial decision, members of the Constitutional Convention chose to protect the slave trade and preserve slavery. One African American who had already taken matters in her own hands was Mumbet, a slave in Massachusetts and the widow of a Revolutionary War soldier. In 1781, she sued for her freedom on the grounds that "all were born free and equal." Her court victory proved a landmark in New England. Proudly, she took the name Elizabeth Freeman.

Ratification and the Bill of Rights

■ *Why was a bill of rights expected by citizens, omitted by the drafters of the Constitution, and later added?*

Committed nationalists now faced their most difficult task: winning public acceptance for an alternative structure that defied existing law. The proposed constitution ignored the fact that the Articles of Confederation—the document governing the United States at the time—could be amended only with the approval of all thirteen states. Instead, the text drafted in Philadelphia stated that ratification (acceptance through voting) by conventions in any nine states would make the new document take effect in those places. Moreover, the proposed ratification process left no room for partial approval or suggested revisions. Each state, if it wanted to enter the debate at all, had to accept or reject the entire proposed frame of government as offered.

THE CAMPAIGN FOR RATIFICATION

The Confederation Congress had acquiesced in allowing the convention to occur in the first place. Most congressional representatives had expected the meeting to produce proposals for amending the current government, not discarding it. But now that the Philadelphia conclave had ended, the Congress sitting in New York City balked at endorsing the revolutionary document. To avoid a lengthy and troublesome debate, proponents of the new constitution urged Congress simply to receive the frame of government as a possible proposal and then transmit it to the states without an endorsement. Congress did so on September 28, 1787, and the document's advocates portrayed the unanimous vote as an expression of approval.

Supporters had no time to lose because Pennsylvania's assembly was set to adjourn the next day. An early victory in that large and central state would be crucial for building momentum, so they rushed the congressional letter of transmittal from New York to Philadelphia. There, the assembly faction dominated by Robert Morris won a hasty vote to schedule a state ratifying convention. Over the next three months, Pennsylvania towns and counties elected delegates, a convention met, and the state voted to approve the new plan. Delaware had already approved it unanimously on December 7. New Jersey and Georgia promptly followed suit. By the end of January, Connecticut had also ratified. Other states called elections and scheduled conventions. Only Rhode Island, which had not sent delegates to the drafting convention, refused to convene a meeting to debate ratification.

By seizing the initiative early, the proponents of the new framework shaped the terms of debate. The drafters, anything but a cross-section of society, worked to portray themselves as such. They noted that their document began with the ringing phrase "We the people of the United States," a last-minute addition by Gouverneur Morris of New York. And Madison told the public that the text sprang from "*your* convention."

> *By seizing the initiative early, the proponents of the new framework shaped the terms of debate.*

Most important, in a reversal of logic and contemporary usage, the nationalists who supported the new constitution took for themselves the respected name of **Federalists.** They gave their opponents, a diverse assortment of doubters and critics, the negative-sounding term **Anti-Federalists.** The Federalists then used their ties to influential leaders to wage a media war for public support. They wrote letters, prepared pamphlets, and published essays praising the proposed constitution.

The strongest advocacy came from the pens of Alexander Hamilton and James Madison. The two men composed eighty essays for the New York press under the pen name *Publius.* John Jay added five more, and in the spring of 1788 the collection appeared as a book titled *The Federalist.* In the most famous piece, "Number 10," Madison challenged the widely accepted idea that a republic must be small and compact to survive. Turning the proposition

DOCUMENT

James Madison
Defends the
Constitution

around, he argued that minority opinions would fare better in a large nation, where diverse competing interests would prevent a unified majority from exerting control.

DIVIDING AND CONQUERING THE ANTI-FEDERALISTS

Opponents of the new plan were on the defensive from the start. Many had supported some government change, and most conceded the presence of economic difficulties. But the Federalists' dire predictions of impending chaos struck them as exaggerated. "I deny that we are in immediate danger of anarchy," one Anti-Federalist writer protested.

DOCUMENT

Patrick Henry, Against Ratification of the Constitution

Richard Henry Lee, president of the Confederation Congress, condemned the Federalists as a noisy "coalition of monarchy men, military men, aristocrats and drones." Other prominent figures joined him in opposition: George Clinton in New York; Luther Martin, Samuel Chase, and William Paca in Maryland; and Patrick Henry, George Mason, and Benjamin Harrison in Virginia. Though not always sufficiently forceful or committed, such notables became the spokespeople for a far wider array of skeptics.

Many opponents of the proposed constitution protested the plan's perceived threat to local political power. Despite Madison's reassurances in *Federalist* Number 10, they believed that local and state governments represented voters more fairly and responded to their needs and concerns more quickly than a distant national authority could. For some critics of the proposed constitution, this belief in local control expressed a radical democratic principle; for others it represented their provincial bias. In short, Anti-Federalists were too diverse to speak with a single voice. They included subsistence farmers living far from any navigable river or urban market, and war veterans who feared that their influence in republican government would be diminished by the

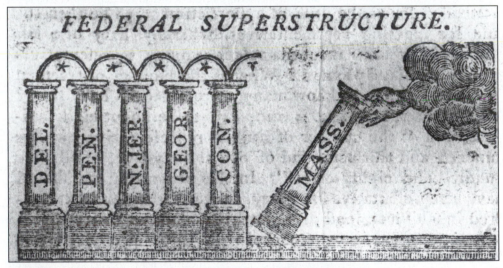

■ In 1788 newspapers tracked ratification of the new "federal superstructure" state by state. Massachusetts ratified the proposed Constitution in March—apparently aided by the Hand of God! New Hampshire provided the "ninth and sufficient pillar" in June, followed by Virginia four days later.

"Grand Federal Processions"

The essays contained in *The Federalist Papers* circulated widely and helped to build the case for ratification of the newly drafted Constitution, but well-organized parades provided the broadest demonstrations of support. These large and orderly public events were carefully planned, handsomely executed, and well publicized in the popular press. Predictably, two of the largest "Grand Federal Processions" were staged in Philadelphia and New York, where pro-ratification forces were strong.

Philadelphia's celebration on July 4, 1788, got underway with the ringing of church bells. A mounted trumpeter leading the vast procession proclaimed a "New Era," and judges carried a copy of the new Constitution. New York City's parade three weeks later was designed to help win ratification from a divided state convention meeting in Poughkeepsie. It featured diverse artisans, such as bakers who served cake to the crowd.

These events had the desired effect of conveying a message of Federalist patriotism and unity. "Rank for a while forgot all its claims," observed Philadelphia's Benjamin Rush, "and Agriculture, Commerce and Manufactures, together with the learned and mechanical professions, seemed to acknowledge, by their harmony and respect for each other, that they were all necessary to each other, and all useful in cultivated society."

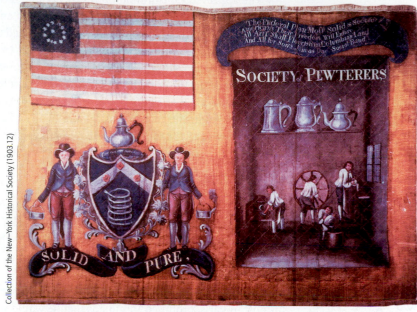

Collection of the New-York Historical Society (1903.12)

■ In New York City's parade urging ratification, on July 23, 1788, the Society of Pewterers carried this elaborate silk banner. A rhyme in one corner proclaims that under the proposed constitution, "All Arts Shall Flourish in Columbia's Land, And All Her Sons Join as One Social Band."

Envisioning History

QUESTIONS

1. Why would the involvement of diverse urban artisans such as butchers, tanners, sailmakers, and bakers have delighted Federalist organizers of pro-ratification parades?

2. Explain the patriotic double meanings behind these artisan slogans on parade banners: "Both Buildings and Rulers Are the Work of Our Hands" (Bricklayers); "With the Industry of the Beaver We Support Our Rights" (Hat Makers); "Solid and Pure" (Society of Pewterers).

proposed system. Many indebted people also opposed ratification, fearing that a strong national government would favor the interests of bondholders and foreign creditors ahead of the economic well-being of ordinary citizens.

If Anti-Federalists were numerous in the remote countryside, Federalists predominated in coastal commercial centers. Using a variety of tactics, they pressed their advantages in the fight to control state ratifying conventions. They lured prominent Anti-Federalist delegates with hints of high office, and they ridiculed vocal opponents as Shaysite extremists. In state after state, they forged coalitions linking commercial farmers living near towns and rivers with aspiring artisans and city-based entrepreneurs.

Through intensive politicking, the Federalists won approval in Massachusetts in February 1788, but only by a thin margin (187 votes to 168 in the ratifying convention). This commitment from "the Bay State" helped to sway Maryland in April, South Carolina in May, and New Hampshire in June. The Federalists could now claim the nine states needed to implement their plan, and in July they staged celebrations to hail the new Constitution of the

United States. In town after town, a "Grand Federal Procession" marched through the streets behind floats and banners, designed by groups of self-assured artisans, proud of their trades and of their prominent place in shaping the new republic.

The approved Constitution promptly became the law of the land. But in Massachusetts, advocates had triumphed only by promising to add an explicit bill of rights that gave written protection for valued civil liberties. The Federalists had to provide similar assurances during the summer to secure slim majorities in Virginia (89 to 79) and New York (30 to 27). North Carolinians had voted down the proposed frame of government at their first ratifying convention because it lacked a bill of rights. A second North Carolina convention, called in 1789, withheld approval until a bill of rights had actually been introduced into the first federal Congress as proposed amendments to the Constitution. In 1790, Rhode Island narrowly voted approval for the new framework (34 to 32) rather than risk being left in economic and political isolation.

ADDING A BILL OF RIGHTS

Abby Aldrich Rockefeller Folk Art Museum, Williamsburg, VA. Colonial Williamsburg Foundation (Acc. 1935.301.4 [slide 1989–1731])

In a society consisting of almost 3 million people, the franchise remained a limited privilege, open primarily to white men with property. All told, only about 160,000 voters throughout the country took part in choosing representatives to the state ratifying conventions. And only about 100,000 of these people—less than 7 percent of the entire adult population—cast votes for delegates who supported the Constitution. Federalists knew, therefore, that they would have to fulfill their pledge to incorporate a bill of rights. Madison, goaded by Jefferson from his post in Paris, promised Virginians that he would push to include the assurance of specific rights as amendments to the Constitution. In making this promise, he had two main motives. First, he hoped to ensure his own election to the nation's new House of Representatives. Second, he wanted to stave off the prospect that discontented states would call a second national convention "for a reconsideration of the whole structure of government."

In compiling a list of protections, or bill of rights, Madison drew from scores of proposals for explicit amendments put forward by the state ratifying conventions. He selected those, mostly dealing with individual rights, that could pass a Federalist-dominated Congress and would not dilute any of the proposed new government's powers. He set aside suggestions for limiting the government's right to impose taxes, raise a standing army, or control the time and place of elections. True to his word, Madison pushed twelve less controversial statements through the Congress as constitutional amendments, despite congressional apathy and opposition. Within two years, three-fourths of the states ratified ten of these short but weighty pronouncements. Hence, the first ten amendments—the **Bill of Rights**—quickly became a permanent part of the U.S. Constitution.

Many of the protections provided by the Bill of Rights harked back to lessons learned in earlier struggles with Parliament. The ten amendments guarded the right of the people to bear arms, limited government power to quarter troops in private homes, and banned unreasonable searches and seizures. They also guaranteed crucial legal safeguards by ensuring the right to trial by jury, outlawing excessive bail and fines, and prohibiting "cruel and unusual punishments." The First Amendment secured freedom of speech and of the press, protected people's right to assemble and petition, and prohibited Congress from meddling in the exercise of religion. By securing these freedoms, Madison engineered a final set of compromises that ensured the acceptance and longevity of the Constitution he had done so much to frame.

Conclusion

The long War for Independence had exhausted the new nation. Managing the difficult task of demobilization (disbanding the army) and reconstruction consumed American energy and resources in the 1780s. So did the new western domain, where Americans had to balance prospects for national expansion against the military threats posed by the European empires and Native American groups that claimed the region. Also, economic differences set aside during the war quickly reemerged; questions of wealth and property loomed large.

Therefore, when Confederation leaders imposed unprecedented taxes to pay off the war bonds gathered up by wealthy speculators, irate farmers and veterans protested that Congress was gouging "the Many" to enrich "the Few." These numerous dissenters pressured state governments to provide debt relief and issue paper money. But wealthy creditors reacted forcefully. These like-minded men maneuvered to create a new and stronger central government that could support their interests and override state-level economic measures favoring the common people. Sidestepping the existing government, they drafted a new constitution at a closed convention in Philadelphia in 1787.

By 1789, America's established leaders had campaigned successfully for ratification of the new constitution, in the face of bitter and varied opposition. Calling themselves Federalists, they had regained a secure grip on the reins of power, which had nearly slipped from their hands during the tumultuous 1770s. But the fierce debate over ratification of the Constitution raised fresh uncertainties about the long-term survival of the union. Much hinged on selection of the first president. Inevitably, George Washington emerged as the overwhelming favorite to become the first chief executive of the new republic.

CHRONOLOGY: 1783–1789

1783	Treaty of Paris.
	Newburgh Conspiracy is thwarted.
	Society of the Cincinnati is formed.
1785	Land Ordinance of 1785.
1786	Shays' Rebellion in Massachusetts.
1787	Constitutional Convention meets in Philadelphia.
	Constitution of the United States is drafted and signed.
	Northwest Ordinance creates Northwest Territory.
1788	Publication of *The Federalist*.
	Ratification of the Constitution.
	Madison agrees to draft Bill of Rights.
1789	George Washington is elected the first president of the United States.

For Review

1. Why did the prospect of a Newburgh Conspiracy and the creation of the Society of the Cincinnati upset many Americans?

2. How would Indians in the Mississippi Valley in the 1780s have viewed the "empire of liberty" envisioned by John Adams?

3. For the numerous debtors during the postwar economic depression of the 1780s, what factors worked for, and against, their interests?

4. To what extent is the genius of the American Constitution found in its unique, innovative structure of checks and balances?

5. If the Constitution's crucial "three-fifths clause" had been a "five-fifths clause" instead, who would have benefited?

6. Did leading nationalists exaggerate the difficulties of the 1780s to suit their agenda, or did they save the new union in a dire situation? Explain.

Created Equal Online

For more *Created Equal* resources, including suggestions on sites to visit and books to read, go to **MyHistoryLab.com**.

In 1786, artist Gilbert Stuart painted this portrait of Mohawk leader Joseph Brant, born Thayendanegea.

concerted campaign against Indians in the area that is present-day Ohio, Indiana, and Michigan. Under the leadership of Miami chief Little Turtle (Michikinikwa), and with support from the British, this Ohio Confederacy temporarily held off the advances of the American army.

The Ohio Confederacy offers some intriguing parallels to the coalition of colonies during the Revolution and to the union of the states afterward. Before the Revolution, Benjamin Franklin had marveled at the cohesion of the Six Nations (the precursor of the confederacy), drawing inspiration from the Indians' example. He noted, "If Six Nations of Ignorant savages" could create a union, then thirteen colonies led by white men should be able to do so also.

Joseph Brant pointed to the lesson that the Indians learned from the United States in creating the Ohio Confederacy: with political unity came military strength. Indians, like the colonists, sought to overcome regional and cultural differences among themselves. In both cases, disparate groups found common ground in their fight against a single enemy—Great Britain in the case of the thirteen colonies, the United States in the case of the Ohio Confederacy.

Members of the Ohio Confederacy soon discovered that their federation could not function as a completely independent political unit. In the early 1790s, the Indians relied heavily on the British for guns and artillery. And many Indians came to depend increasingly on trade with Europeans.

From 1775 to 1800, the Northwest Territory—the Great Lakes region west of the Appalachian Mountains and east of the Mississippi River—remained a vast **middle ground,** where Indian villagers coexisted with British traders and French trappers. The cultures of these groups intermingled. But the incursion of European American settlers into this middle ground disrupted Indian hunting practices. Violence escalated in an endless cycle of raids and retaliation. The U.S. citizens who settled in the area that is today Kentucky, Ohio, Indiana, and Michigan—the trans-Appalachian West—were the vanguard of the new, expanding republic. At the same time, they drew the army of the infant nation into a costly, bloody war.

Native Americans residing in the Northwest Territory in the 1790s included peoples who had long occupied the Great Lakes region and the upper Midwest, such as the Miami, Potawatomi, Menominee, Kickapoo, Illinois, Fox, Winnebago, Sauk, and Shawnee. Also present were refugees from the East: Ottawa, Ojibway, Wyandot, Algonquin, Delaware, and Iroquois displaced by the Revolutionary War. As they resettled in villages, they managed to retain some elements of their cultural identity, but in the seven years immediately after the Revolution, thousands died in Indian–white clashes in the region.

By encouraging European Americans to stake their claim to the area, the Northwest Ordinance inflamed passions on both sides.

What caused this violence? By encouraging European Americans to stake their claim to the area, the Northwest Ordinance inflamed passions on both sides: whites' determination to occupy and own the land and Indians' equal determination to resist this incursion. In 1790, under orders from President Washington, Brigadier General Josiah Harmar led a force of about 1,500 men into the Maumee River valley in the northwest corner of modern-day Ohio. Orchestrating two ambushes in September, Miami chief Little Turtle and his men killed 183 of Harmar's troops, driving the general back in disgrace. The next year, Washington chose General Arthur St. Clair to resume the fight. But when St. Clair's men met Little Turtle's warriors in November 1791 near the upper Wabash River, the Americans suffered an even greater defeat, losing over 600 men.

Washington tried once more to find a commander equal to Little Turtle. This time he chose General Anthony Wayne, a Revolutionary War hero dubbed "Mad Anthony" for his bold recklessness. Wayne mobilized a force of 3,000 men and constructed a string of new forts as well. At the battle of Fallen Timbers in August 1794, near present-day Toledo, hundreds of Indians perished before Wayne's forces. The withdrawal of British

■ **MAP 9.3**   **Western Land Claims of the States**

Several of the original thirteen colonies, including Massachusetts, Connecticut, New York, Virginia, South Carolina, North Carolina, and Georgia, claimed land west of the Appalachian Mountains. By 1802, these states had ceded their western lands to the federal government. The Land Ordinance of 1785 provided that this expanse be auctioned off in parcels no less than 640 acres each, with a minimum price of $1 per acre—too expensive for many family homesteaders, thus opening the way for investors to purchase and profit. Hoping to raise money through land sales, the federal government did not object to speculation.

later generations. With backing from wealthy investors, the Ohio Company quickly bought up tracts of land and then sold parcels to family farmers at inflated rates. A similar venture was initiated in Georgia in 1795, when speculators bribed state legislators for the right to resell huge tracts to the west of the state, land that the state did not even own. The state legislature passed the so-called Yazoo Act (named for a Georgia river) because of these bribes. The act resulted in the defrauding of thousands of buyers, whose land titles were worthless.

By protecting slavery and opening new territory to European American settlement, the new nation condemned southern blacks to a legal bondage that stood in stark contrast to revolutionary principles. Many settlers relied on slave labor. By the late eighteenth century,

support helped doom the Ohio Confederacy. On August 3, 1795, 1,100 Indian leaders met at Fort Greenville (in western Ohio) and ceded to the United States a vast tract of Indian land: all of present-day Ohio and most of Indiana. Little Turtle helped negotiate the agreement.

PATTERNS OF INDIAN ACCULTURATION

White newcomers in the Northwest Territory swiftly made clear their belief that men should farm and herd sheep and cattle, while women should milk cows, raise chickens, tend the garden, spin thread, and weave cloth. However, Indian groups differed in their responses to the various attempts to persuade—or force—them to "acculturate" by adopting novel customs. At first, all learned from each other, as newly arrived settlers and indigenous peoples traded foodways, folk remedies, and styles of dress, adopting foreign habits while still retaining some old ways. Little Turtle himself chose among European American cultural traits; he drank tea and coffee, kept cows, and shunned leather breeches in favor of white men's clothing. The fact that his wife made butter suggested that she was skilled in the ways of European American homemakers.

> *The migration of whites into Indian hunting grounds rapidly depleted their game supply and devastated their crop fields.*

Adopting some habits of European Americans—for example, liquor consumption—amounted to self-destruction. Alcohol was a prized trade item. Moreover, European Americans and Indians often used it to lubricate political negotiations and cultural rituals. Yet conflicts over liquor, and tensions vented under the influence of liquor, became increasingly common—and deadly. Some Indian leaders, including Joseph Brant and Little Turtle, came to view the drinking of alcohol as a full-blown crisis among their people. Both believed that Indians must reject the white man's bottle if they were to survive.

But liquor was only one piece of a larger cultural puzzle, as the experience of the Cherokee, Chickasaw, Choctaw, Creek, and Seminole Indians in the southeastern United States revealed. The migration of whites into Indian hunting grounds rapidly depleted their game supply and devastated their crop fields. Unable to hunt efficiently for food, many in these groups took up new forms of agriculture after the Revolution, and they became known to whites as the Five Civilized Tribes. Women, who had traditionally tended crops using hoes, gave way in the fields to men, who used plows provided by the federal government. Protestant missionaries encouraged Indian women to learn to spin thread and weave cloth. For more than a generation, the willingness of these southern tribes to accommodate themselves to European American law and divisions of labor allowed them to stay in their homeland and retain key elements of their cultural identity.

In southwest and far west borderland areas, Spanish officials met with mixed success in their attempts to convert Indians to Christianity and encourage them to engage in sedentary farming. The Spanish established missions, which served as economic outposts of Spain in California and the Southwest. These missions produced large amounts of wheat, corn, and beans, and they were also major stock-raisers of sheep and cattle. Without the missions, the Spanish *presidios* (forts) and *pueblos* (towns) would have perished. But the missions were also the means of converting and acculturating Indians.

For example, between 1772 and 1804, Spanish priests established nineteen missions among the Chumash, hunter-gatherers living in permanent villages along the California coast. When large numbers of the Indians moved to these settlements, they forfeited their traditional kin and trade networks, and their distinctive culture began to fade. Birth rates plummeted due to disruptions in family life (more women than men lived in the missions), and mortality rates increased dramatically as contact with the Spanish introduced new diseases.

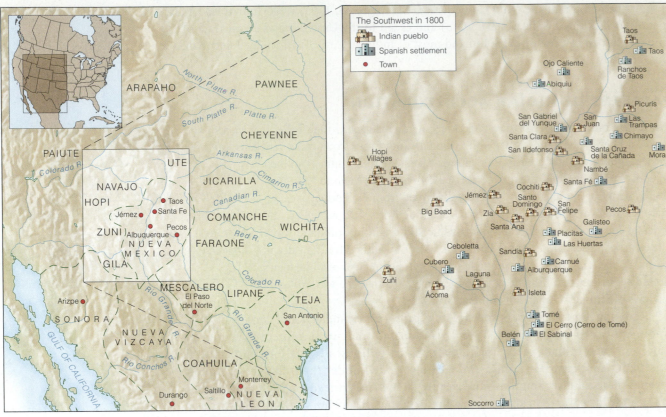

■ **M A P 9 . 2   The Southwest in 1800**
This map shows the pastoral and mountain borderlands (present-day north-central New Mexico) in 1800. Within this region, Spanish colonists and nomadic and pastoral Indian societies were often hostile to one another. But on an everyday local level, these groups engaged in a lively trade. Items of exchange included not only horses, guns, sheep, and buffalo hides, but also women and children captives. Men on both sides recognized the value of women captives in particular as symbols of male power.

In contrast, along the Texas Gulf Coast, the Spanish made little headway in their efforts to bring the Karankawa Indians into the missions. Members of this nomadic tribe arrived at the mission gates only when their own food reserves were low; in essence, the Karankawa simply included the missions in their seasonal migrations between the Gulf Coast and the coastal plain. The West represented a fluid, unsettled region where cultures collided and reconfigured themselves.

LAND SPECULATION AND SLAVERY

The West was not necessarily a place of boundless economic opportunity for all people who settled there. When European Americans poured into the trans-Appalachian West after the Revolution, they often carried alcohol and guns, staples of trade among all groups. These items proved a lethal mix, injecting violence into commercial and diplomatic relations among a variety of cultural groups. Land speculation and slavery helped the West come to resemble society on the eastern seaboard, with its hierarchies based on class, ethnicity, and race.

Eager investors and creditors thwarted many homesteaders' quest for cheap land. Schemes such as the Ohio Company of Associates foreshadowed the significance of land speculation in shaping patterns of settlement and property ownership further west in

Kentucky slaves numbered 40,000—more than 18 percent of the state's total population. In isolated settlements, where farmers owned just one or two slaves, African Americans faced a kind of loneliness unknown on large plantations in the East.

Patterns of land use directly affected the spread of slavery into the West. Despite eastern planters' use of European soil conservation techniques (crop rotation, use of manure as fertilizer), many of them had to contend with depleted soil in the upper South. Generations of tobacco growers had worn out the land, depriving it of nutrients. As a result, many growers were forced to abandon tobacco. Some of them moved west into Indian lands in the Mississippi Territory to cultivate cotton. The scarcity of labor motivated slave owners to push workers to the limits of their endurance. Slaves cleared potential farmland, rooted out tree stumps, and prepared the ground for cultivation. Once cotton could be planted, these same slaves worked in gangs under the sharp eye of a white overseer or black driver. Men, women, and children labored as human machines, planting, hoeing, and harvesting as much cotton as quickly as possible.

> *Whites in the western territories preserved and adapted slavery to extract financial profit from new areas of settlement.*

Many free people of color also found a less than hospitable welcome in the West. In 1802, delegates to the first Ohio territorial convention moved to restrict blacks' economic and political opportunities, even though fewer than 400 were living in Ohio at the time. Although slavery was outlawed in Ohio and other territories, blacks still lacked the right to vote. Soon after Ohio became a state in 1803, the legislature took steps to prevent the in-migration of free blacks altogether. In 1803, the territorial legislature of Indiana passed a "black law" prohibiting blacks or Indians from testifying in court against white people. Black families in the Northwest Territory were also vulnerable to kidnapping: some white men seized free blacks and sold them as slaves to plantation owners in the South.

Whites in the western territories preserved and adapted slavery to extract financial profit from new areas of settlement. The institution of slavery thrived in the West, revealing that few black people could claim that the West offered them new opportunities. For many other Americans, however, the post-Revolutionary period brought new challenges and opportunities in the realms of religion, work, and gender roles.

Shifting Social Identities in the Post-Revolutionary Era

■ *What kinds of traditional hierarchies were challenged by different groups of Americans in the wake of the Revolution? How successful were those challenges?*

The nation's founders had argued for an egalitarian society, one in which people prospered according to their talents and ambition. Of course, their definition of egalitarianism included only white men. Still, it was a revolutionary idea and led to challenges of social hierarchies after the Revolution. These hierarchies included the patriarchal (male-headed) family, established Protestant denominations, power systems based on social standing, and ideas about race and gender. Ordinary men and women penned letters to local newspapers, glorifying common laborers and questioning the claim to power of "the marchent, phesition [physician] the lawyer and divine [minister] and all the literary walkes of life, the Jutical & Executive oficeers & all the rich who live without bodily labour." This letter writer's creative spelling suggests that even people lacking in formal education felt free to voice their opinions on political issues of the day.

In the early nineteenth century, voluntary reform organizations multiplied across the nation, transforming the professions, the religious landscape, slavery, the rights of women, and a host of other American institutions. As these groups proliferated in the

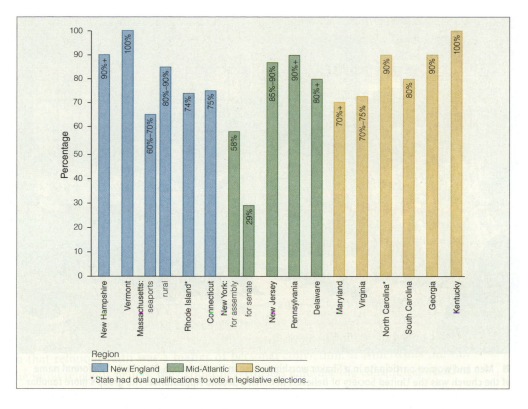

■ **FIGURE 9.2** **Percentage of White Men Eligible to Vote in the United States, 1792**

Source: Robert J. Dinkin, *Voting in Revolutionary America: A Study of Elections in the Original Thirteen States, 1776–1789* (Westport, CT: Greenwood Press, 1982), 36–39.

years immediately after the Revolution, both the possibilities and limitations of reform became clear. Some groups—for example, white working men—sought to advance their own self-interest without showing much concern for the plight of African American laborers. In other cases, people banded together to target the behavior of a specific group: drunkards, slave owners, the irreligious, or prostitutes. These moral reform groups welcomed diversity among members, as long as new converts supported the cause.

THE SEARCH FOR COMMON GROUND

As people identified a common causes, a variety of groups emerged. Manumission and temperance societies had appeared during the Revolution. Other kinds of associations sprang up and multiplied after the war. For example, in southwestern Pennsylvania, tax resisters formed the Mingo Creek Society. The organization offered mediation services for citizens who felt "harassed with suits from justices and courts, and wished a less expensive tribunal." In New York, fifteen women formed the Society for the Relief of Poor Widows and Small Children. Often, free people of color in the North and South created new churches designated as "African," a testament to a shared heritage that predated their transportation to America and enslavement.

Americans redefined the family to accommodate new circumstances and ideas. Whites who chose to live in Indian villages felt they had found new families. Wrote Mary Jemison, a captive and then willing member of the Seneca, "It was my happy lot to be accepted for adoption." She described her initiation ceremony in these terms: "I was received by the two squaws to supply the place of their brother in the family; and I was ever considered and treated by them as a real sister, the same as though I had been born of their mother."

In some instances, the family metaphor extended to religious ties. Members of Baptist and Methodist congregations referred to themselves as brothers and sisters. They called their preachers "elder brother" or, in some places in the South, "Daddy." The Shakers,

Jefferson lived in an age when revolutionary enthusiasm was sweeping the western world. Challenges to slavery had rocked Europe; France outlawed slavery in 1794, although Napoleon later reinstated it. Abolition had also transformed the Western Hemisphere with the successful rebellion of the Saint-Domingue slaves in 1791. The United States provided the political theory and rhetoric to inspire abolitionists around the globe, but within the new nation, the debate over the institution of slavery continued to rage. The southern states, in particular, took decisive steps to solidify the institution within their own boundaries.

PROTECTING AND EXPANDING THE NATIONAL INTEREST

As president, Jefferson reconsidered his original vision of the United States: a compact country in which citizens freely pursued modest agrarian interests without interference from the national government or distractions from overseas conflicts. Indeed, during his years in office, the federal government moved toward increasing its power and the country grew in size.

Just before Jefferson assumed the presidency, the Federalist-dominated Congress had strengthened the national court system by passing the Judiciary Act of 1801. The act created sixteen circuit (regional) courts, with a judge for each, and increased support staff for the judicial branch in general. President Adams appointed these judges (called midnight judges because they were appointed right before Jefferson took office). Before stepping down, Adams had also appointed Secretary of State John Marshall as chief justice of the Supreme Court.

Adams's last-minute acts had long-term consequences. Marshall remained on the bench for thirty-four years. He presided over the court when it rendered its landmark **Marbury v. Madison** decision in 1803, which established the judiciary's right to declare acts of both the executive and legislative branches unconstitutional. This right, called judicial review, empowered the Supreme Court to decide whether an act of Congress was illegal. *Marbury v. Madison* established that Congress did not have the power to modify the Supreme Court's original jurisdiction as stated in the Constitution. Chief Justice Marshall wrote: "It is emphatically the province and duty of the judicial department to say what the law is."

The European powers continued their operations in the territory west of the United States.

In the realm of international affairs, Jefferson asserted his own authority. Challenges from foreign powers prompted the Democratic-Republican president to take bold steps to protect U.S. economic and political interests abroad and along the country's borders. In 1801, Jefferson's administration launched a war against Barbary pirates in North Africa when Tripoli (modern-day Libya) demanded ransom money for kidnapped American sailors. (Together, the North African kingdoms of Tunis, Tripoli, Algeria, and Morocco were known as the "Barbary States.") The war against Tripoli, which spanned four years, revealed the extent of U.S. trade interests even at this early point in the nation's history. The United States signed a peace treaty with Tripoli in 1805 and paid $60,000 for the release of the American captives.

At the beginning of the nineteenth century, the European powers continued their operations in the territory west of the United States. In 1801, Napoleon persuaded the king of Spain to secretly cede the trans-Mississippi region called Louisiana to France. Retaining control of New Orleans, Spain denied the United States the right to use that city as a depository for goods awaiting shipment. In 1803, Jefferson sent his fellow Virginian, and prominent Anti-Federalist, James Monroe to Paris. Together with American ambassador Robert Livingston, Monroe set out to secure American trading rights in New Orleans. To the Americans' surprise, Napoleon agreed to sell the whole area to the United States. Frustrated by his inability to quell the Saint-Domingue revolt, Napoleon believed that the money would help fund future wars against England. At the time, Louisiana included most of the territory between the Mississippi and the Rocky Mountains—a total of 828,000 square miles. The United States agreed to pay $15 million for the Louisiana Purchase.

The Louisiana Purchase reversed the roles of Jefferson and his Federalist rivals. The president now advocated territorial expansion, but his opponents remained suspicious of the move. Devoted to a strict interpretation of the Constitution, Jefferson traditionally favored limiting federal authority. Yet he sought to justify the purchase by pointing out that it would finally rid the area of European influence. He proposed shifting Indians from the Mississippi Territory (part of present-day Alabama and Mississippi) to the West so that American newcomers could have the eastern part of the country to themselves. For their part, the Federalists feared that Louisiana would benefit mainly agrarian interests and eventually dilute New England's long-standing political influence and power. They suspected Jefferson of attempting to expand the influence of his own political party.

Neither the Democratic-Republicans nor the Federalists expressed much concern about the fate of the many Indian and Spanish-speaking inhabitants of Louisiana. All these peoples became residents, if not citizens, of the United States when the Senate approved the purchase in October 1803.

Conclusion

In the years immediately after the war, the American Revolution had far-reaching effects, both abroad and at home. In France in 1789, King Louis XVI's attempt to raise taxes provoked armed resistance among ordinary people, who claimed the right to create a new constitution for the country. Many French Revolutionaries were inspired by the American colonists' revolt against what they claimed were unfair policies of taxation. In the coming generations, emerging countries all over the world would echo the American revolutionary rhetoric of freedom in their own struggles against colonial oppression and government tyranny.

At home, Americans continued to challenge authority in many forms during the decade of the 1790s. In western Pennsylvania, debtors interfered with the work of federal tax collectors in the Whiskey Rebellion, just as Patriots had confronted British customs officials two decades earlier. Anglican clergy in the South and Congregational clergy in the North saw an erosion of their power, as Protestant denominations began to multiply and flourish. Throughout the country, African Americans sought to put into practice the ideals of the Revolution by arguing against slavery and in favor of universal emancipation. In the case of abolitionism, the Founders had unleashed a political movement that they neither approved nor anticipated.

By opening more western lands to European American migration, the Revolution had contrasting effects on different groups. In the West, Indian refugees from the East regrouped but found themselves vulnerable to federal troops bent on eliminating the American Indian

CHAPTER CHRONOLOGY: 1789–1803

1789	Judiciary Act of 1789 establishes national court system.
1790	Congress restricts citizenship to "free white persons."
	Northern states take steps to abolish slavery.
1791	Bill of Rights is ratified.
	Slaves revolt in Saint-Domingue (Haiti).
	Samuel Slater constructs first spinning machine on U.S. soil.
	Bank of the United States is chartered.
1792	Washington is reelected president.
	Mary Wollstonecraft publishes *A Vindication of the Rights of Woman*.
1793	Washington issues Neutrality Proclamation.
	Eli Whitney invents the cotton gin.
1794	U.S. troops defeat forces of Ohio Confederacy.
	Whiskey Rebellion takes place in Pennsylvania.
1796	John Adams is elected president.
1797	XYZ Affair stirs anti-French sentiment.
1798	Quasi War waged with France (to 1800).
	Alien and Sedition Acts curb political dissent.
1800	Thomas Jefferson is elected president.
1801	War waged against Barbary pirates.
1803	Jefferson buys Louisiana Purchase.
	Marbury v. Madison asserts that judiciary can declare laws unconstitutional.

presence there. Soon, the region west of the Appalachian Mountains became a major battle-ground, as white farmers sought to own and cultivate the land that a multicultural mix of traders had occupied before.

During the last decade of the eighteenth century, the United States was not as independent of European influence as it hoped to be. Tensions between France and England continued to shape both the foreign and the domestic policy of the new nation. Some politicians admired the British system of hierarchy and order, while others believed that egalitarian, revolutionary France offered a model for the United States.

The election of Democratic-Republican Thomas Jefferson as president in 1800 provoked fear among Federalists. However, this peaceful transfer of power did not result in a radical challenge to the nation's goals. In fact, Jefferson supported the continuation of certain policies—such as federal support for the institution of slavery and for the displacement of Indians from their homelands. Moreover, the chief executive at times seemed to draw inspiration from the Federalists, who sought to centralize and expand federal authority. He presided over the creation of a national court system, and he expanded the boundaries of the new nation through the Louisiana Purchase in 1803. In the process, Jefferson implicitly acknowledged the Federalists' contention that the United States must develop a strong national government to meet the challenge of changing times.

By stating in his inaugural address, "We are all Republicans, we are all Federalists." Jefferson suggested that American political leaders of both parties shared essentially the same views about the role of government and the importance of economic opportunity for ordinary people. Most office holders also expressed suspicion of groups that professed religious beliefs that lay outside the mainstream of Protestantism. They considered slavery not a moral issue, but a political issue that individual states must address. They united behind the idea that Indians, blacks, and women should have no formal voice in governing the nation.

Despite these common principles, the post-Revolutionary era saw the rise of two opposing camps—those favoring local control and those supporting federal authority. Many people defined political interests in "either-or" terms: *either* the French system of political equality *or* the British monarchy; *either* the individual states *or* the federal government; *either* the farm *or* the factory. Such thinking promoted a narrow view of the United States, a society of great economic and ethnic diversity.

Despite this ideological split, the new nation gave white men opportunities practically unknown in the rest of the world. Regardless of their background, many white men could aspire to own property and to participate in the political process. The federal government supported economic growth by facilitating territorial expansion, technological innovation, and the protection of private property. As much for the prosperity it promoted as for the noble ideas it nourished, the Revolution continued to inspire liberation movements within the United States and throughout the world.

For Review

1. What were the limitations of the "either-or" clash of ideas between the Federalists and the Democratic-Republicans? How might an enslaved Southerner, or a member of one of the Five Civilized tribes, have perceived this political debate?

2. Choose three different groups and describe the ways the legacy of the Revolution affected their postwar experiences. Consider, for example, these issues: legal status, religious beliefs, labor, community life, and culture.

3. How did relations with European countries shape political debates in the United States between 1789 and 1803? In what ways had the new nation not fully achieved its independence?

4. Many of the Founding Fathers were suspicious of political parties. What developments in the decade following the war would have confirmed or dispelled those suspicions?

5. In political terms, at least, the United States emerged from the Revolution as a unified nation. In what ways did regional distinctions challenge the notion—or ideal—of unity among all Americans?

Created Equal Online

For more *Created Equal* resources, including suggestions on sites to visit and books to read, go to **MyHistoryLab.com.**

Chapter 10

Defending and Expanding the New Nation, 1804–1818

CHAPTER OUTLINE

- **British Aggression on Land and the High Seas**

- **The War of 1812**

- **The Era of "Good Feelings"?**

- **The Rise of the Cotton Plantation Economy**

Charles B. J. F. Saint Memin, *Captain Meriwether Lewis*, 1807. Collection of the New–York Historical Society (Neg. 1971.125)

■ Captain Meriwether Lewis posed in Indian dress for this watercolor completed in 1807 by French artist C. B. J. Févret de Saint-Mémin.

In early November 1804, a group of soldiers worked feverishly to construct a rough military garrison on the north bank of the Missouri River, near several Mandan Indian villages and just west of modern Washburn, North Dakota. The soldiers knew they had to work quickly. Within a month, winter would descend on the northern Great Plains, and the temperature would plummet. In fact, not long after Fort Mandan was completed, the temperature registered 45 degrees below zero Fahrenheit.

The garrison provided shelter for the members of the **Lewis and Clark Expedition**, a party of exploration led by Meriwether Lewis and William Clark. Both captains in the U.S. Army, Lewis and Clark had been commissioned by President Thomas Jefferson to explore the upper reaches of the newly acquired Louisiana Territory, which had doubled the size of the country. With the ultimate goal of reaching what is today Oregon, their party spent the winter at Fort Mandan and joined the buffalo hunts and nightly dances sponsored by their hosts, the Mandan Indians. Between November 1804 and March 1805, Lewis and Clark also found time to record their observations on all manner of things natural and cultural. In their journals and their letters to President Jefferson, they described the language of the Hidatsa Indians and the beadwork of the Arikara, the medicinal properties of native plants, and the contours of the Missouri River. In a shipment prepared for the president, they included deer horns, pumice stones, and the pelt of a white weasel. Among an assortment of live animals, only a magpie and a prairie dog survived the journey to Washington, D.C.

Lewis and Clark's trek took 28 months to complete and covered 8,000 miles. Along the way, the two men assured the Indians they met that their expedition's purpose was purely scientific. However, Jefferson had also commissioned them to chart a waterway passage to the Northwest. The president hoped to divert the profitable fur trade of the far Northwest away from British Canada and into the hands of Americans by locating a river connecting the Northwest directly to eastern U.S. markets. Jefferson also instructed Lewis and Clark to initiate negotiations with various Indian groups, to pave the way for miners and ranchers to move into the area.

Throughout their journey, Lewis and Clark expressed awe of the magnificence of the land—its physical beauty and its commercial potential. While camped at Fort Mandan, Lewis described the Missouri: "This immence river so far as we have yet ascended waters one of the fairest portions of the globe, nor do I believe that there is in the universe a similar extent of country, equally fertile, well watered, and intersected by such a number of navigable streams." When the expedition's official report was published in 1814, it caused a sensation. Americans swelled with pride at the bounteous expanse called the upper Louisiana.

Lewis and Clark's party consisted of a diverse group of people, including British and Irish enlisted men, and Lewis's African American slave, York. At Fort Mandan, the group picked up Toussaint Charbonneau, a French Canadian, and his fifteen-year-old wife, Sacajawea, a Shoshone Indian. The explorers came to rely on Sacajawea's skills as an interpreter. And because women never traveled with Plains Indian war parties, Sacajawea's presence reassured suspicious Native Americans that the goal of the expedition was peaceful. White men were fond of boasting that "they were great warriors, and a powerful people, who, if exasperated, could crush all the nations of the earth." Indians heard these threats frequently and so were not inclined to look kindly upon an expedition of white men.

Lewis and Clark failed in their mission to locate a commercial route across the Rocky Mountains; the terrain proved too rugged. However, by sponsoring this and other major exploration parties, the federal government signaled its intention to help European Americans move west. The expedition also revealed that control of western waterways would be crucial to America's attempt to explore the interior of the continent and to establish trading relations with the Indians. The exploitation of waterways and water power proved a key component in the new nation's economic growth and development. In sum, the Lewis and Clark expedition yielded information that furthered westward migration, commercial development, and scientific knowledge about the western landscape.

During the first two decades of the nineteenth century, the United States faced a number of challenges from within and outside its borders, challenges that had long-lasting political and economic effects. Indians in general were a persistent threat to the new nation. Indeed, in the

William Clark, *Eulachon (T. Pacificus)*, 1806, Voorhis Journal #2. William Clark Papers, Missouri Historical Society Archives

■ Lewis and Clark were not only explorers; they were also pioneering naturalists committed to gathering, recording, and studying plants and animal life in the West. William Clark drew this sketch of a eulachon, also called a candlefish, as part of his journal entry for February 25, 1806. Pacific Indians dried the oily fish and used it as a torch.

MAP

The Louisiana Purchase

Great Lakes region, various tribes maintained political and military alliances with the British in Canada. During this period, the United States faced its most severe test to date: a war with Great Britain that raged from 1812 to 1815. The war did not resolve all the disagreements between the two nations, and it revealed some unexpected vulnerabilities in the new nation's defenses. Yet overall, for the United States, the effects of this "Second American Revolution" were far reaching. The conflict eliminated the British from the Northwest once and for all. Its military heroes, including Andrew Jackson and William Henry Harrison, went on to illustrious political careers. The war also spurred industrialization and stimulated commerce. In the South, the cotton plantation system began to shape the political and economic life of the entire region.

Some Europeans who visited the United States during these years criticized Americans for their crudeness and their lack of accomplishment in literature, architecture, road building, and manners. Yet after the War of 1812, American patriotism soared. The country now stretched from New Orleans to the Canadian border—an enormous expanse blessed with rich natural resources. Its military leaders were the equal of, if not superior to, the finest European officers. However, some Americans began to see a threat to their sense of themselves as a unique people. That threat—the expansion of human bondage—would come not from the outside but from within their own borders.

British Aggression on Land and the High Seas

■ *What were the domestic and international consequences of Britain's persistent challenges to U.S. territorial sovereignty and trade relations with other nations?*

In the election of 1804, Democratic-Republican Thomas Jefferson and his vice-presidential running mate, George Clinton, a former governor of New York, easily bested their Federalist opponents, Charles C. Pinckney and Rufus King. Jefferson had gained widespread favor among the voters through the Louisiana Purchase, and his decision to repeal the federal excise tax on whiskey that had so angered farmers in the West secured his popularity. On the eve of his second term, he no doubt imagined himself examining the specimens and reading the reports that Lewis and Clark sent back from the West. Yet the ongoing squabbling between France and England and the increasing aggression of the British navy toward American sailors demanded his attention.

These developments overseas preoccupied Jefferson during his second term in office. England and France continued to challenge each other as the reigning powers of Europe. In 1805, the British navy, under the command of Lord Nelson, defeated the French and Spanish fleets in the Battle of Trafalgar off the coast of Spain. That same year, France reveled in its own triumph on land when Napoleon conquered the Austrian and Russian armies at the Battle of Austerlitz. Supreme on the seas, England in 1806 passed the Orders in Council, which specified that any country that wanted to ship goods to France must first send them to a British port and pay taxes on them. Many Americans believed that England's policies amounted to acts of military and economic aggression against the United States.

TABLE 10.1		
The Election of 1804		
Candidate	**Political Party**	**Electoral Vote**
Thomas Jefferson	Democratic-Republican	162
Charles C. Pinckney	Federalist	14

■ **MAP 10.1** **Lewis and Clark Expedition, 1803–1806**

This map, showing the route of the Lewis and Clark Expedition, suggests the importance of interior water-ways in facilitating travel and exploration in the West. Spain feared, rightly, that the Americans would use western rivers to establish trade links with the Indians and thereby challenge Spain's northern border with the United States.

Source: From Stephen Ambrose, *Undaunted Courage.*

THE EMBARGO OF 1807

Not content to control trade across the Atlantic as decreed by the 1806 Orders in Council, the British also seized sailors from American ships, claiming that these men were British seamen who had been lured away from their own vessels by American captains promising them higher wages. In some cases these claims were probably true. However, U.S. political leaders charged that an estimated 6,000 U.S. citizens had been seized by the British navy between 1808 and 1811, including an unknown number of African Americans, many of whom were working as mariners. Seafaring appealed to free men of color because it paid good wages; in the early nineteenth century, black mariners' pay equaled that of their white counterparts. In this line of work, a man's skill, not the color of his skin, determined the nature of his job. With limited economic opportunities on shore, black sailors accepted the danger and long absences from home. However, neither black nor white sailors had bargained for enforced service in His Majesty's Royal Navy.

Seizure, or impressment, reminded Americans of the period before the Revolution, when British "press gangs" prowled the docks of American port cities and seized colonial merchant sailors. In 1807, the tensions over impressment erupted into violence. Just ten miles off the shore of Virginia, the American ship *Chesapeake* came under attack from a British vessel. British naval officers claimed that the Americans were harboring four British deserters. In the ensuing exchange of cannon fire, three Americans were killed and eighteen wounded. Jefferson demanded that England leave American sailors and ships alone, but he was rebuffed.

President Jefferson decided to place an embargo on all exports to the European powers in an effort to force those nations to respect the rights of Americans on the high seas. The move aroused intense opposition in Federalist-dominated New England, where the regional economy depended heavily on foreign trade. The **Embargo Act of 1807** passed by Congress halted the shipment of goods from the United States to Europe. Because Europe—including England—relied heavily on American grain and timber, Jefferson hoped that the move would force England to respect American independence. The president saw this measure as preferable to either war with or capitulation to England, but the New England states, which were particularly hard hit by the embargo, saw the matter quite differently. As the effects of the embargo took hold, the New England grain growers saw the markets for their products dry up, and the timber industry suffered when local shipbuilding ground to a standstill. Southern tobacco and cotton planters faced similar hardship because of the embargo. By 1808, some of them had joined with Northerners to circumvent the embargo by moving their goods through Canada and then to Europe.

Yet Jefferson held his course. He prodded Congress to enforce the unpopular act, but his efforts provoked a backlash. Ordinary citizens compared him to George III, and New England politicians threatened to take their states out of the union. Despite all the uproar, the embargo did benefit Americans in some ways. Specifically, it encouraged New Englanders to rely more on goods produced locally and less on foreign imports. Jefferson had advocated a policy that had an unanticipated effect: it promoted industrialization at home. At the same time, the embargo seemed only to intensify, not lessen, tensions between England and the United States.

ON THE BRINK OF WAR

The Embargo of 1807 was one of many challenges American political leaders faced during the first decade of the nineteenth century. Both the Federalists and the Democratic-Republicans suffered a blow to their leadership in 1804. That year, the Federalist party lost Alexander Hamilton at the hand of his rival, Aaron Burr. Both successful New York attorneys, the two men had risen together through the political ranks in the 1780s and 1790s. Burr served as Jefferson's running mate in the election of 1800; four years later he ran for governor of New York. Incensed by a report that Hamilton had claimed he was "a dangerous man, and one who ought not to be trusted with the reins of government," as well as "still more despicable rumors," Burr challenged his antagonist to a pistol duel in Weehawken, New Jersey, in July 1804. (Many European American men, especially in the South, considered dueling a means to preserve their honor in response to a perceived insult leveled at them or at a family member.) Hamilton, mortally wounded in the affair, died the next day, and Burr's political career fell into ruins. In 1807 he stood trial for treason, charged with conspiring to create an empire for himself out of the territory Spain held west of the Mississippi. Acquitted of the charges, he nevertheless fled the United States for Europe.

Jefferson, declining to run for a third presidential term in 1808, left the stage as well soon after the inauguration of the new president, James Madison. Congress repealed Jefferson's embargo and replaced it with the Non-Intercourse Act, which eased the complete ban on exports to Europe. This measure permitted American exporters to ship their goods to all European countries except for France and England, still at war with one another. New Englanders opposed even this limited embargo.

Meanwhile, the Federalists' influence in Congress was waning. The partisan division within Congress—the Federalists, with their emphasis on a strong national government, against the localist Democratic-Republicans—gradually eased. That division had emerged in response to the ratification of the Constitution and debates over the direction of the new nation. By 1810, a new split had emerged—between young, hotheaded representatives from the West and their more conservative seniors from the eastern seaboard. The western group, or **war hawks,** called on the nation to revive its former glory, by force if necessary. Americans must uphold U.S. honor, they declared, by opposing European, especially British,

TABLE 10.2		
The Election of 1808		
Candidate	**Political Party**	**Electoral Vote**
James Madison	Democratic-Republican	122
Charles C. Pinckney	Federalist	47
George Clinton	Democratic-Republican	6

claims to military dominance. The war hawks also yearned to vanquish the Indians who impeded settlement of the area west of the Mississippi.

Looking eastward, the war hawks saw an England determined to defile the honor of their young nation. In 1810, Congress passed legislation called Macon's Bill No. 2. Under its provisions, if either France or England agreed to resume trade with the United States, then the Americans would resume trade with that country and refuse to trade with the other. France's emperor Napoleon seized this offer to reestablish economic ties with the United States. Outraged, England began to contemplate war not only with its archenemy, France, but also with the upstart United States. The new nation had positioned itself directly in the middle of a conflict between the two major European powers.

Looking westward, the war hawks saw an equally threatening menace: the rise of an ominous Indian resistance movement that blended military strength with native spirituality. The movement was led by Shawnee brothers Tecumseh and Tenskwatawa. Tenskwatawa, also known as the Prophet, claimed that he had a vision in which he received a message from the world's creator. In the Prophet's words, the creator stated that European Americans "grew from the scum of the great water, when it was troubled by an evil spirit and the froth was driven into the woods by a strong east wind." The Prophet declared to other Indians, "They are numerous, but I hate them. They are unjust; they have taken away your lands, which were not made for them."

In 1808, the two brothers founded Prophet's Town in Indiana. They envisioned a sovereign Indian state and the preservation of Native American culture. Tenskwatawa spoke of a time and place where Indians would reject alcohol and scorn "the food of whites" as well as the "wealth and ornaments" of commercial trade. Tecumseh set out to deliver the message to as many Indian groups as possible, traveling the broad swath of territory from Florida to Canada.

In his journey south, Tecumseh found the Creek nation in Muskogee Territory particularly receptive to his message of Indian solidarity. By that time the Creek had lost millions of acres of land to the Americans. Tecumseh deputized a relative, Seekaboo, to remain with the Creek and instruct them in the religion of Tenskwatawa. He could not know that, within a few years, Tenskwatawa's message would spark armed conflict between the Creek and American troops.

Meanwhile, in 1809, the territorial governor of Indiana, William Henry Harrison, plied a group of Indian leaders with liquor, then got them to agree to sell 3 million acres to the U.S. government for just $7,600. Upon hearing of the deal, Tecumseh decried a new form of American aggression: "treaties" between U.S. officials and Indians who lacked the authority to sell their people's homeland. "All red men," Tecumseh proclaimed, must "unite in claiming a common and equal

The Library of Congress

■ This lithograph of the Prophet (Tenskwatawa) was based on an 1824 painting of the Shawnee mystic and holy man. Early in life, he suffered an accident with bows and arrows, losing his right eye. He and his older brother Tecumseh called on all Indians to resist the appropriation of their lands by whites and to renounce the way of life followed by whites, including the use of liquor. After the Indians' defeat at the Battle of Tippecanoe in 1811, the Prophet retreated to Canada. He returned to the United States in 1826. By that time he no longer wielded influence as a leader of the Shawnees.

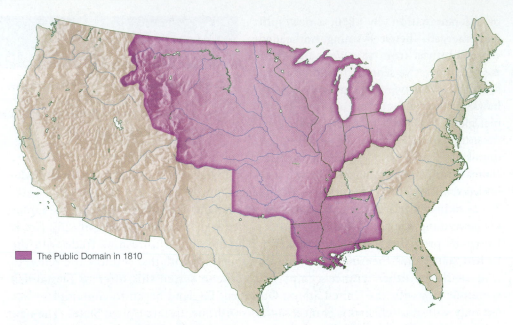

■ **MAP 10.2** **The Public Domain in 1810**

This map indicates the expanse of western lands owned by the U.S. government in 1810, after the Louisiana Purchase. American war veterans received land warrants in return for military service in the Revolutionary War and the War of 1812. A warrant entitled the bearer to settle a specific number of acres of unoccupied land. Warrants could be transferred, sold, and traded like stocks and bonds. After the War of 1812, the government issued 29,186 land warrants for a total of 4.8 million acres.

Source: After Charles O. Paulin, *Atlas of Historical Geography,* Plate 57.

right in the land, as it was at first, and should be yet; for it never was divided, but belongs to all, for the use of each."

In November 1811, Harrison led 1,000 U.S. soldiers in an advance on Prophet's Town. But before they could reach the settlement, several hundred Shawnee under the command of Tenskwatawa attacked their camp on the Tippecanoe River. The Indians suffered a sound defeat, and Harrison burned Prophet's Town to the ground. A Potawatomi chief, Shabonee, who fought at the Battle of Tippecanoe, later recalled the false sense of superiority that had inspired the Indians' doomed attack on Harrison and his men. According to Shabonee, the Indians believed "the white soldiers are not warriors. Their hands are soft. Their faces are white. One half of them are calico [fabric] peddlers. The other half can only shoot squirrels." Warriors or not, the Americans had a distinct advantage over the Indians: better guns. Clearly, military technology, not just determination, would shape the western conflict. Yet in the ensuing war, the Americans faced not just Indian foes, but also one of the mightiest military forces in the world—the British army and navy.

The War of 1812

■ *What were the political and economic interests of the United States, the Indian tribes, and Great Britain and why did those divergent interests clash during the War of 1812?*

The defeat of the Shawnee at Tippecanoe only inflamed western war hawks' passions and stiffened their resolve to break the back of Indian resistance. But to achieve this goal, the United States would have to invade Canada and eliminate the British arms suppliers who had been trading with the Indians. Claiming the mantle of patriotism, western and southern members of the House of Representatives agitated for a war that would eliminate both the

British threat on the high seas and the Canada-based Indian–British alliance. These Americans wanted a war that would win for them a true independence once and for all. "On to Canada! On to Canada!" became the rallying cry of the war hawks.

In a secret message sent to Congress on June 1, 1812, President Madison listed Americans' many grievances against England: the British navy's seizure of American citizens, the blockades of American goods, and continued conflict "on one of our extensive frontiers," the result of "savages" who had the backing of British traders and military officials. Madison left it up to Congress whether the nation would continue to endure these indignities or would act "in defense of their natural rights." Seventeen days later, the House voted 79 to 49 and the Senate voted 19 to 13 to declare war on England and, by extension, the western Indians.

The **War of 1812** united Americans behind a banner of national expansion. But at the same time, it exposed dangerous divisions between regions of the country and between political viewpoints. Many New Englanders saw the conflict as a plot by Virginia Democratic-Republicans primarily to aid France in opposition to England and to add agrarian (that is, slave) states to the Union. In an ironic twist, the New England Federalists—usually staunch defenders of the national government—argued that states should control their own commerce and militias.

TABLE 10.3		
The Election of 1812		
Candidate	**Political Party**	**Electoral Vote**
James Madison	Democratic-Republican	128
De Witt Clinton	Federalist	89

DOCUMENT

Pennsylvania Gazette, "Indian Hostilities"

PUSHING NORTH

Although the Americans were better armed and organized than the western Indians, they were at a disadvantage when they took on the soldiers and sailors of the British Empire. The United States had not invested in the military and thus was ill-prepared for all-out war. The American navy consisted merely of a fleet of tiny gunboats constructed during the cost-conscious Jefferson administration. The charter for the Bank of the United States had expired in 1811, depriving the country of a vital source of financial credit. Suffering from a drop in tax revenues as a result of the embargo on foreign trade, the nation lacked the funds to train and equip the regular army and the state militias. Nevertheless, in the fall of 1812, the Americans launched an ambitious three-pronged attack against Canada, striking from Niagara, Detroit, and Lake Champlain. All three attempts failed miserably.

Lacking united, enthusiastic support on the home front, the U.S. offensive got off to a bad start. Yet some people, even in Federalist New England, believed that all Americans should support the war, regardless of the potential outcome. Writing from a Federalist stronghold in December 1812, Abigail Adams (the wife of former president John Adams) acknowledged to a correspondent that her home state of Massachusetts "had much to complain of" because the war had severely disrupted trade. However, she added, "that cannot justify [Massachusetts] in paralyzing the arm of Government [that is, opposing federal trade policies], when raised for her defense and that of the nation." She warned against "a house divided against itself," which she believed could be the nation's undoing.

In the West, the British moved to take advantage of divisions between Indians and Americans. In late 1812, Tecumseh (who had accepted a commission as a brigadier general in the British army) and British General Isaac Brock captured Detroit. Indians also participated in England's successful raid on Fort Dearborn (Chicago). In at least two cases, when U.S. soldiers marched into Canada, they lost their advantage when state militia members refused to cross the border. Leaders of these militias claimed that their sole purpose was to defend their states from attack, not invade foreign territory.

■ **MAP 10.3   The Northern Front, War of 1812**

Much of the fighting of the War of 1812 centered in the Great Lakes region. It was there, the war hawks charged, that the British were inciting Indians to attack American settlements. Conducted in 1812 and 1813, the campaign against Canada was supposed to eliminate the British threat and, some Americans hoped, win Canadian territory for the United States.

Yet the Americans scored some notable successes in 1813. That September, Commodore Oliver H. Perry defeated a British fleet at Put-in-Bay on Lake Erie. Exhilarated, he famously declared, "We have met the enemy and they are ours." But Perry's victory came at a steep price. Shortly before the engagement, about a third of all the officers and men in the American fleet had fallen victim to a typhus epidemic. And then at the end of the day's battle, of the 100 men who had reported for duty that morning, 21 were dead and more than 60 wounded.

Perry's hard-won victory forced the British back into Canada, over Tecumseh's objections. General William Henry Harrison followed in hot pursuit. British Colonel Henry Proctor marched his troops to eastern Ontario, leaving Tecumseh to try holding the Americans at bay. At the Battle of the Thames (that October), Harrison defeated the Indians. Many perished, Tecumseh among them. A group of Kentucky soldiers skinned what they mistakenly believed to be his corpse. His body was never found.

Later that autumn, an American campaign against Montreal failed. The Americans trudged back into New York State, the British close behind them. Flush with their victory in Montreal, the British captured Fort Niagara and set Buffalo and other nearby towns aflame.

By mid-1814, the English and their allies had also crushed Napoleon in Europe. This success freed up 15,000 British troops, who promptly sailed for North America. Still, in July 1814 the Americans, under the leadership of Major General Jacob Brown and Brigadier General Winfield Scott, managed to defeat the British at the Battle of Chippewa, across the Niagara River from Buffalo. But by the end of that year, the Americans had withdrawn to their own territory and relinquished their goal of invading and conquering Canada. The arrival of fresh British troops forced the Americans to defend their own soil.

FIGHTING ON MANY FRONTS

For the United States, the most humiliating episode of the war came with the British attack on the nation's capital. On August 24, 1814, the British army, backed by the Royal Navy, sailed into Chesapeake Bay. At the Battle of Bladensburg, Maryland, they scattered the American troops they encountered. The Redcoats then advanced to Washington, where they torched the Capitol building and the White House, causing extensive damage to both structures.

Residents of the capital city had received word that the British were advancing. On Sunday, August 21, public officials frantically packed up their books and papers. Private citizens gathered up their furniture and other belongings and left town. By Tuesday, the city stood nearly empty. As a ragtag American force succumbed to the British, President Madison "retired from the mortifying scene, and left the city on horseback." His aides and some military officers accompanied him. As it turned out, he escaped just in the nick of time: by Wednesday

The Library of Congress

■ The U.S. Capitol lies blackened and in ruins after British forces burned it in August 1814.

flames had engulfed not only the Capitol but also Madison's residence. Disorganized, hungry, and hot, the American troops had put up scant resistance. An eyewitness reported, "Our army may with truth be said to have been beaten by fatigue, before they saw the enemy."

Yet the Americans rallied, pursued the British, and bested them at the Battle of Baltimore. This victory inspired an observer, Francis Scott Key, to write "The Star Spangled Banner" as he watched "the bombs bursting in air" over Baltimore's Fort McHenry. The Americans scored another crucial victory in September, when U.S. naval commander Thomas McDonough crushed the British fleet on Lake Champlain near Plattsburgh, New York.

DOCUMENT

Dolley Payne Madison to Lucy Payne Todd (1814)

In the Southeast, Tecumseh's message of Indian unity had resonated with particular force among Native Americans once the war broke out. Some Cherokee and Choctaw cast their lot with the United States. A minority among the Creek was emboldened by Tenskwatawa's message, "War now. War forever. War upon the living. War upon the dead; dig up their corpses from the grave; our country must give no rest to a white man's bones." By 1813, a group of warriors called Red Sticks (for their scarlet-painted weapons) stood ready to do battle with U.S. forces. Yet they faced opposition from some of their own people, the White Sticks, who counseled peace. The Red Sticks finally decided to attack Fort Mims, north of Mobile.

In response, Andrew Jackson, leader of the Tennessee militia, received a commission as major general. His mission was to retaliate against the Indians. Jackson speculated in Indian lands in Mississippi Territory, and he called Native Americans "blood thirsty barbarians." Even in a country where anti-Indian sentiment ran high, his views were extreme. After the attack on Fort Mims, he vowed, "I must destroy those deluded victims doomed to destruction by their own restless and savage conduct." He often boasted about collecting the scalps of all his Indian victims, and he relished his new assignment.

Jackson's 3,500 troops laid waste to Creek territory. Regiments of Cherokee, Choctaw, and Chickasaw Indians, as well as White Sticks, helped the U.S. forces. During a monumental battle in March 1814, more than three-quarters of the 1,000 defending Red Sticks and a number of Indian women and children died at Horseshoe Bend (in modern-day Alabama). Jackson survived the battle thanks to the intervention of a Cherokee soldier. Some U.S. soldiers took their victory to a brutal extreme; they flayed the corpses of their victims and made horse bridles out of their skin.

The Library of Congress

■ This engraving, published in 1814, depicts the bombardment of Fort McHenry by British warships in September of that year. When he witnessed the battle, Francis Scott Key, a Washington lawyer, was aboard a prisoner exchange boat in Baltimore Harbor. He was seeking release of a friend captured by the British. After penning the poem "The Star Spangled Banner," Key set the words to music, using the tune of a popular English drinking song. Congress declared the song the national anthem in 1931.

Yet Jackson insisted on praising his soldiers as a civilizing force. They were only reclaiming the land from a band of savages, he maintained. In a post-battle speech to the men under his command, he declared, "In their places a new generation [of Indians] will arise who know their duties better. The weapons of warfare will be exchanged for the utensils of husbandry; and the wilderness which now withers in sterility . . . will blossom as the rose, and become the nursery of the arts."

In the Treaty of Horseshoe Bend that followed the massacre, the Americans forced the Creek Nation to give up 23 million acres. The remnants of the Red Sticks fled to the swamps of Florida, where they joined additional Creek, other Florida Indians, and numerous fugitive slaves in an emerging group known as the Seminoles (from the Spanish *cimarrones,* or runaway slaves).

Jackson next marched to New Orleans to confront the British. Knowing he would be facing some of Europe's finest soldiers, he assembled 7,000 men, U.S. soldiers and militia from the states of Louisiana, Kentucky, and Tennessee. Two Kentucky regiments consisted of free black volunteers, about 400 men in total. The Battle of New Orleans, fought on January 8, 1815, began with a ferocious assault by British soldiers. But within just half an hour, 2,000 of them lay dead or wounded. The Americans lost only 70. Jackson's backcountry shooters had vanquished the army of Europe's greatest military power.

Later, many Americans associated Andrew Jackson with the war's decisive battle and most glorious victory. But in fact, American and British negotiators had signed a peace agreement that ended the war two weeks before "Old Hickory" defeated the British in New Orleans. (Jackson received his nickname when one of his soldiers called him "tough as hickory.") The Battle of New Orleans might have been a glorious victory for the United States, but it was hardly the decisive battle of the war.

A Government Agent Greets a Group of Creek Indians

Envisioning History

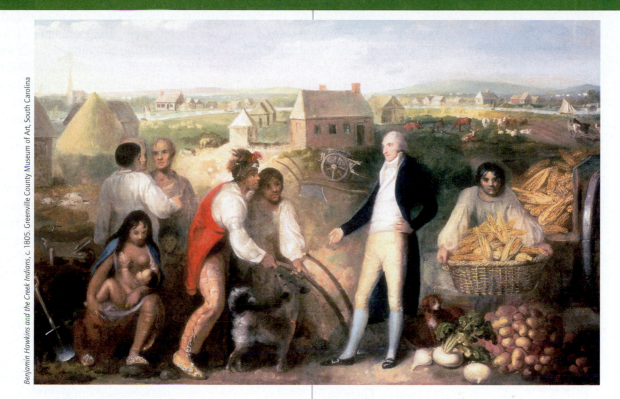

Benjamin Hawkins and the Creek Indians, c. 1805. Greenville County Museum of Art, South Carolina

Southeastern Indians varied widely in their willingness to adopt European American ways. Some Indians argued that the best way to preserve their community and remain on the land of their forebears was to accommodate themselves to white practices of trade and farming and to embrace European dress styles and Christian religious beliefs. Together the Creek, Cherokee, Chickasaw, Choctaw, and Seminole were called the Five Civilized Tribes as a result of their decision to give up hunting in favor of sedentary agriculture. This painting, completed by an unknown artist in 1805, shows a government Indian agent named Benjamin Hawkins meeting with a group of Creek Indians near Macon, Georgia. Hawkins expresses evident satisfaction with the Indians' neat cabins, well-tended fields, flocks of sheep, and bountiful harvest of vegetables.

QUESTIONS

1. In what ways have the Creek pictured here adopted European American ways? (Hint: The Indian men in the foreground are holding the handles of a plow.) In what ways have they retained elements of their traditional culture?

2. What is the significance of various means of conveyance pictured here—the carts and ships?

3. How does the artist seek to represent the role of Hawkins?

4. What elements in the painting suggest that this is a prosperous Creek settlement?

AN UNCERTAIN VICTORY

Before the Battle of New Orleans, in the fall of 1814, President Madison had decided to end the war. He dispatched John Quincy Adams, son of former president John Adams, to the Belgian city of Ghent to start negotiations. Representative Henry Clay and three other American envoys accompanied Adams. At first, British representatives to the meeting made two demands. The Americans, they said, must agree to the creation of an Indian territory in the upper Great Lakes region. They must also cede much of the state of Maine to England. The Americans refused, and the negotiations dragged on.

In the meantime, the New England states had grown increasingly impatient with what they called "Mr. Madison's war." As with the embargo, they saw the effort as a mistake and a threat to their regional commercial interests. In December 1814, Massachusetts, Connecticut, Rhode Island, New Hampshire, and Vermont sent delegates to a gathering in Hartford, Connecticut, to consider a course of action. The delegates demanded that the federal government give their states financial aid to compensate for the revenue they had lost as a result of disrupted trade. Some delegates even hinted that their states wanted to secede from the union. Although most delegates shied away from immediate action, the majority of them apparently wanted to leave open the possibility of secession.

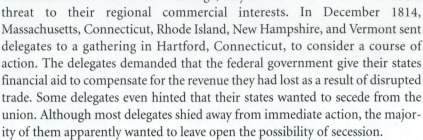

American nationalism came at the expense of vast Indian homelands and thousands of lives on both sides.

Back in Ghent, the British had reversed their initial position by late December. They had lost recent battles in upper New York and in Baltimore and, as always, were still worried about new threats from France. They dropped their demands for territory and for an Indian buffer state in the upper Midwest. They also agreed to an armistice that, in essence, represented a draw: both combatants would retain the same territory they had possessed when the war began. The British made no concessions to the Americans' demands that they stop impressing American sailors and supplying the western Indians with arms or that they revoke the Orders in Council. Still, most U.S. citizens considered the war a great victory for the United States. After Congress ratified the **Treaty of Ghent,** which ended hostilities between the two nations in 1815, the Americans and the British never again met each other across a battlefield as enemies.

DOCUMENT

The Treaty of Ghent (1814)

But some of the American soldiers and sailors who had survived the conflict paid a high price. For example, Benjamin F. Palmer was an American sailor imprisoned in an English jail from 1813 to 1815. There he subsisted on meager rations and witnessed unspeakable cruelties, including the murder of inmates by guards. In all probability, the Treaty of Ghent did not change Palmer's views of the British soldiers' "Brutal & Savage Barbarity." In total, 6,000 American combatants died or suffered wounds in the war. Yet survivors felt that they and their dead fellows had preserved the nation's honor.

Many Indians saw matters quite differently. For them, the War of 1812 had only stiffened white settlers' determination to take native peoples' land. Andrew Jackson would aggressively pursue a national political career. And so the Battle of Horseshoe Bend signaled not only a continuation of bloodshed but also a terrifying sign of things to come. American nationalism came at the expense of vast Indian homelands and thousands of lives on both sides. At the same time, in Washington, the end of the war softened partisan tensions, and lawmakers joined in celebrating the successful defense and the growing prosperity of the young nation.

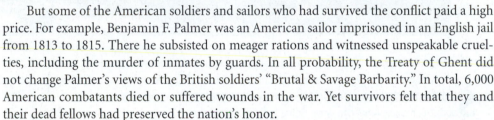

The Era of "Good Feelings"?

■ *Did political and social realities justify the use of the term "the Era of 'Good Feelings'" to describe the period after the War of 1812?*

I n 1816, the Democratic-Republicans nominated James Monroe for president, to run against Federalist candidate Rufus King. Although Monroe only narrowly won his party's endorsement, he soundly defeated King in the general election. Monroe benefited from several developments that had mortally wounded the Federalist party: the War of 1812 victory, presided over by a Democratic-Republican chief executive; the New England Federalists' flirtation with secession (and treason) during the war years; and the strong nationalist tendencies of both the Jefferson and Madison administrations, which had stolen the Federalists' thunder.

Addressing Congress in December 1817, Monroe expressed optimism about the state of the nation. The country's boundaries were secure, and the Indians had little choice but to retreat farther and farther west. The president predicted that, shortly, "Indian hostilities, if they do not altogether cease, will henceforth lose their terror." Equally inspiring, the Americans had once again defied the British Empire and won. Two treaties with Britain—the Rush-Bagot of 1817 and the Convention of 1818—set the U.S.-Canadian border at the 49th parallel and provided that the two countries would jointly occupy the Oregon Territory for ten years.

TABLE 10.4		
The Election of 1816		
Candidate	**Political Party**	**Electoral Vote**
James Monroe	Democratic-Republican	183
Rufus King	Federalist	34

Monroe called on Congress to acknowledge "the vast extent of territory within the United States [and] the great amount and value of its productions" and to expand the construction of roads and canals. (In 1806, Congress had funded construction of a National Road.) It was this "happy situation of the United States," in Monroe's words, that ushered in what some historians call the **Era of Good Feelings,** a period relatively free of partisan political strife. By this time the Federalist party had dissolved, and Monroe faced no real party-based opposition to his administration. Voters continued to disagree over some issues of the day, such as the national bank and internal improvements. Some Northerners believed that slavery was wrong, a conviction that would soon give rise to **sectionalism** (intense political conflict between the North and South). Still, most Americans did not necessarily express their disagreements with each other in the form of bitter partisan wrangling. At the same time, the term "good feelings" may fully apply only to a narrow group of enfranchised citizens, men who shared common beliefs about territorial expansion and economic development.

The War of 1812 yielded little in the way of material gains for the United States or concessions from England. Yet it permanently reshaped American social, political, and economic life. The nation exploited the vulnerable southeastern Indians and hastened their removal from their homeland. Many veterans of the war gained land grants, military glory, and political influence in return for their sacrifices. Although the war had disrupted foreign trade, it also gave home manufacturers a tremendous boost. The textile industry spearheaded a revolution in industry. And a new class of workers—factory operatives (machine tenders)—emerged to symbolize both the promise and the hazards of machines.

PRAISE AND RESPECT FOR VETERANS AFTER THE WAR

American veterans of the War of 1812 won the praise of a grateful nation. Even the British expressed a grudging respect for Americans' fighting abilities. One British naval officer

Gilbert Stuart, *George Washington.* White House Historical Collection (White House Collection, Courtesy), (21)

■ Dolley Madison, wife of President James Madison, helped rescue this famous painting of George Washington by artist Gilbert Stuart when the British invaded Washington in August 1814. The full-length portrait hung in what was then called the President's House. She later wrote a friend that the British attack had rendered her "so unfeminine as to be free from fear." She had hoped to remain in the mansion "if I could have had a cannon through every window, but alas! Those who should have placed them there, fled."

Cherokee Women Petition against Further Land Sales to Whites in 1817

Interpreting History

*I*n traditional Cherokee society, men took responsibility for foreign affairs while women focused on domestic matters, leading to a roughly equal division of labor. However, European American diplomats, military officials, and traders dealt primarily with Indian men. As a result, beginning in the eighteenth century, Cherokee women's traditional influence was eroding within their own communities. In this new world, Indian warriors wielded significant power.

Nevertheless, Cherokee women insisted on presenting their views during the crisis of 1817–1819, when men of the group were deciding whether to cede land to U.S. authorities and move west. The following petition was supported by Nancy Ward, a Cherokee War Woman. This honorific title was bestowed on women who accompanied and attended to the needs of war parties. Ward had supported the colonists' cause during the American Revolution.

In 1987, Wilma Mankiller became the first woman to be elected principal chief of the Cherokee Nation of Oklahoma.

Peter Turnley/CORBIS

Amovey [Tennessee] in Council 2nd May 1817

The Cherokee Ladys now being present at the meeting of the Chiefs and warriors in council have thought it their duties as mothers to address their beloved Chiefs and warriors now assembled.

Our beloved children and head men of the Cherokee nation we address you warriors in council we have raised all of you on the land which we now have, which God gave to us to inhabit and raise provisions we know that our country has once been extensive but by repeated sales has become circumscribed to a small tract, and [we] never have thought it our duty to interfere in the disposition of it till now, if a father or mother was to sell all their lands which they had to depend on which their children had to raise their living on which would indeed be bad and to be removed to another country we do not wish to go to an unknown country [to] which we have understood some of our children wish to go over the Mississippi but this act of our children would be like destroying your

asserted, "I don't like Americans; I never did, and never shall." He had "no wish to eat with them, drink with them, or consort with them in any way." But, he added, he would rather not fight with "an enemy so brave, determined, and alert, and in every way so worthy of one's steel, as they have always proved." To reward U.S. veterans for their service, Congress offered them 160-acre plots of land in the territory between the Illinois and Mississippi Rivers. These grants did much to encourage families to emigrate west and establish homesteads.

Some military heroes of the war parlayed their success into impressive political careers. Andrew Jackson won election to the presidency in 1828 and 1832; William Henry Harrison was elected president in 1840. Countless others earned recognition within their own communities, and European American veterans were not the only ones to gain status and influence as a result of the conflict. For example, a Cherokee leader named the Ridge also earned the gratitude of American officials for his contributions to the war effort. He had accepted the government's attempts to press the Cherokee to adopt European American ways, settling in a log cabin (in northwest Georgia) rather than in a traditional Cherokee dwelling when he married a Cherokee woman named Susanna Wickett in the early 1790s. During the war against the Red Sticks, the Ridge served under Andrew Jackson and earned the title of major. For the rest of his life, the Cherokee leader was known as Major Ridge. His wife devoted herself to tending an orchard, keeping a garden, and sewing clothes, tasks traditionally performed by European American but not Native American women. Eventually, the family prospered and, like some other Cherokee, bought African American slaves. The Ridge family became Christians as well.

mothers. Your mothers your sisters ask and beg of you not to part with any more of our lands, we say ours. [Y]ou are our descendants and take pity on our request, but keep it for our growing children for it was the good will of our creator to place us here and you know our father the great president [James Monroe], will not allow his white children to take our country away for if it was not they would not ask you to put your hands to paper for it would be impossible to remove us all for as soon as one child is raised, we have others in our arms for such is our situation and will consider our circumstance.

Therefore children don't part with any more of our lands but continue on it and enlarge your farms and cultivate and raise corn and cotton and we your mothers and sisters will make clothing for you which our father the president has recommended to us all we don't charge anybody for selling our lands, but we have heard such intentions of our children but your talks become true at last and it was our desire to forewarn you all not to part with our lands.

Nancy Ward to her children[:] Warriors to take pity and listen to the talks of your sisters, although I am very old yet cannot but pity the situation in which you will hear of their minds. I have great many grand children which I wish they to do well on our land.

In addition to Nancy Ward, twelve Cherokee women signed the petition. Their names suggest the varying degrees of assimilation

to white ways on the part of Cherokees in general. Petitioners included Cun, o, ah and Widow Woman Holder, as well as Jenny McIntosh and Mrs. Nancy Fields.

It is unclear what effect, if any, this petition had on Cherokee male leaders. The Cherokee nation did halt land cessions to whites between 1819 and 1835.

QUESTIONS

1. *How and why did motherhood confer authority on Cherokee women?*

2. *What is the significance and meaning of the land in Cherokee culture?*

3. *Does this petition provide evidence for the view that early nineteenth-century Cherokee men and women were adopting elements of European American culture? If so, what elements, and in what ways?*

Source: Cherokee Women to Cherokee Council, May 2, 1817, series 1, Andrew Jackson Presidential Papers, Library of Congress Manuscripts Division, Washington, D.C. Reprinted in Nancy F. Cott, Jeanne Boydston, Ann Braude, Lori Ginzberg, and Molly Ladd-Taylor, eds., *Root of Bitterness: Documents of the Social History of American Women* (Boston: Northeastern University Press, 1996), 177–178.

The Ridge's battlefield experiences earned him the respect of other Cherokee who embraced the "civilization" program that missionaries and government officials promoted. At the same time, the Ridge vehemently resisted U.S. officials' attempts to persuade the Cherokee to give up their lands to whites and move west. Emerging as a leader of the Cherokee nation after the War of 1812, he criticized members of his group who had abandoned their lands in favor of a new life in the West. He declared, "I scorn this movement of a few men to unsettle the nation, and trifle with our attachment to the land of our forefathers." The Ridge believed that his people should adopt some elements of white culture but should also hold fast to their native lands in opposition to white settlers and politicians.

A THRIVING ECONOMY

The War of 1812, along with the Embargo of 1807, stimulated home manufactures—especially the production of cloth and other goods in private households and factories. Home manufacturing resulted in a significant shift in the national economy—from reliance on imported goods to the production of those goods at home. The experiences of one rural Massachusetts family demonstrate the impact this shift had on individuals. Before the war, Lucy Kellogg and her sister worked at home, braiding straw hats to be sold at market. The war ruined their straw business, since economic hardship among New Englanders meant fewer people could afford to buy hats. In response, the sisters invested in cotton looms, which they used to make cloth. They secured cotton thread from the Massachusetts factories that had

Courtesy, American Antiquarian Society

■ This cartoon, c. 1810, reveals two sides to the western emigration question. On the right, a well-dressed Easterner sets out for Ohio. He encounters a dejected, ragged migrant returning home. The men's horses tell a larger story about the failed dreams and hardship endured by many western emigrants. In the caption the artist cautions travelers on "the impropriety and folly of emigrating" from New England to the "Western Wilderness."

sprung up during the war to compensate for the lack of English textile imports. The Kellogg sisters found a ready market for their shirts, gingham dresses, and bed tickings—products that were, in Kellogg's words, "good enough in time of war." Still, their family was restless, moving briefly to New Hampshire but then returning to Worcester, where they resumed farming.

The end of the war saw an upsurge in this kind of internal migration. New Englanders, especially, pushed west in search of new opportunities. Between 1800 and 1820, the population of Ohio grew from 45,000 to 581,000. New means of transportation—and new means to fund them—facilitated the movement of goods, people, and ideas from the East to the West (and, in some cases, back again). Indeed, traveling by stagecoach, wagon, boat, and horseback, Americans seemed to be on the move constantly. In 1807, an entrepreneur named Robert Fulton piloted the *Clermont*, his new kind of boat powered by steam, up the Hudson River from New York City. Steamboats traveled upriver, against the current, ten times faster than keelboats, which had to be pushed, pulled, or hauled by men or mules. Within a few years, such vessels were plying the Mississippi River and its major tributaries.

Improvements in land transportation also stimulated economic growth. The profits that the Philadelphia and Lancaster Turnpike earned by charging travelers tolls inspired other local private corporations to invest in roads. By 1810, several thousand such corporations were building roads up and down the East Coast. Funding came from a variety of sources, both public and private. Philadelphia textile mill owners financed transportation links with the city's hinterland (rural areas to the west) to carry their goods to the largest number of customers. Individual cities also invested in routes westward. The state of Virginia authorized a board of public works to expend funds for roads and other internal improvements. Western politicians flexed their political muscle in 1806 by securing congressional authorization for the building of the Cumberland (later National) Road, which snaked through the Allegheny Mountains and ended at the Ohio River.

The acceleration of commerce in the West, combined with the disruption in trade from Europe that had come with the embargo and war, stimulated manufacturing throughout the United States. Philadelphia's growth proved particularly dazzling. During the War of 1812, the city's craft producers did not have to worry about foreign competition. Local merchant-financiers, who otherwise might have been pouring their money into trade ventures, began to invest in manufacturing. As early as 1808, the city's new factories had compensated for the glass, chemicals, shot, soap, lead, and earthenware that no longer flooded in from England. Philadelphia soon took the lead in production of all kinds, whether carried out in factories, artisans' shops, or private homes. Metalworking, ale brewing, and leather production counted among the array of thriving industries that made Philadelphia the nation's top industrial city in 1815. Still, in 1820, about two-thirds of all Philadelphia workers labored in small shops employing fewer than six people.

TRANSFORMATIONS IN THE WORKPLACE

Even the earliest stages of the Industrial Revolution transformed the way people lived and worked. Some crafts—for example, the production of leather, barrels, soap, candles, and newspapers—expanded from small shops with skilled artisans into larger establishments with unskilled wage earners. In these cases, production was reorganized; now wage earners under the supervision of a boss replaced apprentices and journeymen who had formerly worked alongside a master artisan. These workers performed a single task many times a day instead of using their specialized skills to see a production process through to completion.

While skilled artisans were alarmed at the prospect of being reduced to mere "hands" tending machines, the sons and daughters of many New England farmers eagerly took new jobs in the mills. They appreciated the opportunity to escape close family supervision, to live on their own, and to earn cash wages. Some farm hands and manual laborers considered factory work, no matter how grueling and ill-paid, preferable to plowing fields, digging ditches, and hauling lumber. Chauncey Jerome, a young Connecticut man, lamented that few opportunities were open to him in rural areas: "There being no manufacturing of any account in the country, the poor boys were obliged to let [hire] themselves to the farmers, and it was extremely difficult to find a place where they would treat a poor boy like a human being."

New England rapidly became the center of mechanized textile production in the United States. By the late eighteenth century, Boston shippers were making handsome profits by supplying Alta California (the area from San Diego to present-day San Francisco). These merchants sent New-England-made goods such as cloth, shoes, and tools out west; they then sold Western otter pelts in China, and returned home laden with Chinese porcelains and silks. These profits helped finance New England's mechanized textile industry. By 1813, 76 cotton mills housing a total of over 51,000 spindles were operating within the vicinity of Providence, Rhode Island.

The Granger Collection, New York

■ This engraving, c. 1819, shows women working in an early textile mill. Women and children composed the work force of many early mills. This picture suggests the size of the intricate machinery, which dwarfs the women. For generations women had produced textiles at home, spinning thread and weaving cloth. For all factory operatives, these dark, cavernous places were new kinds of worksites—a striking contrast to the homes, shops, and fields where New Englanders traditionally had worked.

Courtesy, American Antiquarian Society

■ In the early nineteenth century, many skilled artisans worried that economic growth and development would erode their independence. They sought to portray themselves as upright and virtuous citizens and, by extension, superior to poor people who lacked either self-discipline or steady employment. These engravings feature sayings from Benjamin Franklin published in *Poor Richard Illustrated: Lessons for the Young and Old on Industry, Temperance, Frugality & c.*

Faced with a shortage of adult men (many were moving west), New England mill owners sought other local sources of labor. The Rhode Island system of production had relied on child spinners working in small mills. This system gave way to the Lowell model, based in Waltham and Lowell, Massachusetts, which brought young women from the surrounding countryside to work in gigantic mills. Many of the women were eager to earn cash wages and to escape the routine of farm life. Still, New England mill owners realized that they had to reassure Yankee parents that their daughters would find the factories safe, attractive places to work. Mill owners offered the young women housing in dormitory-like boardinghouses staffed by older women, called matrons, who looked after them.

These transformations in the workplace and in social relations disturbed some white male laborers in particular. They feared for their own status as freeborn, proud sons (and grandsons) of the Revolution. To them, the factory represented a loss of independence. In 1806, striking Philadelphia shoemakers charged, "The name of freedom is but a shadow." The court ruled that by joining together to withhold their labor from their employer, these workers were guilty of conspiring to raise their own wages. Some white laborers claimed that they were no longer in charge of their own work lives but instead were condemned to long hours and low pay.

Black men and women continued to suffer the stigma of slavery. Nearly all blacks in the United States were slaves or their descendants. This stigma determined the jobs for which blacks were hired and the pay they received. The 7,500 free blacks who lived in New York City in 1810 were only about 8 percent of the city's total population. But they made up fully 84 percent of all black people in the city (the rest were enslaved children who would not gain their freedom until they became adults). They struggled to earn a living, and they had limited employment options.

One job that was open to them was the dangerous, dirty work of cleaning chimneys. Black men served as master chimney sweeps and employed youths of their own race as assistants and apprentices. In an attempt to control the sweeps, the New York City Council tried to insist that they purchase expensive licenses to ply their trade. In response, a group of master chimney sweeps decried a double standard. Resenting what they considered unreasonably high licensing fees, they declared that they wanted to be treated "in the same manner as you have thought proper to do in respect to Cartmen, porter, measurer &c." To protect themselves, they established their own mutual aid society, the United Society of Chimney Sweeps. Some members asserted their equality with white men of the city by noting that they too had "served in the revolutionary war & some of them received wounds."

Industrialization was not confined to the Northeast; the southern states encouraged the development of textile mills as well. Yet in the South, industrialization had different social consequences. Many owners of southern industrial establishments sought to piece together their labor forces on the basis of the availability of different kinds of labor: enslaved and free, black and white, male and female, young and old. Thus, ironworks, gold and coal mines, brickworks, hemp factories, salt processing plants, and lumber, railroad, and canal camps often employed white men together with blacks, enslaved and free. In southern cities, white artisans concerned about losing their livelihood protested the use of skilled slave labor. But their complaints fell on deaf ears. Most members of city councils and regulatory boards owned slaves and had no intention of giving up their enslaved workers so that white artisans could find jobs.

Southern industry always reflected developments in the plantation economy. For example, when cotton prices rose, slave owners kept their slaves working in the fields. Thus, planters discouraged any kind of large-scale manufacturing that might disrupt the agrarian society they had built so carefully over so many years.

THE MARKET REVOLUTION

As new means of transportation facilitated the movement of ideas, goods, and people, natural barriers separating farms from towns and the West from the East began to crumble. Factory workers quickly and efficiently processed raw materials—leather into shoes, cotton into clothing. Wage earning replaced family labor and indentured servitude as the dominant labor system in the North. Together, all of these rapid economic transformations in the early nineteenth century fueled what some scholars have called the **market revolution.** Driven by improvements in transportation, increasing commercialization, and the rise of factories, powerful economic changes affected ordinary Americans and their everyday routines at home and on the job.

Historians disagree about whether these changes began to appear before the American Revolution or afterward, and whether these changes touched every segment of the population or only people living in or near cities. However, it is clear that, by the mid-nineteenth century, the United States had become a fundamentally different place compared to the colonies on the brink of revolt in 1776. Many people began to make a living and think about the world in ways we now consider "modern."

The gradual changes of the market revolution were driven by investment. Wealthy New England merchants led the way, but a wide variety of private individuals and public institutions were willing to invest their money and energy in new economic opportunities. Profits from foreign trade helped to build the textile factories that dotted the northeastern landscape. States and even towns used the money of taxpayers and private investors to build turnpikes and later to finance canals and railroads. Entrepreneurs pioneered the puttingout system, a form of production (of hats and other forms of clothing, for example) that enlisted the efforts of single women in the cities, as well as farm families during the winter season. These workers received raw materials from a merchant-capitalist and engaged in piecework in return for wages. Combined public–private investment in new forms of business organization and technology spurred American economic growth.

These changes spilled over into American social and religious life, encouraging some people to adopt an optimistic worldview about the possibilities inherent in American life—possibilities that included moving from one place to another, making money by selling new products, altering the natural landscape to make way for canals or factories, and aspiring to buy goods rather than produce goods at home. Foreign visitors often commented on the "restlessness" of Americans, their "acquisitiveness," and their impatience with tradition.

Not all Americans adopted this new way of looking at the world, but almost all groups felt its effects. Slave owners pushed black men, women, and children to work even harder in the fields of the South so that more cotton and rice could be exported to northern and European markets. Western Indians suffered the effects of European American conquest, as whites chopped down forests and cleared the land for farms, violently displacing native populations in the process. In New England textile mills, women and children operated the

D.B. Pawtucket Bridge and Falls, Pawtucket, RI, 1812. Watercolor and ink on paper. Painting. Museum Collection. Rhode Island Historical Society, RHix522

■ Early mills had four possible sources of energy—hands, animals, wind, and water. This water-powered paper mill on Brandywine Creek in northern Delaware, c. 1830, suggests the importance of waterfalls to the early Industrial Revolution. Other mills on the Brandywine manufactured cotton and woolen cloth and produced gunpowder.

machines that produced cloth. These operatives served as the vanguard of the Industrial Revolution in America.

By the second decade of the nineteenth century, America had clearly defined itself as a nation that embraced many different kinds of change in transportation and technology. Yet traditional forms of inequality and hierarchy endured, serving as distinguishing features of the market revolution. Furthermore, in the South, planters persisted in growing staples such as cotton and rice, in the process discouraging industrialization and strengthening the institution of slavery.

The Rise of the Cotton Plantation Economy

■ *How did staple-crop production shape the labor, culture, and family lives of slaves?*

The growth and spread of the cotton economy redefined the institution of slavery, the southern political system, and ultimately all of American history. With the invention of the cotton gin and the acquisition of the Louisiana Territory, cotton production boomed, and the enslaved population expanded. In 1790 plantations produced 3,000 bales (about 300 pounds each) of cotton; 20 years later, that number hit 178,000. Beginning in 1808, the United States outlawed the importation of new slaves. However, the astounding profitability of cotton heightened the demand for slave labor. Planters began to rely on the domestic slave trade—the forced migration of slaves from the upper South to the lower South.

The institution of slavery was marked by sharp regional variations, increasingly reflecting the impact of cotton cultivation on local economies. At the same time, the contours of an

Which Nations Transported African Slaves in the Early 1800s?

Article 1, section 9, of the U.S. Constitution stipulates: "The migration or Importation of such Persons as any of the States now existing shall think proper to admit, shall not be prohibited by the Congress prior to the Year one thousand eight hundred and eight." This provision meant that the United States could not outlaw the importation of African slaves until 1808. In 1807, Congress passed a law that officially ended the U.S. trade on January 1, 1808. Nevertheless, a number of European nations continued to transport enslaved Africans to the Western Hemisphere, as shown in this graph.

QUESTIONS

1. Overall, how does the United States compare to European nations in the number of Africans forcibly transported across the Atlantic in the period covered by the graph?

2. What accounts for Portugal's dominance in the trade? (Hint: Brazil was a Portuguese colony.)

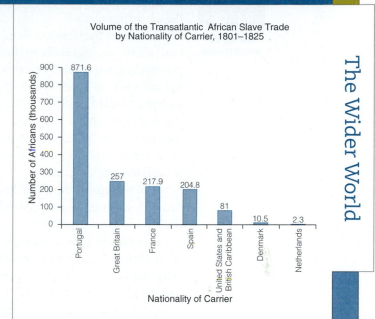

3. Why did the official end of the U.S. international slave trade stimulate domestic trafficking in slaves?

The Wider World

African American culture emerged. This culture had certain characteristics regardless of place, such as strong ties that bound nuclear and extended family members, rich oral and musical traditions heavily influenced by West African customs, and individual and collective resistance to slavery. White people as a group understood little of this culture; they viewed black people primarily as workers who would never become citizens. As U.S. military strength and nationalistic pride grew, southern planters imposed a harsher, more regimented system of slavery on the black population. The tension between the rhetoric of freedom and equality and the reality of slavery would continue to shape southern—and American—life for the next four decades.

REGIONAL ECONOMIES OF THE SOUTH

Throughout the South, shifts in production methods transformed the demographic and economic make-up of specific regions. For example, by the early nineteenth century, the Chesapeake tobacco economy had declined as a result of worn-out lands and falling prices. In its place arose a more diversified economy based on crafts, the cultivation of corn and wheat, and the milling of flour. Owners put enslaved men to work making barrels and horseshoes while forcing their wives, sisters, and daughters to labor as spinners, weavers, dairymaids, personal servants, and livestock tenders.

The lower South states of Georgia and South Carolina also saw their economies change during this period. The indigo export business never recovered from the Revolution, since colonial cultivators of the plant had relied heavily on British subsidies to shore up their profits. European customers now had to turn to Louisiana and Central America for indigo. In contrast, the lowcountry (coastal) South Carolina and Georgia rice economy recovered and flourished after the war. In a particularly rich rice district, All

Plantation and Southern Commerce

Saints Parish, one out of two slaves lived on a plantation with more than a hundred slaves in 1790; thirty years later, four out of five lived on such large establishments. In these areas, the plantation owners often lived elsewhere, and black people constituted almost the entire population.

Adding to the wealth of South Carolina and Georgia was the rapid development of cotton cultivation, especially in the interior, away from the coast. There, prosperous cotton planters began to rival their lowcountry rice-growing counterparts in social status and political influence, and these slaveholders pushed steadily for western expansion. Cotton planters rushed into the Louisiana Territory after 1803. They accelerated an economic process that had begun in the late eighteenth century: the replacement of a frontier exchange economy with plantation agriculture. (Sugar dominated the New Orleans region; cotton, the rest of the lower Mississippi Valley.) By 1800, slaves in lower Louisiana were producing 4.5 million pounds of sugar annually.

The reaches of the lower Mississippi took on an increasingly multicultural flavor. A strong Spanish influence persisted as a vestige of colonial days. Families of French descent (called Acadians) expelled from Nova Scotia, a Canadian province, began to settle in southern Louisiana in 1765. French-speaking planter-refugees and their slaves from revolutionary Saint-Domingue came to New Orleans while the city was still in French hands (1800 to 1803). Between 1787 and 1803, nearly 3,000 slaves arrived from Africa, Spanish West Florida, and the Chesapeake to be sold in New Orleans, followed by even larger numbers of slaves from the North after 1803. Slave owners who settled in Natchez, on the banks of the Mississippi River, grew cotton—and grew rich.

BLACK FAMILY LIFE AND LABOR

The number of enslaved persons in the United States grew from about 717,000 in 1790 to more than 1.5 million in 1820 and continued to increase rapidly over the next four decades. Since importation of Africans ended officially in 1808, these numbers suggest a tremendous rate of natural increase. Some planters continued to buy slaves brought into the country illegally after 1808. But most of the increase stemmed from births. The preferences of both slave owners and slaves account for this development. Southern planters encouraged black women to bear many children. These white men gained new (future) workers when enslaved women gave birth. And many planters believed that slave populations bound together by family ties would be less likely to engage in resistance, such as violent rebellion or running away.

At the same time, enslaved African Americans valued the family as a social unit; family ties provided support and solace for a people deprived of fundamental human rights. Even under harsh conditions, black people fell in love, married (albeit informally, without the sanction of law), had children, and reared families. Despite the lack of protection from local, state, and national authorities, the slave family proved a remarkably resilient institution.

> *Despite the lack of protection from local, state, and national authorities, the slave family proved a remarkably resilient institution.*

The stability of individual slave families depended on several factors, including the size and age of the plantation and the fortunes and life cycle of the slave owner's family. Very large or long-established plantations had more two-parent slave families than did the small or newer holdings, which tended to have more unrelated people. Slave families were broken up when whites died and their "property" was bequeathed to heirs. Slaves might also be sold or presented to other family members as gifts. Many slave families suffered disruption in response to the growing demand for slaves in the fresh cotton lands of Alabama and Mississippi. The forced migration from upper South to lower South necessarily severed kin ties, but slaves often reconstituted those ties in the form of symbolic kin relationships. Families adopted new, single members of the slave community, and the children called these newcomers "Aunt" or "Uncle."

Since plantations functioned as slave labor camps, owners generally showed little or no inclination to take family relationships into account when they parceled out work assignments to men, women, and children. Rather, those assignments, and the conditions under which slaves performed them, reflected the size and crops of a particular plantation. During the period 1790 to 1860, an estimated 75 percent of slaves worked primarily as field hands. On large plantations the division of labor could be quite specialized. Men served as skilled carpenters, blacksmiths, and barrel makers, and women worked as cooks, laundresses, nursemaids, and personal maids.

Rice slaves continued to work under the task system. Each day, after they completed a specific assigned task, they spent their time as they chose, within limits. The women washed clothes and cleaned the living quarters. The men hunted and fished. Both men and women visited friends and worked in their own gardens. Slaves jealously guarded their limited forms of freedom. One white man in Georgia described a slave who had completed his appointed task for the day: "His master feels no right to call on him," leaving him "the remainder of the day to work in his own corn field."

Even in the cotton-growing regions, where blacks labored under the regimented gang system, slaves tried to work for themselves in the little free time they had on Saturday afternoons and Sunday. In Louisiana, one white observer noted that the slave man returning to his living quarters after a long, hot day in the fields "does not lose his time. He goes to work at a bit of the land which he has planted with provisions for his own use, while his companion, if he has one, busies herself in preparing [meals] for him, herself, and their children." Family members who grew or accumulated a modest surplus—of corn, eggs, vegetables—in some cases could sell their wares in a nearby market or to slaves on another plantation.

Some slaves took goods from their master's storeroom and barn and sold or traded them to other slaves or to poor whites. These transactions often took place under the

Francis Guy, Perry Hall Slave Quarters with Field Hands at Work, c.1805. Maryland Historical Society, Baltimore Maryland (86.33).

■ This painting, c. 1805, by Francis Guy is titled *Perry Hall Slave Quarters with Field Hands at Work*. Enslaved workers, organized in a gang, cultivate tobacco on a Chesapeake plantation. After the turn of the century, the center of the plantation staple-crop economy moved south and west. The Chesapeake region of Maryland and Virginia developed a more diversified economy than that of the rich cotton lands of Alabama and Louisiana.

cover of darkness. Planters complained of slaves who stole their cattle, hogs, chickens, sacks full of cotton, farm equipment, and stores of ham and flour. In 1806, planters in lowcountry South Carolina, along the Combahee River, railed against a problem that would grow worse in the coming years: "pedling boats which frequent the river . . . for the purpose of trading with The Negroe Slaves, to the very great loss of the Owners, and Corruption of such slaves." Thus slaves' various forms of labor fell into at least three categories: work performed at the behest of and directly under the supervision of whites, labor performed by and for family members within the slaves' living quarters, and the sale (or sometimes clandestine exchange) of goods with masters, other slaves, and poor whites.

> Taken together, the burdens of work, family, and community life were especially harsh for enslaved women.

Taken together, the burdens of work, family, and community life were especially harsh for enslaved women. Later, the daughter of a slave remembered the labors of her mother with a mixture of pride and bitterness: the older woman "could do anything. She cooked, washed, spun, nursed, and labored in the field. She made as good a field hand as she did a cook." Recalled the daughter, their master said that her mother could "outwork" any slave, male or female, in the county.

At the same time, women were particularly vulnerable to the many and often violent demands of whites in the fields and in the "Big House," the residence of the master and mistress. Hoping to instill fear in their workers, overseers often punished the most vulnerable members of the slave community—elderly persons and pregnant women among them. Frederick Douglass, a Maryland slave who escaped to the North in the 1830s, explained that "the doctrine that submission to violence is the best cure for violence did not hold good as between slaves and overseers. He was whipped oftener who was whipped easiest."

After toiling in the fields, women and young girls would return to their quarters to prepare the evening meal, wash the family's clothes, and tend to the children. Because owners were more likely to separate fathers rather than mothers from their children, women shouldered the bulk of child-rearing responsibilities and dreaded the day when their offspring might be sold away from them.

Tight-knit slave families, which included extended kin relations as well as blood ties, shaped black women's preferences for work assignments. Although white Southerners later in the century would come to glorify the "spoiled" and "petted" house slave, in fact many black women considered manual labor in the fields preferable to domestic service in the Big House. House servants faced almost routine sexual exploitation from masters and masters' sons. In response to these forms of infidelity, a jealous mistress would often take out her frustration and rage not on the men of her own household but on the slave women who worked under her supervision in the parlor and kitchen.

House servants were on call twenty-four hours a day and held to exacting standards in washing and cooking for the white family. For all these reasons, an enslaved woman might prefer arduous field labor, and the opportunity to spend more time with her family, over service in the Big House. Yet whites persisted in viewing black women as workers first and foremost and as family members only incidentally, if at all.

RESISTANCE TO SLAVERY

Enslaved men and women did not always behave according to their masters' demands. In 1817, the New Orleans City Council decreed that slaves could sing and dance at a stipulated place—Congo Square—every Sunday afternoon. Thereafter, a variety of groups came together to make music. These groups included recent immigrants from Saint-Domingue and slaves newly imported from Africa; slaves from neighboring plantations, in town for the day; and free people of color (Creoles), who often blended Spanish and

French classical music traditions. One eyewitness observed that the Congo Square musicians "have their own national music, consisting for the most part of a long kind of narrow drum of various size." In towns and on plantations throughout the South, black people drew from West African musical styles, using drums as well as banjolike instruments, gourd rattles, and mandolins. Over the generations, several uniquely American musical styles flowed from Congo Square and other southern gathering places.

In their artistic expression, dress, hairstyles, and language, slaves sought to preserve their cultural uniqueness and create an existence that slaveholders could not touch. In the South Carolina lowcountry, slaves spoke Gullah. Originally a pidgin—a blend of words and grammatical structures from West African languages and English—Gullah later developed into a more formal Creole language. Slaves throughout the United States also mixed West African religious beliefs with Christianity. Many West African groups believed in a close relationship between the natural and supernatural worlds. In slave quarters, spiritual leaders not only preached a Christianity of equality but also told fortunes and warned away "haunts" (spirits of the dead).

In gatherings of many kinds, enslaved Americans affirmed their bonds with one another and their resistance to bondage. For example, funerals provided opportunities for music and expressions of group solidarity. Many slaves adhered to a view of the world that blended Christian and West African religious elements. This view held that funerals marked a rite of passage for the deceased person. In funeral services and other observances, the rich oral and musical traditions that characterized slave life preserved collective memories of Africa and the lore of individual families and kin networks.

Black resistance to slavery took many forms. Slaves might work carelessly in an effort to resist a master's or mistress's demands. During the course of their workday, some slaves

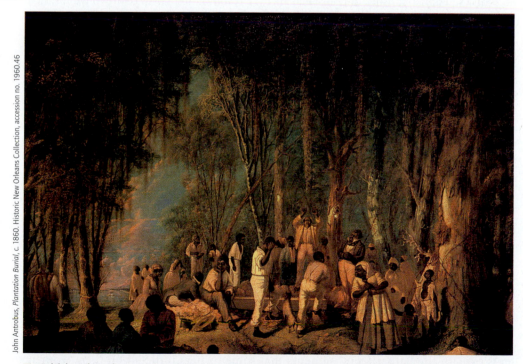

John Antrobus, *Plantation Burial*, c. 1860. Historic New Orleans Collection, accession no. 1960.46

■ British artist John Antrobus titled his 1860 painting *Plantation Burial*. Held at night, after the workday, slave funerals provided an opportunity for the community—including slaves from nearby plantations—to come together in mourning. Planters remained suspicious of such gatherings, which were marked by African musical forms and religious rituals. Whites feared that slaves would conspire under the cover of darkness.

broke hoes and other farm implements. A cook might burn the biscuits, thus spoiling a special dinner party for her mistress. Striking out more directly, the African-influenced "conjurer"—often a woman who had a knowledge of plants and herbs—could wreak havoc on a white family by concocting poisons or encouraging disruptive behavior among slaves.

Slaves also stole goods from their masters and at times stole themselves by running away. (This practice was more common among young, unmarried men than among those who had family obligations.) In plotting their escapes, many blacks took advantage of the ways the natural landscape shaped pathways away from the plantation and out of slavery. In the lowcountry region of South Carolina and Georgia, black men skilled as river pilots stole skiffs and made their way silently through mazes of creeks and inlets to seek freedom in the anonymity of Charleston or Savannah. The built environment of the city, with its narrow alleyways and bustling dock areas, could provide cover for the recent fugitive. In these port cities and in others along the South Atlantic seaboard, some blacks bided their time, hoping to stow away or use forged documents to pass for a free person of color on a steamship, in order to make their way north to Boston or New York. George Washington's slave Ona Judge took advantage of the refuge afforded her by two northern cities—Philadelphia, Pennsylvania, and Portsmouth, New Hampshire.

> *Slave masters and mistresses created a number of myths about the black people they exploited.*

Throughout the southern interior, blacks fled to the swamps, marshes, and forests in an effort to hide out for short or extended periods of time. They lived off the land: fishing, trapping small animals, or scavenging for berries or nuts. In their plans for escape, would-be fugitives had to take into consideration both the obstacles and the potential inherent in their natural environment.

Despite the extraordinary peril involved, some slaves revolted. In St. Charles and St. John the Baptist parishes in Louisiana, an 1811 revolt of 400 slaves cost two whites their lives and left several plantations in flames. The original participants, led by Charles Deslondes, a free man of color, acquired new members as they marched toward New Orleans. U.S. troops cut their advance short, killing 66 of them. In the Southeast in 1817 and 1818, 400 to 600 runaway slaves converged on the swamps of central Florida, uniting with Indian refugees from the Red Stick War. Together, they raided Georgia plantations until Andrew Jackson and his soldiers halted them in April 1818.

To justify their own behavior, slave masters and mistresses created a number of myths about the black people they exploited. Whites had a vested interest in believing that their slaves felt gratitude toward them. Skilled in the so-called deference ritual, some slaves hid their true feelings and acted submissively in the presence of white people. Owners and overseers alike interpreted this behavior as a sign of black contentment.

Yet most whites understood that danger could lurk beneath the surface of the most accommodating slave. Therefore, the prevailing stereotypes of black men and women encompassed two caricatures: "Sambo" and "Mammy" were childlike and grateful, and "Nat" and "Jezebel" were surly, cunning, dangerous, and unpredictable. One Kentucky slave, Susan, was described by a planter in 1822 as "the biggest devil that ever lived." Susan reportedly poisoned a stud horse and set a stable on fire, causing $1,500 worth of damage, after managing to escape from handcuffs.

Although some planters boasted of their fatherly solicitude for their slaves, in fact slave owners harbored deep fears about the men and women they held in bondage. These fears explain the barbaric punishments that some owners inflicted on men, women, and children. Whip-wielding overseers made pregnant women lie down in a trench in the fields, presumably so that the lash would not harm the fetus. Even in "respectable" southern families, slave owners branded, mutilated, and beat enslaved workers for resisting discipline or to deliver a warning to other potentially defiant slaves. In the slave South, American cries of freedom, equality, opportunity, and the blessings of citizenship rang hollow.

Conclusion

During the first two decades of the nineteenth century, the natural landscape shaped the political, military, and economic development of the new nation. Politicians known as "war hawks" believed that American national honor depended on the conquest of Indians in the West and England on the high seas. The War of 1812 represented not only the end of British interference within the continental United States but also the next chapter in the bloody saga of European Americans' acquiring Indian lands through purchase or, more often, forcible seizure. Without British support in the form of troops and guns, Indians in the Great Lakes region suffered devastating losses.

Many Americans owed their livelihoods to the shape of the land or to the riches embedded in it. Powered by water rushing from the hills to the sea, textile mills gave rise to a new class of factory workers. With the annexation of the Louisiana Territory in 1803, the rich lands of the South provided fertile ground for the spread of the slave system. As European Americans migrated west and to the Mississippi Valley, they replaced the trading economy with family farms and plantations, sawmills, and gristmills.

Though enslaved to the brutal demands of plantation economies, African Americans sought to turn the contours of the land to their own advantage. They used rivers, seaports, swamps, and marshes as hiding places and as refuges from slavery. Despite the differences in labor organization characteristic of cotton and rice cultivation, southern blacks developed strong family ties, a vibrant religious tradition, and multiple forms of everyday resistance to the system of slavery.

During this period, dramatic historical developments stirred the spirit of American nationalism. The Louisiana Purchase magnified the natural wealth of the young nation, and the federal government encouraged citizens to exploit that wealth through trade and settlement. The War of 1812 bolstered the American economy by stimulating technological innovation and the growth of manufacturing. Territorial expansion combined with economic development to create new jobs for a burgeoning population. Unlike the rigidly class-conscious nations of Europe, America seemed to offer limitless possibilities—at least for propertied white men, the only people entitled to the full rights of citizenship. Gradually, the two-party system of the Democratic-Republicans and the Federalists dissolved, as the nation secured its boundaries and met the challenge of British aggression. The old models of France and England, a legacy of the Revolution, gave way to new issues reflecting the challenges faced by an industrializing nation.

Southern cotton planters and northern factory owners derived their newfound prosperity from very different sources: staple-crop agriculture on one hand and the emerging industrial system on the other. At the same time, these two groups had much in common. As they expanded their operations, whether sprawling plantations or gigantic mill complexes, they displaced smaller landowners and

CHRONOLOGY: 1804–1818

1804	Lewis and Clark Expedition (1804–1806).
1805	British navy defeats French and Spanish fleets at Battle of Trafalgar.
1806	Congress authorizes funds for construction of National Road.
1807	Jefferson places embargo on all U.S. exports to Europe.
	U.S.S. *Chesapeake* attacked by British vessel.
	Robert Fulton pilots first steamboat up the Hudson River.
1808	Congressional ban on slave trade takes effect.
	Non-Intercourse Act prevents exports to France and England.
	Tecumseh and Tenskwatawa found Prophet Town in Indiana.
1811	Battle of Tippecanoe.
	Revolt of 400 slaves in Louisiana.
1812	War of 1812 begins.
1813	Red Sticks battle U.S. troops at Battle of Horseshoe Bend.
1814	British forces attack Washington, D.C.
1815	Treaty of Ghent ends War of 1812.
	Battle of New Orleans.
1816	Tariff of 1816.
1818	Andrew Jackson battles Seminole in Florida.

raised land prices. Members of both elite groups proved restless entrepreneurs, eager to move around to find the freshest lands and the cheapest labor. Their personal wealth and their political power set them apart from the people under them—the slaves and wage earners—who produced that wealth. And both the southern "lords of the lash" and the northern "lords of the loom" depended on large numbers of slaves to grow cotton. Thus, the fluffy white fiber of the cotton boll is perhaps a most fitting symbol of the emerging American economy. Producing and processing it yielded tangible benefits for a few and created a new, harsher world of work for many.

For Review

1. Who were the war hawks, and why did they emerge as such a potent political force in Congress? Why were most from the West?

2. In 1812, in what ways did the British and Indians see the United States as their common enemy? In what ways did the interests of the British and their Indian allies differ?

3. In the United States, what were the political, social, and economic consequences of the War of 1812?

4. What issues did the War of 1812 resolve? Leave unresolved? Is it accurate to call the war a victory for the United States?

5. Explain the market revolution and its effects on American society. Which groups benefited?

6. What elements of African American culture revealed the slaves' struggle to live life on their own terms, rather than on the terms dictated by white masters and mistresses? Within the plantation, in what ways was the power of slaveholders limited or restricted?

7. Did the United States change substantially between 1812 and 1818? Explain.

Created Equal Online

For more *Created Equal* resources, including suggestions on sites to visit and books to read, go to **MyHistoryLab.com.**

Chapter 11

Society and Politics in the "Age of the Common Man," 1819–1832

■ John Gadsby Chapman painted this portrait of David Crockett in 1834.

CHAPTER OUTLINE

■ The Politics Behind Western Expansion

■ Federal Authority and Its Opponents

■ Americans in the "Age of the Common Man"

■ Ties That Bound a Growing Population

Campaigning for political office in Tennessee in the 1820s was not an activity for the faint of heart. Candidates competed against each other in squirrel hunts, the loser footing the bill for the barbecue that followed. A round of speechmaking often was capped by several rounds of whiskey enjoyed by candidates and supporters alike. Into this boisterous arena stepped a man unrivaled as a campaigner. David Crockett ran successfully for several offices, including local justice of the peace in 1818. He served in the state legislature from 1820 to 1824, and he was elected to the U.S. House of Representatives in 1826, 1828, and 1832. The plainspoken Crockett knew how to play to a crowd and rattle a rival. He bragged about his skill as a bear hunter and ridiculed the fancy dress of his opponents. He condemned closed-door political caucuses (small groups of party insiders who hand-picked candidates) and praised grassroots democracy. Crockett claimed he could out-shoot, out-drink, and out-debate anyone who opposed him. If his opponent lied about him, why, then, he would lie about himself: "Yes fellow citizens, I can run faster, walk longer, leap higher, speak better, and tell more and bigger lies than my competitor, and all his friends, any day of his life." Crockett's blend of political theater and folksy backwoods banter earned him the allegiance of voters like him—people who, though having little formal education, understood the challenges of carving a homestead out of the dense thickets of western Tennessee.

Crockett's raucous brand of campaigning appealed to Westerners—that is, European Americans living just west of the Appalachian Mountains. His social betters might sniff that he was a rough, ignorant man—in the words of one Tennessee political insider, "more in his proper place, when hunting a Bear in the cane Brake, than he will be in the Capital." But newspaper reporters and defeated opponents alike grew to respect his ability to champion ordinary farmers. As a politician, Crockett spoke for debtors, squatters, and militia veterans of the Revolutionary War. He scorned the wellborn in favor of those who could shoot down and skin a wolf.

In 1790, 100,000 Americans (not including Indians) lived west of the Appalachian Mountains; half a century later that number had increased to 7 million, or about four out of ten Americans. During the 1820s, European American settlers in the trans-Appalachian West transformed the style and substance of American politics. Beginning with Kentucky in 1792, western states began to relax or abolish property requirements for adult male voters. Even the English that Americans spoke changed. New terms introduced into the political vocabulary reflected the rough-hewn, woodsman quality of western electioneering: candidates hit the campaign trail, giving stump speeches along the way. They supported their party's platform with its planks (positions on the issues). As legislators, they voted for pork-barrel projects that would benefit their constituents at home. Emphasizing his modest origins, David Crockett became widely known as Davy Crockett. (It is hard to imagine anyone calling the Sage of Monticello Tommy Jefferson.)

Western settlers attacked centralized, eastern-based institutions of wealth and privilege. They scorned a six-person Supreme Court that could overturn the laws of Congress and the individual states. They opposed the privately held Second Bank of the United States, which, its critics charged, enriched its own board of directors at the expense of indebted farmers. And they railed against federally sponsored internal improvements, such as turnpikes and canals, which, many western homesteaders believed, served the interests of well-connected merchants and financiers.

Western voters rejoiced with the 1828 election of Andrew Jackson of Tennessee to the presidency. Here, they claimed, was a person who would battle eastern financiers and at the same time support white settlers' claims to Indian lands in the West. Jackson held out the promise that ordinary people would have a political voice and access to expanding economic opportunities.

During his two terms in office (1828–1836), Andrew Jackson so dominated the American political landscape that historians have called him the symbol of an age and the representative man of his time. Born in humble circumstances, orphaned at age fourteen, Jackson achieved public acclaim as a lawyer, military officer (in the War of 1812), and finally president. In promoting a strong central government, and the authority of the chief executive in particular, he clashed with southern states' rights advocates. Jackson backed up his vision with the use of violence and, at times, contempt for the law, as evidenced in his removal of Indians from the Southeast. Nevertheless, Jackson's view appealed strongly to workers and small farmers who resented what they viewed as entrenched eastern privilege in politics and the economy.

Yet democracy had its limits during this period. White voter participation in presidential elections soared, from 25 percent of eligible voters in 1824 to 50 percent in 1828. Still, most people could not vote. Slaves and American Indians remained barred from even the rudiments of formal citizenship. White married women, who could neither own property nor vote, found themselves second-class citizens. Almost all free people of color, whether in the

DOCUMENT

Davy Crockett, Advice to Politicians (1833)

North, South, or Midwest, likewise lacked basic rights—to vote, serve on juries, or send their children to public school.

Further complicating this age was the rise of distinct social classes. Acquiring great economic and political significance, the class system seemed to mock the idea of equality. The outlines of this system appeared in the 1820s in the Northeast, where business and factory managers received salaries, not hourly wages, and their wives were full-time homemakers and mothers. New forms of popular literature, such as the *Ladies Magazine,* published in Boston, glorified the middle-class family, especially the pious wife and mother who held moral sway over it.

The "Age of The Common Man" was thus rife with irony. Jackson himself embodied many apparent contradictions. An Indian-fighter, he adopted a young Indian boy as his ward. A foe of privilege, he was a slave owner. A self-professed champion of farmers and artisans, he expressed contempt for their representatives in Congress. He also took steps to expand the power of the executive branch. The 1820s in general revealed these larger contradictions as national leaders pursued a more democratic form of politics on one hand and supported a system based on class and racial differences on the other. The resulting tensions shaped American society and politics in the third decade of the nineteenth century.

The Politics Behind Western Migration

■ *How did western expansion affect the nation's politics and economy of the 1820s?*

As the United States gained new territory through negotiation and conquest and as people moved west, these changes were reflected in international and domestic political relations. At the highest levels of politics, President James Monroe warned Europe not to interfere any longer in the Western Hemisphere. Congressional debates over whether Missouri should be admitted to the Union as a slave or free state sent shock waves throughout the country. Of the political conflict over the fate of slavery in the territories, the elderly Thomas Jefferson wrote, "This momentous question, like a firebell in the night, awakened and filled me with terror. I considered it at once as the death knell of the Union."

This migration also led to fundamental changes in the everyday political lives of Americans. As new states were carved out of the West, gaining national influence in Congress, traditional methods of choosing candidates and the old political parties of Democratic-Republicans and Federalists came under fire. Parties began to choose their presidential nominees in conventions, not in caucuses of legislators, and more and more states abolished the requirement that would-be voters and office holders had to own property.

However, the opening of the West to European American settlement, which invigorated white men's democracy, also sowed seeds of economic and political conflict. The newcomers made their way not through empty territory but through Native American homelands. Western debtors' economic distress echoed in eastern centers of finance. Once in the West, most of these settlers faced the same kinds of conflicts that increasingly preoccupied Easterners, especially those between masters and slaves and debtors and creditors.

MAP
Expanding America
and Internal
Improvements

THE MISSOURI COMPROMISE

In 1819, the United States consisted of twenty-two states. Slavery was legal in half of them. Late that year, the territory of Missouri applied to Congress for statehood. This move set off panic in both the North and South because a twenty-third state was bound to upset the delicate balance

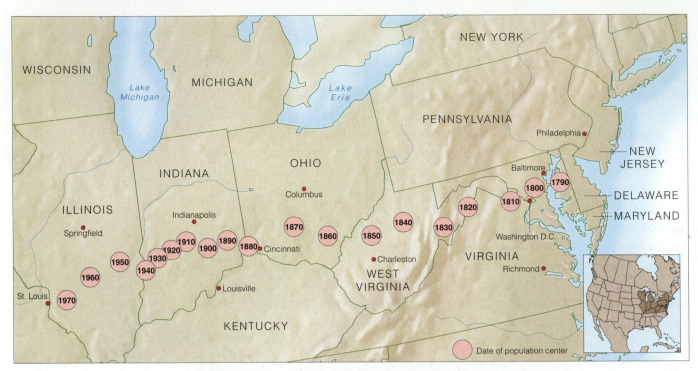

■ **MAP 11.1 The Center of Population Moves West, 1790–1970**

In 1830, most European and African Americans still lived along the eastern seaboard. Yet the statistical center of the country had shifted dramatically westward as settlers moved across the trans-Appalachian West. Migrants from the South sought out the fresh cotton lands of Alabama and Mississippi, while New Englanders created new communities in the upper Midwest. Migration to areas such as Wisconsin and Georgia was contingent on the removal of Indians from those areas, either by treaty or by military force.

of senators between slave and free states. Representative James Tallmadge of New York proposed a compromise: no slaves would be imported into Missouri in the future, and the new state would gradually emancipate the enslaved men and women living within its borders. The Tallmadge Amendment was defeated in the House as Southerners resisted this blatant attempt to limit the spread of slavery. The debate over the future of Missouri occupied Congress from December 1819 to March 1820.

In the Senate, Rufus King of New York claimed that Congress had the ultimate authority to set laws governing slavery. However, his colleague William Pinckney of Maryland retorted that new states possessed the same rights as the original thirteen; they could choose whether or not to allow slavery. Maine's application for admission to the Union suggested a way out of the impasse. Speaker of the House of Representatives Henry Clay of Kentucky proposed a plan calling for Missouri to join the Union as a slave state. At the same time, Maine, originally part of Massachusetts, would become the twenty-fourth state and be designated a free one. In the future, slavery would be prohibited from all Louisiana Purchase lands north of latitude 36°30', an area that included all territory north of present-day Missouri and Kansas. The House and the Senate finally approved the compromise, which maintained the balance between the number of slave and free states.

The day Congress sealed the compromise, Secretary of State John Quincy Adams of Massachusetts walked home from the Capitol with Senator John C. Calhoun of South Carolina. The two men engaged in a muted but intense debate over slavery. Calhoun claimed that the institution "was the best guarantee to equality among the whites." Slavery, he asserted, demonstrated that all white men were equal to one another and superior to all blacks. Unnerved by Calhoun's comments, Adams concluded that the debate over Missouri had "betrayed the secret of [slaveowners'] souls." By reserving backbreaking toil for blacks, wealthy planters fancied themselves aristocratic lords of the manor. Adams confided in his

Slave states
Free states and territories
Open to slavery by Missouri Compromise
Closed to slavery by Missouri Compromise

■ **MAP 11.2 The Missouri Compromise**

Missouri applied for statehood in 1819, threatening the balance between eleven free and eleven slave states. According to a compromise hammered out in Congress, Missouri was admitted as a slave state, and Maine, formerly part of Massachusetts, was admitted as a free state. Slavery was banned above the 36°30' parallel.

diary that night, "They look down upon the simplicity of a Yankee's manners, because he has no habits of overbearing like theirs and cannot treat negroes like dogs."

Adams acknowledged that the compromise had kept the number of slave and free states in balance. Still, he reflected, slavery "taints the very sources of moral principle." Would it not have been better to confront the issue squarely and amend the Constitution in favor of free labor in all new states admitted to the Union? Adams feared that the North-South conflicts over the issue might someday imperil the nation itself. He concluded ominously, "If the Union must be dissolved, slavery is precisely the question upon which it ought to break." Five years later, Adams won the presidency of the United States. Elected separately by the voters, his vice president was none other than John C. Calhoun. Over the next four years, the two men managed to maintain an uneasy political alliance.

WAYS WEST: THE ERIE CANAL

Missouri was just one of the territories west of the Mississippi River where the population had increased during this period. Through land grants and government financing of new methods of transportation, Congress encouraged European American migrants to push their way west and south. The Land Act of 1820 enabled Westerners to buy a minimum 80 acres at a price of $1.25 an acre in cash—even in those days, a bargain homestead. Built with the help of government legal and financial aid, new roads and canals, steamboats, and, after the early 1830s, railroads facilitated migration. Between 1820 and 1860, the number of steamboats plying the Mississippi River jumped from 60 to more than 1,000. Canals linked western producers to eastern consumers of grains and cattle and connected western

LISTEN
"The Erie Canal"

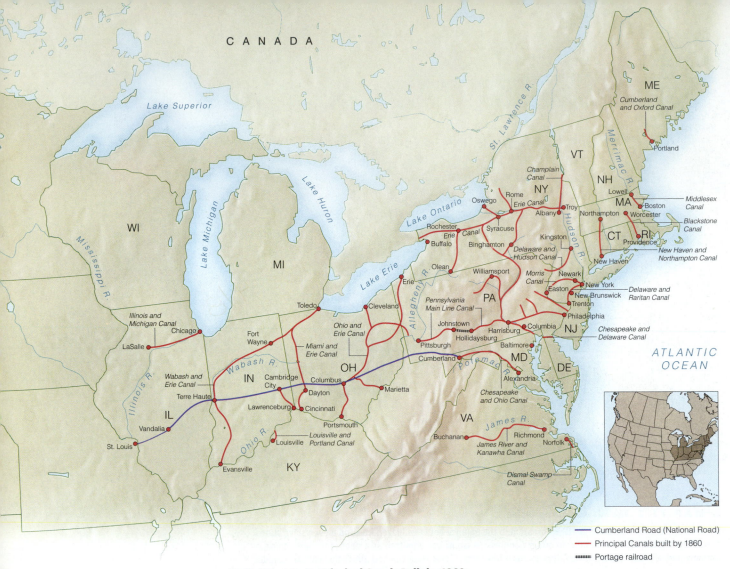

CANADA

Lake Superior

Lake Michigan

Lake Huron

Lake Ontario

Lake Erie

ATLANTIC
OCEAN

Cumberland Road (National Road)
Principal Canals built by 1860
Portage railroad

■ **MAP 11.3 Principal Canals Built by 1860**

Many canals were expensive ventures and, in some cases, engineering nightmares. The Erie Canal had a competitive advantage because it snaked through the Mohawk Valley, the only major level pass through the mountain chain that stretched from Canada to Georgia. In contrast, the Pennsylvania Main Line Canal, which ran from Harrisburg to Pittsburgh, used a combination of inclined planes and steam engines in ten separate locations to haul boats up and down the Allegheny Mountains.

consumers to eastern producers of manufactured goods. Shipping costs and times between Buffalo and New York shrank. Cities such as Rochester and Syracuse, New York, and Cincinnati, Ohio, flourished because of their geographic position along key waterways. Among the most significant of these waterways was the **Erie Canal.**

Begun in 1817, the canal was a marvel in engineering, financial, and social terms. Forty feet wide at the water's surface and 4 feet deep, the "artificial river" ascended 680 feet on its east-west rise and included 83 locks and 18 aqueducts along the way. The 363-mile canal linked the New York cities of Troy and Albany, on the Hudson River, with Buffalo, on the eastern tip of Lake Erie. The waterway allowed farmers throughout the Great Lakes system to send crops and livestock as far east as the Atlantic Ocean, and it allowed East Coast manufacturers to market their products throughout the Midwest.

Yet many people at the time believed that the canal promised more than an economic boon. In their eyes, the project had great political and religious significance as well. Today it is difficult for us to appreciate the excitement and enthusiasm that greeted its opening. The completion of the canal in 1825 was marked by an elaborate celebration called the "Wedding of the Waters." The vision, skill, and hard work that went into building the canal demonstrated "the *spirit and perseverance* of REPUBLICAN FREE MEN," read a capstone on the canal locks at Lockport. Politicians claimed that they had the responsibility to make use of the nation's abundant natural resources. An early supporter of the canal project,

The Granger Collection, New York

■ This drawing of the Erie Canal at Lockport, New York, illustrates two of the ways internal improvements overcame natural barriers to trade and transportation—through canal locks (foreground) and a tall trestle bridge (background).

New York's prominent political leader Gouverneur Morris, promoted this view. He claimed that failing to build the canal would show "a want of wisdom, almost of piety, not to employ for public advantage those means which Divine Providence has placed so completely within our power." Marveling at the intricate lock system, one observer claimed that, aided by technology, humans could now hope to master nature itself: "It certainly strikes the beholder with astonishment, to perceive what vast difficulties can be overcome by the pigmy arms of little mortal men, aided by science and directed by superior skill." Human ingenuity, together with gunpowder and raw human and oxen muscle power, could literally level mountains.

By any measure the state of New York saw a spectacular return on its investment. Though the state had financed the project's whole cost of $7 million on its own, by 1882 it had taken in over $121 million in tolls charged to the users of the waterway. Factories, gristmills, taverns, and inns sprang up along the canal banks, stimulating local economies. Throughout the 1830s and 1840s, approximately 30,000 men, women, and children labored to maintain the canal, operate the locks, and load and pull barges (as many as 3,400 in operation at one time). The prosperity generated by the canal greatly benefited New York City, which emerged as the most important financial center in the country.

The canal also contributed to major social transformations. By making inexpensive manufactured goods accessible to large numbers of people in rural New York and the Midwest, the canal helped to raise the material standard of living of people outside large cities. In the late 1820s, a series of religious revivals swept through western New York, as some people embraced the idea that a new day was dawning, a day when men and women could control their own destiny—even the salvation of their own souls. If ordinary people could now move mountains, was not almost anything possible?

On the other hand, some people believed that prosperity exacted a high price from local communities. A new, unruly mix of boatmen, passengers, and longshoremen changed sleepy farm towns into bustling centers of trade. Not everyone welcomed the change. According to one critic, every settlement along the waterway now boasted "from 3 to 6 groggeries, and all those for the benefit for the traveling public . . . 'Rum, Gin, Brandy, Wine, Beer, Cider, Bread, Milk, and Groceries,' meet the eye every few miles." While some people saw the canal as a sign of progress of religious proportions, others lamented the passing of a traditional, tranquil way of life. Yet virtually everyone would have agreed with the Reverend F. H. Cuming, who spoke at a ceremony marking the completion of the canal in 1825 and proclaimed in awe: "the mountains have been leveled; the vallies have been filled; rivers and gulfs have been formed over them," and in the process, a new river, manmade, was born.

SPREADING AMERICAN CULTURE—AND SLAVERY

These debates did little to keep Americans from pressing west, and they took a variety of routes to get there. In the 1820s, desperate planters moved out of the exhausted lands of the upper South (the states of Virginia and Maryland), the Carolinas, and Georgia, westward into Alabama, Arkansas, Louisiana, and Mississippi. This migration across the Appalachian Mountains furthered the nationalist idea of the "expansion of liberty and freedom," a view held by many whites regardless of political affiliation. Yet it also spread slavery. The sight of slave coffles—groups of men, women, and children bound together in chains, hobbling down a city street or a country road—became increasingly common in this western region. The increase in slaves to the west is evidenced by the increased production of cash crops. In 1821, Virginia, North Carolina, South Carolina, and Georgia produced two-thirds of the nation's cotton crop; the rest came from recently settled areas. Just a dozen years later the proportions shifted: Tennessee, Louisiana, Alabama, Mississippi, and Florida together produced two-thirds of all cotton, and the remaining one-third came from older areas.

European Americans also migrated across the border into Mexican territory. In 1821, Spain approved the application of a U.S. citizen, Moses Austin, to settle 300 American families on 200,000 fertile acres along the Colorado and Brazos river bottoms in southeastern Texas. Austin died soon after, but his son Stephen carried on his legacy. Within two years, the younger Austin had received permission (now from the government of newly independent Mexico) to bring in another 100 families. These settlers, together with squatters, numbered about 1,500 people. Although the Mexican constitution prohibited slavery, some of the new-comers brought their slaves with them, and some free people of color came on their own. All

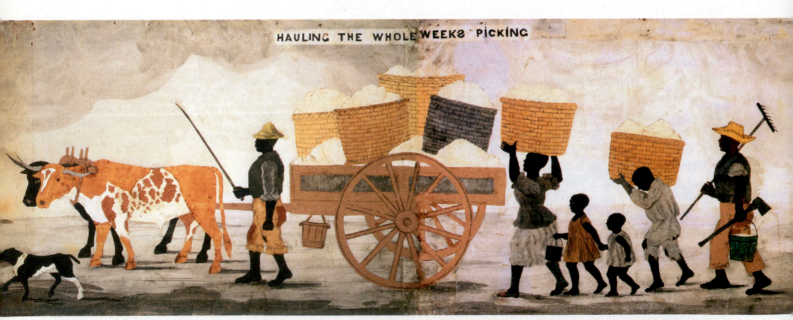

William Henry Brown, *Hauling the Whole Weeks Picking,* 1842. Historic New Orleans Collection (1975.93.1 and 1975.93.2)

■ The rich bottomlands of the Mississippi Delta proved ideal for growing cotton. After the forced removal of the Five Civilized Tribes, slave owners established expansive plantations in the delta. This scene, painted in 1842 by artist William Henry Brown, shows a group of slaves bringing in "the whole weeks picking" of cotton on the Vick plantation near Vicksburg, Mississippi.

The Global Trade in Cotton

In the first half of the nineteenth century, southern planters were integral to the U.S. economy, and cotton represented a significant portion of the nation's exports. Most of the exported cotton was destined for the textile mills of England. Many slaveholders followed world cotton prices closely from year to year; to a great extent, their profits depended on the international demand for cotton. Profits generated by cotton exports allowed planters to buy luxury goods imported from Europe and the North, and to invest in more land and slaves.

Source: Data from Douglas North, *The Economic Growth of the United States, 1790–1860* (Prentice Hall, 1961), p. 233.

Value of U.S. Cotton Exports, 1815–1960

The Wider World

QUESTIONS

1. How does this graph represent the push of cotton planters into the Indian lands of Georgia and other parts of the Southeast, beginning in the early 1830s?

2. Why would British manufacturers be eager to buy U.S. produced cotton?

3. How might the income generated by cotton exports stimulate growth not only in the South but in the North as well?

these migrants from the United States called themselves **Texians** to distinguish themselves from the *Tejanos,* or Spanish-speaking residents of the region. These newly arrived Texians agreed to adopt the Roman Catholic faith and become citizens of Mexico. During the rest of the decade, 900 additional families sponsored by Austin arrived in Texas. They were followed by 3,000 squatters. This mass migration raised well-founded fears among Mexican officials that they would lose authority over the American newcomers within their borders.

THE PANIC OF 1819 AND THE PLIGHT OF WESTERN DEBTORS

In 1819, a financial panic swept across the nation, followed by an economic depression that hit western states and territories particularly hard. The Second Bank of the United States played a major role in triggering this economic downturn, which came to be called the Panic of 1819. Granted a twenty-year charter by Congress in 1816, the bank resembled its predecessor, seeking to regulate the national economy through loans to state and local banks. In 1819, the national bank clamped down on small, local wildcat banks, which had extended credit to many people who could not repay their loans. Many homesteaders were not self-sufficient farmers but producers of staple crops or proprietors of small enterprises. They relied on credit from banks and local private lenders. As a result, the national bank's crackdown on wildcat banks had a devastating impact on western households. Debtors unable to meet their obligations had their mortgages foreclosed, their homes seized, and their crops and equipment confiscated. Ruined by the Panic of 1819, many western farmers developed an abiding hatred of the Bank of the United States and a deep resentment of eastern financiers.

■ MAP 11.4 Mexico's Far Northern Frontier in 1822

This map shows Mexico's far northern frontier in 1822. When Moses Austin died suddenly in 1821, the task of supervising the settlement of migrants from the United States fell to his son Stephen. The Mexican government authorized the younger Austin to act as empresario of the settlement. He was responsible for the legal and economic regulations governing the settlements clustered at the lower reaches of the Colorado and Brazos rivers.

Davy Crockett's own family history suggests the plight of families dependent on bank credit to create homesteads out of western territory. The son of a propertyless squatter, Crockett had an intense fear of debt. Although he campaigned as a hunter and a farmer, he had built several enterprises on land he leased or owned on Shoal Creek in south-central Tennessee: a water-powered gristmill, a gunpowder factory (worked by slaves), an iron ore mine, and a liquor distillery. For each venture, he had to borrow money from local creditors. Spending much of his time away from home, Crockett relied on his wife, Elizabeth, and his children to manage these businesses. (He had three children by his first wife, Polly, who died in 1815, and eventually would have three more with Elizabeth.)

The depression of 1819 cut off Crockett's sources of credit, and in 1822 a flash flood swept away his gristmill and powder factory. Without milled grain, the distillery could no longer operate. Creditors immediately set upon the family, demanding payment of their debts. The Crocketts were fortunate enough to own land they could sell, using the proceeds to repay their debts. Nevertheless, they decided to move farther west, to a remote area on the banks of the Obion River in northwest Tennessee. There they started over. Crockett described the area as a "complete wilderness" (although he noted that it was also "full of Indians who were hunting"). The region still showed the effects of an earthquake that had occurred in 1811. With its downed trees and thick brambles, the fissure-riddled landscape presented challenges to the farmers who ventured there. Once again, Crockett needed bank loans, this time to buy flour and seed for cotton.

Many western settlers engaged in the same sort of cycle: borrowing to improve their land, then selling out and moving on. Unable to pay their debts, the least fortunate among them were thrown in jail. In several states, politicians urged the abolition of debtors' prison. They pointed out that jailing people who owed money did little to ensure that the debt would be repaid. New York state legislators passed such a law in 1831 in response to a group of well-to-do petitioners who argued that debtors' prison was "useless to the creditor—oppressive to the debtor—injurious to both."

Crockett advocated a system that would allow local sheriffs to buy debtors' property at bankruptcy auctions and then sell it back to the former owners. He denounced the bankers and other creditors who "had gone up one side of a creek and down another, *like a [raccoon]*, and pretended to grant the poor people great favors" in making them loans that the moneylenders knew they could not afford to repay. Then these creditors demanded their money and wiped out families, taking their land and livestock. Too often, according to Crockett, the backwoods farmer was burdened by debt and vulnerable to economic depressions and scheming creditors.

The Panic of 1819 caused widespread economic distress. Small farmers who lost their land through foreclosure could not produce crops for the eastern market, contributing to the rise in the price of food. Deprived of credit, small shopkeepers also felt the effects of the economic depression. With rising unemployment, consumers could not afford to buy cloth, and as the demand for cotton fell, southern plantation owners, too, felt the contraction. Within a few years Andrew Jackson would capitalize on the fears and resentments of workers, farmers, planters, and tradespeople as he championed the "common man" in opposition to what debtors called the "eastern monied interests." In doing so, he would transform the two-party system.

THE MONROE DOCTRINE

Despite the troubled economy, James Monroe won reelection easily in 1820. He benefited from the disorganization of his opponents and from the demise of the Federalist party. Congressman John Randolph of Virginia suggested that the voters were unanimous on only one issue: their indifference to Monroe. As it turned out, the president's 231–1 victory in the electoral college was the last chapter in the so-called Era of Good Feelings.

On the international front, Monroe's second term opened on a tense note. Foreign nations continued to claim land and promote their own interests near U.S. borders. The United States remained especially wary of the Spanish presence on its southern and western borders. In 1818, President Monroe authorized General Andrew Jackson to broaden his assault on the Seminole— a group composed of Native Americans and runaway slaves—in Florida. For the previous two years, U.S. troops had pursued fugitive slaves into Spanish-held Florida. Now Jackson and his forces seized the Spanish fort at Pensacola and claimed all of western Florida for the United States. The United States demanded that Spain either suppress the Seminole population or sell all of east Florida to the United States. With the Transcontinental Treaty of 1819, Spain gave up its right to both Florida and Oregon (although Britain and Russia still claimed land in Oregon). In 1822, General Jackson became the first governor of Florida Territory.

Farther north, in 1821 the emperor of Russia forbade non-Russians from entering the territory north of the 51st parallel and the open sea 100 miles off the coast of what is now Canada and Alaska. The Russians had established trading posts up and down that coast, some almost as far south as San Francisco Bay. Meanwhile, rumors circulated that European monarchs were planning new invasions of Latin America.

Fearful of an alliance among Russia, Prussia, Austria, Spain, and France, President Monroe and Secretary of State John Quincy Adams formulated a policy that became a landmark in American diplomatic history. Adams rejected a British proposal that Great Britain and the United States join forces to oppose further Spanish encroachment in Latin America. He convinced Monroe that the United States must

TABLE 11.1		
The Election of 1820		
Candidate	**Political Party**	**Electoral Vote**
James Monroe	Democratic-Republican	231
John Quincy Adams	Democratic-Republican	1

stand alone against the European powers—Spain in the south and Russia in the northwest—if it hoped to protect its own interests in the Western Hemisphere. In his annual message to Congress in December 1823, the president declared that the era of Europe's colonization of the Americas had ceased. Henceforth, Monroe said, foreign nations would not be allowed to intervene in the Western Hemisphere.

DOCUMENT

The Monroe Doctrine
(1823)

The United States conceived the **Monroe Doctrine** as a self-defense measure aimed specifically at Russia, Spain, and Britain. With the Russo-American Treaty of 1824, Russia agreed to pull back its claims to the area north of 54°40', the southern tip of the present-day Alaska panhandle. However, the United States did not have the naval power to back up the Monroe Doctrine with force. The doctrine was at first more a statement of principle than a blueprint for action, intended to discourage European powers from political or military meddling in the Western Hemisphere. The doctrine would have greater international significance in the late nineteenth century, when the United States developed the military might to enforce it.

ANDREW JACKSON'S RISE TO POWER

The election of 1824 provided a striking contrast to the bland affair four years earlier in which Monroe had been elected. In 1824, the field of presidential nominees was crowded, suggesting a party system in disarray. Most notably, all the candidates called themselves "Democratic-Republicans." The label meant little more than the fact that most politicians sought to distance themselves from the outmoded "Federalist" label, which hearkened back to the post-Revolutionary period, rather than pointing forward to the nation's new challenges. Nominees included Secretary of State John Quincy Adams, Representative Henry Clay of Kentucky, and Andrew Jackson, now a senator from Tennessee. Jackson received the highest number of electoral votes (99), but no candidate achieved a majority. As a result, the election went to the House of Representatives.

TABLE 11.2			
The Election of 1824			
Candidate	**Political Party**	**Popular Vote (%)**	**Electoral Vote**
John Quincy Adams	Democratic-Republican	30.5	84
Andrew Jackson	Democratic-Republican	43.1	99
William H. Crawford	Democratic-Republican	13.1	41
Henry Clay	Democratic-Republican	13.2	37

Clay withdrew from the race. He had promised Jackson his support but then endorsed Adams, whom the House subsequently elected. When Adams named Clay secretary of state, Jackson's supporters cried foul. The election, they charged, amounted to nothing more than a corrupt deal between two political insiders.

Haunted by these charges, Adams served his four-year term under a cloud of public distrust. A member of a respected New England family and the son of former president John Adams, the new chief executive had served with distinction in Monroe's cabinet. Still, Adams proved ill suited to the rough-and-tumble world of what came to be called the New Democracy. During his presidency, Adams advocated a greater federal role in internal improvements and public education, a variation on Henry Clay's "American System," a set of policies that promoted a national bank, public funding of canals and turnpikes, and a high tariff to protect domestic manufacturers.

Adams's party, now calling itself the **National Republicans,** faced a formidable challenge in the election of 1828. Having seethed for four long years, Andrew Jackson's supporters (the Democratic-Republicans) now urged "the people" to reclaim the White House. The campaign was a nasty one. Jackson's opponents attacked his personal morality and that of his wife and his mother. Jackson's supporters countered with the charge that Adams was corrupt and that he and his cronies must be swept from office. At campaign rallies, Jacksonians waved about brooms to signal their disgust with the current administration.

A Rowdy Presidential Inauguration

Envisioning History

The presidential inauguration of Andrew Jackson in March 1829 was notable in several respects. Jackson was the first military leader since George Washington to be elected president. For the first time, the inaugural ceremony took place on the east front of the U.S. Capitol building, establishing a tradition that continues to this day. After the ceremony, Jackson and his

The Library of Congress

supporters walked from the Capitol to the White House, where a large party was held.

Some commentators disapproved of what they considered the excessively lively inauguration gala for the president. One critic described the affair this way: "On their arrival at the White House, the motley crowd clamored for refreshments and soon drained the barrels of punch, which had been prepared, in drinking to the health of the new Chief Magistrate. A great deal of glassware was broken, and the East Room was filled with a noisy mob." The president, in danger of being crushed by the crowd, had to flee from the party.

QUESTIONS

1. Does this picture seem to support the critic who referred to inaugural guests as a "motley crowd" and a "mob"? Why or why not?

2. What is the significance of the fact that a wide range of age groups, and both men and women, attended the inaugural festivities?

3. The Jackson inaugural party was the first attended by large numbers of ordinary people. By opening the doors to the White House, do you think that Jackson was sending a signal about the nature of his presidency? If so, what was it?

4. Outgoing President John Quincy Adams attended neither this inauguration nor the party that followed. Why do you think that was so?

5. Modern inaugural festivities include a large number of parties held in various venues throughout the city of Washington, rather than one large gathering at the White House. What does this reveal about the presidency and American culture today?

By the time of the 1828 election, the Democratic-Republicans and their rivals had developed sophisticated national organizations. They sponsored local entertainments such as parades and barbecues. These gatherings brought out the vote and cultivated party loyalty. With the decline of state laws regulating voter qualifications, ordinary people in the South and the West cast ballots for the first time. The "Hero of the Battle of New Orleans" won a stunning victory, accumulating a record 647,292 popular votes. His supporters hailed the well-to-do slaveholder as the president of the "common" (meaning white) man.

DOCUMENT

Andrew Jackson, First Annual Message to Congress (1829)

TABLE 11.3			
The Election of 1828			
Candidate	**Political Party**	**Popular Vote (%)**	**Electoral Vote**
Andrew Jackson	Democratic	56.0	178
John Quincy Adams	National Republican	44.0	83

Jackson's inauguration trumpeted the triumph of a white man's democracy; at the same time, the raucous celebration that followed gave an indication of the tumult that would characterize his presidency. Inspired by the common-man rhetoric of the president-elect, over 20,000 of his supporters thronged the streets of Washington to celebrate the transfer of power. After taking the oath of office at the Capitol, Jackson walked to the White House, and the boisterous crowd followed. Thousands of people invited themselves inside the president's residence, and Jackson at one point found himself jostled by the celebrants, some of them well lubricated by too much alcohol. He soon escaped and decided to spend his inaugural night not in his new home, but in a nearby hotel. Outside his window, the revelry continued through the night. Back at the White House, large numbers of uninvited guests proceeded to wreck furnishings and cause general havoc. Presidential aides scurried to fill tubs with whiskey in order to lure the crowd outside. Some observers reacted with horror, alarmed that Jackson's appeal to the "common man" would bring disorder and dishonor to the nation.

In office, Jackson tightened his party's grip on power by introducing a national political spoils system, a process by which successful candidates rewarded their supporters with jobs and tossed their rivals out of appointed offices. The spoils system let the Democratic-Republicans—now called the **Democrats**—build a nationwide political machine. Not surprisingly, it also provided fertile ground for corruption and fueled the debate over the use and limits of federal authority.

Federal Authority and Its Opponents

■ *How did Jackson expand the power of the presidency? Who supported and who opposed Jackson's policies regarding federal authority?*

When Americans defeated the British in the War of 1812, they ensured the physical security of the new nation. However, the war's end left a crucial question unanswered: what role would the federal government play in a republic of states? During Andrew Jackson's tenure, Congress, the chief executive, and the Supreme Court all jockeyed for influence over one another and over the states. Jackson claimed a broad popular mandate to increase the power of the presidency. He used this power to force Georgia Indians off their land and to end the charter of the Second Bank of the United States.

At the same time, militant southern sectionalists regarded the growth of federal executive and judicial power with alarm. If the president could impose a high tariff on the states and if the Supreme Court could deny the states the authority to govern Indians within their own borders, might not high-handed federal officials someday also threaten the South's system of slavery?

JUDICIAL FEDERALISM AND THE LIMITS OF LAW

In a series of notable cases, the Supreme Court, under the leadership of Chief Justice John Marshall, sought to limit states' power to control people and resources within their own boundaries. In *McCulloch v. Maryland* (1819), the Court supported Congress's decision to grant the Second Bank of the United States a twenty-year charter. The state of Maryland had

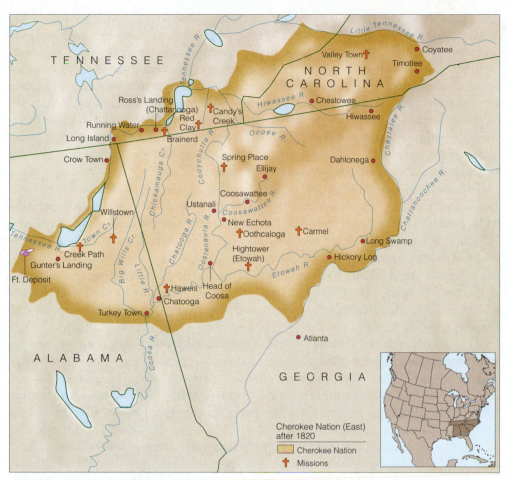

■ **MAP 11.5 The Cherokee Nation After 1820**

This map shows the Cherokee Nation on the eve of removal to Indian Territory (present-day Oklahoma). The discovery of gold in the region sparked a constitutional battle over control of Cherokee land. In 1832, the Supreme Court ruled that the federal government had ultimate authority over Indian nations. The state of Georgia ignored the ruling and sought to enforce its own laws in Cherokee territory.

imposed a high tax on notes issued by the bank. Declaring that "the power to tax involves the power to destroy," the Supreme Court ruled the state's action unconstitutional. The justices held that, although the original Constitution did not mention a national bank, Congress retained the authority to create such an institution. This fact implied that Congress also had the power to preserve it. This decision relied on what came to be called a "loose construction" of the Constitution to justify "implied powers" of the government, powers not explicitly stated in the Constitution.

In 1832, a case involving the rights of the Cherokee Nation brought the Court head to head with President Jackson's own brand of federal muscle-flexing. With the expansion of cotton cultivation into upland Georgia in the early nineteenth century, white residents of that state increasingly resented the presence of their Cherokee neighbors.

At the same time, some Cherokee worked and worshiped in ways similar to European Americans: they cultivated farmland, converted to Christianity, and established a formal legal code. On July 4, 1827, Cherokee leaders met in convention to devise a republican constitution. In the grand tradition of the Patriots of 1776, the group proclaimed the Cherokee a sovereign nation, responsible for its own affairs and free of the dictates of individual (U.S.) states.

By the late 1820s, however, many white people, including the president, were calling for the removal of the Cherokee from the Southeast. The 1829 discovery of gold in the

Georgia hills brought 10,000 white miners to Cherokee territory in a gold rush that the Indians called the "Great Intrusion." President Jackson saw the very existence of the Cherokee Nation as an affront to his authority and a hindrance to Georgia's economic well-being. He resented the fact that the Cherokee considered themselves a sovereign nation, independent of the U.S. president. Jackson, in fact, favored removing all Indians from the Southeast to make way for whites. He declared that Georgia should be rid of "a few thousand savages" so that "towns and prosperous farms" could develop there. In 1830, with the president's backing, Congress passed the Indian Removal Act. The act provided for "an exchange of lands with the Indians residing in any of the states or territories, and for their removal west of the river Mississippi."

Memorial of the Cherokee Nation (1830)

Outraged by this naked land grab, the Cherokee Nation refused to sign the removal treaties specified by Congress as part of the Indian Removal Act. In a petition to Congress in 1830, members of the group declared, "We wish to remain on the land of our fathers. We have a perfect and original right to claim this, without interruption or molestation." In an effort to protect their land titles, the Cherokee first tried to take the case to Georgia courts, but Georgia refused to allow them to press their claim. The Georgia legislature maintained that it had authority over all the Indians living within the state's borders, and that the Cherokee Nation lacked jurisdiction over its own people. The Cherokee Nation appealed to the Supreme Court.

The Cherokee hoped that the Supreme Court would support their position that they were an independent entity, not bound by the laws of Georgia. In a set of cases—*Cherokee Nation v. Georgia* (1831) and *Worcester v. Georgia* (1832)—the Court agreed that Georgia's authority did not extend to the Cherokee Nation. Governor Wilson Lumpkin of Georgia rejected these Supreme Court rulings. Jackson, too, ignored the Court's display of judicial authority. Of the *Worcester* decision, Jackson declared, "John Marshall has made his decision. Now let him enforce it."

> The Georgia legislature maintained that it had authority over all the Indians living within the state's borders.

Some of the president's own supporters protested his determination to deprive landowners—even Indian landowners—of their personal property. Davy Crockett announced that he was voting his conscience and opposing Jackson's Indian removal policy. Declared Crockett, "I believed it was a wicked, unjust measure, and that I should go against it, let the cost to myself be what it might." Nevertheless, in 1832 the president sent troops to Georgia to begin forcing the Indians out of their homeland.

THE "TARIFF OF ABOMINATIONS"

Besides engineering the removal of the Cherokee, Jacksonian Democrats continued the post–War of 1812 policy of high tariffs. In 1828, they pushed through Congress legislation that raised fees on imported manufactured products and raw materials such as wool. Facing a disastrous decline in cotton prices after the Panic of 1819, Southerners protested. To survive, they had to both sell their cotton on the open world market and buy high-priced supplies from New England or Europe. In their view, the higher the tariff on English goods, the less likely the English were to continue to purchase their cotton from southern planters. Southerners dubbed the 1828 legislation the "Tariff of Abominations."

A renewal of the tariff four years later moderated the 1828 rates. But by this time, South Carolina politicians were in no mood to sit back and accept what they saw as the arrogant wielding of federal power. They drew on past precedents in developing a theory called **nullification**—the idea that individual states had the authority to reject, or nullify, federal laws. The Virginia and Kentucky Resolutions of 1798 and 1799 and the Hartford Convention of New England states during the War of 1812 had previously raised this issue of state sovereignty.

The nullification crisis began when politicians led by Senator John C. Calhoun met in a convention in 1832 and declared the tariff "null and void" in South Carolina. But Jackson struck back swiftly. In his Nullification Proclamation of December 10, 1832, he argued that states' rights did not include nullification of federal laws or secession from the Union. The president then sent a token military and naval force to South Carolina to intimidate the nullifiers. Henry Clay, now senator from Kentucky, brokered a compromise agreement: a 10 percent reduction in the Tariff of 1832 over a period of eight years. This compromise finally eased tensions, and the South Carolina nullifiers retreated for the time being. However, they continued to maintain "that each state of the Union has the right, whenever it may deem such a course necessary . . . to secede peaceably from the Union."

THE "MONSTER BANK"

A similar struggle unfolded over the power of the federal government to control a central bank. The repository of federal funds ($10 million), the Second Bank of the United States in the 1830s had thirty branches and controlled the money supply by dictating how state banks should repay their loans: in paper notes or in currency. As a central (though privately held) institution, the bank also aided economic growth and development by extending loans to commercial enterprises.

In 1832, Jackson vetoed a bill that would have renewed the charter of the Second Bank of the United States, which was due to expire in 1836. Somewhat contradictorily, Jackson claimed to represent the interests of small borrowers such as farmers, but he also advocated hard money (currency in the form of gold or silver, not paper or credit extended by banks). Traditionally, small lenders objected to hard money policies, which kept the supply of currency low and interest rates for borrowers high. Jackson also objected to the bank's work as a large commercial institution. For example, he blamed the bank for precipitating the panic and depression of 1819 by withholding credit from small banks, causing them to recall their loans and, in some cases, fail.

Jackson condemned the bank as a "monster" intent on devouring hardworking people and enriching a few eastern financiers. In his veto message to Congress, he fumed, "The humble members of society—the farmers, mechanics, and laborers—who have neither the time nor the means of securing like favors to themselves, have a right to complain of the injustice of their Government." By vetoing the bank bill, Jackson angered members of Congress and his own cabinet. They had urged him to recharter the bank because they believed the credit system was necessary for economic progress and expansion. Convinced that Jackson had overextended his reach, his opponents seized on the issue as a sign of the chief executive's political vulnerability. Harboring presidential ambitions himself, Henry Clay was certain that the bank controversy would prove Jackson's downfall.

However, Clay, the "Great Compromiser," badly miscalculated. Congress upheld Jackson's veto of the national bank (the bank closed when its charter expired in 1836). Nominated for president by the National Republicans in 1832, Clay drew support from merchants who had benefited from Bank of the United States loans and from the sizable contingent of Jackson-haters. Still, Jackson won in a landslide against Clay. The president carried not only his stronghold, the West, but also the South and substantial parts of New York, Pennsylvania, and New England.

TABLE 11.4			
The Election of 1832			
Candidate	**Political Party**	**Popular Vote (%)**	**Electoral Vote**
Andrew Jackson	Democratic	55.0	219
Henry Clay	National Republican	42.4	49
John Floyd	Independent	–	11
William Wirt	Anti-Masonic	2.6	7

While in office, Jackson used his veto power a total of twelve times. All his predecessors *combined* had used it just ten times. When his opponents finally formed a political party in 1834, they called themselves **Whigs,** after the English antimonarchist party. In choosing this name, their intention was to ridicule "King Andrew." In the words of the states' rights advocates, Jackson's high-handed manner was "rather an appeal to the loyalty of subjects, than to the patriotism of citizens." The Whigs opposed the man who had built up the power of the presidency in defiance of Congress and the Supreme Court.

> *Andrew Jackson's expansion of federal power profoundly affected American society and politics.*

Andrew Jackson's expansion of federal power profoundly affected American society and politics. The "age of the common man" produced mixed results for different groups of Americans. On the one hand, greater numbers of white men were able to vote and participate in the political process. The principle of universal manhood suffrage challenged traditional notions that only the wellborn and wealthy were deserving and capable of political leadership and elective office. On the other hand, Native Americans, slaves, free blacks, and women all continued to face inequality and exclusion from the polling place and the jury box. The experiences of these groups highlighted the contradictions in Jacksonian beliefs and policies.

Americans in the "Age of the Common Man"

■ *How did the work of Indians, free and enslaved African Americans, and women change during the "Age of the Common Man"?*

In the early 1830s, a wealthy Frenchman named Alexis de Tocqueville visited the United States and wrote about the contradictions he saw in Jacksonian America. In his book *Democracy in America* (published in 1835), Tocqueville noted that the United States lacked the rigid hierarchy of class privilege that characterized European nations. With universal white manhood suffrage, white men could vote and run for office regardless of their class or religion. However, Tocqueville also noted some sore spots in American democratic values and practices. He commented on the plight of groups deprived of the right to vote; their lack of freedom stood out starkly in the otherwise egalitarian society of the United States. He sympathized with the southeastern Indians uprooted from their homelands. He raised the possibility that conflicts between blacks and whites might eventually lead to bloodshed. He even contrasted the situation of young unmarried white women, who seemed so free-spirited, with that of wives, who appeared cautious and dull. He concluded, "In America a woman loses her independence forever in the bonds of matrimony." Tocqueville saw America for what it was: a blend of freedom and slavery, of independence and dependence.

WARDS, WORKERS, AND WARRIORS: NATIVE AMERICANS

Population growth in the United States—and on the borderlands between the United States and Mexican territory—put pressure on Indian societies. Yet different cultural groups responded in different ways to this pressure. Some, like the Cherokee, conformed to European American ways and became sedentary farmers, and, in some cases, owners of African American slaves. Other Indians were forced to work for whites. Still others either waged war on white settlements and military forces or retreated farther and farther from European American settlements in the hope of avoiding clashes with the intruders.

Nevertheless, prominent whites continued to denigrate the humanity of all Indians. In the 1820s, Henry Clay claimed that Indians were "essentially inferior to the Anglo-Saxon race . . . and their disappearance from the human family will be no great loss to the world." In 1828, the House of Representatives Committee on Indian Affairs surveyed the Indians of the South and concluded that "an Indian cannot work" and that all Indians were lazy and notable for their "thirst for spirituous liquours." According to the committee, when European American settlers depleted reserves of wildlife, Indians as a group would cease to exist.

Members of the Cherokee Nation bitterly denounced these assertions. "The Cherokees do not live upon the chase [for game]," they pointed out. Neither did the Creek, Choctaw, Chickasaw, and Seminole—the other members of the Five Civilized Tribes, so called for their varying degrees of conformity to white people's ways.

Charting a middle course between the Indian and European American worlds was Sequoyah, the son of a white Virginia trader-soldier and a Cherokee woman. A veteran of Andrew Jackson's campaign against the Creek in 1813–1814, Sequoyah moved to Arkansas in 1822, part of an early Cherokee migration west. In 1821, he had finished a Cherokee syllabary (a written language consisting of syllables and letters, in contrast to pictures, or pictographs). The product of a dozen years' work, the syllabary consisted of eighty-six characters. In 1828, the *Cherokee Phoenix*, a newspaper based on the new writing system, began publication in New Echota, Georgia.

Newberry Library, Chicago

■ Artist Charles Bird King painted this portrait of Sequoyah while the Indian leader was in Washington, D.C., in 1828. Government officials honored him for developing a written form of the Cherokee language. He is wearing a medal presented to him by the Cherokee Nation in 1825. He later settled permanently in Sallisaw, in what is today Sequoyah County, Oklahoma.

Sequoyah's written language enabled the increasingly dispersed Cherokee to remain in touch with each other on their own terms. At the same time, numerous Indian cultural groups lost their struggle to retain even modest control over their destinies. In some areas of the continent, smallpox continued to ravage native populations. In other regions, Indians became wards of, or dependent on, whites, living with and working for white families. Some groups who lived close to whites adopted their trading practices. In Spanish California, the Muquelmne Miwok in the San Joaquin delta made a living by stealing and then selling the horses of Mexican settlers.

In other parts of California, Spanish missionaries conquered Indian groups, converted them to Christianity, and then forced them to work in the missions. In missions up and down the California coast, Indians worked as weavers, tanners, shoemakers, bricklayers, carpenters, blacksmiths, and other artisans. Some herded cattle and raised horses. Indian women cooked for the mission, cleaned, and spun wool. They wove cloth and sewed garments.

But even Indians living in or near missions resisted the cultural change imposed by the intruders. Catholic missionaries complained that Indian women such as those of the Chumash refused to learn Spanish. The refusal among some Indians to assimilate completely signaled persistent, deep-seated conflicts between native groups and incoming settlers. In 1824, a revolt among hundreds of newly converted Indians at the mission *La Purisima Concepción* north of Santa Barbara revealed a rising militancy among native peoples.

After the War of 1812, the U.S. government had rewarded some military veterans with land grants in the Old Northwest. Federal agents tried to clear the way for these new settlers by ousting Indians from the area. Overwhelmed by the number of whites, some Indian groups such as the Peoria and Kaskaskia gave up their lands to the interlopers. Others took a stand against the white intrusion. In 1826 and 1827, the Winnebago attacked white families and boat pilots living near Prairie du Chien, Wisconsin. Two years later, the Sauk chief Black Hawk (known to Indians as Ma-ka-tai-me-she-kia-kiak)

DOCUMENT

The Confessions of Nat Turner (1831)

from the Bible, especially the passage "Seek ye the kingdom of Heaven and all things shall be added unto you." Perhaps most disturbing of all, Turner reported that, since 1830, he had been a slave of "Mr. Joseph Travis, who was to me a kind master, and placed the greatest confidence in me; in fact, I had no cause to complain of his treatment to me." Turner's "confessions" suggested the subversive potential of slaves who were literate and Christian and those who were treated kindly by their masters and mistresses.

After the Turner revolt, a wave of white hysteria swept the South. In Virginia near where the killings had occurred, whites assaulted blacks with unbridled fury. The Virginia legislature seized the occasion to defeat various antislavery proposals. Thereafter, all the slave states moved to strengthen the institution of slavery. For all practical purposes, public debate over slavery ceased throughout the American South.

LEGAL AND ECONOMIC DEPENDENCE: THE STATUS OF WOMEN

Regardless of where they lived, enslaved women and Indian women had almost no rights under either U.S. or Spanish law. However, legal systems in the United States and the Spanish borderlands differed in their treatment of white women. In the United States, most of the constraints that white married women had experienced in the colonial period still applied in the 1820s. A husband controlled the property that his wife brought to the marriage, and he had legal authority over their children. Indeed, the wife was considered her husband's possession. She had no right to make a contract, keep money she earned, vote, run for office, or serve on a jury. In contrast, in the Spanish Southwest, married women (both European and native) could own land and conduct business on their own. At the same time, however, husbands, fathers, and local priests continued to exert much influence over the lives of these women.

Although few women earned cash wages in the 1820s, almost all adult women worked.

European American women's economic subordination served as a rationale for their political inferiority. The "common man" concept rested on the assumption that men had the largest stake in society because only they owned property. That stake made them responsible citizens.

Yet women contributed to the economy in myriad ways. Although few women earned cash wages in the 1820s, almost all adult women worked. In the colonial period, society had highly valued women's labor in the fields, the garden, and the kitchen. However, in the early nineteenth century, work was becoming increasingly identified as labor that earned cash wages. This attitude proved particularly common in the Northeast, where increasing numbers of workers labored under the supervision of a boss. As this belief took root, men began valuing women's contributions to the household economy less and less. If women did not earn money, many men asked, did they really work at all?

In these years, well-off women in the northeastern and mid-Atlantic states began to think of themselves as consumers and not producers of goods. They relied more and more on store-bought cloth and household supplies. Some could also afford to hire servants to perform housework for them. Privileged women gradually stopped thinking of their responsibilities as making goods or processing and preparing food. Rather, their main tasks were to manage servants and create a comfortable home for their husbands and children.

In contrast, women in other parts of the country continued to engage in the same forms of household industry that had characterized the colonial period. In Spanish settlements, women played a central role in household production. They made all of their family's clothes by carding, spinning, and weaving the wool from sheep. They tanned cowhides and ground blue corn to make tortillas, or *atole*. They produced their own candles and soap, and they plastered the walls of the home.

Like women's work in general, the labor of wives and mothers in Spanish-speaking regions had great cultural significance. In the Mexican territory of California, Native women servants engaged in backbreaking efforts so that elite wives and daughters could wear snow-white linen clothing. One community member recalled that "certainly to do so was one of the chief anxieties" of well-to-do households: "There was sometimes a great deal of linen to be washed for it was the pride of every Spanish family to own much linen, and the mothers and daughters almost always wore white."

In the Spanish mission of San Gabriel, California, the widow Eulalia Pérez cooked, sewed, ministered to the ill, and instructed children in reading and writing. As housekeeper, Pérez kept the keys to the mission storehouse. She also distributed supplies to the Indians and the *vaqueros* (cowboys) who lived in the mission. She supervised Indian servants as well as soap makers, wine pressers, and olive oil producers. In her spare time, she dipped chocolates and bottled lemonade to be sold in Spain.

At Mission San Diego, Apolonaria Lorenzana worked as a healer and cared for the church sacristy and priestly vestments. From the time she arrived in Monterey at age seven (in 1800) until her death in the late nineteenth century, Lorenzana devoted her life to such labors. Although the priests tried to restrict her to administering the mission hospital, she took pride in her nursing abilities. She also taught herself to read and write. She later recalled, "When I was a young woman in California, I learned alone to write, using the books I saw, imitating the letters on whatever white paper I found discarded."

Indian women also engaged in a variety of essential tasks. Sioux and Mandan women, though of a social rank inferior to men, performed a great deal of manual labor in their own villages. They dressed buffalo skins that the men later sold to traders. They collected water and wood, cooked, dried meat and fruit, and cultivated maize (corn), pumpkins, and squash with hoes made from the shoulder blades of elk. These women worked collectively within a network of households rather than individually within nuclear families.

Many women, regardless of ethnicity, were paid for their work with food and shelter but not money. Nevertheless, some women did work for cash wages during this era. New England women and children, for example, were the vanguard of factory wage-earners in the early manufacturing system. In Massachusetts in 1820, women and children constituted almost a third of all manufacturing workers. In the largest textile factories, they made up fully 80 percent of the workforce.

The business of textile manufacturing took the tasks of spinning thread and weaving cloth out of the home and relocated those tasks in factories. The famous "Lowell mill girls" are an apt example. Young, unmarried white women from New Hampshire, Vermont, and Massachusetts, these workers moved to the new company town of Lowell, Massachusetts, to take jobs as textile machine operatives. In New England, thousands of young men had migrated west, tipping the sex ratio in favor of women and creating a reserve of female laborers. But to attract young women to factory work, mill owners had to reassure them (and their parents) that they would be safe and well cared for away from home. To that end, they established boarding houses where employees could live together under the supervision of a matron—an older woman who served as their mother-away-from-home.

Company towns set rules shaping employees' living conditions as well as their working conditions. In the early 1830s, a posted list of "Rules and Regulations" covered many aspects of the lives of the young women living at the Poignaud and Plant boardinghouse at

■ Although textile production was moving to factories, sewing garments remained a labor-intensive task performed by women at home. The plight of needlewomen became representative of the hazards faced by female workers in the new urban commercial economy of the late eighteenth and early nineteenth centuries. Many women sewed garments that they returned to a "jobber" for payment. The labor, often performed by candlelight in ill-lighted tenements, was tedious and ill paid. Laundry work also took up much of women's time.

Eulalia Pérez Describes her Work in a California Mission, 1823

Interpreting History

Born to Spanish parents in Baja, California, Eulalia Pérez was a widow with five daughters when she became the chief housekeeper for the San Gabriel Mission in the early 1820s. She secured her position by winning a cooking competition between herself and two other Spanish women. Here she gives an account of her many duties in the mission.

I made several kinds of soup, a variety of meat dishes and whatever else happened to pop into my head that I knew how to prepare....

Because of all this, employment was provided for me at the mission. At first they assigned me two Indians so that I could show them how to cook....

The missionaries were very satisfied; this made them think more highly of me. I spent about a year teaching

David Muench/CORBIS

■ Mission San Carlos Borromeo in Carmel, California. Beyond the fountain is the mission's central courtyard. On the left is the *ranchería*, where Indians lived. In this and other missions along the California coast, Indians maintained separate residences in traditional-style dwellings. Even Indians who worked and prayed at the missions attempted to preserve their own customs related to clothing, food, and kin and family relations.

those two Indians. I did not have to do the work, only direct them, because they already had learned a few of the fundamentals.

Lancaster, Massachusetts. The list told the women how to enter the building (quietly, and then hang up "their bonnet, shawl, coat, etc. etc. in the entry") and where to sit at the dinner table (the two workers with greatest seniority were to take their places at the head of the table). Despite these rules, many young women valued the friendships they made with their coworkers and the money they made in the mills. Some of them sent their wages back home so that their fathers could pay off the mortgage or their brothers could attend school.

But not all women wage-earners labored in large mills. In New York City, single women, wives, and widows toiled as needleworkers in their homes. Impoverished, sewing in tiny attics by the dim light of candles, these women were at the mercy of jobbers—merchants who parceled out cuffs, collars, and shirt fronts that the women finished. Other urban women worked as street vendors, selling produce, or as cooks, nursemaids, or laundresses.

The new delineation between men's and women's work and workplaces intensified the drive for women's education begun after the Revolution. If well-to-do women were to assume domestic responsibilities while their husbands worked outside the home, then women must receive their own unique form of schooling, or so the reasoning went. Most

After this, the missionaries conferred among themselves and agreed to hand over the mission keys to me. This was in 1821, if I remember correctly. . . .

The duties of the housekeeper were many. In the first place, every day she handed out the rations for the mess hut. To do this she had to count the unmarried women, bachelors, day-laborers, *vaqueros*. . . . Besides that, she had to hand out daily rations to the heads of households. In short, she was responsible for the distribution of supplies to the Indian population and to the missionaries' kitchen. She was in charge of the key to the clothing storehouse where materials were given out for dresses for the unmarried and married women and children. Then she also had to take care of cutting and making clothes for the men.

Furthermore, she was in charge of cutting and making the vaqueros' outfits, from head to foot—that is, for the vaqueros who rode in saddles. Those who rode bareback received nothing more than their cotton blanket and loin-cloth, while those who rode in saddles were dressed the same way as the Spanish-speaking inhabitants; that is, they were given shirt, vest, jacket, trousers, hat, cowboy boots, shoes and spurs; and a saddle, bridle and lariat for the horse. Besides, each vaquero was given a big silk or cotton handkerchief, and a sash of Chinese silk or Canton crepe, or whatever there happened to be in the storehouse.

They put under my charge everything having to do with clothing. I cut and fitted, and my five daughters sewed up the pieces. When they could not handle everything, the father was told, and then women from the town of Los Angeles were employed, and the father paid them.

Besides this, I had to attend to the soap-house, . . . to the wine-presses, and to the olive-crushers that produced oil, which I worked in myself. . . .

I handled the distribution of leather, calf-skin, chamois, sheepskin, Morocco leather, fine scarlet cloth, nails, thread, silk, etc.—everything having to do with the making of saddles, shoes and what was needed for the belt- and shoe-making shops.

Every week I delivered supplies for the troops and Spanish-speaking servants. These consisted of beans, corn, garbanzos, lentils, candles, soap and lard. To carry out this distribution, they placed at my disposal an Indian servant named Lucio, who was trusted completely by the missionaries.

When it was necessary, some of my daughters did what I could not find the time to do.

QUESTIONS

1. *What were some of the things produced at the mission?*

2. *Why did the position of housekeeper confer such high status?*

3. *What other kinds of workers in the mission does Pérez mention?*

4. *How does this account reveal some of the larger purposes of Spanish missions? In what ways were these missions colonial as well as religious enterprises?*

Source: Eileen Boris and Nelson Lichtenstein, eds., *Major Problems in the History of American Workers*, 2nd ed. (New York: Houghton Mifflin, 2002), 93–95.

ordinary women received little in the way of formal education. Yet elite young women had expanded educational opportunities, beginning in the early nineteenth century. Emma Willard founded a female academy in Troy, New York, in 1821, and Catharine Beecher established the Hartford Female Seminary two years later in Connecticut. For the most part, these schools catered to the daughters of wealthy families, young women who would never have to work in a factory to survive. Hailed as a means to prepare young women to serve as wives and mothers, the schools taught geography, foreign languages, mathematics, science, and philosophy, as well as the "female" pursuits of embroidery and music.

Out of this curriculum designed especially for women emerged women's rights activists, women who keenly felt both the potential of their own intelligence and the degrading nature of their social situation. Elizabeth Cady, an 1832 graduate of the Troy Female Seminary, later went on to marry Henry B. Stanton and bear seven children. But by the 1840s, she strode onto the national stage as a tireless advocate of women's political and economic rights. Still, women of all cultures remained under the control of men even as they contributed to local and national economic development in numerous ways.

Ties That Bound a Growing Population

■ *In what ways did Americans maintain a sense of community in the face of unprecedented migration and population growth?*

Conflicts stemming from racial and gender distinctions proved stubborn throughout this period of territorial expansion. The country's founders had disagreed among themselves about whether democracy could thrive in a large nation, where news necessarily traveled slowly and people remained isolated from their neighbors. Still, by the 1820s few Americans doubted that the nation could grow while preserving its democratic character. In fact, westward expansion seemed to promote democracy, as more ordinary white men than ever participated in the political process.

At the same time, population growth and migration patterns disrupted old bonds of community. When people left their place of birth, they often severed ties with their family and original community. New forms of social cohesion arose to replace these traditional ties. New religions sought to make sense of the changing political and economic landscapes. High literacy rates among the population created a new community of readers, a far-flung audience for periodicals as well as for a new, uniquely American literature. Finally, opinion-makers used the printed word to spread new ideas and values across regional boundaries. These ideas, such as glorification of male ambition, helped knit together scattered segments of the population, men and women who began to speak of an "American character."

NEW VISIONS OF RELIGIOUS FAITH

New forms of religious faith arose in response to turbulent times. During the Indian Wars in the Old Northwest, a Winnebago prophet named White Cloud helped Black Hawk create a coalition of Winnebago, Potawatomi, Kickapoo, Sauk, and Fox Indians. A mystic and medicine man, White Cloud preached against the white man and exhorted his followers to defend their way of life, an Indian way that knew no tribal boundaries. White Cloud, the religious leader, and Black Hawk, the military leader, surrendered together to federal troops on August 27, 1832, signifying the spiritual component in the Indians' militant resistance to whites. Through the rest of the nineteenth century, a number of Indian groups found inspiration, and in some cases common ground, in the teachings of Indian religious leaders.

■ **FIGURE 11.1 Estimated Population of the United States, 1790–1860**
Colonial Times to 1967 (Washington, 1960)

Source: Historical Statistics of the United States, 7.

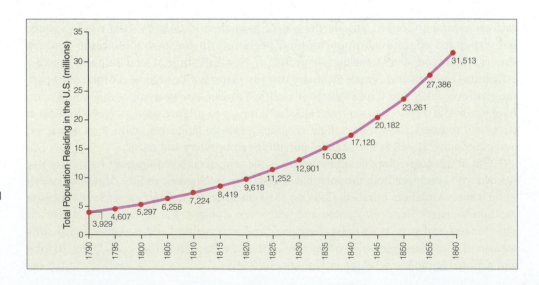

Laurie Platt Winfrey, Inc.

■ The long-lived religious revival called the Second Great Awakening swept through the United States in the 1820s and 1830s. Charles Grandison Finney, an itinerant preacher, helped lead the movement. He urged listeners to consider themselves "moral free agents" with control over their own destinies. Services conducted outdoors, called "camp meetings," provided settings for mass audiences to engage in emotional release and personal testimonials of newly found faith.

New religious enthusiasms took hold in other parts of the country as well. In the late 1820s and early 1830s, the **Second Great Awakening** swept western New York. The fervor of religious revivals so heated the region that people began to call it "the Burned-Over District." Large numbers of people of various Protestant denominations attended week-long prayer meetings, sat together on the "anxious bench" for sinners, and listened, transfixed, as new converts told of their path to righteousness.

What explains this wave of religious enthusiasm? A major factor was a clergyman named Charles Grandison Finney, who managed to tap into the wellsprings of hope and anxiety of the time. A former lawyer, Finney preached that people were moral free agents, fully capable of deciding between right and wrong and doing good in the world. Finney's message had great appeal during this period of rapid social, economic, and technological change. In one sermon, he declared, "The church must take the right ground in regard to politics. . . . The time has come that Christians must vote for honest men." Of course, not all Christians agreed on what constituted the "right ground" in politics. But Finney sought to link the life of the spirit with political and reform efforts, and many men and women responded enthusiastically.

Throughout the country, religious institutions also grappled with questions about slavery. As the fear of possible black uprisings spread, white clergy in the South began to turn away from their former willingness to convert anyone. Instead, they began seeking respectability in the eyes of the well-to-do, slave-owning class. Incorporating masculine imagery into their sermons, they used the language of militant patriotism to distance themselves from the white women, slaves, and free people of color in their congregations. At a western revival in 1824, one itinerant Methodist minister described his military service in the War of 1812; he had helped to vanquish not only the British but also "the merciless savages of the forest, and to secure and perpetuate the liberties secured to us by our forefathers." These preachers strove to reinforce the power of husband over wife, parent over child, and master over slave, relations that defined the typical plantation household.

Elsewhere, some church leaders sought to purge Christianity of what they saw as its too-worldly nature and to revive the earlier, simpler church that Jesus and his disciples had established. On April 6, 1830, a young farmer named Joseph Smith Jr. founded the

More generally, widely distributed newspapers, books, and magazines promoted a set of values that writers claimed described an enduring American character. The ideal American supposedly was ambitious—ready to seize opportunity wherever it could be found—and at the same time devoted to home and family. In fact, these values strongly resembled those adopted by the British middle classes at the same time. Indeed, the United States spawned its own brand of middle-class sensibility called **Victorianism,** after the English queen who reigned from 1837 to 1901.

Five core values defined early American Victorianism. First, was a belief in the significance of the individual. People should be judged on the basis of their character, not on the circumstances of their birth. This belief, however, generally applied only to white men. Second, individuals should have the freedom to advance as far as their talents and ambition took them; no person should claim advantages over others by virtue of a noble title or aristocratic lineage. Third, work was intrinsically noble, whether performed by a canal digger wielding a pick-axe or a merchant using a quill pen. All people, regardless of their trade, deserved to reap the fruits of their labor. Fourth, everyone should exercise self-control and restraint in activities such as drinking and engaging in sexual relations. Finally, men and women occupied separate but complementary spheres. American society could be orderly and stable only if men could find a "haven from the heartless world" of work in their own homes. There, wives tended the hearth and infused the household with their love, self-sacrifice, and religious devotion.

Victorians often saw work as an individualistic endeavor, with men, women, and children earning wages for the number of hours they worked or for each task they performed. However, not all groups embraced Victorian attitudes. The Sioux and Mandan, among other Indian tribes, favored a way of life that valued community over the individual. Likewise, Spanish-speaking settlers of tight-knit adobe pueblos prized the close cooperation of men and women: *compadres* (godfathers) with *comadres* (godmothers). These settlers lived their lives according to the seasonal rhythms of agriculture and stock-raising.

In the South, slaveholders straddled both positions. They idealized both profit-seeking individualism and a traditional way of life based on community ties. These white men and women eagerly raked in the financial gains that flowed from their control over staple-crop agriculture. Yet in their public pronouncements, they scorned the exclusive pursuit of profit. They held their loyalties to family, kin, and community above the crass emphasis on cash that Yankees espoused. As conflicts between Indians and whites revealed, differences in values were far more than theoretical abstractions. Ultimately, they could wreak death and destruction, as Northerners and Southerners soon discovered.

Conclusion

Western settlement infused American politics with raw energy in the 1820s. Andrew Jackson was the first in a long line of presidents who boasted of their humble origins and furthered their careers by denouncing what they called the privileges enjoyed by wealthy Easterners. The western impulse for grassroots politicking shaped political reforms, such as those that abolished property requirements for white male suffrage. The challenges faced by western settlers in establishing homesteads and paying their debts emerged as national, not purely local, issues. Through the sheer force of his personality, Andrew Jackson exemplified these dramatic changes in the political landscape. Almost single-handedly, he extended the limits of executive power and remade the American party system in the process.

Many of the distinctive features of American society in the third decade of the nineteenth century can be traced to the "restlessness" of Americans who had the freedom and desire to move from one place to another. By seeking bank loans to build their family farms, western homesteaders relied on wildcat banks that collapsed in large numbers during the Panic of

1819, leading them to resent and distrust state banks and creditors in general. Believing that Americans had a "destiny" to occupy and control much of the Western Hemisphere, James Monroe's administration conceived the Monroe Doctrine as a way to discourage Russia, Spain, and Britain from blocking United States continental expansion. In the South, land-hungry European Americans used the courts to deprive the Cherokee and other American Indian tribes of their lands. Ironically, by this time the Cherokee had adopted many European American customs; some had converted to Christianity and engaged in farming.

As people moved out west and back again, they replaced traditional social ties with new ones. Religious revivals created new communities of Protestant believers. The increasing circulation of newspapers and magazines allowed even western migrants to subscribe to eastern periodicals and keep informed of the latest dress fashions and child-rearing techniques.

Westward migration had a profound effect on life in the East. The expanded western markets for eastern goods promoted manufacturing in New England and the Mid-Atlantic. When young men migrated west in search of opportunity, eastern textile mill owners turned to young women to serve as machine operatives. New forms of transportation, including canals and steamboats, provided new sources of employment for construction workers and craftsmen. Easterners eagerly read travel accounts, short stories, and novels that portrayed life in the western part of the country. Meanwhile, a new class of western debtors was giving its support to President Andrew Jackson. He denounced the Second Bank of the United States as a "monster" and refused to extend its charter. His bold sense of federal authority gave rise to a new national party, the Jacksonian Democrats; the party claimed support from debtors, workers, and small shopkeepers in all areas of the country.

At the same time, the contradictions in Jacksonian politics became ever more glaring. As the nation expanded its borders and diversified its economy, distinctions between social classes sharpened. Factory workers could not reliably afford to buy the cloth and shoes they produced with machines. Suffrage restrictions, especially those based on property ownership, crumbled under the weight of a Jacksonian ideology of equality. However, a majority of the population remained outside the body politic: women, slaves, and free people of color gained nothing in the way of formal political participation during the "Age of the Common Man."

Most significantly, western migration exposed the fragile political bargain that preserved the institution of slavery. By moving west, European Americans played unwitting roles in the great political drama that would take center stage over the next three decades. Meanwhile, the North and South eyed each other with increasing distrust. And the contrast between those who moved from place to place voluntarily and those who were forced to move became even more striking.

CHRONOLOGY: 1819–1832

1819	Spain cedes Florida to United States.
	Tallmadge Amendment.
	Panic of 1819 triggers economic depression.
1820	Missouri Compromise maintains North–South balance of power.
	Washington Irving, "The Legend of Sleepy Hollow."
1821	Mexico gains independence from Spain.
	Sequoyah completes Cherokee syllabary.
1822	Charleston officials convict and hang blacks in Vesey "plot."
1823	Monroe Doctrine declares Western Hemisphere off limits to Europe.
	Catharine Beecher establishes Hartford Female Seminary.
	Lowell textile mills open.
1824	Erie Canal opens.
1826	American Society for the Promotion of Temperance founded.
1827	Workingmen's party founded in Philadelphia.
1828	*Cherokee Phoenix* begins publication.
1829	Gold discovered on Cherokee lands in Georgia.
1831	Nat Turner leads slave rebellion in Virginia.
	William Lloyd Garrison publishes *The Liberator.*
1832	Nullification crisis.
	Worcester v. Georgia.
	Jackson vetoes Second Bank of the United States.
	Black Hawk War.

For Review

1. Some of Andrew Jackson's supporters declared that his experience as a military leader made him a good candidate for the presidency. In contrast, some of his opponents argued that Jackson's record as a general disqualified him for political leadership. How would you explain and evaluate this debate?

home. On their forty-acre farm, the Torjersens kept swine and produced "tremendous amounts" of wheat, potatoes, beans, cabbages, cucumbers, onions, and many other kinds of vegetables. At the Madison tavern, she had "food and drink in abundance" and dined on the same fare served to the guests: for breakfast, "chicken, mutton [lamb], beef or pork, warm or cold wheat bread, butter, white cheese, eggs, or small pancakes, the best coffee, tea, cream and sugar." For supper she feasted on "warm biscuits, and several kinds of cold wheat bread, cold meats, bacon, cakes, preserved apples, plums, and berries, which are eaten with cream, and tea and coffee." Saehle felt heartbroken to see excess food thrown to the chickens and pigs, for, she wrote, "I think of my dear ones in Bergen, who like so many others must at this time lack the necessaries of life."

Jannicke Saehle was one of more than 13,000 immigrants from Norway, Sweden, and Denmark who arrived in the United States in the 1840s, a sixfold increase over the number of Scandinavians who had arrived the decade before. This migration continued to increase over the course of the nineteenth century. In the 1880s, more than 655,000 Scandinavians, fleeing poverty and military conflict, came to America. Many traveled to Wisconsin and Minnesota, where they farmed small homesteads and found the cold winter climate similar to that of their homeland.

In the rural upper Midwest, clashes between Indians and white settlers shaped the experiences of many immigrants. Newcomers to Minnesota especially did not fare well; there the great Sioux uprising of 1862 resulted in the deaths of hundreds of Indians and immigrant settlers, Swedes and Norwegians prominent among them. However, by the late 1840s, settlers in Wisconsin such as Jannicke Saehle had little reason to fear the Indians whose ancestral lands they occupied; the U.S. Army's destruction of a band of Sauk Indians under the leadership of Black Hawk in 1832 had opened up much of the area to whites.

In the 1830s and 1840s, patterns of settlement and employment among immigrant groups varied widely in the United States. For example, most Irish immigrants lacked the resources to move much farther west than the eastern seaboard ports where they landed. In contrast, many Germans arrived with enough money to buy farmland in the Midwest or take up a trade in eastern cities. Nevertheless, Norwegian immigrants had much in common with other groups that came to the United States in these years. Many relied on compatriots who had already arrived for jobs and housing. The newcomers found employment in expanding regional economies. Communities of immigrants built their own religious institutions and mutual aid societies.

In the 1830s and 1840s, the United States was home to many peoples in motion. Groups of Indians in the Southeast and Midwest and slaves in the upper South were forced at gunpoint to move from one region of the country to another. From western Europe came poor and persecuted groups drawn to the United States by the demand for labor and the promise of religious and political freedom. Some Americans eagerly pulled up stakes and moved to nearby cities or towns in search of better jobs. Migrants with enough resources made the long journey across the Sonoran Desert in the Southwest to California, or to the Oregon Territory in the Northwest.

Population movements and economic change generated new forms of community and group identity. Some immigrants left behind old identities and created new ones for themselves in their new homes. In their native lands, many newcomers to the United States had lived and labored as peasants under the control of aristocratic landlords. Now in America, these immigrants worked as wage-earners or as small farmers. Urban workers founded the National Trades Union, an organization that tried to help laboring people wield political influence. Some women and men who believed in their power to change society banded together for any number of causes—including those that challenged basic institutions such as the nuclear family, slavery, and white supremacy. Some reformers established new communities based on alternative notions of marriage and child-rearing.

Partisan politics also entered a new era. By 1836, the "Second Party" system had emerged, as Jacksonian Democrats squared off against the Whigs on familiar issues, including tariffs and new systems of transportation. The Whigs, a coalition of anti-Jackson forces, sought to craft an economic program that would appeal to the largest number of voters. Less concerned with the purity of their ideas than with success at the ballot box, the Whigs saw their policies as a means to winning elections and not necessarily as ends in themselves.

The choices offered by the Whigs and Democrats failed to represent what many groups saw as their pressing political and economic interests. In response, many Americans turned to violence to advance or defend their causes. The deep-seated resentments or lofty aspirations among various ethnic and religious groups and social classes provoked bloodshed. Urban mobs vented their wrath against African Americans, abolitionists, and Irish immigrants and other Catholics. The government itself sponsored violence, which peaked in the late 1830s with the forced removal of southeastern Indians to the West, and again in the late 1840s, when the United States wrested a vast expanse of land from Mexico. Indeed, within the larger society, physical force seemed to be an acceptable means of resolving disputes; tellingly, politicians of all persuasions followed Andrew Jackson's lead and staked their claim to national leadership on the basis of their records as soldiers, military officers, and Indian-killers.

Although industrial machines such as locomotives and textile looms grew more sophisticated in these years, farming remained the primary occupation for many people. However, when the land refused to yield crops, millions of people had to move on—from the blighted potato fields of Ireland, the rocky soil of New England, or the worn-out cotton fields of the South. In search of new economic opportunities, some people moved into lands belonging to other people. In the territory occupied by native Spanish speakers in Texas or by Indians in the Southeast, people stood ready to fight—and die—for the land.

Mass Migrations

■ *What caused some groups to migrate voluntarily? Why were others forced to move against their will?*

When foreign visitors called Americans a "restless" people, they were referring to patterns of both immigration into and migration within the country. Between 1830 and 1850, 2.3 million immigrants entered the United States, up from a total of 152,000 during the two previous decades. In the 1840s, 1.7 million immigrants arrived. (In 1850 the country's total population stood at 23 million people). Most newcomers came from Ireland, Germany, England, Scotland, and Scandinavia.

Within the United States, individuals and families moved around the country with almost dizzying frequency in search of better jobs. They migrated from rural to urban areas, from one city to another, out west and then back to the east. In Boston, in any one year, about a third of the population left the city to find a new home elsewhere. In the late 1840s, almost half of all urban residents moved within a twelve-month period. For the country as a whole, an estimated one family in five moved every year, and on average every family moved once every five years. Many westward migrants had enough money to move overland and buy a homestead once they arrived in Wisconsin or Oregon. However, much of the population turnover in urban areas stemmed from landless people's relentless quest for higher wages and cheaper places to rent.

Population Change in Ireland, 1841–1851

Percentage of change per county

- +9
- 0
- -13
- -20
- -25

Pauperism in Ireland, 1847–1851

- Over 50% of people living in such poverty as to be declared paupers

■ **MAP 12.1   Population Change in Ireland, 1841–1851**

During the famine of the late 1840s, some counties in Ireland lost more than one-quarter of their population to out-migration. However, emigration rates in some of the very poorest counties were not always high. People there were too poor to pay for passage to the United States. The county of Kerry, in the country's southwestern corner, is an example.

Some people moved because other people forced them to—under the crack of a whip and in manacles. Slave traders in the upper South transported thousands of slaves to the lower South for sale "on the block." Indians underwent a kind of middle passage (the horrific slave-ship voyages between Africa and the Americas) when U.S. soldiers forced them to walk from their homelands in the Southeast to Indian Territory (now the state of Oklahoma). In the less settled West, however, older identities of race and ethnicity sometimes gave way to new identities forged from mixed cultures.

Europeans marveled at Americans' apparent willingness to search out new opportunities. But to some Americans, moving meant the death of dreams and the loss of hope for a better life.

NEWCOMERS FROM WESTERN EUROPE

During this period, hardships in western Europe led to increased immigration to the United States, especially from Ireland and the German states. For the long-suffering people of Ireland, by the early nineteenth century life had become more precarious than ever. Over the generations, small farm plots had been subdivided among heirs to the point that most holdings consisted of fewer than fifteen acres. At the same time, the population of Ireland had grown exponentially—to more than 4 million people in 1800. England treated Ireland like a colony that existed purely for the economic gain of the mother country (or, in the eyes of the Irish, an occupying power). A series of English laws and policies mandated that farmers export most of the island's grain and cattle, leaving the impoverished people to subsist mainly on a diet of potatoes. Then, beginning in 1845, a blight devastated the potato crop. In the next five years, a million people died and another million fled to the United States. The great Irish migration had begun.

Large numbers of poor Irish had settled in the United States even before the potato famine of the mid-1840s. In the 1820s, about 50,000 such immigrants arrived; the following decade saw a spike in numbers to more than 200,000. A more dramatic increase was yet to come. As the 1840s and 1850s unfolded, 1.7 million Irish men, women, and children emigrated to the United States. This exodus continued over the next century as more than 4.5 million Irish arrived. Many immigrants were single women who found work as servants and sent money back to Ireland.

By the 1870s, the Irish constituted fully 20 percent of the population of New York City, 14 percent of Philadelphia, and 22 percent of Boston (the "hub of Gaelic America"). Most Irish immigrants remained along the eastern seaboard, since they lacked the resources to move farther inland. The newcomers quickly formed mutual aid associations and other community organizations. In cities across America, the Sisters of Mercy, a Roman Catholic order founded in Dublin, established homes to provide lodging for single women and day nurseries for the children of working mothers.

The Irish newcomers soon realized that their struggle against poverty, discrimination, and religious persecution would not end in the United States. The large numbers of Irish immigrants who came to America in the 1830s threatened the jobs of native-born Protestants, who reacted with resentment and violence. Employers posted signs outside their doors reading "No Irish Need Apply." Despised for their Roman Catholicism and their supposed clannishness, the Irish competed with African Americans for the low-paying jobs at the bottom of the economic ladder. In 1834, a mob destroyed the Ursuline convent in Charlestown, near Boston, after terrifying the women and children residents and ransacking the building.

Nevertheless, by the 1850s, the Irish had gained a measure of influence in America. They filled many high positions in the Catholic Church and became active in the Democratic party. They maintained that their white skin entitled them to distance themselves from blacks and lay claim to full American citizenship. More than one hundred years later, the election of the first Catholic president of the United States—John Fitzgerald Kennedy of Boston, a descendant of famine-era immigrants on both his mother's and father's side of the family—became a milestone in the Irish American rise to political power.

The hardship endured by the Irish in the early nineteenth century mirrored the political and economic distress of many other people living in Europe at the time. In the revolutions of 1848 in the German states, France, the Austrian Empire, and parts of Italy, people struck out against monarchy and called for constitutional government. The Germans moved in especially dramatic numbers, with more than half a million arriving in the United States between 1831 and 1850. Those numbers exploded in the next few decades, as a failed uprising against the authoritarian Prussian state in 1848 led many German intellectuals, farmers, and workers to flee the region. Across western Europe, rising unemployment and unprecedented population increases made food scarce in both rural and urban areas, stimulating immigration across the Atlantic.

THE SLAVE TRADE

Forced migration of enslaved workers increased during this period as the slave trade became big business. Many wealthy traders made regular trips between the upper and lower South. Traders transported men, women, and children by boat down the eastern seaboard or down the Mississippi River, or chained and forced them to walk as much as twenty miles a day for seven or eight weeks at a time in the chill autumn air. Eventually, slaves stood on the block in the markets of New Orleans, Natchez, Charleston, and Savannah, where white men inspected them for health, strength, and compliance.

MAP

Slavery in the South

Between 1800 and 1860, the average price of slaves quadrupled, revealing a growing demand for bound labor. As many as one out of every ten slave children in the upper South was sold to the lower South (many to cotton planters) between 1820 and 1860. Slave households in Virginia bore the brunt of these forced separations. There, an estimated three-quarters of the people sold never saw their spouse, parents, or children again.

It was sometimes worse if they did. Moses Grandy, standing on a sidewalk one day, saw his wife in chains, in a coffle passing by. He recalled the scene in his 1844 autobiography:

> Mr. Rogerson was with them on his horse, armed with pistols. I said to him. "For God's sake, have you bought my wife?" He said he had; when I asked him what she had done, he said she had done nothing, but that her master wanted money. He drew out a pistol and said that if I went near the wagon where she was, he would shoot me. I asked for leave to shake hands with her which he refused, but said I might stand at a distance and talk with her. My heart was so full that I could say very little. . . . I have never seen or heard from her from that day to this. I loved her as I love my life.

Family members resented being separated from each other as well as the nature of the work itself.

Some cotton planters in the lower South found a new way to exploit their enslaved workforces when gold was discovered in northern Georgia in 1829. Many of the men who actually mined the gold were slaves. Some planters forced their slaves to toil in the gold mines after the cotton crop was harvested in the fall and before the new crop was planted in the spring. In the 1830s, Senator John C. Calhoun of South Carolina sent twenty of his slaves to work in his mine near Dahlonega in Georgia's Lumpkin County. Between 1833 and 1835, each of these black men dug out $500 worth of gold per year.

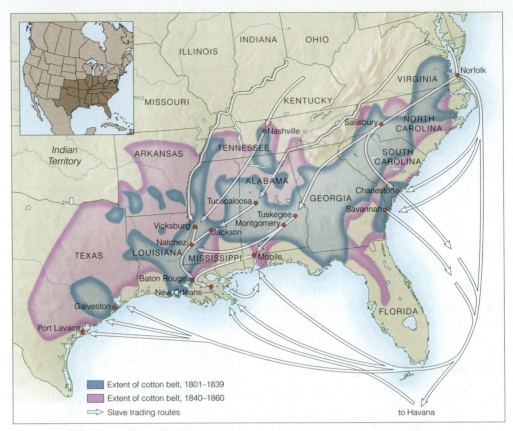

Extent of cotton belt, 1801–1839
Extent of cotton belt, 1840–1860
⇨ Slave trading routes

to Havana

■ **MAP 12.2 Expansion of the Cotton Belt and Slave Trading Routes, 1801–1860**
This map shows the spread of cotton cultivation and routes followed by traders in transporting slaves from the upper South to the new plantations of the Southwest. After Texas won its independence from Mexico in 1836, the new republic legalized slavery. Many white landowners believed that they could not grow cotton without the use of slave labor.

Gold digging in northern Georgia was hard and dangerous; inexperienced miners built tunnels and flimsy shafts that were prone to cave-ins and other hazards. Mindful of the profits that white men derived from their labor, some enslaved men tried to hide nuggets of gold in their hair and clothing, planning to sell them later, but these efforts usually failed.

Voluntary migrations of African Americans formed the counterpoint of the slave trade as runaways and free people of color made their way out of the old slave states. An estimated 50,000 enslaved workers tried to escape each year, but few made it to the North and freedom. Some southern free people of color also headed to northern cities. By 1850, more than half of all Boston blacks had been born outside Massachusetts, with about one-third of those migrants hailing from the South. Slave runaways who lived in fear for their safety and their lives eluded census takers, but by mid-century as many as 600 fugitives lived in Boston.

Regardless of their place of origin, many migrants took up residence with other blacks, who helped ease the newcomers' transition to city life. These boarding arrangements strengthened ties between the enslaved and the free communities. For example, when authorities arrested the runaway George Latimer in Boston in 1842, free blacks in that city took immediate action. They posted signs condemning the police as "human kidnappers." Some tried to wrench Latimer physically from his captors. Still others sponsored protest meetings in the local African Baptist Church and made common cause with white lawyers sympathetic to abolition. Finally a group of blacks and whites raised enough money to buy Latimer from his owner and free him.

Meanwhile, throughout the urban North, whites began eyeing blacks' jobs. Irish immigrants in particular desperately sought work. Skilled black workers found it increasingly difficult to ply their trades as cooks, hotel and boat stewards, porters, brickmakers, and barbers.

An Owner Advertises for His Runaway Slave

Envisioning History

In September 1833, Nathan Cook, the owner of a gold mine in Auraria, Georgia, placed a notice for a runaway slave in a local newspaper, the *Western Herald*. This advertisement is typical for its time. It describes the physical characteristics of the young fugitive and offers a reward for his return. Many ads for runaway servants as well as slaves suggested they had a "down look"—they refrained from looking other people directly in the eye. This ad suggests that Henry ran away not of his own accord but at the "persuasion of some white person." Rather than acknowledge that their own slaves might want, and seize, their freedom, many masters blamed other unknown white people for encouraging enslaved men and women to run away.

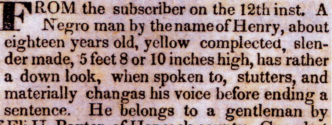

Courtesy of Hargrett Rare Book & Manuscript Library/ University of Georgia Library

RANAWAY, FROM the subscriber on the 12th inst. A Negro man by the name of Henry, about eighteen years old, yellow complected, slender made, 5 feet 8 or 10 inches high, has rather a down look, when spoken to, stutters, and materially changas his voice before ending a sentence. He belongs to a gentleman by the name of Eli H. Baxter of Hancock county, Geo. but was in my employ when he absconded in the neighborhood of Auraria, where I have been opperating on a gold mine, and was brought from North Carolina to this state, by a speculator. It is probable that he has been induced to leave, by the persuasion of some white person. Any person apprehendiug said Negro, and lodging, him in any safe Jail, will be suitably rewarded by dropping a line to E. H. Baxter, of Hancock county, or the subscriber in Auraria, Lumpkin county Geo. NATHAN COOK. Sept 28 —25—3t,

QUESTIONS

1. Although Henry is only eighteen years old, he has been uprooted multiple times. How does the description of him suggest the trauma he has suffered as a result of both his forced removal from North Carolina to Georgia and his work in the gold mines?

2. Cook had hired Henry's time from another man, Eli H. Baxter. What does Henry's running away suggest to us about the experiences of slaves who were hired out to work?

3. Why would Cook prefer to hire Henry, rather than buy a slave, to work in his gold mine?

4. What does Henry's story tell us about larger themes in the history of internal migration during the 1830s and 1840s?

In 1838, 656 black artisans in Philadelphia reported that they had to abandon their work because white customers would no longer patronize them. White factory owners in Philadelphia preferred white laborers. In that same city, a bustling site of machine shops and textile factories, almost no blacks did industrial labor of any kind.

TRAILS OF TEARS

Like enslaved blacks, many Indians were forced to migrate. Throughout the 1830s, the U.S. government pursued the policy of removing Indians from the Southeast by treaty or force. The 1832 Treaty of Payne's Landing, negotiated by the Seminole Indians and James Gadsden, a representative of Secretary of War Lewis Cass, aimed to force the Seminole out of Florida and into Indian Territory (present-day Oklahoma). The federal government promised to give individual Indians cash, plus blankets for the men and dresses for the women, in exchange for their lands. Government authorities also hoped to recapture the large number of runaway slaves who had sought refuge in Seminole villages deep in the swamps of central Florida.

Three years later, many of the Indians had departed for the West. But a small number withdrew deeper into the Everglades and held their ground. They were led by a young man

MAP Native American Removal

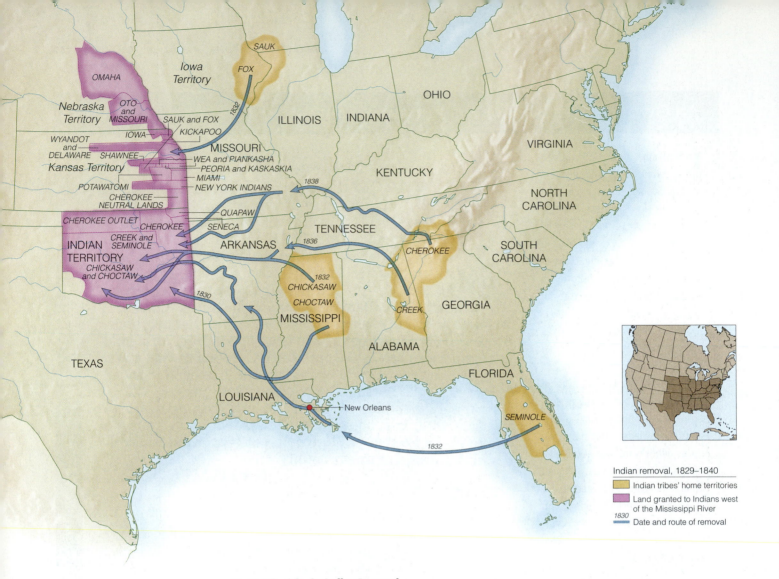

■ **MAP 12.3 Indian Removal**

Indian removal policies forced the Five Civilized Tribes to migrate from the southeast in the 1830s. Other groups from east of the Mississippi, such as the Sauk and Fox, were also obliged to move to the designated Indian Territory, where they crowded longtime Native American inhabitants. Later, many Plains Indians, including the Cheyenne and Comanche, were also forced to move to the region (present-day Oklahoma).

Courtesy American Heritage Center, University of Wyoming

named Osceola, who with his followers waged a **guerrilla war** (based on ambush tactics) against better-armed U.S. troops. Osceola's resistance, called the Second Seminole War, dragged on for seven years. Eventually, the government forced 3,000 Seminole to move west, but not until it had spent $20 million and 1,500 U.S. soldiers had lost their lives.

The Choctaw of the southern Alabama-Mississippi region, the Chickasaw directly to the north of them, the Creek in central Georgia and Alabama, and the Cherokee of North Georgia suffered the same fate in the 1830s. The Creek remained bitterly divided among themselves on the issue of removal, as did the Cherokee. Major Ridge, his son John Ridge, and Elias Boudinot, the leaders of the so-called Treaty Party of the Cherokee Nation, urged their people to give up their homeland and rebuild their nation in the West. The aging Major Ridge had reversed his earlier stance; now he favored migration from Georgia. John Ross and others like him opposed the Ridges and Boudinot. The Cherokee must remain in Georgia at all costs, Ross insisted. He claimed that he spoke for a majority of Cherokee. To silence him, the state of Georgia threw him in prison. Then it concluded negotiations with the Treaty Party, which agreed to sell Cherokee land to the federal government for $5 million. Elias Boudinot said, "We can die, but the great Cherokee Nation will be saved." Within a few years, the Ridges and Boudinot died at the hands of Cherokee assassins.

In 1838, General Winfield Scott, with 7,000 troops under his command, began rounding up the citizens of the Cherokee Nation. U.S. troops held men, women, and children in concentration camps before forcing them to march west. During the period from 1838 to 1839, nearly 16,000 Indians (and their African American slaves) were forced by federal authorities to make a journey from their homeland in the Southeast to western territory. The Indians called this journey the Trail on Which We Cried, also known as the **Trail of Tears.** Four thousand of them died of malnutrition and disease in the course of the 116-day forced march. U.S. troops confiscated or destroyed the material basis of Cherokee culture: sawmills, cotton gins, barns, homes, spinning wheels, meetinghouses, flocks, herds, and the printing press used to publish the *Cherokee Phoenix*. They often forcibly separated families. A soldier who participated in the operation saw children "separated from their parents and driven into the stockade with the sky for a blanket and the earth for a pillow."

U.S. officials claimed that troops had carried out the removal with "great judgment and humanity." However, an internal government report completed in 1841 revealed that the United States had reneged on even its most basic treaty promises. "Bribery, perjury, and forgery, short weights, issues of spoiled meat and grain, and every conceivable subterfuge was employed by designing white men." Many government agents seized goods such as blankets and food intended for Indians and sold these goods for profit. Military authorities suppressed the report, and the public never saw it.

MIGRANTS IN THE WEST

For many native-born migrants seeking a new life west of the Mississippi, the road proved neither smooth nor easy. For example, as the Mormon community moved west from New York, they met with religious persecution. The founder of the church, Joseph Smith, aroused

■ One of the most dramatic western migrations was the Mormons' journey via the Overland Trail, beginning in the spring of 1847. Within five years, more than 10,000 members of the group had made the arduous trek to Utah. This group of Mormon emigrants poses for a group picture not far from their destination of Salt Lake City. Between 1840 and 1860, nearly 300,000 people journeyed overland to Oregon, California, and Utah.

Courtesy American Heritage Center, University of Wyoming

the anger of his neighbors in Nauvoo, Illinois. They took alarm at the Nauvoo Legion, a military company formed to defend the Mormon community. They also heard rumors (for the most part true) that Smith and other Mormon leaders engaged in plural marriage, or polygamy, allowing men to marry more than one wife.

In 1844, this tension came to a head when the Nauvoo Legion destroyed the printing press owned by a group of rebellious church members who objected to what they considered Smith's authoritarian tactics. Civil authorities charged Smith and his brother Hyrum with the destruction of private property and arrested and jailed the two men in the nearby town of Carthage. In June 1844, an angry mob of non-Mormons broke into the jail and lynched the brothers.

By 1847, Brigham Young, who had inherited the mantle of leadership from Smith, determined that the Mormons could not remain in Illinois. Migrants, some of them pushing handcarts loaded with personal belongings, set out for the West. By 1852, 10,000 Mormons had settled in Salt Lake City in what is present-day Utah. With their large numbers and church-inspired discipline, the community prospered. They created an effective irrigation system and turned the desert into a thriving agricultural community.

But the Mormons had not settled an uninhabited wilderness. Around Salt Lake, Canadian trappers, Paiute Indians, and Spanish speakers from New Mexico crossed paths, some to hunt, others to gather roots and berries, herd sheep, or trade captives. A Christmas dinner celebrated near Great Salt Lake around this time revealed the multicultural mix of western life. The guests included Osborne Russell (a European American trader), a Frenchman married to a Flathead woman, and various other intermarried Cree, Snake, and Nez Perce Indians. The group feasted on the meat of elk and deer, a flour pudding, cakes, and strong coffee. After the meal, the women cleared the table. The men smoked pipes and then went outside and shot at targets with their guns.

GOVERNMENT-SPONSORED EXPLORATION

The Lewis and Clark expedition of 1803–1806 was the forerunner of many other U.S. government-sponsored efforts to map unknown territory and make scientific discoveries (see Chapter 10). One of these attempts was the South Seas Exploring Expedition of 1838, also known as the Wilkes Expedition, after its leader, Lt. Charles Wilkes. He commanded a squadron of 6 sailing vessels, 346 men, and 9 scientists and artists. They traveled nearly four years and over 87,000 miles, recording the landscape and wildlife of Antarctica, the South and Central Pacific islands, the California coast, the Pacific Northwest, and Southeast Asia. The expedition was the largest of its kind and also the last to use all-sail vessels.

Like his predecessors Lewis and Clark, Wilkes hoped to advance American diplomatic and economic interests through his explorations. He believed U.S. trade would benefit from the good harbors of the Northwest. He also aimed to provide maps and navigation charts for the U.S. whaling industry.

At the same time, Wilkes's expedition produced scientific discoveries of lasting value. One of the artists accompanying Wilkes was Titian Ramsey Peale, the son of the painter and amateur scientist Charles Willson Peale. A naturalist, painter, and photographer, the younger Peale had, at an early age, explored diverse regions such as Florida, the Rocky Mountains, and Central America. He understood how to study and preserve natural history specimens of animals, plants, and rocks. The samples he gathered on the Wilkes Expedition eventually formed the basis of the collections of the Smithsonian Institution, a museum of natural and social history in Washington, D.C., established by Congress in 1846.

Another expedition, this one overland and sponsored by the U.S. Topographical Corps of Engineers, surveyed the Northwest and aided migrants who eventually settled there. Led by John Charles Frémont, an engineer and mathematician, this 1843–1844 expedition included several Indians and fur trappers. They took precise measurements of the terrain using barometers and field telescopes.

■ MAP 12.4 Western Trails

This map shows the major trails followed by western emigrants in the nineteenth century. Settlers endured long and dangerous journeys. For example, beginning at Independence, Missouri, and stretching to Portland, Oregon, the Oregon Trail was 2,000 miles long. Wagon trains had to traverse rocky terrain, scale mountains, and ford rivers. Along the way, outposts such as Fort Laramie and Fort Hall gave travelers a chance to refresh their supplies, rest their livestock, and repair their wagons. Though resentful of such incursions, Indians rarely attacked large wagon trains.

Frémont's final report had immense practical value for people migrating west, for it mapped the way and provided crucial information about pasture, sources of water, and climate. In addition to detailing plant and animal life, the *Report of Exploring Expeditions to the Rocky Mountains* described a middle ground where Indians spoke fluent Spanish, where whites employed Indian labor to grow their wheat and irrigate their fields, and where German immigrants followed a variety of agricultural pursuits. Like the Lewis and Clark party, the Frémont expedition mapped not an uninhabited "wilderness," but rather territory settled by diverse groups of people.

THE OREGON TRAIL

Protestant missionaries initially settled Oregon beginning in 1834. But in contrast to the Mormons, these northwestern colonists found themselves in the midst of hostile Native Americans. One young doctor and his wife from western New York, Marcus and Narcissa Whitman, established a mission near present-day Walla Walla, Washington. In 1843, the arrival of 1,000 emigrants in Oregon County signaled the beginning of what came to be called the Great Migration.

Missionaries and government officials helped spur the Great Migration of 1843 and spread "Oregon Fever" among economically depressed areas of the Midwest. That region of the country was still reeling from the effects of the Panic of 1837 and the subsequent economic downturn. Peter Burnett was captain of a group of people emigrating from western Missouri for Oregon in the spring of 1843. Burnett and others promised the group that in Oregon they would find not only a fertile land blessed with a mild climate, but also instant prosperity: "And they do say, gentlemen, they do say, that out in Oregon the pigs are running about under the great acorn trees, round and fat, and already cooked, with knives and forks sticking in them so that you can cut off a slice whenever you are hungry."

The **Oregon Trail** was 2,000 miles long. Covering from 12 to 15 miles a day, wagon trains took from four to six months to complete the journey. The natural landscape posed immense obstacles for the travelers. Treacherous river currents swept away whole wagons and their contents. Spring floods and summer droughts prevented the emigrants' livestock from feeding off the Plains grasses. After passing Fort Hall, northwest of Salt Lake City, the going got even rougher, through rocky terrain and uncharted mountains and forests. Emigrants had to rig systems of pulleys and ropes to move their wagons over the Blue Mountains of Oregon. At the end of the day, weary wives and mothers cooked dinner, bathed the children, and washed clothes, while the men plotted the next day's route. Caring for, and bearing, children on the trail was a particular burden borne by migrant women.

TABLE 12.1

Outfitting a Party of Four for the Overland Trail

Area	Item	Amount	Unit Cost ($)	Cost ($)	Weight (lbs.)
Transport	Wagon	1	90.00	90.00	
	Oxen	4 yoke	50.00/yoke	200.00	
	Gear		100.00	100.00	
Food	Flour	600 lb.	2.00/100 lb.	12.00	600
	Biscuit	120 lb.	3.00/100 lb.	3.60	120
	Bacon	400 lb.	5.00/100 lb.	20.00	400
	Coffee	60 lb.	7.00/100 lb.	4.20	60
	Tea	4 lb.	50.00/100 lb.	2.00	4
	Sugar	100 lb.	10.00/100 lb.	10.00	100
	Lard	200 lb.	6.00/100 lb.	12.00	200
	Beans	200 lb.	8.00/100 lb.	16.00	200
	Dried fruit	120 lb.	24.00/100 lb.	28.80	120
	Salt	40 lb.	4.00/100 lb.	1.60	40
	Pepper	8 lb.	4.00/100 lb.	.32	8
	Saleratus	8 lb.	4.00/100 lb.	.32	8
	Whiskey	1 keg	5.00/keg	5.00	25
Goods	Rifle	1	30.00	30.00	10
	Pistols	2	15.00	30.00	10
	Powder	5 lb.	.25/lb.	1.25	5
	Lead	15 lb.	.04/lb.	.60	15
	Shot	10 lb.	.10/lb.	1.00	10
	Matches			1.00	1
	Cooking utensils			20.00	25
	Candles and soap	65 lb.	From home	from home	65
	Bedding	60 lb.	From home	from home	60
	Sewing kit	10 lb.	From home	from home	10
	Essential tools			from home	20
	Clothing			from home	100
			Totals	$589.69	2216

Plains Indians resented the families traveling by wagon train. They believed these families were just one more group—like government scouts and military forces—determined to take their land. Small groups were particularly vulnerable to attacks by Indians. Some wagon trains used oxen because Indians had little interest in the animals, in contrast to horses. Despite the dangers and hardship, the Great Migration continued. In 1845, 3,000 people traveled the Oregon Trail. Two years later the number had increased to almost 5,000. Between the beginning of the Great Migration and 1869, an estimated 50,000 people took the trail to Oregon.

Some settlers established successful homesteads in Oregon, but the settlements founded by missionaries were fragile affairs. Discouraged and overwhelmed by homesickness, Narcissa Whitman eagerly awaited copies of the latest *Mothers' Magazine* sent to her by relatives in the East. After 1843, the influx of newcomers brought her some consolation, but it also brought outbreaks of measles, to which the Native Americans had no immunity. An ensuing epidemic among the Cayuse claimed many lives. In 1847, blaming the missionaries for the deaths of their people, several Indians attacked the Whitman mission, killing twelve whites, including Narcissa and Marcus Whitman.

Like Narcissa Whitman and Mormon women, some women went west with their families for religious reasons. But other women migrants made the journey only reluctantly. Despite hardship back east, they did not want to leave their female kin, who provided them with a network of support throughout their lives. For these reluctant migrants, the journey west and eventual settlement caused deep distress. However, some eventually found satisfaction in making new lives for themselves and their families.

NEW PLACES, NEW IDENTITIES

Like the West, the Midwest and the borderlands between U.S. and Spanish territories were meeting places for many different cultures. Leaving established communities behind, some migrants challenged rigid definitions of who was black, Indian, Hispanic, or European American. Moving from one place to another enabled—or forced—people to adopt new individual and group identities.

People who fell into one racial category in the East sometimes acquired new identities in the West. Some people classified as "black" in the South became "white" outside the region. For example, the commonwealth of Virginia classified the light-skinned George and Eliza Gilliam as black. Beginning their married life near Petersburg, they were well aware of Virginia's tightening restrictions on free people of color and their uncertain future where local officials knew who they were. In 1831, the couple decided to make a new life for themselves in western Pennsylvania. Eliza died in 1838, and George remarried nine years later. He prospered over the course of his lifetime. He worked as a doctor and druggist and invested in and sold real estate. George and his second wife, Frances, eventually moved to Illinois, then finally settled in Missouri.

Deutsches Ledermuseum

■ Plains Indians developed new art forms in response to the westward movement of European American trappers, missionaries, and settlers. Native artists used picture writing to describe violent encounters between Indians and intruders. They etched pictures on sandstone or painted them on cliffs or clothing. These battle pictographs, painted on a Cheyenne buffalo robe (c. 1845), bear similarities to other images produced by Flathead artists. Scholars believe that these drawings formed a language understood by a variety of Indian groups from Canada to the American Southwest.

In 1870, the census listed the value of Gilliam's estate at $95,000 (the equivalent of $2 million today). Public records in Pennsylvania, Illinois, and Missouri listed the family members as white. Outside the slave South, the Gilliams managed to reinvent themselves and embrace opportunities sought by many other Americans in this era of migration.

Throughout the West, migrants forged new identities as a matter of course. For example, many people straddled more than one culture in the western borderlands. In 1828, Mexican military officer José Maria Sanchez described the *Tejano* settlers, who were Spanish-speaking persons, some natives of Mexico and others born in provinces such as *Tejas* (Texas): "Accustomed to the continued trade with the North Americans, they have adopted their customs and habits, and one may say truly that they are not Mexican except by birth, for they even speak Spanish with a marked incorrectness." In other provinces of northern Mexico, European American Protestant traders and travelers mingled with Catholic native Spanish speakers.

Within borderlands, traditional power relationships came under attack as new Spanish-speaking elites emerged and Indian workers resisted oppression by the Spanish. In Alta California, the northern reaches of Mexico, diverse groups of people cohabited. Some landowners, including Indians, mestizos, and blacks, called themselves *gente de razon* (literally, "people of reason"), an ambiguous racial category. They sought to put to work gentiles (unbaptized Indians native to California) and *neofitos* (baptized Indians laboring for Roman Catholic missions). When the Mexican government ended its sponsorship of the mission system in the 1830s, many Indians found themselves in a condition akin to enslavement. For example, in New Mexico, an Indian woman might be considered not just a *crida* (servant), but also a *genizara* (a captive, a spoil of war).

In parts of the West, traditional social identities yielded to new ones, based less on a single language or ethnicity than on a blend of cultures and new ways of making a living from the land. The 1830s and 1840s marked the height of the Rocky Mountain fur trade. The trade could generate huge profits for the eastern merchants who controlled it. Individual trappers fared more modestly, ranging freely across national boundaries and cultures, going wherever the bison, bear, and beaver took them. These men demonstrated a legendary ability to navigate among Spanish, French, European American, and Native American communities.

Westerners coined new terms to describe the people representative of new kinds of cultural identity within trading communities. Some white men became "white Indians," and the children they had with Indian women were called "métis" (mixed bloods). William Sherley "Old Bill" Williams, a convert to the religion of the Osage Indians of the southeastern Plains, was not unusual in the ways he crossed cultural boundaries. He married an Osage woman, and when she died, he wed a New Mexican widow. His third wife was a Ute woman. Williams's life story suggests the ways that Indian and Hispanic women could serve as cultural mediators between native peoples and European American traders.

National Museum of American Art/Art Resource, NY

■ Among all Plains Indians, the Comanche were well known for their use of horses as items of trade and as a means of warfare. Here they show the artist George Catlin the way they use the bodies of their horses as shields in battle. This painting was completed in 1835.

CHANGES IN THE SOUTHERN PLAINS

For Plains Indians such as the Comanche and Kiowa, the horse represented a new way of life. Introduced into North America by Spanish conquistadors in the sixteenth century, the horse enabled Native American groups to hunt, move around, trade, and fight their enemies more effectively and efficiently (see Chapter 5). Horses were easy to feed—they foraged off the Plains grasses—and they became valuable objects of trade. By the early nineteenth century, the Comanche and Kiowa, together with the Cheyenne and Arapaho, had developed a far-flung trading empire that depended on horses for both travel and currency. Throughout the Arkansas basin (the present-day lower Midwest and Southwest), these groups traded horses and mules to European American traders, who in turn supplied people emigrating west along the Santa Fe trail.

Yet the Indians' trading successes came at a high price. The natural environment could not sustain the growing number of horses nor withstand dramatic changes caused by this new form of trade. The needs of their horses began to shape the migratory patterns of the Cheyenne; now they had to spend their winters in the mild river bottoms, where the horses found shelter and water. In the spring, bands were forced to move in search of the open grasslands their horse herds depended on. As the demand for horses grew, so did violence associated with raiding parties. New status distinctions emerged within Indian groups, as a small number of wealthy people—owners of large herds of horses—dominated trade and leadership positions.

As raiding parties traveled long distances to find horses, they relied on increasing numbers of bison to feed themselves. Yet bison and horses coexisted uneasily and competed for natural resources, including water and grasslands. Gradually the number of bison

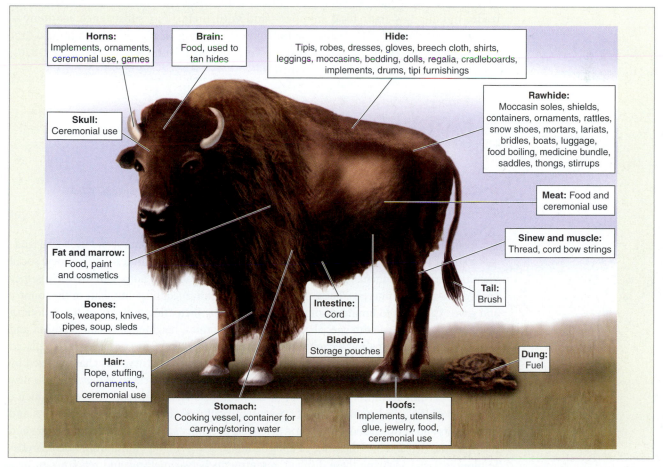

■ **FIGURE 12.1 How Indians Used the Buffalo**

The U.S. and Other Rail Networks Compared

The Wider World

Though a relatively young country, the United States early developed the most extensive railroad network in the world. Railroads contributed to the economy in several ways: They moved people, things, and information quickly and efficiently. They knit together the national economy by transporting manufactured goods from the East to the West and South, cotton from the South to the North, and cattle and grain from the West to the East. In the United States, the rail industry came to serve as a major employer, since it relied on so many people to design and manufacture engines and cars, lay and

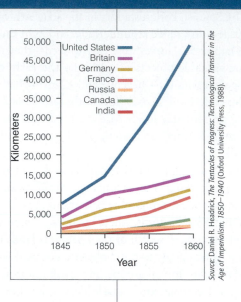

Source: Daniel R. Headrick, The Tentacles of Progress: Technological Transfer in the Age of Imperialism, 1850–1940 (Oxford University Press, 1988).

maintain tracks, work as engineers, and cater to the needs of passengers.

QUESTIONS

1. What factors account for the rapid growth of U.S. railroads? Does the large size of the United States fully explain its development of an extensive rail system?

2. Why, by the 1840s, had railroads surpassed turnpikes and canals as the preferred means of moving large quantities of people and things over long distances?

---

dwindled, causing hardship among southern Plains Indians. More and more reliant on trade, Indians saw their food supplies—and with them their subsistence economy—gradually disappear. By the 1830s, the Indian horse-trading empire was undergoing a dramatic decline, the victim of its own success. The Comanche numbered 20,000 in the 1820s, and only a quarter of that number in the 1860s.

A Multitude of Voices in the National Political Arena

■ *Why did debates over the rights (or lack thereof) of workers, slaves, and immigrants lead to the rise of new political organizations?*

Streams of migration through Indian territory changed both the natural and the social landscape of the West, where diverse peoples forged new social identities—or had new social identities thrust upon them. As various groups moved and made new homes for themselves, they created new political interests. These new interests both enlivened the political life of the country and gave expression to ominous sounds of conflict. The increasing diversity of the American population, combined with specialized regional economies, heightened tensions within and between different groups and sections of the country. The Second Party system, which replaced the Federalist–Anti-Federalist rivalry of the early nineteenth century, was characterized by intense competition between the Jacksonian Democrats and anti-Jackson Whigs. But this new system could not accommodate the old or new conflicts based on race, religion, ethnicity, regional loyalties, and political beliefs. Social and cultural disputes between nativists and immigrants and between abolitionists and defenders of slavery spilled out of the courthouse and the legislative hall and into the streets. Public demonstrations ran the gamut from noisy parades to bloody clashes. During these displays, resentments between ethnic and religious groups, arguments over political issues, and opposition to reformers often blended together.

WHIGS, WORKERS, AND THE PANIC OF 1837

One polarizing force, President Andrew Jackson, did not run for a third term in 1836 due to a bout with tuberculosis. The Democrats nominated his vice president and friend Martin Van Buren of New York. The Whig party, led by Senator Henry Clay and other anti-Jackson congressmen, drew their support from several groups: advocates of Clay's American System (policies that supported a national bank, public funding of canals and turnpikes, and protective tariffs), states' rights Southerners opposed to Jackson's heavy-handed use of national power, and merchants and factory owners in favor of the Second Bank of the United States. **Evangelical Protestants** from the middle classes also joined the anti-Jackson forces; they objected to his rhetoric stressing class differences, because they believed that individual religious conviction, not a group's material status, should shape politics and society. Still somewhat disorganized, these allied groups fielded three candidates: Hugh White of Tennessee, Senator Daniel Webster of Massachusetts, and General William Henry Harrison of Indiana. Benefiting from the Whigs' disarray, Van Buren narrowly won the popular vote but swept the electoral college.

During this period, political candidates of all persuasions in northeastern cities began to court the allegiance of workers aligned with a new trade union movement. People worried about making a living tended to favor the Democratic party, which spoke against class privilege and the wealthy and upheld the tenets of white supremacy. In the late 1820s and early 1830s, a variety of trade organizations had formed to advance the interests of skilled workers (the "producing classes," they called themselves). These unions pressed for a ten-hour workday and the abolition of debtors' prisons. They also objected to paper money (so that workers would receive their wages in hard currency rather than bank notes), and higher wages.

The founding of the **National Trades Union** (NTU) in 1834 made workers more politically visible. The union represented workers as diverse as jewelers, butchers, bookbinders, and factory workers. In Philadelphia in the early 1830s, for example, the local NTU organization, called the General Trades Union, consisted of fifty trade societies and supported a number of successful strikes. Both Whigs and Democrats professed allegiance to the union, but neither party went out of its way to represent the interests of workers over other groups, such as farmers and bookkeepers.

A major economic depression, the **Panic of 1837,** created even larger troubles for the trade union movement. Brought on by overspeculation—in canals, turnpikes, railroads, and slaves—the panic deepened when large grain crops failed in the West. British creditors worsened matters when they recalled loans they had made to American

TABLE 12.2			
The Election of 1836			
Candidate	**Political Party**	**Popular Vote (%)**	**Electoral Vote**
Martin Van Buren	Democratic	50.9	170
William Henry Harrison	Whig		73
Hugh L. White	Whig	49.1	26
Daniel Webster	Whig		14
W. P. Magnum	Independent	—	11

DOCUMENT

Clay, "Defense of the American System"

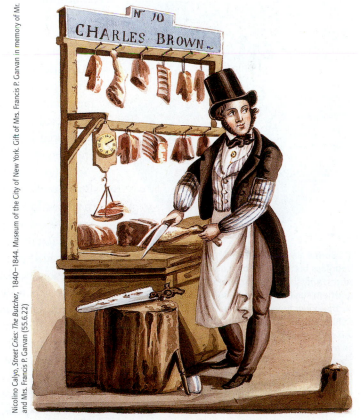

Nicolino Calyo, *Street Cries: The Butcher,* 1840–1844. Museum of the City of New York. Gift of Mrs. Francis P. Garvan in memory of Mr. and Mrs. Francis P. Garvan (55.6.22)

■ In the antebellum period, factory operatives represented only a small percentage of all U.S. workers. Many kinds of skilled craftsmen, such as the butcher pictured here, continued to ply their trades in time-honored ways. Some of these skilled workers formed labor unions affiliated with the National Trades Union.

customers. The depression lasted until the early 1840s and devastated the NTU and its constituent organizations. Up to one-third of all Americans lost their jobs when businesses failed. Those fortunate enough to keep their jobs were in no position to press for higher wages. Not until the Civil War era did members of the laboring classes recapture political momentum at the national level.

SUPPRESSION OF ANTISLAVERY SENTIMENT

DOCUMENT

Garrison, First Issue
of *The Liberator*

Enslaved black workers were also at the center of contention in these years. In 1831, a Boston journalist named William Lloyd Garrison launched the *Liberator,* a newspaper dedicated to "immediate emancipation" of all slaves. Two years later, a group of sixty blacks and whites formed the American Anti-Slavery Society. That same year, Great Britain abolished slavery in the West Indies. This move encouraged like-minded Americans eager to cooperate with their British counterparts to abolish slavery everywhere. In the United States, the abolition movement enlisted the energies of a dedicated group of people who believed not only that slavery was immoral but also that the federal government must take immediate steps to destroy this "peculiar institution."

Both northern free people of color and white women and men provided financial support to the society. All the supporters showed a great deal of courage within a larger American society indifferent to the issue of slavery. Well-to-do black leaders, including Henry Highland Garnet, Charles Lenox Remond, and his sister Sarah Parker Remond, spoke out on behalf of southern blacks in chains. Fugitive slaves, including Frederick Douglass, Solomon Northup, and William and Ellen Craft, electrified northern abolitionist audiences with their firsthand accounts of the brutality of slavery and of their own daring escapes from bondage.

A few white women also became active in the abolitionist cause. Sarah and Angelina Grimké, for example, left the household of their slave-owning father in Charleston, South Carolina, and moved to Philadelphia. The Grimké sisters offended many other whites by speaking before mixed groups composed of men and women, blacks and whites. The Grimkés were struck by what they considered the similar legal constraints of slaves and white women. White men considered both groups unworthy of citizenship rights, childlike in their demeanor, well suited for domestic service, and inherently unintelligent.

Abolitionist activities provoked outrage not only from southern slave owners but also from anti-abolitionists and their allies in Congress—in other words, most northern whites. In Washington, D.C., the House of Representatives imposed a gag rule on antislavery petitions, forbidding them to be read aloud or entered into the public record. Supporters of slavery also resorted to violence. In 1834, a mob of whites attacked a school for young women of color operated by a white teacher, Prudence Crandall, near New Haven, Connecticut. A local paper charged that the school was fostering "levelling [egalitarian] principles, and intermarriage between whites and blacks." The next year in Boston, a mob attacked the *Liberator* founder, William Lloyd Garrison, tying a rope around him and parading him through the streets of that city while onlookers jeered. Antiblack riots broke out in New York City, Philadelphia, and Cincinnati in 1834, and again in Philadelphia in 1842. Indeed white workers attacked blacks so often in the 1830s and 1840s that bricks became known as "Irish confetti" because of the way immigrants used them as weapons.

Still, these dramatic episodes had little noticeable impact on the two major political parties. In 1840, the Democrats renominated Van Buren, although many people blamed him for the depression. Eager to find a candidate as popular as Andrew Jackson, the Whigs selected William Henry Harrison; his supporters called him "Old Tippecanoe" in recognition of his

■ Born a slave in Maryland in 1818, Frederick Douglass became a leading abolitionist speaker, editor, and activist. Not content to condemn southern slaveholders exclusively, he also criticized northern employers for not hiring blacks. Trained as a ship caulker, Douglass faced job discrimination in the shipyards in New Bedford, Massachusetts, where he and his wife, Anna, settled soon after he escaped slavery and they moved north (in 1838).

Library Company of Philadelphia (1835–7/P8658)

■ The artist titled this print *New Method of Assorting the Mail, as Practised by Southern Slave-Holders*. In July 1835, a proslavery mob broke into the U.S. post office in Charleston, South Carolina, and burned abolitionist literature. The sign on the side of the building offers a "Reward for Tappan." The brothers Arthur and Lewis Tappan were wealthy New York City merchants who funded abolitionist activities. Southern slaveholders hoped to stem the north–south flow of abolitionist literature, which took the form of sermons, pamphlets, periodicals, and resolutions.

defeat of Indians at the battle of the same name in 1811. As Harrison's running mate, the Whigs chose a Democratic politician, John Tyler, who had been both governor of and a senator from Virginia. To counter their reputation as well-heeled aristocrats, the Whigs promoted Harrison as a simple, humble man living in a log cabin and drinking hard cider. They rallied around the slogan "Tippecanoe and Tyler Too."

By this time, the Whigs had gained strong support among wealthy southern planters, who worried that Van Buren would not protect their interests in slavery. Harrison won the election, but he contracted pneumonia at his inauguration and died within one month of taking office. Ridiculed as "His Accidency," Tyler assumed the presidency and soon lost his core constituency, Whigs who favored a strong central government, by vetoing bills for both a national bank and higher tariffs. The new president found support among members of the Whig party who were ardent supporters of states' rights. As a result, he proved a poor standard-bearer for the numerous nationalist-minded Whigs. As a former Democrat himself, Tyler learned a hard lesson: that the Whig party was a loose coalition of groups with varying views on a range of issues, rather than a unified party bound to a single idea or principle.

Abolitionists could claim few victories, either real or symbolic, during these years. However, they did take heart from the *Amistad* case. In 1839, the Spanish-owned ship, *Amistad*, carried fifty-three illegally purchased Africans from Havana to another Cuban port. White sailing along the

TABLE 12.3			
The Election of 1840			
Candidate	**Political Party**	**Popular Vote (%)**	**Electoral Vote**
William Henry Harrison	Whig	53.1	234
Martin Van Buren	Democratic	46.9	60
James G. Birney	Liberty	<1	—

Unknown Artist, *La Amistad*, 1840. Gift of Simeon Eben Baldwin, New Haven Colony Historical Society, New Haven, Connecticut (#1972.1)

■ This picture shows the Spanish slave ship, *Amistad*, anchored off the eastern tip of Long Island, in 1839. The slaves, under the leadership of Cinqué, had commandeered the vessel near Cuba. The Africans, charged with murdering the ship's captain, were held in New Haven, Connecticut, until a U.S. Supreme Court ruling led to their release and return to Africa in 1842. Abolitionists hailed the eventual freeing of the *Amistad* captives as one of their few successes in the fight against slavery before the Civil War.

coast, the Africans, under the leadership of a young man named Cinqué, rebelled, killed the captain, and took over the ship. Soon after, U.S. authorities captured the ship off the coast of Long Island. President Van Buren wanted to send the blacks to Cuba. However, a federal district court judge in Hartford, Connecticut, ruled that because the African slave trade had been illegal since 1808, the Africans had been wrongfully enslaved. The U.S. government appealed the case to the Supreme Court.

To raise funds for the *Amistad* case, Philadelphia black leader Robert Purvis paid to have Cinqué's portrait painted; then antislavery activists sold copies for $1 each. In 1841, former president John Quincy Adams argued the Africans' case before the Supreme Court. The Court ruled in their favor. Of the original fifty-three men, women, and children, thirty-five had survived, and they returned to Africa. Slavery advocates and abolitionists alike pondered the question, could the law be used to dismantle slavery?

NATIVISTS AS A POLITICAL FORCE

Immigration, like slavery, aroused strong feelings. Among the active players on the political scene were the **nativists,** who opposed immigration and immigrants. The immigrants who came to the United States were a varied group in terms of their jobs, religion, and culture. Some farmed homesteads in Michigan, and others worked in northeastern factories. But to nativists, these distinctions made little difference: all immigrants were foreigners and thus unwelcome. Some nativists were also **temperance** advocates, calling for the prohibition of alcohol; they objected to the Irish drinking in taverns and the Germans drinking in their *Biergarten*. Protestants worried that large numbers of Catholic immigrants would be loyal to the pope in

Library Company of Philadelphia (59541.D)

■ Taken on May 9, 1844, this daguerreotype is one of the first American photographs to record an urban civil disturbance. A crowd gathers outside Philadelphia's Girard Bank, at the corner of Third and Dock streets. At the time, soldiers called in to quell the riot were occupying the bank. Called the Bible Riots, the clash between Protestant and Catholic workers revealed tensions arising from nativism, temperance activism, and the use of the Protestant version of the Bible in the public schools.

Rome, the head of the Catholic Church, and thus undermine American democracy. Members of the working classes, black and white, feared the loss of their jobs to desperate newcomers who would accept low, "starvation" wages. But nativists objected just as much when immigrants kept to themselves—in their Catholic schools or in their German *Turnverein* (gymnastics clubs). They also complained when immigrants participated in U.S. politics as individual voters and members of influential voting blocs.

Samuel F. B. Morse, the artist and inventor, was among the most vocal nativists. In the early 1840s, he ceased painting portraits and turned his creative energies to developing a form of long-distance electric communication. Congress financed construction of the first telegraph line, which ran from Washington to Baltimore. In May 1844, Morse sent a message in code, "What hath God wrought!" and the modern telegraph was born. The precursor of all later communication innovations, the telegraph revolutionized the spread of information and tied the country together.

Morse was convinced that Catholic immigrants in particular (mostly the Irish) were a grave threat to American democracy. In his book *Imminent Dangers to the Free Institutions of the United States* (1835), Morse charged that Catholics favored "monarchical power" over republican governments. Catholicism was like a cancer, he wrote: "We find it spreading itself into every nook and corner of the land; churches, chapels, colleges, nunneries and convents are springing up as if by magic every where." In his fears, Morse expressed nostalgia for a simpler past, even as his technical ingenuity paved the way for the modern world.

DOCUMENT

Morse, Foreign Immigration

In 1844, an openly nativist political organization, the American party, elected six of its candidates to Congress and dozens of others to local political offices. In 1849, nativists founded the Order of the Star-Spangled Banner. The nativist political groups was also called the Know-Nothing party because it cautioned its members to profess ignorance when asked about its existence.

In some cases, anti-Catholic prejudices in particular helped to justify territorial expansion. Many U.S. Protestants believed the government was justified in seizing the land of Spanish-speaking Catholics in the West. They claimed religious and cultural superiority over Hispanos.

As Protestant explorers, traders, and travelers reported on their experiences in the Southwest, their condemnation of Mexican Roman Catholics set the stage for the U.S. conquest of northern Mexico in the late 1840s. On the other hand, some Protestant nativists objected to U.S. expansion in the West, because they did not want to increase the number of Catholics in the nation.

During this period, nativists formed the short-lived American party to mobilize the native-born working classes against immigrants. Increasingly, Americans believed that the traditional two-party system was incapable of resolving the great social and political issues of the day. As a result, some people also formed new reform organizations to address the deficiencies of the major political parties and to right the perceived moral wrongs of America. Some reformers emphasized personal transformation as the key to lasting social change. Others attempted to agitate through legal channels. Regardless of their cause, all reformers believed they possessed the ability and the responsibility to make America a better place. Yet people continued to disagree about what that "better place" should and would look like.

Reform Impulses

■ *What were the major reform movements of the 1830s and 1840s? What were the various strategies used by reformers to effect social change?*

In August 1841, writer Lydia Maria Child recorded a striking scene in New York City: a march sponsored by the Washington Society, a temperance group, snaked its way through the streets. The procession stretched for two miles and consisted of representatives from "all classes and trades." The marchers carried banners depicting streams and rivers (the pure water favored over liquor) and poignant scenes of the grateful wives and children of reformed drunkards. Stirred by the martial sounds of trumpets and drums, Child wrote that the music was "the voice of resistance to evil." She added, "Glory to resistance! for through its agency men become angels."

Inspired by faith in the perfectibility of human beings and heartened by the rapid pace of technological progress, many Americans set about trying to "make angels out of men," in Child's words. In the process, various reform associations targeted personal habits such as dress and diet, conventional beliefs about sexuality and the status of women, and institutions such as schools, churches, and slavery. Their efforts often brought women out of the home and into public life. Yet not all Americans shared the reformers' zeal. Even those who did rarely agreed about the appropriate means to transform society.

PUBLIC EDUCATION

In the eyes of some Americans, a growing nation needed new forms of tax-supported schooling. As families moved from one area of the country to another, public education advocates pointed out, children should be able to pick up in one school where they had left off in another. Members of a growing middle class wanted to provide their children with schooling beyond basic literacy instruction (reading and writing skills) and had the resources to do so.

Horace Mann, a Massachusetts state legislator and lawyer, was one of the most prominent educational reformers. In 1837, Mann became secretary of the first state board of education. He stressed the notion of a **common school system** available to all boys and girls regardless of class or ethnicity. In an increasingly diverse nation, schooling promoted the acquisition of basic knowledge and skills. But it also provided instruction in what Mann and others called American values: hard work, punctuality, and sobriety.

By the 1840s, public school systems attended by white children had cropped up across the North and the Midwest. Local school boards eagerly tapped into the energies of women as teachers. School officials claimed that women were naturally nurturing and could serve as "mothers away from home" for small children. Furthermore, schools could pay women only a fraction of what men earned. Between the 1830s and 1840s, the number of female schoolteachers in Massachusetts jumped more than 150 percent. In 1846, writer and educator Catharine Beecher created a Board of National Popular Education, which sent unmarried female New England teachers to the Midwest.

Despite the lofty goals of Mann and other reformers, public schooling did not offer a "common" experience for all American children. Almost exclusively, northern white children benefited from public school systems. Slightly more than one-third of all white children attended school in 1830; twenty years later, the ratio had increased to more than one-half. In northern cities, these proportions were considerably higher; there reformers were able to provide elementary-school instruction for relatively large numbers of white children, both immigrant and native-born.

By contrast, few black children had the opportunity to attend public schools. In the South, slave children were forbidden by law to learn to read and write. Recalled one former slave many years later, "dey [owners] didn't teach 'em nothin' but wuk [work]." By the 1830s, schools for even the children of free people of color had to meet in secret. In the North, many black households needed the labor of children to survive, resulting in black school-attendance rates well below those of whites. Throughout the Northeast and Midwest, black children remained at the mercy of local officials, who decided whether they could attend the schools their parents' tax dollars helped support.

All over the country, education remained an intensely grassroots affair, belying the reformers' call for uniform systems. Local communities raised money for the teacher's salary, built the schoolhouse, and provided wood to heat the building. Southern states did not develop uniform public education systems until the late nineteenth century. Lacking local, popular support for tax-supported schooling, poor white children remained illiterate, while wealthy parents hired tutors for their own children or sent them to private academies.

An increase in the literate population resulted in an increased demand for higher education. The number of colleges more than doubled from 46 to 119 between 1830 and 1850.

Albertus del Orient Browere, *Mrs. McCormick's General Store*, 1844. Fenimore Art Museum, Cooperstown, New York (N-0387.55)

■ Artist Albertus Browere titled this 1844 painting *Mrs. McCormick's General Store*. These barefoot boys are getting into trouble. Reformers advocated universal, compulsory schooling as one way to rid street corners of young mischief makers. Had these youngsters lived in the country, they probably would have been working in the fields.

Oberlin College in Ohio (founded in 1833) accepted black men as well as women of both races in 1837. Oberlin and Mount Holyoke, a college for women in Massachusetts (founded in 1837), were unusual for their liberal admission policies. Other forms of education also multiplied. Lyceums—societies offering informal lectures by speakers who traveled from place to place—attracted hordes of adults regardless of their formal education. By the mid-1830s, approximately 3,000 local lecture associations, mostly in New England and the Midwest, were sponsoring such series. In addition, local agricultural fairs offered informal practical instruction to rural people.

> *In rural communities of black and white Southerners, Native Americans, and Mexicans, women continued to practice time-honored ways of midwifery and healing.*

Formal training for professionals such as physicians and lawyers also changed during this period. By the 1830s, almost all states required that doctors be licensed. The only way to attain such a license was to attend medical school, and these schools excluded women. In regions of the country where medical schools appeared, the self-taught midwife gradually yielded to the formally educated male physician. In contrast, in rural communities of black and white Southerners, Native Americans, and Mexicans, women continued to practice time-honored ways of midwifery and healing.

ALTERNATIVE VISIONS OF SOCIAL LIFE

As in education, the crosscurrents of reform showed up clearly in debates about sexuality, the family, and the proper role of women. For example, reformer Sylvester Graham argued that even husbands and wives must monitor their sexual activity. Sexual excess between husband and wife, he claimed, caused ills ranging from headaches, chills, and impaired vision, to loss of memory, epilepsy, insanity, and "disorders of the liver and kidneys." Graham also promoted a diet of special crackers made of wheat flour (now called Graham crackers) and fruit (in place of alcohol and meat) in addition to a regimen of plain living reinforced with cold showers.

Other reformers disagreed with Graham's notion that people must repress their sexuality to lead a good and healthy life. Defying conventional standards of morality, sponsors of a number of experimental communities discouraged marriage-based monogamy (a legal commitment between a man and a woman to engage in sexual relations only with each other) and made child-rearing the responsibility of the entire community, rather than just the child's parents. These communities were communitarian—seeking to break down exclusive relations between husband and wife, parent and child, employer and employee—in an effort to advance the well-being of the whole group, not just individuals within it. These communities were also **utopian,** seeking to forge new kinds of social relationships that would, in the eyes of the reformers, serve as a model for the larger society.

Many of these communities explicitly challenged mainstream views related to property ownership and the system of wage labor as well as rules governing relations between the sexes. The Scottish industrialist and socialist Robert Owen founded New Harmony in Indiana in 1825, basing his experiment on principles of "cooperative labor." In 1826, Owen released his "Declaration of Mental Independence," which condemned private property, organized religion, and marriage. By this time, 900 persons had joined the New Harmony order.

Several other prominent communitarian experiments that challenged conventional marital relations were vehemently criticized, and participants were sometimes physically attacked by their neighbors. Salt Lake City Mormons, who practiced plural marriage, continued to meet intense hostility from outsiders. Another group, the Oneida Community, founded in upstate New York near Utica in 1848 by John Humphrey Noyes, went even further than the Mormons in advocating an alternative to monogamy. At its peak, Oneida consisted of 300 members who endorsed the founder's notion of "complex marriage," meaning communal sexual unions and community-regulated parent–child relations. Charges of adultery eventually forced Noyes to flee the country and seek refuge in Canada.

MAP

Utopian Communities
before the Civil War

NETWORKS OF REFORMERS

Many moral reforms overlapped with and reinforced each other. For example, women's rights advocates often supported temperance. Husbands who drank, they pointed out, were more likely to abuse their wives and children and to squander their paychecks. Angelina and Sarah Grimké gained prominence as both abolitionists and advocates for women's rights. They followed Sylvester Graham's program, and for a short time they sported "bloomers" (loose-fitting pants popularized by dress reformer Amelia Bloomer) in place of cumbersome dresses.

Dorothea Dix spearheaded a major reform effort that gained the support of a variety of politicians and activists. As a young woman, Dix had worked as a teacher and writer. In 1836, she visited England, where she met several prominent British reformers. Five years later she volunteered to teach a Sunday school class for women at an East Cambridge jail not far from Boston. Her first day there, in March 1841, changed her life—and the face of American antebellum reform—forever.

Dix found among the inmates not only women accused of prostitution and vagrancy, but also women who were clearly mentally ill. All of them were miserable, shivering in the cold. Dix was horrified that insane persons were imprisoned with criminals. She set out on a campaign to investigate the conditions under which the mentally ill were confined. Over the next eighteen months, she investigated every prison, almshouse, and asylum in Massachusetts. She kept careful notes, which later formed the basis of her petitions, or "memorials," demanding better treatment for all insane persons. At one place she found people "confined . . . in *cages, closets, cellars, stalls, pens! Chained, naked, beaten with rods,* and *lashed* into obedience." Dix presented her findings to the Massachusetts state legislature. Heartened by the public outcry she had inspired, she widened her investigation to include the states of Rhode Island and New York. In the late 1840s, she traveled to another dozen states in the South, Mid-Atlantic, and Midwest.

Dix found crucial support from several prominent reformers. Massachusetts Senator Charles Sumner, an outspoken abolitionist, and Horace Mann, the driving force behind the common school system, championed her cause. Though associated most famously with the plight of the mentally ill in antebellum America, Dix went on to play a pivotal role in the feminization of the nursing profession during the Civil War when she energetically promoted the use of women as nurses in Union hospitals.

Most striking is the overlap between abolitionism and women's rights. Some middle-class white women contemplated the chains of slaves and saw mirrored in those chains their own legal and social inferiority. They argued that free white women, like enslaved persons, were denied basic legal rights such as the right to own property. Women, like slaves, they suggested, could not aspire to a higher education or positions of religious or political authority; their main purpose in life was to serve (white) men. These reformers often underestimated their own privileges—for example, they never had to worry about their children being sold away from them. Yet the link between the two movements—in both ideas and personnel—was dramatic.

Treated as second-class citizens within the abolitionist movement, many women felt compelled to act. When Elizabeth Cady Stanton and other American women attended the 1840 World Anti-Slavery Convention in London, male leaders of the British and Foreign Anti-Slavery Society relegated the women delegates to a balcony and excluded them from the formal deliberations. Eight years later, Cady Stanton worked with Lucretia Mott,

■ Margaret Fuller was one of the foremost American intellectuals of the antebellum period. Throughout her life she remained conscious of an inner struggle between her passionate self, desiring an active life, and her intellectual self, wanting to engage in study and debate with other scholars. She explored Transcendentalism, feminism, social reform, and finally the revolutionary fervor of Italian nationalism.

a Quaker minister; Susan B. Anthony, a women's rights activist; and other similarly inclined women and men to organize the first women's rights convention in Seneca Falls, New York.

Women's rights advocates made some progress independent of the abolitionist movement. In 1838, both New York and Pennsylvania passed legislation giving married women control over any real property (land) or personal property they brought to marriage. In 1839, Mississippi passed the Married Women's Property Law, intended to protect the fortunes of the married daughters of wealthy planters.

> *Transcendentalists believed in the primacy of the spirit and the essential harmony between people and the natural world.*

Massachusetts resident Margaret Fuller explored many reform impulses of the day during her brief life (1810–1850). Educated in the classics by her father at home in Cambridge, in the 1830s she embraced a new intellectual sensibility called Transcendentalism. Fuller cultivated friendships with two other famous Transcendentalists living in the Boston area: Ralph Waldo Emerson and Henry David Thoreau. Transcendentalists believed in the primacy of the spirit and the essential harmony between people and the natural world. They took their inspiration from European Romantics, who celebrated the beauty of nature in art, music, and literature. In 1845, Fuller published *Woman in the Nineteenth Century*, one of the first feminist works written by an American. "I would have Woman lay aside all thought, such as she habitually cherishes, of being led and taught by men," wrote Fuller. She then embraced the role of investigative journalist, writing about the plight of slaves, Indians, and imprisoned women for the New York *Tribune*.

Some reformers and elected officials believed that the greatest reform movement of all was to expand the boundaries of the United States. They believed that the country should increase its territory and in the process bring more people under the American flag. Yet this "reform" impulse relied not on persuasion or education but on military force. The resulting armed conflict on the nation's borders produced new levels of tension within its borders. Americans could no longer ignore the increasingly divisive issue of slavery.

The United States Extends Its Reach

■ *Why was seizing the land that would become the state of Texas so important to so many Americans?*

Efforts to reform society at home went hand in hand with a determination to expand the nation's borders, especially in the Southwest. In the mid-1840s, the editor of the *New York Morning News* declared that the United States had a "manifest destiny" to "overspread the continent" and claim the "desert wastes." Those inhabiting the "desert wastes"—Mexican settlers and a variety of Indian groups—apparently would have little say in the matter. The term **manifest destiny** soon became a catchall phrase, justifying American efforts not only to conquer new territory but also to seek out new markets for American goods across the oceans.

THE LONE STAR REPUBLIC

In the early 1830s, the Mexican government became alarmed by the growing number of American emigrants to Texas. Worried that the settlers would refuse to pledge allegiance to Mexico, that country closed the Texas border to further in-migration. By 1835, only one out of every eight residents of Texas was a *Tejano* (a native Spanish speaker); the rest, numbering 30,000, hailed from the United States. The U.S.-born Texians, together with some prominent *Tejanos*, had become increasingly well armed and militant. They organized volunteer patrols to attack Indian settlements. These forces became the precursor of the Texas Rangers, a statewide organization of law enforcement officers.

In 1836, the Texians decided to press for independence from Mexico. Only by becoming a separate nation, they believed, could they trade freely with the United States, establish their own schools, and collect and spend their own taxes. The pro-independence Texians included Davy Crockett, who had moved there in 1835. A few months later, Crockett and other armed Texians retreated to a Spanish mission in San Antonio called the Alamo. They were joined by a small group of *Tejanos* who resented Mexico's heavy-handed control of Texas. In March 1836, a military force led by Antonio López de Santa Anna, president of the Republic of Mexico and a general in the army, battled them for thirteen days. All 187 defenders of the Alamo died at the hands of Santa Anna and his men; the Mexican leader lost 600 of his own troops. Historians disagree on whether all of the Alamo defenders died fighting or if some were executed by Mexican soldiers.

In April a force of Texians and their *Tejano* allies, including military leader Juan Seguín, surprised Santa Anna and his men at the San Jacinto River and killed another 600 of them. The victors captured Santa Anna and declared themselves a new nation. Sam Houston, former U.S. congressman from Tennessee and commander in chief of the Texian army, became president of the Republic of Texas (also called the Lone Star Republic) in 1837. Some *Tejanos* who objected to Mexican policies also supported the new republic; these included José Antonio Navarro, Francisco Ruiz, and Lorenzo de Zavala, who became its vice president.

In the northern territories of Mexico, many Spanish speakers had long felt abandoned by the Mexican government, which had made no provisions for their self-government and inhibited trade relations with the United States. Although other Mexican provinces protested the way they were treated by the government, Texas was the only Mexican state to launch a successful rebellion against Mexico.

Texas's independence raised the fears of U.S. abolitionists and imperiled blacks living in the new republic. In contrast to Mexico, which had abolished slavery in 1829, Texas approved a constitution that not only legalized slavery but also prohibited free blacks from living in the country. Greenbury Logan, a black man who owned a farm near Austin, petitioned to stay. He wrote, "Every privilege dear to a free man is taken away." But vigilantes forced him to leave. They also forced out many *Tejanos*. Among them was Juan Seguín, who had helped defeat Santa Anna at the Battle of San Jacinto and was now the mayor of San Antonio. Not until 1981 did another *Tejano*, Henry Cisneros, hold the office of mayor of the city of San Antonio.

THE ELECTION OF 1844

As an independent republic, Texas became a hotly contested political issue in the United States. During the election of 1844, politicians began to debate whether the United States should annex Texas. Van Buren was outspoken in his opposition to the idea. As a result, the frankly expansionist Democrats spurned the former president as a candidate and nominated James K. Polk of Tennessee. They called for "the reannexation" of Texas and the "reoccupation" of Oregon. Their rallying cry became "Fifty-Four Forty or Fight," a reference to their desire to own the area (expressed in terms of its longitude and latitude coordinates) claimed by the British in present-day Canada south of Alaska and west of the Continental Divide. Kentucky congressman Henry Clay received the Whig nomination after he announced he was against the annexation of Texas. But under pressure from Southerners, he later changed his mind, to the disgust of party leaders.

Neither the Democrats nor the Whigs had shown an interest in directly addressing the issue of slavery in the last presidential election. Yet in 1844, the controversy over the annexation of Texas made it impossible for the two parties to ignore the growing controversy over

Max Rosenthal, *Henry Clay*, National Portrait Gallery, Smithsonian Institution/Art Resource NY

■ Henry Clay had a distinguished career as statesman and politician for more than four decades. He was secretary of state under President John Quincy Adams, served as speaker of the House of Representatives for a longer term than anyone else in the nineteenth century, and represented Kentucky in the Senate. A prominent Whig leader, he promoted "the American System" of tariffs and federal subsidies for transportation projects. By 1840, members of both parties were boasting of their (supposed) humble origins. Here Clay is portrayed as the "Old Coon" because the Whigs had adopted the raccoon as their symbol.

TABLE 12.4			
The Election of 1844			
Candidate	**Political Party**	**Popular Vote (%)**	**Electoral Vote**
James K. Polk	Democratic	49.6	170
Henry Clay	Whig	48.1	105
James G. Birney	Liberty	2.3	–

bound labor. Under the banner of the young Liberty party, some abolitionists charged that territorial expansion would mean the continued growth and prosperity of the slave system; they pointed to the public pronouncements of southern planters, who were outspoken in their desire to expand their slaveholdings into the fertile lands of Texas.

For their part, Democrats and Whigs believed, correctly, that most voters would ignore slavery when they cast their ballots. Thus members of both parties tried to silence both sides of the slavery debate. They turned a deaf ear to the proslavery advocates on one hand and squelched northern abolitionist opinion by ignoring petitions to Congress on the other. In the end, Polk won the election. The expansionists had elected one of their most ardent champions to the highest office in the land.

Still, Polk was not interested in going to war with Great Britain over the vast territory of Oregon. In 1846, the two countries reached a compromise. Britain would accept the 49th parallel as the border between Canada and the United States and retain the disputed islands off the coast of Vancouver. The United States settled for one-half of its original claim to Oregon. Thereafter, it was free to turn its full attention to extending its southern and western borders.

WAR WITH MEXICO

Texian leaders wanted to become part of the United States. In 1845, as one of his last acts as president, Tyler invited Texas to become the twenty-eighth state. He also understood that

Joseph Vollmering, *The U.S. Naval Expedition Under Comore. M. C. Perry, Ascending the Tuspan River*, 1848. Amon Carter Museum, Forth Worth, Texas (1976.33.2)

■ This painting shows the U.S. Navy going up the Tuxpan River in Mexico during the U.S.-Mexican War. Located on the Gulf Coast halfway between Vera Cruz and Tampico, Tuxpan was the last significant Mexican port to be seized by U.S. forces by the spring of 1847. Commodore M. C. Perry assembled a formidable force of marines and infantry to take over the town.

MAP 12.5 The U.S.–Mexican War (1846–1848)

During the U.S.–Mexican War, American troops marched deep into the interior of Mexico. General Winfield Scott raised the American flag over Mexico City on September 14, 1847. The treaty that concluded the war was named after the village of Guadalupe Hidalgo, a few miles north of the Mexican capital. The U.S. army withdrew the last of its troops from foreign soil in July 1848.

annexing Texas was a way to goad Mexico into open hostilities; Mexico had warned the United States that such a move would mean war. A joint resolution of both houses of Congress confirmed Texas statehood in December 1845.

The boundaries between Mexico and the new state of Texas remained in dispute. Mexico recognized the Nueces River as the boundary for Texas. In contrast, Texians and U.S. politicians envisioned the boundary a hundred miles to the south at the Rio Grande. Complicating matters further, the new president, James K. Polk, had sent an envoy, John Slidell, to purchase California and a disputed section of Texas from Mexico. Mexico refused the deal. Nevertheless, around this time, Polk wrote in his diary that if he could not acquire all of New Mexico and

Senator John C. Calhoun Warns Against Incorporating Mexico into the United States

In January 1848, Senator John C. Calhoun delivered a speech, addressing his remarks to President Polk and to his fellow law-makers. He urged them to resist calls to incorporate all of a conquered Mexico into the United States. Calhoun favored the spread of slavery into new territories. However, here he expresses the fear that residents of Mexico were incapable of becoming suitable U.S. citizens, for "racial" reasons.

It is without example or precedent, either to hold Mexico as a province, or to incorporate her into our union. No example of such a line of policy can be found. We have conquered many of the neighboring tribes of Indians, but we never thought of holding them in subjection—never of incorporating them into our Union. They have either been left as an independent people amongst us, or been driven into the forests.

I know further, sir, that we have never dreamt of incorporating into our Union any but the Caucasian race—the free white race. To incorporate Mexico, would be the first instance of the kind of incorporating an Indian race; for more than half of the Mexicans are Indians, and the other half is composed chiefly of mixed tribes. I protest such a union as that! . . .

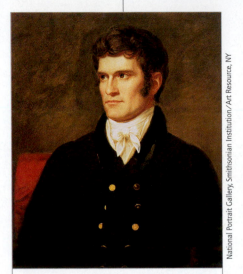

■ Portrait of John C. Calhoun by Charles Bird King, c. 1818–1825.

National Portrait Gallery, Smithsonian Institution/Art Resource, NY

Sir, it is a remarkable fact, that in the whole history of man, as far as my knowledge extends, there is no instance whatever of any civilized colored races being found equal to the establishment of free popular government, although by far the largest portion of the human family is composed of these races. . . . Are we to associate with ourselves as equals, companions, and fellow-citizens, the Indians and mixed race of Mexico? Sir, I should consider such a thing as fatal to our institutions.

Calhoun then moves on to another theme. He disputes the notion that Mexico can begin as a territory and then work its way up to statehood, following the standards Congress set for other western territories.

You can establish a Territorial Government for every State in Mexico, and there are some twenty of them. You can appoint governors, judges, and magistrates. You can give the people a subordinate government, allowing them to legislate for themselves, whilst you defray the cost. So far as the law goes, the thing is done. There is no analogy between this and our Territorial Governments. Our Territories are only an offset of our own people, or foreigners from the same regions from which we came. They are small in number. They are

---

California through diplomatic negotiation, he was determined to obtain them by force. The stage was set for war.

Armed conflict broke out in January 1846. U.S. troops, under the command of General Zachary Taylor (a veteran of wars against Tecumseh, the Seminole, and Black Hawk), clashed with a Mexican force near the mouth of the Rio Grande near Matamoros. Taylor had deliberately moved his troops across the Nueces River into disputed territory; his intention was to provoke an armed response from Mexico. A skirmish ensued, eleven Americans were killed, and Taylor pulled back. Polk used this military action as justification for a declaration of war against Mexico. The president declared, "American blood has been shed on American soil."

Not all Americans supported the war. Transcendentalists such as Henry David Thoreau objected to what they saw as a naked land grab. Refusing to pay taxes for what he considered a war to expand slavery, Thoreau went to jail. Nativists also objected to the war, fearing that the United States would have to assimilate thousands of Indians and Spanish-speaking Roman Catholics. Some members of Congress, including a newly elected U.S. Representative from Illinois named Abraham Lincoln, also condemned Polk's "act of aggression."

DOCUMENT

Corwin, "Against the Mexican War"

incapable of forming a government. It would be inconvenient for them to sustain a government, if it were formed; and they are very much obliged to the United States for undertaking the trouble, knowing that, on the attainment of their majority—when they come to manhood—at twenty-one—they will be introduced to an equality with all other members of the Union. It is entirely different with Mexico. You have no need of armies to keep your Territories in subjection. But when you incorporate Mexico, you must have powerful armies to keep them in subjection. You may call it annexation, but it is a forced annexation, which is a contradiction in terms, according to my conception. You will be involved, in one word, in all the evils which I attribute to holding Mexico as a province. In fact, it will be but a Provincial Government, under the name of a Territorial Government. How long will that last? How long will it be before Mexico will be capable of incorporation into our Union? Why, if we judge from the examples before us, it will be a very long time. Ireland has been held in subjection by England for seven or eight hundred years, and yet still remains hostile, although her people are of kindred race with the conquerors. A few French Canadians on this continent yet maintain the attitude of hostile people; and never will the time come, in my opinion, Mr. President, that these Mexicans will be reconciled to your authority. . . . Of all nations of the earth they are the most pertinacious—have the highest sense of nationality—hold out the longest, and often even with the least prospect of effecting their object. On this subject also I have conversed with officers of the army, and they all entertain the same opinion, that these people are now hostile, and will continue so. . . .

We make a great mistake, sir, when we suppose that all people are capable of self-government. We are anxious to force free government on all; and I see that it has been urged in a very respectable quarter, that it is the mission of this country to spread civil and religious liberty over all the world, and especially this continent. It is a great mistake. None but people advanced to a very high state of moral and intellectual improvement are capable, in a civilized state, of maintaining free government; and amongst those who are so purified, very few, indeed, have had the good fortune of forming a constitution capable of endurance.

Calhoun also warns that "these twenty-odd Mexican States" would eventually have power in Congress. He asks his listeners whether they would want their own states "governed by" these peoples.

QUESTIONS

1. *Why does Calhoun assume that, if the United States incorporates Mexico into its territory, the federal government "must have powerful armies to keep them [Mexicans] in subjection"?*

2. *How might Calhoun's more extreme expansionist colleagues— those in favor of seizing all of Mexico—have countered his arguments against such action?*

Source: Clyde A. Milner, ed., Major Problems in the History of the American West: Documents and Essays (Lexington, MA: D.C. Heath, 1989), 219–221.

Predictably, opponents of slavery were among Polk's most outspoken critics. Soon after the outbreak of war, Representative David Wilmot of Pennsylvania attached an amendment to a bill appropriating money for the war. Called the Wilmot Proviso, the measure declared that "neither slavery nor involuntary servitude shall ever exist" in territories the United States acquired from Mexico. Though a member of the Democratic party, Wilmot spoke primarily as a white Northerner; he wanted to preserve the West for "the sons of toil of my own race and color." Wilmot's views show how racial prejudice and antislavery sentiment coexisted in the minds of many white Northerners. The House approved the proviso, but the Senate did not. Southern Democrats claimed that Congress had no right to deprive slaveholders of their private property anywhere in the nation.

Meanwhile, Polk launched a three-pronged campaign against Mexico. He sent Taylor into northern Mexico and ordered General Stephen Watts Kearny into New Mexico and then into California. Following the third directive of the campaign, General in Chief of the U.S. Army Winfield Scott coordinated an amphibious landing of 10,000 soldiers at Vera Cruz, on the Gulf of Mexico. Mexican forces tried to defend their homeland using guerrilla tactics, but U.S. soldiers overcame them in part by terrorizing civilians. Scott acknowledged that the men under his command had "committed atrocities to make Heaven weep and every American of Christian morals blush for his country. . . . Murder, robbery and rape of mothers and daughters in the presence of tied-up males of the families." Some U.S. soldiers were among those sickened by the sight of atrocities. The San Patricio Soldiers, Irish immigrants who had signed up to fight in the U.S. Army, included 100 men who went over to the Mexican side, rather than engage in the killing and the pillaging of churches and convents.

In September 1847, Mexico City surrendered and the war ended. Mexico had been in no shape to resist superior U.S. firepower. The United States paid for Scott's victory with 13,000 lives and $100 million; the Mexicans lost 20,000 lives. In the Treaty of Guadalupe Hidalgo, approved by the Senate in 1848, Mexico agreed to give up its claims to Texas. The United States gained all of Texas as well as the area west of Texas, comprising present-day New Mexico, Arizona, Utah, Nevada, and California; in all, almost one-half of the territory of Mexico was ceded to the United States under the treaty. Male residents of areas formerly held by Mexico were given one year to decide whether to stay in the United States and become citizens or return to Mexico. They were also entitled to retain their titles to the land, a provision that proved difficult to enforce in the face of European American land hunger.

The U.S. government paid Mexico $18.25 million. Of that amount, $15 million was designated as payment for land lost; the rest was restitution to U.S. citizens who might bring claims against Mexico for damaged or destroyed property during the war. Americans had conflicting views of the treaty. Abolitionists saw it as a blood-drenched gift from American taxpayers to slaveholders. Others argued that Polk had squandered a rare opportunity to seize all of Mexico.

The conflict over Texas finally forced politicians to address the issue of slavery, a subject they had successfully avoided since the Missouri Compromise in 1820. Yet the possibility existed that the current two-party system would mean little in a larger battle that pitted the North against the South. The U.S. victory in the war against Mexico roused the passions of abolitionists and their enemies, and proved that the two-party system could not resolve, or even contain, the greatest political issue of the day.

Conclusion

In the 1830s and 1840s, mass population movements affected almost every aspect of American life. Immigrants from western Europe helped to swell the nation's labor force in Midwestern farming communities and eastern cities. The arrival of the Roman Catholic Irish provoked a backlash among native-born Protestants and spawned a nativist political movement. Groups of people bound together by a particular ethnic identity, religious faith, or set of principles found room to set up their own communities apart from other groups. In contrast, Native Americans such as the Cherokee, together with African American slaves, had little control over their own movements; these groups were forced to move so that white men—modest homesteaders as well as wealthy slaveholders—could prosper.

Reformers in the United States and Europe went back and forth across the Atlantic, exchanging ideas related to women's rights, the abolition of slavery, and utopian communities. More generally, as people, ideas, and things moved around the country at a rapid rate, more Americans believed they had the responsibility and the ability to change the nation. Different reform groups adopted different strategies and goals; in many cases, their causes reflected a growing and diverse population. Labor reformers argued that wage-earners must organize themselves into unions in order to protect themselves from economic downturns such as the Panic of 1837. Public school reformers believed that, regardless of where they lived, children should have access to a common form of education. Temperance reformers looked disapprovingly at immigrants who considered drinking alcohol a social pasttime and not a moral vice. Despite this reform ferment, the Whigs and the Democrats remained aloof from many of the most pressing issues of the day; they sought to avoid large-scale disagreements that would serve to alienate large numbers of voters. As a result, the two parties became increasingly irrelevant as Americans debated among themselves the proper course for the country's future.

The optimism that fueled reform movements spilled over into a newly invigorated American nationalism that encouraged military conquest. As European Americans pushed the boundaries of the country west and south, they clashed with Indians and foreign powers who claimed those lands as their own. Yet some Americans believed the nation must follow a "manifest destiny" to expand its borders the length and breadth of the continent. The Mexican-American War highlighted the restlessness among land-hungry slave owners and antislavery forces alike. The clash over the Wilmot Proviso in particular opened a new chapter in the wider debate over slavery. In considering the proviso, members of Congress gave up their party loyalties as Democrats or Whigs and began to think of themselves as Northerners and Southerners. When Wilmot proclaimed that he wanted to preserve the West for his "own color," he revealed that even antislavery Northerners did not necessarily consider black people as their equals. When Southerners indicated that even the vast expanse of Texas would not satisfy their desire for land, they revealed that the conflict of slavery was about to enter and new and dangerous stage.

For Review

1. Give examples of the ways that migration or immigration led certain groups to change their social or legal identities.

2. Why did so many northerners oppose both slavery and racial equality? (Consider the conflict over the western territories.) What were the various forms of migration that influenced the debate over slavery?

3. What reasons did Americans have for staying in motion during the 1830s and 1840s?

4. Why did some women see their role as social reformers as an extension of their roles as wives and mothers in the home?

5. In what ways did certain reforms of this period overlap with and reinforce one another?

6. Did all opponents of the Mexican War agree with one another? Why or why not?

7. How was slavery intertwined with manifest destiny and the Mexican War?

8. In what ways did sectional tension between the North and South increase during this period? How were those tensions expressed?

CHRONOLOGY: 1832–1848

1833	Great Britain abolishes slavery.
1835	Texas revolts against Mexico.
1836	Congress passes gag rule on antislavery petitions.
	Republic of Texas founded.
1837	Panic of 1837.
1838	Cherokee removal begins; Trail of Tears.
1840	Liberty party founded.
1841	John Tyler assumes presidency after death of William Henry Harrison.
	Supreme Court rules in favor of Amistad Africans.
1844	Mormon leader Joseph Smith killed by mob in Nauvoo, Illinois.
1845	Irish potato famine.
	Frederick Douglass, Narrative of the Life of Frederick Douglass.
	Texas becomes twenty-eighth state.
1846	Great Britain cedes southern part of Oregon Country to United States.
	Mexican-American War begins.
1847	United States wins battles of Buena Vista, Vera Cruz, Mexico City.
1848	Treaty of Guadalupe Hidalgo ends Mexican-American War.
	Women's rights convention in Seneca Falls, New York.
	Popular revolutions sweep Europe.

Created Equal Online

For more Created Equal resources, including suggestions on sites to visit and books to read, go to **MyHistoryLab.com**.

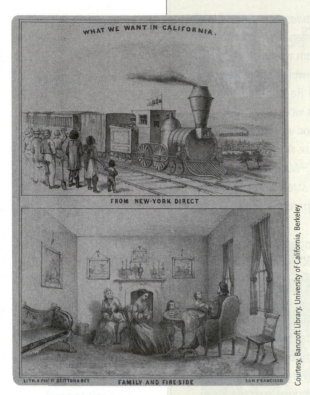

WHAT WE WANT IN CALIFORNIA.

FROM NEW-YORK DIRECT

FAMILY AND FIRE-SIDE

Courtesy, Bancroft Library, University of California, Berkeley

■ This pair of cartoons, titled "What We Want in California," suggests that migrants from the East hoped to reestablish a middle-class ideal in their new home. Above, an Indian family watches the arrival of a train from New York. Below, a European American family relaxes in a well-furnished parlor.

Although the Treaty of Guadalupe Hidalgo guaranteed U.S. citizenship rights to Mexicans, those rights were not enforced under the law. Many Mexicans found themselves vulnerable to violence and land dispossession perpetrated by the growing European American majority. They lacked political voice as well, as delegates to California's constitutional convention in 1849 stipulated that only white *Californios* (descendants of the original Spanish colonists) were entitled to vote, over the objections of the eight *Californios* among the forty-eight delegates in attendance. The majority of delegates also approved a measure prohibiting Indians and blacks from testifying against whites in court.

At midcentury the legal, economic, and cultural tensions among different groups in California mirrored tensions within the country as a whole. Migration into the Midwest accelerated. Slavery shaped life in the South, though most white southerners were not plantation owners. Rapid population growth, the coming together of many different cultures, and dramatic economic changes all fueled the conflict over slavery. The controversy surrounding California statehood revealed that awkward and unjust congressional "compromises" would satisfy neither side in a debate that was becoming increasingly strident and even violent. All over the nation, in the pages of the popular press, on the streets of Boston, in the cotton fields of Alabama, no less than in the courts of California, Americans gradually united around a radical proposition: there could be no compromise on the issue of whether human beings could be held as property.

Regional Economies and Conflicts

■ *To what extent, and in what ways, were U.S. regional economies interdependent by 1860? Were certain regions, or groups of people, outside the emerging national economy?*

It is tempting to view the decade of the 1850s with an eye toward the impending firestorm of 1861. However, in the early 1850s, few Americans could have anticipated the Civil War. At midcentury, the United States was going through a period of rapid transition. New developments such as railroads, the factory system, and more efficient farm equipment led to significant changes in regional economies and began to give shape to an emerging national economy. Continued European American migration into the Midwest, the Great Plains, and the Southwest intensified conflicts over land with Native Americans and Mexicans. Annexation of land in the Southwest and West and the conquest of Indians on the Plains produced wrenching social upheavals for Native Americans in those regions. Meanwhile, Americans continued to wrestle with the role of human bondage in this rapidly changing society. While the South continued to rely on slavery for staple-crop production, a free labor ideology grew stronger in the North.

Territorial expansion in the nineteenth century
Date of territorial acquisition, i.e., 1850
Date of statehood, i.e., *1896*

- Original thirteen states 1783
- Great Britain Cession 1783
- Louisiana Purchase 1803
- Acquired from Great Britain 1818
- Florida Purchase 1819
- Acquired from Great Britain 1842
- Texas Annexation 1845
- Oregon Country 1846
- Mexican Cession 1848
- Gadsden Purchase 1853

■ **MAP 13.1 Territorial Expansion in the Nineteenth Century**

As a result of the Mexican War (1846–1848), the United States won the territory west of Texas by conquest. In 1853, James Gadsden, U.S. ambassador to Mexico, received congressional approval to pay Mexico $15 million for 55,000 square miles in present-day southern Arizona and New Mexico. That year marked the end of U.S. continental expansion.

NATIVE AMERICAN ECONOMIES TRANSFORMED

On the Plains, Indians confronted profound transformations in their way of life. Forced to relocate from the Southeast to Indian Territory (present-day Oklahoma), the Five Southern ("Civilized") Tribes—the Cherokee, Choctaw, Creek, Chickasaw, and Seminole—grappled with the task of rebuilding their political institutions. By the 1850s, the Cherokee had established a new capital at Tahlequah and set up public schools. They founded the Cherokee Female Seminary, with a curriculum modeled after that of an eastern women's college, Mount Holyoke in Massachusetts. They also published a Cherokee newspaper (the *Advocate*) and created a flourishing print culture in their own language.

In the 1850s, U.S. officials negotiated treaties with various Plains Indian groups to enable European Americans to move west without fear of attack. Most migrants were bent on heading straight for California or the Northwest, traversing the Plains, which they called the Great American Desert in the mistaken belief that the absence of trees there demonstrated the infertility of the soil. The Fort Laramie Treaty of 1851 and the Treaty of Fort Atkinson three years later provided that the government could build roads and establish forts along western trails and that, in return, Indians would be compensated with supplies and food for their loss of hunting rights in the region. A young Cheyenne woman, Iron Teeth, recalled "the government presents" to her people in these terms: "We were given beef, but we did not care for this kind of meat. Great piles of bacon were stacked upon the prairies and distributed to us, but we used it only to make fires or to grease robes for tanning." She and her family sought out other items from government trading posts: "brass kettles, coffee-pots, curve-bladed butcher knives, boxes of black and white thread."

MAP

United States Territorial Expansion in the 1850s

As whites moved west in large numbers to "scrape the mountains clean and drain the rivers dry," they disregarded U.S. treaties and tribal boundaries and overran the fragile settlements of Indians. Taking leave of the Fort Laramie conclave of 1851, Cut Nose of the Arapaho declared, "I will go home satisfied. I will sleep sound, and not have to watch my horses in the night, or be afraid for my women and children. We have to live on these streams and in the hills, and I would be glad if the whites would pick out a place for themselves and not come into our grounds." But within a generation, the Plains Indians were besieged by the technology, weaponry, and sheer numbers of newcomers heading west.

LAND CONFLICTS IN THE SOUTHWEST

To the southwest, the United States had gained control over a vast expanse of land, provoking legal and political conflicts over the rights and labor of the people who lived there, both natives and newcomers. Under the terms of the Treaty of Guadalupe Hidalgo, Mexico ceded not only California but also the province of New Mexico, territory that included the present-day states of New Mexico, Arizona, Utah, Nevada, and western Colorado. In 1853, the United States bought an additional tract of land from Mexico, 55,000 acres located in the area south of the Gila River (in present-day New Mexico and Arizona). Overseen by the U.S. secretary of war, a Mississippi planter named Jefferson Davis, the agreement was called the **Gadsden Purchase** (after James Gadsden, a railroad promoter and one of the American negotiators).

In Texas, newly arrived European Americans battled native *Tejanos* (people of Mexican origin or descent) for political and economic supremacy. White migrants from the southern United States brought their slaves with them to the region, claiming that the institution of slavery was crucial for commercial development. German immigrants came to central and east Texas, founding towns with German names such as Fredericksburg, Weimar, and Schulenburg. During the 1850s, commercial farming continued to replace subsistence homesteading as the cattle industry spread and the railroads penetrated the region. Although European Americans monopolized the courts and regional political institutions, *Tejanos* retained cultural influence throughout Texas, dominating the cuisine and styles of music and architecture.

The career of José Antonio Navarro reveals the complex political and cultural history of Texas during this period. Navarro was born in 1795 to a prominent family in San Antonio. Sympathetic to a *Tejano* uprising against Spain in 1813, his family had to flee the escalating violence and seek refuge in the United States. With other *Tejanos*, the Navarro family resented Spanish control of Texas, charging that Spain wanted only to extract as much wealth as possible from the region.

A childhood accident left Navarro lame, and because he could not join his friends in their outdoor activities—hunting, playing—he turned to reading and studying. He gained respect as a scholar and a leader. After his family returned to San Antonio, the young Navarro was elected mayor of the city (in 1822) at the age of twenty-six. He soon became a friend and supporter of Stephen Austin, believing that Americans would help bring prosperity to Texas. A firm believer in local rule, Navarro objected to Mexico's high-handed control of Texas. As a member of the joint state legislature (representing Texas and Coahuila) and later as a representative to the national Mexican Congress, Navarro tried to circumvent antislavery laws. He hoped to encourage U.S. slaveholders to move to Texas. In 1836, Navarro joined with a group of Texians (U.S.-born Texans) and signed Texas's Declaration of Independence from Mexico.

> *In Texas, newly arrived European Americans battled native Tejanos (people of Mexican origin or descent) for political and economic supremacy.*

Austin and Navarro were committed to furthering harmonious relations between Texians and *Tejanos*. Yet Austin's death in 1836 left Navarro with few European American allies. When Texas joined the Union in 1846, Navarro embraced U.S. citizenship, but he deplored the newcomers' aggression in seizing *Tejanos*' land. The Americans' motto seemed to be, "If a *[Tejano]* man will not sell his land, his widow will." Navarro now saw the Americans as the enemies of his family and people. Over the next few years, he watched as *Tejanos* became a minority in San Antonio, and political and economic power shifted to the European Americans. During the course of his lifetime, he had remained loyal to his *Tejano* interests, opposing Spain, then Mexico, and now the United States for this disregard for the principle of local rule. He died in 1871, his dream of *Tejano* equality shattered.

Some Spanish-speaking residents in the Southwest reacted violently when U.S. courts disregarded the land titles held by *Californios* and *Tejanos*. In the early 1850s, California authorities battled Mexican social bandits such as Joaquin Murrieta, who, with his men, raided European American settlements. Murrieta and others argued that they were justified in stealing from privileged European Americans who, they claimed, disregarded the lives and property of Mexicans. In 1859, in the Rio Grande Valley of Texas, tensions between the *Tejano* majority and groups of European American law enforcement officers called the Texas Rangers erupted into full-scale warfare. Juan Cortina, who had fought on the side of Mexico during the Mexican War, orchestrated attacks on European Americans and their property in the vicinity of Brownsville. U.S. retaliation led to Cortina's War, pitting the Mexican leader against a young U.S. colonel, Robert E. Lee. Cortina became a hero to *Tejanos*. "You have been robbed of your property, incarcerated, chased, murdered, and hunted like wild beasts," he declared; "to me is entrusted the work of breaking the chains of your slavery."

The rich print culture developed by Hispanics in the Southwest helped to shape and galvanize public opinion against U.S. seizures of Hispanic lands. For example, in the 1850s, Spanish speakers in southern California published a newspaper dedicated to promoting social justice. Its name was *El Clamor Público* (the Public Clamor).

ETHNIC AND ECONOMIC DIVERSITY IN THE MIDWEST

Compared to the Southwest, the Midwest revealed a distinctive social make-up shaped by the European immigrants and the New Englanders who settled there. The Yankee Strip (named for the northeasterners who migrated there) ran through northern Ohio, Indiana, and Illinois and encompassed the states of Michigan, Wisconsin, and Minnesota. Here migrants from New England settled and established public schools and Congregational churches. Immigrants from western Europe also made a home in this region—the Germans, Belgians, and Swiss in Wisconsin, the Scandinavians in Minnesota. At times cultural conflict wracked even the smallest rural settlements. In some Wisconsin villages, equally matched numbers of Yankees and Germans contended for control over the local public schools, with the group in power posting notices for school board elections in its own language, hoping that its rivals would not show up at the polls.

> *The Midwest revealed a distinctive social make-up shaped by the European immigrants and the New Englanders who settled there.*

The lower Midwest, including the southern portions of Ohio, Indiana, and Illinois, retained strong cultural ties to the southern states, from which many settlers had migrated. Though residing in free states, they maintained broad support for the institution of slavery. In some cases they outnumbered their Yankee counterparts and managed to shape the legal system in a way that reflected a distinct antiblack bias. For example, Indiana's state constitution, approved in 1851, prohibited black people from voting, making contracts with whites, testifying in trials that involved whites, and even entering the state.

Most rural midwestern households followed the seasonal rhythms characteristic of traditional systems of agriculture. However, by the mid-nineteenth century, family farming had become dependent on expensive machinery and subject to the national and international grain markets. John Deere's steel plow (invented in 1837) and Cyrus McCormick's horse-drawn mechanical reaper (patented in 1854) boosted levels of grain production. Improved agricultural efficiency meant that the Midwest, both upper and lower, was fast becoming the breadbasket of the nation.

REGIONAL ECONOMIES OF THE SOUTH

Like the Midwest, the South at midcentury had its own diversity. The South Atlantic states encompassed a number of regional economies. Bolstered by the high price of cotton on the world market, slave plantations prospered in the Black Belt, a wide swath of fertile soil stretching west from Georgia. In many areas of the South, planters concentrated their money and energy on cotton, diverting slaves from nonagricultural labor to toil in the fields. During the 1850s, enslaved Virginia sawmill laborers, South Carolina skilled artisans, and Georgia textile mill operatives all found themselves reduced to the status of cotton hands. In some cases, white laborers took their places in mills and workshops. In other parts of the South, slaves combined field work with nonagricultural work. For example, on expansive low-country South Carolina rice plantations, slaves worked in the fields, but they also processed the raw material, preparing it for market.

Increasingly, northern critics described the South as a land of economic extremes, with wealthy planters enjoying their white-columned mansions while degraded blacks slaved obediently in the fields. The reality was more complicated. Even among whites, there were huge variations in material conditions and daily experiences. A large amount of wealth in land and slaves was concentrated among a small percentage of the white population, and many nonslaveholding whites were **tenant farmers,** leasing their land, mules, and implements from wealthy planters. In some areas as many as one of five farms was operated by tenant farmers; many of these were young men who aspired to become planters and slaveowners themselves some day.

At the same time, about half the total southern white population consisted of yeoman farmers, families that owned an average of fifty acres and produced most of what they consumed themselves (with the occasional help of a leased slave or a wage-earning white person). In upcountry Georgia and South Carolina, yeoman farmers maintained local economies that were little affected by the cotton culture of the great planters in the Black Belt. These families grew what they needed: corn for themselves and their livestock and small amounts of cotton that the women spun, wove, and then sewed into clothing. Men and women alike labored in neighborhood networks of exchange, trading farm produce such as milk and eggs for services such as shoemaking and blacksmithing. Nevertheless, even modest farmers shared with the great planters a southern way of life that prized the independence of white households and the supremacy of whites over blacks.

> About half the total southern white population consisted of yeoman farmers, families that owned an average of fifty acres.

The institution of slavery discouraged immigrants from moving to the rural South in large numbers. German artisans realized that slave labor would undercut their own wages, and Scandinavian farmers understood that they could not compete with large planters in terms of landowning or slave owning. However, the ethnic diversity of southern port cities offered a striking contrast to the countryside, where native-born Protestants predominated. In 1860, 54 percent of all skilled workers and 69 percent of unskilled workers in Mobile, Alabama, were immigrants. On assignment from the *New York Times* in the 1850s, journalist Frederick Law Olmsted noted that in New Orleans, German and Irish workers labored shoulder to shoulder with slave artisans, and although white immigrants "were rapidly displacing the slaves in all sorts of work," it was still possible to glimpse an "Irishman waiting on negro masons."

Throughout the slave states, black people continued to challenge the underpinnings of white supremacy. On the back roads of the plantation counties, late at night, poor workers of both races colluded against the planter elite: slaves swapped hams pilfered from smokehouses and bags of cotton lifted from storehouses for cash and goods offered by landless whites.

Southern blacks were a diverse group. In the cities, masters allowed highly skilled slaves to hire themselves out and keep part of the money they earned for themselves. In their pride of craft and in their relative freedom to come and go as they pleased, these people inhabited a world that was neither completely slave nor completely free. Located primarily in the upper South and in the largest towns, communities composed of free people of color supported churches and clandestine schools, mocking the white notion that all black people possessed a childlike temperament and were incapable of caring for themselves. During the 1850s, the population of free people of color increased from 54,333 to 58,042 in Virginia; in North Carolina the number increased from 27,463 to 30,463. The reality of southern society was not captured by the simple picture of white prosperity and black enslavement. Not all blacks were enslaved field hands, and not all whites were privileged landowners. The widespread mythology masked a more complicated social reality.

A FREE LABOR IDEOLOGY IN THE NORTH

In reaction to the southern slave system, the rural areas of the Northeast and Mid-Atlantic spawned a potent **free labor ideology,** which held that workers should reap what they sow, unfettered by legal systems of slavery and indentured servitude. Free labor advocates glorified the family farmer, the sturdy landowner of modest means who labored according to the dictates of the season and owed his soul—and his vote and the land he tilled—to no master. Nevertheless, the reality that sustained this ideal was eroding in the North during the 1850s.

More and more northerners were earning wages by working for bosses, rather than tilling their own land. Faced with competition from Midwestern farmers and burdened by unfavorable growing conditions imposed by rocky soil and a long winter, New Englanders were migrating to nearby towns and mill villages and to the West. By 1860, the region's textile and shoemaking industries were largely mechanized. From New Hampshire to Rhode Island, growing numbers of water-powered factories perched along the fall line, where rivers spilled swiftly out of the foothills and into the coastal plain. The all-white factory workforce included men and women, adults and children, Irish Catholics and native-born Protestants, failed farmers and young men and women eager to leave the uncertain, hardscrabble life of the countryside for the promise of the mill towns.

Yet the process of industrialization was an uneven one. For example, rural shoemaking workers labored at home, producing shoes for merchant capitalists who provided the raw materials and paid them by the piece. In contrast, in the huge new shoe factories of Lynn, Massachusetts, one worker at a Singer sewing machine achieved the same output as eleven people doing the same task by hand in their homes. In the seaport cities, wage earning had become the norm, although many men and women continued to toil in the hope that they might eventually work for themselves. Thus the seamstress aspired to own a dress shop, the hotel waiter a tavern, the journeyman carpenter a small business.

Maine textile workers, with their shuttles, pose for a formal portrait around 1860. Although women factory workers developed a collective identity distinct from that of middle-class wives, most young, native-born women eventually married and withdrew from the paid labor force. Many male factory workers were skeptical that women could or should play an effective role in labor organizations such as unions. Nevertheless, women workers in a number of industries, including textiles and shoes, formed labor organizations in the antebellum period.

In New York, Boston, Cincinnati, and elsewhere, large numbers of Irish newcomers successfully challenged small numbers of black workers for jobs at the lowest echelons of the labor force. In 1853, fugitive slave Frederick Douglass noted with dismay, "White men are becoming house-servants, cooks and stewards on vessels—at hotels. They are becoming porters, stevedores, hod-carriers, brickmakers, white-washers and barbers, so that blacks can scarcely find the means of subsistence." Stung by the contempt of Yankee Protestants, impoverished Irish Catholics sought to assert their equality through skin color. They distanced themselves from African Americans by claiming a white skin as a badge of privilege over the former slaves, a badge of equality with the native born.

Although northerners in general contrasted themselves to the "backward slave South," their region of the country retained elements of unfree labor systems. New Jersey did not officially emancipate the last of its slaves until 1846, and throughout the North, vestiges of slavery lingered through the mid-nineteenth century. As a group of disproportionately poor people, blacks in New England, the Mid-Atlantic, and the Midwest were vulnerable to labor exploitation, including indentured servitude and a system of "apprenticeship" whereby black children were taken from their parents and forced to work for whites. In Delaware, an African American charged with a petty crime could be "disposed as a servant" by court authorities to the highest bidder for a term of seven years.

Many nonslave workers did not receive pay for their labors. While the measure of a white man was rendered more and more in cash terms, wives and mothers throughout the country performed almost all of their work in the home without monetary compensation. On farms and in textile mills such as those of Pawtucket, Rhode Island, children played a key role in the livelihood of individual households but received little or nothing in cash wages. Some members of the white working classes began to condemn what they called wage slavery, a system that deprived them of what they considered a fair reward for their labors and left them at the mercy of merchant capitalists and factory bosses. These workers charged that they were paid so little by employers, their plight was similar to that of black slaves in the South.

> *Which groups of people were entitled to American citizenship, with all the rights and privileges that the term implied?*

Indeed, although Northerners did not often acknowledge the fact, their own region helped to sustain the institution of southern slavery in several ways: by purchasing raw cotton from planters, by tolerating the system of bondage as long as it was confined to the South, and by implementing their own discriminatory laws that in most states barred blacks from voting and sending their children to public schools.

While different regions developed specialized economies, these regions relied on each other for the production of staple crops and manufactured goods. The result was a national economy. Southern slaves produced the cotton processed in New England textile mills. Midwestern farmers grew the grain that fed eastern consumers. California Forty-Niners discovered the gold that expanded the national currency supply. Yet these patterns of economic interdependence were insufficient to resolve a persistent political question: which groups of people were entitled to American citizenship, with all the rights and privileges that the term implied?

Individualism Versus Group Identity

◼ *In what ways did the American ideal of individualism create tensions with the group stereotypes and prejudices enshrined in 1850s laws and customs?*

In every region of the United States, discriminating ideas and practices began to exert greater force. People were defined ever more strongly on the basis of their nationality, language, religion, and skin color. They were more and more limited in their legal status and the jobs they could obtain. Degrading images of legally vulnerable groups—blacks, Chinese, Hispanics—became a part of popular culture, in the songs people sang and the pictures they saw in books and magazines. Through these means, native-born Americans of British stock sought to distance themselves from people of color and from immigrants.

Paradoxically, some writers also began to highlight the idea of American individualism during this time. Such authors extolled what they considered the universal qualities embedded in American nationhood. They believed that the United States consisted not of distinctive and competing groups, but of a collection of individuals, all bent on pursuing their own self-interest, variously defined. They believed that the "representative" American was ambitious and acquisitive, eager to make more money and buy new things.

Yet not everyone could afford to embrace this optimistic form of individualism. Many who were marginalized found emotional support, and in some cases even political power, in a strong group identity. For example, on the Plains, the Sioux Indians resisted the idea that U.S. officials could carve up territory and sell land to individual farmers at the expense of a people who pursued the buffalo across artificial political boundaries. During negotiations at

George Caleb Bingham, *Raftsmen Playing Cards*, 1847. Saint Louis Art Museum, Ezra H. Linley Fund by exchange (50.1934)

■ Just as American writers explored questions of national identity, American artists portrayed everyday scenes related to the vitality of American enterprise and democracy. This painting, *Raftsmen Playing Cards* (1847), was one from George Caleb Bingham's series of pictures of Missouri rivermen. A contemporary observer speculated that the youth on the right is "a mean and cunning scamp, probably the black sheep of a good family, and a sort of vagabond idler." Large rivers such as the Missouri and Mississippi remained powerful symbols of freedom in the American imagination.

Fort Laramie in 1851, Black Hawk, a leader of the Oglala Sioux, condemned the whites with his understatement, "You have split my land and I don't like it." In contrast to the Plains Indians, who wanted no role in American politics, African Americans and white women strove for full citizenship rights. These groups looked forward to the day when each person was accorded the same rights and was free to pursue his or her own talents and ambitions.

PUTTING INTO PRACTICE IDEAS OF SOCIAL INFERIORITY

Everywhere, European American men sought to achieve or preserve the most stable, well-paying, and appealing jobs for themselves. By promoting ideas related to the inferiority of African Americans, Hispanics, and immigrants, white men could justify barring these groups from the rights of citizenship and landownership as well as from nonmenial kinds of employment. In Texas, Mexican leader Juan Cortina condemned Anglo interlopers whose "brimful of laws" facilitated the seizure of *Tejanos'* land by U.S. law enforcement agents and the courts. In California, U.S. officials justified the exclusion of blacks, Indians, Chinese, and the poorest Mexicans from citizenship rights by claiming that members of these groups were nonwhite, or in the words of one state judge writing in 1854, "not of white blood." (Of course, the concept of "white blood" has no scientific basis; the different blood types—A, B, AB, and O—are found among all peoples.)

The precarious social status of various groups was revealed in patterns of their work. In California, white men pursued opportunities on farms and in factories while increasing numbers of Chinese men labored as laundrymen and domestic servants. Indians toiled as field hands under white supervision. In rural Texas, Anglos established plantations and ranches while more and more Mexicans worked as *vaqueros* (cowboys), shepherds, sidewalk vendors, and freighters. In Massachusetts mill towns, white men and women served as the forefront of

Professor George Howe on the Subordination of Women

Interpreting History

Antebellum southern elites prized what they called "natural" hierarchical social relations: the authority of fathers and husbands over daughters and wives, parents over children, rich over poor, and whites over blacks. According to slaveholders, clergy, and scholars, these relationships provided social stability and ensured that the weak and dependent would receive care from the rich and powerful. In July 1850, George Howe, professor of biblical literature at the Theological Seminary at Columbia, South Carolina, addressed the graduating class of a private women's academy. Howe suggested that the roles of women (elite white women) were enduring and never changing.

■ Louisa McCord was a member of an elite slaveholding family in South Carolina and an ardent supporter of slavery. Though an accomplished essayist, she believed that white women should remain subordinate to their fathers and husbands. In 1856 she wrote, "The positions of women and children are in truth as essentially states of bondage as any other, the differences being in degree, not kind." She added that the "true definition of slavery" thus "applies equally to the position of women in the most civilized and enlightened countries."

The Endowments, Position and Education of Woman. An Address Delivered Before the Hemans and Sigourney Societies of the Female High School at Limestone Springs

The duties of life to all human beings are arduous, its objects are noble—each stage of its progress is preparatory to some other stage, and the whole a preparation to an interminable existence, upon which, in one sense, we are hereafter to enter, and in another, have already entered. Others may slightly regard the employments, trials and joys of the school girl. I am

disposed to put on them a higher value. Our wives, sisters, and our mothers were in the same position yesterday. You will occupy a like [position] with them tomorrow. Whatever of virtue, of patient endurance, of poignant suffering, of useful labor, of noble impulse, of generous endeavor, of influence exerted on society for its good, has been exhibited in their example, in a few short years we shall see exhibited also in yours.

To woman, . . . there must be ascribed . . . acuteness in her powers of perception, . . . instincts . . . and emotions. When these are powerfully excited there is a wonderful vigor and determination of will, and a ready discovery of expedients to accomplish her wishes. She has readier sympathies, her fountain of tears is nearer the surface, but her emotions may not be so constant and

---

an industrial labor force while many African Americans of both sexes and all ages were confined to work in kitchens and outdoors as sweepers, cart drivers, and hawkers of goods.

Despite the divergent regional economies that shaped them, emerging ideologies of racial inferiority were strikingly similar. European Americans persisted in focusing on physical appearances, and they stereotyped all Chinese, Mexicans, and African Americans as promiscuous, crafty, "degraded," and intellectually inferior to whites. They characterized these groups as "cheap labor" who got by with little money: the Chinese supposedly could subsist on rice, Mexicans on beans and *tortillas*, blacks on the "fatback" of the pig. Such prejudices, in places as diverse as Boston, San Antonio, and San Francisco, prevented many people of color from reaching the limits of their own talents in mid-nineteenth-century America.

"A TEEMING NATION"—AMERICA IN LITERATURE

Ideas about ethnic and racial difference coexisted with notions of American individualism, which stressed forms of universal equality. The variety of voices that gave expression to the national ideals of personal striving and ambition suggested the growth, energy, and vitality of the United States in the 1850s. In the Northeast, the writers Ralph Waldo Emerson, Henry David Thoreau, Herman Melville, and Walt Whitman promoted a robust sensibility attuned to the challenges posed by the rigors of both the external world of natural beauty and the inner world of the spirit.

permanent as those of man. She has greater readiness and tact, purer and more noble and unselfish desires and impulses, and a higher degree of veneration for the virtuous and exalted, and when she has found the way of truth, a heart more constant and more susceptible to all those influences which come from above. To the gentleness and quiet of her nature, to its affection and sympathy, that religion which pronounces its benediction on the peace-makers and the merciful, which recommends to them the ornament of a meek and quiet spirit, which, in the sight of the Lord, is of a great price, addresses itself with more force and greater attraction than it addresses man. Born to lean upon others, rather than to stand independently by herself, and to confide in an arm stronger than hers, her mind turns more readily to the higher power which brought her into being. . . .

Providence, then, and her own endowments mark out the proper province of woman. In some cases she may strive for the mastery, but to rule with the hand of power was never designed for her. When she thus unsexes herself she is despised and detested by man and woman alike. England's Queen Victoria at the present moment, if not more feared, is far more beloved in the quiet of her domestic life, than Elizabeth was, the most feared of her female Sovereigns.

Howe ends his address by drawing an implicit comparison between the South and the North. Like many Southerners, he associated the North with labor radicalism, abolitionism, and challenges to the "natural" position of women.

When women go about haranguing promiscuous assemblies of men, lecturing in public, either on infidelity or religion, on slavery, on war or peace—when they meet together in conventions and pass resolutions on grave questions of State—when they set themselves up to manufacture a public opinion for their own advantage and exaltation—when they meet together in organized bodies and pass resolutions about the "rights of woman," and claim for her a voice and a vote in the appointment of civil rulers, and in the government, whether of Church or State, she is stepping forth from her rightful sphere and becomes disgusting and unlovely, just in proportion as she assumes to be a man.

QUESTIONS

1. *Professor Howe clearly believes that men and women are "naturally" different from one another. But do you think he would consider women "inferior" to men? Why or why not?*

2. *Is Howe suggesting here that husband-wife relations are similar to slaveholder-slave relations? Support your response.*

3. *What were the tensions implicit in white women's status, considering that they were neither full citizens like their husbands nor slaves like the workers who toiled on their behalf?*

Source: George Howe, The Endowments, Position and Education of Woman. An Address Delivered Before the Hemans and Sigourney Societies of the Female High School at Limestone Springs, July 23, 1850 (Columbia, SC: I. C. Morgan, 1850), 5, 9, 10–11.

Some forms of literature offered an explicit critique of American materialism. According to Emerson, people were too concerned about material possessions; as he put it, things were "in the saddle," riding everyone. During the 1850s, Thoreau's work became more explicitly focused on nature. In his book *Walden* (1854), he described swimming in the Massachusetts pond of the same name: "In such transparent and seemingly bottomless water, reflecting the clouds, I seemed to be floating through the air as in a balloon." An appreciation of the wonders of nature—wonders that could be felt and tasted, as well as seen—amounted to a powerful force of democratization; anyone and everyone could participate. In turn, Thoreau actively supported the abolition of slavery; his love of nature formed the foundation of his belief in the universal dignity of all people in general and the cause of freedom for black people in particular.

In contrast, other writers celebrated busy-ness, whether in the field or workshop. In the introduction to his book of poetry *Leaves of Grass* (1855), Walt Whitman captured the restlessness of a people on the move: "Here is not merely a nation but a teeming nation of nations. Here is action untied from strings necessarily blind to particulars and details magnificently moving in vast masses." To Whitman, the expansiveness of the American landscape mirrored the American soul, "the largeness and generosity of the spirit of the citizen." His sensuous "Song of Myself" constituted an anthem for all Americans poised, gloriously diverse in their individuality (and their sexuality), to exploit the infinite possibilities of both body and spirit: "I dote on myself, there is a lot of me and all so luscious."

DOCUMENT

"Walden" by Henry David Thoreau

CHALLENGES TO INDIVIDUALISM

Many men and women remained skeptical of—and, in some cases, totally estranged from—the wondrous possibilities inherent in Whitman's phrase, "Me, Me going in for my chances." In northern cities, individualism spawned the kind of creative genius necessary for technological innovation and dynamic economic change, but it had little meaning for Native Americans in the West, most of whom were desperately seeking a collective response to new threats posed by cattle ranchers and the U.S. cavalry. On the Great Plains, groups such as the Pawnee performed ceremonies and rituals that celebrated kinship and village life above the individual.

African Americans in the North forged a strong sense of group identity. Though they rejected notions of white people's "racial" superiority, blacks had little choice but to think of themselves as a group separate and distinct from whites. Their sense of group solidarity was manifested in everyday life and in political rhetoric and action. In northern cities, blacks took in boarders and joined mutual-aid societies in order to affirm the collective interests of the larger black community. In contrast, well-to-do whites were increasingly emphasizing the sanctity of the nuclear family, composed solely of parents and children. Black leaders criticized the racist laws and ideas that affected the lives of black men, women, and children. For example, the charismatic Boston preacher Maria Stewart denounced the twin evils of racial and gender prejudice for condemning all black women to a life of menial labor: "How long shall the fair daughters of Africa be compelled to bury their minds and talents beneath a load of iron pots and kettles? The [white] Americans have practised nothing but head-work these 200 years, and we have done their drudgery."

Bettmann/CORBIS

■ Isabella Baumfree was born into slavery in New York State in 1797. Thirty years later she escaped from bondage and became a preacher. In 1843, she changed her name to Sojourner Truth. A powerful orator, she spoke on behalf of abolitionism and urged white women's rights activists to embrace the cause of enslaved women. Truth sold small cards, called *cartes de visite*, to support herself. On this card, a portrait taken in 1864, she notes that she must sell her image ("the Shadow") to make a living.

Northern blacks furthered a sense of group identity through their own literary societies and newspapers. The purpose of black literary societies, such as the Boston Afric-American Female Intelligence Society, was to educate its members and uphold standards of morality. These groups grew out of the same impulse that led to the founding of African American newspapers during this period. As the black reading public increased, papers such as *Freedom's Journal* and *Colored American* published news from around the world, as well as highlighting biographical sketches of figures such as the poet Phillis Wheatley and Haitian revolutionary Toussaint L'Overture. Frederick Douglass published a series of papers in the 1850s, including the *North Star* (1847–1851), *Frederick Douglass' Paper* (1851–1858), and *Douglass' Monthly* (1858–1860). These publications informed readers of the growing controversy over slavery and also featured book reviews and works of fiction by Charles Dickens, Herman Melville, and Nathaniel Hawthorne, among other writers. The papers promoted the idea that their readers had a special identity not only as black Americans, but also as citizens of a wider literary world.

Similarly, some groups of women embraced a collective identity of womanhood, although the definition of that identity took several forms. For example, in the North, writers such as Catharine Beecher articulated a vision of female self-sacrifice fueled by family obligations and emotional relationships. Beecher declared that self-sacrifice formed the "grand law of the system" by which women should live their lives. Informed by religious devotion and sustained by labors of love in the home, this female world offered an alternative to the masculine individualism necessary to profit-seeking, whether on the family farm or in the bank or textile mill. Yet middle-class women believed they could take pride in rearing virtuous citizens and caring for overworked husbands. Sarah Willis Parton (Fanny Fern) cautioned her readers in a series of sketches published in 1853 (*Fern Leaves from Fanny's Portfolio*) that marriage is "the hardest way on earth of getting a living. You never know when your work is done."

Well-to-do white women in the Northeast yearned to be productive and useful although they stood outside the cash-based market economy. Nevertheless, other groups of women cherished different kinds of aspirations. Organizers of the country's first conference devoted to the status of women, the Seneca Falls Convention held in upstate New York in 1848, derived inspiration from the abolitionist movement and protested the efforts of white men to exclude women from formal participation in it. In their demands for women's rights, Elizabeth Cady Stanton and Lucretia Mott linked the plight of the slave with the plight of free women, arguing that white men exploited and denigrated members of both groups. Stanton, Mott, and others received crucial support from African American leaders such as Sojourner Truth and Frederick Douglass. Delegates to Seneca Falls (including Douglass) approved a document called the "Declaration of Sentiments," modeled after the Declaration of Independence: "We hold these truths to be self-evident: that all men and women are created equal." This group of women thus claimed for themselves a revolutionary heritage and all the rights and privileges of citizenship: to own property in their own names, to vote, to attend schools of higher learning, and to participate "in the various trades, professions, and commerce."

> *Critiques of the dominant culture could at times uphold its lofty ideals while condemning everyday reality.*

Many women, including enslaved workers throughout the South and hard-pressed needleworkers toiling in cramped New York City tenements, could not devote themselves full-time to the care of hearth and home, nor could they aspire to a career of public agitation. In her autobiographical novel *Our Nig; or, Sketches from the Life of a Free Black, in a Two-Story White House, North* (1859), Harriet Wilson wrote bitterly of the fate of women such as her mother, a woman "early deprived of parental guardianship, far removed from relatives . . . left to guide her tiny boat over life's surges alone and inexperienced." Like the book's main character, Alfrado, Wilson herself had suffered at the hands of tyrannical white women employers, but at the end of the story Alfrado achieves a measure of dignity and independence for herself by setting up a small business. She thus offered an explicit challenge to both the arrogance of propertied white men and the homebound sentimentality of wealthy white women.

In sum, there was no single, transcendent American identity in the mid-nineteenth century. Yet critiques of the dominant culture could at times uphold its lofty ideals while condemning everyday reality. In his 1852 speech "The Meaning of July Fourth for the Negro," delivered in Rochester, New York, Frederick Douglass took the country to task for failing to live up to the principles of equality embodied in the Declaration of Independence: "Stand by those principles," he exhorted his listeners, "at whatever cost." His words foreshadowed a great war.

The Paradox of Southern Political Power

■ *Why could white Southerners dominate all three branches of the national government and still perceive themselves on the defensive, under siege?*

At the center of debates about hierarchies and equality, the institution of slavery needed to expand to survive. Decades of intensive cultivation were exhausting the cotton fields in the South. The planter elite was counting on the admission of new territories as slave states to preserve their threatened power in Congress. To slave owners, northern-sponsored efforts to block their expansion amounted to a death sentence for all that the white South held dear. In defense of the slave system, the white South had to mount a strong offense or die.

In the early 1850s, proslavery forces maintained firm control over all branches of the federal government. The presidential election of 1800 showed that the "three-fifths clause" of the Constitution gave disproportionate representation to the slave states, where each slave was counted as three-fifths of a person. By the 1850s, this provision had helped to further slave owners' interests in dramatic ways. Without the clause in place, the Wilmot Proviso, which would have banned slavery in the new state of Texas, would have passed Congress. Conversely, the **Kansas-Nebraska Act** of 1854, which allowed residents of Kansas to decide for themselves whether their state would be slave or free, would have failed. By 1850, slaveholders had dominated the office of the presidency for half a century. Ever since George Washington, presidents elected to a second term had been slaveholders, including Jefferson, Madison, Monroe, and Jackson. From the founding of the nation, eighteen of the thirty-one men who had served as Supreme Court justices had owned slaves. During the 1850s, abolitionists pointed out that six slave states with a combined total population less than that of the free state of Pennsylvania sent a total of twelve senators to Congress. Pennsylvania sent two.

Nevertheless, southern planters felt increasingly defensive as the country expanded westward. They warned against "the abolition excitement," which would necessarily upset the delicate balance between slave and free states. Gradually, this tension between southern strength and southern fears led to the fraying and then unraveling of the Jacksonian

TABLE 13.1

U.S. Population, 1830–1860, by Region, Showing Nativity, Race, and Enslavement

		White			Negro		
Year	Total	Total	Native Born	Foreign Born	Total	Enslaved	Other Races
Northeast							
1860	10,594,268	10,438,028	8,419,243	2,018,785	156,001	18	239
1850	8,626,851	8,477,089	7,153,512	1,323,577	149,762	236	–
1840	6,761,082	6,618,758	–	–	142,324	765	–
1830	5,542,381	5,417,167	–	–	125,214	2,780	–
Midwest							
1860	9,096,716	8,899,969	7,357,376	1,542,593	184,239	114,948	12,508
1850	5,403,595	5,267,988	4,617,913	650,075	135,607	87,422	–
1840	3,351,542	3,262,195	–	–	89,347	58,604	–
1830	1,610,473	1,568,930	–	–	41,543	25,879	–
South							
1860	11,133,861	7,033,973	6,642,201	391,772	4,097,111	3,838,765	2,277
1850	8,982,612	5,630,414	5,390,314	240,100	3,352,198	3,116,629	–
1840	6,950,729	4,308,752	–	–	2,641,977	2,427,986	–
1830	5,707,848	3,545,963	–	–	2,161,885	1,980,384	–
West							
1860	618,976	550,567	406,964	143,603	4,479	29	63,930
1850	178,818	177,577	150,794	26,783	1,241	26	–
1840	–	–	–	–	–	–	–
1830	–	–	–	–	–	–	–

Source: Historical Statistics of the United States, Colonial Times to 1957 (Washington, DC: U.S. Government Printing Office, 1960), 11–12.

An Artist Renders County Election Day in the Early 1850s

Envisioning History

George Caleb Bingham, *County Election*, 1851–1852. Saint Louis Art Museum, Museum Purchases (124.1944)

George Caleb Bingham painted a series of pictures portraying local political customs. Titled *County Election*, this piece was completed in 1851–1852. In 1846, Bingham had lost a campaign to become a congressional representative from Missouri, so he had a political candidate's knowledge of the election process.

The voter expressing his choice before an election official (center right) is a reminder that most state and local elections had open balloting until the late nineteenth century. Throughout the nineteenth century, many voters were accustomed to announcing their choice of candidate in front of a large group of people at the polls. The first U.S. presidential election to require use of the secret ballot was the one held in 1892.

QUESTIONS

1. Besides voting, what other activities are the people in this scene engaged in?

2. What visual evidence suggests that election day brought together a cross-section of white males representing a range of classes and ages?

3. What social groups are conspicuous for their absence from this scene?

4. Do you think Bingham intended this painting to celebrate American democratic traditions? Why or why not?

5. What were some of the implications of the "popular sovereignty" method of deciding whether or not a state should outlaw slavery?

American party system. That system had relied on a truce maintained between Whigs and Democrats on the issue of slavery. A new party, the Republicans, fused the democratic idealism and economic self-interest of native-born Northerners in such a powerful way that white Southerners believed the institution of slavery was in danger of succumbing to the Yankee onslaught. A clash of ideas gradually slipped out of the confines of the polling place and into the realm of armed conflict.

TABLE 13.3			
The Election of 1852			
Candidate	**Political Party**	**Popular Vote (%)**	**Electoral Vote**
Franklin Pierce	Democratic	50.9	254
Winfield Scott	Whig	44.1	42
John P. Hale	Free-Soil	5.0	—

devotion to slavery. This split foreshadowed the end of national political parties and the emergence of regional parties, an ominous development indeed.

EXPANSIONISM AND POLITICAL UPHEAVAL

The interests of southern planters affected not only domestic politics but debates and policies related to foreign affairs as well. Even as Congress was heatedly discussing the Compromise of 1850, Southerners were contemplating ways to extend their reach across and even beyond the continental United States. They wanted to find new, fresh, fertile lands for cotton cultivation, and they hoped to incorporate those lands into the United States. Such expansion would also bolster the political power of slave owners in Congress by someday adding new slave states to the Union.

In 1848, President Polk had made a gesture to buy Cuba from Spain, an offer that was rebuffed but one that did not discourage two privately financed expeditions of proslavery Americans from making forays into Cuba in an effort to seize the island by force on behalf of the United States. In 1854, the American ambassadors to Great Britain, France, and Spain met in Ostend, Belgium, and issued a statement declaring that, if Spain would not sell Cuba, the United States would be justified in taking control of the island. According to the Americans, the Monroe Doctrine gave license to the United States to rid the Western Hemisphere of European colonial powers. Noting that two of the three ambassadors hailed from slave states, abolitionists charged that the Ostend Manifesto was just one more ploy to extend the power of slaveholders throughout the Northern Hemisphere.

In 1855, a young proslavery American adventurer, Tennessee-born William Walker, gathered a band of fifty-eight mercenaries and managed to capture Granada, Nicaragua. Declaring himself president of Nicaragua, Walker encouraged the institution of slavery and won U.S. recognition for his regime in 1856. Walker was driven out of the country a year later.

The Gadsden Purchase of 1853 marked the end of westward land acquisition on the continent, but in a commercial sense, expansion continued past the edge of the continental United States. Americans saw the Pacific Ocean as a trade route and East Asia as a trading partner. Commodore Matthew Perry commanded a fleet of U.S. Navy ships that steamed into Tokyo harbor in 1853. The treaty Perry helped arrange with Japan in 1854 protected American whaling ships, sailors, and merchants in that part of the world and opened the door to an increase in trade later in the century.

By the mid-1850s, the uniting of the continent into what would eventually become the forty-eight contiguous states was a source of sectional tension as well as national pride. Fewer and fewer Northerners supported what they considered proslavery charades, so-called legislative compromises. And the territory of Nebraska, poised on the brink of statehood, forced national lawmakers to confront again the political problem of the expansion of slavery. Once more Senator Douglas from Illinois stepped in to fill the breach. Douglas believed that mutual accommodation between North and South demanded a constant process of negotiation and flexibility on both sides. Thus he argued that the gigantic territory be split into two new states, Kansas and Nebraska, whose respective voters would decide the issue of slavery for themselves. His proposal necessitated that part of the Missouri Compromise of 1820, the part that forbade slavery above the 36°30' line, would have to be repealed.

The Kansas-Nebraska Act became law in 1854, enraging northern Free-Soilers by dismantling the 1820 agreement. They became convinced that what they called the Slave Power Conspiracy would stop at nothing until slavery overran the entire nation. The measure also had a profound effect on the Plains Indians, for it deprived them of fully one-half

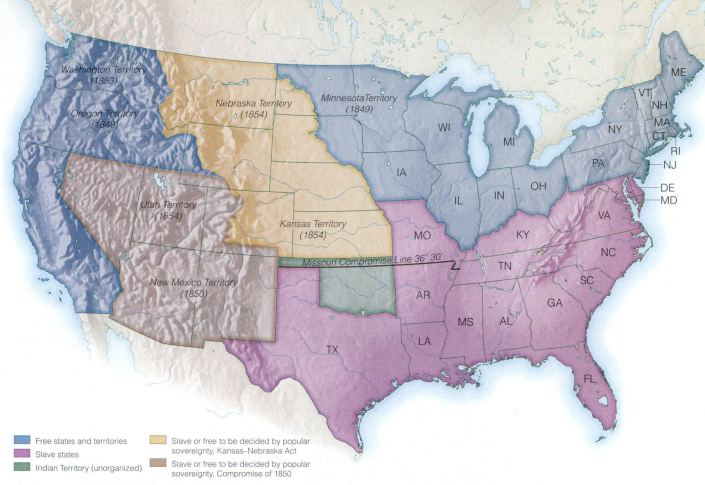

Free states and territories
Slave states
Indian Territory (unorganized)

Slave or free to be decided by popular sovereignty, Kansas–Nebraska Act
Slave or free to be decided by popular sovereignty, Compromise of 1850

■ **MAP 13.3** **The Kansas–Nebraska Act, 1854**

Stephen A. Douglas, senator from Illinois, proposed the Kansas-Nebraska Act of 1854. (Douglas hoped to ensure that any transcontinental railroad route would run through Illinois and benefit his constituents.) To secure southern support for the measure, proponents of the bill repealed the Missouri Compromise of 1820. As a result of the act, settlers displaced many Plains Indians from their lands. In the mid-1850s, the territory of Kansas became engulfed in an internal civil war that pitted supporters of slavery against abolitionists.

the land they had been granted by treaty. Specifically, the act wrought havoc on the lives of Ponca, Pawnee, Arapahoe, and Cheyenne on the southern and central plains. European American settlers poured into the region, provoking Indian attacks. In September 1855, 600 American troops staged a retaliatory raid against an Indian village, Blue Water, in Nebraska, killing 85 Sioux and leading to an escalation in violence between Indians and settlers in the area.

In their impatience with the two major parties, Free-Soilers were not alone in the early 1850s. The nativist American party, or Know-Nothings, condemned the growing political influence of immigrants, especially Roman Catholics. The American party, its ranks filled with former Whigs, tapped into a deep wellspring of resentment against immigrants on the part of urban, native-born workers as well as Protestant farmers anxious about retaining their influence in public affairs. The party wanted to limit the political participation of all foreign-born men by denying them the right to vote, whether or not they became U.S. citizens.

MAP

The Compromise of 1850 and the Kansas–Nebraska Act

THE REPUBLICAN ALLIANCE

The rapid rise of the Know-Nothings further indicated that voters had grown disillusioned with the two-party system. Confirmation of that fact appeared on March 20, 1854, in the small town of Ripon, Wisconsin, when a group of disaffected Whigs created the **Republican party.** One core idea informed the party: that slavery must not be allowed to spread into the western territories. From this base, the Republicans built an organization so powerful that it would capture the presidency within six years.

The genius of the Republican party resided in its ability to create and maintain an alliance between groups with vastly different goals. Now forced by the Fugitive Slave Act of 1850 to serve slaveholders (by returning runaway slaves to them) and fearful of the potential of slaveholding Southerners to capture their party, some northern Democrats cast their lot with the Republicans. From the ranks of antislavery men—the long-suffering adherents of the Liberty and Free-Soil parties—came another wing of the Republicans. These party members openly proclaimed their belief in the power of the federal government to halt the relentless march of slavery and ensure that, throughout the land, free soil would be tilled by free labor, free men and women.

Yet antislavery Republicans were by no means unified on major issues apart from opposition to the extension of slavery. Many Northerners were willing to tolerate slavery as long as it could be confined to the southern states; they cared little or nothing for the rights of black people, slave or free. In fact, in the Midwest, Republicans saw no contradiction in calling for the end of slavery in one breath and for the end of black migration to the area in the next. They feared that as job competitors, blacks would force whites to work for less money than they were accustomed to, or would push whites out of jobs altogether.

From the ranks of the newly formed Illinois state Republican party emerged a formidable leader. Born in 1809 in Kentucky, Abraham Lincoln came from a modest background and followed a checkered path into Illinois Whig politics: from youthful plowhand and log-splitter, to local postmaster and county surveyor, and finally self-taught lawyer and member of the state legislature (1834–1842). Although his six-foot four-inch frame and humble background drew ridicule from wealthy people—a Philadelphia lawyer described him as "a tall rawly boned, ungainly back woodsman, with coarse, ill-fitting clothing"—Lincoln made good use of his oratorical gifts and political ambition in promoting the principles of free soil.

The presidential election of 1856 revealed the full dimension of the national political crisis. The Democrats nominated James Buchanan, a "dough-face" (i.e., proslavery Northerner) from Pennsylvania, with John Breckinridge of Tennessee as his running mate. In their platform they took pains to extol the virtue of sectional compromise on the slavery issue, by this time a very unpopular position. Meanwhile, the enfeebled Whigs could do little but stand by helplessly and declare as their "fundamental article of political faith, an absolute necessity for avoiding geographical parties," another plank decidedly out of favor with a growing number of voters. The Know-Nothings cast their lot with former President Millard Fillmore, offering voters little more than an anti-immigrant platform.

Drawing on former members of the Free-Soil and Whig parties, the Republicans nominated the expedition leader John C. Frémont of California for president. Their platform stated in no uncertain terms the party's opposition to the extension of slavery, as well as Republican support for a transcontinental railroad and other federally sponsored internal improvements such as rivers and harbors. The document also included the bold, noble rhetoric—in favor of "the blessings of liberty" and against "tyrannical and unconstitutional laws"—that would be the hallmark of the Republican party in the decade to come. Buchanan won the election, but Frémont's carrying eleven of the sixteen northern states bode well for the Republican party and ill for the slaveholders' union. In Illinois, Frémont had benefited from the tireless campaigning of Abraham Lincoln, who electrified ever growing crowds of people with the declaration that "the Union must be preserved in the purity of its principles as well as in the integrity of its territorial parts." The founding of the Republican party, with its unabashed pro-Union, antislavery stand, signalled that the days of political compromise on the issue of human bondage were rapidly coming to an end.

TABLE 13.4

The Election of 1856

Candidate	Political Party	Popular Vote (%)	Electoral Vote
James Buchanan	Democratic	45.3	174
John C. Frémont	Republican	33.1	114
Millard Fillmore	American	21.6	8

The Deepening Conflict over Slavery

■ *During the 1850s, what specific events and developments pushed the nation toward armed conflict?*

Only a small subset of Americans—adult white men—participated directly in the formation of new political parties that set the terms for congressional debates over territorial expansion and slavery. Nevertheless, during the 1850s, increasing numbers of ordinary people were drawn into the escalating conflict over the South's "peculiar institution" as some Northerners mounted concerted challenges, violent as well as peaceful, to the Fugitive Slave Act. The western territory of Kansas became a bloody battleground as abolitionists and proslavery forces fought for control of the new state government. Sites of struggle over the slavery issue included the streets of Boston, the Supreme Court of the United States, political rallies in Illinois, and a federal arsenal in Harpers Ferry, Virginia. No longer would the opposing sides confine their disagreements to congressional debates over the admission of new states. Nor would words be the only weapons. The country was rushing headlong into nationwide armed conflict.

THE RISING TIDE OF VIOLENCE

The Fugitive Slave Act of 1850 caused fear and alarm among many Northerners. In response to the measure, some African Americans, hiding in northern cities, fled to Canada, often with the aid of conductors on the Underground Railroad. Abolitionists, white and black, made dramatic rescue attempts on behalf of men and women sought by their self-proclaimed southern owners. In Boston in 1851, a waiter named Shadrach Minkins was seized at work and charged with running away from a Virginia slaveholder. During a court hearing to determine the merits of the case, a group of blacks stormed in, disarmed the startled authorities, and in the words of a sympathetic observer, "with a dexterity worthy of the Roman gladiators, snatched the trembling prey of the slave-hunters, and conveyed him in triumph to the streets of Boston." Shadrach Minkins found safety in Montreal, Canada, and a Boston jury refused to convict his lawyers, who had been accused of masterminding his escape.

DOCUMENT

Benjamin Drew, Narratives of Fugitive Slaves in Canada

The spectacular public rescue of Minkins, and other such attempts, both successful and unsuccessful, brought the issue of slavery into the realm of public performance in northern towns and cities. In 1851, in Christiana, Pennsylvania, a group of blacks violently resisted the attempt of a slaveowner to capture four fugitives. Two years earlier, four slaves had escaped from their master, Edward Gorsuch, who lived in Maryland. The four sought refuge with William Parker, himself a former slave, now living in Christiana, a small town in Lancaster County in the southeastern part of the state. When Gorsuch tracked the men to Christiana in September 1851, he brought with him a posse and a warrant for the fugitives' arrest. But a large group of blacks living in the area quickly armed themselves and converged on the Parker residence. In the ensuing melee, Gorsuch was killed. Federal prosecutors charged more than three dozen men (mostly black) with treason for protecting the fugitives, but a federal jury swiftly acquitted the defendants. The fugitives were never returned to slavery. White Southerners condemned the "Christiana Riot" as one more sign that the North aimed to destroy the institution of slavery, by force if necessary.

Gradually, the war of words over slavery cascaded out of small-circulation abolitionist periodicals and into the consciousness of a nation. In particular, author Harriet Beecher Stowe managed to wed politics and sentiment in a most compelling way. Her novel *Uncle Tom's Cabin* (1852) sold more than 300,000 copies within ten months and a million copies over the next seven years. The book, originally serialized in a magazine, the *National Era*, introduced large numbers of Northerners to the sufferings of an enslaved couple, Eliza and

When Was Slavery Abolished?

The Wider World

1335	Sweden (but not until 1847 in the colony of St. Barthelemy)
1761	Portugal
1791	Haiti, due to a revolt among nearly half a million slaves
1793	Canada, by the Act Against Slavery
1794–1802	France (first time), including all colonies (although abolition was never carried out in some colonies under British occupation)
1811	Spain (and its colonies, though this move was opposed in Cuba and Puerto Rico)
1813	Argentina
1821	Gran Colombia (Ecuador, Colombia, Panama, and Venezuela) through a gradual emancipation plan (Colombia in 1852, Venezuela in 1854)
1823	Chile
1829	Mexico
1833	Great Britain, including all colonies (in effect from 1 August 1834; in East Indies from 1 August 1838)
1835	Mauritius, under the British government.
1848	Denmark, including all colonies
1848	France (second time), including all colonies
1851	Peru
1861	Russia (abolished serfdom)
1863	The Netherlands, including all colonies
1865	United States (abolition occurred in some states before 1865)
1873	Puerto Rico (a colony of Spain)
1880	Cuba (a colony of Spain)
1888	Brazil
1897	Zanzibar (slave trade abolished in 1873)
1910	China

1929	Burma
1936	Ethiopia, by order of the Italian occupying forces
1959	Tibet, by order of the People's Republic of China
1962	Saudi Arabia
1980	Mauritania

This chronology shows when various countries abolished slavery on their own soil or in their colonies. American abolitionists watched foreign antislavery developments with great interest and felt keenly that their own country lagged behind others in outlawing human bondage. During the antebellum period, many U.S. activists maintained ties with their counterparts in Great Britain and other parts of Europe, meeting with them periodically in world antislavery conventions.

QUESTIONS

1. How do you account for the flurry of abolitionist legislation in Europe during the first six or seven decades of the nineteenth century?

2. How do you think slaveholders defended themselves against the abolitionists' charge that the South represented a backward way of life, one that other countries were in the process of rejecting?

3. How was the U.S. case different from that of empire-builders like Great Britain, France, Spain, the Netherlands, and other nations that had colonies?

4. Is it accurate to say that the United States did not outlaw slavery until 1865, considering that the northern states chose to do so in the years after the American Revolution?

George. Slavery's greatest crime, in Stowe's eyes, was the forced severance of family ties between husbands and wives, parents and children.

Southern slaveholders were outraged at Stowe's attempt to portray their way of life as an unmitigated evil. A South Carolina slaveholding woman, Louisa McCord, wrote: "We proclaim it [slavery], on the contrary, a Godlike dispensation, a providential caring for the weak, and a refuge for the portionless." Another Southerner, George Fitzhugh, took this argument to its logical conclusion. In his book *Cannibals All! Or, Slaves Without Masters* (1857), Fitzhugh claimed that civil society demanded the enslavement of the masses, whether white or black: "Some were born with saddles on their backs, and others booted and spurred to ride them—and the riding does them good." Fitzhugh also argued that slaves, who he claimed were cared for by benevolent planters, were better off than northern factory workers, who he asserted were exploited and neglected by indifferent employers.

Meanwhile, the territory of Kansas was becoming engulfed in a regional civil war. Proslavery settlers, aided and abetted by their compatriots (called Border Ruffians) from Missouri, installed their own territorial government at Shawnee Mission in 1855. Opposing these proslavery settlers were the Free-Soilers, some of whom had organized into abolitionist groups, such as the New England Emigrant Aid Company, and armed themselves with rifles.

This dangerous situation soon gave way to terrorism and insurrection on both sides. In 1856, in retaliation for a proslavery raid on the "Free-Soil" town of Lawrence, Kansas, an Ohio abolitionist named John Brown, together with his four sons and two other men, hacked to death five proslavery men at Pottawatomie Creek. The massacre only strengthened the resolve of proslavery advocates, who in the next year drew up a constitution for Kansas that effectively nullified the principle of popular sovereignty over the issue of slavery. Called the **Lecompton Constitution,** the document decreed that voters might approve or reject slavery, but even if they chose to reject it, any slaves already in the state would remain slaves under the force of law. By throwing his support behind the Lecompton Constitution, President Buchanan alienated northern members of his own party, and the Democrats followed the Whigs into North–South factionalism.

The spilling of blood over slavery was not confined to the Kansas frontier. In 1856, Senator Charles Sumner of Massachusetts, an outspoken abolitionist, delivered a speech on the floor of the U.S. Senate condemning "the Crime Against Kansas" (the Lecompton Constitution) and the men who perpetrated it, men he characterized as "hirelings picked from the drunken spew and vomit of an uneasy civilization," men who (like his own colleague Senator Butler of South Carolina) loved slavery the way that degenerates loved their prostitutes. Shortly after this speech, Congressman Preston S. Brooks of South Carolina, a relative of Senator Butler, leapt to the defense of the white South and attacked Sumner on the floor of the Senate, beating him into unconsciousness with a cane. Abolitionists contemplated the necessity of defending themselves and their interests, from the courtrooms of New England and the small towns of the West to the halls of Congress itself.

THE *DRED SCOTT* DECISION

Across the street from the Capitol, proceedings in the Supreme Court were more civil but no less explosive. In 1857, a former slave named Dred Scott sued in federal court, claiming that he was a citizen of Missouri and a free man. Scott maintained that he had become free once his master had taken him onto free soil (the state of Illinois and the territory of Wisconsin). In the case of *Dred Scott v. Sanford* (1857), the Court ruled that residence on free soil did not render a slave a free person, for regardless of their status, black people had "no rights which the white man was bound to respect." With this single decision, Chief Justice Roger B. Taney and the Court threw off the hard-won balance between slave and free states. In effect, the Court declared unconstitutional the Compromise of 1820, which had banned slavery in

Dred Scott

the region north of Missouri's southern boundary, because, the justices held, slave owners could not be deprived of their property without due process. This decision threatened the precarious freedom of the South's quarter million free people of color and extended the reach of slavery into the northern states.

Most white people residing outside the South never read the Court's ruling, but if they had, they probably would have agreed with the justices' claim that, since the earliest days of the Republic, blacks "had been regarded as beings of an inferior order, and altogether unfit to associate with the white race, either in social or political relations." At the same time, northern opinion makers warned that the decision made Northerners complicit in the slave system. Of the "slave power," the *Cincinnati Daily Commercial* thundered, "It has marched over and annihilated the boundaries of the states. We are now one great homogeneous slaveholding community." Even nonabolitionists had good reason to fear the long-term implications of the ruling, for it suggested that the institution of slavery was about to spill out of the confines of the southern states and into the rest of the country. Free white men and women feared competing with slaves in the workplace, whether in the West or East. These concerns increased with the onset of an economic depression in 1857 in the northeastern and midwestern states, as the mining of California gold produced inflation in the East.

THE LINCOLN–DOUGLAS DEBATES

Against this backdrop of economic turmoil and political conflict, the congressional elections of 1858 assumed great significance. In particular, the Senate contest in Illinois pitted the incumbent Democrat Stephen A. Douglas against Republican challenger Abraham Lincoln. In a series of seven public debates, the two men debated the political conflict over slavery as it had been shaped during the tumultuous decade after the Mexican War. Though no friend of the abolitionists, Douglas was quickly falling from favor within the Democratic party; the Supreme Court had nullified his proposal for popular sovereignty in the territories, and he had parted ways from his southern brethren when he denounced Kansas's Lecompton Constitution. Yet in the last debate between Lincoln and Douglas, held in Alton on October 15, 1858, Douglas declared, "I care more for the great principle of self-government, the right of the people to rule, than I do for all the negroes in Christendom."

Lincoln ridiculed the doctrine of popular sovereignty, which he maintained was as thin as the "soup that was made by boiling the shadow of a pigeon that had starved to death." He had no desire to root out slavery in the South, but "I have said, and I repeat, my wish is that the further spread of [slavery] may be arrested, and that it may be placed where the public mind shall rest in the belief that it is in the course of ultimate extinction." According to a reporter present, this last remark provoked great applause. And this was no minor confrontation between two candidates; it is estimated that in six of the seven debates, the two men spoke before crowds exceeding 10,000 people each. Lincoln lost the election (in which blacks were not allowed to vote as a matter of Illinois law), but more significantly, he won the loyalty of Republicans all over the North and put the white South on notice that the days of compromise were over. Meanwhile, with the admission as free states of Minnesota in 1858 and Oregon in 1859, Congress began to reflect a distinct antislavery bias.

HARPERS FERRY AND THE PRESIDENTIAL ELECTION OF 1860

On a Sunday night in October 1859, John Brown and nineteen other men (including at least five African Americans) launched a daring attack on the federal arsenal in Harpers

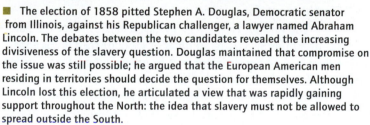
The election of 1858 pitted Stephen A. Douglas, Democratic senator from Illinois, against his Republican challenger, a lawyer named Abraham Lincoln. The debates between the two candidates revealed the increasing divisiveness of the slavery question. Douglas maintained that compromise on the issue was still possible; he argued that the European American men residing in territories should decide the question for themselves. Although Lincoln lost this election, he articulated a view that was rapidly gaining support throughout the North: the idea that slavery must not be allowed to spread outside the South.

The Library of Congress

The Library of Congress

Ferry, Virginia. They had received guns and moral support from some of the North's leading abolitionists, and their plan was to raid the arsenal and distribute arms to slaves in the surrounding area, thereby inciting a general rebellion that, they hoped, would engulf the rest of the South.

In planning this bold raid, Brown relied on funding from well-to-do Northerners who sympathized with his cause. But he had also turned for advice to a thirty-seven-year-old illiterate African American woman. Throughout northern abolitionist circles, Harriet Tubman became known as the "Moses" of her people for her role as one of the most productive "conductors" on the Underground Railroad. Born a slave in Dorchester County, Virginia, she suffered a blow to her head when she was a child. This injury caused her headaches and seizures throughout her life (she perhaps suffered from a form of epilepsy). Tubman herself escaped to Philadelphia in 1849. Over the next decade, she returned to Dorchester County a dozen times and guided as many as seventy friends and relatives to free territory in the North and Canada.

The Ohio Historical Society (al00523)

■ Augustus Washington, son of a former slave, took this picture of John Brown in 1846, thirteen years before the raid on Harpers Ferry, Virginia. A pioneer daguerreotypist, Washington operated a successful studio in Hartford, Connecticut. After the passage of the Fugitive Slave Act in 1850, Washington emigrated with his family to Liberia, an African settlement for American freeborn blacks and former slaves, founded as a republic in 1847.

Brown wanted to enlist Tubman's aid in recruiting former slaves to his small band of men. He also admired her ability to move about freely within slave territory, undetected by slave "patrollers," and he sought information about the informal slave communication network that Tubman knew and used so well. At a meeting with Tubman in St. Catherines, Canada, Brown called her "General Tubman," later claiming that she "was a better officer than most" men. He believed she had the ability to "command an army as successfully as she had led her small parties of fugitives."

Harriet Tubman would later serve as a spy and scout for the Union army during the Civil War. But John Brown's plan for an uprising of southern slaves came to an abrupt end. Soon after Brown initiated the raid, the Virginia militia cornered the band, but not before the insurrectionists had killed seven people (including a free man of color) and injured ten others. Within two days a U.S. Marine force, commanded by Lieutenant Colonel Robert E. Lee, had captured Brown and his surviving followers.

Two weeks later, Brown stood in a Virginia courtroom and declared that his intention indeed had been "to free the slaves." Brown was convicted of several charges: treason against the United States for his raid on the federal arsenal, murder, and inciting an insurrection. On December 2, 1859, before being led to the gallows, Brown handed a scrap of paper to one of his guards: "I John Brown am now quite *certain* that the crimes of this *guilty land: will* never be purged *away:* but with Blood." Brown failed as the instigator of a slave rebellion, but he succeeded as a prophet.

The raid on Harpers Ferry cast a shadow over the party conventions held in the summer of 1860. By then it was apparent that the national party system had all but disintegrated. Southerners in effect seceded from the Democratic party by walking out of their Charleston convention rather than supporting Stephen Douglas as candidate for president. Within a few weeks, representatives of both the northern and the southern wings of the party reconvened in separate conventions in Baltimore; Northerners gave the nod to Douglas and Southerners chose as their standard-bearer John C. Breckinridge, a proponent of extending slavery into the territories and annexing Cuba. Representing the thoroughly discredited strategy of compromise was the candidate of the Constitutional Union party, John Bell of Tennessee.

In Chicago, the Republicans lined up behind the moderate Abraham Lincoln and agreed on a platform that had something for everybody, including measures to boost economic growth (as promoted by Henry Clay's American System earlier in the century): a proposed protective tariff, a transcontinental railroad, internal improvements, and free homesteads for western farmers. The Republicans renounced the Know-Nothings. Lincoln had taken the lead in admonishing Republicans who sought to curtail the voting rights of European immigrants, such as the Germans and Scandinavians. Lecturing members of his own party in Massachusetts, he declared that, since he had denounced the oppression of black people, "I should be strangely inconsistent if I could favor any project for curtailing the existing rights of white men, even though born in different lands, and speaking different languages from myself."

Yet Republicans held out little hope for other groups demanding the rights and protection that flowed from American citizenship. Spanish-speaking residents of California, Chinese immigrants, free people of color throughout the North, Indian tribes from North Carolina to the northwestern states, the wives and daughters of men all over the country—these groups were not included in the Republicans' grand design for a country based on the principles of free labor.

Abraham Lincoln was elected president in 1860, although he received support from only 40 percent of the men who cast ballots. Lincoln won the electoral college, and he also received a plurality of the popular vote. However, ten southern states had refused to list him on the ballot; in that region of the country, he received almost no votes. Stephen Douglas won almost 30 percent of the popular vote; together, Douglas and Breckinridge outpolled Lincoln (2.2 million votes to 1.85 million). Nevertheless, the new president had swept New England, New York, Pennsylvania, and the upper Midwest. The regional interests of North and South took precedence over national political parties.

Lincoln and his party represented the antislavery sentiments of northern family farmers. The South took heed of this dramatic shift in the national political landscape. By the end of 1860, South Carolina had seceded from the Union, and the nation headed toward war.

TABLE 13.5			
The Election of 1860			
Candidate	**Political Party**	**Popular Vote (%)**	**Electoral Vote**
Abraham Lincoln	Republican	39.8	180
Stephen A. Douglas	Democratic	29.5	12
John C. Breckinridge	Democratic	18.1	72
John Bell	Constitutional Union	12.6	39

Conclusion

During his seventh debate with Stephen Douglas, Abraham Lincoln expressed his frustration with the inability and unwillingness of politicians to confront the issue of slavery squarely. Lincoln understood that slavery was the most significant and divisive topic of the day, yet the political system discouraged people from confronting it openly and honestly. Lincoln outlined the excuses used by people who wanted to avoid public discussion of slavery: "You must not say anything about it in the free States, *because it is not here*. You must not say anything about it in the slave States, *because it is there*. You must not say anything about it in the pulpit, because that is religion and has nothing to do with it. You must not say anything about it in politics *because that will disturb the security of 'my place.'* There is no place to talk about it as being wrong, although you say yourself it *is* a wrong." At the same time, Lincoln was speaking for large numbers of Northerners who believed that the national political system was not representing their interests.

In fact, people all over the country came to feel that the institution of slavery had relevance to their lives. In the slave states, black workers remained yoked to a system that denied their humanity and mocked the integrity of their families. In the nonslave states, free people of color understood that northern racial prejudice was but a variation of the slaveholders' theme of domination. New England farm families looking to move west were convinced that western homesteads would not improve their economic security if these homesteads were surrounded by plantations cultivated by large numbers of enslaved workers. Although they expressed little regard for the rights of blacks, enslaved or free, the northern laboring classes feared that the expansion of slavery into the western territories would limit their own economic opportunities; whether shoemakers, wagon drivers, or seamstresses, they could not possibly compete with bound workers in the labor market. The Republicans drew inspiration from the anxieties of all these groups, and the party's platform beckoned toward a future full of hope, a future that would fulfill the long-thwarted promise of the young country as a "republic of equal rights, where the title of manhood is the title to citizenship."

In contrast, southern whites of various classes agreed on a rallying cry that stressed independence from Yankee interlopers and freedom from federal interference. Yet this unifying

war, as threatening to the well-being of the Confederacy as any Yankee sharpshooter in a blue uniform. The charges also suggest that the Confederates were forced to repudiate elements of their own proslavery beliefs, which held that black people were childlike and servile, incapable of acting on their own, and grateful for the guidance and protection of southern whites.

The Pensacola slaves were assigned a defense lawyer, who attempted to show that they had not actually encountered any Union soldiers and so had had no opportunity to divulge information related to Confederate troop movement. Technically, then, they were not guilty of spying. In court, however, the accused men did admit that, ever since President Abraham Lincoln had taken office in early 1861, three white men in the vicinity (a whiskey seller, an employee of the slaves' master, and a shingle maker) had been encouraging them to seek their freedom behind Union lines.

Prosecuting officers believed that "strong measures" were needed to prevent the nefarious activities of "spys whether white or black." These officials therefore were unprepared for the firestorm of criticism that followed the announcement of the verdict. The owner of the slaves, General Jackson Morton, expressed outrage that two of his men were marked for summary execution. In a formal complaint to Confederate authorities, Morton denounced the hearing as "vulgar and improper." By the time the controversy faded, an impressive array of Confederate military officers (from sentinels to a lieutenant, a captain, a colonel, a major general, and a general) had had to justify their actions in convening the trial. The Confederate adjutant and inspector general took time out from more pressing matters to review the case for the secretary of war. In the words of one Confederate official, "The sacrosanctity of slave property in this war has operated most injuriously to the Confederacy." In the end, Peter and William were hanged, and George, Robert, and Stephen received, according to an army commander, "fifty lashes each, well laid on with a rawhide."

Though at a distinct disadvantage compared to the North in terms of troops, supplies, and industrial might, the white South managed to fight on for four long, bloody years. Early on, southern politicians hailed slaves as a tremendous asset, an immense, easily managed labor force that would grow food and dig trenches. Instead, African American men and women became freedom fighters, a source of subversion in the heart of the Confederacy. In October 1862, in response to the crisis of wartime slave management, the Confederate Congress passed a measure that exempted from military service one white man for every twenty slaves on a plantation. Many slave owners used this law to shield themselves or their sons from combat duty. In turn, the Twenty-Negro Law inflamed resentment among non-slave-owning small farmers, who charged that this rich man's war was actually a poor man's fight. Even within the ranks of the elite, conflicts over military strategy and national mobilization policies hobbled the Confederate effort. Many slaveholding women gradually came to see the sacrifice of their husbands, brothers, and sons as too high a price to pay for southern independence.

As defenders of slavery, the Confederates cast themselves as rebels in an age when the principle of individual rights was gaining ground. The citizens of France, Germany, and Italy were agitating on behalf of modern, democratic nation-states, and systems of serfdom and slavery throughout Europe and the Western Hemisphere were under siege. By early 1865, leading southern politicians and strategists had initiated a public debate over the possibility of offering slaves their liberty in return for military service. In acknowledging that African American men might serve as effective soldiers (as 179,000 of them had demonstrated in the Union army), the Confederates undermined their cause. White Southerners were fighting for their own nation, but African Americans were fighting to gain their own country as well.

The Republican conduct of the war on behalf of the North revealed the party's long-range, guiding principles. Yet several groups besides white southerners objected to a strong federal government, one that would weld the country together geographically as well as economically. The Lincoln administration met bitter resistance from Indian tribes as diverse as the Santee Sioux of Minnesota, the Cheyenne of Colorado, and the Navajo and Apache of the Southwest. In northeastern cities, Irish immigrants battled federal draft agents and attacked black women, men, and children, their supposed competitors in the workplace. The Civil War, then, was less a "brothers' war" between the white farmers of the North and South and more a conflict that pitted diverse groups against each other over the issues of slavery, territorial expansion, federal power, and local control. Yet by the end of the war in April 1865, for the time being at least, the Republican vision of a union forged in blood had prevailed, at the cost of nearly 700,000 lives.

Mobilization for War, 1861–1862

■ *How did the North and South prepare for war, and how did those preparations reflect each side's strategy for fighting—and winning—the war?*

On December 20, 1860, less than eight weeks after Abraham Lincoln was elected president of the United States, South Carolina seceded from the Union, determined, in the words of its own Declaration of Independence, to "resume her separate and equal place among nations." By February 1, 1861, Mississippi, Florida, Alabama, Georgia, Louisiana, and Texas (all states dependent on slave-based staple-crop agriculture) had also withdrawn from the United States of America. Three days later, representatives of the seven states met in Montgomery, Alabama, and formed the **Confederate States of America.** They also adopted a constitution for their new nation. Though modeled after that of the United States, this document invoked the power of "sovereign and independent states" instead of "we, the people."

DOCUMENT

Confederate Constitution (1861)

Delegates to the Montgomery convention elected as their president Jefferson Davis, a wealthy Mississippi planter with an impressive record of public service. Davis was a graduate of West Point, a veteran of the Mexican-American War, and a former U.S. congressman and senator. He had also held the position of secretary of war in the Franklin Pierce administration. Chosen vice president was a former Whig from Georgia, Alexander H. Stephens. In devising a cabinet, Davis bypassed some well-known radical secessionists—"fire eaters" such as William Lowndes Yancey of Alabama and Robert Barnwell Rhett Jr. of South Carolina—on the assumption that the builders of a new nation would need skills different from those of the destroyers of an old one.

THE SECESSION IMPULSE

In some respects, the Civil War seems difficult to explain, for the two sides shared a great deal. In both the North and the South, most people were English-speaking Protestants with deep roots in the culture of the British Isles. Together they celebrated a revolutionary heritage, paying homage to George Washington and the other Founding Fathers.

Why, then, was the white South, especially the slave South, so fearful of Abraham Lincoln? Although Lincoln enjoyed a broad electoral college victory, he won only 40 percent of the popular vote in the election of 1860. Political support for Lincoln thus appeared slim, and he did not seem likely to use his authority to move against slavery. He had made it clear that, as president, he would possess neither the authority nor the desire to disturb slavery as it existed in the South. However, he summed up his philosophy before the secession crisis

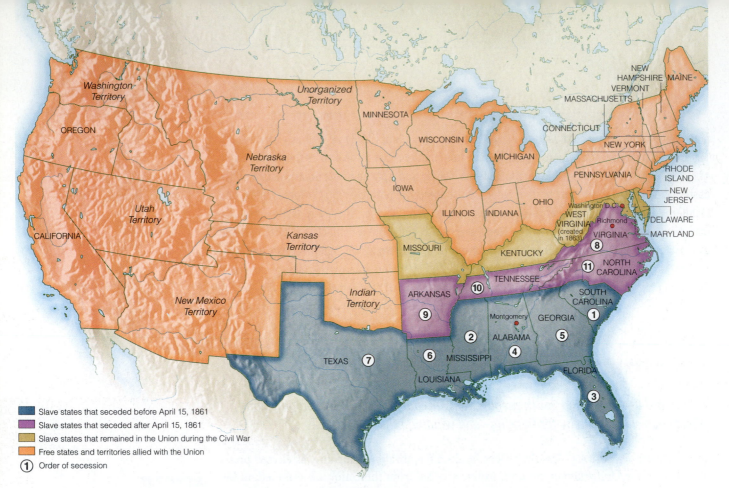

■ **MAP 14.1 The Secession of Southern States, 1860–1861**

The southern states seceded from the Union in stages, beginning with South Carolina in December 1860. Founded on February 4, 1861, the Confederate States of America initially consisted of only that state and six Deep South states. The four upper South states of Virginia, Arkansas, Tennessee, and North Carolina did not leave the Union until mid-April, when Lincoln called for 75,000 troops to put down the civil rebellion. The slave states of Delaware, Maryland, Kentucky, and Missouri remained in the Union, but each of those states was bitterly divided between Unionists and Confederate sympathizers.

this way: "As I would not be a *slave*, so I would not be a *master*. This expresses my idea of democracy. Whatever differs from this . . . is not democracy."

Not surprisingly, then, southern elites felt threatened by Lincoln in particular and the Republicans in general, pointing to the new president's oft-repeated promise to halt the march of slavery into the western territories. Although he was in no position to achieve this goal by executive order, Lincoln did have the power to expand the Republican base in the South by dispensing patronage jobs to a small group of homegrown abolitionists. He could also make appointments to the Supreme Court as openings became available. The Republican party was not a majority party; it was a sectional party of the North and the upper Midwest. But this sectional party had managed to seize control of the executive branch of government, tipping the antebellum balance of power between slave and free states decisively in favor of the North. Slave owners feared that John Brown's 1859 raid on the federal arsenal at Harpers Ferry, Virginia, was just the first in a series of planned attacks on the slave South (see Chapter 13).

Two last-ditch efforts at compromise failed to avert a constitutional crisis. In December 1860, as South Carolina was seceding and other states were preparing to join it, neither northern Republicans nor lower South Democrats showed any interest in a series of proposed constitutional amendments that would have severely curtailed the federal government's ability to restrict the interstate slave trade or the spread of slavery. Called the Crittenden Compromise (after its sponsor, Senator John J. Crittenden, a Whig from Kentucky), this package of proposed amendments was defeated in the Senate on January 16, 1861. A peace conference, organized by the Virginia legislature and assembled in

February, revised the Crittenden Compromise, but key players were missing: the seven Confederate states and five of the northern states. Congress rejected the conference's recommendations at the end of February. By this time many Americans, radicals and moderates, Northerners and Southerners, were in no mood to compromise on the issue of slavery, especially its extension into the West.

In his inaugural address of March 4, Lincoln appealed to the South to refrain from any drastic action, invoking the historic bonds of nationhood, the "mystic chords of memory, stretching from every battle-field, and patriot grave, to every living heart and hearthstone." For the most part Lincoln's plea for unity fell on deaf ears. However, among the Southerners who initially resisted the secessionists' call to arms was the West Point graduate and Mexican-American War veteran Robert E. Lee of Virginia. Later, after Virginia seceded, Lee cast his lot with the Confederacy: "I cannot raise my hand against my birthplace, my home, my children," he declared. By his home, Lee meant the Commonwealth of Virginia, not the collection of disaffected states.

Indeed, in early April, the Confederacy was a rhetorical powerhouse, full of popular firebrands. But it was also a poor excuse for an independent nation, with only one-third of the U.S. population and almost no industrial capacity. Over the next few weeks, as the seven Confederate states attempted to coax the upper South to join their revolution, Lincoln emerged as an unwitting ally in their effort.

Located in Charleston Harbor, Fort Sumter was one of two Union forts in southern territory, and in the spring of 1861 it was badly in need of supplies. On April 12, Lincoln took the high moral ground by sending provisions but not troops to the fort. The Confederates found the move provocative nonetheless and began firing on the fort. After a thirty-three-hour Confederate bombardment, the heavily damaged fort surrendered without a fight. In response, many white Southerners, such as Mary Boykin Chesnut, the wife of a high-ranking Confederate official, cheered and embraced the "pomp and circumstance of glorious war."

Three days after the capture of Fort Sumter, Lincoln (anticipating a conflict no longer than ninety days) called for 75,000 northern volunteers to quell a civil uprising "too powerful to be suppressed by the ordinary course of judicial proceedings." By the end of the month, he had ordered a blockade of southern seaports. Condemning these moves as acts of "northern aggression," the upper South, including Virginia (deprived of its western part, which now formed a new state called West Virginia), Tennessee, Arkansas, and North Carolina all seceded from the Union by May 20. Grateful for the newfound loyalty of Virginia and eager to appropriate the Tredegar Iron Works in Richmond, the Confederacy moved its capital from the down-at-the-heels Montgomery to the elegant Richmond on May 11.

Certain segments of the southern population early demonstrated that they would withhold their support from the Confederacy. Yeoman farmers in the upcountry, Louisiana sugar planters dependent on world markets for their product, and people in the hill country of east Tennessee all voted for Unionist delegates to their respective state conventions that chose secession. Enslaved black workers, of course, could hardly be

Harper's Weekly, May 4, 1861

■ This drawing, titled *The House-Tops in Charleston During the Bombardment of Sumter*, appeared in the May 4, 1861, issue of *Harper's Weekly*, about three weeks after the event. Many Confederate women sent their husbands and sons into battle with great displays of patriotism. However, those parades and parties often masked deep fears. Noted one woman of her husband's departure, "It has always been my lot to be obliged to shut up my griefs in my own breast."

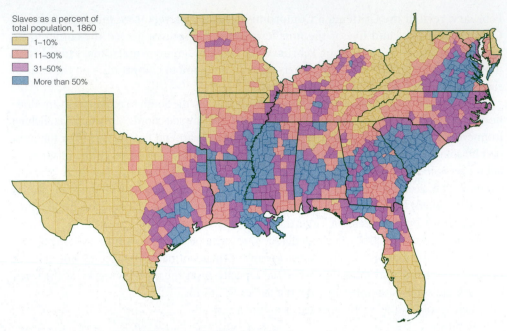

Slaves as a percent of
total population, 1860

- 1–10%
- 11–30%
- 31–50%
- More than 50%

■ **MAP 14.2   Slavery in the United States, 1860**

In the South, the areas of the greatest concentration of slaves were also the areas of greatest support for the Confederacy. During the war, the Appalachian mountain region and the upper Piedmont—the area between the mountains and the broad coastal plain—were home to people loyal to the Union and to people who became increasingly disaffected with Confederate policies as the war dragged on.

counted on to defend those who kept them in bondage. The Border States of Missouri, Kentucky, Maryland, and Delaware remained within the Union, although among their residents were many outspoken people who openly sympathized with the South.

■ General Robert E. Lee turned down President Abraham Lincoln's offer of the field command of the United States Army and chose instead to lead Confederate soldiers in battle.

The Library of Congress

PREPARING TO FIGHT

Poised to battle each other, the South and the North faced similar challenges. Both sides had to inspire—or force—large numbers of men to fight. Both had to produce massive amounts of cannon, ammunition, and food. And both had to devise military strategies that would, they hoped, ensure victory. In early 1861, white Southerners were boasting of the stockpiles of cotton that, if needed, would serve as leverage for military support, diplomatic recognition, and financial assistance from the great European powers. Plantations brimming with hogs and corn, it was expected, would sustain both masters and slaves, in contrast to the North, where cotton mills would lie idle and workers would soon descend to poverty and starvation.

From the beginning of the war, Confederates aimed for a strategy calculated to draw on their strengths. They would fight a purely defensive war with small units of troops deployed around the South's 6,000-mile border. Seasoned officers such as Robert E. Lee and Thomas J. Jackson would lead the charge to crush the Union armies that ventured into Confederate territory. Finally, the South could command 3 million black people (a third of its total population of 9 million), all of whom, it was assumed, would do the bidding of planters and the military. Whereas the North would have to conquer the South to preserve the Union, the Confederacy would only have to survive to win its independence.

A Civil War Encampment

The Library of Congress

Envisioning History

The Civil War was the first war in U.S. history after the advent of photography. Photographers captured not only the war's horrific cost in human lives, but also scenes of the immense military mobilization on both sides. This photo of Camp Northumberland, headquarters of the 96th Philadelphia Infantry, near Washington, D.C., shows Union soldiers in drill formation. Constructing and maintaining camps like this one required considerable time and energy. Soldiers were forced to wield shovels and axes as well as shoulder rifles. Wherever fighting occurred, the landscape was transformed, not only by the fierce battles, but also by the need on the part of Union and Confederate forces to feed and shelter vast armies and to transport them over large expanses of land.

QUESTIONS

1. How does this photograph suggest the different kinds of work needed to establish a large military encampment?

2. Many white men in the Civil War era considered military service a matter of honor. How might these men have reacted to military orders that demanded they perform "fatigue work"—manual labor in support of military operations?

3. What does the drill formation of these troops tell us about battlefield tactics during the Civil War?

4. Why were camps such as this one dangerous breeding grounds for disease?

At first, the North was inclined to think little past the numbers: in 1860, it possessed 90 percent of the manufacturing capacity and three-quarters of the 30,000 railroad miles in the United States. Its population, 22 million, dwarfed that of the South. The North retained control of the (admittedly less than formidable) U.S. Navy and all other resources of the federal government, including a bureaucratic infrastructure to facilitate troop deployment and communication. Its diversified economy yielded grain as well as textiles; it could mobilize a large army and feed it as well.

Early on, the North had a plan, but one that could hardly be dignified by the term *strategy*. It would defend its own territory from southern attack and target Confederate

■ **FIGURE 14.1**
Occupational Categories of Union and Confederate Soldiers

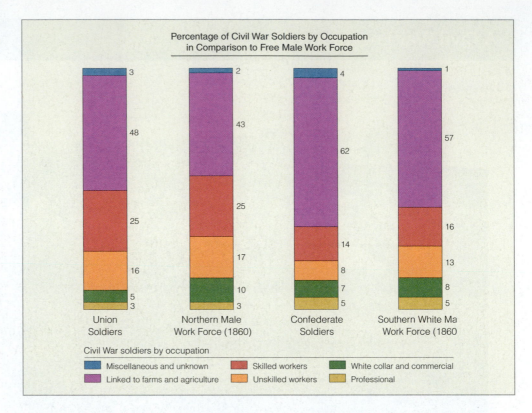

leaders, under the assumption that latent Union sentiment in the South would arise to smash the rebellion before it went too far. Union gunboats positioned along the East Coast and up and down the Mississippi River would seal off the Confederacy from foreign supply lines. The North would also launch a political offensive calculated to undermine Confederate sympathizers by bolstering Unionist sentiment everywhere. Lincoln, for example, continued to appeal to slaveholders loyal to the Union, whether those slaveholders lived in the Border States or deep in the heart of the Confederacy.

Northerners also invoked a Revolutionary heritage to justify their cause. However, they downplayed the issue of unjust taxation and instead stressed the glories of the Union—in Lincoln's words, "the last, best hope of mankind" in an age of kings and emperors.

BARRIERS TO SOUTHERN MOBILIZATION

On July 21, 1861, at Manassas Junction (Bull Run), about thirty miles southwest of Washington, D.C., Union and Confederate forces encountered each other on the field of battle for the first time. This was the fight that earned Thomas "Stonewall" Jackson his nickname and bolstered his reputation, for Union troops skirmished briefly with the enemy and then turned and fled back to the capital, disgraced. In the coming weeks, Northerners gave up the idea that the effort to suppress the rebels would be an easy one, and Lincoln began to reorganize the country's officer corps and fortify its armies.

To win this initial victory, the Confederates had relied on the massing of several huge forces: those of Generals Joseph Johnston and P. G. T. Beauregard, as well as Stonewall Jackson. Consequently, southern military strategists decided they must continue to defend southern territory while going on the offensive against the Yankees (the "offensive-defensive" strategy was used for the duration of the conflict). In other matters, however, the South learned life-and-death lessons more slowly. Only gradually did the central paradox of the Confederate nation become abundantly clear: that a country founded on an agrarian ideal of "states' rights" needed to industrialize its economy and centralize its government operations to defeat the Union.

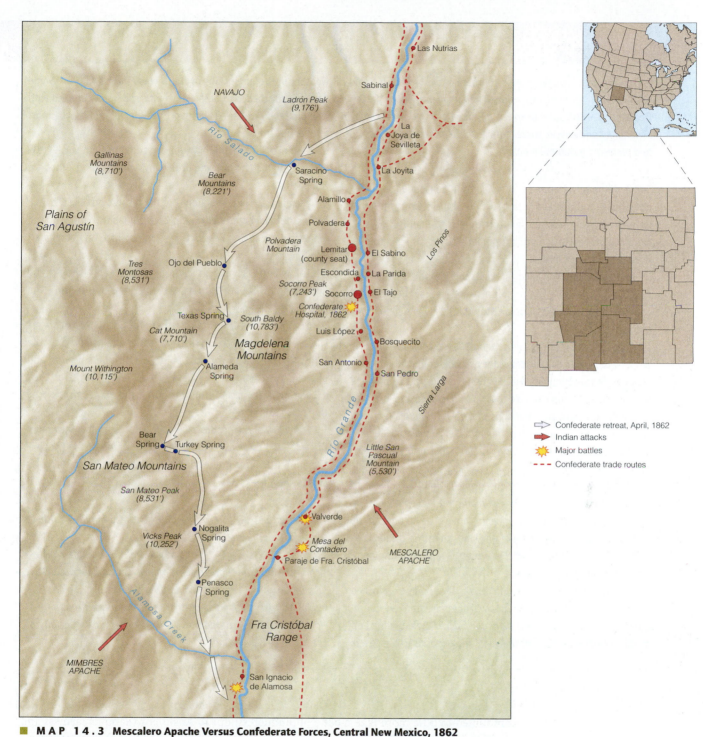

■ MAP 14.3 Mescalero Apache Versus Confederate Forces, Central New Mexico, 1862
The Confederates hoped to conquer the entire Southwest for slavery. In the summer of 1861, a force led by
Colonel John R. Baylor invaded the Mesilla Valley in New Mexico Territory. The Southerners scored a series of
notable successes until defeated at La Glorieta Pass, a battle called the Gettysburg of the West, in March 1862.
This map shows how the Confederates, harried by the Apache and Navajo, retreated from New Mexico.

The first weeks of the war revealed that the South would pursue its antebellum aims of
conquering western territory for slavery. An early victory of Texas forces over Union troops in
New Mexico led to the formation of what slaveholders in that region called the Confederate
Territory of Arizona. Over the next year, the Confederates launched successful assaults on the
cities of Albuquerque and Santa Fe, in present-day New Mexico. However, southern troops

A Virginia Slaveholder Objects to the Impressment of Slaves

During the Civil War, some southern slave owners bitterly resisted Confederate slave impressment policies. On December 4, 1861, John B. Spiece, an Albemarle County, Virginia, slaveholder and lawyer, wrote to the Confederate attorney general and protested government policy.

Dr Sir, Although a stranger to you, yet in consequence of the excitement and distress in this section of the country, in reference to a certain matter; I am constrained to address you, not merely on my own account; but on behalf of a large number of most respectable citizens. . . .

A practice has prevailed for some considerable time in *this* section of the country of impressing into service of the confederate army, the horses wagons and *slaves* belonging to the people.

The "Press masters" will go to their houses, and drag off their property to Just Such an extent as they choose; until it has not only created great excitement and distress; but bids fair to produce wide spread ruin. And I am told that these "Press masters" are paid by the Government the enormous price of *two dollars and fifty cents for each team which they impress;*—hence their anxiety and untiring exertions to increase the number;—thus making thirty or forty dollars pr day—

While I do not controvert the right of the Government to impress into its service *wagons and teams*; yet I do controvert the right to impress *Slaves*—It does seem to me that no one can be impress'd into military service of any kind, unless he is subject to military duty: because this whole business is relating to the Army, and is purely a military matter.—

The people in this section of the country are much attached to their slaves, and treat them in a humane manner—consequently they are exceedingly pained at having them dragged off at this inclement season of the year, and exposed to the severe weather in the mountains of north western Virginia. . . . Some have already died, and others have returned home afflicted with Typhoid fever, which has spread through the family to a most fatal and alarming extent.—

I am a practicing lawyer myself, but these "Press masters" will hear nothing from any one residing amongst the people.—

Therefore Sir, in consequence of the distress produced by the causes before mentioned, I am constrained to write to you; requesting you if you please, to give your opinion upon the questions involved.

To wit—If a man's wagon and team should be impress'd into Service, can his slave be impress'd to drive the said team—

Secondly—If a man has neither wagon or team can his slave be impress'd to drive some other team (*some* of the "Press masters" yield this *last* point, whilst others do not, and contend that they can impress just as many slaves as they choose from any plantation, taking all the negro men if they think proper.)—

Some few of the people have not been able to sow their grain this fall:—and there is deep dissatisfaction amongst the people—therefore I deem it proper and expedient that the authorities should know it—

Spiece goes on to cite the laws of the Commonwealth of Virginia, as amended in 1860, "by which it seems there is no power to impress Slaves." In the absence of Confederate congressional legislation to that effect, he argues, government authorities lack the legal right to take slaves from their owners. Spiece concludes his letter by suggesting that in taking slaves far from their homes, Confederate authorities were endangering the security of the would-be new nation.

amounted to little more than a band of plunderers; in Rio Abajo, for example, farmers and ranchers switched their allegiance to the Union after the rebels raided their homesteads.

Deprived of money raised from customs duties (the U.S. Navy blockade brought a halt to established patterns of overseas trade), the Confederacy relied on floating bonds ($400 million worth), raising taxes, and levying a 10 percent tax on farm produce. The Confederate treasury printed money at a furious rate ($1 billion over the course of the conflict), but its value declined precipitously; near the end of the war, one Confederate dollar was worth only 1.6 cents.

Raising a volunteer army and impressing slave labor (forcing slaves to labor for the military) met with stiff resistance from various quarters of southern society. For yeoman farm families, long defensive of the independence of their own households, Confederate mobilization efforts came as a rude shock. Antebellum Southerners believed that white fathers should protect and retain control over their dependents at all times. Planters expressed

The Library of Congress

■ These slaves are unloading ships at City Point, Virginia. Field hands impressed to work in Confederate factories, on wharves, and in mines experienced a new way of life off the plantation and out of the sight of their owners.

There is also a serious evil in impressing slaves for the service in North western Virginia:—whilst there they get to talking with *Union men* in disguise, and by that means learn the original cause of the difficulty between North & South: then return home and inform other negroes:—not long since one of my neighbors negro men went to his master, and desired to let him go again to the north western army—adding "I wish you to let me go further than I went before["]—I have the honor to be most respectfully your Obt Servt.

It is unknown whether Confederate officials responded to Spiece's letter.

QUESTIONS

1. *How does John Spiece demonstrate his talents as a lawyer in this letter?*

2. *In what ways does Spiece's reaction to slave impressment suggest changes in, or challenges to, southern planters' ideology of paternalism?*

Source: Ira Berlin, Barbara J. Fields, Thavolia Glymph, Joseph P. Reidy, and Leslie S. Rowland, eds., *Freedom: A Documentary History of Emancipation, 1861–1867,* Series 1, Vol. 1, *The Destruction of Slavery* (New York: Cambridge University Press, 1985), 782–783.

a well-founded fear that slaves impressed for a wide range of tasks, whether saltmaking or chopping trees or tending brick kilns, were difficult to control now that plantation discipline had been loosened. When the Confederate call for volunteers failed to produce the number of soldiers (and menial laborers) needed to fight the Union, the Richmond government in March 1862 implemented a military conscription law: all men between ages 18 and 35—later raised to 45—were called up for three years of service. The law exempted certain kinds of workers, such as railroad employees, schoolteachers, miners, and druggists, and allowed the buying of substitutes by draftees who could afford the $300 price for them. This last type of exemption allowed wealthy men to pay someone to fight in their place.

These provisions provoked anger not only among ordinary citizens but also among principled states' rights advocates such as governors Joseph Brown of Georgia and Zebulon Vance of North Carolina. Brown exempted large numbers of men from the draft, claiming that the Confederacy posed a greater threat to states' rights than did the Union. On January 1, 1862, 209,852 southern men were present for duty. Yet the northern force was more than twice as large, with 527,204.

Also complicating the Davis administration's attempts to mobilize for war was the refusal of the Confederates to form a political party system, on the assumption that unity among whites was the highest priority. However, the lack of parties meant that real differences over military and diplomatic strategy were reduced to infighting between shifting groups of elected officials and military men. Davis and members of his cabinet were quick to label dissent of any kind as treasonous, squelching legitimate debate on significant issues. In wartime Richmond, pro- and anti-Davis factions were made and unmade on the basis of rumor, innuendo, and the friendships and feuds among the wives of officers and politicians. In this respect, the white South clung to an outmoded identity as a collection of individuals bound to yield to no person, party, or government.

■ Stand Watie

INDIANS IN THE SERVICE OF THE CONFEDERACY

Just as the Confederates failed in their attempt to use fully the labor of enslaved workers, so they failed to reap much gain from the vaunted military prowess of Indians, especially those in Indian Territory (present-day Oklahoma). In 1861, southern military officials appealed to the Five Tribes for support, promising them arms and protection from Union forces in return. Only gradually and reluctantly did Cherokee leader John Ross commit his men to the Confederacy: "We are in the situation of a man standing alone upon a low naked spot of ground, with the water rising all around him."

More devoted to the Confederate cause was Stand Watie, the brother of one of the Cherokee leaders who signed the original removal treaty. Backed by many Cherokee slaveholders, Stand Watie mobilized young Indian men from several nations as a fighting force on behalf of the Confederacy. Among those responding to the call to arms were Choctaw and Chickasaw men, who formed Company E of the 21st Mississippi Regiment, "the Indian Brigade."

Although Indian Territory was considered of great strategic value to the Confederacy, southern military officials at times expressed frustration with the traditional battle tactics of Indian warriors, who were unused to military encounters that pitted long, straight rows of men on foot against each other. At the Battle of Elkhorn Tavern (Pea Ridge) in March 1862, Indian troops abandoned the battlefield in the face of cannon fire, leading their commander, Albert Pike, to demand that in the future they be "allowed to fight in their own fashion" rather than "face artillery and steady infantry on open ground." Yet most Confederate generals measured Indians by European American standards of what made a "proper" soldier on the battlefield. Many were labeled "undisciplined" and "not very reliable."

By the summer of 1862, the Confederacy had lost its advantage in Indian Territory. The Cherokee and Creek were divided in their loyalties, with some joining Union forces. By this time, the Comanche and Kiowa, resentful of the Confederacy's broken promises (guns and money diverted from them), had joined Union troops and were threatening to invade Texas.

THE ETHNIC CONFEDERACY

Throughout the Confederacy, whites expressed outrage at what they perceived was the North's unfair advantage. These Southerners claimed that their own army consisted overwhelmingly of native-born soldiers—in the words of Mary Boykin Chesnut, "those nearest and dearest [to us]—rank and file, common soldiers." In contrast, they claimed, Union ranks were composed of "crowds of Irish, Dutch, Scotch," and especially Germans. This view was misleading on both counts. Of the 2 million white soldiers and sailors who fought for the North, about 25 percent were immigrants. In contrast, the northern immigrant population amounted to almost a third of all white men of military age. Thus, the foreign-born were actually somewhat underrepresented in the northern army.

Moreover, the Confederacy was more of a multicultural endeavor than many white Southerners realized. Like Native Americans, immigrants and ethnic minorities in the South were divided in their loyalties. A Jewish lawyer and slaveholder, Judah P. Benjamin, served as a cabinet member and trusted adviser to Jefferson Davis. Prominent southern military officers included some from Ireland, Prussia, and France.

Immigrant workmen from southern cities—primarily Germans and Irish—filled the ranks of the Confederate army. Troops drawn from New Orleans included immigrants from Greece, Spain, Cuba, Scandinavia, Scotland, Belgium, and Poland. In that city, a German society founded to aid German immigrants began a monthly subscription series to aid the needy families of southern soldiers; the group sponsored theater performances, fairs, and a spring *Volkfest* (festival) to raise money. Some Louisiana ethnic groups formed their own home guards or volunteer corps. From the northeastern part of the state came the Madison Tips, composed of men who had hailed from County Tipperary, Ireland, and now labored on the Mississippi River levees. In Shreveport, Louisiana, Irish railroad workers formed the Landrum Guards and volunteered for service in the Confederate army.

On the other hand, ethnic loyalties did not rule out disloyalty and dissent within the Confederacy. In Texas, for example, some German immigrants supported abolition. Many of these were political refugees who had fled their native country after the failed revolutions of 1848. Throughout the war, Texas officials remained suspicious of Germans as a group; in 1863, reports that 800 German American men in Colorado, Fayette, and Austin counties were arming themselves to resist the draft law resulted in the jailing of their leaders. Nevertheless, the highest ranks of the Confederate military included immigrants from Germany or men of German heritage.

The *Tejano* community was also split in its loyalties. Some Hispanic men joined the Confederate army not out of conviction but out of fear that they would be sent out of the country if they refused. Others claimed that they were Mexican citizens and so not required to fight for the South. Yet a total of 2,500 Hispanic men joined the Confederate army. Colonel Santos Benavides, who commanded the 33rd Texas Cavalry, became the highest ranking *Tejano* to serve in the rebel army; on the battlefield he was joined by his brothers Refugio and Cristobal, both captains in the regiment.

Among those who fought for the South was the Cuban-born Loreta Janeta Velásquez. Velásquez's husband enlisted in the Confederate cause and was killed early in the war. The young widow then disguised herself as a man and, under the name of Lieutenant Harry T. Buford, fought under General Leonidas Polk during his Kentucky campaign in the early fall of 1861. She was wounded twice and left military service only to begin work as a Confederate spy. Like other women spies, Velásquez used gender stereotypes and expectations to her advantage. (Other women secret agents included Belle Boyd for the Confederates and Elizabeth Van Lew for the Union.) Women spies concealed messages under their skirts and inside elaborate hairdos. They moved back and forth between the North and South because officials on both sides of the conflict were reluctant to challenge a well-dressed woman. In the service of the southern cause, Velásquez carried military documents in her lady's satchel (a large purse) across enemy lines. Posing as a humanitarian, she visited Confederate prisoners in the North and interviewed them about military matters.

Velásquez traveled extensively and rarely missed an opportunity to engage Union officers in conversation. Of one young Union captain she encountered in Baltimore, she remarked: "I courted his friendship." Spinning a (tall) tale about her misfortunes in life, Velásquez gained the confidence of unsuspecting officers. These men were inevitably affected by her "pitiful narrative," Velásquez recalled later; their concern gave her an opportunity to pursue innocent-sounding questions about local troop movements and numbers.

■ This picture shows three Confederate surgeons, along with their African American servant, at a hospital in Lynchburg, Virginia. Confederate officials used enslaved men and women in a variety of capacities—as menial laborers, cooks, and laundresses in army camps, aides in hospitals, railroad hands, and industrial laborers.

University of North Carolina, Southern Historical Collection

■ A Hispanic woman, Janeta Velásquez (right) disguised herself as a soldier named Lt. Harry T. Buford (left) to serve the Confederacy. Later she operated as a spy for the South.

Determined to fight a defensive war, Confederates believed that they need not equal the North in terms of men or resources in order to prevail; they must only show fierce determination in holding their own territory against the onslaught of the invaders. But as the war dragged on, events would suggest that the South had badly miscalculated.

The Course of War, 1862–1864

■ *What obstacles did the South face in defending its territory against northern invaders?*

When the time came to marshal resources in the service of the national state, Northerners were at a distinct advantage over the states' rights men who dominated the Confederacy. Not only did the Union have more resources, but the Republicans' support for the centralization and consolidation of power also facilitated the war-mobilization process. In Congress, the Republicans took advantage of their new majority status and expanded federal programs in the realm of the economy, education, and land use. However, like Davis, Lincoln encountered vehement opposition to his wartime policies from some quarters. Meanwhile, on the battlefield, Union losses were mounting. The United States confronted an uncertain fate.

THE REPUBLICANS' WAR

Worried about disloyalty in the vicinity of the nation's capital, on April 27, 1861, Lincoln gave General Winfield Scott the power to suspend the writ of habeas corpus (a legal doctrine designed to protect the rights of people arrested) in Baltimore. By the end of the year, this policy, which allowed the incarceration of people not yet charged with a crime, was being applied in almost all of the loyal United States. Chief among those targeted were people suspected of interfering with war mobilization of men and supplies. Democrats stepped up their opposition to the president, denouncing him as a tyrant and a dictator. Meanwhile, from the other side of the political spectrum, abolitionists expressed their frustration with the administration's conciliatory policy toward the South in general and toward Unionist

TABLE 14.1

Ohio Men Drafted for Military Service Who Reported for Duty or Hired Substitutes

Occupation	Failed to Report	Exempted for Cause	Commuted or Hired Substitute	Held to Service
Unskilled Laborer	25%	45%	24%	6%
Skilled Laborer	25%	44%	22%	9%
Farmer and Farm Laborer	16%	34%	31%	19%
Merchant, Manufacturer, Banker, Broker	23%	46%	29%	2%
Clerk	26%	48%	24%	2%
Professional	16%	49%	29%	6%

slaveholders in particular. Lincoln insisted that his objective was "to save the Union, and . . . neither to save or destroy slavery."

Wartime manufacturing and commerce proved a boon to entrepreneurs. In Cleveland, a young commission-house operator named John D. Rockefeller was earning enough money to hire a substitute to serve in the army for him. In the middle of the war, he shifted his business from selling grain, fish, water, lime, plaster, and salt to refining the crude oil (used in kerosene lamps) recently discovered in western Pennsylvania. War profiteers seized opportunities in both the North and the South. In 1862, the *Southern Cultivator*, a magazine published in Augusta, Georgia, ran an article titled "Enemies at Home," denouncing the "vile crew of speculators" who were selling everything from corn to cloth at exorbitant prices.

The Republicans' willingness to centralize wartime operations led in 1861 to the formation of the U.S. Sanitary Commission. This agency recruited physicians, trained nurses, raised money, solicited donations, and conducted inspections of Union camps on the front. During the war, as many as 20,000 white and black women served as nurses, cooks, and laundresses in Union military hospitals. Black women worked primarily in the latter two categories. A long-time advocate of reform on behalf of the mentally ill during the antebellum period, Dorothea Dix served as superintendent of nurses.

The Republicans believed that the federal government should actively promote economic growth and educational opportunity, and they enacted measures previously thwarted by Democratic presidents and Congresses. In July 1862, the **Homestead Act** granted 160 acres of western land to each settler who lived on and made improvements to the land for five years. Congress also passed the **Morrill Act,** which created a system of land-grant colleges. (Many of these colleges eventually became major public universities, including Colorado State University, Kansas State University, and Utah State University.) Also approved in 1862, the **Pacific Railroad Act** appropriated to the Union Pacific and the Central Pacific Railroads a 400-foot right-of-way along the Platte River route of the Oregon Trail and lent them, depending on the terrain, $16,000 to $48,000 per mile.

During the first year and a half of war, Union military strategy reflected a prewar Republican indifference to the rights and welfare of both northern and southern blacks. In September 1861, Lincoln revoked a directive released by General John Frémont that would have authorized the seizure of property and the emancipation of slaves owned by Confederates in the state of Missouri. The president feared that such a policy would alienate slaveholders who were considering switching their allegiance to the Union. Later that fall, the capture of Port Royal, South Carolina, allowed Union soldiers to treat blacks as "contraband of war," denying slaveholders their human property but failing to recognize blacks as free people with rights.

As Union forces pushed deeper into Confederate territory, U.S. officers devised their own methods for dealing with the institution of slavery. By early 1862, the North had set

The Library of Congress

■ By 1862, Northerners were hailing General Ulysses S. Grant for his quick decisions and bold action, declaring that his initials stood for "Unconditional Surrender"—the demand he made upon defeated Confederate armies.

its sights on the Mississippi River valley, hoping to bisect the Confederacy and cut off supplies and men bound from Texas, Arkansas, and Louisiana to the eastern seaboard. In February, General Ulysses S. Grant captured Fort Henry and Fort Donelson on the Tennessee and Cumberland rivers, the Union's first major victory of the war; in April, New Orleans fell to Admiral David Farragut. In New Orleans, General Benjamin Butler attempted to retain the loyalty of Unionist slaveholders by returning runaway slaves to them. This policy was not always greeted with enthusiasm within Union ranks. A Massachusetts soldier, restless under the command of an officer sympathetic to "slave catching brutes," vowed, "I never will be instrumental in returning a slave to his master in any way shape or manner."

Butler also inflamed local Confederates with his "Woman Order" of May 15, 1862, which held that any woman caught insulting a Union soldier should be considered a prostitute and treated as such. As far away as the British House of Commons, members of Parliament condemned the "infamous" conduct of Butler toward what they considered respectable American ladies.

THE RAVAGES OF WAR

In the summer of 1862, the South suffered a hemorrhaging of its slave population, as the movement of Union troops up and down the eastern seaboard opened the floodgates to runaways. In August a group of Liberty County, Georgia, planters claimed that 20,000 slaves (worth $12 to $15 million) had absconded from coastal plantations, many of them holding "the position of Traitors, since they go over to the enemy & afford him aid and comfort" by providing information and erecting fortifications.

■ During the war, many slaves remained on the plantation, biding their time and waiting for an opportunity to escape. The arrival of the U.S. Army into an area prompted many to flee the slave quarters and seek refuge behind Union lines. These refugees are on their way to New Bern, North Carolina, in 1863.

Yet over the course of the summer, the Confederacy persevered on the battlefield, aided by the failure of Union armies to press their advantage. In June, General George McClellan was turned back on the outskirts of Richmond, convincing Lincoln not only of the incompetence of his chief general but also of the value of a less forgiving approach toward the South. In July, intending to pursue a more aggressive strategy against the massive southern military force, Lincoln brought back the boastful General John Pope from the western campaign ("where we have always seen the backs of our enemies") to command the 50,000 troops of the Army of the Potomac.

The second battle of Manassas in late August pitted Pope and the ridiculed "Tardy" George McClellan against Lee and Jackson. (Among Jackson's foot soldiers in that battle were New Orleans's Pelican Company F, a veritable "congress of nations" including native speakers of German, French, and Spanish.) Within five days, the Union had suffered 16,000 casualties out of a force of 65,000, whereas 10,000 in Lee's smaller force of 55,000 had been killed or wounded.

The Civil War Part I: 1861–1862

The summer of 1862 highlighted the difficulties faced by both sides in fighting a war during warm weather (when roads were passable) in the southern swamps and lowlands. More deadly than bullets and cannon to troops were diseases, especially diarrhea, dysentery, typhoid, pneumonia, and malaria. These killers affected major campaigns, including the failed Union attempt to capture Vicksburg in July. Languishing in the swamps near Richmond, one Union soldier wrote in his diary, "The Army is full of sick men."

In other parts of the country, the Union's war against the Confederates spilled over into savage campaigns against Indian tribes. An uprising among the Santee Sioux in Minnesota killed 500 whites before the state militia quashed the rebellion at Wood Lake in the fall of 1862. General James H. Carleton routed the Texas Confederates, who had been occupying New Mexico and Arizona, and then provided what he called a "wholesome lesson" to the Mescalero Apache and Navajo who had been menacing Hispanic villages in the area. Sending his troops out to locate the Mescalero, Carleton ordered, "The men are to be slain whenever and wherever they can be found. Their women and children are to be taken prisoner." Union soldiers captured Apache leader Mangas Colorado and later murdered him (although he had surrendered under a white flag). The Mescalero were forced to accept reservation status at Bosque Redondo in the Pecos River valley. Meanwhile, Colonel Kit Carson conducted a campaign of terrorism against the Navajo, burning *hogans* and seizing crops and livestock, claiming that "wild Indians could be tamed." Many of the survivors undertook the "Long Walk" to Bosque Redondo, a forced march reminiscent of the Cherokee Trail of Tears a generation before.

The bloodiest day of the war occurred on September 17, 1862, on the banks of Antietam Creek in northern Virginia. The Battle of Antietam claimed 20,000 lives and resulted in a Union victory, although it was a dubious victory indeed. Part of the battle took place in a thirty-acre cornfield, where Confederates had hidden themselves. Observing the tips of Southerners' bayonets glistening in the sunlight, General Joseph Hooker and his men mowed them down with firepower "as the grass falls before the scythe," in the words of a newspaper reporter present at the battle. The corpses mingled among the cornstalks presented a grisly sight. Nevertheless, Hooker recalled of the encounter, "The conduct of my troops was sublime, and the occasion almost lifted me to the skies, and its memories will ever remain near me."

■ Kate Cumming of Mobile, Alabama, earned the gratitude of the Confederacy for her work as a hospital matron during the war. Before and during the Civil War, many people believed that respectable women should not work in hospitals. Physicians claimed that women were likely to faint at the sight of blood and were not strong enough to turn patients over in their beds. Yet as the war progressed, more and more northern and southern women defied these stereotypes and served in hospitals as nurses, administrators, and comforters of the ill and dying. Noted Cumming soon after she first entered a hospital, "The foul air from this mass of human beings at first made me giddy and sick, but I soon got over it." Still, in southern hospitals, soldiers and enslaved workers handled much of the direct patient care.

Minnesota Historical Society (Neg. #36339)

■ During August 1862, a bitter conflict between local Sioux Indians and rural homesteaders engulfed southern Minnesota. After U.S. troops suppressed the uprising, Lincoln pardoned many of the warriors, but thirty-eight were hanged at Mankato, Minnesota, on December 26, 1982. As shown here, a crowd gathered to watch the largest government execution in American history, and wagons waited to cart away the corpses. U.S. officials forced the surviving Sioux into reservations in present-day South Dakota.

DOCUMENT

Barton, Memoirs about Medical Life at the Battlefield (1865)

To journalists and soldiers alike, battles could offer stirring sights of long rows of uniformed men arrayed against each other, their arms at the ready, regimental flags unfurled in the wind. Yet for the women of Shepardstown, Maryland, left to clean up after the Antietam slaughter, there was no talk of the glory of war, only a frantic, round-the-clock effort to feed the Confederates and bind their wounds. Surveying the battlefield wreckage, one observer, Maria Blunt, lamented the carnage: the dead, but also men "without arms, with one leg, with bandaged sides and backs; men in ambulances, wagons, carts, wheelbarrows, men carried on stretchers or supported on the shoulder of some self-denying comrade." All over the South, white women established temporary hospitals in barns, private homes, and churches and mourned each human sacrifice to the cause: "A mother—a wife—a sister had loved him."

The extraordinarily high casualty rate in the war stemmed from several factors. Confederates and Federals alike fought with new kinds of weapons (rifles and sharpshooters accurate at up to 1,000 yards) while troops massed in old-style, close formation. Soft minié balls punctured and lodged in limbs, leading to high rates of amputation that in turn fostered deadly infections. One Alabama soldier observed in 1862: "I believe the Doctors kills more than they cour [cure]." In fact, twice as many Civil War soldiers died of disease and infection as were killed in combat.

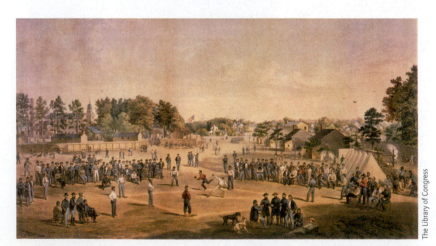

The Library of Congress

■ This painting shows Union prisoners of war playing baseball at Salisbury, North Carolina. Baseball originated in northern working-class communities before the war. It was possible to put in a full day of work and then have time to play a game in the early evening. Southern elite white men scorned baseball, claiming that men of honor did not run—for any reason.

The Library of Congress

■ The bodies of soldiers lay where they fell on September 17, 1862, the single day that claimed the largest number of lives in the Civil War. Like many other battles of the war, Antietam was shaped by the physical features of the battlefield itself, with soldiers on both sides seeking cover in small groves of trees and behind rocks, road ruts, and fences made of stone and wood.

THE EMANCIPATION PROCLAMATION

Appalled by the loss of life but heartened by the immediate outcome of Antietam, Lincoln took a bold step. In September he announced that on January 1, 1863, he would proclaim all slaves in Confederate-controlled territory free. Lincoln used the Emancipation Proclamation not only to bolster northern morale by infusing the conflict with moral purpose but also to further the Union's interests on the battleground by encouraging southern blacks to join the U.S. Army. The measure left slavery intact in the loyal Border States and in all territory conquered by the Union. Consequently, nearly 1 million black people were excluded from its provisions. Skeptical of the ability of blacks and whites to live together, Lincoln remained committed to the colonization of freed blacks outside the United States (in Central America or the West Indies).

In the congressional elections of 1862, the Democrats had picked up strength in New York, Pennsylvania, and Ohio and carried Illinois. The lower Midwest in general harbored large numbers of Democrats who opposed the war (especially now that it was an "abolition war") and called for peace with the South; these so-called Copperheads disrupted Union enlistments and encouraged military desertions. The Emancipation Proclamation electrified abolitionists, but the war effort and the growing casualties were taking their toll among the laboring classes. Especially aggrieved were the working people who paid higher taxes (relative to those paid by the wealthy) to keep the war machine running, and the dockworkers and others who lost their livelihoods when trade with foreign countries ceased. Their resentment boiled over in the summer of 1863.

PERSISTENT OBSTACLES TO THE CONFEDERACY'S GRAND STRATEGY

From the beginning of the war, the North's effort to blockade 3,500 miles of southern coastline met with fierce resistance on the high seas. The South made up in resourcefulness what it lacked in a navy, relying for supplies on swift steamers manned by privateers. (British arms smuggled onto remote southern beaches could bring up to 700 percent in profits.) Seemingly invincible Confederate ships such as the ironclad *Merrimack* and the well-fortified British-built warships *Alabama* and *Florida* prowled the southeastern seaboard, sinking Union vessels and protecting the blockade runners. Nevertheless, by December 1861, Union forces had established beachheads in Confederate territory up and down the East Coast.

In November 1861, Union naval forces intercepted a British packet ship, the *Trent,* and seized two Confederate diplomats, James Mason and John Slidell, who were en route to London and Paris, where they planned to plead the South's case in a bid to gain diplomatic recognition. To avoid a rift with England, Lincoln and Secretary of State William H. Seward released the two men. In the process, Mason and Slidell lost whatever influence they might have had with European governments, and Lincoln enjoyed the praise of the British public for his moderation in handling the *Trent* affair.

> By December 1861, Union forces had established beachheads in Confederate territory up and down the East Coast.

More generally, Confederate hopes for diplomatic recognition foundered on the shoals of European politics and economics, in England and in the Western Hemisphere. English textile mills drew on their own immense prewar stockpiles of raw cotton and sought out new sources of the fiber in Egypt and elsewhere. Also, English workers flexed their political muscle in a successful effort to forestall recognition of the slaveholders' nation. Early in the war, the Confederates recognized the strategic importance of Mexico, both as a trade route for supplies and as a means of access to ports. In approaching Mexican President Benito Juárez for aid in late 1861, however, Confederate envoy John T. Pickett discovered that, although Mexicans still smarted from their defeat on their own land thirteen years before, the Juárez administration remained an ally of the United States.

By the summer of 1862, Britain and France were inclined to mediate peace in favor of Confederate independence, for the two powers assumed that the South's impressive victories in Virginia and Tennessee signaled a quick end to the war. Nevertheless, the Confederacy's autumn setbacks of Antietam and Perryville (in Kentucky), combined with the ennobling rhetoric of the proposed Emancipation Proclamation, proved that the Union was still very much alive. The diplomatic recognition the white South so desperately craved remained elusive.

The Other War: African American Struggles for Liberation

■ *In what ways did black people, northern and southern, enslaved and free, shape the course of the fighting?*

From the onset of military hostilities, African Americans, regardless of whether they lived in the North or the South, perceived the Civil War as a fight for freedom. Although they allied themselves with Union forces, they also recognized the limitations of Union policy in ending slavery. Therefore, blacks throughout the northern and southern states were forced to take action to free themselves as individuals, families, and communities. Twenty-year-old Charlie Reason recalled his daring escape from a Maryland slave master and his decision to join the famous 54th Massachusetts Infantry composed of black soldiers: "I came to fight *not* for my country, I never had any, but to gain one." Soon after the 54th's assault on Fort Wagner (outside Charleston Harbor) in July 1863, Reason died of an infection contracted when one of his legs had to be amputated. Wherever they lived, black people fought in countless ways to gain a country on their own terms.

THE UNFOLDING OF FREEDOM

Black people served as combatants in the war in ways that whites could neither anticipate nor fully appreciate. One noteworthy example is that of an enslaved woman named Nancy Johnson. For Johnson and her family, freedom unfolded only gradually, over the course of the war years. Later in life she would describe her own wartime journey out of slavery and into freedom as a series of novel, potent encounters with individual white people on the Liberty County, Georgia, rice plantation where she and her family lived.

One night, she and her husband, Boson Johnson, harbored an escaped Union prisoner of war, conveying him to safety the following day. Later she marveled that the Northerner had "sat in my room"—a remarkable occurrence, considering that, before the war, "white people didn't visit our house." Soon after, her master's grandson threatened to kill Boson Johnson if Nancy did not reveal the fugitive soldier's whereabouts. In a desperate bid to protect her family, she told the white man a boldfaced lie—"that I had seen nothing." In the course of the conflict, Nancy and Boson Johnson sheltered and fed others they considered their allies—deserters from the Confederate army, poor whites the couple "befriended . . . because they were on our side." These white men "were opposed to the war & didn't own slaves & said they would rather die than fight."

Other wartime confrontations with whites boded ill for the Johnsons and future generations of African Americans. As Union troops began to encroach on southeastern Georgia in December 1864, Nancy Johnson's master approached her and begged her to stay on the plantation—a slave owner pleading with a slave to work! But she "told him if the other colored people were going to be free that I wanted to be." She left the plantation, only to return a short time later. At that point her mistress accosted her, demanding to know "if I had come back to behave myself & do her work & I told her no that I came to do my own work." The white woman ordered Nancy to continue weaving cloth, "like a '*nigger*,'" prompting the black woman to retort "no[,] that I was free."

Nancy eventually agreed to weave forty yards of dress material, but only on the condition that she be paid for the work. When the cloth was woven and the white woman refused to pay, Nancy Johnson repeatedly demanded the money due her. Out of the crucible of war had emerged a new set of personal and public relationships. Here was a black woman demanding wages from her former mistress, and here was a former mistress shedding the veneer of paternalism and doing her best—cajoling, intimidating, making promises—to get a black woman back to the weaver's loom.

In January 1865, Union soldiers under the command of Brigadier General Judson Kilpatrick raided the plantation where the Johnsons lived. The soldiers made off with a huge stock of the family's belongings—dishes, tubs, kettles, bed linens, rice, lard, hogs, chickens, a horse, and even clothes. Years after the fact, Nancy Johnson could still vividly recall the chaotic scene: white men "starved & naked almost," shooting livestock, overturning corncribs, grabbing everything they could carry, including her young son who had been guarding wagons of provisions—"the soldiers took the wagons & the boy, & I never saw him any more." Among the raiding party Nancy Johnson recognized the soldier she and Boson had rescued earlier. When she approached him, he told her "he tried to keep them from burning my house but he couldn't keep them from taking everything we had." She protested to individual soldiers about the amount of food they were taking: "I told one of the officers we would starve." Of the white man who stole her children's clothes, she had a hard time believing that "a Yankee person would be so mean." Within a day and a half the troops were gone, leaving Nancy and Boson Johnson to pick up the pieces of their old life and begin a new one as best they could.

> *Black people served as combatants in the war in ways that whites could neither anticipate nor fully appreciate.*

We have no independent way to verify Nancy Johnson's dramatic story, which she recounted years later in an effort to prove her family's support for the Union Cause. But her story does confirm broad themes related to the experiences of African Americans during the Civil War. Many blacks sought to aid Union forces. The war disrupted labor relations on the plantation, as customary patterns of disciplining and controlling slaves dissolved in the chaos of war. When black people sought to work for themselves, they severed the bonds of slavery and seized freedom on their own terms. These transformations in the system of bondage helped to undermine the Confederacy.

ENEMIES WITHIN THE CONFEDERACY

DOCUMENT

Chesnut, A Confederate Lady's Diary (1861)

Slaveholding whites were shocked when they could not always count on the loyalty of "petted" domestics. Soon after the war began, South Carolina's Mary Boykin Chesnut expressed unease about the enigmatic behavior of one of her trusted house slaves, Laurence, asking herself of all her slaves, "Are they stolidly stupid or wiser than we are, silent and strong, biding their time?" A few months later, Chesnut's cousin was murdered while sleeping, bludgeoned by a candlestick; the cousin's slaves William and Rhody were charged with the crime. One of Chesnut's woman friends remarked of her own mulatto servant: "For the life of me, I cannot make up my mind. Does she mean to take care of me—or to murder me?" Now rising to the surface, such fears put whites on alert, guarding against enemies in their midst.

Yet no single white man or woman could halt the tide of freedom. Given the chance to steal away at night or walk away boldly in broad daylight, black men, women, and children left their masters and mistresses, seeking safety and paid labor behind Union lines. Throughout the South, black people waited and watched for an opportunity to flee from plantations, their actions depending on the movement of northern troops and the disarray of the plantations they lived on.

In July 1862, the Union's Second Confiscation Act provided that the slaves of rebel masters "shall be deemed captives of war and shall be forever free," prompting Union generals to begin employing runaway male slaves as manual laborers. Consequently, military authorities often turned away women, children, older adults, and the disabled, leaving them vulnerable to spiteful masters and mistresses. For black men pressed into Union military service and menial labor, and for their families still languishing on plantations, "freedom" came at a high price indeed.

■ Many southern black men experienced freedom as soldiers for the Union army. They embraced the era's rituals of manhood, including shouldering arms and participating in dress parades. Assembling in formation in Beaufort, South Carolina, in 1864, these soldiers belong to the 29th Regiment, U.S. Colored Troops.

The Library of Congress

THE ONGOING FIGHT AGAINST PREJUDICE

In the North, the Emancipation Proclamation spurred the enlistment of blacks in the Union army and navy. Eventually, about 33,000 northern blacks enlisted, following the lead of their brothers-in-arms from the South. For black soldiers, military service opened up a wider world. Some learned to read and write in camp, and almost all felt the satisfaction of contributing to a war that they defined in stark terms of freedom versus slavery. They wore their uniforms proudly.

Union wartime policies revealed, however, that African Americans would continue to fight prejudice on many fronts. Some northern whites approved recruiting blacks, reasoning that for each black man killed in battle, one white man would be spared. Until late in the war, black soldiers were systematically denied opportunities to advance through the ranks and were paid less than whites. Although they showed loyalty to the cause in disproportionate numbers compared with whites, most blacks found themselves barred from taking up arms at all, relegated to work deemed dangerous and degrading to whites. They intended to labor for the Union, but in the words of a black soldier from New York, "Instead of the musket it is the spade and the Whelbarrow and the Axe cuting in one of the horable swamps in Louisiana stinking and misery." For each white Union soldier killed or mortally wounded, two died of disease; the ratio for blacks was one to ten.

Harriet Beecher Stowe Center, Hartford, CT

Many northern military strategists and ordinary enlisted men showed indifference at best, contempt at worst, for the desire of black fugitives to locate lost loved ones and begin to labor on their own behalf. In the course of the war, Union experiments with free black labor—on the South Carolina Sea Islands under the direction of northern missionaries, and in Louisiana under the direction of generals Nathaniel Banks and Benjamin Butler—emphasized converting the former slaves into staple-crop wage workers under the supervision of Yankees. Some of these whites, in their eagerness to establish "order" in former Confederate territory, saw blacks only as exploitable labor—if not cannon fodder, then hands to dig ditches and grow cotton.

Former slave Susie King Taylor recalled the heady, dangerous days of 1862, when she fled from Savannah and found refuge behind Union lines off the coast of Georgia. Despite receiving little pay for her labors for the First South Carolina Volunteers (later known as the 33rd United States Colored Cavalry), Taylor gained a great deal of satisfaction from her work on behalf of the Union cause and the black soldiers who fought for it. She conducted a school for black children on St. Simons Island and performed a whole host of tasks for the soldiers, from cleaning rifles to washing clothes and tending the ill. She understood that her own contributions to the war effort showed "what sacrifices we can make for our liberty and rights."

The Emancipation Proclamation did not materially change the day-to-day experiences of any slaves within southern territory, though many derived hope from the Union's new-found commitment to the abolition of bondage. That commitment changed the nature of the war from 1863 onward.

■ Laura Towne and three of her pupils pose for a picture on Saint Helena Island, South Carolina, in 1866. A native of Pennsylvania, Towne traveled to the South Carolina Sea Islands in April 1862, soon after they were occupied by Union forces. She and her companion and fellow teacher Ellen Murray epitomized the hundreds of idealistic northern women who volunteered to teach southern black people of all ages during and after the Civil War. Declared Towne on her arrival in the South, "We've come to do antislavery work, and we think it noble work and mean to do it earnestly."

Battle Fronts and Home Fronts in 1863

■ *How did developments on the battlefield affect politics in both the North and South?*

In 1863, the North abandoned the strategy of conciliation in favor of an effort to destroy the large southern armies and deprive the Confederacy of its slave labor force. By this time the war was causing tremendous hardship among ordinary whites in the South. Meanwhile, Lincoln found himself caught between African American freedom fighters who resented the poor treatment they received from many white commanders, and white Northerners who took their opposition to the war in general and the military draft in particular into the streets. Deprivation at home and the mounting casualty rates on the battlefields were reshaping the fabric of American society, North and South.

DISAFFECTION IN THE CONFEDERACY

The Civil War assaulted Southerners' senses and their land. Before the war, slave owners and their allies often contrasted the supposed tranquility of their rural society with the rude, boisterous noisiness of the North. According to this view, the South was a peaceful place of contented slaves toiling in the fields, whereas the North was the site of workers striking, women clamoring for the vote, and eccentric reformers delivering street-corner harangues.

The war exploded on the southern landscape with ferocious force, and the rumble of huge armies on the march shook southern society to its foundations. For the first time, many Southerners smelled the acrid odor of gunpowder and the stench of rotting bodies. They heard the booms of near and distant cannon and the mournful sounds of church bells tolling for the dead. They saw giant encampments of soldiers cover what used to be cotton fields. Seemingly overnight, both armies constructed gorge-spanning train trestles and huge riverside docks and warehouses, all in preparation for conflict. As soldiers withdrew from the battlefield, they left behind a scarred and blood-spattered land, cornfields mowed down, fires raging in their wake.

Women from Virginia to Alabama protested a Confederate 10 percent "tax-in-kind" on produce grown by farmers.

These sights and sounds were especially distressing to Southerners who objected to the war as a matter of principle or because of its disastrous effects on their own households. Scattered throughout the South were communities resistant to the policies of what many ordinary whites considered the Richmond elite—the leaders of the Confederacy. In western North Carolina, a group calling themselves Heroes of America declared their loyalty to the Union. In northern Mississippi, the "Free State of Jones [County]" raised troops for the Union army. Throughout the rural South, army deserters were welcomed home by their impoverished wives and children; it is estimated that during much of the war, as many as one-third of all Confederate soldiers were absent without leave at any particular time.

Groups of poor women resisted the dictates of the Davis administration, which was perceived as representing wealthy men and women who flaunted an extravagant wartime lifestyle of lavish dinners and parties. Women from Virginia to Alabama protested a Confederate 10 percent "tax-in-kind" on produce grown by farmers. Food shortages reached crisis proportions. In April 1863, several hundred Richmond women, many of them wives of Tredegar Iron Works employees, armed themselves with knives, hatchets, and pistols and ransacked stores in search of food: "Bread! Bread! Our children are starving while the rich roll in wealth."

Whereas some white women resisted the Confederacy, others leaped to the fore to provide essential goods and services to the beleaguered new nation. Virginia's Belle Boyd kept track of Union troop movements and served as a spy for Confederate armies. Poor women took jobs as textile factory workers, and their better-educated sisters found employment as clerks for the Confederate bureaucracy. Slaveholding women busied themselves running plantations, rolling bandages, and knitting socks for soldiers. Still, many women thought their labors were in vain. Of the Confederacy's stalled progress, Georgia's Gertrude Thomas noted, "Valuable lives lost and nothing accomplished."

THE TIDE TURNS AGAINST THE SOUTH

In the fall of 1862, Lincoln replaced General McClellan with General Ambrose E. Burnside and then General Joseph ("Fighting Joe") Hooker. In early May 1863, Lee and Jackson encountered Hooker at Chancellorsville, Virginia. The battle left Hooker reeling, but it also claimed the life of Jackson, mistakenly shot by his own men on May 2 in the early evening twilight. The South had lost one of its most ardent champions.

Lee decided to press his advantage by invading Pennsylvania and, it was hoped, encouraging northern Peace Democrats and impressing the foreign powers. The ensuing clash at Gettysburg was a turning point in the war. Drawn by reports of a cache of much-needed shoes, Confederate armies converged on the town, in the south-central part of the state, across the border from Maryland. Union forces pursued the southern troops. In a three-day

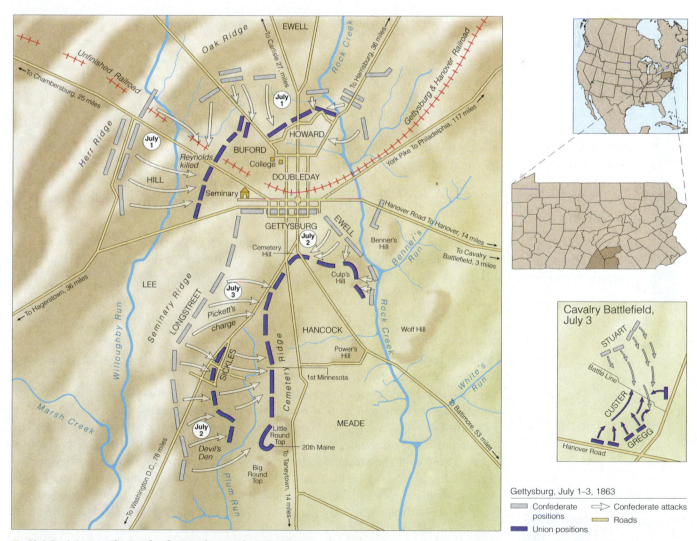

■ **MAP 14.4** **The Battle of Gettysburg, July 1–3, 1863**

The three-day battle of Gettysburg was a turning point in the war. This map shows that Confederate soldiers made repeated assaults on Union lines. Lee's confidence in this strategy was misplaced, and some of his own staff recognized it. Recalled General James Longstreet of the third day of fighting: "My heart was heavy. I could see the desperate and hopeless nature of the charge and the hopeless slaughter it would cause.... That day at Gettysburg was one of the saddest of my life."

The Wider World

Deaths of Americans In Principal Wars, 1775–1991

War	Number Serving	Total Deaths	Battle Deaths	Other Deaths*	Wounded, Not Mortally
Revolutionary War 1775–1783	175,000–200,000	25,674	7,174	18,500	8,241
War of 1812 1812–1815	286,730	2,260	2,260	–	4,505
Mexican War 1846–1848	78,718	13,283	1,733	11,550	4,152
Civil War 1861–1865, Union	2,213,363	364,511	140,414	224,097	281,881
Civil War, Confederate	750,000–1,250,000	258,000	94,000	164,000	622,511
Spanish-American War 1898	306,760	2,446	385	2,061	1,662
World War I 1917–1918	4,734,991	116,516	53,402	63,114	204,002
World War II 1941–1945	16,112,566	405,399	291,557	113,842	671,846
Korean War 1950–1953	5,720,000	36,574	33,741	2,833	103,284
Vietnam War 1964–1973	8,744,000	58,209	47,424	10,785	153,303
Persian Gulf War 1990–1991	2,225,000	382	147	235	467

*Includes deaths from disease.

This table compares the number of American soldiers killed and wounded in the Civil War with figures for Americans killed and wounded fighting foreign foes in other wars. Note that these figures do not include the number of American foreign allies and enemies killed in combat during these wars.

QUESTIONS

1. How do you account for the tremendous difference in the number of American troops killed in the Revolutionary War as opposed to the Civil War?

2. Why are the rates of death from disease so high in many of these conflicts?

3. How do the figures for the Civil War compare to the figures for all other wars combined?

4. Given the tremendous loss of life during the Civil War, how would you characterize the significance of that conflict in American history?

5. Should the number of slaves who died of disease while working on Confederate fortifications be included in this table? If so, under what category?

---

battle that began on July 1, the 92,000 men under the command of General George G. Meade were arrayed against the 76,000 troops of Robert E. Lee.

Gettysburg later came to represent the bloody consequences of a war fought by men with modern weapons under commanders with a premodern military sensibility. On the last day of the battle, the men under Major General George Pickett moved slowly into formation, passing hastily dug graves and the fragments of bodies blown to bits the day before. At 3 p.m., a mile-wide formation of 15,000 men gave the rebel yell and charged three-quarters of a mile across an open field to do battle with Union troops well fortified behind stone walls. Within half an hour, Pickett had lost two-thirds of his soldiers and all 13 of his colonels. The battle's three-day toll was equally staggering: 23,000 Union and 28,000 Confederate soldiers wounded or killed. Fully one-third of Lee's army was dead or wounded.

What made the soldiers of both sides fight on under these conditions? Some remained devoted to a cause. Others cared less about the Confederacy or the Union and more about proving their manhood and upholding their family's honor. Still others sought to avenge comrades slain in battle or to conform to standards of discipline drilled into them. Some prayed merely to survive.

DOCUMENT

Brewster, Three
Letters from the Front
(1862)

The Union victory at Gettysburg on July 3, 1863, brought rejoicing in the North. The next day General Ulysses S. Grant captured Vicksburg on the Mississippi River, a move that earned him the rank of lieutenant general. Within a year Lincoln appointed him supreme commander of the Union armies.

CIVIL UNREST IN THE NORTH

Not all segments of northern society joined in the celebration of Union victories. Even principled supporters of the war effort were growing weary of high taxes and inflated consumer prices, not to mention the sacrifices of thousands of husbands, sons, and brothers. In May, federal soldiers had arrested the defiant and outspoken Copperhead Clement Vallandigham at his home in Dayton, Ohio. Subsequently convicted of treason (he had declared the conflict "a war for the freedom of blacks and the enslavement of whites"), Vallandigham was banished to the South.

Following a military draft imposed on July 1, 1863, the northern white working classes erupted. Enraged at the wealthy who could buy substitutes, resentful of the Lincoln administration's high-handed tactics, and determined not to fight on behalf of African Americans, white laborers in New York City, Hartford, Troy, Newark, and Boston (many of them Irish) went on a rampage. The New York City riot of July 11–15 was especially savage as white men directed their wrath against black men, women, and children. Members of the mob burned the Colored Orphan Asylum to the ground and then mutilated their victims before the federal government deployed 20,000 troops to New York to quell the violence and discourage other men from resisting the draft elsewhere. On August 19, the draft resumed.

> *Following a military draft imposed on July 1, 1863, the northern white working classes erupted.*

THE DESPERATE SOUTH

Meanwhile, the South had to contend not only with dissent and disaffection at home but also with the stunning battle and territorial losses it suffered at Gettysburg and Vicksburg. On August 21, 1863, Jefferson Davis proclaimed a day of "fasting, humiliation and prayer." Even as Davis was invoking the name of the Almighty, 450 rebels under the command of William Clarke Quantrill were destroying the town of Lawrence, Kansas (long a hotbed of abolitionist sentiment), and killing 150 of its inhabitants. With the exception of Quantrill and John Singleton Mosby (whose squads of men roamed northern Virginia attacking Union posts and troops in 1863), Confederate military leaders shunned guerrilla warfare, preferring to meet the enemy on a field of honor. The desperate Quantrill raid on Lawrence demonstrated that the Confederate cause was, if not lost, then losing in the late summer of 1863.

Before the year was out, Davis faced other setbacks as well. Grant's successes at Missionary Ridge and Lookout Mountain, in Tennessee, caused both France and England to draw back from offering overt support to the Confederacy in the form of sales of navy warships or diplomatic recognition. The Confederate president had long counted on securing the support of the great European powers; now those hopes were dashed.

Dedicating the national cemetery at Gettysburg on November 19, 1863, Lincoln delivered a short address that affirmed the nation's "new birth of freedom" and its commitment that "the government of the people, by the people, for the people, shall not perish from the earth." Lincoln's speech is one of the great rhetorical masterpieces of American politics. In it he elevated the Civil War from a military conflict exclusively to a great moral struggle against slavery. In the South, more and more whites were flagging in their conviction that the system of bondage was worth the ultimate sacrifice in terms of their own lives and the welfare of their families.

Chivington did not come in peace. That day he and his men massacred 125 to 160 Indians, mostly women, children, and old people, returning later to mutilate the bodies. In response, Sioux, Arapaho, and Cheyenne launched their own campaigns against white migrants traveling the South and North Platte trails. Chivington declared that it was "right and honorable" to kill Indians, even Indian children, using any means.

"FATHER ABRAHAM"

The election of 1864 proceeded without major incident, although Lincoln faced some opposition within his own party. Together with his new running mate, a former slave owner from Tennessee named Andrew Johnson, Lincoln benefited from a string of Union victories won by Admiral David G. Farragut at Mobile, Alabama, and by General Philip Sheridan in Virginia's Shenandoah Valley. As a result, he defeated the Democratic nominee, his own former general, George McClellan, who managed to garner 45 percent of the popular vote. One of the keys to Lincoln's success was the "peace platform" that the Democrats had drafted at their convention the summer before.

TABLE 14.2			
The Election of 1864			
Candidate	**Political Party**	**Popular Vote (%)**	**Electoral Vote**
Abraham Lincoln	Republican	55.0	212*
George B. McClellan	Democratic	45.0	21

*Eleven secessionist states did not participate.

Support among Union soldiers for "Little Mac" dropped precipitously as a result, and Lincoln won three-quarters of the army's vote.

Despite his limited military experience, Lincoln possessed a strategic sense superior to that of many of his generals. He played down his own military experience, making light of his minor part in the Black Hawk War of 1832. In that conflict, he reminisced, he had engaged in "charges upon wild onions . . . [and] bloody struggles with the Musquetoes." However, he cared deeply about ordinary soldiers and talked with them whenever he had the opportunity. In return, Union troops gave "Father Abraham" their loyalty on the battlefield and, especially during the election of 1864, at the ballot box.

SHERMAN'S MARCH FROM ATLANTA TO THE SEA

The South's physical environment—its terrain, natural growth, and climate—shaped the course of the Civil War, and that environment was in turn transformed by the fighting. The Union army's famous march from Atlanta to the sea in the late fall of 1864 reveals the complex interplay of armies and the land.

Occupying the Piedmont city of Atlanta in the summer of 1864, General William Tecumseh Sherman believed that an assault on the Georgia coastline would have tremendous strategic and diplomatic benefits for the Union cause: "If we can march a well-appointed army right through [Confederate] territory, it is a demonstration to the whole world, foreign and domestic, that we have a power which [Confederate President Jefferson] Davis cannot resist. . . . I can make the march, and make Georgia howl!"

The Library of Congress

■ Like other officers in both the Union and Confederate armies, William Tecumseh Sherman had graduated from the United States Military Academy at West Point.

On November 15, Sherman's army left Atlanta, organized in four columns, 60,000 infantry and 5,550 cavalry strong. Along the 285-mile march, the army met only light resistance from a few thousand Georgia militia cavalry commanded by General Joseph Wheeler.

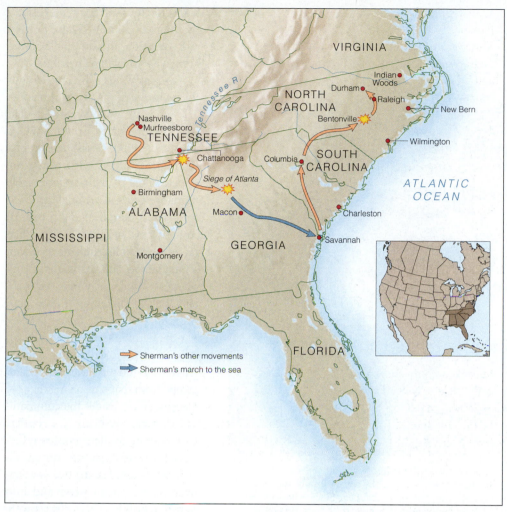

■ **MAP 14.6 Sherman's March to the Sea, 1864–1865**

General William T. Sherman's famous march to the sea marked the final phase of the Union effort to divide and conquer the Confederacy. Sherman's men burned Atlanta to the ground in September 1864. In late December they made their triumphant entry into the city of Savannah. Under a policy of "hard war," Sherman ordered his troops to seize from civilians any food and livestock they could use and to destroy everything else, whether rail lines, houses, or barns. White southerners expressed outrage over these tactics. Still, Sherman never systematically attacked civilians, a characteristic of the Union's "total war" against Native American peoples in the West.

The march itself was an engineering marvel. Confederate forces sought to block the enemy advance by burning bridges, felling trees across roads, and planting land mines along the way. Sherman responded to the challenge by encouraging able-bodied black men, now former slaves, to join the army and work as part of its Corps of Engineers, who had the task of overcoming natural obstacles. These workers, called "pioneers," constructed corduroy roads made with rails or newly cut poles, allowing supply trains to traverse swampland and muddy ground. Sherman's forces could repair bridges quickly, rebuilding a 1,000-foot-long span in as little as three days. They became expert at using pontoons to cross rivers. Pontoons were structures consisting of two boats with a trestle suspended between them. These temporary bridges could be dismantled in as little time as thirty minutes and then reassembled as needed farther down the road.

The Union army also destroyed railroads, leaving the Georgia landscape littered with smoldering, twisted iron ties. Observed John J. Hight, a Union chaplain from New York State: "Our people are making a thorough wreck of them [the railroads]. The rails are torn from the ties, which are then piled, and laid across them. The ties are then fired, and the rails, while red hot in the center, are twisted. A rail, simply bent, can be used again, without being

CORBIS

This photo shows Confederate defenses on the eve of Union forces' assault on Petersburg, Virginia, in mid-summer 1864. The Confederates managed to hold the city until early April 1865. Wrote one Union soldier who survived the battle, "They had some awful and devilish devices and batteries fixed up. Around some of their batteries' earthworks, they drive thick beds of wooden stakes, sharpened to a point and slanting to the front, so that anyone who would charge them might as well charge a sword cane."

taken to the shop for repair, but a twisted bar cannot." These burned and twisted railroad ties became known as "Sherman's hairpins."

Sherman's army became famous for its foraging off the countryside. The general was convinced that large supply trains would slow his advance, and he was determined to impress upon Georgians the hopelessness of their situation. He therefore ordered raiding parties to seize food supplies and livestock from farms along the way. The raiders were indiscriminate in seizing animals, food, and goods from grand planters, modest yeoman farmers, and slaves, including Boson and Nancy Johnson.

If Sherman's march to Savannah depended on overcoming natural barriers, so too did the Confederates' escape from that city, on the night of December 19. Under the command of General William J. Hardee, Confederate soldiers worked feverishly for several days to construct a pontoon bridge leading from the city over the Savannah River and into South Carolina. Their efforts were delayed by fog and by ships running aground in the shallow Savannah River. Eventually engineers managed to fasten together thirty rice flats, each seventy to eighty feet long. Workers laid these flats end to end and then covered them with planks ripped from Savannah River wharves. Later contemplating his successful evacuation of the city, with his army intact and many civilians in tow, Hardee wrote: "Though compelled to evacuate the city, there is no part of my military life to which I look back with so much satisfaction." Hardee's pride in his pontoon bridge came at a high price; Sherman's capture of Savannah amounted to a death knell for the Confederacy.

THE LAST DAYS OF THE CONFEDERACY

MAP

The Civil War Part II: 1863–1865

After presenting Lincoln with the "Christmas gift" of Savannah in December, Sherman took his 60,000 troops north, slogging through swamps and rain-soaked terrain to confront the original secessionists. Later, he recalled with satisfaction, "My aim then was to whip the rebels, to humble their pride, to follow them to their inmost recesses, and make them fear and dread us." By mid-February, South Carolina's state capital, Columbia, was in flames. African American troops were among the triumphant occupiers of the charred city.

In the spring of 1865, Confederate leaders betrayed their desperation by initiating a debate over whether to arm slaves to fight for southern independence. At the beginning of the war, southern whites had believed that military service was an honor reserved for white men. But by early 1865, some political and military leaders, including Robert E. Lee, argued that the Confederacy should offer slave men the option of fighting in return for their freedom and the freedom of their families. However, the Confederate Congress never acted on this proposal.

By early April 1865, Grant had overpowered Lee's army in Petersburg, Virginia. Withdrawing, Lee sent a telegram to Davis, who was attending church in Richmond, warning him that the fall of the Confederate capital was imminent. Davis and almost all other whites fled the city. Arriving in Richmond on April 3, only hours after the city had been abandoned by Confederate officials and troops, was the commander in chief of the Union army, Abraham Lincoln. Flanked by a group of ten sailors, Lincoln calmly walked the streets of the smoldering city (set afire by departing Confederates). Throngs of black people greeted the president, exclaiming, "Glory to God! Glory! Glory! Glory!" When a black man kneeled to thank Lincoln, the president said, "Don't kneel to me. That is not right. You must kneel to God only, and thank Him for the liberty you will enjoy hereafter."

On April 9, Lee and his demoralized and depleted army of 35,000 found themselves outnumbered by Grant and Meade, and Lee surrendered his sword at Appomattox Courthouse in northern Virginia. Lee had rejected a plea by one of his men that the army disband and continue to fight a guerrilla war in the woods and hills. The general predicted that such a force "would become mere bands of marauders," destroying the countryside and with it what was left of the fabric of southern society.

The city of Charleston, South Carolina, lies in ruins after its defeat at the hands of Sherman's army in February 1865. This photo, taken in April, shows the shell of the city's famed Circular Church in the center.

The Library of Congress

Union officials assured rebel soldiers of protection from future prosecution (for treason) and allowed the cavalry to keep their horses for use in spring planting. When the ragtag members of the Stonewall Brigade—soldiers who had entered the war with Stonewall Jackson four years before—came forward to lay down their arms, the Union army gave them a salute of honor, acknowledging their bravery. However, this scene set the stage for the not-too-distant future, when the North and South reaffirmed their ties based on a shared "whiteness" in opposition to African Americans.

One of the last casualties of the war was Abraham Lincoln. Watching a comedy with his wife, Mary, at Ford's Theater in Washington on the night of April 14, 1865, Lincoln was assassinated by John Wilkes Booth, a Confederate loyalist fearful that the president was bent on advancing "nigger citizenship." Lincoln lingered through the night but died the next morning. Booth was caught and shot within a matter of days. Of the departed president, Secretary of War Edwin M. Stanton said: "Now he belongs to the ages."

Conclusion

Rather than asking why the South lost the Civil War, we might wonder why it took the North four years to win it. Despite all the political dissent and social conflict in the white South, despite the crumbling of the institution of slavery and the lack of support from the European powers, the Confederacy was able to mobilize huge armies under the command of brilliant tacticians such as Lee and Jackson. The war was fought on the battlefield by regiments of soldiers, not on the sea by navies or in the countryside by guerrillas. Therefore, as long as Confederate generals could deploy troops and outwit their foes during brief but monumental clashes, the Confederacy could survive to fight another day. The South had as its immediate goal the slaughter of as many Yankees as possible. Meanwhile, the North staggered under the

CHRONOLOGY: 1860–1865

1860 South Carolina secedes from Union.

1861 Confederate States of America is formed.

Civil War begins.

1862 Minnesota (Santee) Sioux uprising.

Congress passes Homestead, Morrill, and Pacific Railroad acts.

Union victory at the Battle of Antietam.

1863 Emancipation Proclamation.

Richmond Bread Riots.

Union victory at Battle of Gettysburg with heavy losses on both sides.

Northern antidraft riots.

Lincoln delivers Gettysburg Address.

1864 Fort Pillow massacre of African American (Union) soldiers in western Tennessee.

Sand Creek (Colorado) massacre of Cheyenne and Arapaho.

Sherman's March to the Sea.

Lincoln reelected president.

1865 Confederacy is defeated.

Lincoln assassinated.

weight of mobilizing large numbers of soldiers in enemy territory and supplying them with the necessary resources far from home.

The South had entered the war armed with a states' rights ideology that held that all whites in the region were unified in support of slavery, and that black people were passive and childlike in their dependence on whites. The course of the war exposed the fallacy of this ideology. Even at the outset of the war, white Southerners differed in their support for the Confederacy, and as the conflict dragged, many poor whites believed they were sacrificing more for the cause than were their social betters. Blacks proved aggressive in fighting for their freedom, wreaking havoc on plantation discipline and on southern military strategy. And too, many Confederates were forced to accept the fact that in order to fight the war successfully, principled states' rights supporters must yield to those politicians advocating a more centralized effort in behalf of mobilizing for war and fighting the enemy.

In terms of soldiers' lives lost—620,000—the Civil War was by far the costliest in the nation's history. At the end of the war, the Union was preserved and slavery was destroyed. Yet, in their quest for true freedom, African Americans soon learned that military hostilities were but one phase of a wider war, a war to define the nature of American citizenship and its promise of liberty and equality. Thus April 1865 marked not so much a final judgment as a transition to new battlefields.

For Review

1. Despite the claims of white leaders, the South was not unified in fighting the Civil War. Identify three different social groups within the South and discuss why they either initially withheld their support for the Confederacy, or why their initial support for the cause gradually eroded over the course of the fighting.

2. What were the North's advantages over the South in terms of centralizing military, political, and economic operations during the war? Given those advantages, why did the Confederacy nevertheless believe it could win the war?

3. What were the effects, and limitations, of the Emancipation Proclamation in shaping the course of the war? In shaping southern and black communities during the war?

4. How did developments on the northern home front reflect the priorities of the Republican party?

5. In what ways did the war challenge white southerners' traditional beliefs about the role of slavery—and slaves—in southern society?

6. What accounts for the long duration of the Civil War and the very high mortality rates among military personnel during the conflict? Why did neither Jefferson Davis nor Abraham Lincoln seek a negotiated settlement to avoid further bloodshed?

Created Equal Online

For more *Created Equal* resources, including suggestions on sites to visit and books to read, go to **MyHistoryLab.com**.

Chapter 15

Consolidating a Triumphant Union, 1865–1877

■ In Savannah, African American Sunday School pupils pose for photographer William Wilson in 1890. After the Civil War, many southern black communities created, or enlarged and solidified, their own institutions, including schools and churches.

Courtesy of the Georgia Historical Society, William Wilson Collection

CHAPTER OUTLINE

■ The Struggle over the South

■ Claiming Territory for the Union

■ The Republican Vision and Its Limits

The day of jubilee had come at last! In late December 1864, African American men, women, and children rejoiced when the troops of Union General William Tecumseh Sherman liberated Savannah, Georgia. The city's black community immediately formed its own school system under the sponsorship of a new group, the Savannah Education Association (SEA). The association owed its creation to the desire of freedpeople of all ages to learn to read and write. A committee of black clergy began by hiring fifteen black teachers and acquiring buildings (including the Old Bryan Slave Mart) for use as schools. By January 10, 1865, Savannah blacks had raised $800 to pay teachers' salaries, enabling several hundred black children to attend classes free of charge.

Following hard on the heels of the Union army, a group of northern white missionaries arrived in Savannah to seek black converts for two Protestant denominations, the Presbyterians and the Congregationalists. On the first day of school, in January 1865, these northern newcomers watched a grand procession of children wend its way through the streets of Savannah. The missionaries expressed amazement that the SEA was an entirely black-run organization. These whites had believed the former slaves incapable of creating such an impressive educational system.

In March 1865, the federal government, under the auspices of the newly formed Bureau of Refugees, Freedmen, and Abandoned Lands (Freedmen's Bureau), agreed to work with missionaries to open schools for black children throughout the former Confederate states. In Georgia, missionaries and government officials soon became alarmed that black leaders were willing to accept financial aid from them but not willing to relinquish control of SEA schools to the whites in return. The Northerners were also distressed by the militancy of certain local black leaders. One of these leaders was a former fugitive slave, Aaron A. Bradley, who arrived in Savannah from Boston in late 1865. Armed with a pistol and bowie knife, he began urging other blacks to free themselves from all forms of white power.

In an effort to wrest control of the SEA from Savannah blacks, northern missionaries and agents of the Freedmen's Bureau decided to withhold funds from the association. By March 1866, the city's black community, swollen by a refugee population, was no longer able to support its own schools. Northern whites took over SEA operations, and the association ceased to exist.

Almost a year earlier, on April 11, 1865, President Abraham Lincoln had appeared on the balcony of the White House to announce that the Union forces were victorious, the Confederate States of America defeated. Four years before, southern slaveholders had organized a rebellion against the federal government; their aim was to preserve slavery in the wake of the election of a Republican, antislavery president. The Civil War claimed nearly 700,000 American lives—more than all other conflicts (before or since) in American history combined. Yet the military defeat of the rebels did not resolve fundamental problems related to black people's status in the South or in the nation at large. Contemplating the difficult task ahead of the United States, Lincoln declared in that speech on April 11, just a few days before he was assassinated, "We must simply begin with, and mould from, disorganized and discordant elements."

During the months and years immediately after the war, a major conflict raged between supporters of African American rights and supporters of southern white privilege. Republican congressmen hoped to *reconstruct* the South by enabling African Americans to own their own land and to become full citizens. Southern freedpeople sought to free themselves from white employers, landlords, and clergy and to establish control over their own workplaces, families, and churches. In contrast, President Andrew Johnson appeared bent on *restoring* the antebellum power relations that made southern black field laborers dependent on white landowners. For their part, many southern whites were determined to prevent blacks from becoming truly free and equal citizens. Most former rebels remained embittered about the outcome of the war and vengeful toward the freedpeople.

The Civil War hardened the positions of the two major political parties. The Republicans remained in favor of a strong national government, one that promoted economic growth. The Democrats tended to support states' efforts to manage their own affairs, which included regulating relations between employers and employees, whites and blacks.

After the war, western economic development presented new challenges. In order to open the West to European American miners and homesteaders, the U.S. army clashed repeatedly with Native Americans. On the Plains and in the Northwest, Indians resisted white efforts to force them to abandon their nomadic way of life and take up sedentary farming. William Tecumseh Sherman, Philip H. Sheridan, and George Custer were among the U.S. military officers who had commanded troops in the Civil War and now attempted to subdue the Plains Indians and to promote white settlement. Sherman declared, "We must act with vindictive earnestness against the Sioux, even to their extermination, men, women and children." The former head of the Freedmen's Bureau, General Oliver O. Howard, oversaw the expulsion of Chief Joseph and his people, the Nez Perce, from their homeland in Southeast Washington's Walla Walla Valley in 1877.

U.S. soldiers also contributed to the building of the transcontinental railroad. A former Union military officer, Grenville Dodge, served as chief civil engineer for the Union Pacific Railroad, supervising huge workforces of immigrant laborers. The railroad industry was a potent symbol of postwar

U.S. nationalism. It also represented a robust, Republican-sponsored partnership between private enterprise and the federal government. Between 1862 and 1872, the government gave the industry subsidies that included millions of dollars in cash and more than 100 million acres of land. On the Plains, U.S. soldiers protected Union Pacific Railroad land surveyors against the retaliatory raids conducted by Indians who were enraged by this incursion into their territory and by the government's failure to abide by its treaties.

The Republicans' triumph prompted dissent from those people who feared that the victorious Union would serve the interests of specific groups such as men, employers, and white property owners. Some women's rights activists, for example, felt betrayed by the suggestion that this was "the hour of the Negro [man]." These women were not willing to wait indefinitely for their own voting rights. At the same time, in the bustling workshops of the nation's cities, many workers realized that they remained at the mercy of employers bent on using cheap labor. The founding of the **National Labor Union** in 1866 revealed that members of the laboring classes had a national vision of their own, one that valued the efforts of working people to earn a decent living for their families.

At great cost of human life, the Civil War decisively settled several immediate and long-standing political conflicts. The southern secessionists were defeated, and slavery as a legal institution was destroyed. Nevertheless, the relationship between federal power and group rights remained unresolved, leading to continued bloodshed between whites and Indians on the High Plains, as well as in the former Confederate states between Union supporters and diehard rebels. During the postwar period, now called the **Reconstruction era,** federal government officials attempted to complete the political process that the military defeat of the South had only begun: the consolidation of the Union, North and South, East and West. This process encompassed the nation as a whole.

The Struggle over the South

■ *How did various groups of northerners and southerners differ in their vision of the postwar South?*

The Civil War had a devastating impact on the South in physical, social, and economic terms. The region had lost an estimated $2 billion in investments in slaves; modest homesteads and grand plantations alike lay in ruins; and gardens, orchards, and cotton fields were barren. More than 3 million former slaves eagerly embraced freedom, but the vast majority lacked the land, cash, and credit necessary to build family homesteads for themselves. Hoping to achieve social and economic self-determination, African American men and women traveled great distances, usually on foot, in efforts to locate loved ones and reunite families that had been separated during slavery. At the same time, landowning whites considered black people primarily as a source of agricultural labor; these whites resisted the idea that the freedpeople should be granted citizenship rights.

In the North, Republican lawmakers disagreed among themselves how best to punish the defeated but defiant rebels. President Abraham Lincoln had indicated early that after the war the government should bring the South back into the Union quickly and painlessly. His successor wanted to see members of the southern planter elite humiliated but resisted the notion that freedpeople should become independent of white landowners. In Congress, moderate and radical Republicans argued about how far the government should go in ensuring the former slaves' freedom.

WARTIME PRELUDES TO POSTWAR POLICIES

Wartime experiments with African American free labor in Union-occupied areas foreshadowed these bitter postwar debates. As early as November 1861, Union forces had occupied the Sea Islands off Port Royal Sound in South Carolina. In response, wealthy cotton planters fled to the mainland. Over the next few months, three groups of northern civilians landed on the Sea Islands with the intention of guiding blacks in the transition from slave to free labor. Teachers arrived to create schools, and missionaries hoped to start churches. A third group, representing Boston investors, also settled on the Sea Islands to assess economic opportunities. By early 1862, they decided to institute a system of wage labor that would reestablish a staple crop economy and funnel cotton directly into northern textile mills. The freed slaves, however, preferred to grow crops for their families to eat rather than cotton to sell, relying on a system of barter and trade among networks of extended families. Their goal was to break free of white landlords, suppliers, and cotton merchants.

Meanwhile, in southern Louisiana, the Union capture of New Orleans in the spring of 1862 enabled northern military officials to implement their own free (nonslave) labor system. General Nathaniel Banks proclaimed that U.S. troops should forcibly relocate blacks to plantations "where they belong"; there they would continue to work for their former owners in the sugar and cotton fields, but now for wages supposedly negotiated annually. The Union army would compel blacks to work if they resisted doing so. In defiance of these orders, however, some blacks went on strike for higher wages, and others refused to work at all. Moreover, not all members of the Union military relished the prospect of forcing blacks to work on the plantations where they had been enslaved. Thus, federal policies returning blacks to plantations were contested even within the ranks of the army itself.

The Lincoln administration had no hard and fast reconstruction policy to guide congressional lawmakers looking toward the postwar period. In December 1863, the president outlined his Ten Percent Plan. This plan would allow former Confederate states to form new state governments once 10 percent of the men who had voted in the 1860 presidential election had pledged allegiance to the Union and renounced slavery. Congress instead passed the Wade-Davis Bill, which would have required a majority of southern voters in any state to take a loyalty oath affirming their allegiance to the United States. By refusing to sign the bill before Congress adjourned, Lincoln vetoed the measure (through a **pocket veto**). However, the president approved the creation of the Bureau of Refugees, Freedmen, and Abandoned Lands, or **Freedmen's Bureau,** in March 1865. The bureau was responsible for coordinating relief efforts on behalf of blacks and poor whites loyal to the Union, for sponsoring schools, and for implementing a labor contract system on southern plantations. At the time of his assassination, Lincoln seemed to be leaning toward giving the right to vote to southern black men.

PRESIDENTIAL RECONSTRUCTION, 1865–1867

When Andrew Johnson, the seventeenth president of the United States, assumed office in April 1865 after Lincoln's death, he brought his own agenda for the defeated South. Throughout his political career, Johnson had seen himself as a champion of poor white farmers in opposition to the wealthy planter class. A man of modest background, he had been elected U.S. senator from Tennessee in 1857. He alone among southern senators remained in Congress and loyal to the Union after 1861. Lincoln first appointed Johnson military governor of Tennessee when that state was captured by the Union in 1862 and then tapped him as his running mate for the election of 1864.

H. P. Moore/Collection of the New-York Historical Society, Neg. #37497

■ Residents of Edisto Island, one of the Sea Islands off the coast of South Carolina, pose with a U.S. government mule cart immediately after the Civil War. U.S. troops captured the island in November 1861. The following March, the government began to distribute to blacks the lands abandoned by their former masters. In October 1865, President Andrew Johnson halted the program. A group of angry and disappointed blacks appealed to the president, claiming, "This is our home, we have made these lands what they are." After meeting with the group, General Oliver O. Howard noted, "I am convinced that something must be done to give these people and others the prospect of homesteads."

Soon after he assumed the presidency, Johnson disappointed congressional Republicans who hoped that he would serve as a champion of the freedpeople. He welcomed back into the Union those states reorganized under Lincoln's Ten Percent Plan. He advocated denying the vote to wealthy Confederates, though he would allow individuals to come to the White House to beg the president for special pardons. Johnson also outlined a fairly lenient plan for readmitting the other rebel states into the Union. Poor whites would have the right to vote, but they must convene special state conventions that would renounce secession and accept the Thirteenth Amendment abolishing slavery. Further, they must repudiate all Confederate debts. The president opposed granting the vote to the former slaves; he believed that they should continue to toil as field workers for white landowners.

Initiated by presidential proclamation at the end of May 1865, the pardoning process revealed a great deal about Andrew Johnson as both a Southerner and a Republican politician.

■ President Andrew Johnson.

He personally considered appeals from 15,000 men, all of whom were required to apply directly to the president for a pardon; these men included those who had served as high-ranking Confederate officials and who owned taxable property worth $20,000 or more. Of humble origins himself, Johnson relished the sight of the wealthiest Southerners nervously crowding his office and seeking his pardon—at times hundreds of men in a single day. With these pardons, Johnson aimed to humble a group of southern leaders he considered arrogant—he wanted to "punish and impoverish them," he said. He also hoped to win support for his own reelection from southern poor whites, men who approved of his effort to humiliate the planter elite. One former Tennessee politician who had known Johnson for many years believed that if "Johnson were a snake, he would lie in the grass to bite the heels of rich men's children."

While he was in office, Johnson sought to reassure Southerners that he believed blacks needed "the care and civilizing influence of dependence upon the white race." Indeed, many former rebels gradually came to see Johnson as their postwar political ally; they hoped that he would counter the power of what they called vengeful Yankee "fanatics." The former Confederate secretary of the treasury, Christopher Memminger, noted that Johnson "held up before us the hope of a 'white man's government' and it was natural that we should yield to our old prejudices."

Johnson also argued that individual states should make their own laws on black suffrage. Many Northerners agreed. Indeed, northern states seemed eager to impose upon the defeated South provisions that they themselves would not accept. In 1865, only five New England states (of all northern states) allowed blacks to vote. That year, three state referenda on the issue—in Minnesota, Wisconsin, and Connecticut—failed to win voter approval. Almost all northern Democrats opposed black suffrage, but many of their Republican neighbors shared the same views. During the summer of 1865, Pennsylvania Republicans proclaimed that any discussion of black voting rights was "heavy and premature."

Johnson failed to anticipate the speed and vigor with which former Confederate leaders would move to reassert their political authority. In addition, he did not gauge accurately the resentment of congressional Republicans, who thought his policies toward the defeated South were too forgiving. The southern states that took advantage of Johnson's reunification policies passed laws that instituted a system of near slavery. Referred to as **Black Codes,** they aimed to penalize "vagrant" blacks, defined as those who did not work in the fields for whites, and to deny blacks the right to vote, serve on juries, or in some cases even own land. The Black Code of Mississippi restricted the rights of a freedperson to "keep or carry fire-arms," ammunition, and knives and to "quit the service of his or her employer before the expiration of his or her term of service without good cause." The vagueness of this last provision threatened any blacks who happened not to be working under the supervision of whites at any given moment. People arrested under the Black Codes faced imprisonment or forced labor.

DOCUMENT

The Mississippi Black Code

At the end of the war, congressional Republicans were divided into two camps. Radicals wanted to use strong federal measures to advance black people's civil rights and economic independence. In contrast, moderates were more concerned with the free market and private property rights; they took a hands-off approach regarding former slaves. But members of both groups reacted with outrage to the Black Codes. Moreover, when the legislators returned to the Capitol in December 1865, they were in for a shock: among their new colleagues were four former Confederate generals, five colonels, and other high-ranking members of the Confederate elite, including former Vice President Alexander Stephens, now under indictment for treason. All of these rebels were duly elected senators and representatives from southern states. In a special session called for December 4, a joint committee of fifteen lawmakers (six senators and nine members of the House) voted to bar these men from Congress.

By January 1865, both houses of Congress had approved the Thirteenth Amendment to the Constitution, abolishing slavery. The necessary three-fourths of the states ratified the measure by the end of the year. However, President Johnson was becoming more openly defiant of his congressional foes who favored aggressive federal protection of black civil rights. He vetoed two crucial pieces of legislation: an extension and expansion of the Freedmen's Bureau and the Civil Rights Bill of 1866. This latter measure was an unprecedented piece of legislation. It called on the federal government—for the first time in history—to protect individual rights against the willful indifference of the states (as manifested, for example, in the Black Codes). Congress managed to override both vetoes by the summer of 1866.

In June of that year, Congress passed the Fourteenth Amendment. This amendment guaranteed the former slaves citizenship rights, punished states that denied citizens the right to vote, declared the former rebels ineligible for federal and state office, and voided Confederate debts. This amendment was the first to use gender-specific language, guarding against denying the vote "to any of the male inhabitants" of any state.

Even before the war ended, some northerners had moved south, and the flow increased in 1865. Black and white teachers volunteered to teach former slaves to read and write. Some white Northerners journeyed south to invest in land and become planters in the staple-crop economy. White southern critics called all these migrants **carpetbaggers.** This derisive term suggested that the Northerners hastily packed their belongings in rough bags made of carpet scraps—a popular form of luggage at the time—and then rushed south to take advantage of the region's devastation and confusion. To many freedpeople, whether they worked for a carpetbagger or a Southerner, laboring in the cotton fields was but a continuation of slavery.

Some former southern (white) Whigs, who had been reluctant secessionists, now found common ground with northern Republicans who supported government subsidies for railroads, banking institutions, and public improvements. This group consisted of some members of the humbled planter class as well as people of more modest means. Southern Democrats, who sneered at any alliances with the North, scornfully labeled these whites **scalawags** (the term referred to a scrawny, useless type of horse on the Scottish island of Scalloway).

Soon after the war's end, southern white vigilantes launched a campaign of violence and intimidation against freedpeople who dared to resist the demands of white planters and other employers. The Ku Klux Klan, begun by a group of Tennessee war veterans, soon became a white supremacist terrorist organization that spread to other states. In May 1866, violence initiated by white terrorists against blacks in Memphis, Tennessee, left forty-six freedpeople and two whites dead; in July, a riot in New Orleans claimed the lives of thirty-four blacks and three of their white allies. Vigilantes attacked blacks who tried to vote or to challenge planters who cheated their workers. Men in disguise broke into the homes of blacks at night, whipping and beating women as well as men. These bloody encounters demonstrated the lengths to which ex-Confederates would go to reassert their authority and defy the federal government.

Back in Washington, Johnson condemned the Fourteenth Amendment and traveled around the country, urging the states not to ratify it. He argued that policies related to black suffrage should be decided by the states. The president maintained that the time had come for reconciliation between the North and South. (The amendment would not be adopted until 1868.)

Congressional Republicans fought back. In the midterm election of November 1866, they won a two-thirds majority in both houses of Congress. These numbers allowed them to claim a mandate from their constituents and to override any future vetoes by the president. Moderates and radicals together prepared to bypass Johnson to shape their own reconstruction policies.

THE POSTBELLUM SOUTH'S LABOR PROBLEM

While policymakers maneuvered in Washington, black people throughout the postbellum (postwar) South aspired to labor for themselves and gain independence from white

A Southern Labor Contract

Interpreting History

The Library of Congress

■ After the Civil War, many rural southern blacks, such as those shown here, continued to toil in cotton fields owned by whites.

After the Civil War, many southern agricultural workers signed labor contracts. These contracts sought to control not only the output of laborers but also their lives outside the workplace.

On January 1, 1868, the planter John D. Williams assembled his workers for the coming year and presented them with a contract to sign. Williams owned a plantation in the lower Piedmont county of

Laurens, South Carolina. He agreed to furnish "the said negroes" (that is, the three black men and two black women whose names were listed on the document) with mules and horses to be used for cultivating the land. The workers could receive their food, clothing, and medical care on credit. They were allowed to keep one-third of all the corn, sweet potatoes, wheat, cotton, oats, and molasses they produced.

overseers and landowners. Yet white landowners persisted in regarding blacks as field hands who must be coerced into working. With the creation of the Freedmen's Bureau in 1865, Congress aimed to form an agency that would mediate between these two groups. Bureau agents encouraged workers and employers to sign annual labor contracts designed to eliminate the last vestiges of the slave system. All over the South, freed men, women, and children would contract with an employer on January 1 of each year. They would agree to work for either a monthly wage, an annual share of the crop, or some combination of the two.

According to the Freedmen's Bureau, the benefits of the annual labor contract system were clear. Employers would have an incentive to treat their workers fairly—to offer a decent wage and refrain from physical punishment. Disgruntled workers could leave at the end of the year to work for a more reasonable landowner. In the postbellum South, however, labor relations were shaped not by federal decree but by a process of negotiation that pitted white landowners against blacks who possessed little but their own labor.

For instance, blacks along the Georgia and South Carolina coast were determined to cultivate the land on which their forebears had lived and died. They urged General Sherman to confiscate the land owned by rebels in the area. In response, in early 1865, Sherman issued Field Order Number 15, mandating that the Sea Islands and the coastal region south of

Presumably, they would pay their debts to Williams using proceeds from their share of the crop.

According to the contract, Williams's workers promised to

bind them Selves to be steady and attentive to there work at all times and to work at keeping in repair all the fences on Said plantation and assist in cuting and taking care of—all the grain crops on Said plantation and work by the direction of me [Williams] or my Agent. . . .

And should any of them depart from the farm or from any services at any time with out our approval they shall forfeit one dollar per day, for the first time and for the second time without good cause they shall forfeit all of their interest in the crop their to me the enjured person—they shall not be allowed to keep firearms or deadly wapons or ardent Spirits and they shall obey all lawful orders from me or my Agent and shall be honest—truthful—sober—civel—diligent in their business and for all wilful Disobedience of any lawful orders from me or my Agent drunkenness moral or legal misconduct want of respects or civility to me or my Agent or to my Family or any elce, I am permitted to discharge them forfeiting any claims upon me for any part of the crop. . . .

Moses Nathan	1 full hand
Jake Chappal	" "
Milly Williams	$\frac{1}{2}$ " "
Easter Williams	" "
Mack Williams	" "

At the end of the contract is this addition:

We the white labores now employed by John D. Williams on his white plains plantation have lisened and heard read the foregoing Contract on this sheet of paper assign equal for the black laborers employed by him on said place and we are perfectly Satisfied with it and heare by bind our selves to abide & be Governed & Controwed by it

Wm Wyatte	1 full hand
John Wyatte	1 full hand
Packingham Wyatte	$\frac{1}{2}$ " "
Franklin Wyatte	$\frac{1}{2}$ " "
R M Hughes	1 full hand
B G Pollard	1 full hand
George Washington Pollard	1 full hand

To sign the contract, all of the blacks and two of the whites "made their marks," signing with an "X" because they were illiterate.

QUESTIONS

1. *In what ways did sharecropping differ from wage labor?*

2. *Do you see evidence that family or kin members worked together on Williams's plantation?*

3. *What is the significance of the contract addendum signed by white laborers?*

Source: Rosser H. Taylor, "Postbellum Southern Rental Contracts" [from Furman University library, Greenville, South Carolina], *Agricultural History* 17 (1943): 122–123.

Charleston be divided into parcels of forty acres for individual freed families. He also decreed that the army might lend mules to these families to help them begin planting. Given the provisions of this order, many freed families came to expect that the federal government would grant them "forty acres and a mule."

As a result of Sherman's order, 20,000 former slaves proceeded to cultivate the property once owned by Confederates. Within a few months of the war's end, however, the War Department bowed to pressure from the white landowners and revoked the order. The War Department also provided military protection for whites to return and occupy their former lands. In response, a group of black men calling themselves Commissioners from Edisto Island (one of the Sea Islands) met in committee to protest to the Freedmen's Bureau what they considered a betrayal. Writing from the area in January 1866, one Freedmen's Bureau official noted that the new policy must be upheld but regretted that it had brought the freedpeople in "collision" with "U.S. forces."

In other cases, the Freedmen's Bureau opposed changes sought by African Americans, such as the ability of women to care for their children at home full-time. In April 1866, a white planter in Thomson, Georgia, wrote to a local Freedmen's Bureau official and complained that the black wives and mothers living on his land had refused to sign labor contracts. The planter explained, "Their husbands are at work, while they are nearly idle as it is possible for them to be, pretending to spin—knit or something that really amounts to nothing." These "idle" women posed a threat to plantation order, the white man asserted.

> *Who should toil in the fields of the South? And under what conditions should they labor?*

Women who stayed home to care for their families were hardly idle. Yet Freedmen's Bureau agents and white planters alike tended to define productive labor (among blacks) as work carried out under the supervision of a white man in the fields or a white woman in the kitchen. During the postwar period, a struggle ensued. Who should toil in the fields of the South? And under what conditions should they labor?

The physical devastation wrought by the war gave these questions heightened urgency. Most freedpeople understood that first and foremost they must find a way to provide for themselves. However, they thought of freedom in terms of welfare for their family rather than just for themselves as individuals. Men and women embraced the opportunity to live and work together as a unit; for many couples, their first act as free people was to legalize their marriage vows. Black women shunned the advice of Freedmen's Bureau agents and planters that they continue to pick cotton. These women withdrew from field labor whenever they could afford to do so. Enslaved women had been deprived of the opportunity to attend to family life. Now freedwomen sought to devote themselves to caring for their families.

During its brief life (1865 to 1868), the Freedmen's Bureau compiled a mixed record. The agency's most formidable challenge was its effort to usher in a new economic order in the South—one that relied on nonslave labor but also returned the region to prewar productivity levels in terms of planting and harvesting cotton. The Freedmen's Bureau established elementary schools and distributed rations to southerners who had remained loyal to the Union, blacks and whites alike. The Freedmen's Bureau's functions in the areas of education and labor represented a new and significant federal role in the realm of social welfare, yet the agency did not have the staff or money necessary to effect meaningful change. The individual agents represented a broad range of backgrounds, temperaments, and political ideas. Some were former abolitionists who considered northern-style free labor "the noblest principle on earth." These men tried to ensure safe and fair working arrangements for black men, women, and children. In contrast, some agents had little patience with the freedpeople's drive for self-sufficiency. While some bureau offices became havens for blacks seeking redress against abusive or fraudulent labor practices, others had little impact on the postwar political and economic landscape. For agents without means of transportation (a reliable horse), plantations scattered throughout the vast rural South remained outside their control. Because white landowners crafted the wording and specific provisions of labor contracts, the bureau agents who enforced such agreements often served the interests of employers rather than laborers.

DOCUMENT

Southern Skepticism of the Freedmen's Bureau (1866)

In fact, for the most part, postwar freedpeople pressed for their labor rights independently of the federal government. Their efforts took a dramatic form along the coastline of Georgia and South Carolina, where thousands of slaves had toiled in the muck-filled rice fields before the war. With the revocation of Sherman's Field Order Number 15, black laborers sought to negotiate with white landowners who wished to maintain rice cultivation in the region. Rice culture necessitated an intricate network of ditches, dams, and sluice gates; together these improvements amounted to a complicated hydraulic system. This system allowed for the periodic flooding of rice fields with fresh water from local canals and rivers. Resisting the heavy, hot, muddy work of conventional rice culture, and wishing to spend more time on their own crops, blacks forced landowners to institute labor-saving measures. These measures included the use of mules to pull rakes in order to clean out weed-choked ditches, and the use of wagons to carry rice from the fields to the barn. Some planters turned to other groups of workers—for example, Irish men who came out to the coast from the city of Savannah—whom they hired on a seasonal basis.

However, rice farming required year-round work to keep ditches, fences, and canals in good working order, jobs that seasonal workers could not or would not do. For their part, the freedpeople preferred to engage in subsistence farming and to fish and hunt to support their families. Gradually lowcountry planters realized they lacked the large, subordinate labor force that would make their rice competitive with the rice grown in other parts of the country and the world. In the low-country rice regions, then, black people's desire for economic autonomy, combined with the unhealthful and disagreeable nature of rice culture, transformed the local economy.

> *Freedpeople preferred to engage in subsistence farming and to fish and hunt to support their families.*

In the cotton regions of the South, freedpeople resisted the near-slavery system of gang labor that planters tried to enforce right after the war. Instead, extended families came together in groups called squads to negotiate collectively with landowners. Gradually, squads gave way to sharecropping families. The outlines of share-cropping, a system that defined southern cotton production until well into the twentieth century, were visible just a few years after the Civil War. Poor families, black and white, con-tracted annually with landlords, who advanced them supplies, such as crop seed, mules, plows, food, and clothing. Fathers directed the labor of their children in the fields. At the end of the year, many families remained indebted to their employer and, thus, entitled to nothing and obliged to work another year in the hope of repaying the debt. If a sharecropper's demeanor or work habits displeased the landlord, the family faced eviction.

DOCUMENT

A Sharecrop Contract

Single women with small children were especially vulnerable to the whims of landlords in the postbellum period. Near Greensboro, North Carolina, for example, when planter Presley George Sr. settled the year's accounts with his field worker Polly at the end of 1865, Polly was charged $69 for corn, cloth, thread, and board for a child who did not work. By George's calculations, Polly had earned exactly $69 for the labor she and her three children (two sons and a daughter) performed in the course of the year, leaving her no cash of her own. Under these harsh conditions, freedpeople looked to each other for support and strength.

BUILDING FREE COMMUNITIES

Independence in the workplace was not the only concern of freedpeople. Soon after the war's end, southern blacks set about organizing themselves as an effective political force and as free communities devoted to their own social and educational welfare. Differences among blacks based on income, jobs, culture, and skin color at times inhibited communal institution building. Some black communities found themselves divided by social status, with blacks who had been free before the war (including many literate and skilled light-skinned men) assuming leadership over illiterate field hands. In New Orleans, a combination of factors contributed to class divisions among people of African heritage. During the antebellum period, light-skinned freedpeople of color, many of whom spoke French, were much more likely to possess property and a formal education than were enslaved people, who were dark-skinned English speakers. After the Civil War, the more privileged group pressed for public accommodations laws, which would open the city's theaters, opera, and expensive restau-rants to all blacks for the first time. However, black churches and social organizations remained segregated according to class.

For the most part, postbellum black communities united around the principle that free-dom from slavery should also mean full citizenship rights: the ability to vote, own land, and educate their children. These rights must be enforced by federal firepower: "a military occupa-tion will be absolutely necessary," declared the blacks of Norfolk, "to protect the white Union men of the South, as well as ourselves." Freedpeople in some states allied themselves with white yeoman farmers who had long resented the political power of the great planters and now saw an opportunity to use state governments as agents of democratization and economic reform.

LISTEN

"Free at Last"

TABLE 15.1

Comparison of Black and White Household Structure in 27 Cotton-Belt Counties, 1870, 1880, 1900

1870 (N = 534)

Single Person %	Nuclear %	Ext. %	Aug. %	Ext./Aug. %	(Unrelated Adults %)	Total	
3.1	80.7	14.4	1.4	.3	.3	290	**Black**
2.1	71.3	7.4	17.6	1.2	.4	244	**White**
2.6	76.4	11.0	8.8	.7	.4	534	

1880 (N = 672)

Single Person %	Nuclear %	Ext. %	Aug. %	Ext./Aug. %	(Unrelated Adults %)	Total	
3.7	74.2	13.6	5.9	1.7	.8	353	**Black**
3.1	62.7	13.5	15.7	5.0	.0	319	**White**
3.4	68.8	13.5	10.6	3.3	.4	672	

1900 (N = 643)

Single Person %	Nuclear %	Ext. %	Aug. %	Ext./Aug. %	(Unrelated Adults %)	Total	
5.7	64.9	22.9	4.0	1.7	.8	353	**Black**
3.4	65.2	19.0	10.7	1.7	.0	290	**White**
4.7	65.0	21.2	7.0	1.7	.5	643	

Single person: one person living alone.
Nuclear: father, mother, and children.
Ext.: extended family consisting of parents, children, and kin.
Aug.: augmented household consisting of family and nonfamily members (boarders, servants, hired hands).
Ext./Aug.: combination of extended and augmented.
Unrelated adults: more than one unrelated adult living together.

Source: Jacqueline Jones, *Labor of Love, Labor of Sorrow: Black Women, Work and the Family from Slavery to the Present* (1985). Based on a sample of households (in selected cotton staple counties in Alabama, Florida, Georgia, Louisiana, Mississippi, North Carolina, South Carolina, and Texas) listed in the 1870, 1880, and 1900 federal population manuscript censuses.

Networks of freedpeople formed self-help organizations. Like the sponsors of the Savannah Education Association, blacks throughout the South formed committees to raise funds and hire teachers for neighborhood schools. Small Georgia towns, such as Cuthbert, Albany, Cave Spring, and Thomasville, with populations no greater than a few hundred, raised up to $70 per month and contributed as much as $350 each for the construction of school buildings. Funds came from the proceeds of fairs, bazaars, and bake sales; subscriptions raised by local school boards; and tuition fees. In the cash-starved postbellum South, these amounts represented a great personal and group sacrifice for the cause of education.

All over the South, black families charted their own course. They elected to take in orphans and elderly kin, pool resources with neighbors, and arrange for mothers to stay home with their children. These choices challenged the power of former slaveholders and the influence of Freedmen's Bureau agents and northern missionaries and teachers. At the same time, in seeking to attend to their families and to provide for themselves, southern blacks resembled members of other mid-nineteenth-century laboring classes who valued family ties over the demands of employers and landlords.

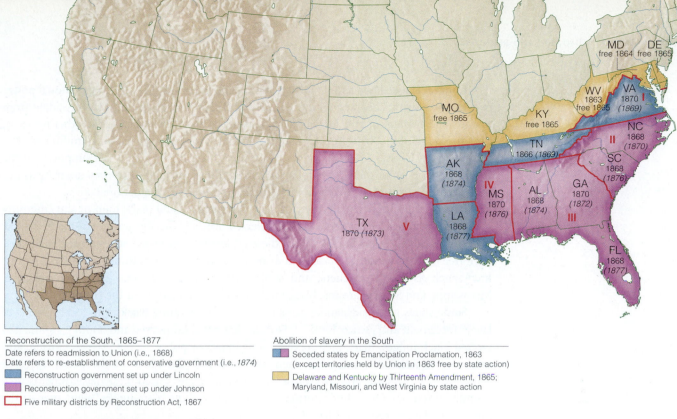

Reconstruction of the South, 1865–1877

Date refers to readmission to Union (i.e., 1868)
Date refers to re-establishment of conservative government (i.e., *1874*)

- ▬ Reconstruction government set up under Lincoln
- ▬ Reconstruction government set up under Johnson
- ▭ Five military districts by Reconstruction Act, 1867

Abolition of slavery in the South

- ▬ Seceded states by Emancipation Proclamation, 1863 (except territories held by Union in 1863 free by state action)
- ▬ Delaware and Kentucky by Thirteenth Amendment, 1865; Maryland, Missouri, and West Virginia by state action

■ **MAP 15.1   Radical Reconstruction**

Four of the former Confederate states—Louisiana, Arkansas, Tennessee, and Virginia—were reorganized under President Lincoln's Ten Percent Plan in 1864. Neither this plan nor the proposals of Lincoln's successor, Andrew Johnson, provided for the enfranchisement of the former slaves. In 1867, Congress established five military districts in the South and demanded that newly reconstituted state governments implement universal manhood suffrage. By 1870, all of the former Confederate states had rejoined the Union, and by 1877 all of those states had installed conservative (i.e., Democratic) governments.

Tangible signs of emerging black communities infuriated most southern whites. A schoolhouse run by blacks proved threatening in a society where most white children had little opportunity to receive an education. Black communities were also quick to form their own churches, rather than continue to occupy an inferior place in white churches. Other sights proved equally unsettling: on a main street in Charleston, an armed black soldier marching proudly or a black woman wearing a fashionable hat and veil, the kind favored by white women of the planter class. These developments help to account for the speed with which whites organized themselves in vigilante groups, aiming to preserve "the supremacy of the white race in this Republic."

CONGRESSIONAL RECONSTRUCTION: THE RADICALS' PLAN

The rise of armed white supremacist groups in the South helped spur congressional Republicans to action. On March 2, 1867, a coalition led by two radicals, Senator Charles Sumner of Massachusetts and Congressman Thaddeus Stevens of Pennsylvania, prodded Congress to pass the Reconstruction Act of 1867. The purpose of this measure was to purge the South of disloyalty once and for all. The act stripped thousands of former Confederates of voting rights. The former Confederate states would not be readmitted to the Union until they had ratified the Fourteenth Amendment and written new constitutions that guaranteed black men the right to vote. The South (with the exception of Tennessee, which had ratified the Fourteenth Amendment in 1866) was divided into five military districts. Federal troops were stationed throughout the region. These troops were charged with protecting Union personnel and supporters in the South and with restoring order in the midst of regional political and economic upheaval.

MAP

Reconstruction

Congress passed two additional acts specifically intended to secure congressional power over the president. The intent of the Tenure of Office Act was to prevent the president from dismissing Secretary of War Edwin Stanton, a supporter of the radicals. The other measure, the Command of the Army Act, required the president to seek approval for all military orders from General Ulysses S. Grant, the army's senior officer. Grant also was a supporter of the Republicans. Both of these acts probably violated the separation of powers doctrine as put forth in the Constitution. Together, they would soon precipitate a national crisis.

During the Reconstruction period, approximately 2,000 black men of the emerging southern Republican party served as local elected officials, sheriffs, justices of the peace, tax collectors, and city councilors. Many of these leaders were of mixed ancestry, and many had been free before the war. They came in disproportionate numbers from the ranks of literate men, such as clergy, teachers, and skilled artisans. In Alabama, Florida, Louisiana, Mississippi, and South Carolina, black men constituted a majority of the voting public.

Some states made substantial gains in terms of integrating blacks into local systems of law enforcement and justice. By 1872, Florida, Arkansas, Louisiana, and South Carolina had elected black judges. Black men served as city chiefs of police in Tallahassee, Florida, and Little Rock, Arkansas, and black men made up half the ranks of the police force in Montgomery, Alabama, and Vicksburg, Mississippi. Whites found these developments profoundly unsettling. One white attorney observed that calling black jurors "gentlemen of the jury" was "the severest blow I have felt."

Throughout the South, 600 black men won election to state legislatures. Still, nowhere did blacks control a state government, although they did predominate in South Carolina's lower house. Sixteen black Southerners were elected to the U.S. Congress during Reconstruction. Most of those elected to Congress in the years immediately after the war were freeborn. However, among the nine men elected for the first time after 1872, six were former slaves. All of these politicians exemplified the desire among southern blacks to become active, engaged citizens.

■ This drawing by famous political cartoonist Thomas Nast depicts the first black members of Congress. Left to right, front row: Senator Hiram Revels of Mississippi (the first African American to serve in the U.S. Senate), Representatives Benjamin S. Turner of Alabama, Josiah T. Walls of Florida, Joseph H. Rainey of South Carolina, Robert B. Elliott of South Carolina. Back row: Representatives Robert G. DeLarge of South Carolina, Jefferson Long of Georgia.

THE FIRST COLORED SENATOR AND REPRESENTATIVES.
In the 41st and 42nd Congress of the United States.

Newly reconstructed southern state legislatures provided for public school systems, fairer taxation methods, bargaining rights of plantation laborers, racially integrated public transportation and accommodations, and public works projects, especially railroads. All new state constitutions guaranteed black civil rights and most recognized the right of married women to hold property in their own names. With the exception of Louisiana, every new southern state constitution included a household exemption—from $1,500 to $5,000 worth of property that could not be seized by creditors. Many of these Republican-dominated legislatures were shaped by the drive to further economic development in the largely rural, agricultural South. Black and white Republicans agreed that tax breaks and subsidies to railroads would provide jobs and update the South's transportation system.

Nevertheless, the legislative coalitions forged between northerners and southerners, blacks and whites, were uneasy and, in many cases, less than productive. Southern Democrats (and later, historians sympathetic to them) claimed that Reconstruction governments were uniquely corrupt, with some carpetbaggers, scalawags, and freedpeople vying for kickbacks from railroad and construction magnates. In fact, whenever state legislatures sought to promote business interests, they opened the door to the bribery of public officials. In this respect, northern as well as southern politicians were vulnerable to charges of corruption. In the long run, southern Democrats cared less about charges of legislative corruption than about the growing political power of local black Republican party organizations.

In Washington in early 1868, President Johnson forced a final showdown with Congress. He replaced several high military officials with more conservative men. He also fired Secretary of War Stanton, in apparent violation of the Tenure of Office Act. Shortly thereafter, in February, a newly composed House Reconstruction Committee impeached Johnson for ignoring the act, and the Senate began his trial on March 30. The president and Congress were locked in an extraordinary battle for political power.

The final vote was thirty-five senators against Johnson, one vote short of the necessary two-thirds of all senators' votes needed for conviction. Nineteen senators voted to acquit Johnson of the charges. Nevertheless, to win acquittal, he had had to promise moderates that he would not stand in the way of congressional plans for Reconstruction. Johnson essentially withdrew from policymaking in the spring of 1868. That November, with Republicans urging Northerners to "vote as you shot" (that is, to cast ballots against the former Confederates), Ulysses S. Grant was elected president.

Political reunion was an uneven process, but one that gradually eroded the newly won rights of former slaves in many southern states. By the end of 1868, Arkansas, North Carolina, South Carolina, Louisiana, Tennessee, Alabama, and Florida had met congressional conditions for readmission to the Union, and two years later, Mississippi, Virginia, Georgia, and Texas followed. The Fifteenth Amendment, passed by Congress in 1869 and ratified by the necessary number of states a year later, granted all black men the right to vote. However, in some states, such as Louisiana and Georgia, reunification gave Democrats license to engage in wholesale election fraud and violence toward freed men and women. In 1870–1871, a congressional inquiry into the Klan exposed pervasive and grisly assaults on Republican schoolteachers, preachers, and prospective voters, black and white. The Klan also targeted men and women who refused to work like slaves in the fields. In April 1871, Congress passed the Ku Klux Klan Act, which punished conspiracies intended to deny rights to citizens. But Klan violence and intimidation had already taken their toll on Republican voting strength.

Resenting the political power of both black and white Republicans, Louisiana Democrats unleashed a wave of violence during the 1875 elections. When the state's governor appealed to

TABLE 15.2			
The Election of 1868			
Candidate	**Political Party**	**Popular Vote (%)**	**Electoral Vote**
Ulysses S. Grant	Republican	52.7	214
Horatio Seymour	Democratic	47.3	80

President Grant for military troops to quell the bloodshed, Grant replied: "The whole public are tired out with these autumnal outbreaks in the South, and the great majority now are ready to condemn any interference on the part of the Government." In the absence of law enforcement, the Democrats swept to victory in 1875.

■ This formal portrait of Blanche K. Bruce conveys his status as a wealthy and powerful politician.

The ibrary of Congress

THE REMARKABLE CAREER OF BLANCHE K. BRUCE

The career of Blanche K. Bruce reveals the opportunities and limitations faced by an emerging black leadership during Reconstruction. Born a slave in 1841, this light-skinned mulatto spent much of his childhood working on a tobacco farm in central Missouri. He learned to read at an early age and acquired an interest in plantation management. After the war began, Bruce managed to escape from slavery. He eventually settled in Hannibal, Missouri, where he established the first school for blacks and worked as a printer's helper. In 1866, he enrolled in Oberlin College in Ohio. Though he worked hard, sawing wood to pay tuition, he could not afford to continue his formal education.

In 1867, Bruce attended a political rally in Mississippi. He became convinced that the state, especially the Delta region, afforded both economic and political opportunity. He quickly rose up the local political ranks, starting as voter registrar in Tallahatchie County, serving as sergeant at arms of the state legislature, and then tax assessor, sheriff, and member of the board of levee commissioners for Bolivar County. Bruce soon earned a reputation for fairness and honesty in public service. In 1872, he served simultaneously as education superintendent, sheriff, and tax collector in Bolivar County. He had established himself as the most powerful black politician in the Delta. Meanwhile, Bruce began to buy houses and parcels of land in the county; by the 1880s, he was a wealthy man.

Blanche K. Bruce won support from the Republican-dominated state legislature in his bid to run for the U.S. Senate in 1874; a year later he was elected to that seat. As a U.S. senator, Bruce demonstrated an interest in navigation improvements and flood control of the Mississippi River. He was one of a few legislators to condemn discrimination against Chinese immigrants in California, expressing "a large confidence in the strength and assimilative power of [our] American institutions." When he lost his Senate seat in 1881, Bruce and his wife moved to Washington, D.C. There he held a series of federal patronage jobs and became a member of the city's African American elite. Ultimately, his rise to wealth and political power distanced him from poorer blacks. His four-decade odyssey from slavery to the fashionable salons of the nation's capital revealed the promise, as well as the limitations, of Radical Reconstruction.

During Reconstruction, the struggle over the South showed that different groups of Americans had different priorities for former Confederates and former slaves. Depending on their political leanings, people disagreed over the way the former Confederate states should eventually be readmitted to the Union. However, most Republicans saw the reconstruction of the South as only one step in a sweeping effort to weld the whole country into a single economic, political, and cultural unit.

Claiming Territory for the Union

■ *What human and environmental forces impeded the Republican goal of western expansion?*

While blacks and whites, northerners and southerners clashed over power in the South, poet Walt Whitman celebrated the "manly and courageous instincts" that propelled a brave, adventurous people west. Whitman hailed the march across the prairies and over the mountains as a cavalcade of progress. He and other Americans believed that the postbellum migration fulfilled a mission of national regeneration begun by the Civil War. Kansas's population grew by 240 percent in the 1860s, Nebraska's by 355 percent.

To unite the entire country was the Republican ideal. The railroads in particular served as vehicles of national integration. When the Central Pacific and Union Pacific Railroads met at Promontory Point, Utah, in 1869, the hammering of the spike that joined the two roads produced a telegraphic signal received simultaneously on both coasts, setting off a national celebration.

Meanwhile, regular units of United States cavalry, including two regiments of blacks, were launching attacks on Indians on the Plains, in the Northwest, and in the Southwest. Between 1865 and 1890, U.S. military forces conducted a dozen separate campaigns against western Indian peoples and met Indian warriors in battle or attacked Indian settlements in more than 1,000 engagements. In contrast to African Americans, who adamantly demanded their rights as American citizens, defiant western Indians battled a government to which, they steadfastly maintained, they owed no allegiance.

The National Archives

■ At Promontory Point near Ogden, Utah, workers joined the tracks linking the Central Pacific (its wood-burning locomotive, *Jupiter*, is on the left) with the Union Pacific (whose coal-burning engine No. 119 is on the right). This photo was taken during the May 10, 1869, celebration marking the completion of the transcontinental railroad. According to one eyewitness, the crowd included Indians, Chinese and Irish immigrants, European Americans, and Mexicans "grouped in picturesque confusion." Yet this official photo shows little evidence of the Chinese workers who helped engineer and build the Central Pacific line.

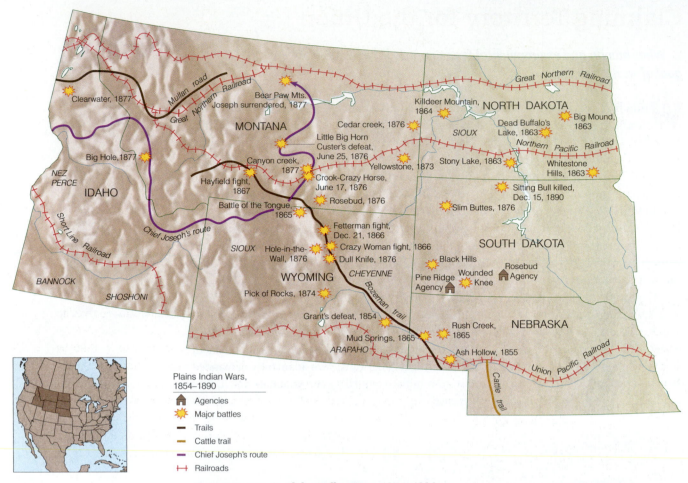

■ **MAP 15.2 Plains Indian Wars, 1854–1890**

Between 1854 and 1890, many of the conflicts between Indians and U.S. troops occurred along either railroad lines or trails used by European American settlers. For example, the Sioux, Cheyenne, and Arapaho fiercely resisted travelers along the Bozeman Trail running from Colorado to Montana.

FEDERAL MILITARY CAMPAIGNS AGAINST WESTERN INDIANS

In 1871, the U.S. government renounced the practice of seeking treaties with various Indian groups. This change in policy opened the way for a more aggressive effort to subdue native populations. In 1848, the United States had acquired a vast amount of western territory as a result of the Mexican-American War. As a result, the U.S. government abandoned its policy of pushing Indians ever farther westward. Instead, officials expanded the reservation system, an effort begun in the antebellum period to confine specific Indian groups to specific territories.

On the Plains, clashes between Indians and U.S. soldiers persisted after the Civil War. In 1867, at Medicine Lodge Creek in southern Kansas, the United States signed a treaty with an alliance of Comanche, Kiowa, Cheyenne, Arapaho, and Plains Apache. This treaty could not long withstand the provocation posed by wagon-train trails, such as the Bozeman, and the railroad. The year before, the Seventh U.S. Cavalry, under the command of Lieutenant Colonel George Custer, had been formed to ward off Indian attacks on the Union Pacific, snaking its way across the central Plains westward from Kansas and Nebraska. In November 1868, Custer destroyed a Cheyenne settlement on the Washita River, in present-day Oklahoma. The settlement's leader was Black Kettle, who had brought his people to reservation territory after the Sand Creek Massacre in Colorado in 1864. Custer's men murdered women and children, burned tipis, and destroyed 800 horses. Sickened by the scene, one

Two Artists Memorialize the Battle of Little Big Horn

Kicking Bear, *Battle of Little Big Horn*, c.1890. Courtesy of the Southwest Museum of the American Indian, Autry National Center, Los Angeles (1026.G.1)

Bettmann/CORBIS

Envisioning History

These pictures both portray the Battle of Little Big Horn in June 1876. In that clash, Lieutenant Colonel George Custer and his force of 264 U.S. soldiers attacked 2,500 Sioux and Cheyenne on the banks of the Little Big Horn River in Montana. During the battle, often referred to as "Custer's last stand," the Indians killed all of Custer's troops. The illustration below is from a book celebrating the life of Custer, which was published soon after the battle. At the time, the nation was in the midst of commemorating the centennial of its birth.

The picture above, a painting completed in 1890 by the Sioux artist Kicking Bear, also memorializes the battle. The figure in yellow buckskin at the left is Custer. In the upper-left corner are ghostlike figures, in the form of outlines of human shapes, meant to represent the spirits of the dead. At the center of the painting, Kicking Bear placed the figures of Sitting Bull, Rain-in-the-Face, Crazy Horse, and himself.

QUESTIONS

1. What are the differences in the composition of these two pictures? What are the similarities?

2. What is the significance of the term "Custer's last stand," and how is that term illustrated here?

3. What was the larger national context in which each of these artistic renderings was completed? How did that context shape the way each artist chose to portray the battle?

4. How do you account for the differences in the way horses are portrayed in each picture?

army officer later wrote sarcastically of the "daring dash" on the part of "heroes of a bloody day." The soldiers left piles of corpses scattered among the smoldering ruins of the village.

A series of peace delegations to Washington, several led by Red Cloud of the Sioux, produced much curiosity among whites but no end to the slaughter of people or animals in the West. Indians continued to attack the surveyors, supply caravans, and military escorts that preceded the railroad work crews. Lamenting the loss of his people's hunting grounds to the railroad, Red Cloud said, "The white children have surrounded me and have left me nothing but an island."

The Apache managed to elude General George Crook until 1875. Crook employed some of these Apache to track down the war chief Geronimo of the Chiricahua. Like many other

Geronimo and Natiche
Surrender (1886)

Indian leaders, Geronimo offered both religious and military guidance to his people. He believed that a spirit would protect him from the white man's bullets and from the arrows of Indians in league with government troops. Yet Geronimo was tricked into an initial surrender in 1877, and he was held in irons for several months before gaining release and challenging authorities for another nine years.

In 1874, Custer took his cavalry into the Black Hills of the Dakotas. Supposedly, the 1868 Treaty of Fort Laramie had rendered this land off-limits to whites. Custer's mission was to offer protection for the surveyors of the Northern Pacific Railroad and to force Indians onto reservations as stipulated in the 1868 treaty. However, the officer lost no time trumpeting the fact that Indian lands were filled with gold. This report prompted a rush to the Black Hills, lands sacred to the Sioux. Within two years, 15,000 gold miners had illegally descended on Indian lands to seek their fortunes. The federal government proposed to buy the land, but leaders of the Sioux, including Red Cloud, Spotted Tail, and Sitting Bull, spurned the offer. "The Black Hills belong to me," declared Sitting Bull. "If the whites try to take them, I will fight."

During the morning of June 25, 1876, Custer and his force of 264 soldiers attacked a Sun Dance gathering of 2,500 Sioux and Cheyenne on the banks of the Little Big Horn River in Montana. Custer foolishly launched his attack without adequate backup, and he and all his men were easily overwhelmed and killed by Indian warriors, led by the Oglala Sioux Crazy Horse and others. Reacting to this defeat, U.S. military officials reduced the Lakota Sioux and Cheyenne to wardship status, ending their autonomy.

> *"The Black Hills belong to me," declared Sitting Bull. "If the whites try to take them, I will fight."*

Indians throughout the West maintained their distinctive ways of life during these turbulent times. Horse holdings, so crucial for hunting, trading, and fighting, varied from group to group, with the Crow wealthy in relation to their Central Plains neighbors the Oglala and the Arikara. Plains and Plateau peoples engaged in a lively trading system. They exchanged horses and their trappings (bridles and blankets) for eastern goods such as kettles, guns, and ammunition. Despite their differences in economy, these groups held similar religious beliefs about an all-powerful life force that governed the natural world. People, plants, and animals were all part of the same order.

Even in the midst of brutal repression, Indian cultural traditions survived and in some cases flourished. On the West Central Plains and the Plateau, among the Crow, Shoshone, Nez Perce, and other tribes, women developed a new, distinctive style of seed beadwork characterized by variations of triangular patterns. These designs, made of beads selected for their quality and consistency, adorned leggings, gauntlets, and belt pouches. In these ways, the decorative arts were endowed with great symbolic meaning. When a wife embellished moccasins with patterns signifying her husband's military achievements, handicrafts assumed political as well as artistic significance.

THE POSTWAR WESTERN LABOR PROBLEM

In 1865, the owners of the Central Pacific Railroad seemed poised for one of the great engineering feats of the nineteenth century. In the race eastward from California, they constructed trestles spanning vast chasms, and roadbeds traversing mountains and deserts. Government officials in Washington were eager to subsidize the railroad. What the owners lacked was a dependable labor force. The Irish workers who began the line in California struck for higher wages in compensation for brutal, dangerous work. These immigrants dropped their shovels and hammers at the first word of a gold strike nearby—or far away. As a result, in 1866 the Central Pacific decided to tap into a vast labor source by importing thousands of Chinese men from their native Guandong province.

The Chinese toiled to extend the railroad tracks eastward from Sacramento, California, up to ten miles a day in the desert, only a few feet a day in the rugged Sierra Nevada Mountains. In nerve-wracking feats of skill, they lowered themselves in woven baskets to implant nitroglycerine explosives in canyon walls. Chinese laborers toiled through snowstorms and blistering heat

Carleton Watkins/Union Pacific Museum

■ Chinese construction workers labor on the Central Pacific Railroad, c. 1868. Many Chinese immigrants toiled as indentured laborers, indebted to Chinese merchant creditors who paid for their passage to California. Isolated in all-male work camps, crews of railroad workers retained their traditional dress, language, and diet. After the completion of the transcontinental railroad in 1869, some immigrants returned to China and others dispersed to small towns and cities throughout the West.

to blast tunnels and cut passes through granite mountains. With the final linking of the railroad in Utah in 1869, many Chinese sought work elsewhere in the West.

Signed in 1868, the Burlingame Treaty, named for Anson Burlingame, an American envoy to China, had supposedly guaranteed government protection for Chinese immigrants (most of whom were men) as visitors, traders, or permanent residents within the United States. Yet the treaty did not stop U.S. employers, landlords, and government officials from discriminating against the Chinese.

By 1870, 40,000 Chinese lived in California and represented one-quarter of the state's wage-earners. They found work in the cigar, woolen-goods, and boot and shoe factories of San Francisco; in the gold mining towns, now as laundry operators rather than as miners as they had before the Civil War; and in the fields as agricultural laborers. White workers complained of unfair competition from this Asian group that was becoming increasingly integrated into the region's economy.

Responding to these complaints, in 1870 Congress passed the Page Act. The act was intended to determine whether immigration from "China, Japan, or any Oriental country, is free and voluntary." Besides prohibiting Chinese forced laborers from entering the country, the Page Act prohibited the entry of any women who were prostitutes. This law placed the burden on Chinese women immigrants to prove that they were not prostitutes, slowing the immigration of single women as well as those married to Chinese men already in the country.

By this time, Hispanic workers had become the primary unskilled labor force in Los Angeles and surrounding areas. These workers were employed in the developing urban and service economies of southern California. Another labor group, California Indians, remained trapped in the traditional agricultural economy of unskilled labor. Whites appropriated Indian land and forced many men, women, and children to work as wage-earners for large landowners. Deprived of their familiar hunting and gathering lands, and wracked by disease and starvation, California Indians suffered a drastic decline in their numbers by 1870, from 100,000 to 30,000 in twenty years.

By the early 1870s, western manufacturers were faltering under the pressure of cheaper goods imported from the East by rail. At the same time, the growth of fledgling gigantic agricultural businesses opened new avenues of trade and commerce. Located in an arc surrounding the San Francisco Bay, large ("bonanza") wheat farmers produced huge crops and exported the grain to the East Coast and to England. These enterprises stimulated the building of wharves and railroad trunk lines and encouraged technological innovation in threshing and harvesting. Western enterprises had a growing demand for labor, whatever its skin color or nationality.

LAND USE IN AN EXPANDING NATION

The Union's triumph in 1865 prompted new conflicts and deepened long-standing ones over the use of the land in a rich, sprawling country. In the South, staple-crop planters began to share political power with an emerging elite, men who owned railroads and textile mills. Despairing of ever achieving antebellum levels of labor efficiency, some landowners turned to mining the earth and the forests for saleable commodities. These products, obtained through extraction, included phosphate (used in producing fertilizer), timber, coal, and turpentine. Labor in extractive industries complemented labor in the plantation economy. Sharecroppers alternated between tilling cotton fields in the spring and harvesting the crop in the fall, while seeking employment in sawmills and coal mines in the winter and summer.

As European Americans settled in the West and Southwest, they displaced natives who had been living there for generations. For example, the U.S. court system determined who could legally claim property. Western courts also decided whether natural resources such as water, land, timber, and fish and game constituted property that could be owned by private interests. In the Southwest, European American settlers, including soldiers who had come to fight Indians and then stayed, continued to place Mexican land titles at risk. Citing prewar precedents, American courts favored the claims of recent squatters over those of long-standing residents. In 1869, with the death of her husband (who had served as a general in the Union army), Maria Amparo Ruiz de Burton saw the large ranch they had worked together near San Diego slip out of her control. The first Spanish-speaking woman to be published in English in the United States, Ruiz de Burton was a member of the Hispanic elite. Nevertheless, she had little political power. California judges backed the squatters who occupied the ranch.

As they controlled more land and assumed public office, some European Americans in the Southwest exploited their political connections and economic power. In the process, they managed to wield great influence over people and vast amounts of natural resources. In the 1870s, the so-called Santa Fe Ring wrested more than 80 percent of the original Spanish grants of land from

Robert Benecke, photographer. DeGolyer Library, Southern Methodist University, Dallas, Texas, Ag1982.86.60

■ With this 1870 photograph, the Kansas Pacific Railroad advertised the opportunity for western travelers to shoot buffalo from the comfort and safety of their railroad car. The company's official taxidermist shows off his handiwork. Railroad expansion facilitated the exploitation of natural resources while promoting tourism.

Spanish-speaking landholders in New Mexico. An alliance of European American lawyers, businesspeople, and politicians, the Santa Fe Ring defrauded families and kin groups of their land titles and speculated in property to make a profit. Whereas many ordinary Hispanic settlers saw land—with its crops, pasture, fuel, building materials, and game—as a source of livelihood, the Santa Fe Ring saw land primarily as a commodity to be bought and sold.

Seemingly overnight, boom towns sprang up wherever minerals or timber beckoned: southern Arizona and the Rocky Mountains west of Denver, Virginia City in western Nevada, the Idaho-Montana region, and the Black Hills of South Dakota. In all these places, increasing numbers of workers operated sophisticated kinds of machinery, such as rock crushers, and labored for wages. When the vein of ore was exhausted or the forests depleted, the towns went bust.

Railroads facilitated not only the mining of minerals but also the growth of the cattle-ranching industry. By 1869, a quarter of a million cattle were grazing in Colorado Territory. Rail connections between the Midwest and East made it profitable for Texas ranchers to pay cowboys to drive their herds of long-horned steers to Abilene, Ellsworth, Wichita, or Dodge City, Kansas, for shipment to stockyards in Chicago or St. Louis. Large meatpackers, such as Swift and Armour, prepared the carcasses for the eastern market.

Cattle drives were huge; an estimated 10 million animals were herded north from Texas alone between 1865 and 1890. They offered employment to all kinds of men with sufficient skills and endurance. Among the cowhands were African American horsebreakers and gunmen and Mexicans skilled in the use of the *reata* (lasso). Blacks made up about 25 percent and Hispanics about 15 percent of all cowboy outfits. Tracing the evolution of the Chisholm Trail, which linked southern Texas to Abilene, from Indian path to commercial route, one observer wrote in 1874, "So many cattle have been driven over the trail in the last few years that a broad highway is tread out, looking much like a national highway." Yet this new "national highway" traversed Indian Territory (present-day Oklahoma), lands supposedly promised to Indians forever.

WATCH

Cowboys and Cattle

In knitting regional economies together, federal land policies were crucial to the Republican vision of a developing nation. Yet a series of land use acts had a mixed legacy. The Mineral Act of 1866 granted title to millions of acres of mineral-rich land to mining companies, a gift from the federal government to private interests. In 1866, Congress passed the Southern Homestead Act to help blacks acquire land, but the measure accomplished little and was repealed in 1876. The Timber Culture Act of 1873 allotted 160 acres to individuals in selected western states if they agreed to plant one-fourth of the acreage with trees. Four years later, the Desert Land Act provided cheap land if buyers irrigated at least part of their parcels.

The exploitation of western resources raised many legal questions: Must ranchers pay for the prairies their cattle grazed on and the trails they followed to market? How could one "own" a stampeding buffalo herd or a flowing river? What was the point of holding title to a piece of property if only the timber, oil, water, or minerals (but not the soil) were of value? The Apex Mining Act of 1872 sought to address at least some of these issues. This law legalized traditional mining practices in the West by validating titles approved by local courts. According to the law, a person who could locate the apex of a vein (its point closest to the surface) could lay claim to the entire vein beneath the surface. The measure contributed to the wholesale destruction of certain parts of the western landscape as mining companies blasted their way through mountains and left piles of rocks in their wake. It also spurred thousands of lawsuits as claimants argued over what constituted an apex or a vein.

> *The Mineral Act of 1866 granted title to millions of acres of mineral-rich land to mining companies.*

It was during this period that a young Scottish-born naturalist named John Muir began to explore the magnificent canyons and mountains of California. Viewing nature as a means for regenerating the human spirit, Muir emphasized a deep appreciation of the natural world. He contrasted nature's majesty with the artificial landscape created by and for humans. In the wilderness, there is nothing "truly dead or dull, or any trace of what in manufactories is called

Colorado Historical Society (CHS.J 2067)

■ Chicago photographer Thomas J. Hine titled this stereograph "Old Faithful in Action, Fire Hole Basin." It is the first photograph of the eruption of the famous Yellowstone geyser. Costing 15–25 cents each, stereographs were a popular form of entertainment in middle-class households beginning in the 1860s. The stereoscope merged two identical photos to form a single three-dimensional image. Widely distributed stereographs of scenic natural wonders boosted western tourism.

rubbish or waste," he wrote; "everything is perfectly clean and pure and full of divine lessons."

Muir believed that the need to protect breathtaking vistas and magnificent stands of giant redwoods compelled the federal government to act as land-policy regulator, and he was gratified by the creation of the National Park system during the postwar period. By this time, pressure had been building on the federal government to protect vast tracts of undeveloped lands. Painters and geologists were among the first Easterners to appreciate the spectacular vistas of the western landscape. In 1864, Congress set aside a small area within California's Yosemite Valley for public recreation and enjoyment. Soon after the war, railroad promoters forged an alliance with government officials in an effort to block commercial development of particularly beautiful pockets of land. In the late 1860s, the invention of the Pullman sleeping car—a luxurious hotel room on wheels—helped spur tourism, and thus the drive to protect areas of natural beauty from farming, lumbering, stock raising, and mining. Northern Pacific railroad financier Jay Cooke lobbied hard for the government to create a 2-million-acre park in what is today the northwest corner of Wyoming. As a result, in March 1872, Congress created Yellowstone National Park. Tourism would continue to serve as a key component of the western economy.

Muir and others portrayed the Yosemite and Yellowstone valleys as wildernesses, empty of human activity. In fact, both areas had long provided hunting and foraging grounds for native peoples. Since the fifteenth century, Yellowstone had been occupied by the people now called the Shoshone. This group, together with the Bannock, Crow, and Blackfoot, tried to retain access to Yellowstone's meadows, rivers, and forests after it became a national park. However, U.S. policymakers and military officials persisted in their efforts to mark off territory for specific commercial purposes, while Indians were confined to reservations.

BUYING TERRITORY FOR THE UNION

Before the Civil War, Republicans had opposed any federal expansionist schemes that they feared might benefit slaveholders. However, after 1865 and the outlawing of slavery, some Republican lawmakers and administration officials advocated the acquisition of additional territory. Secretary of State William Seward led the way in 1867 by purchasing Alaska from Russia. For $7.2 million (about 2 cents an acre), the United States gained Alaska—and 591,004 square miles of land. Within the territory were diverse indigenous groups—Eskimo, Aleut, Tlingit, Tsimshian, Athabaskan, and Haida—and a small number of native Russians. Though derided at the time as "Seward's icebox," Alaska yielded enough fish, timber, minerals, oil, and water power in the years to come to prove that the original purchase price was a tremendous bargain.

> *For $7.2 million (about 2 cents an acre), the United States gained Alaska—and 591,004 square miles of land.*

The impulse that prompted Johnson administration support for the Alaska purchase also spawned other plans for territorial acquisitions. In 1870, some Republicans joined with Democrats in calling for the annexation of the Dominican Republic. These members of Congress argued that the tiny Caribbean country would make a fine naval base, provide investment opportunities for American businesspeople, and offer a refuge for southern freedpeople.

However, influential Senator Charles Sumner warned against a takeover without considering the will of Dominicans, who were currently involved in their own civil war. Some members of Congress, in a prelude to foreign policy debates of the 1890s, suggested that the dark-skinned Dominican people were incapable of appreciating the blessings of American citizenship. In 1871, an annexation treaty failed to win Senate approval.

In facilitating western expansion, Republicans upheld the ideal that prosperity would come to all people who worked hard. Indians were not part of the Republican vision of western prosperity. But other groups also questioned the Republican vision as it affected their own interests.

The Republican Vision and Its Limits

◼ *What were some of the inconsistencies in, and unanticipated consequences of, Republican notions of equality and federal power?*

After the Civil War, victorious Republicans envisioned a nation united in the pursuit of prosperity. All citizens would be free to follow their individual economic self-interest and enjoy the fruits of honest toil. In contrast, some increasingly vocal and well-organized groups saw the expansion of legal rights, in particular giving black men the right to vote, as only initial, tentative steps on the path to an all-inclusive citizenship. Women, industrial workers, farmers, and African Americans made up overlapping constituencies pressing for equal political rights and economic opportunity. Together they challenged the mainstream Republican view that defeat of the rebels and destruction of slavery were sufficient to guarantee prosperity for everyone.

Partnerships between government and business also produced unanticipated consequences for Republicans committed to what they believed was the collective good. Some politicians and business leaders saw these partnerships as opportunities for private gain. Consequently, private greed and public corruption accompanied postwar economic growth. Thus, Republican leaders faced challenges from two very different sources: people agitating for civil rights and people hoping to reap personal gain from political activities.

POSTBELLUM ORIGINS OF THE WOMAN SUFFRAGE MOVEMENT

After the Civil War, the nation's middle class, which had its origins in the antebellum period, continued to grow. Dedicated to self-improvement and filled with a sense of moral authority, many middle-class Americans (especially Protestants) felt a deep cultural connection to their counterparts in England. Indeed, the United States produced its own "Victorians," the term for the self-conscious middle class that emerged in the England of Queen Victoria during her reign from 1837 to 1901.

At the heart of the Victorian sensibility was the ideal of domesticity: a harmonious family living in a well-appointed home, guided by a pious mother and supported by a father successful in business. Famous Protestant clergyman Henry Ward Beecher and his wife were outspoken proponents of this domestic ideal. According to Eunice Beecher, women had no "higher, nobler, more divine mission than in the conscientious endeavor to create a *true home.*"

Yet the traumatic events of the Civil War only intensified the desire among a growing group of American women to participate fully in the nation's political life. They wanted to extend their moral influence outside the narrow and exclusive sphere of the home. Many women believed they deserved the vote and that the time was right to demand it.

In 1866, veteran reformers Elizabeth Cady Stanton, Susan B. Anthony, and Lucy Stone founded the Equal Rights Association to link the rights of white women and African Americans. Nevertheless, in 1867, Kansas voters defeated a referendum proposing suffrage for both blacks and white women. This disappointment convinced some former abolitionists that the two causes should be separated—that women should wait patiently until the rights of African American men were firmly secured. Frederick Douglass declined an invitation to a women's suffrage convention in Washington, D.C., in 1868. He explained, "I am now devoting myself to a cause [if] not more sacred, certainly more urgent, because it is one of life and death to the long enslaved people of this country, and that is: negro suffrage." But African American activist and former slave Sojourner Truth warned: "There is a great stir about colored men getting their rights, but not a word about the colored women; and if colored men get their rights, and not colored women get theirs, there will be a bad time about it."

In 1869, two factions of women parted ways and formed separate organizations devoted to women's rights. The more radical wing, including Cady Stanton and Anthony, bitterly denounced the Fifteenth Amendment because it gave the vote to black men only. They helped to found the National Woman Suffrage Association (NWSA), which argued for a renewed commitment to the original Declaration of Sentiments passed in Seneca Falls, New York, two decades earlier. They favored married women's property rights, liberalization of divorce laws, opening colleges and trade schools to women, and a new federal amendment to allow women to vote. Lucy Stone and her husband, Henry Blackwell, founded the rival American Woman Suffrage Association (AWSA). This group downplayed the larger struggle for women's rights and focused on the suffrage question exclusively. Its members supported the Fifteenth Amendment and retained ties to the Republican party. The AWSA focused on state-by-state campaigns for women's suffrage.

In 1871, the NWSA welcomed the daring, flamboyant Victoria Woodhull as a vocal supporter, only to renounce her a few years later. Woodhull's political agenda ranged from free love and dietary reform to legalized prostitution, working men's rights, and women's suffrage. (In the nineteenth century, free love advocates denounced what they called a sexual double

The Library of Congress

■ The *Daily Graphic,* a New York City newspaper, carried this caricature of Susan B. Anthony on its June 5, 1873, cover. The artist suggests that the drive for women's suffrage has resulted in a reversal of gender roles. Titled "The Woman Who Dared," the cartoon portrays Anthony as a masculine figure. One of her male supporters, on the right, holds a baby, while women activists march and give speeches. On the left, a female police officer keeps watch over the scene.

When Did Women Get the Vote?

1893	New Zealand
1906	Finland
1913	Norway
1915	Denmark
1917	Canada
1918	Austria, Estonia, Germany, Hungary, Poland, Latvia, Russian Federation
1919	Belarus, Luxembourg, Netherlands, Ukraine
1920	Albania, Czech Republic, Slovakia, United States
1921	Armenia, Sweden
1928	Ireland, United Kingdom
1929	Romania
1930	Turkey, South Africa (whites)
1931	Spain, Sri Lanka
1932	Brazil, Thailand, Uruguay
1934	Cuba
1937	Philippines
1945	Croatia, Indonesia, Italy, Japan, Slovenia, Togo
1946	Cameroon, Guatemala, Liberia, Panama, Venezuela, Viet Nam, Yugoslavia
1947	Argentina, Mexico, Pakistan, Singapore
1948	Belgium, Israel, Niger, Republic of Korea, Suriname
1949	Chile, China, Costa Rica
1950	Barbados, Haiti, India
1955	Cambodia, Ethiopia, Honduras, Nicaragua, Peru
1962	Algeria, Australia, Monaco, Uganda, Zambia
1971	Switzerland
1972	Bangladesh
1974	Jordan
1980	Iraq
1984	South Africa (coloureds and Indians)
1990	Samoa
1994	South Africa (blacks)
2005	Kuwait

This chronology shows the year in which certain countries granted women the same voting rights as men. In the United States, women first pressed for suffrage in an organized way at the women's rights convention in Seneca Falls, New York, in 1848. At that time, many people (including many women) considered women's suffrage to be a radical idea. After the Civil War and the enfranchisement of African American men in 1867, more American women began to agitate for the right to vote.

This chronology does not reveal key themes in the global history of women's suffrage. First, many countries divided citizenship rights into a number of different components. For example, women in Norway won the right to run for election (the British would say "stand for election") in 1907, but not the right to vote until six years later. Second, some countries legally enfranchised women but did not enforce that right. In theory, all U.S. women had the right to vote in 1920, but in fact, the federal government did not guarantee that right to African American men or women until 1965. Third, a number of countries initially put literacy or other conditions on women's right to vote. The dates above indicate when, in those cases, restrictions were lifted. And finally, some local entities allowed women the right to vote before the national government sanctioned that right. For example, in the United States, some localities and some western states enfranchised women before 1920.

QUESTIONS

1. Which country enshrined in law "racial" differences among women for the purposes of suffrage?

2. What do you think accounts for the relatively large numbers of countries to enact women's suffrage during and after the two world wars of the twentieth century—1918–1919, and 1945–1946?

3. What assumptions about women account for the fact that some countries allowed women the right to run for office before granting them the right to vote?

The Wider World

standard, one that glorified female chastity while tolerating male promiscuity.) In 1872, Woodhull spent a month in jail as a result of zealous prosecution by vice reformer Anthony Comstock, a clergyman who objected to her public discussions and writings on sexuality. Comstock assumed the role of an outspoken crusader against vice. A federal law passed in 1873, and named after him, equated information related to birth control with pornography, banning this and other "obscene material" from the mails.

Susan B. Anthony used the 1872 presidential election as a test case for women's suffrage. She attempted to vote and was arrested, tried, and convicted. By this time, most women suffragists, and most members of the NWSA for that matter, had become convinced that they should focus on the vote exclusively; they therefore accepted the AWSA's policy on this issue. In the coming years, they would avoid other causes with which they might have allied themselves, including black civil rights and labor reform.

WORKERS' ORGANIZATIONS

Many Americans benefited from economic changes of the postwar era. Railroads, mines, and heavy industry helped fuel the national economy and in the process boosted the growth of the urban managerial class. In the Midwest, many landowning farmers prospered when they responded to an expanding demand for grain and other staple crops. In Wisconsin, wheat farmers cleared forests, drained swamps, diverted rivers, and profited from the booming world market in grain. Yet the economic developments that allowed factory managers and owners of large wheat farms to make a comfortable living for themselves did not necessarily benefit agricultural and manufacturing wage-workers.

Wisconsin Historical Society, WHi (D32) 821

■ A Norwegian immigrant extended family in the town of Norway Grove, Wisconsin, poses in front of their imposing home and up-to-date carriage in this photograph taken in the mid-1870s. Linking their fortunes to the world wheat market, these newcomers to the United States prospered. Wrote one woman to her brother back home in Norway, "We all have cattle, driving oxen, and wagons. We also have children in abundance."

Indeed, during this period, growing numbers of working people, in the countryside and in the cities, became caught up in a cycle of indebtedness. In the upcountry South (above the fall line, or Piedmont), formerly self-sufficient family farmers sought loans from banks to repair their war-damaged homesteads. To qualify for these loans, a farmer had to plant cotton as a staple crop, to the neglect of corn and other foodstuffs. Many sharecroppers, black and white, received payment in the form of credit only; for these families, the end-of-the-year reckoning yielded little more than rapidly accumulating debts. Midwestern farmers increasingly relied on bank loans to purchase expensive threshing and harvesting machinery.

Several organizations founded within five years of the war's end offered laborers an alternative vision to the Republicans' brand of individualism and nationalism. In 1867, Oliver H. Kelly, a former Minnesota farmer now working in a Washington office, organized the National Grange of the Patrons of Husbandry, popularly known as the **Grange**. This movement sought to address a new, complex marketplace increasingly dominated by railroads, banks, and grain elevator operators. The Grange encouraged farmers to form cooperatives that would market their crops and to challenge discriminatory railroad rates that favored big business.

Founded in Baltimore in 1866, the National Labor Union (NLU) consisted of a collection of craft unions and claimed as many as 600,000 members at its peak in the early 1870s. The group welcomed farmers as well as factory workers and promoted legislation for an eight-hour workday and the arbitration of industrial disputes. William Sylvis, a leader of the Iron Molders' International Union in Philadelphia and the second president of the NLU, sounded twin themes that would mark national labor union organizing efforts for generations to come. He called for an alliance of black and white workers. Yet at the same time, Sylvis defended the practice of excluding blacks from positions of leadership on the job and in the union. Impatient with such pronouncements, Isaac Myers, a black ship caulker from Baltimore, helped found the short-lived and small Colored National Labor Union in Washington, D.C., in 1868. Myers offered a view of citizenship that differed from white Republicans' exclusive emphasis on the franchise: "If citizenship means anything at all," the black labor leader declared, "it means the freedom of labor, as broad and universal as freedom of the ballot."

> *In 1873, a nationwide economic depression threw thousands out of work and worsened the plight of debtors.*

In 1873, a nationwide economic depression threw thousands out of work and worsened the plight of debtors. Businesspeople in agriculture, mining, the railroad industry, and manufacturing had overexpanded their operations. The freewheeling loan practices of major banks had contributed to this situation. The inability of these businesspeople to repay their loans led to the failure of major banks. With the contraction of credit, thousands of small businesses went bankrupt. The NLU did not survive the crisis.

However, by this time, a new organization had appeared to champion the cause of the laboring classes in opposition to lords of finance. Founded in 1869 by Uriah Stephens and other Philadelphia tailors, the Knights of Labor eventually aimed to unite industrial and rural workers, the self-employed and the wage earner, blacks and whites, and men and women. The Knights were committed to private property and to the independence of the farmer, the entrepreneur, and the industrial worker. The group banned from its ranks "nonproducers," such as liquor sellers, bankers, professional gamblers, stockbrokers, and lawyers.

This period of depression also laid the foundation for the Greenback Labor party, organized in 1878. Within three years after the end of the Civil War, the Treasury had withdrawn from circulation $100 million in wartime paper currency ("greenbacks"). The government also ceased coining silver dollars in 1873, despite the discovery of rich silver lodes in the West. With less money in circulation, debtors found it more difficult to repay their loans. To add insult to injury, the Resumption Act (1875) called for the government to continue to withdraw paper "greenbacks." Thus, hard money became dearer, and debtors became more desperate. In 1878, the new Greenback Labor party managed to win 1 million votes and elect fourteen candidates to Congress. The party laid the foundation for the Populist party that emerged in the 1890s.

Several factors made coalition building among American workers difficult. One was the nation's increasingly multicultural workforce. Unions, such as the typographers, were notorious for excluding women and African Americans, a fact publicized by both Frederick Douglass and Susan B. Anthony, to no avail. In 1869, shoe factory workers (members of the Knights of St. Crispin) went on strike in North Adams, Massachusetts. They were soon shocked to see seventy-five Chinese strikebreakers arrive by train from California. Their employer praised the new arrivals for their "rare industry." The shoemakers' strike collapsed quickly after the appearance of what the Massachusetts workers called this "Mongolian battery." Employers would continue to manipulate and divide the laboring classes through the use of ethnic, religious, and racial prejudices.

POLITICAL CORRUPTION AND THE DECLINE OF REPUBLICAN IDEALISM

Out of the new partnership between politics and business emerged an extensive system of bribes and kickbacks. Greedy politicians of both parties challenged the Republicans' high-minded idealism.

In the early 1870s, the *New York Times* exposed the schemes of William M. "Boss" Tweed. Tweed headed Tammany Hall, a New York City political organization that courted labor unions and contributed liberally to Catholic schools and charities. Tammany Hall politicians routinely used bribery and extortion to fix elections and bilk taxpayers of millions of dollars. One plasterer employed on a city project received $138,000 for two days' work. After the *Times* exposé, Tweed was prosecuted and convicted. His downfall attested to the growing influence of newspaper reporters.

Another piece of investigative journalism rocked the political world in 1872. In 1867, major stockholders of the Union Pacific Railroad had formed a new corporation, called the Crédit Mobilier, to build railroads. Heads of powerful congressional committees received shares of stock in the new company. These gifts of stock were bribes to secure the legislators' support for public land grants favorable

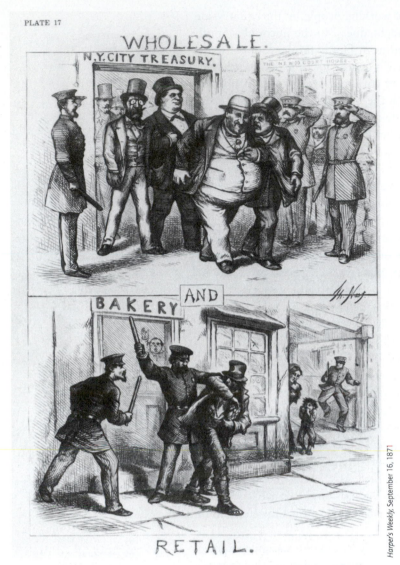

PLATE 17

Harper's Weekly, September 16, 1871

In 1871, Thomas Nast drew a series of cartoons exposing the corruption of New York City Democratic boss William M. Tweed and his political organization, Tammany Hall. In this drawing, published in *Harper's Weekly,* Nast depicts Tweed and his cronies engaging in a "wholesale" looting of the New York City treasury with the assistance of compliant police officers. Those same officers stand ready to crack down on the impoverished father who robs a bakery to feed his family. By portraying Tweed as an enemy of the poor, Nast ignored the fact that the political boss gained a large following among immigrant voters.

TABLE 15.3			
The Election of 1872			
Candidate	Political Party	Popular Vote (%)	Electoral Vote
Ulysses S. Grant	Republican	55.6	286
Horace Greeley	Democratic, Liberal Republican	43.9	66

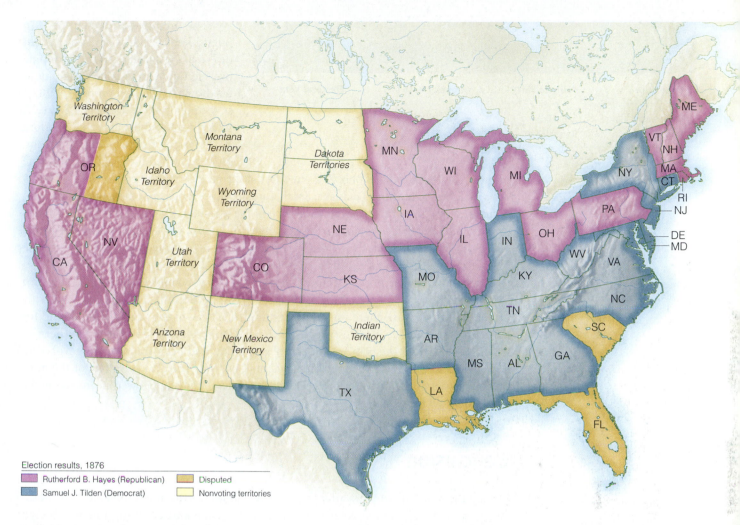

■ **MAP 15.3   The Compromise of 1877**

During the presidential election of 1876, returns from South Carolina, Florida, and Louisiana (the only states that remained under Republican control) were disputed. Under a compromise reached by Republicans and Democrats in Congress, Republican Rutherford B. Hayes became president and Congress removed all federal troops from the South.

Election results, 1876

- Rutherford B. Hayes (Republican)
- Samuel J. Tilden (Democrat)
- Disputed
- Nonvoting territories

to the new corporation. The *New York Sun* exposed a number of the chief beneficiaries in the fall of 1872, findings confirmed by congressional investigation. Among the disgraced politicians was Grant's vice president, Schuyler Colfax.

The 1872 presidential election pitted incumbent Grant against the Democratic challenger, *New York Tribune* editor Horace Greeley. Many Republicans, disillusioned with congressional corruption and eager to press forward with civil service reform, endorsed the Democratic candidate. Greeley and his Republican allies decried the patronage (or "spoils") system by which politicians rewarded their supporters with government jobs. Nevertheless, Grant won the election.

By 1872, after four bloody years of war and seven squandered years of postwar opportunity, the federal government seemed prepared to hand the South back to unrepentant rebels. The North showed what one House Republican called "a general apathy among the people concerning the war and the negro." The **Civil Rights Act of 1875** guaranteed blacks equal access to public accommodations and transportation. Yet this act represented the final, half-hearted gesture of radical Republicanism. The Supreme Court declared the measure unconstitutional in 1883 on the grounds that the government could protect only political and not social rights. White Southerners reasserted their control over the region's political economy.

TABLE 15.4			
The Election of 1876			
Candidate	**Political Party**	**Popular Vote (%)**	**Electoral Vote**
Rutherford B. Hayes	Republican	48.0	185
Samuel J. Tilden	Democratic	51.0	184

The presidential election of 1876 intensified public cynicism about deal making in high places. A dispute over election returns led to what came to be known as the Compromise of 1877. In the popular vote, Democrat Samuel J. Tilden outpolled Republican Rutherford B. Hayes, a former Ohio governor. However, when the electoral votes were counted, the Democrat had only 184, one short of the necessary number. Nineteen of the 20 votes in dispute came from Louisiana, South Carolina, and Florida, and these three states submitted two new sets of returns, one from each of the two main parties. A specially appointed congressional electoral commission, the Committee of Fifteen, was charged with resolving the dispute. It divided along partisan lines. The eight Republicans outvoted the seven Democrats to accept the Republican set of returns from Florida.

To break the logjam, the Democrats agreed that Hayes could assume office in return for the withdrawal of all remaining federal troops from the South. The Republicans tacitly agreed that their work there was finished and that blacks in the region should fend for themselves. Hayes declined to enforce the Civil Rights Act of 1875. White Southerners were free to uphold the principle of states' rights that had been traditionally invoked to deny blacks their rights in the region. Thus the Civil War failed to solve one of the most pressing issues of the day—the relation between federal and state power in protecting the rights of individuals.

Conclusion

During the dozen or so years after the Civil War, both northern Republicans and southern Democrats registered a series of spectacular wins and crushing losses. Though humiliated by the Union victory, southern whites eventually won the freedom to control their own local and state governments. As landlords, sheriffs, and merchants, they defied the postwar federal amendments to the Constitution and deprived African Americans of basic citizenship rights. By the end of Reconstruction, northern Republicans had conceded local power to their former enemies. Even an aggressive nationalism, it turned out, could accept traditional southern hierarchies: white over nonwhite, rich over poor.

Yet the Civil War was not only a fight between whites. During the conflict, black people had served as combatants in the struggle for freedom. They saw the war in different terms than did northern white Republicans and southern white Democrats. After the war, blacks pursued full citizenship rights while attempting to maintain institutional and cultural autonomy from white people regardless of political affiliation. In their quest, freed men and women met with mixed success. They gained the status of citizens under federal amendments to the Constitution, and black men gained the (formal) right to vote. Yet white Republicans, both in Congress and in southern state legislatures, proved to be disappointing allies to blacks who found themselves, increasingly, at the mercy of white vigilantes and other terrorist groups. During the Reconstruction period, blacks consolidated their families, established their own churches, and sought to work on their own terms in the fields. Yet lacking money and credit, they found it difficult to buy land and in the process achieve true independence from white landowners, bankers, and politicians.

At the end of Reconstruction, Republicans remained in firm control of national economic policy. The white South had secured its right to conduct its own political affairs, but the Republican vision of economic growth and development had become the law of the land. This vision was a guiding principle of historic national and, increasingly, international significance. Economic innovation in particular proved to be a force of great unifying power, stronger even than all the federal military forces deployed during and after the Civil War.

For Review

1. In what ways did African Americans and western Indians differ in their view of the federal government? How were those differences revealed in the military and political arenas after the war?

2. Was the Civil War a turning point in women's history? Why or why not?

3. Andrew Johnson was a Republican, and yet he and congressional Republicans engaged in a bitter fight during Reconstruction. Why?

4. In what ways did the outcome of the Civil War challenge the power of states' authority over their own economy and people? Was the war a clear victory for federal authority? Why or why not?

5. Did all workers share the same interests after the war? Choose three groups of workers and describe the challenges they faced during Reconstruction.

6. What did freedom mean to southern black people after the war? What were the limits on their freedom?

7. In what ways was or was not the effort to subdue the Plains Indians after 1865 an extension of the Civil War?

Created Equal Online

For more *Created Equal* resources, including suggestions on sites to visit and books to read, go to **MyHistoryLab.com.**

CHRONOLOGY: 1865–1877

1865	Freedmen's Bureau is formed.
	Lincoln is assassinated; Andrew Johnson becomes president.
	Thirteenth Amendment abolishing slavery is ratified.
1866	Civil Rights Act of 1866.
	Ku Klux Klan is organized.
1867	U.S. purchases Alaska from Russia.
	Reconstruction Act of 1867.
	Ratification of Fourteenth Amendment protecting civil rights.
1868	Johnson is impeached and acquitted.
	Fourteenth Amendment is ratified.
1869	Transcontinental Railroad is completed.
	National Woman Suffrage Association and American Woman Suffrage Association are formed.
	Knights of Labor is founded.
1870	Fifteenth Amendment enfranchising black men is ratified.
1871	Ku Klux Klan Act.
1873	Onset of economic depression.
1874	Congress passes Civil Rights Act.
1876	Battle of Little Big Horn.
	Contested presidential election between Rutherford B. Hayes and Samuel J. Tilden.
1877	Compromise of 1877.

The Declaration of Independence

The Articles of Confederation

The Constitution of the
United States of America

Amendments to the Constitution

Presidential Elections

In Congress, July 4, 1776

The Unanimous Declaration of the Thirteen United States of America

When, in the course of human events, it becomes necessary for one people to dissolve the political bonds which have connected them with another, and to assume, among the powers of the earth, the separate and equal station to which the laws of nature and of nature's God entitle them, a decent respect to the opinions of mankind requires that they should declare the causes which impel them to the separation.

We hold these truths to be self-evident: That all men are created equal; that they are endowed by their Creator with certain unalienable rights; that among these are life, liberty, and the pursuit of happiness; that, to secure these rights, governments are instituted among men, deriving their just powers from the consent of the governed; that whenever any form of government becomes destructive of these ends, it is the right of the people to alter or to abolish it, and to institute new government, laying its foundation on such principles, and organizing its powers in such form, as to them shall seem most likely to effect their safety and happiness. Prudence, indeed, will dictate that governments long established should not be changed for light and transient causes; and accordingly all experience hath shown that mankind are more disposed to suffer, while evils are sufferable, than to right themselves by abolishing the forms to which they are accustomed. But when a long train of abuses and usurpations, pursuing invariably the same object, evinces a design to reduce them under absolute despotism, it is their right, it is their duty, to throw off such government, and to provide new guards for their future security. Such has been the patient sufferance of these colonies; and such is now the necessity which constrains them to alter their former systems of government. The history of the present King of Great Britain is a history of repeated injuries and usurpations, all having in direct object the establishment of an absolute tyranny over these states. To prove this, let facts be submitted to a candid world.

He has refused his assent to laws, the most wholesome and necessary for the public good.

He has forbidden his governors to pass laws of immediate and pressing importance, unless suspended in their operation till his assent should be obtained; and, when so suspended, he has utterly neglected to attend to them.

He has refused to pass other laws for the accommodation of large districts of people, unless those people would relinquish the right of representation in the legislature, a right inestimable to them, and formidable to tyrants only.

He has called together legislative bodies at places unusual, uncomfortable, and distant from the depository of their public records, for the sole purpose of fatiguing them into compliance with his measures.

He has dissolved representative houses repeatedly, for opposing, with manly firmness, his invasions on the rights of the people.

He has refused for a long time, after such dissolutions, to cause others to be elected; whereby the legislative powers, incapable of annihilation, have returned to the people at large for their exercise; the state remaining, in the mean time, exposed to all the dangers of invasions from without and convulsions within.

He has endeavored to prevent the population of these states; for that purpose obstructing the laws for naturalization of foreigners; refusing to pass others to encourage their migration hither, and raising the conditions of new appropriations of lands.

He has obstructed the administration of justice, by refusing his assent to laws for establishing judiciary powers.

He has made judges dependent on his will alone, for the tenure of their offices, and the amount and payment of their salaries.

He has erected a multitude of new offices, and sent hither swarms of officers to harass our people and eat out their substance.

He has kept among us, in times of peace, standing armies, without the consent of our legislatures.

He has affected to render the military independent of, and superior to, the civil power.

He has combined with others to subject us to a jurisdiction foreign to our constitution, and unacknowledged by our laws, giving his assent to their acts of pretended legislation:

For quartering large bodies of armed troops among us;

For protecting them, by a mock trial, from punishment for any murder which they should commit on the inhabitants of these states;

For cutting off our trade with all parts of the world;

For imposing taxes on us without our consent;

For depriving us, in many cases, of the benefits of trial by jury;

For transporting us beyond seas, to be tried for pretended offenses;

For abolishing the free system of English laws in a neighboring province, establishing therein an arbitrary government, and enlarging its boundaries, so as to render it at once an example and fit instrument for introducing the same absolute rule into these colonies;

For taking away our charters, abolishing our most valuable laws, and altering fundamentally the forms of our governments;

For suspending our own legislatures, and declaring themselves invested with power to legislate for us in all cases whatsoever.

He has abdicated government here, by declaring us out of his protection and waging war against us.

He has plundered our seas, ravaged our coasts, burned our towns, and destroyed the lives of our people.

He is at this time transporting large armies of foreign mercenaries to complete the works of death, desolation, and tyranny already begun with circumstances of cruelty and perfidy scarcely paralleled in the most barbarous ages, and totally unworthy the head of a civilized nation.

He has constrained our fellow-citizens, taken captive on the high seas, to bear arms against their country, to become the

No Bill of Attainder or ex post facto Law shall be passed.

No Capitation, or other direct, Tax shall be laid, unless in Proportion to the Census or Enumeration herein before directed to be taken.

No Tax or Duty shall be laid on Articles exported from any State.

No Preference shall be given by any Regulation of Commerce or Revenue to the Ports of one State over those of another: nor shall Vessels bound to, or from, one State, be obliged to enter, clear, or pay Duties in another.

No Money shall be drawn from the Treasury, but in Consequence of Appropriations made by Law; and a regular Statement and Account of the Receipts and Expenditures of all public Money shall be published from time to time.

No Title of Nobility shall be granted by the United States: And no Person holding any Office of Profit or Trust under them, shall, without the Consent of the Congress, accept of any present, Emolument, Office, or Title, of any kind whatever, from any King, Prince, or foreign State.

Section 10

No State shall enter into any Treaty, Alliance, or Confederation; grant Letters of Marque and Reprisal; coin Money; emit Bills of Credit; make any Thing but gold and silver Coin a Tender in Payment of Debts; pass any Bill of Attainder, ex post facto Law, or Law impairing the obligation of Contracts, or grant any Title of Nobility.

No State shall, without the Consent of the Congress, lay any Imposts or Duties on Imports or Exports, except what may be absolutely necessary for executing its inspection Laws: and the net Produce of all Duties and Imposts, laid by any State on Imports or Exports, shall be for the Use of the Treasury of the United States; and all such Laws shall be subject to the Revision and Controul of the Congress.

No State shall, without the Consent of Congress, lay any Duty of Tonnage, keep Troops, or Ships of War in time of Peace, enter into any Agreement or Compact with another State, or with a foreign Power, or engage in War, unless actually invaded, or in such imminent Danger as will not admit of delay.

Article II

Section 1

The executive Power shall be vested in a President of the United States of America. He shall hold his Office during the Term of four Years, and, together with the Vice President, chosen for the same Term, be elected, as follows:

Each State shall appoint, in such Manner as the Legislature thereof may direct, a Number of Electors, equal to the whole Number of Senators and Representatives to which the State may be entitled in the Congress: but no Senator or Representative, or Person holding an Office of Trust or Profit under the United States, shall be appointed an Elector.

The Electors shall meet in their respective States, and vote by Ballot for two Persons, of whom one at least shall not be an Inhabitant of the same State with themselves. And they shall make a List of all the Persons voted for, and of the Number of Votes for each;

which List they shall sign and certify, and transmit sealed to the Seat of the Government of the United States, directed to the President of the Senate. The President of the Senate shall, in the Presence of the Senate and House of Representatives, open all the Certificates, and the Votes shall then be counted. The Person having the greatest Number of Votes shall be the President, if such Number be a Majority of the whole number of Electors appointed; and if there be more than one who have such Majority, and have an equal Number of Votes, then the House of Representatives shall immediately chuse by Ballot one of them for President; and if no Person have a Majority, then from the five highest on the List the said House shall in like Manner chuse the President. But in chusing the President, the Votes shall be taken by States, the Representation from each State having one Vote; A quorum for this Purpose shall consist of a Member or Members from two thirds of the States, and a Majority of all the States shall be necessary to a Choice. In every Case, after the Choice of the President, the Person having the greatest Number of Votes of the Electors shall be the Vice President. But if there should remain two or more who have equal Votes, the Senate shall chuse from them by Ballot the Vice President.

The Congress may determine the time of chusing the Electors, and the Day on which they shall give their Votes; which Day shall be the same throughout the United States.

No person except a natural born Citizen, or a *Citizen of the United States, at the time of the Adoption of this Constitution,* shall be eligible to the Office of President; neither shall any Person be eligible to that Office who shall not have attained to the Age of thirty five Years, and been fourteen Years a Resident within the United States.

In Case of the Removal of the President from Office, or of his Death, Resignation, or Inability to discharge the Powers and Duties of the said Office, the Same shall devolve on the Vice President, and the Congress may by Law provide for the Case of Removal, Death, Resignation or Inability, both of the President and Vice President, declaring what Officer shall then act as President, and such Officer shall act accordingly, until the Disability be removed, or a President shall be elected.

The President shall, at stated Times, receive for his Services, a Compensation, which shall neither be encreased nor diminished during the Period for which he shall have been elected, and he shall not receive within that period any other Emolument from the United States, or any of them.

Before he enter on the Execution of his Office, he shall take the following Oath or Affirmation:—"I do solemnly swear (or affirm) that I will faithfully execute the Office of President of the United States, and will to the best of my Ability, preserve, protect and defend the Constitution of the United States."

Section 2

The President shall be Commander in Chief of the Army and Navy of the United States, and of the Militia of the several States, when called into the actual Service of the United States; he may require the Opinion, in writing, of the principal Officer in each of the executive Departments, upon any Subject relating to the Duties of their respective Offices, and he shall have Power to grant Reprieves and Pardons for Offences against the United States, except in Cases of Impeachment.

He shall have Power, by and with the Advice and Consent of the Senate, to make Treaties, provided two thirds of the Senators present concur; and he shall nominate, and by and with the Advice and Consent of the Senate, shall appoint Ambassadors, other public Ministers and Consuls, Judges of the supreme Court, and all other Officers of the United States, whose Appointments are not herein otherwise provided for, and which shall be established by Law: but the Congress may by Law vest the Appointment of such inferior Officers, as they think proper in the President alone, in the Courts of Law, or in the Heads of Departments.

The President shall have Power to fill up all Vacancies that may happen during the Recess of the Senate, by granting Commissions which shall expire at the End of their next Session.

Section 3

He shall from time to time give to the Congress Information of the State of the Union, and recommend to their Consideration such Measures as he shall judge necessary and expedient; he may, on extraordinary Occasions, convene both Houses, or either of them, and in Case of disagreement between them, with Respect to the Time of Adjournment, he may adjourn them to such Time as he shall think proper; he shall receive Ambassadors and other public Ministers; he shall take Care that the Laws be faithfully executed, and shall Commission all the officers of the United States.

Section 4

The President, Vice President and all civil Officers of the United States, shall be removed from Office on Impeachment for, and Conviction of, Treason, Bribery or other high Crimes and Misdemeanors.

Article III

Section 1

The judicial Power of the United States, shall be vested in one supreme Court, and in such inferior Courts as the Congress may from time to time ordain and establish. The Judges, both of the supreme and inferior Courts, shall hold their offices during good Behaviour, and shall, at stated Times, receive for their Services, a Compensation, which shall not be diminished during their Continuance in Office.

Section 2

The judicial Power shall extend to all Cases, in Law and Equity, arising under this Constitution, the Laws of the United States, and Treaties made, or which shall be made, under their Authority;—to all Cases affecting Ambassadors, other public Ministers and Consuls;—to all Cases of admiralty and maritime Jurisdiction;—to Controversies to which the United States shall be a Party;—to Controversies between two or more States;—between a State and Citizens of another State;—*between Citizens of different States;*—between Citizens of the same State claiming Lands under Grants of different States, and between a State, or the Citizens thereof, and foreign States, Citizens or Subjects.

In all Cases affecting Ambassadors, other public Ministers and Consuls, and those in which a State shall be Party, the supreme Court shall have original Jurisdiction. In all the other Cases before mentioned, the supreme Court shall have appellate Jurisdiction, both as to Law and Fact, with such Exceptions, and under such Regulations as the Congress shall make.

The Trial of all Crimes, except in Cases of Impeachment, shall be by Jury; and such Trial shall be held in the State where the said Crimes shall have been committed, but when not committed within any State, the Trial shall be at such Place or Places as the Congress may by Law have directed.

Section 3

Treason against the United States, shall consist only in levying War against them, or in adhering to their Enemies, giving them Aid and Comfort. No person shall be convicted of Treason unless on the Testimony of two Witnesses to the same overt Act, or on Confession in open Court.

The Congress shall have Power to declare the Punishment of Treason, but no Attainder of Treason shall work Corruption of Blood, or Forfeiture except during the Life of the Person attainted.

Article IV

Section 1

Full Faith and Credit shall be given in each State to the public Acts, Records, and judicial Proceedings of every other State. And the Congress may by general Laws prescribe the Manner in which such Acts, Records and Proceedings shall be proved, and the Effect thereof.

Section 2

The Citizens of each State shall be entitled to all Privileges and Immunities of Citizens in the several States.

A Person charged in any State with Treason, Felony, or other Crime, who shall flee from Justice, and be found in another State, shall on Demand of the executive Authority of the State from which he fled, be delivered up, to be removed to the State having Jurisdiction of the Crime.

No Person held to Service or Labour in one State, under the Laws thereof, escaping into another, shall, in Consequence of any Law or Regulation therein, be discharged from such Service or Labour, but shall be delivered up on Claim of the Party to whom such Service or Labour may be due.

Section 3

New States may be admitted by the Congress into this Union; but no new State shall be formed or erected within the Jurisdiction of any other State; nor any State be formed by the Junction of two or more States, or Parts of States, without the Consent of the Legislatures of the States concerned as well as of the Congress.

The Congress shall have Power to dispose of and make all needful Rules and Regulations respecting the Territory or other Property belonging to the United States; and nothing in this Constitution shall be so construed as to Prejudice any Claims of the United States, or of any particular States.

Section 4

The United States shall guarantee to every State in this Union a Republican Form of Government, and shall protect each of them against Invasion; and on Application of the Legislature, or of the Executive (when the Legislature cannot be convened) against domestic violence.

Article V

The Congress, whenever two thirds of both Houses shall deem it necessary, shall propose Amendments to this Constitution, or, on the Application of the Legislatures of two thirds of the several States, shall call a Convention for proposing Amendments, which, in either Case, shall be valid to all Intents and Purposes, as Part of this Constitution, when ratified by the Legislatures of three fourths of the several States, or by Conventions in three fourths thereof, as the one or the other Mode of Ratification may be proposed by the Congress; Provided *that no Amendment which may be made prior to the Year One thousand eight hundred and eight shall in any Manner affect the first and fourth Clauses in the Ninth Section of the first Article;* and that no State, without its Consent, shall be deprived of its equal Suffrage in the Senate.

Article VI

All Debts contracted and Engagements entered into, before the Adoption of this Constitution, shall be as valid against the United States under this Constitution, as under the Confederation.

This Constitution, and Laws of the United States which shall be made in Pursuance thereof; and all Treaties made, or which shall be made, under the Authority of the United States, shall be the supreme Law of the Land; and the Judges in every State shall be bound thereby, any Thing in the Constitution or Laws of any State to the Contrary notwithstanding.

The Senators and Representatives before mentioned, and the Members of the several State Legislatures, and all executive and Judicial Officers, both of the United States and of the several States, shall be bound by Oath or Affirmation, to support this Constitution; but no religious Test shall ever be required as a Qualification to any Office of public Trust under the United States.

Article VII

The Ratification of the Conventions of nine States, shall be sufficient for the Establishment of this Constitution between the States so ratifying the Same.

Done in Convention by the Unanimous Consent of the States present the Seventeenth Day of September in the Year of our Lord one thousand seven hundred and Eighty seven and of the Independence of the United States of America the Twelfth[†] IN WITNESS whereof We have hereunto subscribed our Names,

George Washington
President and Deputy from Virginia

Delaware	*South Carolina*	*New York*
George Read	John Rutledge	Alexander Hamilton
Gunning Bedford, Jr.	Charles Cotesworth Pinckney	
John Dickinson	Charles Pinckney	*New Jersey*
Richard Bassett	Pierce Butler	William Livingston
Jacob Broom		David Brearley
	Georgia	William Paterson
Maryland	William Few	Jonathan Dayton
James McHenry	Abraham Baldwin	
Daniel of St. Thomas Jenifer		*Pennsylvania*
Daniel Carroll	*New Hampshire*	Benjamin Franklin
	John Langdon	Thomas Mifflin
Virginia	Nicholas Gilman	Robert Morris
John Blair		George Clymer
James Madison, Jr.	*Massachusetts*	Thomas FitzSimons
	Nathaniel Gorham	Jared Ingersoll
North Carolina	Rufus King	James Wilson
William Blount		Gouverneur Morris
Richard Dobbs Spraight	*Connecticut*	
Hugh Williamson	William Samuel Johnson	
	Roger Sherman	

[†]The Constitution was submitted on September 17, 1787, by the Constitutional Convention, was ratified by conventions of the several states at various dates up to May 29, 1790, and became effective on March 4, 1789.

Amendment I

Congress shall make no law respecting an establishment of religion, or prohibiting the free exercise thereof; or abridging the freedom of speech, or of the press; or the right of the people peaceably to assemble, and to petition the Government for a redress of grievances.

Amendment II

A well regulated Militia being necessary to the security of a free State, the right of the people to keep and bear Arms, shall not be infringed.

Amendment III

No Soldier shall, in time of peace be quartered in any house, without the consent of the Owner, nor in time of war, but in a manner to be prescribed by law.

Amendment IV

The right of the people to be secure in their persons, houses, papers, and effects, against unreasonable searches and seizures, shall not be violated, and no Warrants shall issue, but upon probable cause, supported by Oath or affirmation, and particularly describing the place to be searched, and the persons or things to be seized.

Amendment V

No person shall be held to answer for a capital, or otherwise infamous crime, unless on a presentment or indictment of a Grand Jury, except in cases arising in the land or naval forces, or in the Militia, when in actual service in time of War or public danger; nor shall any person be subject for the same offense to be twice put in jeopardy of life or limb; nor shall be compelled in any criminal case to be a witness against himself, nor be deprived of life, liberty, or property, without due process of law; nor shall private property be taken for public use, without just compensation.

Amendment VI

In all criminal prosecutions, the accused shall enjoy the right to a speedy and public trial, by an impartial jury of the State and district wherein the crime shall have been committed, which district shall have been previously ascertained by law, and to be informed of the nature and cause of the accusation; to be confronted with the witnesses against him; to have compulsory process for obtaining witnesses in his favor, and to have the Assistance of Counsel for his defence.

Amendment VII

In Suits at common law, where the value in controversy shall exceed twenty dollars, the right of trial by jury shall be preserved, and no fact tried by a jury, shall be otherwise re-examined in any Court of the United States, than according to the rules of the common law.

Amendment VIII

Excessive bail shall not be required, nor excessive fines imposed, nor cruel and unusual punishments inflicted.

Amendment IX

The enumeration in the Constitution, of certain rights, shall not be construed to deny or disparage others retained by the people.

Amendment X*

The powers not delegated to the United States by the Constitution, nor prohibited by it to the States, are reserved to the States respectively, or to the people.

Amendment XI
[Adopted 1798]

The Judicial power of the United States shall not be construed to extend to any suit in law or equity, commenced or prosecuted against one of the United States by Citizens of another State, or by Citizens or Subjects of any Foreign State.

Amendment XII
[Adopted 1804]

The Electors shall meet in their respective states, and vote by ballot for President and Vice President, one of whom, at least, shall not be an inhabitant of the same state with themselves; they shall name in their ballots the person voted for as President, and in distinct ballots the person voted for as Vice President, and they shall make distinct lists of all persons voted for as President, and of all persons voted for as Vice President, and of the number of votes for each, which lists they shall sign and certify, and transmit sealed to the seat of the government of the United States, directed to the President of the Senate;—The President of the Senate shall, in the presence of the Senate and House of Representatives, open all the certificates and the votes shall then be counted;—The person having the greatest number of votes for President, shall be the President, if such number be a majority of the whole number of Electors appointed; and if no person have such majority, then from the persons having the highest numbers not exceeding three on the list of those voted for as President, the House of Representatives shall choose immediately, by ballot, the President. But in choosing the President, the votes shall be taken by states, the representation from each state having one vote; a quorum for this purpose shall consist of a member or members from two-thirds of the states, and a majority of all the states shall be necessary to a choice. And if the House of Representatives shall not choose a President whenever the right of choice shall devolve upon them, before *the fourth day of March* next following, then the Vice President shall act as President, as in the case of the death or other constitutional disability of the President.—The person having

---

*The first ten amendments (the Bill of Rights) were ratified and their adoption was certified on December 15, 1791.

the greatest number of votes as Vice President, shall be the Vice President, if such number be a majority of the whole number of Electors appointed, and if no person have a majority, then from the two highest numbers on the list, the Senate shall choose the Vice President; a quorum for the purpose shall consist of two-thirds of the whole number of Senators, and a majority of the whole number shall be necessary to a choice. But no person constitutionally ineligible to the office of President shall be eligible to that of Vice President of the United States.

Amendment XIII
[Adopted 1865]

Section 1

Neither slavery nor involuntary servitude, except as a punishment for crime whereof the party shall have been duly convicted, shall exist within the United States, or any place subject to their jurisdiction.

Section 2

Congress shall have power to enforce this article by appropriate legislation.

Amendment XIV
[Adopted 1868]

Section 1

All persons born or naturalized in the United States, and subject to the jurisdiction thereof, are citizens of the United States and of the State wherein they reside. No State shall make or enforce any law which shall abridge the privileges or immunities of citizens of the United States; nor shall any State deprive any person of life, liberty, or property, without due process of law; nor deny to any person within its jurisdiction the equal protection of the laws.

Section 2

Representatives shall be apportioned among the several States according to their respective numbers, counting the whole number of persons in each State, excluding Indians not taxed. But when the right to vote at any election for the choice of electors for President and Vice President of the United States, Representatives in Congress, the Executive and Judicial officers of a State, or the members of the Legislature thereof, is denied to any of the male inhabitants of such State, being twenty-one years of age, and citizens of the United States, or in any way abridged, except for participation in rebellion, or other crime, the basis of representation therein shall be reduced in the proportion which the number of such male citizens shall bear to the whole number of male citizens twenty-one years of age in such State.

Section 3

No person shall be a Senator or Representative in Congress, or elector of President and Vice President, or hold any office, civil or military, under the United States, or under any State, who, having previously taken an oath, as a member of Congress,

or as an officer of the United States, or as a member of any State legislature, or as an executive or judicial officer of any State, to support the Constitution of the United States, shall have engaged in insurrection or rebellion against the same, or given aid or comfort to the enemies thereof. But Congress may by a vote of two-thirds of each House, remove such disability.

Section 4

The validity of the public debt of the United States, authorized by law, including debts incurred for payment of pensions and bounties for services in suppressing insurrection or rebellion, shall not be questioned. But neither the United States nor any State shall assume or pay any debt or obligation incurred in aid of insurrection or rebellion against the United States, or any claim for the loss or emancipation of any slave; but all such debts, obligations and claims shall be held illegal and void.

Section 5

The Congress shall have power to enforce, by appropriate legislation, the provisions of this article.

Amendment XV
[Adopted 1870]

Section 1

The right of citizens of the United States to vote shall not be denied or abridged by the United States or by any State on account of race, color, or previous condition of servitude.

Section 2

The Congress shall have power to enforce this article by appropriate legislation.

Amendment XVI
[Adopted 1913]

The Congress shall have power to lay and collect taxes on incomes, from whatever source derived, without apportionment among the several States, and without regard to any census or enumeration.

Amendment XVII
[Adopted 1913]

The Senate of the United States shall be composed of two Senators from each State, elected by the people thereof, for six years; and each Senator shall have one vote. The electors in each State shall have the qualifications requisite for electors of the most numerous branch of the State legislatures.

When vacancies happen in the representation of any State in the Senate, the executive authority of such State shall issue writs of election to fill such vacancies: *Provided,* That the legislature of any State may empower the executive thereof to make temporary appointments until the people fill the vacancies by election as the legislature may direct.

This amendment shall not be so construed as to affect the election or term of any Senator chosen before it becomes valid as part of the Constitution.

Amendment XVIII
[Adopted 1919, repealed 1933]

Section 1

After one year from the ratification of this article the manufacture, sale, or transportation of intoxicating liquors within, the importation thereof into, or the exportation thereof from the United States and all territory subject to the jurisdiction thereof for beverage purposes is hereby prohibited.

Section 2

The Congress and the several States shall have concurrent power to enforce this article by appropriate legislation.

Section 3

This article shall be inoperative unless it shall have been ratified as an amendment to the Constitution by the legislatures of the several States, as provided in the Constitution, within seven years from the date of the submission hereof to the States by the Congress.

Amendment XIX
[Adopted 1920]

The right of citizens of the United States to vote shall not be denied or abridged by the United States or by any State on account of sex.

Congress shall have power to enforce this article by appropriate legislation.

Amendment XX
[Adopted 1933]

Section 1

The terms of the President and Vice President shall end at noon on the 20th day of January, and the terms of Senators and Representatives at noon on the 3d day of January, of the years in which such terms would have ended if this article had not been ratified and the terms of their successors shall then begin.

Section 2

The Congress shall assemble at least once in every year, and such meeting shall begin at noon on the 3d day of January, unless they shall by law appoint a different day.

Section 3

If, at the time fixed for the beginning of the term of the President, the President elect shall have died, the Vice President elect shall become President. If a President shall not have been chosen before the time fixed for the beginning of his term, or if the President elect shall have failed to qualify, then the Vice President elect shall act as President until a President shall have qualified; and the Congress may by law provide for the case wherein neither a President elect nor a Vice President elect shall have qualified, declaring who shall then act as President, or the manner in which one who is to act shall be selected, and such person shall act accordingly until a President or Vice President shall have qualified.

Section 4

The Congress may by law provide for the case of the death of any of the persons from whom the House of Representatives may choose a President whenever the right of choice shall have devolved upon them, and for the case of the death of any of the persons from whom the Senate may choose a Vice President whenever the right of choice shall have devolved upon them.

Section 5

Sections 1 and 2 shall take effect on the 15th day of October following the ratification of this article.

Section 6

This article shall be inoperative unless it shall have been ratified as an amendment to the Constitution by the legislatures of three fourths of the several States within seven years from the date of its submission.

Amendment XXI
[Adopted 1933]

Section 1

The eighteenth article of amendment to the Constitution of the United States is hereby repealed.

Section 2

The transportation or importation into any State, Territory, or possession of the United States for delivery or use therein of intoxicating liquors in violation of the laws thereof, is hereby prohibited.

Section 3

This article shall be inoperative unless it shall have been ratified as an amendment to the Constitution by conventions in the several States, as provided in the Constitution, within seven years from the date of the submission hereof to the States by the Congress.

Amendment XXII
[Adopted 1951]

Section 1

No person shall be elected to the office of the President more than twice, and no person who has held the office of President, or acted as President, for more than two years of a term to which some other person was elected President shall be elected to the office of the President more than once. But this Article shall not apply to any person holding the office of President when this Article was proposed by the Congress, and shall not prevent any person who may be holding the office of President, or acting as President, during the term within which this Article becomes operative from holding the office of President or acting as President during the remainder of such term.

Section 2

This article shall be inoperative unless it shall have been ratified as an amendment to the Constitution by the legislatures of three-fourths of the several States within seven years from the date of its submission to the States by the Congress.

Amendment XXIII
[Adopted 1961]

Section 1

The District constituting the seat of Government of the United States shall appoint in such manner as the Congress shall direct:

A number of electors of President and Vice President equal to the whole number of Senators and Representatives in Congress to which the District would be entitled if it were a State, but in no event more than the least populous State; they shall be in addition to those appointed by the States, but they shall be considered, for the purposes of the election of President and Vice President, to be electors appointed by a State; and they shall meet in the District and perform such duties as provided by the twelfth article of amendment.

Section 2

The Congress shall have power to enforce this article by appropriate legislation.

Amendment XXIV
[Adopted 1964]

Section 1

The right of citizens of the United States to vote in any primary or other election for President or Vice President, for electors for President or Vice President, or for Senator or Representative in Congress, shall not be denied or abridged by the United States or any state by reason of failure to pay any poll tax or other tax.

Section 2

The Congress shall have the power to enforce this article by appropriate legislation.

Amendment XXV
[Adopted 1967]

Section 1

In case of the removal of the President from office or his death or resignation, the Vice President shall become President.

Section 2

Whenever there is a vacancy in the office of the Vice President, the President shall nominate a Vice President who shall take the office upon confirmation by a majority vote of both houses of Congress.

Section 3

Whenever the President transmits to the President pro tempore of the Senate and the Speaker of the House of Representatives his written declaration that he is unable to discharge the powers and duties of his office, and until he transmits to them a written declaration to the contrary, such powers and duties shall be discharged by the Vice President as Acting President.

Section 4

Whenever the Vice President and a majority of either the principal officers of the executive departments or of such other body as Congress may by law provide, transmit to the President pro tempore of the Senate and the Speaker of the House of Representatives their written declaration that the President is unable to discharge the powers and duties of his office, the Vice President shall immediately assume the powers and duties of the office as Acting President.

Thereafter, when the President transmits to the President pro tempore of the Senate and the Speaker of the House of Representatives his written declaration that no inability exists, he shall resume the powers and duties of his office unless the Vice President and a majority of either the principal officers of the executive department or of such other body as Congress may by law provide, transmit within four days to the President pro tempore of the Senate and the Speaker of the House of Representatives their written declaration that the President is unable to discharge the powers and duties of his office. Thereupon Congress shall decide the issue, assembling within 48 hours for that purpose if not in session. If the Congress, within 21 days after receipt of the latter written declaration, or, if Congress is not in session, within 21 days after Congress is required to assemble, determines by two-thirds vote of both houses that the President is unable to discharge the powers and duties of his office, the Vice President shall continue to discharge the same as Acting President; otherwise, the President shall resume the powers and duties of his office.

Amendment XXVI
[Adopted 1971]

Section 1

The right of citizens of the United States, who are 18 years of age or older, to vote shall not be denied or abridged by the United States or any state on account of age.

Section 2

The Congress shall have the power to enforce this article by appropriate legislation.

Amendment XXVII
[Adopted 1992]

No law, varying the compensation for the services of the Senators and Representatives shall take effect, until an election of Representatives shall have intervened.

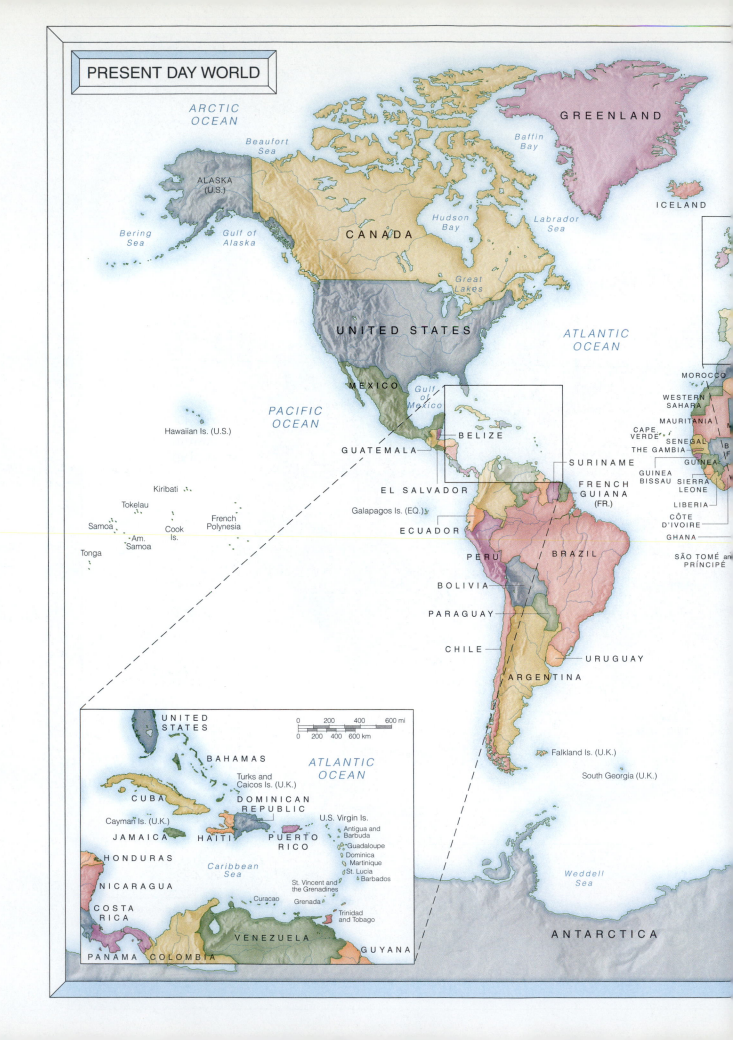

PRESENT DAY WORLD

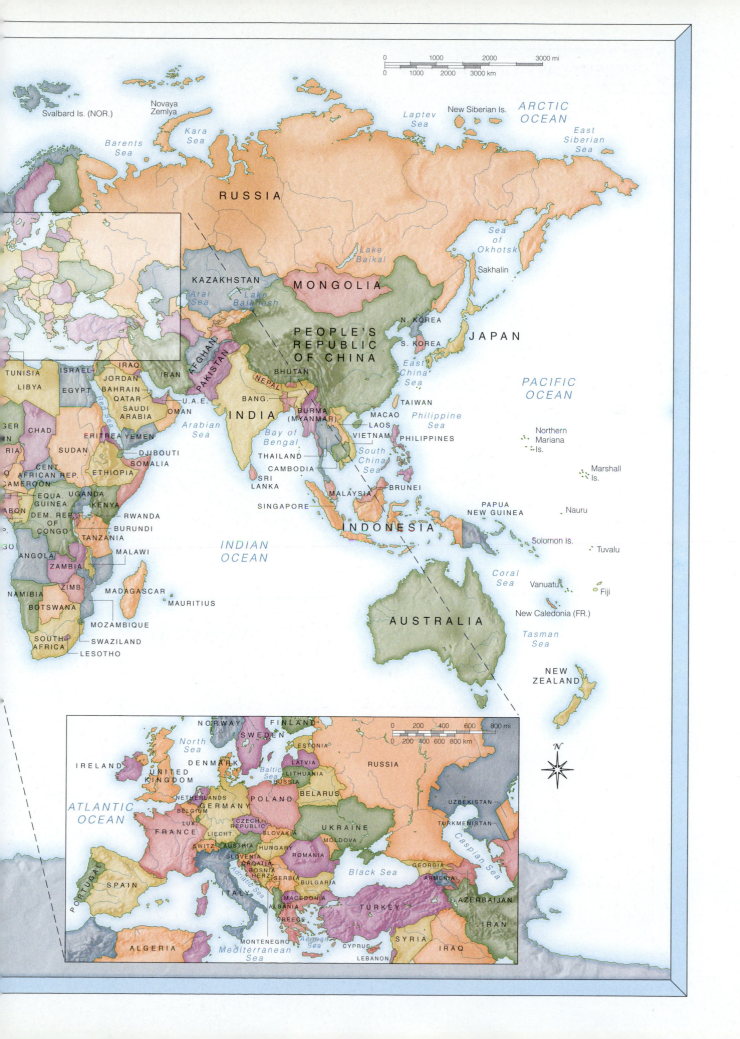

RUSSIA

ARCTIC OCEAN

Svalbard Is. (NOR.)
Novaya Zemlya
Barents Sea
Kara Sea
Laptev Sea
New Siberian Is.
East Siberian Sea

Sea of Okhotsk
Sakhalin

KAZAKHSTAN
Aral Sea
Lake Balkhash
Lake Baikal

MONGOLIA

N. KOREA
S. KOREA
JAPAN

PEOPLE'S REPUBLIC OF CHINA

TUNISIA
LIBYA
ISRAEL
JORDAN
IRAQ
IRAN
AFGHAN.
PAKISTAN
BHUTAN
NEPAL
BANG.
East China Sea

EGYPT
BAHRAIN
QATAR
SAUDI ARABIA
U.A.E.
OMAN
YEMEN
Red Sea

GER
CHAD
RIA
SUDAN
ERITREA
DJIBOUTI
SOMALIA

Arabian Sea

INDIA

BURMA (MYANMAR)
TAIWAN
MACAO
LAOS
VIETNAM
Philippine Sea

PACIFIC OCEAN

Northern Mariana Is.

Marshall Is.

CENT. AFRICAN REP.
CAMEROON
ETHIOPIA
EQUA. GUINEA
UGANDA
KENYA
ABON
DEM. REP. OF CONGO
RWANDA
BURUNDI
TANZANIA
GO

Bay of Bengal
THAILAND
CAMBODIA
SRI LANKA
South China Sea
MALAYSIA
BRUNEI
SINGAPORE

PAPUA NEW GUINEA
Nauru

ANGOLA
ZAMBIA
MALAWI
ZIMB.
MADAGASCAR
MAURITIUS

INDIAN OCEAN

INDONESIA

Solomon Is.
Tuvalu

NAMIBIA
BOTSWANA
MOZAMBIQUE
SWAZILAND
SOUTH AFRICA
LESOTHO

Coral Sea
Vanuatu
Fiji
New Caledonia (FR.)

AUSTRALIA

Tasman Sea

NEW ZEALAND

0   1000   2000   3000 mi
0   1000   2000   3000 km

NORWAY
FINLAND
SWEDEN
North Sea
IRELAND
DENMARK
ESTONIA
LATVIA
LITHUANIA
RUSSIA
Baltic Sea
RUSSIA
UNITED KINGDOM
NETHERLANDS
GERMANY
POLAND
BELARUS

ATLANTIC OCEAN

BELGIUM
LUX.
FRANCE
LIECHT.
CZECH REPUBLIC
SLOVAKIA
UKRAINE
MOLDOVA
SWITZ.
AUSTRIA
HUNGARY
SLOVENIA
CROATIA
ROMANIA
UZBEKISTAN
TURKMENISTAN

PORTUGAL
SPAIN
ITALY
Adriatic Sea
BOSNIA HERZ.
SERBIA
BULGARIA
MACEDONIA
ALBANIA
GREECE
MONTENEGRO
Aegean Sea
Black Sea
GEORGIA
ARMENIA
AZERBAIJAN
Caspian Sea

TURKEY
CYPRUS
SYRIA
IRAN
IRAQ
LEBANON

ALGERIA
Mediterranean Sea

0   200   400   600   800 mi
0   200   400   600   800 km

N

affirmative action   Policies designed to improve the educational and employment opportunities of historically underrepresented groups such as women and African Americans. *p. 864*

Alien and Sedition Acts   Laws enacted by the Federalist-dominated Congress in 1798 to limit the speech of their critics and to make it more difficult for immigrants to become citizens. *p. 270*

Allies   Members of an alliance, such as the military coalition led by the United States, the Soviet Union, and Great Britain during World War II. *p. 719*

almshouse   A privately financed home for the poor; a poorhouse. *p. 153*

American Federation of Labor (AFL)   A union of skilled craft workers organized by Samuel Gompers, in 1886; advocated higher wages and better working conditions and focused its organizing efforts primarily on skilled white men. *p. 546*

anarchists   Persons who reject all forms of government as inherently oppressive and undesirable. *p. 545*

Archaic period   The second long stage of North American habitation, covering about 7,000 years, from roughly 8000 to 1000 BCE (or from 10,000 to 3,000 years ago). During this period, inhabitants adapted to diverse local environments, gathering plants and hunting smaller animals than during the previous Paleo-Indian period. *p. 7*

archipelago   A group of islands, such as the Hawaiian archipelago. *p. 14*

asiento   A contract negotiated by the Spanish crown (between 1595 and 1789) with other European powers such as Portugal, France, England, and the Netherlands to provide a fixed number of slaves annually to Spain's American colonies for a set payment. *p. 106*

Axis   A political alignment or alliance, such as the military coalition between Germany, Italy, and Japan during World War II. *p. 716*

Babel   A city described in the Bible where constructing a tower was made impossible by the confusion of varied languages. This term from Chapter 11 of the Book of Genesis is used to describe any scene of clamor and confusion. *p. 138*

baby boom   The period of increased U.S. childbirths from roughly the early 1940s to the early 1960s. *p. 920*

barracoon   An enclosure or barrack used for the confinement of slaves before their forced deportation from the African coast. *p. 116*

Bill of Rights   A set of amendments assuring basic rights, proposed by James Madison to help ensure acceptance of the newly drafted Constitution, and based on suggestions from the states. Ten of the twelve items passed by Congress were ratified by the states in 1791; these first ten amendments to the Constitution became known as the Bill of Rights. *p. 260*

Black Codes   Legislation passed by southern state lawmakers in 1865 to reassert white control over blacks by limiting their freedom of movement, political rights, and economic opportunity. *p. 462*

black power   The slogan used by young black nationalists in the mid- and late 1960s. *p. 821*

"bloody shirt"   A partisan rallying cry used to stir up or revive sectional or party animosity after the American Civil War; for example, post–Civil War Republicans "waved the bloody shirt," associating some Democrats with a treasonous acceptance of secession during the war, while opponents had spilled their blood for the Union. *p. 517*

Boston marriages   Unions of two women based on long-term emotional bonds in which the women live together as if married to each other. *p. 618*

braceros   Mexican nationals working in the United States in low-wage jobs as part of a temporary work program between 1942 and 1964. (The *bracero* program was established by an executive agreement between the presidents of Mexico and the United States, providing Mexican agricultural labor in the Southwest and the Pacific Northwest.) *p. 725*

Bull Moosers   Supporters of Theodore Roosevelt in the 1912 presidential election when he broke from the Republican party and ran as a third-party candidate on the ticket of the Progressive (or Bull Moose) party. *p. 596*

burgess   A representative elected to the popular branch of the colonial legislature in either Virginia or Maryland. *p. 56*

Cajuns   The Louisiana word for French-speaking people Acadians (from Nova Scotia) who were forced to move south in 1755 during the French and Indian War. Many of these refugees eventually settled in French Louisiana, where they have had a lasting impact on the culture. *p. 146*

capitalism   The now almost worldwide economic system of private ownership of property and profit-seeking corporations. *p. 682*

carpetbaggers   A negative term applied by Southerners to Northerners who moved to the South after the Civil War to pursue political or economic opportunities. *p. 463*

Central Powers   A World War I alliance of Germany, Austria-Hungary, Italy, and the Ottoman Empire (Italy withdrew in 1915). *p. 623*

checks and balances   The rules controlling interactions among the executive, legislative, and judicial branches of government, making up a novel system designed to prevent any single branch from overreaching its powers, as set forth in the Constitution in 1787. *p. 254*

Chinese Exclusion Act   Congressional legislation passed in 1882 to bar most Chinese workers from entering the United States. *p. 501*

civic organizations   Membership organizations that exist to further the public life and welfare of a community. *p. 784*

Civil Rights Act of 1875   Congressional legislation that guaranteed black people access to public accommodations and transportation; the Supreme Court declared the measure unconstitutional in 1883. *p. 487*

civil service reform   Measures designed to eliminate the spoils system in government hiring, in favor of maintaining professional standards in public service. *p. 520*

coffle   A procession or train of enslaved prisoners, bound together for travel (from the Arabic word for "caravan"). *p. 116*

Cold War   The conflict and competition between the United States and the Soviet Union (and their respective allies) that emerged after 1945 and lasted until 1989. *p. 745*

colonialism   The centuries-old system of mostly European nations controlling and governing peoples and lands outside of Europe. *p. 757*

Columbian exchange   The two-way interchange of plants, animals, microbes, and people that occurred once Christopher Columbus established regular contact by sea between Europe and the New World. *p. 21*

comfort women   Women, mostly Chinese and Korean, forced into sexual slavery by Japanese troops during World War II. *p. 731*

common school system   Tax-supported public education to provide elementary schooling free to young children. *p. 380*

communism   A totalitarian form of government, grounded in the theories of German philosopher Karl Marx and the practices of V. I. Lenin in Russia, that eliminated private ownership of property in supposed pursuit of complete human equality; the system of government also featured a centrally directed economy and the absolute rule of a small group of leaders. *p. 745*

Compromise of 1850   Congressional legislation that provided that California would enter the Union as a free state that year, and that New Mexico and Utah would eventually submit the slavery question to their voters. As part of this compromise, the federal government abolished the slave trade in Washington, D.C. *p. 395*

Confederate States of America   The would-be new nation formed in February 1861 by seven southern states—South Carolina, Mississippi, Florida, Alabama, Georgia, Louisiana, and Texas—in a bid for independence from the United States of America. By late spring 1861, the Confederacy also included Virginia, Arkansas, Tennessee, and North Carolina. *p. 425*

consumer economy   an economic system in which most people work for wages, which they use to purchase manufactured goods and foodstuffs. *p. 651*

containment   During the Cold War, the U.S. policy of trying to halt the expansion of Soviet and communist influences. *p. 756*

coverture   French term for the dependent legal status of a woman during marriage. Under English law, the male family head received legal rights, and his wife lost independent status, becoming, in legal terms, a *femme covert*. *p. 85*

czar   The monarch (king) of Russia before the 1917 revolution. *p. 624*

Dawes Act   Congressional legislation (formally the Dawes Severalty Act) passed in 1887, eliminating common ownership of Indian tribal lands in favor of a system of private property. The law hastened the decrease in the number of Indian-held acres, from 138 million acres in 1887 to 78 million thirteen years later. *p. 521*

Democratic-Republicans   The political party that emerged after the Revolution to oppose the Federalists' support for a strong central government; favored states' rights and the agrarian way of life. Thomas Jefferson, a leader of the Democratic-Republicans, was elected president in 1800. *p. 264*

Democrats   Members of the Democratic party, a political party descended from the Democratic-Republican party of the early national period and formed under the leadership of Andrew Jackson, who assumed the presidency in 1829. The party favored local and state (rather than federal) control of economic issues, but beginning in the 1930s, under the leadership of President Franklin D. Roosevelt, the party advocated more robust federal intervention in social welfare as well as economic development. *p. 340*

détente   The lessening of military or diplomatic tensions, as between the United States and the Soviet Union. *p. 841*

diaspora   The dispersion of a population abroad, whether forced or voluntary. The term is often applied to Jewish settlement outside the eastern Mediterranean region and to the spread of Africans across the Americas due to the Atlantic slave trade. *p. 134*

don't ask, don't tell   A policy established by the Clinton administration allowing gays and lesbians to serve in the military so long as they do not disclose their sexual orientation. *p. 911*

Dred Scott V. Sanford   The 1857 case in which the Supreme Court held that residence on free soil did not render a slave a free person, for black people, enslaved and free, had (in the words of the court) "no rights which the white man was bound to respect." *p. 417*

Dust Bowl   The plains regions of Oklahoma, Texas, Colorado, and New Mexico affected by severe drought in the 1930s. *p. 687*

Edmonds Act   Congressional legislation passed in 1882 and aimed at Utah Mormons; it outlawed polygamy, stripped polygamists of the right to vote, and provided for a five-member commission to oversee Utah's elections. *p. 520*

electoral college   An intricate system in which each state appoints electors, equal in number to its representation in Congress, to elect the president and vice president. The electoral college is a provision of the Constitution (Article II, Section 1) because the framers were unwilling to approve the direct election of president and vice president. *p. 255*

emancipation National or state-sponsored program to free slaves. *p. 437*

Embargo Act of 1807 A law passed by Congress, at the urging of President Thomas Jefferson, to halt the shipment of U.S. goods to Europe in response to British military and naval aggression. *p. 302*

encomienda The Spanish *encomienda* system, imposed in Spain's American empire, requiring Indian communities to supply labor or pay tribute to a local colonial overlord (identified as an *encomendero*). *p. 44*

Entente The alliance of Britain, France, and Russia, later joined by Italy and the United States, during World War I. *p. 622*

Era of Good Feeling A term used by historians to describe the presidency of James Monroe (1816–1820), when partisan tensions eased among voters and their political leaders. *p. 311*

Erie Canal Waterway linking the New York cities of Troy and Albany, on the Hudson River, with Buffalo, on the eastern tip of Lake Erie; in the 1820s, the opening of the Erie Canal revolutionized trading between the Midwest and East Coast and established New York City as the most important financial center in the United States. *p. 332*

established churches Religious denominations that receive special favors, financial or otherwise, from state governments. *p. 282*

family wage A level of income sufficient for an individual worker, usually a man, to support a spouse and family through a single salary. *p. 705*

fascism A form of right-wing dictatorship exalting nation and race above the individual. *p. 715*

Federalists A coalition of nationalist leaders who favored creating a stronger central government to replace the Articles of Confederation in the late 1780s; the strongest essays endorsing their proposed new Constitution were entitled *The Federalist Papers*. *p. 257*

feminism The belief that women and men are of equal value and that gender roles are, to a considerable degree, created by society rather than being simply natural. *p. 839*

flappers Young women in the 1910s and 1920s who rebelled against the gender conventions of the era with respect to fashion and behavior. *p. 651*

flotilla Any sizeable fleet of ships, or, more specifically, a naval term for a unit consisting of two or more squadrons of small warships. *p. 164*

free trade International economic relations characterized by multinational investment and a reduction or elimination of tariffs. *p. 912*

free labor ideology The ideas, represented most forcefully by the antebellum Republican party, that workers should profit from their own labor and that slavery is wrong. *p. 401*

Freedmen's Bureau Federal agency created by Congress in March 1865 and disbanded in 1869. Its purposes were to provide relief for Southerners who had remained loyal to the Union during the Civil War, to support black elementary schools, and to oversee annual labor contracts between landowners and field hands. *p. 460*

Fugitive Slave Act of 1850 Congressional legislation that required local and federal law enforcement agents to retrieve runaways no matter where they sought refuge in the United States. *p. 410*

globalization The process of integration—economic, but also cultural—of different parts of the world into a more unified system of trade and communication. *p. 17*

Grange An organization founded by Oliver H. Kelly in 1867 to represent the interests of farmers by pressing for agricultural cooperatives, an end to railroad freight discrimination against small farmers, and other initiatives. Its full name was National Grange of Patrons of Husbandry. *p. 485*

Great Awakening The interdenominational Christian revival that swept Britain's North American colonies between the 1730s and the 1750s, inspired at first by the preaching of Jonathan Edwards and George Whitefield. *p. 155*

Great Migration The movement of African Americans out of the South to northern cities, particularly during World War I. *p. 635*

Great Society In the 1960s, President Lyndon Johnson's programs for reducing poverty, discrimination, and pollution, and for improving health care, education, and consumer protection. *p. 809*

guerrilla war A conflict fought not on the basis of conventional warfare but by mobilizing small groups of fighters who attack and harass superior forces. *p. 366*

gun control The legal regulation of firearms. *p. 919*

Haymarket bombing A labor protest held in Chicago's Haymarket Square that erupted in violence on May 4, 1886. A bomb blast killed eight people, including several policemen, and the incident marked the decline of the Knights of Labor, associated in the minds of many Americans with violent labor protest. *p. 545*

headright System in which English colonial governments granted a fixed amount of land, usually fifty acres, to any head of household for every family member or hired hand that person brought into the colony. Sometimes fewer acres were granted for women and children on the grounds that they would clear and plant less land. *p. 56*

hobo Migrant worker or poor and homeless vagrant who traveled on trains from location to location, usually in search of employment. *p. 686*

Holocaust The name given to the Nazi genocide against the Jews during World War II. Six million Jews were murdered. *p. 714*

Homestead Act Legislation passed in 1862 that granted 160 acres of land free to each settler who lived on and made improvements to government land for five years. *p. 437*

Hoovervilles   Shantytowns, named for President Hoover and occupied largely by people who lost their homes and farms during the Great Depression. *p. 676*

horticultural   Pertaining to the art and science of growing fruits, vegetables, and ornamental plants. *p. 8*

Iberian   Relating to Europe's Iberian Peninsula, the location of Spain and Portugal. *p. 16*

imperialism   The policy of extending a nation's authority by territorial acquistion (through negotiation or conquest) or by the establishment of political or economic control over other nations. *p. 558*

indenture   A document binding one person to work for another for a given period of time. Indentured servants received food, shelter, and clothing, plus "freedom dues" when their terms of service ended to help them get started independently. *p. 108*

Interstate Commerce Act   Congressional legislation passed in 1887 mandating that railroads charge all shippers the same freight rates and refrain from giving rebates to their largest customers; established the Interstate Commerce Commission to enforce the new legislation and oversee and stabilize the U.S. railroad industry. *p. 521*

Iroquois League   A Native American confederacy, located in central New York, originally composed of the Cayuga, Mohawk, Oneida, Onondaga, and Seneca Indians and later including the Tuscarora. *p. 49*

Islamist   Pertaining to an ideology promoting the creation of governments based on a fundamentalist interpretation of Islamic law. *p. 871*

isthmus   A narrow strip of land connecting two larger land areas (such as the isthmus of Panama). *p. 25*

jihadist   A Muslim engaged in what is seen as holy war in behalf of Islam. *p. 933*

Jim Crow   The name given to the set of legal institutions that ensured the segregation of nonwhite people in the South. *p. 532*

juke joint   A small, inexpensive establishment where patrons could eat and drink or dance to music from a jukebox. *Juke* is a word of West African origin popularized by African Americans in the Sea Islands of South Carolina. *p. 651*

kachina   An Indian religious system, inspired by Mesoamerican traditions, and present in the American Southwest for more than 800 years; the kachina cult used masks for group performances associated with rain, curing, fertility, warfare, and the ancestors. Among many Pueblo and Hopi Indians, this tradition was epitomized by kachina (or katsina) dolls. *p. 44*

Kansas-Nebraska Act   Congressional legislation passed in 1854 that divided Nebraska Territory into two states, Kansas and Nebraska, whose respective voters would decide for themselves whether to allow slavery. A compromise brokered by Senator Stephen Douglas of Illinois, this act angered abolitionists because it repealed the Compromise of 1820, which had banned slavery north of the Missouri Compromise line of 36°30'. *p. 408*

Kentucky and Virginia Resolutions   Resolutions issued by two state legislatures in 1798 in response to the Alien and Sedition Acts passed by Congress; proclaimed that individual states had the right to declare such measures "void and of no force." *p. 271*

Knights of Labor   A secret order founded in 1869 to organize productive people, regardless of their race, religion, sex, ethnicity, or regional affiliation; blended a critique of the late nineteenth-century wage system with the belief in dignity and a call for collective action, especially among workers. Its high point came in 1886 with the organizing of unions, including some that were biracial, throughout the country. *p. 525*

laissez-faire   A belief in little or no government interference in the economy. *p. 517*

League of Nations   International organization founded in 1919 as a forum to resolve conflicts between nations. It was replaced by the United Nations in 1945. *p. 645*

Lecompton Constitution   A Kansas state constitution drawn up by proslavery advocates in 1857; sought to nullify the doctrine of popular sovereignty in the state, decreeing that even if voters rejected slavery, any slaves already in the state would remain enslaved under the force of law. *p. 417*

Lewis and Clark Expedition   A "corps of discovery" commissioned by President Thomas Jefferson in 1804 to explore the newly acquired Louisiana Territory. Led by Meriwether Lewis and William Clark and lasting twenty-eight months, the party reported on an array of subjects, including the cultural practices of western Indians and the natural features of the land, but failed to find a water route that would connect the Pacific Northwest to eastern markets. *p. 298*

manifest destiny   The idea, first promoted in the 1840s, that the United States had a God-given right to expand its territory; used to justify territorial growth, expansion of economic markets, and conquest. *p. 384*

manumission   A formal emancipation from slavery; the act (by an individual owner or government authority) of granting freedom to an enslaved person or persons. *p. 127*

Marbury v. Madison   An 1803 Supreme Court decision establishing the right of the judiciary to declare acts of both the executive and legislative branches unconstitutional. *p. 292*

market revolution   The combined effects of transportation innovation, technological change, and economic growth, especially during the first half of the nineteenth century. *p. 317*

Marshall Plan   U.S. economic assistance to western Europe for rebuilding after World War II, 1948–1952. *p. 756*

McCarthyism   The political campaign led by Senator Joseph McCarthy (R-Wisconsin) to blame liberals at home for setbacks to U.S. interests abroad, due to what he considered liberals' sympathies with communism. *p. 770*

mercantilism   A commercial policy that sought to achieve economic self-sufficiency and a favorable balance of trade (often by planting colonies) in order to promote a country's prosperity, strength, and independence in the seventeenth and eighteenth centuries. *p. 72*

Mesoamerica   The transitional region between North and South America, composed of Mexico and Central America. p. *8*

mestizo   A person of mixed European and American Indian ancestry. *p. 79*

Mexican Cession   Territory ceded by Mexico to the United States as a result of the 1848 Treaty of Guadalupe Hidalgo; the 530,000 square miles constituted almost half of the territory of Mexico. *p. 395*

middle ground   The geographical region occupied by diverse cultural groups engaged in trade. *p. 276*

middle passage   For European slave ships, the middle passage was the second of three legs in the triangular round-trip voyage from Europe to Africa to America and back to Europe. For enslaved Africans, the middle passage came to mean not only the transatlantic journey itself, but the entire process of removal from an African homeland and ultimate sale to an American master. *p.114*

militarism   A policy of aggressive military preparedness that exalts the use of force as a solution to international problems. *p. 748*

military-industrial complex   The term used by President Dwight D. Eisenhower to describe the military arms industry. *p. 793*

monetary policy   Government policies designed to affect the national economy through bank lending policies, interest rates, and control of the amount of money in circulation. *p. 265*

Monroe Doctrine   Policy announced by President James Monroe in 1823 that the era of European colonization of the Americas had ceased; warned foreign powers, especially Russia, Spain, and Britain, that the United States would not allow them to intervene in the Western Hemisphere. *p. 338*

Morrill Act   Legislation passed by Republican Congress in 1862 to create a system of agricultural (land-grant) public colleges. *p. 437*

most-favored-nation status   A designation allowing countries to export their products to the United States with tariffs no greater than those levied against most other nations. *p. 914*

mulatto   A person of mixed European and African ancestry; the first-generation offspring of a Caucasian and a Negroid parent. *p. 79*

National Labor Union   An alliance of craft unions founded in 1866 to represent the interests of workers, including the eight-hour day and arbitration of industrial disputes. *p. 459*

National Republicans   A political party, led by John Adams in the 1820s, that favored a greater federal role in funding internal improvements and public education; forerunner of the Whigs, formed in opposition to President Andrew Jackson. *p. 338*

national security state   The reorientation of the U.S. government and its budget after 1945 toward a primary focus on military and intelligence capabilities. *p. 764*

National Trades Union   Organization formed in 1834 to help workers gain greater political influence. *p. 375*

nativists   American citizens born in the United States who oppose further immigration, especially from anywhere outside northwestern Europe. *p. 378*

New Deal   Programs President Franklin Delano Roosevelt put together to address the problems of the Great Depression and to provide relief to Americans in need; during his campaign for president, he promised the nation a "new deal." *p. 682*

New Democrats   Members of the Democratic party, many of them organized in the Democratic Leadership Council, who espouse center to center-right policies. *p. 910*

Nisei   Japanese Americans born in the United States of Japanese immigrant parents. *p. 722*

NSC-68   The 1950 directive of the National Security Council that called for rolling back, rather than merely containing, Soviet and communist influences. *p. 764*

nullification   The doctrine that a state has the right to ignore or nullify certain federal laws with which it disagrees. *p. 342*

Okies   Migrants from Oklahoma who left the state during the Dust Bowl period in search of work. *p. 688*

Oregon Trail   A 2,000-mile-long trail used by people from the Midwest to establish new homesteads in the Oregon Territory following the Panic of 1837. *p. 370*

outsourcing   The export of jobs to countries where the cost of labor is cheaper. *p. 899*

pachucos   Young Mexican American men who expressed attitudes of youthful rebellion in the 1940s. Many wore the Zoot Suit, also fashionable among urban African Americans. *p. 737*

Pacific Railroad Act   Legislation that granted to the Union Pacific and the Central Pacific railroads cash subsidies and a 400-foot right of way along the Platte River route of the Oregon Trail. *p. 437*

Paleo-Indians   The earliest human inhabitants of North America, who first migrated to the continent from Siberia more than 15,000 years ago; faced with a warming climate and the disappearance of many large game animals roughly 10,000 years ago (8000 BCE), they learned to hunt smaller animals and adapted to varied local conditions during the Archaic Period (to c. 1000 BCE). *p. 6*

Panic of 1837   Economic crisis and depression caused by a combination of overspeculation—in bridges, canals, and turnpikes—and a large failure of grain crops in the West. *p. 375*

Pendleton Act   Congressional legislation passed in 1883; established a merit system for federal job applicants and created the Civil Service Commission, which administered competitive examinations to candidates in certain job classifications. *p. 520*

pest house   In colonial times, a shelter to quarantine those possibly infected with contagious diseases (such as newcomers arriving in American ports from Africa or Europe) to prevent the spread of shipborne pestilence. *p. 122*

planned obsolescence   A concept whereby producers intend for their products to eventually become obsolete or outdated and require replacement, thus perpetuating a cycle of production and consumption. *p. 665*

Plessy v. Ferguson   The 1896 case in which the Supreme Court decided that states could segregate public accommodations by race. *p. 562*

pocket veto   An indirect veto of a legislative bill made when an executive (such as a president or governor) simply leaves the bill unsigned, so that it dies after the adjournment of the legislature. *p. 460*

political machine   A group that effectively exercises control over a political party, usually at the local level and organized around precincts and patronage. *p. 653*

popular sovereignty   The idea that residents of a state should be able to make decisions on crucial issues, such as whether or not to legalize slavery. *p. 410*

Populists   Agrarian reformers who formed the Populist, or People's party, a major (third) political party that emerged mostly in the Midwest and South in the late 1880s to address the needs of workers and farmers in opposition to government monetary policies and big business. The party faltered after its presidential candidate, William Jennings Bryan, lost in the 1896 election. *p. 537*

presidio   A military garrison in an area under Spanish control. *p. 173*

privateer   A ship (or a crew member) licensed to harass enemy shipping in wartime. *p. 95*

producer economy   An economic system dominated by individuals who are self-producers of manufactured goods and foodstuffs rather than employees working for wages. *p. 651*

Progressivism   A notion of political reform central to the "Progressive Era" (the first two decades of the twentieth century), when urban reformers with a faith in progress sought to address local and national social problems through political and civic means. *p. 591*

quitrent   A fixed rent paid annually by a tenant to a proprietor or landowner. *p. 86*

race suicide   A fear articulated by Theodore Roosevelt and others that the low birthrate of Anglo-Saxon Americans, along with the high birthrate of immigrants from southern and eastern Europe and elsewhere, would result in a population in which "inferior" peoples would outnumber the "American racial stock." *p. 615*

Real Whigs   Radical theorists in eighteenth-century England who stressed that power corrupts and criticized mainstream Whig views of "balanced" government; their calls for vigilance and virtue among citizens won favor in the American colonies. *p. 183*

Reconstruction era   The twelve years after the Civil War when the U.S. government took steps to integrate the eleven states of the Confederacy back into the Union. *p. 459*

redemption system   An eighteenth-century arrangement in which potential migrants in Europe signed up with an agent who agreed to pay for their Atlantic passage. Reaching America, the newcomer signed a pact to work for several years for an employer. In exchange for much-needed labor, the employer agreed to pay back the shipper, "redeeming" the original loan that had been made to the immigrant "redemptioner." *p. 144*

red lining   A business practice in which lending institutions deny credit to racial or ethnic minorities who live in poor neighborhoods. *p. 782*

Red Scare   Post–World War I repression of socialists, communists, and other left-wing radicals ("Reds"). *p. 648*

regressive tax   A tax that decreases in rate as the base increases, so that someone with a large holding pays a relatively small amount. A fixed tax of $100 is regressive, since persons with $1,000 or $1 million shoulder very different relative burdens. This is the opposite of a progressive tax, where those with less pay at a lower rate. *p. 185*

Regulators   In the 1760s, owners of small farms in North Carolina's Piedmont, lacking adequate political representation in the colony, banded together to protect their interests, oppose unjust taxes, and "regulate" their common affairs. *p. 185*

Republican mother   A wife and mother whose primary role is caring for and socializing future citizens (her children); an ideal favored by some elites after the American Revolution. *p. 285*

Republican party   Founded in 1854, this political party began as a coalition of Northerners who opposed the extension of slavery into the western territories. *p. 413*

rescate   In the colonial Southwest, the organized process of tribute in which Spaniards paid a ransom to Indians for the release of captives that one tribe had taken from another. The ransomed Indians often became Christians working as servants in Spanish households. Some captives were Hispanic settlers captured in raids. *p. 140*

Restoration   Period beginning in 1660, when Charles II became king, restoring the British monarchy after the brief experiment of the Puritan Commonwealth, until the end of the Stuart family dynasty in 1688. *p. 83*

rogue nations   A label used by the U.S. government to refer to nations it considers hostile, unpredictable, and potentially dangerous. *p. 924*

Rosie the Riveter   A heroic symbol of women workers on the homefront during World War II. *p. 733*

sachem   Algonquin Indian term for a Native American leader or chief. *p. 88*

scalawag   A negative term applied by southern Democrats after the Civil War to any white Southerner who allied with the Republican party. *p. 463*

Second Great Awakening A series of Protestant religious revivals that began in the 1790s and continued through the 1820s. Prominent revivalists such as Charles Grandison Finney sought to link the life of the spirit with political action and reform efforts. *p. 353*

Second New Deal The agenda of policies and programs initiated by President Franklin Delano Roosevelt beginning in 1935 that was intended to strengthen the lot of American workers while simultaneously preserving the capitalist system. *p. 696*

sectionalism Intense political conflict between North and South in the nineteenth-century United States. *p. 311*

separation of powers The constitutional doctrine upholding the independence of each of the three branches of the federal government: executive (president), legislative (Congress), and judicial (Supreme Court). *p. 254*

Sherman Anti-Trust Act Congressional legislation passed in 1890 outlawing trusts and large business combinations. *p. 522*

sit-down strike A strategy employed by workers agitating for better wages and working conditions in which they stop working and simply sit down, thus ceasing production and preventing strikebreakers from entering a facility to assume their jobs. *p. 707*

sit-in A form of civil disobedience in which activists sit down somewhere in violation of law or policy in order to challenge discriminatory practices or laws. The tactic originated during labor struggles in the 1930s and was used effectively in the civil rights movement in 1960. *p. 792*

Social Darwinism A late nineteenth-century variation on the theories of British naturalist Charles Darwin, promoting the idea that only the "fittest" individuals will, or deserve to, survive (i.e., the idea that society operates on principles of evolutionary biology). *p. 522*

Social Gospel A reform movement around the end of the twentieth century that stressed the responsibility of religious organizations to remedy a wide range of social ills related to urban life. *p. 551*

social stratification The schematic arrangement of a population into a ranking of horizontal of social layers (strata), or an identifiable hierarchy of classes within a society. *p. 11*

socialism A form of government in which the means of production are owned collectively and managed by the state. *p. 542*

Sons of Liberty Secret societies of American colonists that successfully resisted Parliament's 1765 Stamp Act; their agitations continued over the ensuing decade. *p. 180*

speakeasies Establishments where alcohol was illegally sold during the Prohibition era. *p. 654*

suffrage The right to vote. *p. 254*

Sunbelt The band of states from the Southeast to the Southwest that experienced rapid economic and population growth during and after World War II. *p. 769*

tariff A government tax on imported goods. *p. 265*

Tejanos Spanish-speaking residents of the Mexican state of Texas. Today many Mexican Americans in Texas refer to themselves as Tejanos as a point of cultural and state pride. *p. 335*

temperance A social movement embracing either total opposition to alcohol consumption or support for its moderate use. *p. 240*

tenant farmer A farmer who pays a landowner for use of the land in cash or with a share of the crop. In the South, tenant farmers often owned their own mules (for plowing), in contrast to sharecroppers, who did not. *p. 400*

Texians The name used by Euro-Americans who lived in the Mexican state of Texas. *p. 335*

theocracy A government by officials who are regarded as divinely guided. *p. 870*

three-fifths clause The policy asserted in Article I, section 2, of the U.S. Constitution that in apportioning representatives and direct taxes among the states according to population, each slave would count as "three fifths of all other Persons." Section 2 of the Fourteenth Amendment (1868) did away with the three-fifths clause. *p. 256*

tithe A levy or donation (generally a tenth part) given to provide support, usually for a church. *p. 31*

total war The attacking of both military and civilian targets. *p. 725*

Townsend Plan A proposal by Dr. Francis Townsend in 1934 for a 2 percent national sales tax that would fund a guaranteed pension of $200 per month for Americans older than age 60. *p. 701*

Trail of Tears The name Cherokee Indians gave to their forced removal from the Southeast to the West in 1838 and 1839 as part of the federal government's Indian removal policy. During the journey, U.S. troops destroyed the material basis of Cherokee culture and separated many families; over 4,000 Indians died. *p. 367*

Treaty of Ghent Peace treaty signed by the United States and Great Britain in 1815, ending the War of 1812. *p. 310*

trickle-down economics An economic concept whereby the government aids the wealthiest strata as well as large corporations in the belief that the benefits of this aid will "trickle down" to the middle and lower classes. *p. 659*

Truman Doctrine President Truman's policy of containment, articulated in a March 1947 speech. *p. 756*

trusts A combination of firms or corporations created for the purpose of reducing competition and controlling prices throughout an industry. *p. 500*

Underground Railroad A secret network of abolitionists developed during the antebellum period to help slaves escape and find refuge, many in the North or in Canada. *p. 410*

unicameral legislature A legislative body that has only one chamber, or house. *p. 86*

utopian Relating to communities organized to strive for ideal social and political conditions; utopians intend that their communities should serve as a model to the larger society. *p. 382*

Victorianism   Middle-class, chiefly Protestant, ideology popular during the reign of Britain's Queen Victoria (1837–1901). Victorians professed social values such as self-control, sexual restraint, and personal ambition. *p. 356*

war hawks   Politicians who favor specific forms of military action as a tool of U.S. foreign policy. *p. 303*

War of 1812   A military and naval conflict that pitted U.S. forces against the British and their Indian allies. The end of the war eliminated the post-Revolutionary British threat to U.S. sovereignty. *p. 305*

war on drugs   The global campaign spearheaded by the federal government to eliminate the production of illegal drugs and their importation into the United States, and its domestic counterpart in which drug violations are treated harshly by the legal and criminal justice system. *p. 902*

Watergate   The Washington, D.C., hotel-office complex where agents of President Nixon's reelection campaign broke into Democratic party headquarters in 1972; Nixon helped cover up the break-in, and the subsequent political scandal was called "Watergate." *p. 842*

welfare reform   The legislative campaign in the 1960s through the 1990s to abolish Aid to Families with Dependent Children in favor of a program that sets limits on the amount of time a poor family can receive government aid (culminating in the Temporary Aid to Needy Families Act of 1996). *p. 912*

welfare state   A nation in which the government provides a "safety net" of entitlements and benefits for citizens unable to economically provide for themselves. *p. 683*

Whigs   A national political party formed in 1834 in opposition to the presidency of Andrew Jackson and his policy of expanding the power of the president. The Whigs favored congressional funding for internal improvements and other forms of federal support for economic development. *p. 344*

Whiskey Rebellion   Protest in 1794 by western Pennsylvania farmers and grain distillers who objected to a high federal tax on the whiskey they produced. *p. 268*

Wobblies   Members of the Industrial Workers of the World (IWW), a radical labor union formed in 1905. *p. 611*

yellow journalism   Newspaper articles, images, and editorials that exploit, distort, or exaggerate the news in order to inflame public opinion. *p. 579*

Credits

Part Opener 1

Page 2: Laurie Platt Winfrey, Inc.

Chapter 1

Page 8: Lee Boltin Picture Library
Page 17: (Top) © Charles E. Rotkin/CORBIS
Page 17: (Bottom) Museum of the History of Science, Oxford, Oxfordshire, UK/Bridgeman Art Library
Page 18: Topkapi Serail-Museum/AKG Photo
Page 36: Courtesy of Map Collection, Yale University Library
Page 38: (Top) © Charles E. Ratkin/CORBIS
Page 38: (Center) Courtesy Map Collection, Yale University Library
Page 38: (Bottom) Lee Boltin Picture Library

Chapter 2

Page 39: Leonard Harris/Stock, Boston, Inc.
Page 41: Courtesy of the John Carter Brown Library at Brown University
Page 50: Harry Engels/Photo Researchers, Inc.
Page 67: The Granger Collection, New York
Page 68: (Top) The Granger Collection, New York
Page 68: (Bottom) Leonard Harris/Stock, Boston, Inc.

Chapter 3

Page 72: Réunion des Musées Nationaux/Art Resource, NY
Page 75: Courtesy Texas A & M University, Nautical Archaeology
Page 76: (Bottom) Thaw Collection, Fenimore Art Museum, Cooperstown, NY
Page 76: William L. Clements Library, University of Michigan
Page 99: (Bottom) © Copyright the Trustees of the British Museum
Page 100: Thaw Collection, Fenimore Art Museum, Cooperstown, NY

Part Opener 2

Page 102: The Menil Collection, Houston

Chapter 4

Page 104: Voyage Pittoresque dans le Bresil, Rugendas plate 10, 2nd part. The Newberry Library, Chicago
Page 106: (Top) © Copyright the Trustees of the British Museum (1982, 1-12.1)
Page 109: Albert and Shirley Small Special Collections Library, University of Virginia
Page 110: Chicago Historical Society, ICHi-x.1354
Page 124: (Bottom) Museum Volkenkunde, Leiden, The Netherlands (360–5696)
Page 134: (Top) Voyage Pittoresque dans le Bresil, Rugendas plate 10, 2nd part. The Newberry Library, Chicago
Page 134: (Bottom) Chicago Historical Society, ICHi-x.1354

Chapter 5

Page 139: (Bottom) Charm, c. 1870, Potawatomi, Founders Society Purchase. Photograph ©1992 The Detroit Institute of Arts (81.614)
Page 153: © Science Museum Pictorial/Science & Society Picture Library, London
Page 154: Gustavus Hesselius, "Tishcohan," 1735. Courtesy of the Historical Society of Pennsylvania (HSP) Collection, Atwater Kent Museum of Philadelphia.
Page 158: Attributed to Mary Leverett Denison Rogers, "Harvard Hall." Courtesy of the Massachusetts Historical Society, MHS #427
Page 163: © Pat & Chuck Blackeley
Page 166: (Top) Gustavus Hesselius, "Tishcohan," 1735. Courtesy of the Historical Society of Pennsylvania (HSP) Collection, Atwater Kent Museum of Philadelphia (1834.1).

Chapter 6

Page 167: Courtesy, American Antiquarian Society
Page 169: Hunterian Museum and Art Gallery, University of Glasgow
Page 182: Peabody Essex Museum. Photograph by Mark Sexton
Page 196: (Top) Peabody Essex Museum. Photograph by Mark Sexton
Page 196: (Bottom) Courtesy, American Antiquarian Society

Chapter 7

Page 203: Henry Gray, "The Morning After the Attack on Sullivan's Island, June 1776." Gibbes Museum of Art/Carolina Art Association, 1907.002.0001
Page 207: The Library of Congress
Page 213: Collection of the Museum of Early Southern Decorative Arts, Old Salem Museum and Gardens (Acc. #3119)
Page 218: The Library of Congress
Page 230: Chicago Historical Society, ICHi-x.1937.36
Page 232: (Top) "Old Salem Inc.; Collection of the Museum of Early Southern Decorative Arts" (Acc. #3119)
Page 232: (Bottom) The Library of Congress

Chapter 8

Page 233: CORBIS
Page 238: Courtesy of the American Numismatic Society
Page 250: Anchorage Museum of History and Art (4.81.68.9)
Page 256: Susan Anne Livingston Ridley Sedgwick, "Elizabeth 'Mumbet' Freeman," 1842. Courtesy of the Massachusetts Historical Society (MHS image #0028)
Page 260: Abby Aldrich Rockefeller Folk Art Museum, Williamsburg, VA, Colonial Williamsburg Foundation, (Acc. #1935.301.4 [slide 1989–173])
Page 261: (Top) Courtesy of the American Numismatic Society
Page 261: (Bottom) Abby Aldrich Rockefeller Folk Art Museum, Williamsburg, VA, Colonial Williamsburg Foundation, (Acc. #1935.301.4 [slide 1989–173])

Chapter 9

Page 262: Courtesy of Florida Stage. Photograph by Susan Lerner.
Page 267: (Top) Paul Rocheleau Photography
Page 267: (Bottom) The National Archives
Page 276: Gilbert Stuart, "Joseph Brant," 1786. Fenimore Art Museum, Cooperstown, New York (N-199.61). Photo by Richard Walker
Page 293: (Top) The National Archives
Page 293: (Bottom) Gilbert Stuart, "Joseph Brant," 1786. Fenimore Art Museum, Cooperstown, New York (N-199.61). Photo by Richard Walker

Part Opener 4

Page 296: Smithsonian Institution, American Art Museum/Art Resource, NY

Chapter 10

Page 302: Courtesy, JPMorgan Chase Archives (NEG #1077-26-1)
Page 307: The Library of Congress
Page 314: (Bottom) Museum of Spanish Colonial Art, Collections of the Spanish Colonial Arts Society, Inc., Santa Fe, NM. Bequest of Alan and Ann Vedder. Photograph by Jack Parsons
Page 315: The Granger Collection, New York
Page 325: William Clark, "Eulachon (T. Pacificus)," 1806, Voorhis Journal #2. William Clark Papers, Missouri Historical Society Archives

Chapter 11

Page 327: John Gadsby Chapman, "Davy Crockett," date unknown. Art Collection, Harry Ransom Humanities Research Center, The University of Texas at Austin (neg. #65.349)

Page 332: Collection of David J. and Janice L. Frent

Page 346: Courtesy of the American Numismatic Society

Page 355: Courtesy, Dartmouth College Library

Page 357: (Top) Courtesy of the American Numismatic Society

Page 357: (Bottom) Collection of David J. and Janice L. Frent

Chapter 12

Page 359: Museum Collections, Minnesota Historical Society (Neg. #6640)

Page 376: Samuel J. Miller, "Frederick Douglass," 1847–52. Major Acquisitions Centennial Endowment, 1996.433. Photograph © The Art Institute of Chicago

Page 380: The Newberry Library, Chicago

Page 383: Bettmann/CORBIS

Page 391: Samuel J. Miller, "Frederick Douglass," 1847-52. Major Acquisitions Centennial Endowment, 1996.433. Reproduction © The Art Institute of Chicago

Part Opener 5

Page 392: Winslow Homer, "Young Union Soldier: Separate Study of a Soldier Giving Water to a Wounded Companion," 1861. Cooper-Hewitt, National Design Museum, Smithsonian Institution. Gift of Charles Savage Homer, Jr. (1912-12-110). Photo by Ken Pelka

Chapter 13

Page 394: Courtesy of the California History Room, California History Section, California State Library, Sacramento, California. Mines & Mining: Gold: Scenes from Dag. #3 "Head of Auburn Ravine," Neg. #912

Page 395: Michael Freeman/CORBIS

Page 401: American Textile History Museum, Lowell, Massachusetts

Page 404: Georgia Historical Society, Savannah, Georgia. D.M. Wright Papers, #1277, Box 36, Folder 286

Page 410: Collection of David J. and Janice L. Frent

Page 417: Harriet Beecher Stowe Center, Hartford, CT

Page 422: (Top) Michael Freeman/CORBIS

Page 422: (Bottom) Harriet Beecher Stowe Center, Hartford, CT

Chapter 14

Page 423: Chicago Historical Society, ICHi-22172

Page 434: University of Oklahoma, Western History Collections, Phillips Collection (#1459)

Page 435: Courtesy, The Museum of the Confederacy, Richmond Virginia

Page 439: Courtesy, The Museum of the Confederacy, Richmond Virginia

Page 456: Chicago Historical Society, ICHi-22172

Chapter 15

Page 463: Antique Textile Resource, Bethesda MD

Page 473: (Top) Iris & B. Gerald Cantor Center for Visual Arts, Stanford University (1998.115)

Page 475: (Top) Kicking Bear, "Battle of Little Big Horn," c.1890. Courtesy of the Southwest Museum of the American Indian, Autry National Center, Los Angeles, (1026.G.1)

Page 489: (Top) Antique Textile Resource, Bethesda MD

Page 489: (Bottom) Iris & B. Gerald Cantor Center for Visual Arts, Stanford University (1998.115)

Index

Note: Italicized page numbers indicate tables or illustrations that are not discussed in the text on that page. Maps are indicated by an italicized page number followed by (map).

A

Abbey, Edwin, *221*
Abenaki Indians, 98
Abolition movement, 128, 376, *377*, 383–384, *406*, 410. *See also* Slavery
Abstinence movement, 282
Academies for young ladies, 285
Acadians, 146, 156, 320
Accault, Michel, 76–77
Acoma pueblo, 43, *44*
Act Concerning Religion (Maryland), 66
"Act for the Government and Protection of the Indians," 395
Adams, Abigail, *184,* 286, 305
Adams, John
  and American experiment, 240
  and bicameral system, 254
  Continental Congress and, 207
  as diplomat, 229–231
  elected president, 265
  and election of 1800, 289
  as Federalist candidate for president, 269
  and individual demands for liberty, 184–185
  and Massachusetts constitution, 218–219
  seizure of sloop owned by, 190
  Supreme Court appointments of, 292
  Tea Act and, 192
  and XYZ Affair, 270
Adams, John Quincy, 309–310, 330–331, 337–338, 378
Adams, Samuel, 188–189, 195, 237
Adams, Will, 40
Administration of Justice Act, 192–193
Advertisements and advertising
  for runaway slaves, *365*
Advocate (Cherokee newspaper), 397
Aesoamerican calendar, 11
Affluence. *See* Wealth
Africa, 72, *115, 116* (map), 199. *See also* African Americans
African American fiddlers, 124
African American newspapers, 406
African Americans. *See also* Free blacks; Lynchings; Slaves
  Black Codes in postwar southern states, 462
  black law of Indiana and, 280
  in British colonies, 145
  caricatures off, 324

citizenship rights and, 396, 488
civil rights and, 471
in Civil War, 443–445
class divisions among, in New Orleans, 467
communities of, 467, 469
as cowhands, 479
culture of, 319
education, access to, 381
as field hands, *464*
as freedom fighters, 424, 446
jobs of, in the North, 347
leaders, militancy of, 458
legal and social standing of, 107
literary societies of, 406
massacre of soldiers at Fort Pillow, 451
New Light ministers and, 159
in New Netherland, 52
Thomas Paine's view on, 207
in postbellum South, 463
in postwar America, 459
punishment for petty crimes, 402
response to Fugitive Slave Act (1850), 415
and Revolutionary War, 204–205, 222–223, 272
right to vote guaranteed, *483*
as sailors, 301
and self-sufficiency, 465–466
sense of group solidarity, 406
and slavery, 271, 274
social status of, in 1850s, 403
street demonstrations by, 182
struggles for liberation, 442–445
suffrage and, 462
Sunday School pupils, *457*
traditions preserved by, *290*
value on family, 320
voluntary migrations of, 364
in War of 1812, 308
African American women, 322, 465–466
African-American Female Intelligence Society, 406
African musical instruments, 124
Africans, 24, 103, 105, 123, 155
African slaves, 56, 104–105, 110, *112, 118* (map), *411* (map)
Age of the Common Man, 327–329, 344–351
Alabama (ship), 442
Alamo, the, 82, 385
Alaska. *See also* Russian Alaska
  colonial contact along coast of, 168
  expeditions to, 172
  explorations of, *173* (map)
  land bridge, Siberia to, 3
  purchase of, 481
  U.S. purchase from Russia, 480–481

Albany, New York, 85
Albany Congress of 1754, 193
Albany Plan, 161
Albemarle Sound, 99
Albuquerque, New Mexico, 80
Alcohol, 277, 303. *See also* Temperance movement
Aleutian Islanders, 172
Aleut people, 481
Alexander, Mary Spratt Provoost, 145
Alexandria, port of, 148
Algonquin Indians, 49, 50, 276. *See also* Ohio Confederacy
Alien and Sedition Acts, 270–271
Allen, Ethan, 203
All Saints Parish, 319–320
Almshouses, 153
Alta California, 315, 372
America, in the millennium before Columbus, *10* (map)
American Anti-Slavery Society, 376
American Bottom, 14
American character, 311–312, 317, 352, 356, 404
American Colonization Society, 346–347
American democracy, contradictions in, 344
American Department, 188
American Dictionary of the English Language (Webster), 239
American Duties Act (1764), 178
American independence, terms of, 231. *See also* Declaration of Independence
American Indians. *See* Native Americans
American (Nativist) party, *422*
American party, 379, 413, *414*
American Renaissance, 355
American Revolution. *See* Revolutionary War
Americans, earliest, 3
American Spelling Book (Webster), 239
American War in Vietnam. *See* Vietnam War
American Woman Suffrage Association (AWSA), 482
Amherst, Jeffery, 164, 175–177
Amistad case, 377–378
Amistad (ship), *378*
Anabaptists, 62
Anasazi Indians, *10* (map), 11–13
Ancient America, 5–9
André, John, 226–227
Andrew (slave), 190
Andros, Sir Edmond, 92
An–Choi, 395
Anglican Church (Church of England), 32, 57, 58, 156, 282–283

Anglo-Dutch Wars, 84
Aniaga (African prince), 114–115
Annapolis, port of, 148
Anne (Queen of England), 93
Anthony, Susan B., 384, 482, 483, 486
Anti-abolitionists, 376
Anti-Federalists, 257–260. *See also* Democratic-Republicans
Antinomian Crisis, 62
Antislavery sentiment, 248, 376–378
Antrobus, John, *323*
Anza, Juan Bautista de, 173, 174, *174* (map)
Apache Indians
    and horses, 138
    Father Santa Ana and, 81, 137, 425, 474, 475–476
        and Pueblo Revolt, 79–80
        in San Antonio, 136
Apalachee, 83
Apex Mining Act (1872), 479
Appalachian Mountains, 223, 334
Apprenticeship, of black children, 401–402
Arabella (ship), 59–60, 109
Aramepinchone (Marie), 76–77
Arapaho Indians, 373, 413, 451–452, 474
Archaic Indians, 8, 9
Archaic period, 7–8
Ardra, slave trading depot at, 117
Arikara Indians, 299, 476
Aristotle, 183
Arizona, 81, 82
Arkansas, and reconstruction, *469* (map)
Ark (ship), 66
Arnold, Benedict, 203, 206, 215, 226–227
Arson, by slaves, 123
Arteaga, Ignacio de, 173, *173* (map)
Articles of Confederation, 217–218, 234, 253, 257
Artifacts of human habitation, *6*
Artisan-politicians, 283–284
Artisans, 263, 267, 283, 315, *316*
Asher, Gad, 272
Asher, Jeremiah, 272
Ashkenazi Jews, 156
Ashley-Cooper, Anthony, 87
Asiento contract, 106, 114
Atahualpa, murder of, 27
Athabaskan people, 481
Atlanta, Georgia, *453*
Atlantic chart, *18*
Atlantic coastal settlements, 87–93
Atlatl, 7
Attucks, Crispus, 190
Auburn Ravine, panning for gold in, *394*
Austin, Moses, 334, *336*
Austin, Stephen, 334, *336*, 398

Ayllón, Lucas Vásquez de, 28, *33* (map)
Azores islands, 17, *18*
Aztec Indians, *10* (map), 11, 25–27

B
Babel, ancient tale of, 165
Bacon, Nathaniel, 90–91, 111
Bacon's Rebellion, 87, 89–91, 111, *134*
Bad Axe River massacre, 346
Balboa, Vasco Núez de, 25
Baldwin, F. L., *423*
Baltimore, Lord, 65–66
Baltimore, port of, 148
Bambara, Samba, 125
Banjo, African, 124
Bank of the United States, 265, 305
Bank of the United States, Second, 335, 343
Banks, 335–336, 343–344. *See also individual banks*
Banks, Nathaniel, 445, 460
Bannock Indians, 480
Baptists, and family metaphor, 281
Baranov, Alexander, 172
Barbados island, 114
Barbary wars, 292
Barracoons, 116
Barré, Isaac, 179, 180
Bartram, John, *240*
Bartram, William, 239, *240*
Baseball, *440*
Battle pictographs, *371*
Battles. *See also specific war*
    of Almanace, 185
    of Austerlitz, 300
    on Lake Champlain, *49*
    of Little Big Horn, *475*
    of Trafalgar, 300
Baumfree, Isabella (Sojourner Truth), *406, 407*, 482
Baxter, Eli H., *365*
Bayard, Judith, 52
Baylor, John R, *431*
Beauregard, P. T. G., 430
Beaver hats, 230
Beaver Wars, 50
Beecher, Catharine, 351, 381, 406–407
Beecher, Eunice, 482
Beecher, Henry Ward, 482
Beissel, Conrad, 155
Belcher, Andrew, 96
Bell, John, 420
Belle (ship), 74, 75
Benavides, Cristobal, 435
Benavides, Refugio, 435
Benavides, Santos, 435
Benezet, Anthony, 130
Benjamin, Judah P., 435

Bering, Vitus, 171–172, *173* (map)
Beringia, 6
Bering land bridge, 6
Berkeley, John, 86
Berkeley, Sir William, 89–91, 90, 91
Berryman, Hugh, 4
Bethabara, North Carolina, 150
Bettering House, 154, 289
Bias. *See* Discrimination; Prejudices
Bible, 58
Biddle, Grace, 288–289
Bight of Biafra, 117
Bigler, Henry William, 394
Bill of Rights, U.S., 260, *261*, 264
Bingham, George Caleb, *409*
Birth control, 483
Birthrates, 143
Bison jumps, 7
Black Americans. *See* African Americans
Blackbeard, *96*
Black Belt, 399–400
Black Codes, 462
Blackfoot Indians, 138, 480
Black Hawk (Sauk chief), 345, 352, 360
Black Hawk (Sioux chief), 402
Black Hawk War, 346
Blackheath encampment, *147*
Black Hills, 476
Black Kettle (Cheyenne chief), *451*, 474–475
Blackwell, Henry, 482
Blockades, 427, 441–442
Bloomers, 383
Blue Water raid, 413
Blunt, Maria, 440
Boardinghouses, for mill girls, 349–350
Boardman, Elijah, *265*
Board of Customs for British North America, 188
Board of National Popular Education, 381
Book of Mormon, 354
Boom towns, 479
Boone, Daniel, 223, 242–243
Booth, John Wilkes, 455
Border Ruffians, 417
Bosque Redondo reservation, 439
Boston, Massachusetts
    deepwater port at, 148
    gap between rich and poor, 96
    Irish population in, 362
    in Revolutionary War, *196*, 205–206
    runaway slaves in, 364
    as seaport, 167
    shipyards of, 95
    Stamp Act repeal celebrations in, 182
Boston Marathon, 103
Boston Massacre, 186–187, 189–190, *190*
Boston Port Act (1774), 192–193

Boston revolt, 92

Boston Tea Party, 167, 168, 192–193, *196*

Boudinot, Elias, 366

Bougainville, Louis Antoine de, 169, *196*

Bound workers, types of, 271. *See also* Slaves

Bourgmont, Etienne, 140

Bowdoin, James, 252

Boycotts, 188–189, 193, 199

Boyd, Belle, 435, 446

Bozeman Trail, *369* (map), 474, *474* (map)

Braddock, Edward, 162

Bradford, William, 57

Bradley, Aaron A., 458

Bradstreet, Anne Dudley, 60–61

Brandywine Creek, Delaware, *318*

Brant, Joseph (Thayendanegea), 164, 225, 275, 276, *276*

Brant, Molly, 164

Bray, Thomas, 128–129

Brazil, 134

Bread riots, 446

Breckinridge, John C., 414, 420, 421

Breed's Hill, 205–206

Britain

  and American Civil War, 442

  armed forces expenses (1775–1782), *217*

  attack on U.S. Capitol, 307

  and Canada, 234

  cessions of, *397* (map)

  colonialism of, *196*

  conflicts with France and U.S., 217, 303

  conquests of New France, *162* (map), 164–165, 176

  contract to supply African slaves to Spanish colonies, *134*

  domestic opposition to conflict in America, 217

  economic and military aggression against U.S., 300

  formal union of England and Scotland, 98

  impressment of American sailors, 267

  negotiating end to America's War for Independence, 229–231

  North American colonies of, *143*, 175–176

  Ohio Confederacy, support for, 267

  Oregon Territory compromise, 386

  Pacific explorations by, 169, *202* (map)

  possessions of (1775), 199

  Proclamation Line, 177

  promises to black Loyalists, 203

  Royal Army's struggle to control Boston, 205–206

  tensions between U.S. and, following Revolutionary War, 267

  transatlantic slave trade and, *118–119* (map), *319*

  Treaty of Ghent and, 309–310

  war with American colonies, 300

  war with Spain, 126

British Caribbean, and Transatlantic African slave trade, *319*

British colonies, *194* (map)

  economic regions of, *149* (map)

  expansion of, 98

  in mid-18th century, *181* (map)

  non-English newcomers in, 145

  population structure by gender and age, *144*

  settlements in mid-18th century, *162* (map)

  as societies with slaves, 151

  southern limit of, *132* (map)

  transatlantic slave trade, 18th century, *118–119* (map)

British forts, *275* (map)

British imports, prohibition of, 195

British military forces, 206, 208–209, 209–210, 222, 223, 229

British military troops, shots fired at Lexington by, 195

British model of government, 264

British ships, 114

British slavery regime, *132* (map)

British slave trade, 109

British West Indies, 248–249, 251

Brock, Isaac, 305

Brooks, Preston S., 417

Browere, Albertus, 381

Brown, Jacob, 306

Brown, John, 191, 418–420, *420*

Brown, John (Ohio abolitionist), 417

Brown, Joseph, 433

Brown, Moses, 267

Brown, William Henry, *334*

Brown (Providence merchant), 249

Bruce, Blanche K., *472*, 472

Bryant, William Cullen, 355

Buccaneers, 95, 97

Buchanan, James, 414, 417, *422*

Buffalo (bison), 373–374, *478*

Buford, Harry T. (Loreta Janeta Velásquez), 435

Bunker Hill, *196*

Burgoyne, John, 210, 214–215

Burke, Aedanus, 238

Burlingame, Anson, 477

Burlingame treaty, 477

Burnett, Peter, 370

Burnside, Ambrose E., 447

Burr, Aaron, 289, 302

Burroughs, George, 94, 94–95

Bush-Brown, H. K., 163

Business and businesses, 267. *See also* individual companies

Butler, Benjamin, 438, 445

Butler, John, 225

Butler, Pierce, 254

Byrd, William, 112–113

C

Cabeza de Vaca, álvar Núñez, 28, 29, *33* (map)

Cabot, John, 20–21

Cactus Hill, Virginia, 6, *6*

Caddo Indians, 141

Cadillac (founder of Detroit), 78

Cady, Elizabeth, 351, 383, 407, 482

Cahokia, Illinois, 14, 78

Cajuns, 146

Calhoun, John C., 330, 331, 343, 363, 388–389

California. *See also individual cities*

  coastal colonization by Spain, 172–175

  denial of citizenship rights in, 396

  Foreign Miners Tax, 395

  immigrants in, 477

  migration to, 360, *396*, *422*

  right to vote, 396

  statehood of, 395, 410

California Trail, *369* (map)

Californios, 396, 398

Calvert, George (Lord Baltimore), 65–66

Calvert family, 93

Calvin, John, 31, 58

Calvinist doctrine, 31

Calvinists, 31, 58

Cambridge, Massachusetts, *60*

Camp meetings, *353*

Camp Northumberland, *429*

Canada, 203, 231, 234, 241

Canal diggers, 283

Canals, 331, *332*

Canary islands, 17, *18*

Cape Coast Castle, West Africa, 84, 117

Cape St. Vincent, *18*

Cape Town, 47

Caravels, 17, *18*

Caribbean region, 18, *24*, 105–106, *319*

Caribs, 24–25

Carleton, Guy, 230

Carleton, James H., 439

Carlisle, Lord, 217

Carlisle Commission, 217

Carlos III (King of Spain), 173

Carlos II (King of Spain), 76

Carmel, California, *350*

Carolina colony, 85, 87

Carolina Piedmont, 150

Carolinas, the, *98* (map)

Carpenters Hall, Philadelphia, 193

Carpetbaggers, 463

Carson, Kit, 439

Carter, Robert, 274

Carteret, Sir George, 86

Carthage, Illinois, 368

Cartier, Jacques, 28, *33* (map)

Cary's Rebellion, 99

Cass, Lewis, 365, 410

Casualties in principal wars, *448*

Cathay, 15

Catherine of Aragon, 32

Catherine the Great (Empress of Russia), 234

Catholic Church, 58, 106, 363

Catholic immigrants, 156

Catholicism, 73–74, 379

Catholic missionaries, in Congo-Angola, 117

Catholic missions in Spanish Florida, *46* (map), 78

Catholics, 66, 77, 91, 363, 379

Catlin, George, *372*

Cato's Letters: Essays on Liberty (Trenchard and Gordon), 183–184

Cattle drives, 479

Cattle ranching, in Florida, 47, 82

Cayuga Indians, 225. *See also* Iroquois Confederacy

Cayuse Indians, 371

Census, 255, 263

Central Pacific Railroad, 473, *473*, 476–477

Chaco Canyon, 12

Champlain, Samuel de, 49

Chandeliers, 206

Chapman, John Godsby, *327*

Charbonneau, Toussaint, 299

Charles II (King of England), 83, 85, 86, 91, 114

Charles I (King of England), 54, 59, 63, 65, 83

Charleston, South Carolina, 126, 148, 182, *455*

Charlestown (Charleston), South Carolina, 87, 205–206

Charles V (Emperor of Spain), 28

Charts of early explorations, *29, 30*

Chase, Samuel, 258

Checks and balances, 254

Cheraw District, South Carolina, 210–211

Cherokee Female Seminary, 397

Cherokee Indians, 100. *See also* Five Civilized Tribes

and acculturation, 277, 344

confiscation of culture, 367

deerskin trade, 150

division of labor and, 287

gold discoveries on land of, 341–342

James Grant's slaughter of, 175

home territory of, 313, *341, 366* (map)

in Indian Territory, 312, 397

and literacy, 345

in Revolutionary War, 201, 223

in service of the Confederacy, 434

War of 1812 and, 307, 309

Cherokee Nation Treaty Party, 366

Cherokee Phoenix (newspaper), 345

Cherokee War Woman, 312

Chesapeake Bay, 53–54, 107, 148, *149* (map), 151–152

Chesapeake Bay colonies, 64–68, *98* (map)

Chesapeake region, *65* (map), 112, *121* (map), 122

Chesapeake (ship), 301

Chesnut, Mary Boykin, 427, 434, 444

Cheyenne Indians
horses of, 373

Kansas-Nebraska Act and, 413

at Little Big Horn, 476

massacre of, at Sand Creek, 451–452

massacre of, on Washita River, 474–475

Plains Indian Wars and, *475*

Father Santa Ana and, 425

Treaty of Medicine Lodge Creek, 474

Chickasaw Indians, 139, 277, 307, 309, *366* (map), 434. *See also* Five Civilized Tribes

Chief Joseph, route of, *474* (map)

Child, Lydia Maria, 380

Child labor, 401–402

Children of the street, shipment to Jamestown, 56

Chimney sweeps, 316

China, overseas exploration and trade by, 15, 249

Chinese immigrants, 395, 403, 476–477, 486

Chippewa Indians, 225

Chisholm Trail, 479

Chivington, John M., 451–452

Choctaw Indians, 125, 277, 307, 309, *366* (map), 434. *See also* Five Civilized Tribes

Christiana riot, 415

Christian crusades, 16

Christian immigrants, 156

Christianity, 58–59, 94, 127, 155, 158–159

Chronometer, 153, 170

Chumash Indians, 277, 345

Churches, established, 282

Church of England (Anglican Church), 32, 57, 58, 156, 282–283

Church of Jesus Christ of Latter-day Saints (Mormons), 353–354, 367–368, *369* (map)

Church of San Miguel, 45

Cincinnati Club, 238

Cincinnati Daily Commercial, 418

Cincinnatus, 238

Cinqué, rebellion of, 378

Circular Church, Charleston, South Carolina, *455*

Circular Letter, 188

Cisneros, Henry, 385

Citizenship
economic independence and, *266*

ideal of, in post-Revolutionary America, *286*

limited to free white males, 271, 272, 328

meaning of, to postbellum black communities, 467

slaves barred from, 328

Citizenship rights
African Americans and, 488

limitations of, 420–421

people of "white blood" and, 403

in Treaty of Guadalupe Hidalgo, 396

in various countries, *483*

women and, 328

Civil rights, African Americans' fight for, 471

Civil Rights Acts, 487, 488

Civil Rights Bill, 463

Civil War. *See also* Civil War battles
African Americans as soldiers in, 445, *450*

battle fronts and home fronts, 446–450

casualties of, 440, 445, *448*

effect of, on political parties, 458

immigrants in, 434–435

manufacturing and commerce during, 436–437

North's blockade of southern coastline, 441–442

Pelican Company F, 439

physical environment of the South, 452–454

policy of "hard war," 450–455

preparations for, 428–430

ravages of, 430–438

Sherman's field order revoked, 465

and social transformations, 443

soldiers, occupations of, *430*

southern mobilization for, 430–434

suspension of habeas corpus during, 436

Union loyalists in the south, 427–428

Union officers' methods of dealing with slavery, 437–438

Union soldiers, *429*
Union soldiers, occupational categories of, *430*
unrest in the North, 449
women as secret agents in, 435
Civil War battles
  Antietam, 439–440, *441*
  Bull Run, First, 430
  Elkhorn Tavern, 434
  Fort Pillow, *450,* 451
  Fort Wagner, 442, *450*
  Gettysburg, *447*
  La Glorieta Pass, *431*
  Manassas, second, 439
  Petersburg, *454*
Clark, George Rogers, 225–226
Clark, William, 298–299
Class system in U.S., 329
Clay, Henry, 309–310, 330, 338, 343, 345, 375, 385
Clay, Joseph, 248
Clermont (steamboat), 314
Cliff Palace, *12*
Clinton, George, 258, 300
Clinton, Sir Henry, 208, 217, 223, 226, 229–230
Clovis, New Mexico, 5
Clovis people, predecessors to, 6–7
Clovis points, 5
Coercive Acts, 192–193, 195
Coffin, Levi, *411*
Coffles, *115,* 116
Colbert, Jean-Baptiste, 72, 74
Colfax, Schuyler, 487
College of New Jersey (Princeton University), 158
College of William and Mary, 158
Colleges. *See also specific college names*
  land-grant, 437
Colonial conflicts of mid-18th century, 161
Colonial economies, 148
Colonial epidemics, 143
Colonial families, and wars in England, 95
Colonial governments, 103
Colonialism, 240–241, 338. *See also individual nations*
Colonial workers, skin color of, 110
Colonists, shared identity as Americans, 166, 168, 183
Colonization, and mixing of ethnic groups, 137–138
Colorado, Mangas, 439
Colorado Territory, 479
Colored American, 406
Colored National Labor Union, 485
Colored Orphan Asylum, 449
Color quebrados, 271

Columbia, as term, 239
Columbia, South Carolina, 239, 454
Columbian Exchange, 21–22, 82
Columbia River, origin of name, 249
Columbia (ship), *248,* 249
Columbia University, 239
Columbus, Bartholomew, 18
Columbus, Christopher, 3, 18–20, *20–21* (map), 239
Comanche Indians
  horses and, 81, 139–140, *372, 373*
  and Treaty of Medicine Lodge Creek, 474
  as Union troops, 434
  Wichita and, 141
Comanchería, 140–141
Combat veterans. *See* Veterans
Command of the Army Act, 470
Committee of Fifteen, 488
Committee of Five, *207*
Committee of Public Safety, 193
Committee on Postponed Matters, 255
Committees of Correspondence, 191
Committee to Alleviate the Miseries of the Poor, 154
Common school system, 380
Common Sense (Paine), 207
Communitarians, 382
Communities and community
  African American, 457–458, 469
  Mormon, 367–368
  Native Americans' value of, over individual, 356
  new forms of, 360
  Oneida, 382
  sense of, 352
Company towns, 349
Complex marriage, 382
Compromise of 1820, *Dred Scott* decision and, 417–418
Compromise of 1850, 395, 410–412, *422*
Compromise of 1877, *487* (map), 488
Comstock, Anthony, 483
Concessions and Agreements, West Jersey, 86
Conestoga Indians, 177
Confederacy
  capital of, 427
  central paradox of, 430
  defeat of, 450–455
  disaffection in, 446–447
  hopes for diplomatic recognition, 442
  Indians in service of, 434
  last days of, 454–455
  multicultural character of, 435
  strategy of, 428–430
  strengths of, 455–456
Confederate Army, *431,* 446, 450–453
Confederate press masters, 432

Confederate soldiers, occupational categories of, *430*
Confederate States of America, 244, 425
Confederate surgeons, *434*
Confederate Territory of Arizona, 430
Confederate treasury, 432
Confederation Congress, 218, 256, 257
Confessions of Nat Turner, The (Gray), 347
Congo Square, 322–323
Congregational Church, in New England, 156
Congregationalism, 58
Congregationalist missionaries, 457
Congress, U.S., 272, 302–303, *470*
Congressional electoral commission, 488
Conjurers, 324
Connecticut, 243–244, 257, 272, *279* (map), 346
Connecticut colony, 88
Connecticut Wits, 239
Constitution, U.S.
  amendments to (*See also* Amendment *number*)
  in chronology, *261*
  fears of opponents of, 258
  loose construction of, 341
  ratification of, 199, 257–260
  ratifying conventions, 257
  southern whites and postwar amendments to, 488
  for white men with property, 260
Constitutional Convention, 253–256, *261*
Constitutional Union party, 420, *421*
Continental Army
  African Americans soldiers in, 272
  dissidents within, 235–237
  enlistment terms, 213–214
  Foreign officers in, 220–222
  formation of, 202
  mutinies and strikes in, 226
  retreat toward Philadelphia, 212
Continental Congress, 168, 202–204, 207, 215, 217–218, 234
Continental Navy, 223
Contraception, 483
Conway, Thomas, 220
Conway Cabal, 220
Cook, James, 169–171, *173* (map), *196*
Cook, Nathan, *365*
Cooke, Jay, 480
Coolies, 395
Cooper, James Fenimore, 355
Copley, John Singleton, *219*
Copperheads, 441, 449
Copyright laws, 239
Corn, 67, 81, 151
Cornwallis, Charles, 213, 226–229
Coromantee (Akan) people, 125

Coronado, Francisco Vásquez de, 30, *33* (map)
Corps of Engineers, 453
Corruption, 471, 478–479, 481, 486–488
Cortés, Hernán, 26–27
Cortina, Juan, 399, 403
Cortina's War, 399
Cotton, John, 62
Cotton belt, *364, 468*
Cotton fields, *464*
Cotton gin, 267
Cotton mills, 315
Cotton plantation economy, 267, 280, 318–325
Cotton production, 199, 334
Cotton trade, *335*
Councils for Trade and Plantations, 85–86
Counter-reformation, 31, 32, 50
Country-born slaves, 120
Country marks, *104*
County Election (Bingham), *409*
County of Kerry, Ireland, *362*
Coverture, 85
Coyotes, 271
Craft, Ellen, 376
Craft, William, 376
Crandall, Prudence, 376
Crazy Horse, *475*, 476
Crédit Mobilier, 486–487
Creek Indians. *See also* Five Civilized Tribes
    and acculturation, 277
    deerskin trade, 150
    home territory of, *366* (map)
    and Treaty of Horseshoe Bend, 308
    War of 1812 and, 307, 309
Creoles, 322–323
Crittenden, John J., 426
Crittenden Compromise, 426
Crockett, David "Davy," 327–328, 335–336, 342, 385
Crockett, Elizabeth, 336
Cromwell, Oliver, 83
Crook, George, 475–476
Crow Indians, 476, 480
Crown Point, Lake Champlain, 164
Crozat, Antoine, 78
Cuba, 412
Cuffee (slave), 126
Culpeper, John, 99
Culpeper's Rebellion, 99
Cultural conflict, 399
Cultural diffusion, 17
Cultural identity, migrants and, 372
Cultural values in America, 238–240, 354–356
Cumberland Road (National Road), 314, *332*

Cuming, F. H., 333–334
Cumming, Kate, *439*
Currency
    demand for reforms in, 252
    Hamilton's monetary policies, 265
    hard money policies, 343
    of U.S., 250–251
    withdrawn from circulation, 485
Currency Act, 178, *196*
Custer, George, 458, 474–475
Customs Act, 188
Customs officials, absentee, 178
Cutler, Manasseh, 247
Cut Nose (Arapaho), 397–398

D

Da Gama, Vasco, 18, *20–21* (map)
Daily Graphic (newspaper), *482*
Dampier, William, 97
"Danger of an Unconverted Ministry, The" (Tennent), 158
Danish immigrants, 360
Darien, Panama, 25
Daughters of Liberty, 189, 199
Davidson, George, *248*
Davis, Jefferson, 398, 425, 449, 455
Dawes, William, 195
Debtors' prison, 336–337
Declaration of Independence, 168, 199, 207–208
Declaration of Independence, The (Trumbull), *208*
Declaration of Rights, 194–195
Declaration of Sentiments, 407, 482
Declaratory Act (1766), 182, *196*
Deer Island, 88
Deerskin trade, 108, 150
De Grasse, François, J. P., 228
De Kalb, Johann, 220
DeLarge, Robert G., *470*
Delaware Indians, 154, 224, 257–258, 276. *See also* Ohio Confederacy
Delaware River, Washington's crossing of, 213
Delaware River valley, English settlement in, 85
Democracy in America (Tocqueville), 344
Democratic-Republicans, 264–267, 269–271, 289, 338
Democratic party
    challenges to, by Free-Soil party, 410
    Irish immigrants and, 363
    loss of white southerners from, 420
    on scalawags, 463
    in Second Party system, 360–361
    supporters of, 375
Denmark, *118–119* (map), *319*
Denton, Vachell, 109

Desert Land Act, 479
Deslondes, Charles, 324
De Soto, Hernando, 28–29, *33* (map)
Detroit, Michigan, 78, 177. *See also* Fort Detroit
Dias, Bartolomeu, 18
Diaspora, 134
Dickinson, John, 187–188
Direct election, 255
Discourse for a Discovery for a New Passage to Cathay (Gilbert), 36–37
Discrimination. *See also* African Americans; Prejudices
    and American individualism, 402
    Union wartime policies and, 445
Disease, *21–22, 22,* 448
Distilleries, 152
District of Columbia, 239, 395
Dix, Dorothea, 383, 437
Dodge, Grenville, 458
Dollar. *See* Currency
Domesticated animals, 8
Domínguez, Father, *174* (map)
Dominican Republic, 481
Doolittle, Amos, *195*
Dorchester Heights, 206
Dough-faces, 414
Douglas, Stephen A., 410, 412, 418, *419,* 420–421, *422*
Douglass, Anna, *376*
Douglass, Frederick, 322, 376, 401, 406–407, *482,* 486
Dove (ship), 66
Draft, Confederate, 433
Draft riots (1863), 449
Dragging Canoe, 223, 243
Drake, Sir Francis, *33* (map), 35, 37, 41, 54
Drinker, Elizabeth, 289
Dueling, 302
Dunmore, Lord, 203, 205, 208
Dutch, 51, 56, 85, 106
Dutch East India Company, 47
Dutchman's Point, *275* (map)
Dutch Reformed Church, 31, 85
Dutch Republic, 215
Dutch West India Company (DWIC), 51, 52
Duties, *196*
Dwight, Timothy, 239

E

Earl, Ralph, *265*
East Florida, 165, *194* (map)
East India Company, 191
East Jersey, 86
Economic changes of postbellum era, 484
Economic depressions, 247–248, 335, 485

Economic development, 458
Economic diversity, 274, 399–400
Economic growth, 267, 481
Economy, national, 285, 313–314, 402
Edenton, North Carolina, 193
Edenton Ladies' Tea Party, 193
Edict of Nantes, 49, 74, 91, 145
Edisto Island Commissioners, 465
Edisto Island residents, *461*
Edo (Tokyo), Japan, 40
Education. *See also* Schools; *specific school names*
    access to, 285–287, 351, 381–382
    higher, 381
    public, 380–382
Edwards, Jonathan, 157–158
Eldrige, Elleanor, 288
Election fraud, 471
Election of black officials, 470
Electoral college, 255
Eliot, John, 63
Elizabeth I (Queen of England), 32, 54
Elliott, Robert B., *470*
Elmina, Ghana, 18, 114, 117
Emancipation Proclamation, 441, 445
Embargo Act, 301–302, 305
Emerson, Ralph Waldo, 404–405
Empress of China (ship), 249
Enclosure movement, in England, 35, 53
Encomienda system, 44, 79, 81
Endowments, Position and Education of Woman, The (Howe), 404–405
Energy. *See specific types of energy*
England. *See also* Britain
    ambitions of, 40
    American empire of, 83–87
    and Atlantic slave trade, 114
    brutality toward Indians, 64
    colonization by, 43, 47
    colonizaton in America, 53–57
    enclosure movement in, 35, 53
    expansion by, 34–35
    and Gulf of Mexico, 77
    national economy, in 1600s, 59
    as a nation–state, 32
    North American colonies of, *48*
    Parliament, dissolution of, 91
    and St. Augustine, 82
    union of Scotland and, 98
    warfare under reign of William and Mary, 93
English Barbados, slavery in, 134
English Civil War, 63
English common law, 56
English East India Company, 47
English–Spanish competition, *132* (map)
English Jamaica, slavery in, 134
English Quakers, 52
English rule, married women and, 85

English settlement, by 1650, *65* (map)
English Turn, 77
English Whigs, 183
Enlightenment, 155
Enslavement, 106, 117
Ephrata Community, 155
Epidemics, colonial, 143. *See also specific illnesses*
Equality, in post-Revolutionary period, 291
Equal Rights Association, 482
Era of Good Feelings, 310–318, 337
Erie Canal, 331–334, *332*
Eriksson, Leif, 15
Erik the Red, 15
Escalante, Father, *174* (map)
Eskimo mother and baby, *35*
Eskimo people, 481
Esteban (North African), 28, 29
Ethiopian Regiment, 205, 233
Ethnic diversity, 263, 399, 400
Etowah, Georgia, 14
Eulachon (candlefish), *299*
Europe, 114–115, 144
European colonizers, 3, *53* (map), 398, 478
European immigrants, 103, 399
European outposts, 114
European power, expansion of, 292
European Renaissance, overseas exploration and, 24
European revolutions, 363
European voyages to Alaska, *173* (map)
Evangelical Christians, 159, 375
Exclusion, 382
Expansion. *See* Territorial expansion
Expansionists, 385–386
Extractive industries, 478

F

Factories, early use of word, 114
Factory workers, 267, 349. *See also* Textile industry
Family, redefinition of, following Revolutionary War, 281–282
Family businesses, 267, 348
Family metaphor, 281–282
Family values, 320–321, 363, 465–466
Farmers. *See also* Sharecroppers; Tenant farmers
    demand for money reforms, 252
    Midwestern, 485
    Panic of 1819 and, 337
    and power of the few, 284–285
    small, and American Revolution, 263
    and whiskey tax, 268
Farm frontier, 154
Farming, 361, 401, 466–467

Farragut, David G., 438, 452
Fascines, 206
Federal government. *See also* United States (U.S.) government agencies
    balanced, 183
    and a central bank, 343
    expanded powers of, 292
    exploration sponsored by, 368–369
    implied power of, 341
    Indian removal policies, *366*
    objections to a strong, 424–425
    role of, following War of 1812, 340
    and treaty promises to Native Americans, 367
    violence sponsored by, 361
Federalist, The, 257–259, 261
Federalist party, 264–267
    and bill of rights, 260
    dissolution of, 310–311
    and election of 1800, 289
    Thomas Jefferson and, 293–294
    resentments against policies of, 269
    support of proposed constitution, 257
Federal lands, in the West, 274
Federal power, expansion of, under Andrew Jackson, 344
Federal taxes, 268
Female academies, 285, 351
Female seminaries, 351, 397
Ferdinand of Aragon (King of Spain), 18
Ferguson, Patrick, 226
Fertility rates, 285
Feudalism, 87
Field labor *vs.* house service, 322
Fifteenth Amendment, 471, 482
"Fifty-four Forty or Fight," 385
Fillmore, Millard, 410, 414
Finney, Charles Grandison, 353, *353*
Firearms, 141
First Amendment, 260, 282–283
First Continental Congress, 193
Fiscal policies of Confederation Government, 247–248
Fishing industry, 152
Fitzhugh, George, 415–416
Five Civilized Tribes, 277, 309, *334*, 345, *366*, 396–397
Flathead Indians, *371*
Florida. *See also* Spanish Florida
    borderland conflict in, 82–83
    ceded to British by Spain, 103
    claimed for Spain by Ponce de León, 25
    competing claims for, 32–34
    fall of British at Pensacola, 226
    Andrew Jackson's capture of, 337
    Spain and, 241
    as Spanish colony, 78–79
Florida purchase, *397* (map)

Florida (ship), 442
Folsom, New Mexico, 5
Folsom points, 5
Foreign Anti-Slavery Society, 383
Foreign Miners Tax (California), 395
Foreign trade, 302, 317
Forrest, Nathan Bedford, 451
Fort Caroline, 33
Fort Christina, 52
Fort Deadborn, *275* (map), 305
Fort de Chartres, 78
Fort Defiance, *306* (map)
Fort Detroit, 225, *275* (map)
Fort Donelson, 438
Fort Duquesne, 161, 164
Fort Erie, *306* (map)
Fort Frontenac, 164
Fort George, *306* (map)
Fort Greenville, 276
Fort Hall, *369* (map)
Fort Henry, 438
Fort Laramie, *369* (map)
Fort Laramie Treaty, 397, *422*
Fort Louis, 78
Fort Loyal, 76
Fort Mackinac, *306* (map)
Fort Mandan, 298
Fort McHenry, 307, *308*
Fort Meigs, *306* (map)
Fort Michilimackinac, 225
Fort Mims, 307
Fort Molden, *306* (map)
Fort Mose, 125, *126, 132* (map), 133
Fort Necessity, 161
Fort Niagara, 164, 225, *275* (map), 306,
     306 (map)
Fort Orange, 51, 85
Fort Oswego, *275* (map)
Fort Pillow, *450*, 451
Fort Pitt, 164, 177
Fort Rosalie, 78
Fort Smith, *369* (map)
Fort St. George, 54, *132* (map)
Fort Stanwix, 201
Fort Stephenson, *306* (map)
Fort Sumter, 427
Fort Ticonderoga, 203
Fort Toulouse, 78, 100
Fort Wagner, 442, *450*
"Fort Wilson" Riot, 220
Forty-Niners, 394, 395, *422*
Foundation builders, 3
Fourteenth Amendment, 463, 469
Fox Indians, 225, 276, 346, 352, *366* (map)
France. *See also French entries*
     ambitions of, 40
     and the American interior, 72–78
     and American Revolution, 201, 222,
          228–229

British colonies acquired from, *181*
     (map)
colonial capital of, in New Orleans,
     125–126
colonization by, 43, 47
forts of, 71, *73* (map)
Jay's treaty, retaliation for, 269–270
and North American empire, 159
Pacific explorations by, 169
posts of, 78
slave traffic from Loango and
     Cabinda, 117
southern strategy of, 76
tensions between Britain and, 217, 300
tensions between U.S. and, 266–267
and Transatlantic African slave
     trade, *319*
transatlantic slave trade, 18th century,
     118–119 (map)
U.S. alliance with, 213–217
Franciscan friars, 43
Franciscan missionaries, 26–27, 43, 44,
     81, 173
     in Spanish Florida, 45–46
Franklin, attempted state of, *242*
     (map), 243
Franklin, Benjamin, 138, 143, 150, 192
     Albany Plan, 161
     and alliance with France, 215
     and bicameral legislature, 255
     Continental Congress and, 207
     as diplomat, 229–231
     in Philadelphia, 155
     on Six Nations, 276
     on Society of the Cincinnati, 238
Franklin tree, *240*
Free African Society, 273
Free blacks
     in American population, *272*
     Industrial Revolution and, 316
     lynching of, 346
     in northern colonies, 127
     reenslavement of, 280, 395
     restrictions on, 272–273, 280, 288,
          328, 385
     in southern population, 346
     threat of, to white southerners, 127
     treatment of, in the North, 199, 272
     as Union laborers, 445
Freedmen's Bureau, 350, 457–458,
     463–466
Freedom, meaning for former slaves, 466
Freedom fighters, 125
Freedom's Journal, 406
Free-Soil party, 410, 412, 417
Free labor ideology, 401–402
Free love advocates, 19th-century,
     482–483
Freeman, Elizabeth (Mumbet), 256

Free men, in Bacon's Rebellion, 111
Free people of color, 346–348, 400, 468.
     See also Free blacks
Free State of Jones County, 446
Free states and territories, *331*
Frémont, John C., 368–369, 414, 437
French and Indian War (Seven Years'
     War), 103, 160, 167, 175, 177
French colonists, 160–161
French Company of the Indies, 125
French explorations, *73* (map)
French forts, 160–161
French Guadeloupe, 134
French Huguenots, 32–34, 49, 53, 74
     Louis XIV and, 72
     prohibition against emigration by,
          145–146
French Louisiana, 122
French model of government, 264
French population in America, 160
French Protestants, *34*, 49
French Revolution, 266–267, 293
French Saint Domingue, 134
French Senegal, 164–165
French settlements, 141
French settlements, in mid-18th century,
     162 (map)
French traders, 141
Freneau, Philip, 239
Frobisher, Martin, *35*, 36–37
Fugitive Slave acts, 263, 410–411, 414,
     415, *422*
Fugitive slave commissioners, 410–411
Fugitive Slave Law (California), 395
Fuller, Margaret, *383*, 384
Fulton, Robert, 314
Fur trade, 48–50, 52, 89–90, 299, 372
     Russian, 171

G

Gálvez, Bernardo de, 226
Gabriel rebellion, 264
Gadsden, James, 365, *397*
Gadsden Purchase, *397* (map), 398,
     412, *422*
Gage, Thomas, 177, 192–193, 195–196,
     204–206
Galloway, Joseph, 193, 195
Galloway Plan, 194
Garcés, Father, 173–174, *174* (map)
Garrison, William Lloyd, 376
Gaspée (customs boat), destruction of,
     190–191
Gates, Horatio, 215, 220, 226–227, 236
Gays. *See* Homosexuals and
     homosexuality
Gender roles
     in post-Revolutionary America, *286*

General Court, 60
Generall Historie of Virginia, New-England, and the Summer Isles, The (Smith), 58
General Society of Mechanics and Tradesmen, 283
General Trades Union, 375
Genêt, Citizen Edmund, 267
Genizaros, 271, 288
Genocide
    of Spanish against West Indian population, 24
Gente de razon (people of reason), 372
George III (King of England), 192–193, 202, 240–241
    appointment of Grenville, 177
    in *The Times,* 176
George (runaway slave), 424–425
Georgia
    antislavery stance of, 133
    Atlanta, *453*
    Constitution ratified by, 257
    economy of, 319–320
    expansion of slavery into, *132* (map)
    as experimental colony, *131*
    gold digging in, 363
    growing season in, 148–149
    land claims of, 242, *279* (map)
    launched as nonslave colony, *134*
    law enforcement in Cherokee territory, *341*
    John Ross imprisoned by, 366
    as royal colony, 133
    runaway slaves, 324
    Savannah, *453,* 454, 457–458
    slave code of, 133–134
    slavery curtailment opposed by, 256
    Yazoo claim of, 242
Georgia colony, 130
Germain, Lord George, 209–210, 230
German Americans, 263
German-speaking immigrants, 147
German immigrants, *147,* 360, 363, 398, 435
German pietists, 156–157
German Protestants, 86–87
Germantown, 214
Germany
    and British War against American colonies, 210
Geronimo (Chiricahua), 475–476
Gerry, Elbridge, 254, 256, 270
Gibson, Edward, 128
Gilbert, Sir Humphrey, 36
Gilliam, Eliza, 371–372
Gilliam, Frances, 371–372
Gilliam, George, 371–372
Global circumnavigation, 249

Global conflict, 162–165
Global expeditions, *20–21* (map)
Globalization
    Portugal and first step into, 16–17
Global navigation, 153
Glorious Revolution in England, 87, 91–93
Gnadenhutten massacre, 234, *245* (map)
Godey's Lady's Book (magazine), 355
Godwyn, Morgan, 110
Gold
    discoveries of, 341–342, 394, *422,* 476
    mining of, 363, 394–395
Gold Coast, Africa, *116* (map), 117
Gordon, Thomas, 183–184
Gorée Island, 117
Gorsuch, Edward, 415
Government, federal. *See* Federal government
Graham, Sylvester, 382
Grain cultivation, 154
Granada, Nicaragua, 412
Grand Banks, 152
Grand Federal Processions, 259–260
Grandy, Moses, 363
Granges, 485
Grant, James, 175
Grant, Ulysses S., 438, 449, 455, 470–471, *486,* 487
Grantham, Thomas, 111
Gravier, Jacques, 76–77
Gray, Robert, *248,* 249
Gray, Thomas, 347
Great Awakening, 155–157
Great Basin, 174
Great Britain. *See* Britain
Great Lakes region, 275–277, *306* (map)
Great Migration, 369–371
Great Plague (1665), *84,* 108
Great Plains, 168
Great Swamp Fight, 88
Great Wagon Road, 148, *149* (map)
Great War. *See* World War I
Greeley, Horace, *486,* 487
Greenback Labor party, 485
Greene, Nathaniel, 227–228
Greenland, Norse settlements in, 15
Green Mountain Boys, 203
Green Spring faction, 90
Green Spring Plantation, 89, *90*
Greensted, William, 104
Greenwich, England, 153
Grenville, Robert, 177–179
Grid system of surveys, 244–245, *246* (map)
Grimké, Angelina, 376, 383
Grimké, Sarah, 376, 383
Grotius, Hugo, 41
Guadeloupe, 164

Guerrilla warfare, 243, 365, 449
Gulf of St. Lawrence, 28
Gullah language, 323
Gun frontier meets horse frontier, 141, *142* (map)
Guy, Francis, *321*

H
Haida people, 481
Hakluyt, Richard, 37, 54
Hale, John P., *412*
Hale, Sarah, 354
Half freedom, 52
Half Moon (ship), 50
Hamilton, Alexander
    as abolitionist, 240
    and Confederation finances, 236
    and Constitutional Convention, 253–254, 257
    death of, 302
    Jefferson compared to, 265
    Revolutionary War and, 221
    and Whiskey Rebellion, 268
Hamilton, Henry, 224, 226
Hancock, Dolly, *168*
Hancock, John
    and Boston Tea Party, 167
    boycott against British goods and, 188–189
    Declaration of Independence and, 168, 208
    Revolutionary War and, 195, 201
    Stamp Act repeal celebrations by, 182
    Tea Act and, 192
Hannibal, Missouri, 472
Hardee, William J., 454
Hard money policies, 343
Harlem, 85
Harmar, Josiah, defeat of, *275* (map), 276
Harpers Ferry, Virginia, 418–420
Harper's Weekly, 427, 486
Harrington, James, 86, 87
Harrison, Benjamin, 258
Harrison, John, 153, 170
Harrison, William Henry "Old Tippecanoe"
    advance on Prophet's Town, 304
    death of, while president, 377
    elected as president, 312
    nomination of, by Whigs, 376
    War of 1812 and, 300, 303, 306
    Whig party and, 375
Hartford, Connecticut, 60
Hartford Convention, 342
Hartford Female Seminary, 351
Harvard College (University), *60, 62,* 158
Havana, Cuba, 164
Hawaiian Islands, 168, 169, 171

Hawkins, Benjamin, 309
Hawkins, John, 35
Hayes, Rutherford B., *487, 488*
Hays, Mary "Molly Pitcher," 221
Head-Smashed-In, 7
Headright system, 113
Hemings, Sally, 289
Henrietta Maria (Queen of England), 59
Henry, Patrick, 180, 191, 194, 258
Henry IV (King of France), 49
Henry (Prince of Portugal), 16, *16, 20–21*
    (map), *38*
Henry VIII (King of England), 32, 34
Henry VII (King of England), 20–21
Hereditary racial slavery system, 112
Heretics, 32
Heroes of America, 446
Hessians, 210
Hewes, George, 167, 168, 192
Hickey, Thomas, 211
Hidatsa Indians, 299
Higginson, Humphrey, 105
Higher education, 381. *See also*
    individual colleges and universities
Hight, John J., 453–454
Hillsborough, Lord, 188–189, 191
Hine, Thomas J., *480*
Hispanics, 399. *See also* Mexicans and
    Mexican Americans
Hispaniola (Haiti and Dominican
    Republic), 18
Hochelaga, 28
Hodges, William, *170*
Hogarth, William, *130, 176*
Hohokam Indians, *10* (map), 12
Holland, 40, 47, *48,* 222. *See also* Dutch
Homestead Act (1862), 437
Homesteaders, 335
Homosexuals and homosexuality
    charges against von Steuben, 220–221
Honor wives, 288
Hooker, Joseph, 439, 447
Hopewell Indians, *10* (map), 13–14
Hopkins, Elizabeth, 39
Hopkins, Stephen, 39
Horse frontier meets gun frontier,
    142 (map)
Horses
    Native Americans and, 373–374, 476
    Pueblo Indians and, 81
    reappearance of, 21, *22*
    as sacrifice, 137, 138
    spread of, across the West, 103,
        138–142
Horticultural societies, 8
House Committee on Indian Affairs, 345
Household industry, 267, 348
Household structure, in the cotton
    belt, *468*

House of Burgesses, 56
House Reconstruction Committee, 471
Houston, Sam, 385
Howard, Oliver O., 458, *461*
Howe, George, 404–405
Howe, Richard, 210–211
Howe, William, 205–206, 210–214, 217
Hudson, Henry, 50
Hudson River, 209–210
Hudson's Bay Company, 85
Hughson, John and Sarah, 126
Huguenots, 31
Human ancestors, earliest, 3, 5–6
Hunt, William, 109
Huronia, 50
Huron Indians, 49, 50, 163
Husband, Herman, 185
Hutchinson, Anne, 61–63
Hutchinson, Thomas, 182, 191, 193

I
Iberian peninsula, 16
Iberville, *73* (map)
Iberville, Bienville d', 70, 77, 78
Iberville, Pierre le Moyne d', 70,
    77–78
Iceland, colonization of, 15
Ideal American, 356
Identity and identities, 371–372
Illinois, 246, *275* (map)
Illinois Country, 78
Illinois Indians, 76, 276
Immigrants
    from 1830 to 1850, 361
    in the Civil War, 434–435
    Protestant, from Switzerland, 99
    Western European, 362–363
Immigration. *See also individual source*
    nations and regions
    opposition to, by nativists, 378–380
    and population growth, 144
    to southern states discouraged by
        slavery, 400
Impeachments, 471
Imperialism
    limits of, 167–169
Impressment, 267, 301, 432
Inca empire, 9
Inca Indians, *10* (map)
Indebtedness
    and debtors' prison, 336–337
    following Revolutionary War, 199,
        236, 245, 247–248, 251
    loans, and cycle of, 485
    national, 265
Indentured servants, 108, 112
Independence movements. *See*
    Nationalist movements

Indiana, 246, *275* (map), 277, 280
Indian agencies, *474* (map)
Indian Bible, 63
Indian Brigade, 434
Indian College, *60, 63, 88*
Indian-British alliance, in War of
    1812, 305
Indian pueblos, *278* (map)
Indian raiding parties, 177
Indian Removal Act, 342
Indian reservations, 474. *See also*
    individual reservations
Indian Reserve, under British Rule,
    194 (map)
Indians. *See* Native Americans
Indian Territory, 199, *366* (map),
    434, 479
Indian Wars, 352
Indigo, 123, 150, 319
Individualism, 402, 404–405, 406–407
Industrialization
    Embargo Act and, 302
    in Philadelphia, 314
    process of, 401
    in the South, 316–317
Industrial Revolution, 267, 311, 314–317
Ingersoll, Thomas, 128
Inland commerce, 148
Inquisition, 32
Inter Caetera (papal bull), 18–19
Interracial marriage, 272
Intolerable Acts (1774), 193
Ireland, 15, 35, 362
Irish Catholics, displacement of, 147
Irish confetti, 376
Irish immigrants, 360, 364, 401, 476
Irish migration, 362
Iron Teeth (Cheyenne), 397
Iroquois Confederacy, 49–50, 99, 161,
    163, 225, 275–277
Iroquois Indians, 49, 76, 164, 201, 243
Iroquois settlements, *162* (map)
Irving, Washington, 355
Isabella of Castile (Queen of Spain), 18
Islam, 16
Itinerant ministers, 158–159
Izard, Alice, 286

J
Jackson, Andrew "Old Hickory"
    and the "common man," 337
    elected president, 312, 328, 343–344
    inauguration of, 339–340
    and Nullification Proclamation, 343
    political career of, 310
    as president, 297
    rejection of Supreme Court
        ruling, 342

and tuburculosis, 375
veto of bill to recharter Second Bank
    of United States, 343
victory over British at New
    Orleans, 308
views on Native Americans, 307
War of 1812, 300
Jackson, Thomas J. "Stonewall,"
    428–430, 447
Jacksonian American party system,
    408–409
Jacksonian Democrats, 374
James (Duke of York), 85, 86
James II (King of England), 87, 91, 92
James I (King of England), 54, 56, 64
James River, 54
Jamestown colony, 54–55, 56, 64, 90
Japan
    isolationist policy of, 42
Jay, John, 229–231, 240, 257, 269
Jay Treaty, 269–270
Jefferson, Thomas
    Alien and Sedition Acts and, 271
    as candidate for president, 269
    compared to Hamilton, 265–266
    Continental Congress and, 207
    on divisiveness of slavery, 329
    on early Chesapeake housing, 67
    elected president, 289–290, 294, 300
    and Embargo Act, 302
    as enigma, 290–292
    John Ledyard and, 250
    Lewis and Clark Expedition, 298–299
    Notes on the State of Virginia,
        239–240
    plan for Western territory, 244–245,
        244 (map)
    Proclamation Line and, 177
    Stamp Act and, 180
    and Tea Act, 191
    and territorial expansion, 293
    and two-party system, 265
    on Washington's response to military
        dissidents, 238
Jemison, Jane, 163
Jemison, Mary, 163, 281
Jemison, Thomas, 163
Jemmy (Stono Rebellion leader), 126
Jeremiah, Thomas, 204, 208
Jerome, Chauncey, 315
Jesuit missionaries, 33–34, 50, 81
Jesuits (Society of Jesus), 32
    removal of, from Spanish
        America, 173
Jewish ghetto, in New Amsterdam, 52
Jewish immigrants, 18, 156
    in New Amsterdam, 52
Jobbers, 350
Jobs, 364

Johnson, Andrew, 462
    in 1864 election, 452
    campaign against Fourteenth
        Amendment, 463
    land distribution to former slaves
        halted by, 461
    in postbellum South, 458
    as president, 460–463
    and purchase of Alaska, 481
    showdown with Congress, 471
Johnson, Boson, 443, 454
Johnson, Nancy, 443, 454
Johnson, Sir William, 164
Johnson, Thomas, 165
Johnston, Joseph, 430
Jolliet, Louis, 74
Jolliet and Marquette explorations,
    73 (map)
Jones, John Paul, 222–223
Joseph James (ship), 203
Joutel, Henri, 75
Juarez, Benito, 442
Judge, Ona, 262, 324
Judicial federalism, 340–342
Judiciary acts, 264, 292
Jupiter (locomotive), 473

K
Kamchatka peninsula, 171–172
Kansas-Nebraska Act (1854), 408, 412,
    413 (map)
Kansas Pacific Railroad, 478
Kansas Territory, 413 (map), 417
Karankawa Tribe, 278
Kaskaskia, Illinois, 77, 78
Kaskaskia Indians, 345
Kealakekua Bay, Hawaii, 171
Kearny, Stephen Watts, 388
Kellogg, Lucy, 313–314
Kelly, Oliver H., 485
Kemmelmeyer, Frederick, 268
Kendrick, William, 249
Kennedy, John F., 363
Kennewick Man, 4
Kentucky, 274, 280
Kentucky and Virginia Resolutions, 271
Kentucky Resolution (1799), 342
Key, Elizabeth "Bess," 104–105
Key, Francis Scott, 307, 308
Key, Thomas, 104
"Key of Liberty, The" (Manning),
    284–285
Kickapoo Indians, 276, 346, 352
Kicking Bear (Sioux), 475
Kidnapping, 108, 109
Kieft, Willem, 52
Kieft's War, 52
Kilpatrick, Judson, 443

King, Charles Bird, 345, 388
King, Rufus, 300, 310, 330
King George's War, 160
King Philip's War, 87
King William's War, 76, 93, 94–95, 161
Kino, Eusebio, 80 (map), 81
Kiowa Indians, 373, 434, 474
Kivas, 12, 45
Knights of Labor, 485
Know-Nothing party, 413, 414
Knox, Henry, 205–206, 236–237,
    238, 252
Knoxville, Tennessee, 239, 241
Kocherthal, Joshua von, 145
Kodiak Island, 172
Korean War, 448
Kosciusko, Thaddeus, 220
Koshkonong, Wisconsin, 359
Ku Klux Klan Act, 471
Ku Klux Klan (KKK), 463, 471

L
Labor, 321. See also Child labor
Laborers, 271, 445
Labor force, 316, 463–467, 476–478, 486
Labor organizations, 283
Labor unions. See also specific union
    organizations
    women and, 401
Ladies Magazine, 329, 354–355
Lady Washington (ship), 249
Lafayette, Marquis de, 213, 215, 220, 229
Lagos, slave trading depot at, 117
La Harpe, 73 (map)
Lake Texcoco, 11
Lakota Sioux, 476
Lancaster, Pennsylvania, 155
Land Act (1820), 331–334
Land cessions by Native Americans to
    U.S. government, 312–313
Land claims, Native American resistance
    to, 242–243
Land-grant colleges, 437
Land grants to war veterans, 312, 345
Land Ordinance (1785), 244–245, 261,
    279 (map)
Landowners, in postbellum South, 464
Landrum Guards, 435
Land speculation in the west, 278–280
Land transportation, and economic
    growth, 314
Land use acts, 479
Land use patterns, 280, 478–480
Lane, Ralph, 37
L'Anse aux Meadows, Newfoundland, 15
Lansing, John, 254
La Salle, René-Robert Cavelier, Sieur de,
    73 (map), 74, 139

Las Casas, Bartholomé de, 24, 35
Last of the Mohicans, The (Cooper), 163
Last of the Mohicans, The (Cooper), 355
Lateen sails, 17, *18*
Latimer, George, 364
Latitude, determination of, 153
Laud, William, 59
Laundry work, *349*
Laurence (slave), 444
Laurens, Henry, 182, 201
Lawrence, Kansas, 449
Lawson, John, *98* (map), 99
Lawsuit, by African American slave, 256
Leaves of Grass (Whitman), 405
Lecompton Constitution, 417
Lecture associations, 382
Ledyard, John, 250
Lee, Charles, 220
Lee, Richard Henry, 191, 258
Lee, Robert E., 399, 420, 427, 428–430,
    447–448, 454–455
"Legend of Sleepy Hollow, The"
    (Irving), 355
Leisler, Jacob, 92–93
Leisler's Rebellion, 93
Lenni-Lenape (Delaware) Indians, 86
Le Sueur, Marguerite Messier, 70–71
Le Sueur, Pierre-Charles, 70–71
Letchworth, William, 163
Letters from an American Farmer
    (Crèvecoeur), 240
Lewis, Meriwether, 298–299
Lewis and Clark Expedition, 250,
    298–299, *301* (map), 368
Lexington, Kentucky
    westward expansion and, 241
Liberal Republican party, *486*
Liberation, 204
Liberator (newspaper), 376
Liberia, 347
Liberty, individual demands for, 184
Liberty party, 386
Liberty (sloop), 188–189
    seizure by Newport citizens, 190
Lincoln, Abraham, *419*
    assassination of, 455
    elected president, 421, *452*
    Emancipation Proclamation, 441
    Gettysburg Address, 449
    inaugural address of, 427
    and Andrew Johnson, 460–461
    opposition to war against
        Mexico, 388
    and pocket veto, 460
    on popular sovereignty, 418
    as Republican party leader, 414
    and surrender by Confederacy, 455
    suspension of habeas corpus, 436
    threat of, to southern elites, 425–426

Lincoln-Douglas debates, 418, 421
Literary endeavors and values, 234–235,
    354–356, 404–405
Little Turtle (Michikinikwa), 276–277
Livestock farming, 82, 149
Livingston, Robert, 85, 207, 292
Loans, and cycle of indebtedness, 485
Lobos, 271
Locke, John, 87, 207
Logan, Greenbury, 385
London fire, 84, 108
Lone Star Republic (Republic of Texas),
    384–385
Long, Jefferson, *470*
Long Island, English settlement of, 53
Longitude, calculation of, 153
Longitude Act, 153
Longstreet, James, *447*
Long Walk, 439
Lorenzana, Apolonaria, 349
Lost Colony of Roanoke, 37
Louisburg, 161, 164
Louisiana. *See also individual cities*
    economy of, 319
    France and, 292
    French people in, 160
    naming of, 74
    reconstruction and, *469* (map)
    settlement in, 320
    slave plots in, 125
    Spain and, 241
Louisiana colony, 77–78, 103
Louisiana Democrats, 471–472
Louisiana Purchase, 293, 325,
    397 (map)
Louisiana Territory, 199, 298, 320
Louisville, Kentucky, 239, 241
Louis XIV (King of France) "Sun King,"
    72, 72–74, 76, 77, 91, 145
Louis XVI (King of France), 215, 293
L'Overture, Toussaint, 406
Lowell model of production, 316
Lowell textile mills, 349
Loyalists, 167, 199
Loyal Nine, 180
Loyola, Ignatius, 32
Lumber, 67
Lumpkin, Wilson, 342
Luther, Martin, 31
Lynchings, of Mormons, 368
Lyon, Matthew, 270–271

M

Mabila, 28–29
Macon's Bill No. 2, 303
Madagascar, 116
Madeira islands, 17, *18*
Madison, Dolly, *311*

Madison, James, *311*
    Alien and Sedition Acts and, 271
    and bill of rights, 260
    on divisive effects of slavery, 256
    elected president, 302
    and Massachusetts constitution, 219
    retreat from Washington, D.C., 307
    and U.S. Constitution, 253, 257
    and the Virginia Plan, 255
    and War of 1812, 305
Madison Tips, 435
Magellan, Ferdinand, *20–21* (map), 25, 27
Magna Carta, 183
Mail delivery, *283*
Maine, 92, 330, *331*
Maize agriculture, 8–9, 13–14
Malacca, 47
Malcontents, 133
Male privilege, in New England, 153
Mallet, Paul, 159
Mallet, Pierre, 159
Mandan Indians, 298, 349, 356
Mandingos, 109
Manhattan Island, purchase of, by
    Dutch, 51
Manifest destiny, 384
Mankiller, Wilma, 312
Mann, Horace, 380, 383
Manning, C. William, 284–285
Manufacturing, 267, 314
Manumissions, 127, 273–274, 346
Maps, allegorical, 36
Marblehead, Massachusetts, 152
Marbury v. Madison, 292
Margate, David, 204
Marina, Doña, 26
Marion, Francis, 226, 227
Maritime law, 41
Maritime shipping, 72
Market economy, women and, 288–289
Market revolution, 317–318
Marquesas Islands, 169
Marquette, Jacques, 74
Marrant, John, 124
Marriage
    complex, 382
    forbidden by Shakers, 282
    interracial, 272
    polygamy, 367, 382
Married Women's Property Law
    (Mississippi), 384
Marshall, John, 270, 292, 340
Martin, Joseph Plumb, 236–237
Martin, Luther, 254, 258
Martinique, 164
Maryland, 65–66, *65* (map), 110, 113,
    122, 260, 274
Mary of Orange, 91
Maslov-Bering, Aleksandri, *172*

Mason, Biddy, 395
Mason, George, 218, 256, 258
Mason, James, 442
Massachusett language, 63
Massachusetts
    and bill of rights, 260
    direct tax on citizenry, 252
    Humane Society, 240
    land claims of, 244, *279* (map)
    Provincial Congress at Concord, 193
    ratification of proposed
        Constitution, *258*
    rebellion, 248
    settlers of, 63
    and Stamp Act, 180
    state constitution, 218–219
    state navy of, 222
    treatment of free blacks, 272
Massachusetts Bay Colony, 58–59, 88, *89*
    (map), 107
Massachusetts Charter, 92, 193
Massachusetts Government Act, 193
Massachusetts Provincial Congress, 195
Massachusetts Regulation, 252
Massasoit (Wampanoag sachem), 39,
    57, 88
Mass migrations, 361–374
Matagorda Bay, 74, 75
Mather, Cotton, 88, 95, 128
Maumee River valley, Ohio, 276
Mayan Indians, 10–11, *10* (map)
Mayflower Compact, 39–40, 57
Mayflower (ship), 39, 57
Mayhew, Jonathan, 156
McClellan, George B., 439, 447, 452
McCord, Louisa, *404*, 415
McDonald, Elizabeth, 145
McDonough, Thomas, 307
McGillivray, Alexander, 231, 243
Meade, George G., 448, 455
"Meaning of July Fourth for the Negro,
    The" (Douglass), 407
Measles epidemic, 371
Medical schools, 382
Melville, Herman, 404
Memminger, Christopher, 462
Menéndez de Avilés, Pedro, 33–34
Menominee Indians, 276
Mental illness, 383
Mercantilism, 72
Mercer, Hugh, *212*
Mercer, William, *212*
Merrimack (ship), 442
Mesa Verde National Park, *12*
Mescalero Apache Indians, *431, 439*
Mesoamerica, 8, 9, 10–11
Messier, Jean-Michel, 70
Messier, Marguerite, 70–71, 78
Mestizos, 20, 79, 271

Metacom's War (King Philip's War), 87,
    87–88, *89* (map), 93
Methodists, 281
Métis (mixed blood), 372
Mexican Cession, 390, 395, *397* (map)
Mexican-American War, 386–390, *387*
    (map), *448*
Mexicans and Mexican Americans
    as cowhands, 479
    as laborers, 477
    land titles, loss of, 478
    print culture of, in the Southwest, 399
    social status of, in 1850s, 403
Mexico territory, 334–335, *336, 387*
    (map), 390
Miami Indians, 225, 276. *See also* Ohio
    Confederacy
Michigan, 246, *275* (map)
Micmac Indians, 28
Middle class, following Civil War,
    481–484
Middle colonies, as economic region, *149*
    (map), 154
Middle passage, 114, 117–120
Migration, ancient ice-age, *7*
Migrations, internal
    to California, 360, *396*
    forced, 320, 329, 361–362,
        363–364, *366*
    Great, 369–371
    postbellum, 473
    transportation and, *331*
    western, 314, 329–340, *369* (map),
        371–372
Migrations, international
    from England, 54, 56, 59–61
    from Europe, 156
Military conscription, Civil War, 433, 437
Military dissidents, following
    Revolutionary War, 235–237
Military technology in Battle of
    Tippecanoe, 304
Military units
    29th Regiment, U.S. Colored
        Troops, *444*
    33rd U.S. Colored Cavalry (First
        South Carolina Volunteers), 445
    54th Massachusetts Infantry, 442
Military veterans. *See* Veterans
Mills, energy sources for, *318*
Mineral Act (1866), 479
Mingo Creek Society, 281
Mining, 479
Ministers, shortage of, 158
Minkins, Shadrach, 415
Minnesota, 360
Minnesota Territory, *413* (map)
Minuit, Peter, 51
Minutemen, 193, 195, 202

Missionaries
    Congregationalist, 457
    in Mexico, 26–27
    in New England, 63, 88
    Oregon settlement by, 369
    in Savannah, 457–458
Missions, *336, 341, 372. See also specific
    missions*
Mission San Carlos Borromeo, Carmel,
    California, *350*
Mission San Francisco del Espada, San
    Antonio, *136*
Mississippi, Black Code of, 462
Mississippian culture, 9, 13–14
Mississippian earthwork, *13*
Mississippian Indians, *10* (map)
Mississippi Delta, 334
Mississippi River, 241
Mississippi Territory, 280, 293
Mississippi Valley, 74, 78, 199, 240–241
Missouri, admitted to statehood, *331*
Missouri Compromise, 329–331, 412,
    413 (map)
Missouri River, 299
Mittelberger, Gottlieb, 145
Moale, John, *151*
Mobile, Alabama, 70, 78, 226, 400
Moche Indians, 9, *10* (map)
Moctezuma, 26
Mogollon Indians, *10* (map), 12
Mohawk Indians, 88, 164, 225. *See also*
    Iroquois Confederacy; Ohio
    Confederacy
Mohawk Valley, New York, 147
Mohegan Indians, 63
Molasses, 178
Monetary policies, 265
Money. *See* Currency
Monroe, James, 246, 253, 292, 310, 311,
    329, 337
Monroe Doctrine, 337–338
Monster bank, 343–344
Montcalm, Marquis de, 163, 164
Monterey, California, 173
Monterey Bay, 41
Monte Verde, Chile, 6
Montgomery, Richard, 204, 206
Montreal, 50, 164–165
Moody, Deborah, 62
Moore, James, 82–83
Moravians, 150
Morgan, Daniel, 215, 227–228
Mormons (Church of Jesus Christ of
    Latter-day Saints), 353–354, 367–368,
    369 (map)
Moroni (angel), 354
Morrill Act (1862), 437
Morris, Gouverneur, 257, 332
Morris, Robert, 236, 248–249, 254, 257

Morse, Jedidiah, 239
Morse, Samuel F. B., 379
Morton, Jackson, 424
Mosby, John Singleton, 449
Moscovy Company, 35
Mothers' Magazine, 371
Mothers of 19th century, idealized, *355*
Mott, Lucretia, 383–384, 407
Mottrom, John, 104
Mound-building centers, Mississippian, 13–14
Moundville, Alabama, 14
Mount Holyoke, Massachusetts, 382
Mourning wars, 50
Mozambique, 116, *116* (map)
Mrs. McCormick's General Store (Browere), 381
Muir, John, 479–480
Mulattos, 79, 271
Muquelmne Miwok, 345
Murray, Ellen, *445*
Murray, Judith Sargent, 286
Murrieta, Joaquin, 399
Muskets, 141
Muslims, forced from Spain, 18
Myers, Isaac, 485

N

Nantucket whaling industry, 152, 248
Napoleon, 292–293, 300, 303, 306
Narragansett Indians, 62, 63, 88, 98
Narrative of the Life of Mary Jemison, A (Seaver), 163
Narváez, Pánfilo de, 28, *33* (map)
Nash, Francis, 239
Nashville, Tennessee, 239, 241
Nast, Thomas, *470, 486*
Natchez, Louisiana, 320
Natchez Indians, 125
Natchez Trace, *242* (map)
Natchitoches, Louisiana, 78, 137
National anthem, *308*
National debt, 265
National Era (magazine), 415
National Grange, 485
National highway, 479
Nationalist movements, 252
National Labor Union (NLU), 459, 485
National Park Service, 480
National Republicans, 338
National Road (Cumberland Road), 314, *332*
National Trades Union, 360, 375
National Woman Suffrage Association (NWSA), 482
Nation-state, emergence of modern, 31

Native Americans
18th-century towns and trails of, *245* (map)
acculturation of, 277–278, 344
in Age of the Common Man, 344–346
in British colonies, 145
celebration of kinship by, 406
Chesapeake Bay colonists and, 64
Christian, 88
citizenship rights demanded by, 396
of coastal Carolina, 98
of coastal North Carolina, *37*
colonialism and, 241
Creek orator, *243*
cultural traditions of, 476
economies of, 396–398
enslavement of, 108
epidemics and, 46, 233–234
European contact with, in the Northeast, *53* (map)
European expeditions and, 3
exploitation and relocation of, 311
expulsion of, 458
federal military campaigns against, 474–476
fight for independence from European encroachment, 168
forced migrations of, 329, 361–362, *366*
fur trade and, 49
in Great Lakes region, 299–300
horses and, 103, 138–139, 373–374
hunting grounds of, 277
Lewis and Clark Expedition and, 299
in Louisiana, 78
massacred by colonists, 88
of New England, 63, 88
New Light ministers and, 159
Ohio and, *245* (map)
in the Old Northwest, 243–245
in the Old Southwest, 242–243
Pacific tribes, and candlefish, *299*
peace delegations to Washington, 475
Proclamation Line and, 240–241
reassignment of homelands, in Treaty of Paris, 165
Republican vision of prosperity and, 481
reserved to, under British rule, *181* (map)
resistance movement, 303
retaliation against Jeffery Amherst, 176
revolt of, at mission *La Purisima Concepción,* 345
revolts by, in Spanish Florida, 47
Revolutionary War and, 199, 223, 231
roles of women, 312, 349
Russian trappers and, 172

as Satan's helpers, 95
slaughter of, by de Soto, 28–29
as slaves, 90, 99, 122
social status of, in 1850s, 403
southeastern groups, *242* (map), 309
Spanish missions and, 350–351
spiritual component in resistance to whites, 352
in Texas and Florida, 82
threat of, at Catholic missions, 349
traditional roles, weakening of, 287–289
tribal creation stories, 5
U.S. army clashes with, 458
U.S. cavalry attacks on, 473
value of community over individual, 356
value of treaty promises made by U.S., 367
Nativists, 378–380, 388
Naturalization laws, 271
Natural resources
exploitation of, 479
Nauvoo Legion, 367–368
Navajo Indians
James Carlton and, 439
and horses, 81
and Pueblo Revolt, 79
settlements of, *80* (map)
Spanish and, 81–82
Naval stores, 150
Navarro, José Antonio, 385, 398
Navigation acts (England), 83–84, 92, 178
Nebraska Territory, *413* (map)
Needleworkers, *349, 350*
Negro Act (South Carolina), 123
Negro Act (Virginia), *134*
Negro Election Day, 273
Negro Law (South Carolina), 126
Nelson, Lord, 300
Neolin (Delaware Indian prophet), 177
Netherlands, *118–119* (map), *319*
New Albion (California), 35
New Amsterdam, 51, 52–53, 84–85, 156
New Bedford, Massachusetts, 248
New Bern, North Carolina, 99, 147, *186*
Newburgh, establishment of, 146
Newburgh Conspiracy, 235–237, 261
New Democracy, 338
New Ebenezer, Georgia, 147
New England
colonies of, 145
Dominion of, 92
economic disadvantages of, 152
as economic region, *149* (map)
gap between rich and poor, 96
houses of, 66
merchants of, *265,* 317

mill owners of, 316
peace in frontier villages, 98
population of, in 1660s, 66
religious status in, 107
shipbuilding in, 152
War of 1812 and, 310
white men eligible to vote in 1792, *281*
women of, 349
New England Emigrant Aid Company, 417
New France (Canada), 48–49, 50, 73, *162* (map)
New Hampshire, 86, 252, *258*, 260
New Harmony order, 382
New Jersey
  College of (Princeton University), 158
  Constitution ratified in, 257
  as a royal colony, 86
  slaves emancipated in, 401
  treatment of free blacks, 272
  voting rights for free blacks revoked, 346
  voting rights for women, 199, 263
  Washington's visit to, 266
  women and girls of Trenton, *266*
New Jersey Plan, 255
New Light preachers, 158–159
New Mexico
  Confederate retreat from, *431*
  racial and ethnic diversity of, 44
  and slavery, 395, 410
  Spanish census of, 271
  as Spanish colony, 78–79
  survival of, 44–45
  Union troops defeated in, 430–431
  U.S. attempted purchase of, 387–388
New Mexico Territory, 43, *413* (map)
New Netherland, 50, 51, 84–85, 107
New Orleans, Louisiana
  in 1700s, *160*
  class divisions in, 467
  establishment of, 137
  Spanish control of, 292
  Union capture of, 438
New Orleans's Pelican Company F, 439
New Paltz, 53
Newport, Rhode Island, 156
New Spain, colonial pattern in, 44
Newspaper reporters, and corruption, 486
Newspapers, and American literary tradition, 355
New Sweden, 52, *65* (map)
News wives, 90
New Voyage Round the World, A (Dampier), 97
New Voyage to Carolina, A (Lawson), 99
New York
  and bill of rights, 260
  and Declaration of Independence, 208
  deepwater port at, 148

Dutch in, 263
enslaved people in, 121–122
Erie Canal investment, 333
growth in mid-18th century, 154
land claims of, 244, *279* (map)
naming of, 85
ouster of Dominion officials, 92–93
as royal province, 92
voting rights for free blacks revoked, 346
New York City
  British attempt to capture, 209–211
  draft riots, 449
  Erie Canal and, 333
  fire in, 126
  foreign-born population of, 362
  Grand Federal Procession in, 259
  licensing fees of, 316
  non-English newcomers in, 145
  slave revolt, *134*
New Yorkers, French, 145
New York harbor, 50
New York Slave Plot, 126
New York Sun (newspaper), 487
New York Times (newspaper), 486
Nez Perce Indians, 138, 476
Non-Intercourse Act, 302
Nonimportation movement, 189
Nootka Indians, 249
Norfolk, port of, 148
North, Baron Frederick, 189
North, enslaved people in, 121–122
North, Lord, 190, 191, 193, 212, 229
North America
  colonies by nationality, *48*
  exploration of, *33* (map)
  imperial map of, redrawn, 165
  rivalry to establish control of continent, 169
  slavery in, 134
North Briton (periodical), 178
North Carolina, *149* (map), 150, 185, 186, 260, *279* (map)
Northerners, 414, 463
Northern Iroquoian Indians, *10* (map)
Northup, Solomon, 376
Northwest Coast Indians, 173
Northwest Ordinance (1787), 245–247, 256, *261,275* (map), 276
Northwest Territory, 241, 274, *275* (map), 276, *279* (map)
Norway Grove, Wisconsin, *484*
Norwegian immigrants, *359*, 360, *484*
Notes on the State of Virginia (Jefferson), 240
Nova Scotia, 203
Noyes, John Humphrey, 382
Nuevomexicanos, 288
Nugent, Polly, 288–289
Nullification Proclamation, 342–343, 343

O
Oberlin College, Ohio, 382, 472
Occaneechi Indians, 90
Oceana (Harrington), 86, 87
Ochelaga, *30*
Ocracoke Island, *96*
Oglala Sioux, 476
Oglethorpe, James, 130–133, *134*
Ohio, 231, 246, *275* (map), 277, 280
Ohio Company, 247, 278–279
Ohio Company of Virginia, 161
Ohio Confederacy, 263, 267, 275–276
Ohio River, 240–241
Ohio Valley Indians, 243
Ojibway Indians, 276
Old Faithful, *480*
Old Lights, 158–159
Old Northwest, 241, 243–245, 246–247
Old Southwest, 241–243
Old Spanish Trail, *369* (map)
Oliver, Andrew, 180
Olmec Indians, 9
Olmsted, Frederick Law, 400
Omaha Indians, 141
Oñate, Juan de, *42* (map), 43–44
Oneida Indians, 225, 382. See also Iroquois Confederacy
Onondaga Indians, 225. See also Iroquois Confederacy
"On the Equality of the Sexes" (Murray), 286
Opechancanough (Pamunkey tribe), 64–65, 68
Order of the Star-spangled Banner (Know-Nothing party), 379
Orders in Council (Great Britain), 300, 301
Oregon Territory (Country), 311, 360, 386, *397* (map), *413* (map)
Oregon Trail, 369–371, *369* (map), 437
Orinoco River, 20
Orinoco tobacco, 56
Osage Indians, 141
Osborn, Sarah, 229
Osceola, and guerrilla war, 365
Ostend Manifesto, 412
Ottawa Indians, 225, 276
Our Nig, or, Sketches from the Life of a Free Black (Wilson), 407
Outer Banks, 37, 150
Overland Trail, *370*
Owen, Robert, 382

P
Paca, William, 258
Pacific exploration, 169–171
Pacific Ocean, 25
Pacific Railroad Act (1862), 437

Page Act (1870), 477
Paine, Thomas, 207, 213, 219
Paleo-Indian period, 6, 7
Palmer, Benjamin F., 310
Pamlico Sound, 27, 99
Pamunkey Indians, 64–65
Panic of 1819, 335–337
Panic of 1837, 370, 375
Paoli, Pasquale, 185
Paper mill, *318*
Pardo, Juan, 33, *33* (map)
Pareja, Francisco de, 45
Parker, William, 415
Partisan politics, 360–361
Parton, Sarah Willis (Fanny Fern), 407
Paterson, William, 255
Patriotism, 300
Patriots' Day, 103, *195*
Patronage system, 184
Pawnee Indians, 141, 413
Peace of Westminster (1674), 84
Peale, Charles Willson, *205*, 239, 368
Peale, James, *286*
Peale, Titian Ramsey, 368
Pelican (ship), 70–71
Penn, Thomas, 154
Penn, William, 86–87, 154
Pennsylvania
    German-born people in, 263
    German-speaking immigrants in, 147
    German immigrants in, 86–87
    government of, under colonial rule, 86
    print culture of Philadelphia, 355
    ratification of Constitution, 257
    religious toleration in, 156
    state constitution of, 219
    voting rights for free blacks
        revoked, 346
Pennsylvania Dutch, 148
Pennsylvania Main Line Canal, *332*
Pensacola, Florida, 226, 423–424
People of color, 271–274, 280. *See also*
    specific ethnicities
Peoria Indians, 78, 345
Pequot War, 63
Pérez, Eulalia, 349, 350–351
Perkins, Carter, 395
Perkins, Robert, 395
Perkins, Sandy, 395
Perry, Matthew C., *386*, 412
Perry, Oliver H., 306
*Perry Hall Slave Quarters with Field
    Hands at Work* (Guy), *321*
Persian Gulf War, *448*
Pest house, 122
Peterborough, New Hampshire, 200–201
Peter (runaway slave), 424–425
Peters, Clairy, 203
Peters, John, 203

Peters, Sally, 203
Peters, Thomas, *202*, 203
Petersburg, siege of, *450*
Philadelphia, Pennsylvania
    commercial dynamism of, 155
    deepwater port at, 148
    German immigrants in, 86–87, 148
    growth in mid-18th century, 154
    industrialization in, 314
    print culture of, 355
    Stamp Act repeal celebrations in, 182
Philip II (King of Spain), 32, 35, 40
Philip of Anjou, 76
Philippe, Michel, 77
Philippines
    British conquest of, 164
    Spanish expeditions to, 27
Philip V (King of Spain), 78
Photography, 429
Pickens, Andrew, 226
Pickett, George, 448
Pickett, John T., 442
Pictographs, *371*
Piedmont farm families, 185
Pierce, Franklin, 411, *412*
Pietism, 156–157
Pike, Albert, 434
Pima Indians, 81
Pinckney, Charles C., 270, 289, 300
Pinckney, William, 330
Pine forests, 150
Pirates, 95, 97, 270
Pitt, William, 164–165, 176, 179, 182
Pizarro, Francisco, 27
Place names, following end of
    Revolutionary War, 238–239
Plains Indians, 371, 402–403, 412–413
Plains Indian Wars, *474* (map)
Plains of Abraham, 164–165
Plantation Burial (Antrobus), *323*
Plantation Duty Act (1673), 84
Plantation economy, 199, 267, 280, 317,
    318–325
Plantation system of agriculture, 150,
    151–152
Planters, southern, 113, 124–125, 127, 128
Plants, domestication of, 8
Plumer, William, 289
Plymouth Colony, 39–40, 56–57, 88, *89*
    (map), 92
Pocahontas, 64
Pocket veto, 460
Poignaud and Plant boardinghouse,
    Lancaster, 349–350
Pointe-au-Fer, *275* (map)
Political activists, 355
Politics
    American, influence of Westerners
        on, 328

and erosion of rights of former
    slaves, 471
power of southerners in, 407–414
western migration and changes in, 329
Polk, James K., 385, 386, 387–388, 412
Polly (sharecropper), 467
Polo, Marco, 15, *20–21* (map)
Polygamy, 367, 382
Polynesians, 14, 169
Ponca Indians, 413
Ponce de León, Juan, 25, *33* (map)
Pontchartrain, Comte de, 77
Pontiac Indians, 168
Pontiac's Rebellion, 176, 177, *181* (map)
Pontoon bridges, 453, 454
Poor, as Devil's people, 96
Pope, John, 439
Popé, and Pueblo Revolt, 79–80
Popham, George, 54–55
Popular sovereignty, 410, 417, 418
Population center, *330*
Population growth, 143, 297, *352, 408*
Population structure by gender
    and age, *144*
Populist party (People's party), 486
Pornography, 483
Portage railroad, *332*
Portolá, Gaspar de, 173, *174* (map)
Port Royal Sound, 33, *34*
Portugal, *319*
    Brazil under control of, 106
    consolidation of, with Spain, 40
    enslavement of African infidels, 106
    maritime exploration of, 16
    slave trade, 47, 117, *118–119* (map)
    Treaty of Tordesillas, 20
Postbellum era
    economic changes in, 484
    Andrew Johnson and, 458
    labor force in the South, 463–467
    land use patterns in, 478–480
    migration in, 473
    women's suffrage movement in,
        481–484
Post-traumatic stress disorder, 120
Potawatomi Indians, 276, 346, 352
Potomac Company, 283–284
Pottawatomie Creek massacre, 417
Poverty Point culture, 9
Power, abuse of, 183
Powhatan, Chief, 64
Powhatan Confederacy, 64, 64–65, *65* (map)
Powhatan Indians, 54
"Prairies, The" (Bryant), 355
Praying towns, 88
Prejudices. *See also* Discrimination
    against African Americans, 274, 399
    against Catholics, 363, 379
    of Protestants, 379–380

Presbyterian ministers, 158
Presbyterian missionaries, 457–458
Presbyterians, 31
Presidential pardons, 461–462
Presidential power, 340, 344
Presidential selection method, 255
Presidents, as slaveholders, 408
Presidios, 173, *336*
Presley, George, Sr., 467
Press-gangs, 267, 301, 432
Prester John, 16, *18*
Priber, Christian, 129–130, 138
Prime meridian, 153
Princeton University (College of New
    Jersey), 158
Printing presses, 31, 155
Private-public partnerships,
    458–459, 481
Privateers, 95, 223, 441–442
Proclamation Line, 177, 240–241
Proclamation of Neutrality, 267
Proclamations by colonial grand juries,
    210–211
Proctor, Henry, 306
Production, 315–317
Productivity, 466
Prohibition, 131
Property ownership, 219, 246, 254
Prophet, the (Tenskwatawa), 303, *303*, 307
Prophet's Town, 303
Proportional representation, 255
Proslavery lobby, 133
Protestant denominations, 156
Protestantism, *282*, 379–380
Protestant missionaries, 369, 457–458
Protestant Reformation, 31–37, 54, 58, 106
Protestants
    English, 57, 76–77
    German-speaking, 156–157
    as immigrants, 147
    march on St. Mary's City, 93
    origins of name, 31
Providence, Rhode Island, 62, 152, 347
Public domain, *304* (map)
Public education, 380–382
Publius (Hamilton and Madison), 257
Pueblo Bonito, *12*
Pueblo Indians, 30, 43, 44–45, 79–81
Pueblo Revolt, *45, 80* (map)
Puget, Peter, 234
Pulaski, Casimir, 220
Pullman Palace Car Co., 480
Punch, John, 107
Puritan experiment, 57–63
Puritan Revolution in England, 83
Puritans, 31, 58, 59–61, 63, 66
Purvis, Robert, 378
Puttingout system, 317
Pyke (Captain), 109

Q
Quakers, 86, 130
Quantrill, William Clarke, 449
Quaqua, 290
Quartering Act, 178, 188, 192–193
Quasi War, 270, *270*
Quebec, 49, 164–165, *166,194* (map)
Quebec, the Capital of New France
    (Johnson), *165*
Quebec Act (1774), 193
Queen Anne's War, 93, 95, 98
Quetzalcoatl, 11
Quivira, 30

R
Race, notions of, 105
Race-based slavery, 103, 105–108,
    109–110, 130, 144
Race riots, 347, 376
Racial categorization, 271
Racial difference theories, 403–404
Railroad lines, *474* (map)
Railroads, *374*, 453, 473, 479
Rain-in-the-Face, *475*
Rainey, Joseph H., *470*
Raleigh, Walter, 37
Ranchéria, 350
Randolph, Edmund, 256
Randolph, John, *337*
Ranney, William, 200, *236*
Ratification progress, in newspapers, *258*
Real Whigs, 183, 184, 186–187,
    189–190
Reason, Charlie, 442
Reconstruction
    emerging black leadership during, 472
    government corruption, charges of, 471
    of the South, 458–459, *469* (map)
Reconstruction Act (1867), 469
Red Cloud (Sioux), 475–476
Redemption system, for indentured
    servants, 144–145
Red Sticks, 307, 308, 312
Reform movements, 380–384
Reform organizations, 280–281
Regional divisions in U.S., 305
Regional economies, 103, 148, 319–320,
    399–401
Regional vice-admiralty courts, 178, 188,
    194 (map)
Regulator Movement, 185, 186–187
Reign of Terror, 266–267
Religious affiliation, 353
Religious beliefs and traditions, 323,
    352, 476
Religious conflict, 31
Religious denominations, *282. See also*
    specific denominations

Religious liberty, 282
Religious persecution, 367–368
Religious revivals, 353
Religious toleration, 155–156
Remond, Charles Lenox, 376
Remond, Sarah Parker, 376
Renaming the landscape, 238–239
Rensselaer, Kiliaen van, 51–52
Report of Exploring Expeditions to the
    Rocky Mountains (Frémont), 369
Representation, proportional, 255
Representative legislature, in Jamestown, 56
Republican Mothers, 284–287
Republican party
    black men in, 470
    creation of, 413–414
    opposition to slavery, 409
    threat of, to southern elites, 425–426
    vision of prosperity, following Civil
        War, 481–488
Resolution (ship), 170
Restoration Era, 83
Resumption Act (1875), 485
Return from a Boarding School
    (engraving), *287*
Revels, Hiram, *470*
Revenue acts, 178, 186–188
Revere, Paul, 189–190, 194, 195
Revivals, 157
Revolutionary ideals, 262–264
Revolutionary War. *See also*
    Revolutionary War battles
    overview of, 199–201, *209* (map)
    African Americans and, 204–205, 222
    American casualties in, *448*
    beginnings of, 167
    demobilization process, 236–237
    final phase of, 229–231
    in global context, *202* (map), 217
    in the North, *216* (map)
    opening volley of, *195*
    at sea, 222–223
    smallpox epidemic and, 233–234
    in the South, 226–227, *227* (map)
    Spain and, 215
    in the West, *224* (map)
    women in, 221
Revolutionary War battles
    Bunker Hill, 201, 205–206
    Camden, 226
    Concord Bridge, 103
    Cowpens, 228
    Fallen Timbers, *275* (map), 276
    Fishing Creek, 226
    Guilford Courthouse, 228
    King's Mountain, 226
    Long Island, 211
    Monmouth, 220
    Princeton, *212*

Revolutionary War battles (cont.)
  Thames, 275 (map)
  Tippecanoe, 275 (map)
Rhett, Robert Barnwell, Jr., 425
Rhode Island
  following Revolutionary War, 251
  laws limiting involuntary service, 107
  ratification of proposed
    Constitution, 260
  Revolutionary War and, 222
  separation of church and state, 156
  slaves in, 127
Rhode Island colony, 88, 89 (map)
Rhody (slave), 444
Rice economy, 319
Rice farming, 122, 150, 321, 466–467
Rice zone in West Africa, 116 (map)
Richelieu, Cardinal, 49, 50
Richmond, Virginia, 148
Ridge, John, 366
Ridge, Major (the Ridge), 312–313, 366
Rio Grande valley, 43, 138
"Rip Van Winkle" (Irving), 355
Riverside trading centers, 148
Road building, following War of 1812, 314
Robert (runaway slave), 424–425
Roberval, 28
Rockefeller, John D., 436–437
Rockingham, Lord, 182
Rocky Mountain fur trade, 372
Rolfe, John, 56, 64
Roman Catholics. See Catholics
Ross, John, 366, 434
Rouensa (Illinois Chief), 76
Royal Adventurers into Africa, 84
Royal African Company (RAC), 84, 109,
    114, 117, 132, 134
Royal charters, 85
Ruiz, Francisco, 385
Ruiz de Burton, Maria Ampara, 478
Rum, 152
Runaway slaves
  advertisement for, 365
  in Boston, 364
  during Civil War, 423–424,
    438–439, 444
  Georgia and, 324
  in Northwest Ordinance of 1787, 247
  Treaty of Payne's Landing and, 365
Rupert (Prince), 114
Rush, Benjamin, 259
Russell, Osborne, 368
Russia, 199, 210, 337
Russian Alaska, 169, 171–172, 173
    (map), 234
Russian-American Company, 172
Russian fur traders, 103
Russian fur trappers, 172
Russo-American Treaty (1824), 338

S

Sacajawea, 299
Saehle, Jannicke, 359–360
Sagadahoc River, 54
Sagres, Portugal, 16–17
Sahagúernardino de, 26–27
Sailing, deep–sea, 15
Sailors, 273, 301, 310
Saint-Mémin, C. B. J. Févret de, 298
Salem, Massachusetts, 94–95
Salt Lake City, Utah, 368
Saltwater slaves, 109, 120
Sampson, Deborah (Robert Shurtleff), 221
San Antonio, Texas, 136, 137
San Antonio de Valero, 82
Sanchez, José Maria, 372
Sand Creek massacre, 451
San Diego mission, 349
San Francisco Bay, 173
San Gabriel Mission, 173, 174, 233,
    349, 350–351
San Jose, 173
San Juan River basin, 12
San Marcos, St. Augustine, 82
San Patricio Soldiers, 390
San Saba Mission, 140
San Salvadore, 18
Santa Ana, Father, 136–138
Santa Anna, Antonio Lopez de, 385
Santa Fe, New Mexico, 44, 140
Santa Fe Ring, 478–479
Santa Fe Trail, 369 (map)
Santee Sioux Indians, 424–425, 439, 440
San Xavier del Bac mission, 81
São Tomé island, 106
Saratoga, British surrender at, 215
Sassamon, John, 88
Saukamappee (Cree Indian), 141
Sauk Indians, 225, 276, 352, 360,
    366 (map)
Savage, Edward, 168
Savannah, Georgia, 131, 453, 454,
    457–458
Savannah Education Association (SEA),
    457–458
Scalawags, 463
Scandinavian immigrants, 360
Scarification, 104
Schenectady, founding of, 53
Schools. See also Education; specific
    school names
  for African Americans, 457–458,
    468, 472
Schuyler, Philip, 203–204, 243
Scioto Company, 247
Scotland, immigrants from, 146
Scots-Irish immigrants, 146–147
Scott, Dred, 417–418
Scott, William "Long Bill," 200–201

Scott, Winfield, 306, 366, 387, 388–389,
    411, 412, 436
Scottish Highlanders, 133
Scottish Presbyterians, 147
Scurvy, 28, 170
Seafaring, 301
Sea Islands, 460, 464–465
Seasoning, of saltwater slaves, 120
Seaver, James, 163
Secession of southern states, 425–428,
    426 (map)
Second Bank of the United States,
    335, 343
Second Confiscation Act (1862), 444
Second Continental Congress,
    202–204, 207
Second Great Awakening, 353
Second Party system, 374
Second Seminole War, 365
Secret ballot, 409
Sectionalism, slavery and, 311
Securities, 250, 251–252
Security Act (Charleston), 126
Seekaboo, 303
Seguin, Juan, 385
Seminole Indians, 277, 308, 309, 365, 366
    (map). See also Five Civilized Tribes
Senate, U.S., first black member of, 470
Seneca Indians, 163, 177, 225. See also
    Iroquois Confederacy
Senegambia, 116 (map), 117
Separation of blacks and whites, 113
Separation of church and state, 62, 156
Separation of powers, 219, 254, 470
Separatists, 57, 58
Sephardic Jews, 52, 156
Sequoyah, 345
Serapis (frigate), 223
Serpent Mound site, Ohio, 13
Serra, Junípero, 173
Servants, skin color and terms of
    service, 107
Seventh U.S. Cavalry, 474
Seven Years' War (French and Indian
    War), 103, 160, 167, 175, 177
Seward, William H., 442, 480–481
Sewell, Samuel, 128
Sexual abuse, 322
Sexual behavior, 282, 382
Seymour, Horatio, 471
Shabonee, 304
Shakers, 281–282
Sharecroppers, class divisions and, 467
Shawnee Indians, 224, 276, 304. See also
    Ohio Confederacy
Shays, Daniel, 252
Shays Rebellion, 251–252, 261
Sheep, 45, 81
Shelburne, Earl of, 230

Shelikov, Grigorii, 172
Shenandoah Valley, Virginia, 147
Sheridan, Philip H., 452, 458
Sherman, Roger, 207
Sherman, William T., 452–454, 458, 464–465
Sherman's hairpins, 454
Shipbuilding, 152
Shipping, 331
Shoe factory workers, 486
Short, Mercy, 95
Shoshone Indians, 138, 476, 480
Siberia to Alaska land bridge, 3
Sierra Leone, 203
Sioux Indians
    communal way of life, 356
    expansion of, 141–142
    and Iroquois Confederacy, 225
    at Little Big Horn, 476
    Plains Indian Wars and, 475
    response to Sand Creek massacre, 452
    role of women, 349
    uprising of, 360
Sisters of Mercy, 362
Sitka, Alaska, 172
Sitting Bull (Tatanka Iyotake), 475, 476
Six Nations, 276. See also Ohio Confederacy
Skin color
    and competition for jobs, 364
    as distinguishing marker, 107–108, 113
    and identity, 371–372
    and privilege, 401
    slavery and, 105
    and social status, 403
Slater, Samuel, 267
Slave Coast (Bight of Benin), 116 (map), 117
Slave coffles, 334
Slave drum, 124
Slave-based societies, 103
Slave-trading voyage, 106
Slave families, 320–321, 363
Slave funerals, 323
Slaveholders, 204, 290, 324, 356, 408
Slave labor camps, 110–111
Slave labor system, 127, 130
Slave markets, 363
Slave revolts, 125–126, 134, 324, 347
Slavery
    in 1860s U.S., 428 (map)
    John Quincy Adams on, 330–331
    conflict over, 329, 415
    cotton plantation economy and, 199, 267, 280, 318–325
    expansion into western territories, 421
    extent of, in 1819, 329

in Fundamental Constitutions of Carolina, 87
Industrial Revolution and stigma of, 316
and insecurity of English colonies, 132–133
in Kentucky, 280
land use patterns and spread of, 280
legalization of, in Georgia, 134
in Lincoln-Douglas debates, 421
Mexican-American War and, 390
Missouri Compromise, 331
in the North, 401
Northerners' support of, 402
and Northwest Ordinance (1787), 256
in Ohio, 280
popular sovereignty and, 410
preserved by Constitutional Convention, 256
prohibition of, north of Ohio River, 246
refusal of Congress to exclude, from new states, 245
religious institutions and, 353
resistance to, 322–325
spread of, 334–335
in Texas, 385
and Texas annexation controversy, 385–386
truce on, 408–409
Turner revolt and end of debate, 348
violence over issue of, 415–417
western expansion of, 274–280
white women and, 404
Slavery, abolition of, 271, 272, 376, 416, 469 (map)
Slaves
    in Age of the Common Man, 346–348
    barred from citizenship, 328
    births of, 320
    brutality against, 324
    as contraband of war, 437
    cultivating tobacco, 321
    economic diversity among, 400
    and election of 1800, 289
    and Emancipation Proclamation, 441
    exploitation of, in gold mines, 363
    forced migrations of, 361–362
    funerals of, 323
    hauling cotton, 334
    hired out to work, 365
    in horticultural society, 8
    impressment of, by Confederate Army, 432
    labor of, 321–322
    legal killing of, 113
    Native Americans as, 83
    in North America, 121 (map)
    owned by Native Americans, 312

percentage of 1860 population, 428 (map)
population of, by region, 408
populations of, in the North, 127
as prisoners, 115
in proportional representation, 255–256
punishment of, 322
religious beliefs of, 323
resistance of, in Bacon's Rebellion, 134
resistance patterns, 123
supply of, to Spanish colonies, 134
as surgeons' servant, 434
theft by, 324
unloading ships, 433
white servants vs., in Virginia, 113
Slave trade, 248, 256, 320, 363–364
    on the African coast, 115–117
    from Africa to Caribbean, 25
    Atlantic, during 18th century, 118–119 (map)
    England and, 84
    expansion of, 113
    forced migrations of, 114
    Portugal and, 17, 117
    Stuyvesant and, 52
    transatlantic, 35, 100, 108, 118–119 (map)
    transatlantic African, 319
Slave unrest, 125
Slidell, John, 387–388, 442
Smallpox, intentional spread of, to Native Americans, 177
Smallpox epidemics, 26, 50, 206–207, 214, 233–234, 235 (map)
Smith, Hyrum, 368
Smith, John, 54, 58, 64
Smith, Joseph, 367–368
Smith, Joseph, Jr., 353–354
Smithsonian Institution, 368
Snuff, 151
Social covenant, 96
Social hierarchies, 8, 280, 403–405
Social identities, cultural blending and, 372
Societies with slaves vs. slave societies, 151
Society for Promoting Christian Knowledge, 128
Society for the Promotion of the Manumission of Slaves, 240
Society for the Propagation of the Gospel in Foreign Parts (SPG), 128
Society for the Relief of Poor Widows and Small Children, 281
Society of Friends, 52, 86
Society of the Cincinnati, 238, 253, 261
Soil depletion, tobacco and, 68, 280

Solomon, Job Ben (Simon), 109

Solon, 254

Some Considerations on the Keeping of Negros (Woolman), 130

"Song of Myself" (Whitman), 405

Sons of Liberty, *180*, 180–182, 185, 190, 191–192, 283

South

enslaved people in, *121* (map)

lower, enslaved people in, 122

political power of, 407–414

wealth per person in 1770s, 152

white men eligible to vote in 1792, *281*

South Carolina

absence of civil government, 185

abundance of, 146–147

Africans, importation of, 148

economy of, 319–320

enslaved people in, 122

growing season in, 148–149

Gullah language in, 323

hereditary race slavery system, 110

import duty on African arrivals, 127

labor camps in, 122

land claims of, *279* (map)

nonsupport of curtailment of slavery, 256

and nullification, 342–343

ratification of proposed Constitution, 260

rice growers in, 122–123

runaway slaves, 324

secedes from Union, 425

and slavery during Revolutionary War, 222

Stamp Act resistance in, 182

and Stono Rebellion, 126

South Carolina and Georgia as economic region, *149* (map)

Southern Alliance. *See* National Farmers' alliances

Southern Homestead Act (1866), 479

Southern land debates, 242–243, *242* (map)

Southern Overland Trail, *369* (map)

Southern states, disproportionate representation of, in 1800s, 290

South Seas Exploring Expedition (Wilkes Expedition), 368

Southwest Territory, *278–279* (map), 398–399. *See also* Old Southwest

Spain

African men and explorations of, 106–107

British colonies acquired from, *181* (map)

in California, 169

census of New Mexico, 271

colonies of, 78–82, *132* (map)

control of western lands by, 234

domination of, west of Mississippi, 169

enslavement of African infidels, 106

exploration and settlement of the Americas, 23–30

influence in lower Mississippi area, 320

introduction of horses, 373

land claims, *242* (map)

and Lewis and Clark Expedition, *301* (map)

Louisiana Territory acquired by, 199

missions of, *73* (map)

Native American allies of, 241

New World empire of, 40–47

North American colonies of, *48*

presence on southern and western U.S. borders, 334, 337

and Revolutionary War, 201, 215, 222, 231

settlements of, *73* (map)

slave traffic from Loango and Cabinda, 117

St. Augustine established by, *38*

and Transatlantic African slave trade, *319*

Treaty of Tordesillas, 20

war with Britain, 126

Spanish Armada, 32

Spanish colonization, *80* (map), 106, *278* (map)

Spanish-American War, *448*

Spanish-language materials, 355

Spanish-speaking settlers, 348–349, 356

Spanish explorations, *42* (map), *174* (map)

Spanish Florida, 45–47, *46*, 122

Spanish introductions to New Mexico, 45

Spanish land titles lost to squatters, 478–479

Spanish Louisiana, *181* (map), *194* (map)

Spanish missions, 79, 82, 277, 345, 350–351

Spanish slave traders, 377–378

Spanish territory (1610), *42* (map)

Spear, Chloe, 288

Spectral evidence, 94

Speculators in paper holdings, 249, 251–252

Sperm whale industry, 273

Spice trade, 15, 18

Spiece, John B., 432

Spiro, Oklahoma, 14

Spoils system, 340

Spotted Tail, 476

Springfield, Connecticut, 60

Spy, The (Cooper), 355

Squanto, 39, *39*–40, 57

Squatters' claims, 478

St. Augustine, Florida, 33, *38*, 45, 107, 125

St. Charles Parish, Louisiana, 324

St. Clair, Arthur, *275* (map), 276

St. Denis, *73* (map)

St. John de Crèvecoeur, Hector, 240

St. John the Baptist parish, Louisiana, 324

St. Lawrence River, 74

St. Lawrence Valley, 78

St. Marie, 50

St. Mary's City, Maryland, 66

St. Thomas Protestant Episcopal Church, Philadelphia, 273

Stadacona, 28

Staines, John, 263

Stamp Act, 179, 180, *181* (map)

Standing armies, 189–190

Stands-in-Timber, John, *139*

Stanton, Edwin M., 455, 470, 471

Stanton, Elizabeth Cady, 351, 383, 407, 482

Stanton, Henry B., 351

"Star Spangled Banner, The" (Key), 307, *308*

State constitutions, 218–219

State governors, 219

Statehood, Northwest Ordinance and, 246–247

State legislatures, 219, 254, 470, 471

State militias, 220, 269

States' power, 340

States' rights

in Articles of Confederation, 218

ideology of, 456

Andrew Jackson and, 328

Thomas Jefferson and, 265

in Kentucky and Virginia Resolutions, 271

Statistical center of the country, *330*

Steam Cotton Manufacturing Company, 267

Steamships, 314, 359

Stephen (runaway slave), 424–425

Stephens, Alexander H., 425, 462

Stephens, Uriah, 485

Stereographs, *480*

Stevens, Thaddeus, 469

Stewart, Maria, 347, 406

Stone, Lucy, 482

Stonewall Brigade, 455

Stono Rebellion, 125, *126,134*

Stowe, Harriet Beecher, 415–416

Strait of Gibralter, *18*

Strait of Magellan, 25

Straumfjord (L'Anse aux Meadows), Newfoundland, 15

Strikebreakers, 486

Stuart, Gilbert, *276*, *311*
Stuart, James, 54
Stuart dynasty, 83, 87
Stuyvesant, Judith Bayard, 52
Stuyvesant, Peter, 52, 85
Suffolk Resolves, 195
Suffrage, 254–255, 344. *See also* Voting
    rights; Women's suffrage
Sugar Act (1764), 178
Sugar production, 106, 115, 320
Sugar revolution, 106
Suicide, by enslaved people, 125
Sullivan, John L., 225, 252
Sullivan's Island, 122, 208–209
Summary View of the Rights of British
    America A (Jefferson), 193
Sumner, Charles, 383, 417, 469, 481
Sumter, Thomas, 226, 227
Sunshine law, 86
Supreme Court
    John Adams's appointments to, 292
    Alien and Sedition Acts and, 270–271
    Dred Scott decision, 417–418
    justices as slaveholders, 408
    and states' power, 340
    support for Cherokee Nation, 342
Surfboarders, *171*
Susan (Kentucky slave), 324
Susquehannock Indians, 89, 90
Sutter, John, 394
Sutter's mill, gold discovery at, 394
Sweden, colonies of, *48*
Swedish immigrants, 360
Swiss Reformation, 31
Sylvis, William, 485

T

Tahlequah, 397
Taino Indians, 24–25
Talleyrand, Charles, 270
Tallmadge, James, 329
Tallmadge Amendment, 329
Tammany Hall, 486, *486*
Taney, Roger B., 417–418
Taos Trail, *369* (map)
Tappan, Arthur, *377*
Tappan, Lewis, *377*
Tariffs
    of abominations, 342–343
    on imported goods, 265
Tarleton, Banastre, 226, 228
Taxation
    Civil War and, 441, 446
    federal, 268
    following Revolutionary War, 265
    by Massachusetts, 252
    regressive, 95, 185
Taylor, Susie King, 445

Taylor, Zachary, 388, 410
Tea Act (1773), 191–192
Teach, Edward "Blackbeard," 95
Tea tax, 191–192
Tecumseh, 303, *303*, 305, 306, 307
Tejanos, 334, 372, 384–385, 398, 435
Tejas Indians, 82
Telegraph, 379
Temperance movement, 240, 378, 383
Tenant farmers, 185, 400
Tennent, Gilbert, 158
Tennent, William, 158
Tennessee, 274, 327, *469* (map)
Tenochtitlán, Mexico, 11, *25* (map),
    26–27
Ten Percent Plan, 460, 461, *469* (map)
Tenskwatawa (the Prophet), 303,
    303, 307
Tenure of Office Act (1867), 470, 471
Teotihuacan, Mexico, 11
Territorial expansion
    19th-century, *397* (map)
    effects of, 297
    following Revolutionary War, 234,
        240–241
    Thomas Jefferson as advocate of, 293
    in mid-1840s, 384–386
    into Mississippi Territory, 280
    Republican support for, following
        Civil War, 480–481
    southern planters' push for, 412–413
    western, from southern states,
        242–243
Territorial governments, 246, 388
Territory ceded by Mexico, *387* (map)
Terror and terrorism
    against Navajo, 439
    reign of, 266–267
    by U.S. soldiers, 388–389
Terrorists, 463
Teton Sioux Indians, 141
Texas
    annexation area, *397* (map)
    annexation controversy, 385–386
    borderland conflict in, 82–83
    independence of, from Mexico,
        384–385, 398
    origins of name, 82
    slavery in, *364*
    southern boundary of, prior to
        1836, *336*
    Spanish claims to, 82
    statehood of, 387
    white migrants to, 398
Texas Rangers, 384, 399
Texians, 334, 384
Textile industry, 311, 315, *349*, *401*
Thanksgiving, 57
Thirteenth Amendment, 462–463

Thomas, Gertrude, 447
Thoreau, Henry David, 388, 404–405
Thoughts on Government (Adams), 219
Three-fifths clause, 255–256,
    289–290, 408
Ticonderoga, capture of, 164
Tilden, Samuel J., *487* (map), 488, *488*
Timber Culture Act (1873), 479
Times, The (Hogarth), 176
Timucua, 82
Timucuan language, 45
"Tippecanoe and Tyler Too," 377
Tirsch, Ignacio, *175*
Tishcohan, *154*
Tituba, 94
Tlingit Indians, 172, 481
Tobacco economy, 56, 67–68, 89,
    109–110, 110, 111, 319
Tobacco production, 151
Tobacco trade, 89
Tocqueville, Alexis de, 344
Tokugawa dynasty, 40, 42
Tolsey, Alexander, 109
Toltec Indians, *10* (map), 11
Tories, 167
Torjersen family, 359–360
Total war, 450
Tourism, *478*, 480
Touro Synagogue, Newport, Rhode
    Island, *156*
Towne, Laura, *445*
Townshend, Charles, 187–188
Townshend Revenue Act, 187–188
Townships, 244
Trade
    European goods, *115*
    Hopewell Indian network, 13–14
Trail of Tears, 365–367
Transcendentalism, 384, 388
Transcontinental railroad,
    458–459, *473*
Transcontinental Treaty, 337
Trans-Appalachian West, 274–275,
    276, 328
Transportation
    and market revolution, 317
    and migration, 331
Travis, Joseph, 348
Treaties
    with Britain, 269, 311
    Burlingame, 477
    Kansas-Nebraska Act and violations
        of, 412
    with Native Americans, 243, 367,
        397, 459
    Russo-American, 338
    Tecumseh on, 303–304
    Transcontinental, 337
    U.S. changed policy, 474

Treaty at Utrecht, 98
Treaty of Fort Atkinson, 397
Treaty of Fort Laramie, 397, 476
Treaty of Ghent, 309–310
Treaty of Guadalupe Hidalgo, *387*, 390, 395, 396, 398
Treaty of Horseshoe Bend, 308
Treaty of Medicine Lodge Creek, 474
Treaty of Paris, 160, 165, 243, 261
Treaty of Payne's Landing, 365
Treaty of San Lorenzo, 269
Treaty of Tordesillas, 20
Treaty with Japan, 412
Trenchard, John, 183–184
Trenton, New Jersey, *266*
Trent (ship), 442
Tripoli, war against, 292
Troy Female Seminary, 351
Trumbull, John, *208, 243*
Truth, Sojourner (Isabella Baumfree), *406*, 407, 482
Tryon, William, 185
Tryon's Palace, *186*
Tsimshian people, 481
Tubman, Harriet, 419–420
Tudor dynasty, 32
Tunica Indians, 141
Turner, Benjamin S., *470*
Turner, Nat, 347, *347*
Turquoise, 11
Tuscarora Indians, 99, 225. *See also* Iroquois Confederacy
Tuxpan, Mexico, *386*
Tweed, William M. "Boss," *486, 486*
Twenty-Negro Law, 424
Two-party system, 263, 360–361, 380, 410
Tyler, John, 377, 386
Typhus epidemic, 306
Typographers, 486

U

Uncle Tom's Cabin (Stowe), 415–416
Underground Railroad, 410, *411* (map), 415, 419–420
Unicameral legislature, 86
Union, readmission of Confederate states to the, 471
Union Pacific Railroad, 458–459, 473, *473*, 486
Unions. *See* Labor unions
United Nations of Indians, 434
United Society of Believers in Christ's Second Appearance (Shakers), 282
United Society of Chimney Sweeps, 316
United States-Canadian border, 311

United States (U.S.)
    boundaries negotiated with Great Britain, 231
    Capitol in 1814, *307*
    legislature, 254, 255
    population structure by gender and age, *144*
    southern boundary granted by Britain, 241
    and Transatlantic African slave trade, *319*
    transatlantic slave trade, 18th century, *118–119* (map)
United States (U.S.) government agencies
    Freedmen's Bureau, 350, 457–458, 463, 464, 465–466
    Sanitary Commission, 437
    territory, *387* (map)
    Topographical Corps of Engineers expedition, 368–369
United States (U.S.) military. *See also* Continental Army
    Army in clashes with Native Americans, 360, 458
    birth of Marine Corps, 270
    birth of Navy, 222–223, 270
    creation of Army, 202–203
    on Tuxpan River, *386*
    in War of 1812, 305
Urban managerial class, 484
Urrutia, Turibio de, 136–137
Ursuline convent, Charlestown, 362
U.S. military
    troops withdrawn from South, 488
Utah, 395, 410, *413* (map)
Ute Indians, 81, 138
Utopian experiments, 155, 382

V

Valdez, Maria Rita, 395
Vallandigham, Clement, 449
Valley Forge mural, *221*
Van Angola, Anna, 107
Van Blarenberghe, Louis Nicolas, *229*
Van Buren, Martin, 375, 376, 385, 410
Vance, Zebulon, 433
Vancouver, George, 233–234
Van Lew, Elizabeth, 435
Van Rensselaer, Alida Schuyler, 85
Vaqueros, outfits of, 351
Vargas, Diego de, 80
Velásquez, Loreta Janeta, 435, *436*
Vera Cruz, 26
Vergennes, Comte de, 215, 230–231
Vermont statehood, 247
Verrazano, Giovanni da, 27, *29,33* (map), 54
Versailles, France, 231

Vesey, Denmark, 346
Vesey plot, 346
Vespucci, Amerigo, 20
Veterans
    of 1812 War, 311–313
    land warrants granted to, *304* (map)
    of Revolutionary War, 236–237
Vice-admiralty courts, 178, 188, *194* (map)
Vick Plantation, *334*
Victorianism, 356, 481–482
Victoria (ship), 25–26
"Victory or Death" code phrase, 213
Vietnam War
    American casualties in, *448*
Vigilantes, white, 463, 469
Vikings, 3, 15
Vindication of the Rights of Woman, A (Wollstonecraft), 284
Vinland colony, Newfoundland, 15
Virginia, *98* (map)
    antislavery proposal defeated, 348
    Bacon's Rebellion in, 89–91
    bill of rights in, 260
    England's claim, 54
    and first republican state constitution, 218
    free people of color, restrictions on, 127
    House of Burgesses, 191
    land claims of, 243–244, *279* (map)
    laws of, on separation of whites and blacks, 113
    manumission ban lifted, 273–274
    Negro Act of 1705, 113
    population of, in 1660s, 66
    ratification of proposed Constitution, *258*
    and reconstruction, *469* (map)
    as a royal colony, 64
    skin color and laws of, 107
    slavery in, 110, 122, 222
    tobacco exports, 67
Virginia Company, 54–55, 56–57, 64–65
Virginia Declaration of Rights, 218, 256
Virginia militia, free blacks in, 124
Virginia Plan, 255
Virginia Resolution, 342
Virginia Resolves, 180
Virginia (ship), 54
Vizcaíno, Sebastián, 41–43, *42* (map)
Von Kocherthal, Joshua, 146–147
Von Steuben, Friedrich, 220–222
Voting rights. *See also* Women's suffrage
    in California, 396
    Constitutional Convention and, 254–255
    for free blacks, 346
    property requirements for, 246

reduction in limits on, in state constitutions, 219
revoked by Berkeley, 89
white men and, *281*

W

Wachovia, North Carolina, 150
Wade-Davis Bill (1864), 460
Wage earning, 317, 401
Wage slavery, 402
Walden (Thoreau), 405
Walker, David, 346
Walker, William, 412
Walker's Appeal to the Coloured Citizens of the World (Walker), 346
Walking Purchase, 154
Walls, Josiah T., *470*
Wall Street, New York, 51
Wampanoag Indians, 87, 98
Wamsutta, 88
Ward, Nancy, 312–313
War hawks, and War of 1812, 303, 304–305
War of 1812, 300, 304–310, *306* (map), 325, *448*
War of 1812 battles
    Baltimore, 307
    Bladensburg, 307
    Chippewa, 306
    Detroit, 305
    Horseshoe Bend, 307, 310
    New Orleans, 308
    Thames, 306
    Tippecanoe, 304
War of American Independence. *See* Revolutionary War
War of Spanish Succession, 76, 78, 93, 98
War of the League of Augsburg, 93
War profiteers, in Civil War, 437
Wars, American casualties in, *448*
War veterans. *See* Veterans
Washington, Augustus, *420*
Washington, D. C., 410
Washington, George, *205,311*
    attack on French soldiers at Fort Duquesne, 161
    as commander of Continental Army, 204, 213–214
    Constitutional Convention and, 253
    defeat at Fort Necessity, 162
    elected president, 261, 264
    farewell address, 269
    Fugitive Slave Act and, 263
    Ona Judge and, 262–263
    manumission by, 273–274
    and military dissidents at Newburgh, 237

Northwest Ordinance and, 276–277
Proclamation Line and, 177
Proclamation of Neutrality, 267
retreat toward Philadelphia, 212
Society of the Cincinnati and, 238
struggle to control Boston, 205–206
in Trenton, New Jersey, 266
two-party system and, 264–265
use of name for streets and towns, 239
Whiskey Rebellion and, 268–269
Washington, Martha Custis, 262
Washington Society, 380
Washington Territory, *413* (map)
Watie, Stand, 434, *435*
Wayne, Anthony "Mad Anthony," 276–277
Wealth
    distribution of, in U.S. and Europe (1798), *291*
    percent of, owned by adult males, *291*
    per person in 1770s, 152
    presidential pardons for Confederates and, 461–462
    sources of, following Revolutionary War, 248–249
Webber, John, *171*
Webster, Daniel, 375
Webster, Noah, 239–240
Wesley, John, 157
West Africa, 84, *107,116* (map), 290
West Central Africa (Congo-Angola), *116* (map), 117
Western Herald (newspaper), *365*
Western land claims, *279* (map)
Western life, multicultural mix of, 368
Western migration, *314,* 329–340, *330,* 360, *369* (map)
Western plains, 138
"Western Planting" (Hakluyt), 37
Western settlers, 328
Western territories, Northwest Ordinance and, 246–247
Western trails, *369* (map)
West Florida, British-ruled providence of, *194* (map)
West Indies
    abolition of slavery in, 376
    British, restrictions on trade with, 248–249
    English migration to, 59
    middle passage and, 114
    slavery-based colonial societies in, 112
    slavery in, 134
    Spanish arrival in, 24–25
West Jersey, 86
Whaling industry, 152, 248, 273
Wheat, 151

Wheatley, Phyllis, 406
Wheeler, Joseph, 452
Whig party. *See also* Real Whigs
    composition of, 463
    presidential candidates of, 376, 377, 385, 410, 411
    in presidential elections, *412,* 414
    in Second Party system, 360–361, 374
    support for, 375
Whipple, Josiah, 263
Whiskey Rebellion, *268,* 268–269, 293
White, Hugh, 375
White, John, 35, 37
White Antelope (Indian chief), *451*
White Cloud (Winnebago prophet), 352
White Eyes, 224
Whitefield, George, 155, 156–157, 158
White Indians, 372
White Sticks, 307
White supremacist terrorist organizations, 463
White supremacy doctrine, 274–280
Whitman, Marcus and Narcissa, 369, 371
Whitman, Walt, 404–405, 406, 473
Whitney, Eli, 267
"Whole World as a Clover Leaf, The," 36
Whydah, trading depot at, 117
Wichita Indians, 141
Wickett, Susanna, 312
Wildcat banks, 335
Wilkes, Charles, 368
Wilkes, John, 178, 185
Wilkes Expedition, 368
Willard, Emma, 351
William III (King of England) (William of Orange), 87, *91,* 92
William (King of England), 75–76, 93
Williams, John D., 464
Williams, Roger, 61–63, 62
Williams, William S. "Old Bill," 372
William (slave), 424–425, 444
Wilmot, David, 388
Wilmot Proviso, 388, 408, 410
Wilson, Harriett, 407
Wilson, James, 220, 236, 254
Wilson, William B., *457*
Windward Coast, Africa, *116* (map), 117
Winnebego Indians, 276, 345, 346, 352
Winslow, Anna, 189
Winthrop, John, 59–61, 62
Wisconsin, 246, *275* (map), 360, 399
Witchcraft trials, in Salem Village, 94–95
Wolfe, James, 164–165
Wollstonecraft, Mary, 284–285
Woman Order, 438

Women. *See also* African American women
  antislavery work of, *445*
  in Civil War, 435, *439*
  collective identity embraced by, 406–407
  Confederate, 446–447
  economic subordination of, 348
  educational opportunities for, 285–287, 351, 382
  in Jamestown, 56
  labor unions and, *401*
  lack of benefits for, under Constitution, 199
  as migrants, 371
  in New England economy, 152–153
  nonelite, 287–289
  in the Revolutionary War, 221
  roles of, in regional economies, 395
  second-class citizenship, 328
  status of, in Age of the Common Man, 348–351
  subordination of, 404–405
  as teachers, 380–381
  in textile industry, *315*
  as wage earners, 350

Women in the Nineteenth Century (Fuller), 384
Women's rights, 383, 384
Women's Rights Convention, Seneca Falls, New York, 384, 407, *483*
Women's rights movement, 286
Women's suffrage, 481–484, *482, 483*
Woodhenge, 14
Woodhull, Victoria, 482–483
Woolman, John, 129–130
Wool production in England, 35
Work, delineation between men's and women's, 350–351
Workers' organizations, 484–488
World Anti-Slavery Convention (1840), 383
World diagram, 36
World War I, *448*
World War II, 366, *448*
Writ of habeas corpus, suspension of, 436
Wyandot Indians, 276
Wyck, Jan, *91*

X

XYZ affair, 270

Y

Yakutsk, 250
Yale University (College), 158
Yamasee Indians, 99
Yamasee War, 99–100
Yancey, William Lowndes, 425
Yanktonai Sioux Indians, 141
Yates, Robert, 254
Yazoo Act (1795), 279
Yazoo claim, of Georgia, 242
Yellow fever epidemic, 71
Yellowstone National Park, 480
Yeomen farmers, 400, 467–468
York, burning of, 94–95
York (Lewis's slave), 299
Yorktown, siege of, 229
Yosemite valley, 480
Young, Brigham, 368
Yuma Indians, 174, 175

Z

Zavala, Lorenzo de, 385
Zheng He, 15, *20–21* (map)
Zoffary, Johann, *112*
Zuni pueblos, 30
Zwingli, Ulrich, 31